BREWER STATE
LIBRARY
TUSCALOOSA

Y0-BRI-684

DISCARDED

E
322
.S642
Vol.2

Smith, Page

John   Adams.

DATE DUE			
MAR 1 '84			
DEC 2 1 1988			
JAN 2 2 1990			
JUN 10 '95			
JUL 1 3 2009			

DISCARDED

JOHN ADAMS

DISCARDED

JOHN ADAMS

II
1784–1826

PAGE SMITH

GREENWOOD PRESS, PUBLISHERS
WESTPORT, CONNECTICUT

Copyright © 1963 by Page Smith

Reprinted by permission
of Doubleday & Co., Inc.

Library of Congress Catalogue Card Number 77-88941

SBN 8371-2348-8

PRINTED IN UNITED STATES OF AMERICA

JOHN ADAMS

XLIV

At the end of July word reached Adams at The Hague that Abigail and Nabby had finally arrived. The letter from Abigail had made him "the happiest man upon earth," he wrote. He felt twenty years younger. It was a mortification to him not to be able to come for her himself, but he felt obliged to wait for word from Paris. In his place he sent "a son who is the greatest traveler of his age, and without partiality . . . as promising a youth as is in the world." For John every hour would be a day until they were together, "Yours with more ardor than ever. . . ."[1]

No sooner had he dispatched John Quincy than Adams received news that Jefferson had arrived in France. He decided at once to join Abigail, Nabby, and John Quincy in London and go with them to Paris to meet Jefferson and begin the work of the commission.

Several weeks after her arrival in London, Abigail was sitting in the drawing room of her apartment surrounded by callers when John Briesler came puffing up the stairs. "Young Mr. Adams is come," he announced with a delighted grin.

"Where, where is he?" from Abigail and Nabby.

"In the other house, madam; he stopped to get his hair dressed."

Abigail restrained her impatience. In a few minutes a young man came in, slender, of medium height, with a fresh, fair complexion and a face of unusual delicacy and intelligence. At first Abigail did not recognize her own son, the boy she had parted with more than four years ago, and then, as he came toward her, she saw his eyes, wide-set and beautiful, familiar and beloved. The sight of him touched her to tears—her son, in the wonderful vibrancy of young manhood, full, it seemed, of all the gifts of the spirit, of all goodness and grace and beauty. Abigail gave free rein to her mother's pride as she watched her son and daughter together. "Were I not their mother," she wrote Mary Cranch, telling her of the reunion, "I would say a likelier pair you will seldom see in a summer's day."

On August 4, Adams left The Hague to join his family and three days later he and Abigail met at the Adelphi Hotel. They were by romantic standards an odd pair of lovers. Short and stout with two grown children, their passion sat a little awkwardly upon them, made them, after twenty years of marriage and almost ten years of separation, suddenly shy and a little ill at ease. All the ache and agony of the separation were somehow comprehended in the moment of their meeting, the demons of loneliness exorcised, the pain of exile healed. The air in the comfortable drawing room of the Adelphi Hotel was charged with emotions that lay too deep for words. Perhaps Abigail, writing to Mary Cranch, said as much as could be said: "You know, my dear sister, that poets and painters wisely draw a veil over those scenes which surpass the pen of the one and the pencil of the other."

An hour or so later when Nabby came in she saw an unfamiliar hat on the apartment table with two small books in it. The whole apartment seemed strangely altered. "Has Mamma received letters that have determined her departure? When does she go? Why are all these things moved?" she asked Esther Field, all in a rush.

"No, ma'am," Esther replied, delighted with her secret, "she has received no letter, but goes tomorrow morning."

"Why is all this appearance of strangeness?" Nabby persisted. "Whose hat is that in the other room? Whose trunk is this? Whose sword and cane?" And then it struck her. "My father's! Where is he?"

"In the room above."

Nabby rushed up the stairs, knocked softly at John's door, and had her own tender reunion. "Sure I am, I never felt more agitation of spirits in my life," she wrote in her journal; "it will not do to describe."[2]

They all set out next day, crossed the Channel at Dover, and began the long trip by stagecoach to Paris. From the first Abigail and Nabby felt that they were in an alien country. "There is certainly a great difference," Nabby noted, "in favor of England; the country is by no means equal to it." The soil was not as well cultivated and the little villages through which the coach passed seemed "the most wretched habitations of man." Not one house in ten had glass in the windows; wooden shutters must serve instead. The dirt of ages stained the farmhouses and the coaching stations and the ladies remained in the carriage rather than dismount amid so much filth. Everything looked unkempt. Even the two French postillions attending the coach wore ragged, out-at-the-elbows liveries and great unpolished jack boots that gave them an indescribably comic air. In the fields along the highway they saw whole families at work—men, women, and young children. The English yeoman farmers had an alert, independent spirit which reminded Abigail of the farmers of New England, but the French peasants seemed a different breed of men—lumpish and heavy, dulled by the unvarying routines of farm life.

At almost every town there was a customs official whose duty it was to search all travelers to make sure they paid a duty on anything they had with them which had not been manufactured in France, but the bribe of half a crown was readily accepted in lieu of opening their baggage for the official to rummage through.

At Chantilly, Adams stopped at the château of the Prince de Condé to take his family through the grounds that he had visited three years before. They saw and smelled the Prince's hunting dogs, were shown his private theater where he produced and acted in plays for the entertainment of his friends, fed the enormous golden carp, and walked through the "groves and arbors . . . winding woods and vales, banks and rivers," past innumerable fountains and statues—the chariot of Venus drawn by doves, a statue of Cupid, one of Psyche. At the end of one of the gardens was the Pavillion of Venus decorated in chintz, surrounded by four fountains. In the "English garden" was a replica of an English cottage, perfect in detail down to ornamental plows and farm utensils. Beside it was an ancient, rustic barn—"a little dirty place, with old windows and little doors," but inside was an elegant room, the furniture covered with pink silk and fringed with silver braid and tassels, the walls hung with handsome paintings.

From Chantilly it was a short stage to Paris where they lingered a day or two. Abigail was no more impressed with the city than with the French countryside. Its smell, pungent, pervasive, overwhelming, made up of a thousand odors, stupefied her. "It is the dirtiest place I ever saw," she wrote Lucy Cranch. "There are some buildings and some squares which are tolerable; but in general the streets are narrow, the shops, the houses inelegant and dirty, the streets full of lumber and stone." Boston was as much superior in her eyes to Paris as London was to Boston.

After several days of sight-seeing the Adamses rode out to Auteuil where Thomas Barclay had rented a house for them—the mansion of the Count de Rouault. The stables were somewhat run down and the spacious garden ragged and untidy but the whole estate, bordered by the Bois de Boulogne and looking down on the Seine and the city itself, had an unmistakable elegance. The salon on the left of a handsome entrance hall was, Abigail noted, "about a third larger than General Warren's hall"; the dining room was on the right of the hall, and each room had large "French doors" opening onto a charming garden and a courtyard.

With all its elegance the mansion was a housekeeper's nightmare, full of quirks and eccentricities. There were some thirty bedrooms and numerous odd apartments. The floors were of red tile which could not be scrubbed with water. To clean them a manservant with brushes strapped to his feet whirled around the room, "dancing here and there like a Merry Andrew." The house, moreover, was incompletely furnished. There were no decent tables and no rugs for the cold, hard floors; no bed linens or table linen, few kitchen utensils and no table silver. Abigail had to order three dozen spoons and forks to be made of silver, a tea set, and china for the table. Everything she wanted was twenty or thirty per cent higher in Paris than in Boston. A dozen handsome wineglasses cost three guineas and other prices—for wood, coal, cloth, and so on—were correspondingly high. There were, in addition, dozens of French domestic implements whose use Abigail had first to discern and then master. Most maddening of all was her discovery that she must employ a vast corps of servants. "Each servant," she wrote Cotton Tufts, "has a certain etiquette and one will by no means intrude upon the department of the other." The coachman would do nothing but care for the carriages and horses; the cook would only cook and not think of washing a dish; the business of the *maître d'hôtel* was to purchase food and other items for the family, "and oversee that nobody cheats but himself." With a swarm of servants Abigail had to inquire constantly: "Pray why is not this or that done?" And the answer: "O, this not the business of their department, that belongs to the *femme de chambre;* and this to the *cuisine femme!*"

As a *coiffeuse* Abigail employed a nineteen-year-old girl, Pauline, who refused to dust the bedroom because "it is not de fashion, it is not her business." Abigail was about to dismiss the girl when inquiries convinced her that she would have to pay much more for a replacement. At least Pauline talked a little English and consented to sew, which was something to be grateful for. Abigail was pleased and touched by Esther Field's report that she had heard Pauline muttering, "Ah, *mon Dieu*, it is provoking." Esther had asked what provoked her. "Why," Pauline answered, speaking of Nabby, "Mademoiselle look so pretty, I, so *mauvais.*"

The *frotteur* who polished the floors, the *valet de chambre,* a job filled by John Briesler, and the *femme de chambre,* Esther Field, completed the staff of eight domestics. Excepting the Americans, Abigail wrote resentfully to Cotton Tufts, they were "a pack of lazy wretches who eat the bread of idleness" and "are saddled upon you to support and maintain for the purpose of plundering you." With such a swarm there was no one to do the wash, and if John Briesler and Esther had not done triple duty, the mistress of the house would have had to hire a half dozen more. Abigail was also dismayed by the disposition she found to cheat. Everywhere she was importuned for tips, the "perquisite of office (of insolence it should be)," she noted. Everyone—the waiter, the postillion, the hostler, the chambermaid—had his hand out. It was degrading and repugnant.

Abigail was also put out at the "tyranny of fashion" established by the French to which everyone must conform. Even the porters and washerwomen, she noted, had their hair powdered and dressed every day. "Such is the *ton,*" she added wryly. John Briesler and Esther were jeered at by the other servants until Abigail urged them to give way. Esther, good New England girl that she was, had several crying spells at the prospect of getting herself up like such a fool, but she consented at last, and the two of them appeared, red and self-conscious but *à la mode*. "To be out of fashion," she wrote Mary Cranch, "is more criminal than to be seen in a state of nature, to which the Parisians are not averse."[3]

The day after their arrival at Auteuil the Adamses dined with Thomas Barclay. Thomas Jefferson and his daughter were also guests and Abigail and John were delighted to see the Virginian. Adams remembered the younger man affectionately from their service together in Congress and from their work on the committee for drafting the Declaration of Independence. Jefferson was an excellent conversationalist, witty and entertaining, with a range of interests as wide as Adams' own. He had a Southerner's gift for graceful compliments and flattering attention to the ladies, and Abigail and Nabby were charmed with his manners and his good humor. The Virginian, with clothes that appeared several sizes too small for his long limbs, sprawled in a chair or couch with "a loose shackling air" about him and talked most entertainingly.

The next day Adams' old friends, the three abbés, Chalut, Arnoux, and Tersan, called to pay their respects. They were like three kind, ancient aunts full of compliments for the ladies, proffering their help, pleased to have their American friend back, exclaiming over his handsome family. They insisted that Nabby speak French with them and she did her best in her halting, copybook fashion, blushing most fetchingly over her mistakes. The abbés were charmed and declared that they should be her preceptors.

Abigail, harassed though she was by her corps of domestics, was full of contentment. She wished for nothing better than to keep house, walk in the garden or the Bois, sit in her little writing room, reading or sewing, or writing to her friends in America. The proximity of her husband was a perpetual joy. It came upon her a dozen times a day and made her heart leap each time—the sudden awareness that he was nearby, in his study or chamber, within reach of her voice, or on a walk from which he would soon return.

The daily routine at Auteuil was a pleasant one. Abigail lay in bed until the fire had been made in her chamber by Briesler. When the chill was off the room she dressed, tidied up, went to Nabby's chamber and roused her, then knocked at John Quincy's door. Together the family sat down to a sturdy New England breakfast, salted with lively conversation. After breakfast John retired to read or write, Abigail to darn stockings or sew, Nabby to her own room to translate Telemachus from French to English, John Quincy to his Tacitus and Horace. At twelve Adams put down his books and papers, took his cane, and set out for a brisk walk through "his" woods, the paths and byways of the Bois de Boulogne. Abigail from her room could watch him striding along until he entered the gate of the woods and disappeared from sight. While he was gone the ladies had their hair dressed and took the occasion to practice their French on Pauline.

John was always back by two when the family dined and after lunch, or more properly dinner, they went their separate ways. Adams often walked the mile to Passy to confer with Franklin and Jefferson; Abigail generally visited John Quincy to chat or to have him read aloud to her. Nabby usually joined them, and sometimes, provoked by John Quincy's teasing ways, brother and sister tussled and romped like exuberant children.

The afternoons were short and a bell soon summoned them all to tea, an American ritual which they faithfully observed. As soon as tea was over and the table cleared, it was covered with "mathematical instruments" and books. John and John Quincy settled down and, in Abigail's words, "you hear nothing till nine o'clock but of theorems and problems, bisecting and dissecting tangents and segments." (Father and son made their way systematically through geometry—eight books of Euclid in Latin—through plain trigonometry, through algebra, through decimals, fractions, arithmetical and geometrical proportions and conic sections.) After the lesson the gentlemen often joined the ladies in a game of whist "to relieve their brains," and the family retired to bed at ten.

Idyllic as all this was, Abigail professed to be a little put out by her husband. In Braintree he had entered readily into all of her domestic problems—whether to have turkey or goose for Thanksgiving, whether the serving girl was too free with the hired hand, whether to paint or paper the drawing room—but now he was very much the statesman. He "loves to have everything as it should be," she wrote Dr. Tufts, "but does not wish to be troubled about them," and indeed declared, a little too grandly, Abigail thought, that he had no time to think about domestic matters. He even left it to Abigail to carry on the negotiations to buy the Alleyne house in Braintree, which was a mansion, at least by comparison with the Adams farmhouse. She could hardly face the prospect of returning to the farm's cramped quarters after living in the Auteuil château. There was more to it than just space. She was reminded, she told Tufts, of the story of Queen Elizabeth who, visiting the house of one of her ministers, expressed surprise at how small it was. "May it please Your Majesty," said the minister, "the house is big enough for the man, but you have made the man too big for the house."[4]

At Auteuil, Abigail entertained Franklin and Jefferson, Thomas Barclay, and Commodore John Paul Jones, the latter cockier than ever after his spectacular victory over the *Serapis*. The abbés came almost daily to go through their pleasant ritual of teaching French to Nabby and to talk with Abigail and John about thoroughly worldly matters. A less welcome visitor was the Abbé Thayer, the renegade son of the Boston Thayers, who had become a convert to Roman Catholicism and an abbé to boot. He visited in his habit and lectured Abigail and John on the glories of the Roman Church. Adams listened silently if sourly until the abbé began to quiz him on the Bible and "rail at Luther and Calvin." This was too much for John, who brought the presumptuous young man up short. He had no idea, he told him curtly, of accepting him as his father confessor. As far as his own religious beliefs were concerned he took the view that he was not accountable to anyone but his Maker. He did not, furthermore, care to hear either Calvin or Luther spoken of in such a manner; Thayer or no Thayer, he had no intention of being either catechized or converted.

At Franklin's for dinner Abigail met for the first time the famous Madame Helvétius. That lady, entering the drawing room very much at home, "with a careless, jaunty air," and seeing two strange women, "bawled out, 'Ah! *mon Dieu*, where is Franklin? Why did you not tell me there were ladies here? How I look!'" She grasped at "a chemise made of tiffany, which," Abigail reported, "she had on over a blue lute-string . . . which looked as much upon the decay as her beauty."

Disconcerted, Madame Helvétius ran out of the room, apparently seeking the doctor, and returned just as Franklin entered by another door. Before the fascinated gaze of Abigail and Nabby, she ran forward to meet him, caught him by the hand with the cry "*Hélas!* Franklin," and gave him a kiss upon each cheek and another on his forehead. At the dinner table she sat between the doctor and Adams and monopolized most of the conversation, frequently locking her hand with Franklin's, "and sometimes spreading her arms upon the backs of both the gentlemen's chairs, then throwing her arm carelessly upon the doctor's neck."

Abigail's face told very plainly what she thought of Madame's behavior. She was inclined to set her down as "a very bad one" despite her age and widowhood. After dinner the lady courted further disapproval, throwing herself down on the settee, "where she showed more than her feet." There she made a great to-do over a little yelping lap dog which she covered with kisses, and when the animal wet the floor Madame wiped up the puddle with her chemise. "Thus," wrote Abigail to Lucy Cranch, "you see, my dear, that manners differ exceedingly in different countries." To Dr. Tufts she wrote in a somewhat racier spirit that Franklin, hugged and kissed so frequently by the lady, "cannot be averse to the example of King David, for if embraces will tend to prolong his life and promote the vigor of his circulation he is in a fair way to live the age of an antediluvian."[5] Despite her knowledge of Franklin's perfidy (or at least what her husband considered to be such) and his notorious immorality, Abigail was not entirely immune to the wicked doctor's charm. She enjoyed his wit and his conversation and observed with amusement his forays among the ladies.

One of Abigail's pleasantest surprises was the Frenchmen. She had somehow thought of them as oily, insinuating, licentious characters, bent on doing a woman out of her good name; bent, to put it bluntly, on seduction and addicted to loose living. She found them charming—gracious, attentive, full of compliments and courtesies, quite unlike the abrupt and matter-of-fact American males. The gentlemen always stood with their swords and their small silk hats clamped under their arms, and generally shut the ladies off from the fire. The talk was never general but invariably tête à tête. They had certainly the gift of making women deeply conscious of their womanliness, of surrounding them, plain or beautiful, young or old, with a kind of aura of desirability. To have a Frenchman enter the room was to feel at once involved in a kind of romantic drama, to be conscious of one's appearance, and to dare to anticipate, if one was wearing a becoming hat or a charming frock, a compliment upon it. Abigail, who loved to flirt, found herself in a world where flirtation was simply a part of the character of social life. She even caught herself wishing a little guiltily that American men might be, at least in their attitude toward ladies, a little more like Frenchmen.

Abigail also found the French ladies, on closer acquaintance, most appealing. They were "very easy in their manners, eloquent in their speech, their voices soft and musical and their attitude pleasing. I fancy they must possess the power of persuasion and insinuation beyond any other females."[6] Certainly they were a dramatic contrast to the matter-of-fact, rather masculine English ladies.

Abigail, the product of a society which in its simple effort to survive had abandoned the graces for the essentials, which had imposed on the naked will the terrible burden of sustaining the order of civilized life, encountered as her husband had done the strange seduction of French culture. Supported by layers of custom and traditions, by established orders that seemed to sustain themselves, by lines and limits that placed everyone with an almost mathematical exactitude in his or her respective place, this culture paradoxically freed people to be more expressive, more responsive, more natural and in some ways more human. Like John, she noted that the peculiar style of the men and women of Paris was not simply an attribute of the upper classes but extended down to the chambermaid, the hairdresser and the shopgirl—it was a quality that distinguished Parisiennes from all other members of the human race, a gracefulness of movement, an air of elegance, an animation "communicated to every feature of the face and to every limb of the body."

Slowly, or perhaps for her with surprising speed, Abigail grew accustomed to the strange habits of the French. Dining at Franklin's, she had been shocked to see the gentlemen, when the partridges were passed, smell them before they put them on the plates of their dinner partners, and she felt only slightly reassured when she was told that this was a courtesy to make sure the meat had not spoiled. But she soon came to accept the practice as part of the code of etiquette and even the sight of a French lady putting her arms "wrapterously . . . around a gentleman" and kissing him in public she came to consider "as a thing of mere course. . . . I can even see," she confessed, "that the rouge gives an additional splendor to the eyes."[7]

But the sexual immorality of the French she could not reconcile herself to nor did she try. Every instinct was offended by the casual way in which married men took mistresses and married women lovers. There were, in short, some customs which might well be transplanted to American soil and there were others which would lead her to repeat the words of the church service: "Good Lord deliver us; good Lord save thy people."

One startling evidence of the French attitude toward sex was the Hôpital des Enfants-Trouvés, the foundling home, run by nuns. Abigail visited the Hôpital and found the experience both painful and pleasing. It was painful in the extreme to see so many illegitimate babies abandoned by their mothers, the fruit of "debauchery and baseness," but it was pleasing to see the care and attention given the children, the large, clean, airy rooms, the neat and efficient sisters.

Abigail was told that one half the children born in Paris each year were illegitimate. This one home received six thousand foundlings a year, another over five thousand, and fifteen thousand were sent into the provinces "at nurse." It was so common for mothers, wed and unwed, to abandon their children that in certain parts of Paris small boxes were provided with covers in which unwanted infants could be deposited and then collected and brought to the Hôpital des Enfants-Trouvés. The Hôpital had four wet nurses on constant duty in each ward "for the youngest and weakest of the children," but infants were often brought in "so chilled with the cold and so poorly clad" that the nurses "could not bring them to any warmth, or even make them swallow." Writing her sister Eliza about her visit to the Hôpital, Abigail concluded with the lines, "Where can they hope for pity, peace or rest/Who move no softness in a parent's breast?"[8]

In the quiet life at Auteuil, Nabby and John Quincy discovered each other. Nabby was a year older than her brother and very much in love; John Quincy fancied himself in love with Monsieur Dumas' daughter; a hopeless passion, it seemed, for he was far too young to even think of marriage, and that nubile lady was not likely to wait ten years for her young admirer to grow up. So they had everything important in common. Having known each other only as children, they fell very much in love in a perfectly proper way. They went sight-seeing in Paris and to the Comédie du Bois de Boulogne, where Nabby found the actors and actresses "only tolerable." They went shopping together, read poetry and

novels to each other, and found mutual solace in recounting the tribulations of their respective romances.

Nabby wrote regularly, long, detailed letters, to Royall Tyler, and
Abigail, proud of her daughter's success in the fashionable world of Paris,
could not forbear to boast a little of the figure she cut: "The old abbés
who are Mr. Adams' particular friends call her *une ange*," she wrote
Tyler, and Madame Helvétius, meeting her at Dr. Franklin's, had thrown
herself into a chair with the exclamation, "*Mon Dieu, qu'elle est belle,
une belle figure, Monsieur Adams*. . . . . Parisian dress," Abigail added,
"with American neatness gives an advantageous appearance."[9]

Abigail and Nabby, with the guidance of the two Johns, extended
their range of visits and sight-seeing trips. They drove to the Dauphin's
palace and there with a large crowd of visitors peered at the royal infant
playing in the garden with a toy shovel, attended by a Duchess and three
ladies in waiting.

The rage of Paris were the balloon ascents. It seemed as if man had
at last conquered the air. Soon he might ride it as freely as he rode the
oceans and the land. The more daring envisioned fleets of balloons whisk-
ing their passengers hither and yon in a fraction of the time taken by
cumbersome coaches. The Adamses made up an expedition to Paris to
witness an ascent at the Tuileries. There they surrendered their tickets
at the gate and entered the great garden crowded with some ten thousand spectators. The balloon, made of silk taffeta, was shaped like an egg.
Below it hung a handsomely painted "gallery" for the balloonists.
Promptly at eleven o'clock it was moved from its moorings in the trees
to a launching site in the center of the gardens. The privilege of holding
the mooring ropes was reserved to some of the most distinguished men in
France; dukes and counts had vied for the honor. As the ropes were cut,
the balloon began to rise in a flutter of pennants and bright streamers,
slowly at first, then more rapidly, with a breath-taking buoyancy. A great
sigh of pleasure came from the crowd, awed and exhilarated at the sight
of their own species sharing the air with birds. The balloon hung for a
time in the middle distance as the aeronauts experimented with their
ballast, then it rose once more and, carried by a gentle wind, dwindled to
a gay dot on the horizon.

In the American colony of Paris, Mr. William Bingham and his beautiful bride were conspicuous. Bingham, who had made a fortune during
the Revolution, had married a sixteen-year-old beauty. With his lovely
wife in tow he was the first of a long succession of socially ambitious
Americans who were to come to Europe, seeking introductions at the
courts of royalty. Since beauty in women is irresistible, Mrs. Bingham was
looked at, talked about, admired, invited everywhere, and made her way
into the highest circles. She was only two years older than Nabby and

they soon became close friends. There was much visiting back and forth at Auteuil and at the Binghams' handsome apartments in Paris. The play *Figaro* by Beaumarchais, then at the Comédie Française, was the talk of the city. The more it was denounced as vulgar and scandalous, the more people flocked to see it. Even John and Abigail succumbed, and though they agreed with the general verdict—that it was an inconsequential trifle, "a piece of studied deception and intrigue," which by presenting a charming courtesan as the central character taught bad morals—they enjoyed the drama. That was, after all, one of the French talents: to make the scandalous gay and amusing.

Another of the great sights of Paris was the dance, the ballet. The first performance that Abigail attended shocked her. The dress and beauty of the dancers, she confessed, was enchanting, but no sooner did the dance commence, she wrote, "than I felt my delicacy wounded and I was ashamed to be seen to look at them." The dancers, clothed in the flimsiest silk and gauze with short petticoats, leaping into the air "with their feet flying and as perfectly showing their garters and drawers as though no petticoat had been worn," Abigail wrote her sister, "was a sight altogether new to me." To the Puritan lady, the body was a perilous thing, the home of dark passions and desires. If the face was a mask, the body should, in the same spirit, be shrouded. The feeling was not born of prudery but of an awareness of the body's extraordinary power, its dangerous magnificence. From its founding Puritan New England had been abnormally sensitive to dancing. It had seen it, not as the exuberant human counterpart to the harmony of the spheres, but as a kind of abandoned play which invited the senses to break through the restraints of will and become license and lechery. The danger, of course, had not been an imaginary one. To rob the dance of its mad, bacchanalian elements took considerable time and ingenuity, and required formalities as rigid as those of the Church or the law.

But Abigail, a sensualist herself, was quickly won over. The dancers were, to be sure, of a marvelous gracefulness, "as light as air, and as quick as lightning." If her moral instincts sounded the alarm, her senses were charmed, and she soon confessed to Mary Cranch that "repeatedly seeing these dances has worn off that disgust which I at first felt, and . . . I see them now with pleasure." Yet the pleasure was tinged with uneasiness, for, characteristically, she could not forget "the tendency of these things, the passions they must excite, and the known character . . . which is attached to an opera girl. . . . And O!" she added, "the music, vocal and instrumental, it has a soft, persuasive power and a dying sound." The singers were "clad in all the most pleasing and various ornaments of dress . . . singing like cherubs to the best tuned instruments, most skillfully handled, the softest, tenderest strains; every attitude corresponding with the music." It was almost enough to convert a New England lady into a French one.[10]

At Jefferson's invitation they all went to the convent where his daughter was receiving her education to witness two novices taking the veil. Here, where they touched the rich and moving pageantry of a culture alien to their own, mother and daughter were in spite of themselves deeply moved and disturbed by the beautiful, dignified ritual of a church which they had been taught to regard with suspicion and distrust. Nabby wrote in her journal a detailed account of the ceremony—the lighted candles, the simple, flowing gowns of the postulants, the shaving of their heads, the chants, the forms and orders of the service, the girls prostrate on the floor before the altar, the abbess dressing them in the robes of the order, the music, the holy water, the incense; all devilish contrivances to ensnare the senses, Nabby reminded herself, but she wept nonetheless.

In November the Marquise de Lafayette returned to Paris from her country estate and Abigail went to call upon her and her charming family. George Washington Lafayette was five, and Virginia two. The Marquise, "sprightly and agreeable," met Abigail at the door and, as the latter wrote to her sister, "with the freedom of an old acquaintance and rapture peculiar to the ladies of this nation," caught her by the hand and kissed her soundly on both cheeks. Abigail was both embarrassed and pleased. She was perpetually astonished at the "ease of manners" and the naturalness of great French ladies. It was in the sharpest possible contrast to the New England reserve to which she was accustomed, but Abigail took an immediate fancy to the sweet and gracious Marquise. In contrast to many ladies of high rank, Abigail noted, she gave her time and her devotion to her children and her husband. The Marquis was visiting in the United States and when the Marquise came to dine with the Adamses in Auteuil she was so informally attired that Abigail reflected no American woman would have thought of dining out "so little dressed." But when a Virginia lady, sitting next to Abigail, whispered, "Good heavens! how awfully she is dressed," Abigail sprang at once to the defense of her new friend. "The lady's rank," she whispered coldly, "sets her above the formalities of dress." While Abigail had to admit that the Marquise was a little overrouged, and perhaps too casually dressed, she admired her neatness and style.

On New Year's Day the foreign ministers, by tradition, paid their respects to the King. Every branch of the royal family must be visited and presents must be given to all the servants of the court. "If you miss one of these harpies," Abigail wrote Cotton Tufts, "they will follow you from Versailles to Paris." The servants of the Adams household all expected New Year's gifts, and in addition there was the clerk of the parish, the newspaper carrier—Abigail did not know where it was to end. These extortions made her more American than ever.[11]

The feast days and fast days, the saints' days, the holy days were a puzzle to Abigail. It complicated the life of a housekeeper to be constantly fretted by such concerns. Le jour des rois, a major feast day, was celebrated on January 25. The day before it was the French custom to make a large meat pie into which was put one bean. When the pie was divided the person who got the bean reigned as king or queen in the household the following day.

The pie was baked and at dinner the family took turns helping themselves to slices and searching for the ennobling bean. Nabby took the first slice but, "poor girl, no bean, and no queen." John Quincy was next and equally unsuccessful though he took an uncommonly large slice and dissected it with mathematical precision. Abigail followed her son, declaring emphatically that she had no cravings for royalty, and again, no bean. Thereupon John, who had been silently gnawing his chicken bone, seized the remaining half of the pie, slashed it to pieces with his knife, scattering crumbs far and wide, and captured the elusive bean. "And thus," he declared, brandishing his knife, "are kingdoms obtained." But the butler who had watched the performance denied him the title—the laws of the pie left it to chance, not force, to decide the succession, he said firmly, and John was forced to abdicate.[12]

The winter was mild (there was only one brief but blessed New England style snowstorm) and the spring was dry. The result was a drought that blighted the young grass and caused "such a scarcity of herbage," Abigail wrote to Isaac Smith, "that the poor people in many places have been obliged to kill their cattle to prevent their starving." But at least the drought had silenced the French agitation against American trade with the West Indian possessions of France. Abigail found the ducks, geese, and turkeys "very indifferent" and very expensive. Even stuffed with truffles they made poor fare, in her view. Fish was also dear—she paid three gold louis for a turbot and ten livres for an eel, but the capons and poulards were the best in the world.

Both Abigail and John, obliged to live on the meager dole of Congress, complained that people were not concerned with whether a man was "qualified for his office, but [with] how many domestics and horses" he kept. "If he is not able to support an army of them, all of whose business it is to rob and plunder," Abigail wrote indignantly, "he is considered as a very small person indeed." When the Dutch minister came to dinner he arrived in a coach driven by six horses and was attended by five liveried servants. Such displays made Abigail "wish to return to America where frugality and economy are or ought to be considered as virtues."[13]

Amid all the attractions of Paris and the pleasures of country life at Auteuil, Abigail missed her Braintree relatives and friends. Her inability to speak French was a blight on her social life and despite the frequent excursions to the city she was often lonely in the big, cold house. She worried about her little charities and benefactions in Braintree and wrote Dr. Tufts to add to the list of the poor who received regular contributions from her the wife of John Hayden. "I wish it was in my power to enlarge the sums and increase the number," she added.

She yearned for news of home and waited impatiently for a packet of letters from Boston. When they arrived at last—letters from Charles and Tommy, Richard Cranch and Mary, Eliza Shaw and Dr. Tufts—the family was all together in the drawing room at Auteuil, John in his easy chair beside the table reading Plato; Abigail entertaining herself with the *Letters of an American Farmer;* Nabby sitting pensively on a stool by the fire. John Quincy was the postman and he delivered the precious bundle to his father who, to tease, cut the cords with maddening deliberation and unwrapped the letters, peering at each one through his glasses while everyone fidgeted with impatience. "Here is one for you, my dear, and here is another; and here, Miss Nabby, are four, five, upon my word, six, for you and yet more for your mamma." While Nabby, blushing with pleasure, gathered hers up and fled the room, he added ruefully, "Well, I fancy I shall come off but slenderly. One only for me."

When the next batch of letters from America arrived, Abigail and John were alone at Auteuil. Nabby and John Quincy had gone to Paris to a play. As Briesler entered the room with a packet in his hands, Abigail cried out at once, "From America! I know they are from America!" and seized her scissors to cut the cords that bound them. Sorting them out, Abigail tucked away Nabby's letters from Royall Tyler. Some time later the barking of Caesar, the dog, and the ringing of the gate bell announced the children's return and in a few minutes Nabby appeared, rosy and glowing from the ride through the cold night air, followed by John Quincy, his hands filled with rulers, calipers, protractors, pen and paper for his mathematics lesson. Abigail, full of her surprise, played out the little drama. Was Nabby cold? Had they enjoyed the plays? What had they seen? Molière. A variety of his plays at the Palais Royal. Finally, "Come take off your cloak and I will give you a New Year's present. . . . Off went the cloak in an instant." Abigail reported. "Then I dealt the letters one by one, at every one Miss calling out for more, until I had exhausted the budget." Nabby devoured their contents but so jealously that Abigail could "hardly get a peep at a single line. . . . . I believe you will think by my thus trifling that I am imbued with the frivolity of the nation," Abigail added in her letter to Tyler describing the scene.[14]

From Mary Cranch she got news of family matters. Mary had opened the house to get some of John's clothes, but the moths had gotten to the woolens and everything was wrinkled and musty from having been laid away so long. In addition most of the clothes were out of style. Royall

Tyler was a model of industry, shut away in his room with dozens of books from Adams' library for a week together, scarcely interrupting his studies to eat. Although he was an erratic letter writer himself, he fretted over not receiving enough letters from Nabby. He would, he told Mary, rather receive a number of short letters than one volume. "One letter from the heart and sent in *season* was worth all of them," Mary replied pointedly. To which he replied that he had no excuse for not writing more often and looked so miserable that Mary could find no answer.[15]

Eliza Shaw wrote that Charles and Tommy were making good progress in their studies. They were also taking singing and dancing lessons, and Charles, grown so tall that Abigail would hardly recognize him, excelled. He danced, Abigail's sister wrote, "exquisitely," adding, "You know what an ear he has for music. . . . He is grace in all his motions and attitudes." His habit of hanging his head was much improved. At the end of dancing class the pupils had had a ball in the new assembly room and it fell to Charles, as the most accomplished dancer, to have the honor of opening it with Sally White in a minuet. "I find the misses all like to have him for a partner," his proud aunt wrote. In a few months he would be going up to the university to enter as a freshman. Thomas was a "very good child" who did not "want for fondling because you are absent," Eliza assured Abigail. "He has had many a kind stroke and kiss upon that account. . . . I think his natural roughness is much worn off."[16]

XLV

WHILE Abigail and Nabby explored the attractions of Paris and its environs, John labored with Franklin and Jefferson at Passy on drafts of the commercial treaties which the three men had been commissioned to negotiate with twenty European powers. It was a tedious task although the commissioners worked together amicably enough. "We proceed with wonderful harmony, good humor, and unanimity," Adams wrote Gerry, and to Dana he confessed, "The Dr. is very gracious, never so much so since he was born, at least since I knew him."[1]

In Jefferson John felt he had discovered a kindred spirit. Arthur Lee had written a caustic warning against his fellow Virginian: "His genius is mediocre, his application great, his affectation greater, his vanity greater than all." But from the first Adams found him a thoroughly congenial companion. The catholicity of Jefferson's tastes delighted him; their conversations ranged from the principles of government (on which he found his friend a little shaky) to the question of natural versus revealed religion; from the principle which made warm air rise to problems of aesthetics. "Jefferson is an excellent hand," he wrote Gerry. "You could not have sent a better. He appears to me to be infected with no party, passions or national prejudices, or any partialities but for his country." To Lee he replied firmly that his new partner was "an old friend and coadjutor whose character I studied nine or ten years ago and which I do not perceive to be altered. The same industry, integrity, and talents," he added, "remain without diminution."[2]

Two subjects were much on Adams' mind in these months: the adequacy (or inadequacy) of the Articles of Confederation as a government for the United States; and the progress of Congress in raising funds first of all to meet the interest on its foreign debt and then to pay off the principal of both foreign and domestic debts. Payment of interest on the French and Dutch loans was the most immediate problem and here Adams became once more involved in a series of desperate, last-minute, stopgap measures. As the time for the payment of each interest installment approached and no money appeared from Congress, Adams would grow increasingly apprehensive. If the interest was passed, the unfilled balance of the Dutch loan would suffer and American credit and American prestige would fall precipitously. He was alarmed at the news that Gouverneur Morris had advised Marbois that France should draw on the Dutch bankers for the interest of ten million livres on the French loan and he wrote hastily to Congress to warn them that Messrs. Willink and Staphorst did not have sufficient funds to meet the interest payments on the French loan and that drafts of them would in all probability be returned.

In addition to interest of nearly a million and a half pounds sterling on the French debt and that to the Dutch bankers of another half million, there were the expenses of the commissioners of Congress which must be met. There seemed no possibility of raising such sums in America. "Therefore," Adams wrote somberly, "we must not only forgo great future advantages, but violate contracts already made, and faith already pledged, and thereby totally ruin our credit if not expose the property of our merchants to be frozen abroad." It was that or borrow more money in Europe. Holland was the only place where money could be procured. If interest on the Dutch loan became delinquent, there would be no further credit in that country and America would be, in consequence, "absolutely desperate."[3]

Adams was concerned by reports from his American correspondents that there was a strong faction in Congress that was opposed to sending any ministers or ambassadors from the United States to European courts. This was a degree of provincialism that infuriated him. "The project of doing without ministers in Europe," he wrote Elbridge Gerry, "is as wild and impracticable as any in the flying island of Lagado—you will find yourselves obliged to have ministers and ambassadors, too, to support them like other ministers and ambassadors." When Congress "has ruined and discouraged us who are now here and driven us home in despair it will not be three years afterwards," he added, "before you will send a number of ambassadors to Europe with six or eight thousand pounds a year."[4]

John saw disturbing evidences of the spirit of isolationism in two of his closest friends, Francis Dana and Elbridge Gerry. Francis Dana wrote him a letter full of fear of foreign influences in the United States. Congress should send no ministers to European courts, he argued, because these courts would in turn send ministers of their own who would plot and intrigue to undermine American independence and embroil the United States in European quarrels. They would, moreover, by high living and dissolute behavior, set an unhappy example for the citizens of the new nation. He was opposed also to giving Congress any further powers.[5] It seemed to Adams that the cancer of interstate jealousy was growing and there was little indication that Congress would act with boldness and resolution on any issue—debts, negotiations with Great Britain, commercial arrangements, a permanent naval and military establishment, or even their own powers and authority.

Gerry likewise was adamant. "I am not of your opinion respecting either the policy or necessity of having ministers perpetually at any of the courts of Europe. . . . I never wish to see Congress surrounded by foreign ministers. I never shall hope to see the vicious policy of foreign courts introduced to ours," he wrote. And the ubiquitous William Gordon expressed his concern about the subversive efforts to strengthen the Union which he had observed. "I am not for being betrayed under that plea," he told Adams, "into a violation of the Confederation and the great fundamentals upon which it was established, and into a mode of congressional government that, by not suiting the northern climate . . . will after a time bring on fresh wars and fighting among ourselves."[6]

John's friend and Harvard classmate, Tristram Dalton, with a sharper sense of the real danger, wrote him that Massachusetts was so jealous of the powers of Congress that the General Court had instructed its delegates to work for the abolition of Robert Morris' office and the replacement of the financier by a rotating treasury board made up of members from all the states. "It appears to me impossible," Dalton wrote, "that the U. States can continue long, as such, in this unsettled situation." Dalton, in disgust at the unwillingness of his state to pay its bills or to support a vigorous government, had resigned as Speaker of the House.[7]

A more pressing problem for Adams was that of the Barbary pirates. The Emperor of Morocco and the Bey of Algiers extorted large sums from the European powers to purchase immunity from piratical attacks upon their merchants' vessels. These two improbable potentates confiscated cargoes, held passengers of captured vessels for ransom, and sold common sailors as slaves. There were two schools of thought about what America should do—pay tribute or go to war. Adams was firmly on the side of tribute. The Mediterranean was important to American commerce. War against the Barbary powers would be expensive and inconclusive. It would cost many times the yearly exaction and would during its course put a stop to United States trade in the area. If it was the intention of Congress to pay the annual levies, money should be raised and a treaty negotiated as quickly as possible. So Adams advised the new Secretary of Foreign Affairs, John Jay.[8]

Adams was also troubled by the fact the commissioners were not meeting with the success in negotiating treaties that he had anticipated. Those nations that were not allies of France seemed afraid of the Americans, he wrote Dana; moreover the merchants of the seaport cities and several of the provincial Parlements of France had protested vigorously at an edict of the King allowing United States vessels to trade with the French West

Indian islands; and the British refused to negotiate until they should have an American minister. He remained convinced that it was essential to have a minister at the British court even though it was quite possible that nothing would be accomplished in terms of a treaty agreement. If a minister failed, America could not be worse off than before the experiment. On the contrary, the country would be "better prepared to enter unanimously into measures of retaliation, renunciation, prohibition, or discouragement. . . . We are wrong to neglect or delay the exchange of ambassadors, of some denomination or other, with that Court."9

While Adams pushed the Prussian treaty to a conclusion and busied himself with the duties of the commission, Congress debated his future.

Finally, reluctantly, that body came to accept the notion of appointing a minister to the Court of St. James. The merchants were almost unanimous in clamoring for more favorable commercial arrangements. There was the matter of the slaves carried off by the British when they evacuated New York; there were the frontier posts still in the hands of British troops; the matter of the debts and the Tories—points of friction that every day grew more raw and irritated. Yet as soon as the delegates had ventured on this slippery ground, tempers and voices rose dangerously. Some members, including a number of New Yorkers and some of the Southern delegates, were opposed to Adams on the grounds that "being totally averse to the slave trade" he would not exert himself to obtain restitution for the slaves taken off by the British in violation of the treaty; others opposed him on the ground that, since he believed that justice required that British creditors have a right to try to recover lawful debts, he would not "be assiduous in executing the instructions of Congress for discharging the American merchants from payments of the interest that accrued during the war, and for postponing the payments of the principal for three years after the signing of the preliminaries for the peace."

But perhaps the most basic ground for opposition was personal. Many of the delegates disliked Adams. He could count as his enemies all the supporters of Franklin and Silas Deane plus those members who simply had a constitutional suspicion and dislike of New Englanders. The Southerners thought of him as the champion of New England fisheries and commerce. His onetime ally, Henry Laurens, had written disparagingly of him in recent letters. He had enemies left over from his days in Congress when his outspokenness and quick temper had offended tender sensibilities. For all those who felt a personal animosity toward Adams, the "private" journal (with its reference to the Spanish ambassador's calling him "the Washington of diplomacy") which he had rashly directed into Livingston's hands, and the transparent letter which he had written to the Secretary of Foreign Affairs outlining the qualifications of an ambassador to the Court of St. James, were potent weapons.

It was not safe, they argued, to trust an important diplomatic post to a man of such overweening vanity. The astute British ministers would play upon it like virtuosi and make him their own creature. The journal and the letter showed "traits of a weak passion, to which a minister ought never to be subject." Adams' supporters listened unhappily to these attacks. Their answer was that, whatever Adams' personal eccentricities, no man had served his country longer or more effectively. His accomplishments must argue his cause.

After a warm discussion, Adams and John Rutledge were both placed in nomination for the post of ambassador to the Court of St. James. Adams seemed certain to carry the election, but in a last-minute move Robert Livingston, the recently retired Secretary of Foreign Affairs, was also nominated. Livingston was a far more dangerous opponent than Rutledge. He had the wholehearted support of the Franklin-Vergennes faction and strength in the South as well as in his own state of New York. On the first ballot Adams got five states, Livingston four, and Rutledge two. Since a majority of the states was required, the election was deadlocked. For two days the alignments stood through further debates and balloting while Adams' backers worked to reconcile his opposers. The Northern states, they pointed out, would never surrender the negotiation of a commercial treaty into the hands of a Southerner. Livingston, aside from his tenure as Secretary of Foreign Affairs, had performed services in no way comparable to those of Adams. New Englanders would consider it a slap in the face if one of their most distinguished sons and one of the United States' most experienced diplomats was passed over for a comparative novice. It would seem to the world a repudiation not only of Adams but of the treaty he had helped to negotiate.

Gradually the Adams partisans, led by Elbridge Gerry, Arthur Lee, and Francis Dana, made their way by persistence and persuasiveness, and perhaps even more by the growing awareness of the delegates that there was really no reasonable alternative. They must swallow Adams if they choked. At last nine states out of the eleven present in Congress were mustered to Adams' side, and early in February he was elected first American ambassador to the Court of St. James, the post on which he had set his heart.[10]

As secretary to Adams in the legation, Congress seemed inclined to elect Colonel William Stephens Smith, formerly aide-de-camp to General Washington and member of an influential New York family. Before he would accept young Smith, Gerry, with his colleague Rufus King of Newburyport, gave him a sharp cross-examination. The Colonel had strong ties to New Yorkers who were hostile to Adams. He must pledge himself to support the American minister loyally and to avoid anything that might savor of intrigue against him, such as writing about the affairs of the ministry or Adams' execution of his duties to friends in America. They would only support him, in brief, as long as he supported Adams faithfully. The Colonel gave his interrogators satisfactory assurances, and Gerry noted that no officer in the army was thought of more highly by Washington than Colonel Smith, young as he was. He had had "a liberal education," and Gerry judged him "a sensible man and a polite one."[11]

Adams' instructions directed him to insist in "a respectful but firm manner" that the British should immediately vacate all the posts within the limits of the United States; to remonstrate against the British violation of the seventh article of the treaty of peace by carrying off the Negro slaves from New York, many of whom were refugees from Southern masters who had found their way to the city during the British occupancy; to "represent to the British ministry the strong and necessary tendency of their restrictions on our trade to incapacitate our merchants . . . to make remittances to theirs. You will represent in strong terms the losses which many of our and also of their merchants will sustain, if the former be unseasonably and immoderately pressed for the payment of debts contracted before the war."[12]

It was a kind of minor tragedy that word of his triumph, when it reached Adams, should be soiled by the unhappy details of the debate that preceded it; it was characteristically tactless of Gerry to divulge everything in a lengthy letter which included an account of the attack on Adams for his "weak passion," vanity. Stung to the quick, John made a response so remarkably and transcendentally Adamsean that one can only be astonished. He sat down and wrote for his distant friend a history and analysis of vanity, or at least that special division of it which applied to those involved in foreign affairs.

"According to all that I have read . . . of morals or seen of manners," he began, "there are, in mankind, various kinds of vanity, and every gradation of the passions." There was first of all the vanity of mere show which attempted to dazzle by "magnificence." This species of vanity frequently changed the whole character of a people because it turned them from the simplicity and frugality on which a republic must rest. Adams could never be accused of this vanity. In contrast to such vanity, there was the vanity of the "genuinely benevolent" who do good, in part at least, because they expect to be appreciated and supported for so doing. Washington's vanity, for instance, led him to conform to an ideal type of leader because he knew that only as such a leader could he win the admiration of the American people. Then there was the vanity that was marked by boasting of wealth, birth, power, learning, or virtue. Such vanity was "never indulged in . . . by a cunning politician."

Then, finally, there was the vanity which, although it might be considered a weakness, rose "from the testimony of a good conscience. . . . . When a man," Adams continued, "is conscious of services and exertions from the purest principles of virtue and benevolence" and sees his "labors

crowned with transcendent success there arises a satisfaction and sometimes a transport which he would be very wise indeed if he can at all
times conceal." Indeed, it might be argued that it was hypocrisy to try to
do so. The gentlemen of Congress apparently thought that a public
minister ought never to have "the weak passion," and he agreed
with them in principle, but where would they find a minister without a
fault? Certainly vanity was "a scurvy folly" which he despised and dis-
dained, even though he might have been guilty of it, but it was equally
the case, since the issue had been raised, that some of the greatest men
and the greatest ministers in history had been "horribly infected with it."
There were, of course, innumerable examples from antiquity; it was the
classic vice of ancient heroes and statesmen. More recently one might
name Sully and Clarendon, the Duke of Marlborough, Sir William
Temple, the Earl of Chatham, Turgot, Necker, and Bolingbroke. One
could indeed argue that vanity and greatness went together, or at least a
keen sense of one's worth, of one's capacities and powers. And, strangely
enough, foreign ministers seemed to be some of the most prominent victims of "this childish, boyish passion."

Adams was finally persuaded by his logic that vanity—if he had it,
which he was not entirely willing to concede but could not flatly deny
(because a denial would, if anything, involve him in still greater vanity)—
was a positive attribute, one might almost say an essential quality in a
foreign minister, and if the delegates to Congress had had any sense they
would have perceived it without Adams having to point it out to them.
The only man Adams knew who claimed to be free from vanity was
Franklin and he in his heart was "the vainest man and the falsest character I have ever met with in life." As for his rivals for the office—Livingston
and Rutledge—both men had at least as much of the weak passion as
Adams himself. "These criticisms smell," he wrote in a final burst of
indignation, "as rank as the ripeness of rabbit's tail, of French politics."

The "piddlers may nibble at inadvertences, at unguarded expressions
in times of great agitation of mind or at excesses of joy," but Adams would
pay no heed to them. Then, at last catching himself busy at the old work
of self-justification, knowing that there was no justification except in the
eyes of God, knowing that this exegesis of vanity was the work of a
proud and stubborn and inordinately sensitive man, with that insight
into himself which redeemed him, he added, "When a man is hurt he
loves to talk of his wound, and I know of no other way to account for this
long letter." Having written, he felt better; he did not send the letter, but
it remained among his papers, a cry of pain and outrage.[13]

The letter that he actually sent to Gerry was a restrained and carefully
composed epistle affirming his determination to uphold the wishes of
Congress, alluding to the charge of "the weak passion" in passing, and
assuring his friend that the only thing near his heart was "an arrangement

with England to mutual satisfaction so as to prevent war . . . and I am persuaded, he added, "that a settlement with Spain, harmony with France, and agreement with all the other courts and nations of Europe would follow it."[14] As for the appointment of Colonel Smith as secretary, even though he was a "Knight of the Cincinnatus" he would receive every kindness and consideration from Adams. To Richard Henry Lee he wrote, "I perceive I have lately received a trouncing in Congress, and perhaps not wholly unmerited."[15]

Writing to his friend Jay, now Secretary of Foreign Affairs, about his appointment, he spoke of the need for strong action by Congress if Great Britain was to be dealt with effectively. The British were boasting that all the prophecies of the loss of American trade as a consequence of the Revolution had proved groundless. At the end of the war all the nations of Europe had competed for the commerce of the United States, but the superior abilities of the British manufacturers, the cheaper prices and better articles, the greater capital and better credit facilities of the British had drawn American trade inevitably to British ports. The British had indeed to a large extent come to monopolize American commerce once more. Such, Adams continued, was "the pride and arrogance" of the British, and "such . . . the feeble means and forces of your minister, that his hopes are fainter than his fears. . . . There is no evil under the sun which I dread so much as another war, not so much from a fear of our enemies as from the foibles of our friends."[16]

If he wrote circumspectly to Jay and to his friends in Congress about his appointment, expressing in rather formal terms his gratitude, his hopes and fears for his mission, his determination to do his best and his willingness that the office might have gone to someone else, John quite let himself go in a letter to Mercy Warren. The time had come at last, he wrote, when the United States of America were to have a minister at the Court of Great Britain, "a time foretold by the prophets and seers and dreamers of dreams." The child grown to a sturdy man was to approach the parent as an equal. His only regret was that the task had not fallen to someone better equipped than he. He would certainly meet with enough problems and dilemmas "to try the strongest nerves." There were "groups upon groups of Tories and refugees . . . in the variety of their shapes and shades of their colors, the numbers of emissaries from other parts of Europe, the concourse of unexceptionable Americans, the impassioned English, Scotch and Irish all watching his motions and most of them wishing and contriving his fall."[17]

Now that Adams had obtained at last the prize which he had so coveted, he set out, of course, to convince the world and himself that he had not really wanted it so much after all. He engaged in the usual interior dialogue (and frequently exterior, too) about his motives and ambitions and about the positive and negative aspects of his new assignment. He, and more especially Abigail, would find life pleasanter in England, but he realized that he would be far more vulnerable to criticism from Congress as an ambassador to England than as a commissioner to negotiate European treaties and he had an ever tender concern for his reputation. The task would be a difficult and arduous one; the British would resent and doubtless snub him, but he was determined to be unflinching in his advocacy of the cause of his country. Above everything else there was what might be called the symbolic nature of his mission. It was this of which the Count de Vergennes spoke when Adams went to Versailles to announce his appointment to the French minister.

Vergennes, bland and smiling, expressed his felicitations, to which Adams replied politely that the mission probably merited compassion more than felicitation "because . . . it is a species of degradation in the eyes of Europe, after having been accredited to the King of France, to be sent to any other court." The Count bowed: "But permit me to say it is a great thing to be the first ambassador from your country to the country you sprang from. It is a mark." John affected an indifference that could hardly have deceived the shrewd Count. He cared little for such matters, he replied. His only concern was the difficulty, not the honor, of the service.

John took pleasure also in the remarks of a foreign minister who, congratulating him upon his appointment, said, "You have been often in England?"

"Never," Adams answered, "but once in November and December 1783."

"You have relations in England, no doubt?"

"None at all."

"How can that be? You are of English extraction?"

"Neither my father or mother, grandfather or grandmother, great-grandfather or great-grandmother, nor any other relation that I know of, or care a farthing for, has been in England these one hundred and fifty years; so that you see I have not one drop of blood in my veins but what is American."

"Ay, we have seen proof enough of that," his interrogator replied dryly.

"I was vain enough to be pleased with it," Adams wrote in his diary.[18]

There were numerous details to attend to before Adams could depart for England. His commission to negotiate European treaties remained in force and he decided that he could maintain contact with Jefferson by correspondence. He was still technically minister to the United Provinces and was uncertain about how he should properly take leave of their high mightinesses and the Stadtholder. He and Abigail decided to ship John Quincy back to Boston so that he could enter the junior class at Harvard and graduate with classmates his own age. On the twelfth of May the young man left Auteuil for L'Orient to embark for America weighed down with dozens of letters of introduction from his proud father.

It was a difficult parting; they were so much of one spirit, father and son. John Quincy had been his father's personal secretary for almost a year; they had studied together, walked together in the Bois and discussed politics and diplomacy by the hour. It was a cruel wrench to give him up, but the presence of Abigail and Nabby reconciled John to his loss and he found pleasure in anticipating his son's successes in America. Surely everyone would succumb to a young man so handsome, so learned, so traveled, and so wise for his years.

John Quincy's parting with Nabby was deeply affecting to both of them. They had lived in an intimacy all the closer for their years of separation. They had so recently discovered each other that it was heart-rending to part; both promised, as a special pledge of their devotion, to write daily to each other and John Quincy went off bearing letters and tender messages to Royall Tyler. It was Nabby's dearest wish that her brother and her fiancé might become fast friends. She had received no letters from her lover in recent months and she charged her brother to exact assurances that his ardor had not cooled.

It was difficult also to leave Auteuil in the delicate beauty of spring. The garden was coming into bloom, the fishpond and fountain had just been put in order and the noise of cascading water was a grace note in the mild evening air. "The forest trees are new clad in green," Abigail wrote her sister, "several beautiful rows of which form arched bowers at the bottom of our garden." She confessed to Charles Storer that the thought of her impending departure caused her "some pain . . . for it is, as we say, a dying leave when we quit a place with no thought of ever returning."[19] John wrote to Charles Dumas, "What shall I do in London for *my* garden, *my* park, *my* river, and *my* plain? You see I call all the environs of Auteuil *mine*, and with good reason, for I will lay a wager they have given me more pleasure in the last nine months than they ever afforded their legal and royal proprietors for a century."[20]

But the greatest loss was the company and conversation of Jefferson. While Adams consoled himself with the prospects of a correspondence of "friendship, confidence, and affection," Abigail wrote Mary, "I shall really regret to leave Mr. Jefferson. He is one of the choice ones of the earth."[21]

On the twentieth of May the Adamses set out for Calais—John, Abigail, Nabby, and Esther Field in the carriage, Esther with the bird cage on her lap containing Abigail's songbird, John Briesler mounted beside the coachman. The servants, whom Abigail had grown fond of, lazy though they were, gathered on the steps to wave farewell and weep with Gallic emotion at the departure of their strange American master and mistress.

Abigail's bird fluttered so alarmingly in its cage that she decided to leave it with the weeping Pauline and its bestowal brought another cascade of tears from the girl.

From Auteuil the little party rode through a normally verdant country-side sadly seared by drought. "The country is a heap of ashes," John wrote to Jefferson, ". . . all sorts of grain is short, thin, pale, and feeble." There were no peas, no salad, no vegetables to be had at the inns and posthouses along the road. The sheep and cattle browsed forlornly "like droves of walking skeletons." Jefferson's going-away present had been a copy of his recently published book *Notes on the State of Virginia* which had been privately printed in an edition of two hundred copies for distribution to his friends. John, Abigail, and Nabby relieved the tedium of their trip by reading aloud from it. "It will do its author and his country great honor," Adams wrote. "The passages upon slavery are worth diamonds. They will have more effect than volumes written by mere philosophers." The only criticism that the ladies had to offer was that he should have mentioned West and Copley as having a secure place among his list of American geniuses, "because they think them the greatest painters of the age." Jefferson replied that the departure of the Adams family had left him "in the dumps," adding, "My afternoons hang heavily on me."[22]

For Abigail, who missed her songbird acutely, the Channel crossing brought an unexpected bonus. The rough waters made a young French-man seasick and Abigail ministered so skillfully to him that he insisted on her accepting two songbirds of his own as an expression of his gratitude.

XLVI

O<small>N THE</small> twenty-fifth of May, John and his entourage arrived in
London and made for the Adelphi. They found, however, that the
hotel was filled, and indeed so was every other. They had arrived at
a bad time. Parliament was sitting, it was the King's birthday, and the
music of Handel was being performed at Westminster Abbey. They finally
found an apartment at the Bath Hotel in Piccadilly and moved in, bag
and baggage. John had hardly time to get his bearings before he was
greeted by an editorial in the *Public Advertiser* which addressed him as
"His Excellency John Adams (honest John Adams), the ambassador of
America," and exclaimed: "An ambassador from America! Good heavens,
what a sound! The Gazette surely never announced anything so extraordinary before. . . . This will be such a phenomenon in the *corps
diplomatique* that 'tis hard to say which can excite indignation most, the
insolence of those who appoint the character, or the meanness of those
who receive it." The American refugees—"very desperate, bitter, and
venomous," Abigail called them—spread the rumor that Adams would
never be received by the King. The upstart minister of a treacherous
and ungrateful nation would be left to cool his heels at the Bath Hotel,
they predicted.

As soon as they were settled in the hotel Adams notified Lord
Carmarthen, the Secretary of State for Foreign Affairs, of his arrival. The
minister replied, inviting Adams to come to his home at Grosvenor Square
or to his office the following day. Adams went to Grosvenor Square where
he was "admitted in an instant and politely received." He showed
Carmarthen his commission and left him a copy and the Secretary
informed him that he would be presented to the King "in his closet" the
following Wednesday, and at that time should deliver his letter of
credence from the United States of America.

The master of ceremonies, Sir Clement Cotterell, who called on Adams
to brief him on matters of etiquette in his presentation to the King,
told him that it was customary for foreign ministers to address both Their

Majesties in terms "as complimentary as possible." Although he professed to consider it a chore, Adams was pleased at the opportunity to deliver a formal address. He spent much time on a speech which he hoped would be a milestone in the reconciliation of the two nations. Into it went all his admiration and affection for the country out of whose womb America had been born and under whose protection it had grown to manhood; he thus abandoned himself to emotions by no means inappropriate to the occasion.

He would assure His Majesty of the unanimous disposition of the United States "to cultivate the most friendly and liberal intercourse" between His Majesty's subjects and their own citizens. "The appointment of a public minister from the United States to Your Majesty's court will form," he wrote, "an epoch in the history of England and of America." He thought himself "more fortunate than all my fellow citizens in having the distinguished honor to be the first to stand in Your Majesty's royal presence in a diplomatic character." It was his sincerest wish to be "instrumental in recommending my country, more and more, to Your Majesty's royal benevolence; and of restoring an entire esteem, confidence and affection, or, in better words, the old good nature and good humor between people who, though separated by the ocean and under different governments, have the same language, a similar religion, and kindred blood."

There was a touch of simple vanity in the speech and the perfect tactfulness of genuine feeling. John went over it with Abigail and, reassured by her approval, committed it to memory.

The time was short before his presentation and besides the speech there were a number of things to be done. At the advice of the British minister in Paris, John had bought a handsome new coat for the occasion. Abigail checked a dozen times the various articles of apparel—his black silk breeches and silk stockings, his buckled shoes, his sword, his sash, his hat, and finally his wig, which must be carefully dressed and powdered. On the morning of the presentation Briesler took special pains with his toilet. Abigail and Nabby approved the results and pronounced him handsome and distinguished-looking to a fault. His nervousness was quite apparent as he fidgeted with his sword and gloves. Sir Clement called for him and took him to Lord Carmarthen's office in Cleveland Row. The Foreign Secretary then carried Adams with him in his coach to the court and ushered him to the antechamber, "very full of ministers of state, lords, and bishops, and all sorts of courtiers." The Dutch and Swedish ministers, perhaps noticing Adams' agitation came up to chat and in a few minutes Carmarthen returned to escort him to the King's closet. The door was closed after him and Adams found himself alone with the King and the Foreign Secretary. He bowed the three times that etiquette required—at the door, again halfway into the room, and a third time standing directly before His Majesty. It was a strange and dramatic confrontation—two short, stout men, both rather choleric, stubborn and strong-willed, sharing a certain emotional instability and a native shrewdness and wit. They were both great talkers and both, in their hearts, farmers. They both lived in worlds where they felt frequently that every man's hand was turned against them. One was the King of the most powerful nation in the world, the other's permanent rank that of a provincial lawyer and farmer. It was the New England farmer who represented victory and the King who had been forced to accept defeat. The name of Adams, John or Samuel, had been a stench in the nostrils of George III for almost twenty years and now an Adams stood before him, ambassador from those colonies which not so long ago had been the King's special treasure.

Both men were agitated and ill at ease. Adams, obviously nervous, ("I felt more," he wrote later, "than I did or could express") delivered his speech as best he could and the King listened "with a most apparent emotion . . . very much affected" and replied with a tremor in his voice: "Sir—the circumstances of this audience are so extraordinary, the language you have now held is so extremely proper and the feelings you have discovered so justly adapted to the occasion, that I must say that I not only receive with pleasure the assurance of the friendly dispositions of the United States, but that I am very glad the choice has fallen upon you to be their minister. . . . I will be very frank with you," the King continued slowly, rather haltingly, searching out his words. "I was the last to consent to the separation; but the separation having been made, and having become inevitable, I have always said, as I say now, that I would be the first to meet the friendship of the United States as an independent power."

Then in a more informal spirit the King asked Adams if he had come most recently from France. "Yes, Your Majesty." The King gave his short, barking laugh. "There is an opinion among some people that you are not the most attached of all your countrymen to the manners of France." Adams was disconcerted at the remark, but he adopted the King's light air and answered: "That opinion, sir, is not mistaken; I must avow to Your Majesty I have no attachment but to my own country."

"An honest man will never have any other," the King replied.

The King spoke a few words to Lord Carmarthen and then turned and bowed to Adams, signifying that the audience was at an end. The American retreated, walking backward with as much grace as he could affect, bowed a last time at the door, and withdrew. As he left the room the master of ceremonies joined him and led him "through the apartments . . . several stages of servants, gentlemen porters and underporters, roaring out like thunder . . . 'Mr. Adams' servants, Mr. Adams' carriage.'"[1]

The long-dreamed-of moment was over; triumph and ordeal, Adams had come through with credit to himself and his country. He was much heartened by the King's friendly reception; it augured well for the success of his mission. Back at the Bath Hotel he gave the anxiously waiting ladies a detailed account of his presentation: how the King had replied to his address, what the King wore, his manner and so on.

On the day after his presentation Adams went to court for the King's birthday. In contrast to the punctilio of the French monarch on such occasions, Adams observed that the King had some personal word for each one of the hundreds of people who paid their respects to him. Having expressed his own felicitations and received a gracious reply, Adams stationed himself near the Spanish ambassador and listened, fascinated, to the King's conversation. He was an informed and interesting talker with a flair for epigram. Adams heard him say to the Spaniard in first-rate French that one of the troubles with the world was that the great enemy of "the good" was "the better," and John applied the phrase to the folly of the King's ministers in prevailing on him to try to replace "the good" with "the better" in America.

The Handel festival, which had just started, reminded the King of his passion for the works of that musician. To Handel, he declared, he owed the greatest happiness of his life. He remembered the composer well from the days of his own youth and he recalled his prophecy: "That young man will preserve my music." Recounting the conversation later to Abigail and Nabby over a pot of tea in their apartment at the Bath Hotel, Adams declared he had never heard such talk at a court. He marveled that the King had the energy to take personal notice of so many hundreds of people and to talk unconcernedly and delightfully to particular individuals in the midst of the vast crush that surged around him.

Having had his appetite whetted, Adams, who loved good talk and was most anxious to relieve the tedium of court routine, took advantage of every opportunity at St. James either to engage the King in conversation or to station himself where he could overhear the King talking to others. In one conversation the King deplored the decadence of the modern age. For himself, he believed in order and regularity. He always rose at five o'clock in the morning—the first person up in the cold, drafty palace during the winter months—and usually made his own fire. The man not capable of helping himself, he told his sympathetic listener, was a slave. He even shaved himself, he confided, and dressed his own "scratch wig." John, of course, was charmed. George was a man after his own heart. As Adams had no fund of small talk, the King's facility dazzled him and he put him down as "the greatest talker in Christendom," adding, "It is but justice to say that it was agreeable and instructive to hear . . . His Majesty said as many things which deserved to be remembered as any sage I ever heard." From one who had conversed with many of the greatest philosophers, statesmen, and litterateurs of the day, this was high praise.

The next court ceremony was Adams' presentation to Queen Charlotte. Again he prepared a gracious speech, expressing his pleasure at making his court "to a great Queen whose royal virtues, talents, and accomplishments have ever been acknowledged in America . . . as an example to Princesses, and the glory of her sex. . . . Permit me, madam," he continued, "to recommend to Your Majesty's royal goodness a rising empire and an infant, virgin world. . . . Another Europe, madam, is rising in America. . . . To a philosophical mind like Your Majesty, there cannot be a more pleasing contemplation than this prospect of doubling the human species and augmenting at the same time their prosperity and happiness. It will in future ages be the glory of these kingdoms to have first planted that country; and to have there sown those seeds of science, of liberty, of virtue, and permit me, madam, to add, of piety, which alone constitute the prosperity of nations and the happiness of the human race."

Adams was less successful with the Queen than he had been with the King. She, poor lady, doubtless held him responsible for many of the King's sleepless nights and temper tantrums, and she was startled and annoyed by his presumptuous suggestion that the future glory of England would be that she had spawned America. She answered almost curtly, thanking him for his "civilities" and declaring, "I am glad to see you in this country."[2]

While Adams bustled about making official calls, Abigail and Nabby went to hear Handel's *Messiah* at Westminster Abbey. "It was sublime beyond description," Abigail wrote Jefferson. "I most sincerely wished for your presence as your favorite passion would have received the highest gratification." Listening, Abigail could easily imagine she was among angels, auditor of a heavenly choir.[3]

The presentation of Abigail and Nabby at court was the next order of official business. Custom required it and Abigail set about the preparations, directing her dressmaker to make her a gown that should be "elegant, but plain as I could possibly appear, with decency." The result was a dress of "white lutestring, covered and trimmed with white crepe, festooned with lilac ribbon and mock point lace over a hoop of enormous extent." Ruffled cuffs, a dress cap with lace lappets, two white plumes and a lace handkerchief, pearl pins, earrings and necklace completed her "rigging," as she put it. When the day arrived for the presentation she and Nabby set off handsomely if plainly attired with wreaths of flowers in their hair.

At the court Abigail was introduced to Lord Carmarthen and the Swedish and Polish ministers; Count Sarsfield paid his compliments, as did the Baron Lynden, the Dutch minister. The only lady present whom

Abigail knew was the Countess Effingham, whose husband had resigned his commission in the British army rather than serve against the Americans. Abigail, Nabby, and the three daughters of the Marquis of Lothian, who were to be presented at the same time, were placed in a circle in the crowded drawing room. The King entered and proceeded around to the right accompanied by a lord in waiting who introduced those being presented to the King while the Queen with a lady in waiting went to the left. The King's practice of speaking to each person and the large number present made the ceremony a lengthy one. When George III came to Abigail she removed her right glove. The King, looking "very jovial and good-humored," "saluted" her left cheek and then asked if she had taken a walk that morning. Abigail, recalling her painstaking preparations to go to court, was tempted to reply that she had been too busy getting dressed, but she replied, "No, sire."

"Don't you love walking?" the King pressed her.

"No, I fear I am rather indolent in that respect," she answered, thinking a little ruefully of her plumpness. The King bowed and passed on.

It was two hours more before the Queen and the Princess Royal reached Abigail. As in the interview with Adams, the Queen seemed embarrassed and ill at ease and Abigail herself felt uncomfortable. The Queen asked politely enough if she had found a house that suited her and if she liked its location and the Princess, as Abigail wrote her sister, "looked compassionate and asked me if I was not much fatigued." The Princess Augusta, who followed her older sister, asked Nabby if she had visited England before and spoke to her "with . . . the ease and freedom of an old acquaintance." In Abigail's opinion the Princesses, dressed in black and silver silk with "their heads full of diamond pins," were "pretty rather than beautiful, well shaped, with fair complexions" and a marked resemblance to their father. But the Queen, in purple, was neither well shaped nor handsome and the ladies of the court, in contrast to those at Versailles, were in general "very plain, ill shaped, and ugly."[4] It did not seem to her that fine feathers made fine birds. "I found the court like the rest of mankind," she wrote John Quincy, "mere men and women, and not of the most personable kind neither." She and Nabby were as elegantly and neatly if not as richly attired as anyone and made as good an appearance. "I had vanity enough," Abigail noted, "to come away quite self-satisfied. . . . I will not strike my colors to many of them."[5] But the four hours of standing were an ordeal and Abigail could not forbear to reflect, "What a fool do I look like to be thus accoutered and stand here for four hours together, only to be spoken to by royalty."

Nabby, taking her cue from Abigail, wrote scornfully to John Quincy of the "ridiculous ceremony." Like her father, she rather took a fancy to the King and found the Queen a "haughty, proud, imperious dame . . .

excessively mortified to see our family at her drawing room." The Prince of Wales looked "stuffed."

The illness of Lord Carmarthen delayed Adams' conference with the Foreign Secretary for several weeks. Meanwhile he received from Tristram Dalton a graphic account of the condition of New England trade. When British ships had sailed into Boston Harbor fully loaded and American vessels half empty—a dramatic illustration of the effect of British commercial policy—"the spirit of '75 had revived," and the North End mobs with John Hancock at their head had rioted and threatened the life and property of several British agents in the city. Trade was finding its way, Dalton wrote, from Boston to Nova Scotia. British ships carried off American products to British ports while American ships and crews, denied a part in such trade, rotted at anchor. The prohibitive duty that Parliament had imposed on American whale oil in an effort to reserve the industry to British ships and sailors was ruining seaport towns which had depended on the whale fishery for their livelihood. Boston itself, Dalton informed Adams, was riddled with jealousy and suspicion. The merchants excluded from British trade were jealous of those who still managed to carry on some. The farmers, feeling the pinch, suspected the tradesmen and merchants of exploiting them. Dalton felt that the situation was an explosive one and that remedies of some kind were urgently needed.[6]

The same word came to Adams from James Sullivan, who noted that the suggestion that Congress be given more power to regulate American commerce and impose retaliatory restrictions on British trade was coldly received in New England. Congress, it was feared, would use the power to raise an army and a navy and "coerce the people." To the argument that the United States would "never be happy at home or respectable abroad until we are united by a corporeal relation and under one system of government," the answer was given that it was possible to preserve "our federal relation and . . . [support] the separate sovereignty of the states." The Northern states, Sullivan wrote, were jealous of the Southern. They foresaw the Union growing through the addition of states in the South, additions that would give the South control over the Union, and they professed to be afraid "that their system of politics, should we ever consolidate our governments, will reduce the Union to a vile aristocracy or disunite the federated powers." Much, therefore, depended on Adams' negotiation. Perhaps an unsuccessful outcome might be more helpful to the cause of good government than a successful one, since it was Sullivan's guess that "a little more calamity may drive us into the necessity of entertaining more national ideas."[7]

A letter from Stephen Higginson, one of Boston's leading merchants, contrasted New England before the war to its present state. Whale oil shipped to London had been a major item which had brought back hard-cash remittances. New England rum had gone to Newfoundland, Nova Scotia, and Quebec and brought back bills of exchange upon Britain which could be used to pay for British imports. The New Englanders had built new ships which carried salt fish to the West Indies, took on products of the islands, carried them to London and then ships and cargoes were sold to British merchants. All the salt fish that was not carried to the Indies was traded to Spain and Portugal. Pot- and pearlash had gone to London.

Since the peace, Higginson wrote, remittances to Britain had largely been in the form of rice and tobacco. Higginson, like many others, pointed out that Americans could not pay their debts to the British as long as they had an unfavorable balance of trade. New England must have an outlet for its rum so that its merchants could bring back molasses from the Indies. If Adams' negotiations failed, Higginson wrote, "despair and discontent will very generally appear in our seaport towns."[8]

Adams replied, warning the merchants that they must depend upon themselves rather than upon him or upon Great Britain. Everything must be done to revive the whale fishery "which is our glory" and to search out other markets. With Jefferson, Adams had enlisted Lafayette in an effort to get a contract for American whale oil, which was superior to all other whale oils because, while other fishermen brought back their whales and rendered them on shore, allowing the oil to become rancid, the Americans extracted the oil at sea and brought it home pure and fresh. In Adams' lyrical description, American spermaceti oil "preserves its fluidity in the cold, gives a bright, clear and glorious flame; burns till nine o'clock in the morning and is cheaper." It could be burned in street lights, in churches, and in homes in the form of "beautiful spermaceti candles."[9]

When Carmarthen recovered from his indisposition Adams was summoned to the office in Cleveland Row. There Carmarthen assured him that the King and his ministers were anxious to cultivate "the most cordial friendship" with America and to try to "dissipate every little animosity" that might exist between the citizens of the United States and Great Britain. Adams replied in a similar spirit and then enumerated for the Foreign Secretary a list of six critical issues between the two countries which needed to be clarified or resolved.

First and most pressing was the matter of the posts within the territory of the United States which remained in the hands of the British. The second was the exportation of Negroes and other American property from New York when the British evacuated that city, items which the British had bound themselves by the seventh article of the treaty not to carry off. The third was the tendency of the restrictions on American trade "to incapacitate our merchants to make remittances" to their British counterparts. Still another was the sore point of the payment of debts contracted before the war, more specifically the question of interest on those debts during the war and the need of American merchants for extension of the time of repayment. Finally there was the matter of captures made by British vessels after the beginning of the armistice period in February 1783, and the liquidation of the charges of the prisoners of war.

In Adams' view, outside of the complicated problem of commercial regulations, the points of contention could be readily settled. The debts were perhaps the most pressing issue, and here the tardiness of the British in fulfilling their treaty engagements, Adams argued, was the principal obstacle. If the posts were evacuated, the Negroes restored or paid for, compensation given for the ships seized after the armistice, and the charges of the prisoners liquidated, the American debtors would be better able to meet their obligations. The posts still in British hands shut off Americans from a rich fur trade, the loss of the slaves deprived their masters of a source of revenue, and so on. For his own part he was sure from what he knew of the character of the people of the United States, and from all the information he could gather, "that nothing lay with greater weight upon their minds than the payment of their debts; that they thought their moral characters and their reputations as men, as well as their credit as merchants, [were] concerned in it." That at least was Adams' view of how the American debtors ought to feel. The fact was that many of them, especially the Southern planters, who made up a very large body of debtors, had no such feelings and wished only to find a way to evade payment. But Adams spoke in good faith. He could not imagine that Americans with a profound respect for the sanctity of property would try to welch on their debts.

He placed the blame squarely on the British, pointing out that the restrictions imposed by Parliament on American trade made it impossible for Americans to earn the "remittances" to repay their debt. At the conclusion of the war both British and American merchants had incurred further obligations on the assumption that the trade with America would flow back into the old channels. But Parliament had directed otherwise. All kinds of "obstructions, restrictions, and imposts" had been laid on American exports to Great Britain. "Neither rice, tobacco, pitch, tar, turpentine, ships, oil, nor other articles" which formerly had been a source of remittances could now be carried to British ports by American vessels. The trade with the West Indies, the other great source of remittances, was likewise obstructed. The British, therefore, in pressing for the immediate payment of all debts due their merchants, were imposing an impossible condition that could only bring ruin to American and

British merchants alike. The British, in effect, were demanding repayment while blocking the means of repayment.

Carmarthen listened closely and with apparent sympathy to Adams' recital. He thought things might be reconciled in time but there would be "many rubs. . . . . Passion and private interest would sometimes be in [the] way on both sides." Adams must give him the American propositions in writing so that they could be more fully considered. When Adams pressed Carmarthen on the matter of the evacuation of the posts, His Lordship was evasive. That question, too, must be more fully considered by the King's ministers.

There was one moment of embarrassment for Adams in the interview when the Foreign Secretary mentioned the report of the riot at Boston against English agents. Adams replied that the unfortunate episode simply demonstrated how much British mercantile policy was an obstacle to the restoration of good feeling between the two nations.

Despite the agreeable manner of the Foreign Secretary, Adams found, as he wrote Jay, "a reserve which convinces me that we shall have no treaty of commerce until this nation is made to feel the necessity of it." The British reasoned in this manner, Adams noted: "*Cui bono?* to what end a treaty of commerce when we are sure of as much American trade as we have occasion for without it? The experiment had been tried, and the Americans have found that they cannot supply themselves elsewhere; there must be a *quid pro quo;* and what have the United States to give in exchange for the liberty of going in their own ships to our sugar colonies and our colonies upon the continent?"

The proper answer to these "smart reasoners," Adams observed, was: "The Americans allow Britons to come in their own vessels to all their ports in this United States, and this is more than a *quid* for your *quo.* This is true reciprocity; and while we allow you this liberty, we have a right to demand it in return."

"But," replies the Briton, "you cannot avoid this; you have no government; you cannot agree to prohibit our ships and goods or to lay duties upon them."

"These ignorant sophisms of the Britons will never be confuted to any effect," Adams added, "until vigorous measures are taken by all the states in concert." He saw everywhere evidence that the British were both arrogant and complacent. Their policy was built on the assumption that the American states could not act in concert. They professed to care little for American commerce in any event. "They say," Adams noted, "that the progress of the fine arts in this kingdom has given to their manufactures a taste and skill and to their productions an elegance, cheapness, and utility so superior to any others that the demand for their merchandises from all parts of Europe is greater than ever."[10]

It did not bode well for the American cause that the Tories were pampered and made much of. Silas Deane and Joseph Galloway appeared to have the ear of the ministry and the general sentiment of the public was hostile to the United States. "The people," Adams wrote, "are deceived by numberless falsehoods industriously circulated by gazettes and conversation." The nation, indeed, seemed quite in the temper to go to war with the United States and only a lack of money and the resistance of the court prevented armed conflict. Adams despaired of accomplishing anything until the states should combine to exert a federal control of commerce, "for," he added, "I really believe it must come to that. . . . I have no hopes of a treaty before next spring, nor then without the most unanimous concurrence of all our states in vigorous measures, which shall put out of all doubt their power and will to retaliate."[11]

Adams continued to bombard Lord Carmarthen with demands for evacuation of the posts and compensation for the Negroes carried off by Clinton, but to no avail. Carmarthen, suave and affable, turned aside Adams' queries or simply ignored them.

While Adams proposed strong action by Congress as the only means of prevailing on the British ministers to modify their restrictions on American trade, Jay was writing from New York, "It gives me great pain to have occasion so often to repeat that the irregular attendance of the members of Congress has, for a long time past, prevented their paying a seasonable attention to their foreign affairs; for there have been very few, and those very short, intervals in which nine states were represented in Congress this year."[12]

Below the level of diplomatic negotiation, the Adamses lived an active and pleasant life. John himself professed to pine for his woods at Auteuil and deplored the English weather, writing to Jefferson that "the smoke and damp of this city is ominous to me," and complaining of the odors of "kitchens, cellars, stables, and servants' apartments . . . [which] pours directly on the passenger on foot. Such whiffs and puffs assault you every few steps as are enough to breed the plague if they do not suffocate you on the spot." But it was plain that he preferred London to Paris and England to France.[13] Abigail was unreserved in her delight with English things and English ways. She wrote Jefferson glowingly of the splendor of London, the elegance of the hackney coaches, and the comfort and convenience of English life. Jefferson, who had made himself a Frenchman, replied stoutly, declaring his preference for "the polite, self-denying, feeling, hospitable, good-humored people of this country and their amiability in every point of view, (though it must be confessed our streets are somewhat dirty, and our fiacres rather indifferent)" over "ten such races of rich, proud, hectoring, swearing, squibbing, carnivorous animals as those among whom you are . . . I . . . love this *people*," he wrote, "with all my heart, and think that with a better religion and a better form of government . . . their condition and their country would be most enviable."[14]

Abigail was prompt and eloquent in rebuttal. She had the advantage, she pointed out, of having visited both countries, while Jefferson knew only France. If he were to come to England, she assured him, "as husbandman you would be delighted with its appearance, the rich verdure of the fields and the high cultivation of the lands." Moreover in manufacturing "this country can boast a superiority over their Gallican neighbors." She was ready to concede that when one considered "the social affections" the English showed up poorly in comparison with the French. In addition the English were hopelessly insular. "They possess," Abigail noted, "in general a much greater narrowness of sentiment and they cannot allow their neighbors half the merit they really deserve—they affect to despise the French and hate the Americans." It was also true that the English stage had a "heavy, uncouth" air about it quite unlike the "Parisian ease and grace."

It was similarly indisputable that English manners were bad. In "civility of behavior, politeness of manners, true hospitality and benevolence," England had "much more need of going to America to learn them than our country has of any embellishment this can bestow," Abigail wrote an American friend. She had heard "more narrow prejudice, more illiberality of sentiment . . . since my residence here," she added, "than I ever saw or heard in America in my whole life." It seemed clear to Abigail that "all the contracted sentiments which we ever possessed with respect to other countries we imbibed from this [one] when we reverenced her and her sentiments as our parents."

Moreover Abigail found in England a "wretchedness and oppression enough . . . to make a wise man mad." Yet with all this she preferred England to France although she was often tempted to declare the contrary "on purpose to mortify the pride of this people, who are really, in point of civility to strangers and good breeding, not to be compared with their neighbors [the French] whom they so contemptibly despise."[15] Furthermore, the English social forms were less pleasing, at least to the ladies, than the French. Abigail objected strongly to gatherings where the ladies sat "in a cluster" talking about clothes and food and servant problems and the gentlemen collected by themselves in another part of the room to discuss the state of the stock market and review politics. After the mixing of the sexes that characterized French social affairs, such segregation seemed to her quite uncivilized.

Abigail also found the custom of passing food formal and ridiculous. It wasted time and impeded the conversation. The English were great toasters; a meal could not pass without toasts to the King, to Anglo-American solidarity, to the ladies, to this and to that. After dinner the ladies withdrew and left the gentlemen at table with their port and cigars and walnuts, and this Abigail, who so enjoyed masculine conversation and masculine minds, resented. To be herded off to the drawing room like some inferior order of being irritated her intensely. Sometimes the company went from the dining table to the card table, which also seemed a dull pastime to Abigail. Finally, English cookery could not compare to that of the French. John grumbled constantly over the half-cooked vegetables and raw meat that seemed to exhaust the culinary resources of English cooks and contrasted such fare to the inspired sauces and noble garnishings that distinguished French cooking. It was the difference between art and a kind of gross fueling of the body. (Jefferson, replying to Abigail's complaints about English food, suggested that it was the quantity of raw meat eaten by the British which rendered "their character insusceptible of civilization. I suspect," he continued, "that it is in their kitchens and not in their churches that their reformation must be worked.")

Another British characteristic that both the Adams ladies resented was that of staring. The British were the greatest starers Abigail had ever seen. It was part of their insolence and bad manners. Lady Lucy Lincoln, who lived across the street, was one of the worst offenders; Abigail, not to be outcountenanced, stared back with equal hauteur.

The fact was that the staring was simply a manifestation of the thing that in Abigail's view poisoned much of English life—snobbery. "They think much more of their titles here than in France," she wrote Eliza Shaw. The titled Englishman was often arrogant and condescending while in France people of the highest rank were often "the best bred and the politest people." The British feelings of superiority, Abigail noted, "lead them to despise all other nations." Conscious of her own preference for things American, she was determined to avoid the narrowness of spirit so conspicuous in the British. "In the cultivation of the arts and improvement in manufactures they greatly excel us," she confessed to Eliza Shaw, "but we have a native genius, capacity, and ingenuity equal to all their improvements, and much more general knowledge diffused amongst us." This was most striking in the lower orders of society. "You can scarcely form an idea," she told her sister, "how much superior our common people, as they are termed, are to those of the same rank in this country. Neither have we that servility of manners which the distinction between nobility and citizens gives to the people of this country."[16]

The class distinctions, indeed, were the most unpleasant aspect of England to John as well as to Abigail. A natural aristocracy of talents was one thing. That was simply recognition and respect for ability and accomplishment. But hereditary distinctions were odious. They warped and distorted relations between people of different classes and encouraged the English provincialism that so offended them both.

Another aspect of the English class system that annoyed them was the barrier it raised against ability and ambition in the lower orders of society. Abigail could not forbear to contrast England with America, "a young, a flourishing, a free, and, I may add, a virtuous country, uncontrolled by a royal mandate, unshackled by a military police, unfearful of the thundering anathemas of ecclesiastical power, where every individual possessed of industry and probity has a sure reward for his labor, uninfested with thousands of useless vermin whom luxury supports upon the bread of idleness."[17]

"In houses also, in furniture, in gardens and pleasure grounds, and in equipage, the wealth of France and England is displayed to a high pitch of grandeur and magnificence," she wrote Mary Cranch. But when she reflected "upon the thousands who are starving, and the millions who are loaded with taxes to support this pomp and show, I look to my happier country with an enthusiastic warmth, and pray for the continuance of that equality of rank and fortune which forms so large a portion of our happiness."[18]

To Eliza Shaw she wrote that Europe "is all lost in ceremony, parade, and venality." It was her most devout wish that "a general spirit of liberality [would] prevail and all mankind . . . be considered as one nation equally entitled to our regard as brethren of the same universal parent, and virtue [and] learning creating the only marks of distinction with us." But perhaps, she added, "this is wishing for more than mankind are capable of attaining till the millennium or the thousand years in which we are told the just shall reign upon earth."[19]

Yet despite her efforts to be impartial it seemed to Abigail that the European birds "have not half the melody of ours. Nor is their fruit half so sweet, nor their flowers half so fragrant, nor their manners half so pure, nor their people half so virtuous." She had, she protested, none of that small-minded national prejudice "of conceiving all that is good and excellent comprised within the narrow compass of the United States." The "Universal Parent" had dispensed His blessing throughout all creation, and neither seas nor mountain barriers could "contract the benevolence and good will of the liberal mind which can extend itself beyond the limits of country and kindred, and claim fellowship with Christian, Jew, or Turk." Even so, America was best.[20]

The combativeness of the British appalled Abigail. "Forgiveness of injuries is no part of their character," she wrote Jefferson, "and scarcely a day passes without a boxing match." Even in genteel Grosvenor Square, Abigail had been shocked to see ten-year-old boys stripped to the waist, fighting until the blood flowed freely, surrounded by spectators who cheered them on, "stimulating them to continue to fight, and forcing every person from the circle who attempted to prevent it. Bred up with such manners and principles," she added, "who can wonder at the licentiousness of their manners and the abuse of their pens?"[21]

The English ladies were supposed to have creamy complexions and handsome bearing, but even these virtues Abigail was unwilling to concede. She saw as many bad complexions as good ones and far more protuberant teeth than comported with a high standard of beauty. The Duchess of Devonshire, a famous beauty, was much too masculine to Abigail's way of thinking. Lady Salisbury was "small and genteel" but her complexion was bad. Lady Talbot was the fairest of all, but even she could not compare to Anne Bingham, whose husband, having conquered Paris with his American beauty, had moved on to London to pit her against the English belles, and whom Abigail never tired of looking at and praising—her animation, "the elegance of her form, and the affability of her manners."[22]

When all was said and done, England was clearly the favorite of both Abigail and her husband. But she would concede to Jefferson French superiority in manners and in the art of living, and above all in that most important feminine sphere, fashions. She commissioned the Virginian to order her four pairs of shoes from her Paris shoemaker, who would have her last. Two of them were to be satin and two faille silk of any color so long as it was fashionable. She would also like an epergne for the center of her table like the one that they had had in the house at Auteuil and which he would doubtless remember.[23]

ARLY in July the family moved into the house on Grosvenor Square near Hyde Park, which Abigail described to her sister as rather like Boston Common, only "much larger and more beautified with trees." The town house of Lord North faced the Adams residence. Thus, Abigail wrote Mary Cranch, it was clear that she had "not taken sides with Lord North but [was] still opposite to him."[1]

The house itself was handsome and spacious. On the first floor a dining room which held fifteen persons opened off a large hall. Beyond the dining room was a small sitting room where the family usually established itself after dinner, and beyond that was John's office. Over the dining room was a formal drawing room and opening off it a little room that Abigail made into a parlor in which they breakfasted and had tea. Next to it was a large sunny room which served as Adams' library and where he did most of his work. The family bedrooms were on the third floor with a fine view out over the city—a charming piece of garden, the roofs of the surrounding houses, and a forest of chimneys. The servants were domiciled on the fourth floor.

To Abigail's dismay she found she must employ an even larger staff than had bedeviled her at Auteuil. There was Mr. Spiller, the butler, a benign tyrant who presided over the other domestics; there was a footman, a German, "an honest, quiet, stupid kind of creature"; a cook; a coachman who, it turned out, was too fond of the bottle, fell off the coach driving John home one night, and had to be replaced by a stout fellow who talked an incomprehensible Cockney at a mile a minute; and a platoon of maids—upstairs, downstairs, chamber, and whatever.

Abigail's personal maid dressed her hair, looked after all the linen in the house, and sewed. The butler's business was "to take care of the wine, to market for the family, to keep the weekly accounts, to see to the table and sideboard." The housemaid made the beds and cleaned the house from the top of the kitchen stairs to the third floor. The two footmen rode behind the carriage, waited at table, polished the furniture, and answered the door. "All the doors have to be locked at all times," Abigail wrote Mary Cranch, "and you can only gain access by knocking or ringing a bell," a dramatic contrast to Braintree where no one thought of locking any door and you came and went as freely in the homes of friends as in your own house. The kitchen maid washed the silver and dishes and cleaned below stairs. Mr. Spiller suggested that Abigail should have a housekeeper, laundry maid, and porter to complete the roster of a well-run household, but she flatly refused. She felt imposed upon enough already.

The house on Grosvenor Square soon became headquarters for the American colony in London. John Quincy's friend, William Vans Murray, was a frequent visitor along with the Copleys, Paradises, Temples, Charles Bulfinch, John Trumbull, Benjamin West, and a young painter named Mather Brown. Copley had been a student of West's, and Trumbull and Brown had both come to London to study with the master. West was especially pleased with Trumbull. "I know of no young man," he declared, "who promises so much as he." Trumbull had launched himself on a heroic scene of the battle of Bunker Hill and West was delighted with it. If it was well received the young New England artist planned to paint a number of the dramatic episodes in the history of America.

One day West turned up bursting with excitement. Among a pile of old canvases in a picture cleaner's attic he had found one that struck his eye and that he had purchased for twenty guineas. When it was cleaned he found it was Titian's *Death of Actaeon*. He had already been offered a thousand pounds for the treasure.[2]

Adams took a special liking to young Mather Brown. The least talented of the group, he seemed determined to supply his deficiencies through sheer determination. He begged John to let him try his skill on a portrait, and Adams, warning him that it was a task which in his opinion at least had defeated the brilliant brush of Copley, consented to sit. The result turned out to be one of those happy coincidences of artist and subject. Brown, earnest and straightforward, quite without artistic tricks and without guile, put down a direct and expressive representation of his sitter. It was a much better likeness than that achieved by more sophisticated painters. Adams was delighted and Brown as proud as punch. Encouraged by the success of John's portrait, Abigail and Nabby sat for the young artist and again the results were much applauded. The likeness of Abigail was admirable in John's view, and he declared that the painter had exactly captured Nabby's "mixture of drollery and modesty."

The number of painters among the close circle of Adams' friends was not coincid nce. Art and architecture, the history of painting, and the theory of aesthetics were among his lifelong preoccupations. Everywhere he went in his travels he sought out the work of the masters in public or private collections.

The foreign ministers visited Grosvenor Square soon after the Adamses moved in and were "very civil," but Adams thought them a mediocre lot compared with the diplomats of The Hague and Versailles. One of his closest friends among the ministers came to be the Spanish ambassador, the Chevalier del Campo, "a very ugly man" with squinting black eyes, but with a fund of excellent conversation. Another was the Baron Lynden, Dutch minister, whom John had known at The Hague. Although Abigail called him "a sad, womanish kind of a man" and commented on his dirty linen, unshaven face, and untidy appearance, her husband treasured him for his bright and entertaining talk and his general erudition.

General Oglethorpe, the founder of the colony of Georgia, like a figure out of history, came to visit the Adamses. He was almost a hundred years old, tall and thin as a reed, his mind as sharp as it had been half a century earlier when he led his motley band of settlers to America.

The learned Dr. Jebb, an eccentric scientist and a warm supporter of America, soon became one of Adams' closest friends. They exchanged writings on law and politics and talked hours on end about political and social man, his nature and his destiny; about theology, science, art, and the progress of the race. Mrs. Jebb was a "great politicianess," which delighted Abigail, and the two ladies ranged over the American Revolution, the Irish and Polish questions, and the state of the European powers "with much animation."[3]

One of the Adamses pleasantest diversions was their weekly Sunday trip to Hackney to hear Dr. Richard Price, the radical English divine who had written a book praising the American Revolution. Abigail wrote John Quincy that she would willingly go much farther "to hear a man so liberal and so sensible and so good as he is. He has a charity which embraces all mankind and a benevolence which would do good to all of them."[4]

Among the American transients who passed through London, Adams took a special fancy to Major Langborn of Virginia. "This gentleman, who is rich," Adams noted in his diary, "has taken the whim of walking all over Europe after having walked over most of America. His observations are sensible and judicious. He walks forty-five or fifty miles a day." The Major pleased and flattered Adams by remarking that nowhere had he seen country superior to that between New York and Boston. "He is in love with New England, admires the country and its inhabitants," John noted. Langborn deplored the fact that his own Virginians were not as thrifty, industrious, and enterprising as their Northern cousins; Adams in turn offered him his receipt "for making a New England in Virginia." The meeting-house and school-house and training field were the scenes where New England men were formed, Adams told him. These institutions molded "the virtues and the talents of the people . . . their temperance, patience, fortitude, prudence, and justice, as well as their sagacity, knowledge, judgment, taste, skill, ingenuity, dexterity, and industry."[5]

The occasional meetings with Tory refugees from New England were painful to John and Abigail. For John the most heart-rending encounter was with Jonathan Sewall. He had known and loved Jonathan Sewall "as his own soul." Since their paths had parted fifteen years before, Adams had gone on to become one of the leading men of a new nation and Sewall had suffered one disappointment after another, coming finally to live the pitiful, marginal life of an exile in England. When John and Abigail heard that Sewall and his wife were in the city they decided at once to go to see them. At the simple Sewall apartment John took his schoolmate's hand in both of his and with an affectionate squeeze asked, "How do you do, my dear old friend?" After an awkward and emotional moment they fell easily into conversation, "just such as might be expected," Sewall wrote, "at the meeting of two old sincere friends after a long separation." A Revolution lay between them—one an honored leader, the other an outcast. That was the strangeness of life which had torn them apart and now brought them together again in a different world; and that was the sad, silent fact that lay behind their talk of old times and old friends. The warmth in Adams flowed to the warmth in Sewall until it seemed as though all that had divided them was an illusion, an ephemera, and they were once more young men sharing their dreams and enthusiasms, their youthful, insatiable appetites for life. They talked and talked, forgetting the time, and as the Adamses left Abigail invited the Sewalls to dine with them at Grosvenor Square.

The visit meant much to the exiled New Englander and his wife who lived for news of their former home. "Adams has a heart formed for friendship and susceptible of its finest feelings," Sewall wrote Judge Lee; "he is humane, generous, and open—warm in the friendly attachments though perhaps rather implacable to those whom he thinks his enemies." If Adams could play backgammon, "I declare I would choose him," he continued, "in preference to all the men in the world for my *fidus Achates* in my projected asylum." He felt that Adams, the diplomat, was restless and frustrated and longed to be back in Braintree. He was not qualified by nature or education, Sewall thought, "to shine in courts"—in terms of general intelligence and the technical requirements of his post he was quite equal to the office, but this was not enough. "He can't dance, drink, game, flatter, promise, dress, swear with the gentlemen, and small talk and flirt with the ladies—in short, he has none of the essential *arts* or *ornaments* which make a courtier—there are thousands who with a tenth part of his understanding, and without a spark of his honesty, would distance him infinitely in any court in Europe."[6] Sewall undoubtedly put his finger on his friend's most conspicuous shortcomings as a diplomat, but

Adams through intelligence and tenacity had accomplished far more than Sewall was aware of.

The sights of London which Abigail, Nabby, and sometimes John took in ranged from St. Paul's to the dancing dogs, the singing duck, and a little horse which beat a drum. The learned pig was another popular attraction but the tumblers of Sadler's Wells made the most strenuous objections to sharing the stage with a pig, learned or otherwise. The tumblers, for a certainty, were an extraordinary sight. The tightrope walker was dressed like a jockey in bright silks with a sash around his waist. He danced along the rope to a musical accompaniment, carrying a long pole, then threw the pole away and did somersaults of such grace and ease that Abigail and Nabby, watching fascinated, had the feeling they could whirl in the air themselves. Another performer called the "Little Devil" danced on the rope with wooden shoes and stood on his head. Most wonderful of all, there was a beautiful girl who performed the same feats and, fortunately, "was well clad . . . with drawers" under her billowing skirt. Even so, as with the French dancers, Abigail felt embarrassed at her gyrations. "Delicacy, modesty, and diffidence," she wrote Lucy Tufts, were "wholly laid aside, and nothing of the woman but the sex left."[7]

When Mrs. Siddons came out of retirement the Adamses were among the glittering company that crowded the theater to see her. She played the part of Desdemona with extraordinary conviction. Nabby wrote her brother, "I did not go into fits—nor swoon, but . . . I never was so much pleased with any person I ever saw upon any theater." She had a wonderfully expressive face which registered every nuance of emotion and a voice "sweet and harmonious" beyond words.

While Nabby was preoccupied by the grace and charm of Mrs. Siddons, her mother was upset at her own reaction to Othello embracing Desdemona. "My whole soul shuddered," she confessed, "when I saw the sooty Moor touch the fair Desdemona." She could not decide whether her reaction arose from "the prejudices of education or from a real, natural antipathy. . . . The liberal mind," she wrote in a firm rebuke to herself, "regards not what nation or climate it springs up in, nor what *color* or complexion the man is of."[8]

In all this there was one persistent, nagging irritation. John was constantly short of funds. Congress simply would not allow its ministers sufficient salary to keep up diplomatic appearances. For Adams, who had no income to speak of to supplement his meager stipend as ambassador, his impecuniousness was a source of constant frustration. He could not do the official entertaining that his position required of him. He had to count every penny and shilling in an effort to avoid bankruptcy. Moreover his pinched financial circumstances became the subject of jokes and witticisms which eventually found their way back to him and hurt his pride, for his country as much as for himself. London journalists—"scrib-

blers"—found him an irresistible target. He was referred to in the press as
"the American commercial agent," "a proscribed rebel," and a bumpkin
lawyer. One writer reported that he had taken Dr. Price as his father
confessor and another declared that he was such a notorious penny
pincher that the other foreign ministers would have nothing to do with
him. Indeed he could not even get credit from the grocers and tradesmen.
"The American minister," a journalist declared, "has not yet paid his
way, that is given a diplomatic dinner to the ministers, because Congress'
paper [money] will not pass here."[9] There was just enough truth in the
latter charges to make Adams smart. The foreign ambassadors, after their
initial visits, had been inclined to avoid him, and despite Abigail's skill
as a manager and housekeeper he was slipping gradually into debt,
which to Adams was like slipping into perdition. But the cruelest barb
was directed at Abigail herself. In an effort to stretch each shilling she had
taken over Mr. Spiller's shopping duties and the *Public Advertiser* declared that she cut a figure like a farmer's wife "going in an old chaise to
market with a little fresh butter."

Finally the day arrived when, money or no money, John and Abigail
resolved they must invite the foreign ministers to dinner. In the midst of
a great bustle presided over by the imperturbable Spiller, Captain Hay
arrived from Boston by way of the West Indies, bringing a giant cod
from New England waters and a hundred-pound turtle from the Indies.
John was delighted. It was providential that such a classic New England
dish as cod should arrive at that particular moment. It would be most
appropriate for the foreign ministers. Grinning like a schoolboy, he told
Nabby he would vow that Mr. Jefferson had received no such bounty in
Paris. She must not let Congress know of it however, he added, for those
penny pinchers would at once reduce his salary.

There was the question of what to do with Abigail and Nabby during
the dinner. The practice on such occasions seemed to be to banish the
ladies, so after a solemn council mother and daughter were packed off
to the Copleys' where they had to sit and fret and wonder if everything
was going as it should.

Their anxieties proved groundless; the dinner was a great success and
Lord Carmarthen was gracious enough to say that he would have enjoyed
dining with the ladies. This remark, when John, pleased as could be over
the whole affair, reported it to them, gave Abigail and Nabby a pang of
regret at having missed the spectacle—John presiding over a table lined
with the ambassadors of the great powers of Europe.

From the moment of his arrival in London, Adams had been involved in
the time-consuming and often tedious routines of diplomacy. Colonel
William Stephens Smith, secretary to the legation, was in the city when
the Adamses arrived. He delivered John's commission and instructions

and took on the duties of his office at once. The Colonel was a handsome, agreeable young man, cheerful and willing but not notably efficient. His responsibilities were not heavy ones—receiving petitioners, arranging appointments, copying correspondence, accompanying the ladies to formal functions in the absence of the ambassador. Although it was certainly not true, as one journalist wrote, that the Colonel could not read or write and that Adams had been forced to send him to night school to learn those basic secretarial accomplishments, the Colonel was longer on charm than on brains. With the aid of his secretary Adams poured forth a great volume of letters, most of them directed to Jay as the Secretary for Foreign Affairs, and he complained that, as always, he got little or no response from Jay or from the individual members of Congress to whom he wrote informally.

Adams' first bit of official business was to dissuade two Scottish merchants from petitioning Parliament on the subject of debts owed them by Americans. The merchants of Glasgow, Adams told them, must realize that the United States was just emerging from a devastating war "in which there had been a great interruption of agriculture and commerce, and a still greater destruction of property, which rendered it difficult for any debtor, and impossible for many, to discharge their debts forthwith." The Americans, he assured his visitors, wished to discharge their debts promptly and honorably. But time and patience would be needed. The merchants went away apparently satisfied and Adams reported his conversation to John Jay.[10]

Refusing to be discouraged by his interview with Carmarthen, Adams continued to press his argument that a reconciliation between Great Britain and the United States would benefit both nations. The issue of the Negro slaves carried off from New York was an especially tender subject. Here it seemed clear enough that the British had violated the specific provision of the treaty.

On the twenty-fourth of August, Adams had a long conference on the subject with Pitt. The minister agreed that the carrying off of the Negroes was contrary to the provisions of the treaty and on this point and on the question of the violation of the armistice he seemed quite ready to accede to Adams' demands. As to the posts, Pitt stated that they were tied to the matter of the debts. "Several of the states had interfered," he said, "against the treaty, and by acts of their legislature had interposed impediments to the recovery of debts." Adams argued that on the critical point of payment of interest during the war American courts and lawyers took the view that the Revolution, which had constituted a social upheaval, had broken all contracts and engagements and that debtors were not therefore responsible for the interest on their debts during the period of the conflict.

Proceeding to a discussion of a treaty of commerce, Adams put forward his thesis that England's best interest lay in a generous commercial policy that would encourage American trade to flow to that country. As things stood the existing acts had the tendency to drive that trade to other European nations.

"But," Pitt answered, "you will allow we have a right."

"Certainly I do," Adams replied, "and you, sir, will allow we have a right too."

"Yes, I do; but you cannot blame Englishmen for being attached to their ships and seamen which are so essential to them."

"Indeed I do not, sir; nor can you blame Americans for being attached to theirs, which are so much fewer and so much more essential to them."

"No, I do not blame them."

"As this was a very sprightly dialogue, and in a very good humor, I thought I might push it a little," Adams wrote Jay, giving an account of the interview. Americans were convinced, he told Pitt, that the British had settled on a policy designed to ruin American trade. This went actually beyond self-interest and was a punitive measure which in many respects worked against the best interests of English merchants and manufacturers. If both English and Americans set out to protect their commerce against each other, all commerce would cease and the trade of both nations would stagnate.

The discussion ranged over the West Indian trade, over the whale fisheries and the advantages of free trade. Pitt listened attentively and said little. Adams had the feeling that the Englishman was not so much hostile as indecisive and unwilling to commit himself, and he left with the conviction that nothing would be done for the present to effect a reconciliation of American and British interests. "I hope the states will be cool," he wrote Jay, "and do nothing precipitately; but I hope they will be firm and wise."[11] Close observation of Pitt did not give Adams an exalted opinion of that young man. Able and gifted he certainly was, but no more so in Adams' opinion than some of the younger members of the Continental Congress. He seemed to the New Englander to be simply a political novice with a job too big for him, a job which he might, to be sure, grow into but which for the present rather confused him. His policy seemed to rest primarily on reconciling parliamentary factions and raising the stocks. Neither promised much for America.[12]

A month later Adams took the occasion of Lord Carmarthen's levee for the foreign ministers to arrive an hour early and once more press his arguments. He opened the conversation by reaffirming his hope that there should soon be a return of confidence between Britain and America. His Lordship assented and Adams paused, hoping he might receive some more positive expression of official intent from which he "could have drawn some conclusion, excited some hope, or started some fresh topic," but

Carmarthen remained silent. Adams then pressed on to the question of the posts. If they remained in British hands the Indians might be encouraged to make war upon the frontier with all the attendant horrors that accompanied such clashes. The Foreign Secretary seemed embarrassed and replied hesitantly that Mr. Pitt meant to retain the posts until the British debts had been paid. "Paid! My Lord," Adams exclaimed, "that is more than ever was stipulated. No government ever undertook to pay the private debts of its subjects. . . . The treaty only stipulated that creditors should meet with no lawful impediment to the recovery of their debt."

Carmarthen's reply was that by placing impediments in the way of collections, as some states had done, the states made themselves responsible for the debts. But he refused to discuss the question further, saying he had no authority, and Adams, as he had done with Pitt, proceeded to an exhaustive analysis of British and American trade and the alternatives which America would be forced to explore if Great Britain remained indifferent or indeed hostile to her commerce. "All this was very patiently and civilly heard, but not a word of answer." Finally, in exasperation, Adams declared that he could not understand the unresponsiveness of the British cabinet. Mr. Pitt, he felt, was candid and intelligent, but the situation was critical and in his view, "if a foundation should be laid of a final alienation between England and America, it would be a deeper stain, a blacker blot upon his administration, than the independence of the United States had been upon that of Lord North."

The Foreign Secretary heard him out with the same imperturbable courtesy and good humor. The handsome, florid face showed no sign of irritation or of agreement. It tried Adams beyond all patience. A rebuff was better than these bland encounters. "This nation," he wrote Jay, "is strangely blinded by prejudice and passion. They are ignorant of the subject beyond conception. There is a prohibition of the truth arising from popular anger. . . . Printers will print nothing which is true without pay," Adams declared, "because it displeases their readers; while their gazettes are open to lies because they are eagerly read and make the papers sell. . . . The rise of the stocks has established Mr. Pitt; and if he were willing, he would scarcely be able to do right until America shall enable him and oblige him." The only thing that all factions seemed to unite upon was a punitive policy against America. Pitt, Adams felt, was "but a tool and an ostensible pageant, a nose of tender virgin wax," who was under the King's lead strings and had no real program of his own. "Fox and his friends and patrons," he wrote, "are ruined by the endless expenses of the last elections and have no longer any spirit or any enterprise. North and his friends were afraid of impeachments and vengeance, and thus lay low"; Shelburne, an Irishman, was too personally unpopular to muster any support.[13]

The result was that in the middle of this factionalism and confusion the King managed to exercise a surprising amount of influence. He seemed to Adams, for all his bluff, open manner, "the most accomplished courtier in his dominions." Entertaining and informed as he was in conversation, he trifled his time and his intelligence away so that on the great issues of state he was as poorly informed as he had been during the period of the Revolutionary crisis. But his great personal popularity with the British people and the flattery that was continually showered upon him were taken by the King as evidence of his wisdom and the rightness of his actions. The more Adams saw of him the more he realized that George III, like so many men in power, was shut off from any direct apprehension of political reality. He was surrounded by people who, judging correctly his pride and obstinacy, told him only what he wished to hear. It was a double tragedy because he alone among those in the government had the resolution and energy to carry out a positive course of action.

One measure of the anti-American sentiment in England was the experience of Adams' friends, the historians Gordon and Ramsay. American publishers had rejected Gordon's work as pro-British, and simply on the basis of rumors that his book had a British bias he had endured numerous calumnies and slanders. That the charges were groundless and that he had actually written a fair and balanced account of the struggle could not be shown, since no printer dared to hazard its publication. Gordon thus arrived in London in the spring of 1786 to try to peddle his history there, but with no better success. The printers to whom he submitted the work felt that it was too pro-American to be acceptable to English readers.

Adams' friend David Ramsay, the South Carolina physician who had served as President *pro tem* of Congress, encountered similar difficulties with his *History of South Carolina during the Revolution,* a book written "in a cool, dispassionate style." The English printer, Dilly, to whom Ramsay had sent a shipment of the books was afraid even to sell them for fear of being prosecuted for libel. Ramsay wrote Adams that, in consequence, the work would be pirated in England and he would get nothing.[14]

From his position in Congress, Ramsay sent Adams a diagnosis of the political situation. In the first five months of the current session there had not been four days when more than eight states had been represented. As a result it was impossible to do anything. With everything to be done there was not even a quorum and Congress, haunted by a sense of futility, was characterized more by acrimony than by wisdom. "A strange languor seemed to prevail," Ramsay wrote. But he dared to hope "we have already reached the point of ultimate depression from which public affairs will revert in a direction contrary to what they have lately been in." Ineptitude and confusion could hardly go further. The states seemed at last convinced that they must give Congress power to establish a uniform "commercial system." There was to be a convention in Annapolis to discuss what might best be done and almost all the states had appointed delegates to attend. A plan would soon be brought into Congress recommending a "continental convention" for the purpose of enlarging that body's power. "Our government," the South Carolinian noted, "hitherto has rather been advisory than an efficient system."[15]

For Adams there were two bright spots in a generally gloomy picture. The Portuguese ambassador, the Chevalier de Pinto, had lately arrived from Lisbon after a long absence and informed Adams that his court had instructed him to enter into discussion with the American looking toward a commercial treaty. Adams was more than willing and the two spent hours discussing the mutual advantages that might be derived from trade between their countries. One stumbling block which the Chevalier pointed out was that Portugal wished to send consuls to America but could not do so with propriety until the United States should send a minister and consul to Lisbon. Adams replied that a projected treaty would cover an exchange of consuls.[16]

Hearing that the Tripolitanian ambassador had inquired why he had not visited him, Adams stopped to leave a card. He was told that the ambassador was at home and would receive him. He was thereupon ushered into a room of oriental magnificence. Two large chairs had been placed before the fire, one for Adams and one for the ambassador. Adams had no Turkish and the minister no English but they managed with a kind of *lingua franca* to carry on a conversation. His Excellency observed that the tobacco grown in Tripoli was too strong, "your American tobacco is better." A servant brought two long pipes, filled and lighted. Adams solemnly took one and placed the bowl upon the carpet, "for," he wrote Jefferson, "the stem was fit for a walking cane, and I believe more than two yards in length." They sat side by side, Turk and New Englander, "and smoked in aweful pomp, reciprocating whiff for whiff . . . until coffee was brought in." Then, following the example of his host, Adams alternately puffed and sipped "with such exactness and solemnity that the two secretaries appeared [to be] in raptures and the superior of them, who speaks a few words of French, cried out in ecstasy, "*Monsieur, vous êtes un Turk!*"

The amenities being thus observed, the ambassador announced: "Tripoli is at war with the United States."

"Oh, I am sorry to hear that," Adams replied coolly, "I had not heard of any war with Tripoli. Certainly America has done no injury to Tripoli, committed no hostility?"

Yes, that was quite true, but there was no treaty and without a treaty there was war, for the Turks and the Africans were lords of the Mediterranean and there could be no navigation there and no peace without a treaty. In other words, though the ambassador did not say it outright, without the payment of large bribes. The meeting was concluded with much bowing and exchange of courtesies. Abdrahaman expressed a desire to return the visit and Adams pressed him to call.

The next Sunday the ambassador came to Grosvenor Square. Nabby, peeping from behind the curtain of an upstairs window, watched him dismount with his retinue—an interpreter, a band of turbaned servants dressed in flowing orange robes bound at the waist, their feet thrust into sandals. The upshot of two hours of affable discussion was that peace with the four states—Algiers, Morocco, Tripoli, and Tunis—would cost the United States a million dollars at least. John was impressed with Abdrahaman's skill as a negotiator. The ambassador, he wrote Jay, was "either a consummate politician in art and address, or he is a benevolent and wise man."[17]

The negotiation with the Tripolitanian ambassador was small compensation for Adams' continued frustration in the main business of his mission. Abigail put the best face on British intransigence when she wrote Cotton Tufts: "Thus is this nation driving us into greatness, obliging us to become frugal, to retrench our luxuries, to build a navy, to have a great number of seamen."[18]

Adams wrote Richard Henry Lee that there was much anti-American sentiment in Europe as well as in England. A large part of it came from fear that this new element would now intrude itself into all European plans, schemes, and arrangements with its own requirements and its own ambitions. A Spanish minister at Madrid had been heard to say that he wished all America, north and south, under water. "European ministers expect a great deal of trouble from America," Adams noted, "and they all know that she will always prevail; but I hope we are neither so impious," he added, "so inhuman, or so silly, as to wish her annihilated or under water."[19] He could not help reflecting that if all intercourse between Europe and America were cut off Americans would be the happiest people upon earth, and in fifty years the most powerful." European luxuries would only "enfeeble our race of men and retard the increase of population." But, he conceded, "the character of our people must be taken into consideration. They are as aquatic as the tortoises and sea fowl, and the love of commerce, with its conveniences and pleasures, is a habit in them as unalterable as their natures." It was chimerical to wish it otherwise. "We are," he added, "to consider men and things as practical statesmen, and to consider who our constituents are and what they expect of us."[20]

His American correspondents sent Adams discouraging news. There was a jealousy of Congress by the states that gave little hope for strengthening that body. The British restrictions on American trade had alarmed and intimidated the merchants and convinced many people that America would profit most from a long interruption of British trade which would force the United States to become self-sufficient and thus independent of Europe. The isolationist sentiment was very evident. There should be no ties with Europe, no ministers or consuls sent or accepted.[21]

Tristram Dalton, Richard Henry Lee, and James Sullivan wrote of general demoralization and uncertainty. Sullivan admitted that there were those who advocated "the changing of our confederation into one like a consolidated government of the whole" and that this group "grows larger and larger, vainly supposing that our happiness depends more on the form of a union than in frugality."[22] Jay informed Adams that the leading members of Congress from the Southern states threw "cold water" on all ideas of giving Congress the power to regulate trade. "They wish," he noted, "to leave to foreign powers to manage the commerce of the United States." They had no inclination to sacrifice any of their present profits for the sake of their Northern neighbors, and they seemed quite ready to promote "aristocratical measures," whatever they might be.[23]

The report from Charles Storer was more encouraging. He found the people of all the colonies "highly incensed" against the British for retaining the posts, and the Southern delegates to Congress "to be warm and high for navigation acts and reciprocal restrictions." Maryland, he was informed, was about to pass a navigation act similar to that of Massachusetts; New Hampshire had already done so, and Rhode Island and New Jersey had empowered Congress to regulate their commerce. The real issue was whether Congress or the individual states should regulate trade and here the Southerners, as Sullivan had stated, were strongly opposed to giving the regulatory power to Congress. "The bal[ance] between them and us, they say, is against them and therefore they wish to have the staff in their own hands."[24]

Jefferson and Adams joined forces to try to push the negotiations with the Barbary pirates to a conclusion but it was a weary business. The treaty with Prussia alone seemed to make satisfactory progress. Adams' efforts to reach some kind of rapport with the British were complicated by an explosive incident in Boston, where the captain of a British naval vessel was attacked on the streets of the city by two sailors whom he had impressed and cruelly abused during the war. The incident served to harden, if that was possible, British opinion against America, and a series of treaty violations by the British in regard to the United States-Canadian boundary lines further exacerbated American feelings. "We hold conferences upon conferences," Adams wrote Jefferson, "but the ministers either have no plan or they button it up closer than their waistcoats." America was too trusting and naïve. "All foreign nations are taking an ungenerous advantage of our simplicity and philosophical liberality," he complained.[25]

The apparent futility of negotiations with the British ministry, the crushing load of work which had so affected his eyes, the lack of instructions from Jay or from Congress, the little snubs and rebuffs which he had experienced, and above all the ordeal of trying to make ends meet financially, made Adams increasingly restless and anxious to be recalled. He began to talk about the pleasures of Braintree in a way that Abigail and Nabby recognized very well. "Pappa decides *as usual*," Nabby wrote her brother, "that our continuance in Europe will be no longer than the spring . . . if I had not heard him say so ever since we have been [in Europe], I should think more of it."[26]

Adams pressed Carmarthen once more for a definite answer on the posts and after weeks of delay he received a reply which made the government's position clear enough. The fourth article of the treaty respecting the recovery of debts had not been faithfully observed by the United States. In consequence many of the King's subjects had been reduced to "the utmost degree of difficulty and distress." They had not obtained "that justice to which, on every principle of law as well as of humanity, they were clearly and indisputably entitled. . . . . I can assure you, sir," the Foreign Secretary concluded, "that whenever America shall manifest a real determination to fulfill her part of the treaty Great Britain will not hesitate to prove her sincerity . . . depend upon her for carrying every article . . . into real and complete effect." Simply stated, the posts would be held as security for the payment of the debts owed British merchants.[27]

At the end of May, Adams wrote to Jay advising him to pass on to Congress the information that it was "vain to expect the evacuation of the post, or payment for the Negroes, a treaty of commerce, or restoration of prizes—payment of the Maryland or Rhode Island demands, compensation to the Boston merchants, or any other relief of any kind, until these laws [obstructing the collection of British debts in various states] are all repealed—nor will the ministers ever agree to any explanation concerning the interest during the war, or payments by installments." Adams made his own position clear enough, daring "all the clamor that can be raised against me by my friends or by my enemies . . . and of all the consequences that can befall me, for writing my sentiments freely to Congress." The fact was that America had placed itself in a poor light by complaining of "breaches of the treaty when the British court have it in their power to prove upon us breaches of the same treaty of greater importance. My advice then, if it is not impertinent to give it, is that every law of every state which concerns either debts or loyalists, which can be impartially construed as contrary to the spirit of the treaty of peace, be immediately repealed and the debtors left to settle with their creditors or dispute the point of interest at law."[28]

ABIGAIL fretted about the lack of news from home. John Quincy had sailed in May and by September she still had not heard of his arrival in the United States. But on the fifth of September, having spent the evening chatting with Mather Brown and then reading "Barrow upon the government of the tongue," she went to bed and there, settled under the quilted counterpane, she felt the familiar premonition that letters from home were near at hand. The next morning she went down to the "setting parlor" on the second floor with a feeling of anticipation. John and Nabby joined her there for breakfast; the footman brought up the tea urn, still simmering, and placed it on the table beside the pot of chocolate; Mr. Spiller entered, spry and smart in his handsome livery, bowed, and presented an armful of letters. "Up we all jumped," Abigail wrote John Quincy, "your sister seized hold of a letter and cried, 'My brother, my brother!' We were not long opening and perusing, and 'I am so glad,' was repeated from one to another." Abigail was triumphant. Her infallible instinct, she announced to her husband and daughter, had told her as it had often told her before that letters were in the offing. With the family immersed in news from John Quincy and the Braintree relatives and friends, "the chocolate grew cold, the teapot was forgotten, and the bread and butter went down[stairs] uneaten, yet nobody felt the loss of breakfast."

John Quincy, armed with his father's letters, had had a triumphal procession from New York to Boston. He had stayed in the former city with Richard Henry Lee, presently President of Congress, had met Gardoqui, the Spanish minister, talked to Elbridge Gerry, Rufus King, and the Dutch minister, Van Berckels. He had dined at General Knox's with the Massachusetts and Virginia delegates and given them all the information he could about European affairs. "The politicians here," he wrote his father, "wait with great impatience to hear from you. Matters seem to be at a crisis." The New York merchants resented the act of the Massachusetts legislature which had prohibited English vessels from carrying goods to and from ports of that state. "The states have not yet given to Congress the power of regulating their trade," he noted, "but it is almost universally considered here a necessary measure." Richard Henry Lee, who still exercised much influence, was "much against it" however, as were most of the New England delegates.[1]

John Quincy met and dined with Tom Paine and Dr. Witherspoon, the President of the college at Princeton. From all the people he encountered he got the same questions. How were his father and his mother? How did they like Europe? Which country did they prefer? When would they return? He thought, he wrote his mother, of having the answers printed up and then distributing them to the questioners. He had spent several hours with Arthur Lee and had had dinner at Dr. Ramsay's with a large company that included two New York belles—Susan Livingston and Miss Marshall, who was engaged to marry "that swarthy Don," Gardoqui. Nabby had especially enjoined him to write about the American girls he met and he dutifully reported to her that "Miss Livingston passes for a very smart, sensible young lady. She is very talkative, and a little superficial. I cannot say I admire her."

Miss Riche was a famous beauty but had "a good deal of affectation." She played on the harpsichord and wrote songs, but not very well in John Quincy's opinion. Of the Sears girls, Polly and Sally were handsome but engaged; 'Becca was the prettiest of them all. He listened to Miss Eccles, "the best harpsichordist in the city," and visited Miss Alsop, a notorious coquette who "injured her appearance very much by simpering airs." His encounters with the belles of the city had inspired him to write a poem:

> The eye half shut, the dimpled cheek
> And languid look are cuts too weak
> To win the heart of any youth
> Who loves simplicity and truth.

It might be that Boston would do better. But it turned out otherwise. The Boston girls were, if possible, worse. They apparently thought it beneath them to learn "anything but to dance and talk scandal. In this last particular," he noted caustically, "they have attained great perfection." They were, he felt, taken into company too young and encouraged by foolish mammas to think that "if they can talk nonsense very fluently and set very straight and upright, five hours together in one chair, they will be most accomplished women." Miss Debby Perkins he found charming and agreeable, "but amazingly wild." There was in Boston as in New York a kind of glut of pretty girls, and "too many of them," John Quincy wrote, "are also like a beautiful apple that is insipid or disgusting to the taste."

When Abigail read her son's lofty indictment of American girls she replied quite tartly. "They are not at fault; it is their education." Women were what men wished them to be and if American girls were giddy, frivolous, and affected, it was because American men liked them that way. They were "like clay in the hands of the artist—and may be molded to whatever form [men] please." Thus a gentleman who "was severe against the ladies is . . . upon every principle very impolitic—his character is soon established for a morose, severe, ill-natured fellow," swollen with his own importance.[2]

John Quincy, unaware that the engagement between his sister and Royall Tyler was proceeding toward a dissolution, met the latter in the character of a prospective brother-in-law. He bore him all kinds of messages from Nabby, and he was burdened by Nabby's anxious injunctions (about which he kept silent to Tyler) that he try to penetrate the riddle of her fiancé's behavior. John Quincy was attracted to Tyler at once, but he became quickly aware of the young man's unhappiness and dangerous instability. While he enjoyed their hours together, their walks and rides, he grew increasingly uneasy about Tyler's relationship to his sister.

In addition to the letters from John Quincy, there were letters from Mary Cranch and Eliza Shaw, letters full of family news and local gossip, letters that carried Abigail in an instant to the familiar sights and faces of Braintree, that summoned up her remote home so vividly that she alternately laughed and cried as she read. The whole drama of town life unfolded before her: Mr. Bass's son had run off with a loose woman, leaving his wife in the lurch; Tom Field had cut himself with a scythe in the back and shoulder, a dreadful wound that had required fourteen stitches to close; Lucy Jones was being courted by a rustic swain from Weymouth who fancied himself a portrait painter and tried to paint her picture but was so unnerved by her charm that first his hand failed and then his tongue, leaving the courtship to be conducted by mail. Practical, matter-of-fact Lucy in turn had become a coquette, dressing herself most carefully instead of in her usual casual and rather disorderly manner. Mary Cranch had observed her stroll into Whitman's field, in a neat white frock, arrange herself on a rock near where her suitor was raking hay, and begin "to sing to the accompaniment of the birds." But when the poor youth approached, she fled.

The hay was rich and deep in the fields and the Adams garden was producing so plentifully, her sister reported, that Abigail's "sable tenants" almost maintained themselves by selling vegetables. Betsy Palmer was visiting the Cranches. Mary's son, Billy, played the flute and the violin and Betsy sang and played the old spinet which Billy had tuned for her, "a pleasant music for unsophisticated country ears not used to the opera." Mary and Eliza were busy getting Billy Cranch and Charles Adams ready to start in at Cambridge in the fall as freshmen. Acting on Abigail's instruction, Lucy Tufts and Betsy Smith had spent an afternoon in the Adams house picking out furniture for Charles's chamber in Cambridge. After some deliberation they took the tea table and the marble-painted drop-leaf. Mary had made seven linen shirts for the two boys and Eliza had made a suit for Charles out of the cinnamon-colored cloth John had sent from Holland. Most precious of all to Abigail were her sisters' comments on John Quincy. To Mary he looked like both his father and mother. She saw in him his father's diffidence and his mother's animation. He was certainly all that a mother could wish. Eliza also was struck with the strong family resemblance—his eyes, his mouth, even his gestures, sharp and emphatic, reminded her of John.[3]

Abigail was amused by Eliza Shaw's tale of how her husband and Charles had tried to trick her by putting on long faces when they came back from Charles's entrance examinations at Harvard, trying to make her believe that Charles had failed, but she was not taken in. "I could easily discern by their countenances," she wrote, "that joy and satisfaction played sweetly at their heart."

John Quincy, it was discovered, was not proficient enough in Latin and Greek diction to enter Harvard as a sophomore though in most other subjects he was in advance of his class. It was therefore decided that he should study through the winter with Mr. Shaw and enter in the spring as a junior sophister. Mr. Shaw was uneasy about taking him on. He was not sure that he was up to it. It was one thing to prepare a freshman, quite another to equip a student to enter the junior class.[4]

Running through the letters of Mary Cranch to Abigail was the hint that Abigail's head might be turned by all the pomp and circumstance of the world in which she moved, so that she might find it difficult ever to return to the simple, rural life of Braintree. Abigail, for her part, never ceased to protest that she was unspoiled by the high life around her, indeed that she had contempt for it and preferred the "flow of soul and feast of reason" that had always so delighted her at Braintree.

Mary and Eliza had put their heads together frequently about Royall Tyler's strange behavior. He was alternately moody and almost aggressively cheerful. He withdrew to his room for days, hardly spoke, and, when he made an appearance, glowered at the Cranches as though they were his mortal enemies. He never seemed to send off any letters to Nabby, but he displayed her letters around the town and when a friend rebuked him for being so ungallant he declared that he was so proud of Nabby's epistles that he could not forbear to show them off. He got his hands on a packet of letters from Nabby to various members of the family and hid them away, refusing to give up those addressed to Mrs. Guild until her husband came after them. When asked why he had not delivered the letters, Tyler had turned crimson and mumbled that "he had a particular reason for not doing it." "It must be a very particular one indeed," the indignant Mr. Guild replied, "or it will not excuse you from a large breach of trust." The next day Tyler surrendered two of the letters. But Mary Cranch, cleaning his room, noticed a letter addressed to Mrs. Guild with the seal broken on it. He kept a letter from Nabby to Betsy Palmer and only relinquished it when Billy Cranch challenged him directly to say whether or not he had one. Under Billy's prodding he admitted that he did; "he looked a little vexed but went up and got it."

Meanwhile, in London, Nabby was in a turmoil. The long, inexplicable silence of her fiancé filled her with doubt and anxiety and made her so generally miserable that even the sights of the city failed to distract her. John Quincy had been her confidant, the sharer of her secrets and hopes. She missed him terribly—their long walks, the first just a year ago when they had taken a stroll together in Pope's garden at Richmond; their intimate conversations; his reading aloud to her. "I only wish for you and I would esteem myself happy," she wrote. "I have much to regret in thee—more than you can judge—*with all your knowledge of yourself.*" She treasured the edition of the British poets that he had given her, portions of which they had read together; she had a miniature of him hanging over her desk which, although it did not look like him, was some comfort and she wished for a lock of his hair; and be sure it was a lock from his head, she wrote teasingly, and not from his luxuriant eyebrows. She had caught his restlessness, his impulse to roam and wander, and she looked to him to remind her of her "errors, mistakes, and foibles," and "to convince my judgments, guide my opinion."[5]

She was quite at a loss as to what to do about her engagement to Royall Tyler. Complicating everything was the fact that Colonel Smith had fallen in love with her and that she in turn was perilously close to returning his affection. Before the romance with the young secretary could flourish, Nabby must break off with Tyler, whose strange behavior certainly provided her with ample grounds.

Abigail, who had written John Quincy instructing him to look into the Tyler affair and report secretly to her, had looked on Colonel Smith from the moment she first saw him as a possible replacement for her daughter's eccentric fiancé. When she had satisfied herself that the young man was an acceptable suitor, which she did very promptly—(He was "a man of an independent spirit, high and strict sentiments of honor, much the gentleman in his manners and address," she wrote John Quincy)—she abetted the incipient romance in every way she could. The only impediment was the fact that the Colonel was a member of the Society of the Cincinnati, but that was easily circumvented when he assured John and Abigail that he had never worn the insignia of the Society and had joined it more out of regard for General Washington than out of any personal conviction.

With such an attractive alternative lingering in the wings, so to speak, Abigail supported Nabby's decision to write Tyler and break off the engagement. At the same time it was awkward to have the Colonel about the house in the period when Nabby was making the break with Tyler. Providentially, an invitation to journey to Berlin to watch Frederick's review of his army provided the perfect pretext for the Colonel to absent himself. He would go to observe and report on the latest equipment and tactics displayed by Europe's finest soldiers. He was packed off forthwith and Nabby wrote to Tyler to inform him that their engagement was terminated.

Adams, quite unaware of the intrigue going on under his nose, dispatched Smith in all innocence to report on Frederick's grand parade. The Colonel wrote from Paris begging Nabby to plead his cause with her father. Should she confess to him that his secretary had departed "on a quick trip of the heart in pursuit of those affections which make us love each other?" Or should she say that he was fleeing out of a sense of delicacy?[6]

William Smith's letters to Nabby show him a romantic, rather humorless young man, filled with such gallant illusions as one might expect in a properly brought up gentleman whose mature life had been spent in the army. In his handsome, florid hand, he wrote epistles sprinkled with classical references and restrained hints of passion.

Abigail directed the lovers' campaign with the authority of a born strategist. "Prudence," she wrote the Colonel, "dictates silence to me." He would do best to "take a draught of Lethe, and all will be . . . right," she assured him, adding, "There are entanglingments, as Lady G terms them, from which time, the great solacer of human woe, only can relieve us—and time, I dare say, will extricate those I love from any unapproved step into which inexperience and youth may have involved them . . . a word to the wise is sufficient."

When Tyler finally got Nabby's letter breaking off the engagement, he was inconsolable. He showed very plainly by his manner that he suspected Mary Cranch of having written unfavorably of him and so broken up his romance. Mary could hear him weeping in his room. He pulled himself together enough to write to Adams like a sober enough suitor, telling him that he had been busy getting his financial affairs in order and would soon be ready "to exhibit to you the outlines of my pecuniary circumstances: and if you shall judge my situation such as to countenance a speedy connection with your daughter, I shall hope for your consent and advice affecting of it." John Quincy, whom Tyler had met, had impressed him as an excellent young man with "no tincture of what we style 'European frivolity of manners.'" He went on to discuss very learnedly the religious affairs of the state, especially the growing controversy between the Unitarians and the Episcopalians, and sent

Adams a bundle of pamphlets dealing with American issues, and an ancient coin that had been found near Braintree.[7]

John, still unaware of the broken romance, was delighted with the pamphlets and presented the coin to the Society of Antiquaries where, he wrote, it "occasioned a sensation among the learned, and all heads are employed to discover whether the figures are Phoenician, Carthaginian or what." If the coin, which contained what was apparently a compass in one side, was of ancient origin, it might mean that mariners long before the fifteenth century had used a compass. He urged Tyler to continue his researches and promised to try to secure for him the Abbé de Mably's letters and his answer to Gibbon.[8]

Tyler, having written Adams in the character of a prospective son-in-law, whirled gaily about; spoke of himself as still engaged and planning to go to London to clear up a little misunderstanding; bought himself a handsome Philadelphia chaise and spent enough time in Mrs. Veasey's parlor to set tongues in the town wagging. He also made quite a display of wearing a picture of Nabby around his neck and at several houses where he lodged he left it in his bed, came down to breakfast, discovered it was gone, made a great clamor of grief and dismay, and, when it was finally restored to him, expressed "raptures" of delight and kissed the picture of his beloved. Building a windmill was only one of a number of ambitious projects he launched himself on. ("I wonder if the law business is to go by wind also," Mary Cranch wrote sarcastically.) At the raising of the windmill he gave an elegant entertainment of "meat and drinks, a dinner and supper . . . for the large company."[9]

Several times he came into the Cranch living room with his hand trunk, opened it, spread Nabby's letters on the table, and occupied himself reading them very ostentatiously. It always put Betsy into a fury. She wished she dared to sweep the letters up and throw them all in the fire.

In spite of his eccentric behavior, Tyler was one of the most popular men in the town. People responded to his reckless, openhanded ways, the passion he poured into everything he did, the sensitive, vulnerable face, the tousled hair and careless dress. He was a charming man and, while Braintree was uneasy in the presence of charm, it was no more resolute than other communities in resisting it. Moreover there were families in the town who had no liking for the Adamses and they were quite ready to credit the rumor that a haughty girl, her head turned by European manners, had thrown over her American beau.

XLIX

THE celebration of the Queen's birthday drew Abigail and Nabby to court once more. They started dressing after breakfast and by two o'clock they were properly arrayed, Abigail in a satin dress "of the new-fashioned color which is called the Spanish fly," trimmed with black crepe and gold fringe. Nabby was dressed in pink satin with a silver fringe and John wore his ambassador's regalia with his sword strapped to his side. There was such a mob crowding down Piccadilly that Adams' coach skirted around through St. James's Park. In the crush at the palace they were almost squeezed to death. Nabby in her frail pink dress found herself pressed against the ambassador from Algiers, a dirty, turbaned savage who smelled ferociously. Ladies' hoops got entangled, trimmings were ripped from skirts and finery damaged beyond repair. Finally they were carried by the tide of humanity into the drawing room and past the King, who had a polite question for each of them but could do no better with Nabby than to ask what he had asked for the past three months: "Do you get out much in this weather?" "Instructive and improving indeed," Nabby wrote scornfully to John Quincy. It took two more hours to reach the Queen and present congratulations to her. That chore completed, the Adamses rushed home, exhausted, and began to prepare for the ball that was to crown the day's festivities. After a hasty dinner they set out once more for the place where Sir Clement Cotterel, the master of ceremonies, found them excellent seats behind the rail that fenced off the section reserved for foreign ministers and then stationed himself beside Abigail, as he said, "to keep the turnpike" and guard against improper intrusions.

All the press and the wearisome waiting were redeemed for the two Adams women by the excitement that Anne Bingham created. "She shone a goddess, and she moved a queen," wrote Abigail to John Quincy. In the great crush women strained and stretched to get a glimpse of the American beauty and Abigail, her proud sponsor, heard all about her whispers of admiration. The most satisfying query was repeated again and again, "Is she an American?" The ambassador of the Emperor whispered to Adams, "Sir, your country produces exceedingly fine women."

"Ay," Adams replied, bowing, "and men too," presenting to the minister a visiting American, Mr. Chew of Philadelphia, and adding that Mrs. Bingham was not without rivals. The presentation was enlivened by the rumor that the poor foolish Prince had been for several years the suitor of "a widow lady near forty years of age . . . fat, fair and forty," and was secretly and illegally married to her.[1]

At nine the King and Queen entered and went around the circle speaking to those ladies who were to dance. Then the King spoke a few words to the foreign ministers and the Prince of Wales opened the ball with the Princess Royal dancing the minuet. Each couple came up in turn, bowed and curtsied to the King and Queen, and then danced. Nabby refused to be impressed by the pageantry. "The gentlemen and ladies dance better in America," she wrote her brother. The Prince, fat and awkward, fell down on the dance floor, which everyone pretended tactfully not to notice. At eleven the King and Queen retired and the Adamses returned wearily to Grosvenor Square.

As week after week dragged by with no sign of Colonel Smith's return from his journey to Berlin, Adams grew increasingly impatient at the long absence and Nabby confided to her journal, "the Secretary must be out of his senses to remain so long from his duty."[2]

Was she to be jilted by two suitors in succession? Anxious and unhappy, she went with her parents to a Shakespeare Jubilee at the Drury Lane Theater, hoping to get her mind off the absent Colonel. The Jubilee, which lasted for five hours, consisted of a "procession of the principal characters and a representation of the principal scenes of every one of his plays," acted against magnificent settings. It was very well done but the Adamses were exhausted by five hours of sitting and came home at eleven quite surfeited with the Bard. They had hardly settled down in the drawing room when the errant Colonel Smith, whose three-week journey had turned into an absence of more than four months, stuck his head into the room and said to Adams, "Dare I see you, sir?"

He might well ask the question. His absence had thrown a heavy burden on Adams which had been only in part relieved by pressing Nabby into service as a secretary. On the other hand John had by now more than an intimation of Nabby's interest in the Colonel. Smith had brought with him his friend David Humphreys, whose engaging ways and irrepressible high spirits had appealed to Adams when Humphreys had been a frequent visitor to Auteuil; the Colonel presented his friend as a peace offering, although "he was too well grown to st[yle] him a lamb."

Nabby was overjoyed to see her suitor, so handsome and sprightly, and charmed by the skill and aplomb with which he carried off an awkward situation. Now that he was back she realized a little guiltily how much she had missed him. The two men were full of news from Paris, from Jefferson, from the abbés, increasingly frail and saddened by the death of one of their trio, from Mably, even from Petit, the Adamses servant at Auteuil whom they had passed on to Jefferson when they left. In the midst of the reunion Adams did not have the heart to take his secretary to task for his long absence, and the Colonel found himself restored to the good graces of the family.

It was a measure of Nabby's pleasure in having him back that she sat down to write her brother, although in her letter she was careful to refrain from any comment that might suggest a romantic involvement with the wandering Colonel. She wrote on until she heard the watchman call the hour of twelve-thirty and then she ended her letter: "I am going to drink some lemonade—as we used to do at Auteuil—I wish you could sip with me now."[3]

With Colonel Smith back and Nabby's engagement to Royall Tyler officially ended, the new romance moved rapidly toward a conclusion. Smith wrote Abigail a few weeks after his return to ask if he might visit Nabby in the role of a suitor for her hand. Abigail might think his note had better gone to her husband but, he wrote, "I feel more easy in communication with you—and as I do not know that he is acquainted with my sentiments respecting the lady (as well as you are, madam)—it would render a long and formal letter necessary." He knew that he had an advocate in Abigail and that she would be the best champion of his cause with her often unpredictable husband.[4] It turned out as he and Nabby had hoped. Abigail won the concurrence of John. Nabby and William Smith, in effect, became engaged. The wedding would take place in the spring.

A few days after the Colonel's return there was another feast of letters from home. When they came back from dining with some American tourists a beaming John Briesler hurried out to open the carriage door. "Oh, ma'am! there are a thousand letters come!" "Well," John said to Abigail, "now I shall see your eyes glisten. Nobody ever enjoyed a letter more than you." Nabby was up the steps and into the house before her parents had even dismounted from the coach. For the next two hours they all sat in the upstairs sitting room devouring the news from home, especially John Quincy's lengthy reports of friends and family. Even the call of the watchman which invariably put John "in motion for bed" went ignored. The Colonel had to amuse himself by reading or pretending to read the American newspapers that had accompanied the letters, but Abigail's sharp eyes noted that he watched the others covertly, especially Nabby as, flushed and excited, she pored over her brother's epistles. When the footman announced that his carriage was at the door William Smith rose and went a little wistfully to Abigail. Was she planning to write to America soon? Yes, within the week. Would she, he asked hesitantly, remember him to her son? Abigail promised; she would tell John Quincy that his sister and the Colonel were engaged. "Delicacy of sentiment and honor are the striking traits of his character," she wrote John Quincy. He was a complete contrast to Tyler, she assured him, and Nabby was happy and secure in her relationship with the handsome Colonel as she had never been with her erratic and emotional Braintree suitor.[5]

Abigail's principal attention was for the letters from John Quincy. He thoroughly approved of Nabby breaking off her engagement to Tyler. He had liked Tyler personally, but the stories he had heard on every hand of his behavior, he wrote, "excited in my mind such fears as I never wish to feel again. . . . I cannot express how much I was relieved when the news came so unexpectedly of her having so happily freed herself from an inclination which I considered as very dangerous." He himself was working ten hours a day with Mr. Shaw to prepare to enter Harvard in the spring semester. He had found to his chagrin that "if a person has studied *certain books* he may be admitted; but those I had not studied." He felt confident that he was "as well prepared as many of the class" in which he wished to enter; "yet as I had not acquired knowledge from the same sources, the government of the college could not admit me." He had to read with Mr. Shaw four books of Homer, two of Xenophon, the Greek Testament, and John Locke's *Essay on the Human Understanding.* "It shall be the study of my life," he declared, "to follow the instructions and the example of my parents, and the nearer I come to them, the greater share of happiness I shall enjoy." Indeed, he could never sufficiently express his "love and gratitude."[6]

As always Mary Cranch's letters summoned up for Abigail with almost heartbreaking vividness the home and friends she missed so much. Charles, a freshman now at Harvard, had spent his Thanksgiving "vacancy" at the Cranches', bringing with him his chum, Samuel Walters. The two boys had stuffed themselves on Mary's plum pudding and pies and she had sent them back to Cambridge supplied with enough plum cake and cheese to last them until their "winter vacancy" began. The thrifty Dr. Tufts, who was Charles's source of pocket money, doled it out so sparingly that Charles felt always pinched and his indulgent aunt slipped him a few dollars on the side, explaining that the doctor did not realize "how small a young fellow feels without any money in his pocket."[7]

Mary had a new neighbor, a Mrs. Allen, a wonderful Mrs. Malaprop who used "bilious" for "rebellious," "distinguish" for "extinguish" and many other similarly engaging errors that Mary and Abigail would have laughed over until they cried.[8]

On the thirteenth of March, John Quincy, his deficiencies repaired, went up to Harvard to be examined by the President, three professors, and four tutors. Dressed in their gowns, the examiners made a formidable company. They quizzed him on Horace and the *Iliad*, asked him "a number of questions in logic, and in Locke, and several in geography," then gave him a passage in English to translate into Latin. He passed with flying colors, found an apartment in the university with a recent graduate, and began at once to attend Mr. Williams' lectures in Experimental Philosophy, to read Terence and study Euclid.

In the Shaw household John Quincy had shown an inclination to dispute with his elders, a slight touch perhaps of arrogance or superciliousness. In his aunt's opinion "he had imbibed some curious notions, and was rather peculiar in some of his opinions, and a little too decisive and tenacious of them." The truth was that to John Quincy his aunt and uncle sometimes seemed hopelessly provincial and out of date in their ideas. But Eliza Shaw was Abigail's sister and she showed no sign of yielding ground to her self-assured nephew, who obviously thought himself so advanced in his views. Young men, she told him, as close to severity as she ever came, who were very liberal in their youth "came to have very illiberal and contracted ideas in later life. . . . . Opinionatedness was the characteristic of youth which always thought itself right."[9]

At Harvard, John Quincy alarmed his father by his critical attitude. The classes, he wrote, formed four distinct "orders of beings" without any real communication between them. The tutors were too young and ill informed, being scarcely older and sometimes no wiser than the students under their charge. "Their acquirements," he noted sharply, "are not such as an instructor at this university ought to be possessed of." Moreover it was in his opinion unfortunate "so much time should be wasted in prayers and recitation as there is." Yet even with such failings, it was certainly true that Harvard was a much better university than any he had observed in Europe. The "public exercises," he thought, were particularly valuable. All students had to speak in the chapel and recite before their classes. They also had "forensic disputations" in which a question in metaphysics was given out by the tutor for the class to dispute upon, taking alternately one side and then the other. It had fallen to John Quincy to take the affirmative side of the question "Whether the immortality of the human soul is probable from natural reason." The students themselves were "a confused medley of good, bad, and indifferent."[10]

John Quincy's room was furnished with articles from the Braintree house, but he had had to buy "a tea kettle and tea apparatus." His aunt Mary Cranch sent a fine barrel of cider to Cambridge for him and Charles to bottle, thus saving the expense of wine.

John and Abigail were at the same time pleased and uneasy at having John Quincy and Charles in Harvard. While they were, as John put it, "breathing now in the atmosphere of science and literature, the floating particles of which will mix with your whole mass of blood and juices," they were daily exposed, as John well knew from his own days at Harvard, to the grossest kinds of temptation—to excessive drinking, gambling, sexual adventures, any of which could result in their expulsion and in a few years drag them down to the lowest level. "I hope you will guard your brother against that pernicious vice of gaming too much practiced at the university," his mother wrote John Quincy.[11]

As though to remind them of the terrible dangers that lay in wait for the weak or careless, Mary Cranch wrote of the wretched condition of her brother-in-law, Robert Cranch, a drunkard and a ne'er-do-well, without even a decent suit of clothes. Richard was trying to get him a job and put him back on his feet but it was a discouraging business. William Smith, the wastrel brother of Mary and Abigail, was not only a profligate and a heavy drinker but had been accused of having counterfeited money, and although he had been cleared of the charge, he had abandoned his wife and children and was reputed to be living with another woman and ruining his health with drink and dissipation. Mary still dared to hope "that the prayers and efforts of his dying parents will sooner or later have some effect."[12] The Warrens had suffered bitter disappointment and misfortune. Charles, their eldest son, had died in Spain of some brief and virulent disease. The second son, Winslow, so handsome and so promising, the apple of his mother's eye, had been constantly involved in dubious enterprises. He had been pursued for debt, caned his creditor, and was now being sued for two thousand pounds for assault and battery. So, surrounded by examples of disastrous failure within the circle of the immediate family and among their closest friends, it was small wonder that John and Abigail, as well as the boys' aunts, Mary Cranch and Eliza Shaw, had constantly in mind the hazards of life in Cambridge. One slight, thoughtless misstep might carry Charles and John Quincy to irretrievable disaster. Anxious as she was, Eliza Shaw sought to reassure John and Abigail. "His father is *his* oracle," she wrote of their eldest son. "There never was a son who had a greater veneration for a father. . . . In him I see the wise politician, the good statesman—and the patriot in embryo." In her beloved Charles, Eliza beheld "those qualities that form the engaging, the well-accomplished gentleman—the friend of science—the favorite of the misses, and the graces—as well as of the ladies." Thomas Boylston, his aunt thought, was best suited for a military life. He had "a more martial and intrepid spirit . . . a fine natural capacity, a love of business, an excellent faculty in dispatching it." If not as gifted as his brothers, he should certainly be "a useful member of society."[13]

Both Abigail and John wrote the boys by every conveyance, John to exhort them to intellectual attainment, Abigail to warn them to keep their virtue unspotted. To Charles's letter telling of an awakening interest in history, she replied warmly, urging him to persevere. He should read Hubbard's *History of the Indian War* and Neal's and Hutchinson's histories of Massachusetts. They would give him "a just idea of the first settlement of America and the dangers, perils, and hardships which your ancestors encountered in order to establish civil and religious liberty." Although the first settlers had come seeking liberty of conscience, it had to be admitted that they carried with them "much superstition and bigotry, which may be attributed in some measure to the spirit of the times in which they lived and the persecution they had suffered." Persecution, she pointed out, "always tends to narrow the mind and to make it more tenacious of its principles." At the same time they had a "zeal for religion and that strict piety together with the principles of civil liberty which enabled them to brave every hardship and to build them up as a people and lay the foundation for that noble structure which the present generation have founded." Each individual might think of himself as unimportant, as having little to contribute, but this was an immoral point of view. "Everyone is accountable for his conduct," she wrote, "and none is so insignificant as not to have some influence."

As he read history Charles should take careful note of the various actors in that drama, "their views, pursuits, and the consequences of their actions," seeing what an influence "justice, honor, integrity, and reverence for the Deity had upon the nations and kingdoms whenever they predominated." Abigail sealed the letter with wax and placed under it a gold guinea to season her maternal advice.[14]

Adams urged his eldest son not to lead too sedentary a life. "Never fail to walk an hour or two every day." Joel Barlow had sent him his *Vision of Columbus,* an epic poem celebrating the settlement and expansion of America, and Adams was delighted with it. In his opinion it was a work "which would do honor to any country and any age. . . . Excepting *Paradise Lost,* I know of nothing superior in any modern language." In painters and poets, with West and Copley and Trumbull and now with Barlow, America was not "at present outdone by any nation in Europe."[15]

As for the college, Adams had much advice. John Quincy, despite the exclusive "order of beings" in the different classes, should do his best to make as many worth-while friendships as possible among "the most remarkable scholars." He should "drop in upon them frankly, make them a visit in a leisure hour at their chambers, and fall into conversation." He should ask them about their tutors' "manner of teaching, observe what books lie upon their tables, ask questions about the towns they were born in, the schools they were fitted in." He should ask about the Revolution, what good officers came from their town, who their minister was and who their representative in the General Court, who were the leading men, the judges or justices who lived there, the brigade or regiment of militia that the town mustered. "Or fall into questions of literature, science or what you will." He should write down questions to ask his professors, and he must begin to consider where he would study law. He might indeed have already settled upon a master who would take him as a student and a clerk, "or," Adams wrote, "shall I come home and take you into my office? or are you so disgusted with our Greek breakfasts at The Hague and our Euclid suppers at Auteuil as to prefer another preceptor?" Then another warning, "Take care of your health. . . . Never defraud yourself of your sleep, nor of your walk. You need not now be in a hurry."[16]

Abigail rebuked John Quincy for his criticisms of his preceptors. Whatever he thought of their qualifications, he should always "treat them with the respect due their station, and enjoin the same conduct upon your brothers." Since it was not in his power to remedy the evils, he should make the best of them, remembering that "whilst the salaries are so small it cannot be expected that gentlemen of the first abilities will devote their lives to the preceptorship." In consequence, the positions must be filled with young men at the start of their careers who soon left. "You must," she admonished, "be conscious of how great importance it is to youth that they should respect their teachers; therefore whatever tends to lessen them is an injury to the whole society." Lest he puff himself up, Abigail reminded him that he had had unusual advantages. He had traveled more widely than any young man of his age in America; he had never wanted a book that had not been at once supplied him, his "whole time [had] been spent in the company of men of literature and science. . . . . How unpardonable would it have been in you," she added, "to have been a blockhead."[17]

L

Early in 1786, Adams encouraged by the apparent progress of his talks with De Pinto and with Abdrahaman, the Tripolitanian, sent Colonel Smith to Paris to urge Jefferson to come to London to try to push these negotiations to a conclusion.

When Jefferson arrived he was welcomed as a member of the family. He brought presents for Abigail and Nabby and hours of good conversation for Adams. He entered wholeheartedly into the life that centered on Grosvenor Square, accompanied the Adamses to Drury Lane to see Mrs. Siddons in *Macbeth,* and to John Trumbull's studio to gaze in awe at his dramatic depiction of the death of General Joseph Warren at Bunker Hill. The picture was especially moving to John and Abigail, who had known and loved Warren so well. "I can only say," Abigail wrote her sister, "that in looking at it my whole frame contracted, my blood shivered, and I felt a faintness at my heart."[1]

At Abigail's urging Jefferson sat for a portrait by Mather Brown and then presented it to Adams. He accompanied them to court, but when John tried to present his friend to the King, George III turned his back. Adams, as minister from the United States, the King must acknowledge and be courteous to; but there was no code of etiquette requiring him to take notice of the man who had written that insolent and offensive document, the Declaration of Independence. It was an embarrassing moment for Adams; he had presumed too much on the King's friendly manner toward him and exposed Jefferson to a humiliating snub. The rudeness of the King and the "vagueness and evasions" of the Foreign Secretary convinced the Americans that there was no prospect of a commercial treaty.

Jefferson enjoyed the company and conversation of Adams' friends, Dr. Price and Dr. Jebb; investigated and reported on an extraordinary grist mill driven not by water power but by a steam engine that consumed a hundred bushels of coal a day; met Lord Shelburne; and visited the great sights of London.

The city itself, handsomer than Paris, was not, he thought, as handsome a city as Philadelphia, though manufacturing—"the mechanical arts" —was carried "to a wonderful perfection."[2] Jefferson gave special attention to the agriculture of the farm areas adjacent to London and noted that the English soil, though not naturally as fertile as the French, was better manured and therefore more productive. The working people were better off than those of France and more independent. But it was in gardening that the English surpassed "all the earth." Their pleasure in gardening," he wrote John Page, ". . . went far beyond my ideas."

By April, Jefferson and Adams were ready to sign a commercial treaty with the Portuguese ambassador although De Pinto expressed doubts— well founded as it turned out—that the treaty would be ratified because it did not stipulate that American wheat must enter Portugal in the form of grain and be ground to flour in Portuguese mills.

Waiting for De Pinto to receive word from his court, Jefferson and Adams decided to take a tour of English estates and gardens.[3] Aside from his trip to London in 1784, it was Adams' first real vacation since he had come to Europe almost nine years before.

The two friends traversed acres of magnificent lawn and garden, examining the soil, remarking the latest methods of horticulture, talking with gardeners, delighting in the early foliage and in each other's company. For Adams it was the happiest interlude of his European years, a true farmer's vacation, away from the endless demands of his office and the pomp and ceremony of court life.

They made an oddly assorted pair as they traveled about the countryside, the tall, thin Virginia aristocrat and the short, stout New England farmer. Their friendship, in a sense, was a triumph of mind over temperament, for the contrast in character and personality was as marked as their physical disparity. Adams was the more original and imaginative, Jefferson more the representative man; Adams was the system builder, Jefferson the brilliant commentator. In all the vast body of his writings the Virginian never committed himself to an over-all philosophy which took account of man's relation to his fellow men and to God. His writings were, rather, a loose and extended disquisition on the liberal ethos of the eighteenth century. He lived by a set of liberal stereotypes (noble ones to be sure) which could not be easily reconciled with the reality of a disorderly world; perhaps sensing this, he refrained from any systematic examination of the precepts which he professed. The result was a lack of tension in his thought, a liberal blandness. His writings, personal or political, were not studded with the paradoxes and ambiguities which mark real life. Adams, less doctrinaire than his friend, had the Puritan's classic awareness of the tension between the real and the ideal—much of his intellectual energy was expended in trying to bring these two realms into a satisfying harmony, trying to enlarge his cosmology by constant reference to experience.

Jefferson shrank from looking full into the face of man bearing so plainly the stigmata of original sin. When his nephews murdered a Negro slave for breaking a teacup, Jefferson could never bring himself to allude to the episode. He could not indeed comprehend it. But when Adams' son died a drunkard's death in his early thirties, John, distressed as he was, had place in his philosophy for this tragic event. He could even preserve the family letters detailing his son's disintegration, for he knew that life was made up of bitter defeats and failures as well as hard-won successes. Thus while Jefferson maintained a simple and characteristically American optimism, refusing to face the dark spots in the human psyche, Adams oscillated, as we have seen, between hope and despair.

Yet it would be a mistake to overemphasize their differences. They were both men of their country and their age. They believed in man's ability to shape his own future (Adams with strong reservations to be sure); they believed in tolerance, in equality (although they interpreted the word differently), in the rights and obligations of the free citizen, in political freedom, in the efficacy of education, in the dangers of luxury, in the need for strict personal and political morality in a republic, in the superior wisdom and virtue of the yeoman farmer over any other class of society, and in the great destiny of their own country. Perhaps, above all, they both had an insatiable curiosity about the world, human and physical, in which they lived. Certainly they had enough in common to make them most congenial companions.

Jefferson, armed like Adams with Thomas Whately's *Observations on Modern Gardening*, gave particular attention to the styles of the gardens they visited and made careful notes. Chiswick, the estate of the Duke of Devonshire, was disfigured by an octagonal dome, and the gardens were somewhat too formal, almost contrived, without that quality of naturalness which even the most formal garden should display. They had a pond in the center that was poorly integrated with the area around it and contained "an obelisk of very ill effect." Woburn Manor, which belonged to Lord Peters, had four men to tend the farm, four for the "pleasure garden," and four for the kitchen garden. At Wotton, Jefferson noted a Palladian bridge which had escaped Whateley's attention and made a careful amendment in the margin of the guidebook.

Sensitive as he was to the gardens, everywhere it was people who most engaged Adams' interest. While his companion viewed every prospect with the eyes of a landscape architect, analyzing and criticizing, John was content to take his pleasure from a much simpler response to the beauty around them, to the giant trees and yew hedges, the pools and Doric arches, the sweeping vistas and noble prospects. "Superb," "beautiful," "great and elegant," Adams called them. As Jefferson made careful drawings of an Archimedes screw for raising water, Adams chatted with a gardener. While the Virginian recorded the measurements of a formal avenue, Adams instructed the grounds keeper on the principles of true liberty.

In Worcester, the scene of Cromwell's final victory over Charles II in the English Civil War, Adams was indignant to discover that the inhabitants knew nothing of the town's great history. At the tavern he quizzed half a dozen of the local farmers and found them so "ignorant and careless," he wrote impatiently, "that I was provoked and asked, 'And do Englishmen so soon forget the ground where liberty was fought for? Tell your neighbors and your children that this is holy ground; much holier than that on which your churches stand. All England should come in a pilgrimage to this hill once a year.'" His audience of solid, red-faced farmers, unconscious of the incongruity of being lectured to by an American rebel, seemed quite taken with John's exhortation.

In Stratford-upon-Avon, beside the classic English stream, Adams felt once more that he was on holy ground. Shakespeare's grand periods came readily to his mind and to his lips, the magnificent cadences, the words and phrases that were as familiar to him as Scripture. Here was marrow of the English bone. Three doors from the inn where they lodged was the cottage, "as small and mean as you can conceive," where the poet had been born. When their guide pointed out to them an old wooden chair by the chimney where Shakespeare supposedly sat, Jefferson and Adams cut off a chip as a memento, "according to custom," Adams noted apologetically. "There is nothing preserved of this great genius," he wrote in the diary, "which is worth knowing; nothing which might inform us what education, what company, what accident turned his mind to letters and the drama." His name was not even on his gravestone, but "his wit, fancy, his taste and judgment, his knowledge of nature, of life and character are immortal."

Much as the tour pleased him, Adams could not forbear to remark that he hoped it would be "long . . . before ridings, parks, pleasure grounds, and ornamented farms" became fashionable in America. There nature, he wrote, "has done greater things and furnished nobler materials . . . the oceans, islands, rivers, mountains, valleys are all laid out upon a larger scale." Penn's Hill itself, he thought, might be made into something to boast of, but he preferred it in its tangled, rocky state.[4]

By the end of April, Jefferson's projected three weeks' stay had stretched to seven. The Portuguese negotiation had been carried as far as he and Adams could carry it. They met with De Pinto to sign the treaty and a few days later Jefferson departed for Paris, leaving a large hole in the lives of all the Adamses. Abigail missed him as much as John, for he had carried on his gallant mock courtship; had combined compliments and courtesies, discussions of the theater, of art and music, with what was most flattering of all to Abigail, serious conversation on political subjects. He had lighted up the Grosvenor Square house with his charm, his mannered wit, his anecdotes, his endless inquisitiveness about his surroundings. It had been like the delightful days at Auteuil, and when he left it was as though someone had blown out an especially bright and cheerful light.

The warmth and affection of the relationship, to be sure, had been rather more in John and Abigail than in Jefferson. As with most charming men, the Virginian held something of himself in reserve. There was in him an ultimate area, a kind of interior arctic region—remote and lonely and cold. It might be said that Jefferson was so gracious, so affable, so easy to know, that few men ever knew him; Adams, on the other hand, awkward and stiff, often repelled people on slight acquaintance, but when he gave his friendship he gave it as he gave everything without reservation or restraint, abandoning his defenses and opening his heart. It was revealing of the two men that Adams in his letters to Jefferson signed himself, "Yours affectionately"; "With the most cordial esteem, your friend and ser[vant]"; "My dear friend, adieu"; while Jefferson never varied from the correctly formal, "Dear Sir, your most obedient humble servant." Put another way, it might be said that Adams loved Jefferson, while Jefferson liked Adams.

The most immediate excitement in the Adams household was the impending marriage of Nabby and Colonel Smith. There was first the matter of who was to marry them. They could not be married, under English law, by a dissenting minister. It must then be an Anglican priest, a little hard for a good Congregationalist to swallow, but John, who considered himself emancipated, took it in good part. The affable Bishop of St. Asaph, a friend of Dr. Price and Dr. Priestley ("a liberal man," Abigail called him), consented to perform the ceremony. Unstrung by the preparations, Abigail lost sleep and alternately wept at the thought of her only daughter marrying and laughed at her tears. The night before the wedding she slept fitfully and was tormented by an unhappy dream of Royall Tyler.

The service itself, with the stately and moving phrases of the Book of Common Prayer, was soon over and Abigail found solace in the beauty of the bride and the soldierly bearing of the groom. They really made a striking couple. Nabby was graceful and demure with a kind of touching vulnerability. The Colonel had the easygoing good nature of an essentially simple man who has found life very pleasant. He had been spoiled by devoted and indulgent parents, then became a brave soldier and a favorite of General Washington's. Friends had secured an interesting job for him; he had met a lovely girl, his superior's daughter, and married her after a short and dashing courtship. Abigail knew enough about life to have reflected that such a career was not the best preparation to make one's way in a hard world, that Colonel William Smith, who stood up so straight and handsome beside her daughter, had had little occasion to feel the rougher textures of life. If she had such thoughts she loyally suppressed them. The unhappy Tyler affair had perhaps made her less wary than she might otherwise have been. In addition it must be admitted that Colonel Smith was the kind of young man that mothers are especially susceptible to: polite, tactful, with a good family background, "a liberal education," excellent manners and no noticeable vices—as Abigail put it, "of strict honor and unblemished reputation and morals, brave, modest and delicate"—all the things which are supposed to ensure worldly success and marital bliss, but which of course have very little to do with either.

After the ceremony the Bishop of St. Asaph came up to Abigail and assured her: "I have never married a couple with more pleasure because I never saw a fairer prospect of happiness." Abigail was delighted with the Bishop's prognostication.[5] "God bless them and make them as happy as their parents have been thus far through life," she wrote Mary Cranch. Man and wife, Nabby and her husband rode off to their apartments on Wimpole Street. They would maintain their own establishment but dine every day with John and Abigail.

In June, John and Abigail took a trip to Windsor Castle. Abigail was "charmed and delighted with it. . . . . The most luxuriant fancy," she wrote her niece, Lucy Cranch, "cannot exceed the beauties of this place." They approached the castle along a broad, straight road, some three miles in length, lined by a double row of majestic elms. Windsor stood on a hill and from its tower the visitors could see into thirteen counties, a breathtaking view of rolling green hills, of forest and field. The castle itself was furnished with royal opulence and hung with paintings of the "first masters." They saw the Queen's bedchamber: her bed with white satin counterpanes and pea-green, richly embroidered curtains; and a full-length portrait of the Queen and her fourteen children in miniature painted by Benjamin West. The room adjoining the Queen's bedchamber was "the room of beauties," so called because it contained portraits of the fourteen most celebrated beauties of the time of Charles II.

The Royal Observatory was located at Windsor and while Abigail strolled through the extensive gardens John spent hours with Mr. Herschel, the astronomer. The purpose of the trip had indeed been less to see the castle than to meet and talk to Herschel and to look through his telescope at the stars. Unhappily the evening was overcast so that there was no stargazing, but Adams was completely captivated by the astronomer. Prone as he was to sudden and impulsive attachments, he struck if off at once with Herschel who, as he later told Nabby in recounting the highlights of the trip, had not been made "silent or absent by his study," but was a "cheerful and intelligent companion; communicative of his knowledge and very agreeable." He had answered with infinite good humor John's endless questions, had shown him all his apparatus, brought him up to date on the latest observations and altogether charmed him. Nabby, hearing her father's excited account of his visit, watching his flushed and animated face, noted in her journal, "I have never known him to be so much gratified by a visit of any kind before."[6]

The next excursion, which included Nabby and her husband, was if possible even more rewarding. The greatest English patron of Harvard had been Thomas Hollis, a devoted friend of America and of liberty. Hollis had given the college at Cambridge money for a building (John Quincy and Charles were at that very moment lodged in Hollis Hall). More important, he had kept the college library supplied with all the important books on political theory written from a liberal persuasion. As fast as such works appeared in England, Thomas Hollis had shipped them off to Harvard. It had been his hope that the best spirit of English liberty would put its roots deep in American soil; that Algernon Sidney, Locke, Milton, Marchmont Needham, Harrington, and a host of others would imbue the young scholars of Harvard with an ineradicable devotion to free and constitutional government, to the rights of Englishmen as defined and defended by generations of brave and faithful men. As a scholar and one of the foremost intellectuals of his day Hollis had built up a great library of his own and made his house a museum, stocked with antiquities of the Greek and Roman civilizations which he so loved.

On his death his beneficiary, Thomas Brand, "a neat, nice bachelor," a lover of "liberty, benevolence, and philosophy," and a man of the same eccentric, liberal spirit as his patron, took the Hollis name and became a kind of custodian of the Hollis treasures, remaining a friend to America throughout the Revolution and corresponding with American statesmen. Adams and Brand-Hollis had met in London and subsequently exchanged letters; the Englishman invited John and the family to visit him at his manor house in Essex County. With London in the summer doldrums and nothing stirring on the diplomatic scene, Adams decided to make the trip in late July.

He and Abigail rose with the sun, mounted their carriage, picked up Nabby and the Colonel at Wimpole Street and rode out to Rumford where they had a belated breakfast. From Rumford they went on to Thornton and stopped to visit the estate of Lord Petre. They entered the grounds through "a spacious and elegant portal, of the Corinthian order," from whence, Abigail wrote, "a noble prospect is opened to the palace, the bridge, the lake with its valley and other beautiful scenes." On the pediment was a bust of Louis XIV taken by the Duke at Tournai as spoils of war. This, the gardener told the Adamses, he never failed to point out to visiting Frenchmen, who invariably "shrugged their shoulders and *mon-dieu'd.*"

Sixty-three hands were employed during the summer "in mowing, sweeping, pruning, lopping, and in ornamenting the grounds." From a lawn smooth as a looking glass they walked down to the water. The gardens were four miles square. The gardener, "very loquacious and swelled with importance," conducted them around, pointing out recent additions —the temple of Diana, the sculptured group of four river gods in the cascade. The house, John noted, "is vast and the apartments are grand, and the prospects from the windows are extensive and agreeable. The furniture is rich and elegant."

From Thornton they rode on to Essex where the Brand-Hollis estate was located. They approached the house through fields dotted with cattle and sheep, past a grove of trees planted by the elder Hollis which contained, Adams noted, a number of American trees, among them firs growing in a "rude, wild but agreeable manner."

Brand-Hollis met them at the doorway, an odd, perky, cheerful little man who took them on a tour of the manor. They entered a large hall in which stood a number of classic busts, most prominent among them one of Marcus Aurelius and a fine white marble bust of Thomas Hollis. In architecture, Palladio, the Italian Renaissance builder, had been a Hollis favorite and the architect's influence was apparent everywhere in the house.

Over the chimney in the study were three small portraits which, Brand-Hollis told Abigail, depicted his favorite general, philosopher, and writer. Marcus Aurelius was the general, Plato the writer, and Francis Hutcheson, Brand-Hollis' tutor at the University of Edinburgh, the philosopher. The walls were crowded with pictures, good and bad, all celebrating liberty or depicting a heroic episode from antiquity, and statues, busts, curiosities, and mementos filled every nook and cranny. Thomas Hollis' magic liberal insignias had been an owl, a liberty cap, and a dagger, symbolizing liberal wisdom, liberty, and the courage to fight for it—this motif was repeated interminably throughout the house.

One of the prize pieces was a silver cup with a lid in the shape of an owl with two rubies for eyes, a relic of pagan Britain which had been dug up at Canterbury. The attention of the visitors was called to an ebony cabinet inlaid with brass. In this was preserved the heart of Thomas Hollis; his body had been buried ten feet deep in an unmarked grave.

Brand-Hollis lived with his maiden sister, a wispy little woman who was a collector in her own right. Her taste ran to china and she had a piece of every manufacturer in the kingdom, "either a cup or bowl, a mug or a jar." She also had a great variety of singing birds, and a strong interest in good works. She had taken half a dozen poor children from the streets of London, clothed them, and put them in school.

In the dining room Abigail noted with a little sniff of disapproval two nude Greeks, Venus and Adonis, disporting themselves in a voluptuous Rembrandt—"a luxuriant picture for a bachelor."

The library was the *sanctum sanctorum* of this liberal temple; "as select and highly honored friends" the Adamses were admitted. The room was lined with books and crowded with Egyptian, Greek, and Roman antiquities—busts, medals, and coins.

The gardens of the estate stretched some distance from the house. At the end of the formal garden stood a Greek temple, and through the trees beyond, a rustic cottage with a large pond beside it filled with gold-fish. There was a tall cypress at the side of the garden which was named George Washington, and in honor of Nabby's husband, the General's former aide-de-camp, Brand-Hollis christened a smaller one beside it "Colonel Smith."

Staying at the Brand-Hollis mansion, the Adamses took brief excursions into the surrounding countryside, walked the paths and lanes on the estate, and visited adjoining manors. Colonel Smith tried his luck fly fish-ing in a nearby stream and John was flattered by an invitation to visit the gardener's house. The gardener, like his master strongly pro-American, lectured Adams on the American government and its laws and filled him full of gardening lore. He was "bee mad" and had a number of glass hives in which John could see the bees at work. He showed Abigail the queen bee's cell, and she observed with astonishment that he handled "the bees as one would flies without ever being stung." The gardener had devised an ingenious door through which drones could exit from the hive but not return. The bees knew and liked him, he declared, discoursing at length upon their habits, a topic which appealed more to John than to his wife. He "will with great fluency read you a lecture of an hour upon their laws and government," she wrote John Quincy. The gardener, "who is a Son of Liberty," John noted, "and was always a friend of America, was de-lighted with [the] visit. 'Dame,' says he to his wife, 'you have had the greatest honor done you today that you ever had in your life.' "[7]

John, the coachman, showed them through *his* garden where he had a collection of curious flowers "and a little grotto filled with fossils and shells."

The next day John and Abigail set off by carriage to Braintree, some eighteen miles away. "I thought we ought to make a little excursion to the town after which the town in New England where I was born and shall die was originally named," Adams noted in his diary. They rode through good fertile land covered with crops of barley, oats, rye, wheat, and buckwheat to the market town. The church, which was approached through a lane of lime trees, was the principal object of John's interest. It was a fine old Norman building "not much larger than Mr. Cleverly's church at Braintree in New England." Adams prowled through the grave-yard adjoining the church looking for a trace of some English Adams, or some other names common in Braintree, Massachusetts. There were none and the town, "a poor, dirty, miserable village," was "at present," he wrote, "the home only of very ordinary people," who made a precarious livelihood weaving baize cloth in their homes.

They came back from their expedition depressed by the squalor and poverty they had seen, but after dinner their spirits were revived by a lecture from Brand-Hollis "upon antiquities and curiosities." The ebony cabinet containing his benefactor's heart was opened and they saw inside, not the heart, which was encased in wood, but a small shrine containing a bust of Milton surrounded by four or five first editions of his works.

The next day they made their farewells to the kind Miss Brand, as avian as one of her own singing larks, to the "bee-mad" gardener, to John, the coachman, and to Brand-Hollis, custodian of the museum of "enlightenment," packed with liberal treasures, and returned to Grosvenor Square, "much pleased with our visit," as Nabby declared to John Quincy.[8]

Back in London, Adams carried on by letter his debate with Jefferson over whether it was more practical to pay the Barbary pirates their bounty money or to make war against them. Jefferson, the idealist, was for war as the more honest and worthy course; Adams, the realist, felt that war was impractical, that America had neither the ships nor the money to carry on a naval campaign against the Algerians. Indeed, he wrote, it seemed that "neither force nor money will be applied. Our states are so backward that they will do nothing for some years." He would be surprised if they could raise enough money to pay the interest on their European debts, let alone scrape together enough to buy off the rapacious Algerians. "A disposition seems rather to prevail among our citizens to give up all ideas of navigation and naval power, and lay themselves consequently at the mercy of foreigners. . . . Your plan of fighting will be no more adopted than mine of negotiating. This is more humiliating to me than giving the presents would be." The latest word from America was that New Hampshire and Rhode Island had given up their "navigation laws"—that is, their effort to regulate trade—and it must be assumed that without their support Massachusetts would soon follow suit, thus leaving it up to the Annapolis convention to form some system. But even if the convention formed one it would not "be completed, adopted and begin to operate under several years," he added. In the meantime there was little that could be done to negotiate commercial treaties or produce any plan or order in America's relations with European countries.

The only bright spot in a general dreary picture was the ratification of the Prussian treaty by Congress. Adams found it waiting for him when he returned from Hyde and he decided to take Abigail with him to The Hague to exchange the ratified treaty with Baron von Thulemeier and to give Abigail a chance to so some sight-seeing in Holland. They left for The Hague early in August and spent five weeks touring the country and visiting Dutch friends.

The Prince of Orange, at loggerheads with the States-General, had retreated in a huff to Loo so that Abigail could not be presented at court. But she and John were invited to dine with the British ambassador, Sir James Harris, and his beautiful young wife, "ranked with the first of English beauties." Lady Harris, who had been married at seventeen, had four handsome children but "no dignity in her manners, nor solidity in her deportment"; she was rather "of the good-humored giggling class—a mere trifler," Abigail wrote her sister. Later John and Abigail were escorted to see the estate and gardens of Secretary Fagel, "a jaunt of three miles, through a sand like Weymouth Hill," until Abigail "puffed and blowed" and sat down at every opportunity, not thinking the view worth the fatigue.

Abigail found her diversion with Plutarch's *Lives* while John was engaged in business, but the gloomy recital of "tyranny, cruelty, devastation, and horror" that comprised the lives of the Roman emperors gave her bad dreams. She was "haunted every night," she wrote Nabby, "with some of their troubled spirits," and she swore the next time she went traveling to take the cheerful *Don Quixote* with her.[1]

The country charmed Abigail—the dikes lined with willow trees, the flat meadows, canals, brightly painted barges, windmills, brick-paved streets, the neatness and order, the picturesque clothes of the farm people, short petticoats and long short-gowns, the round-eared caps, large straw hats, the "trig neatness of the women" in black tammy aprons and thick quilted coats and russet skirts, with gold bracelets and earrings. "The respect, attention, civility, and politeness" which they received everywhere convinced her that the Dutch were most sympathetic to the principles of the American Revolution. Indeed, the Dutch themselves declared that their connection with America had stirred the dying embers of their own zeal for liberty. They appeared, moreover, "to be a . . . contented, happy people." There were few evidences of poverty, and the cities had many charitable organizations which did justice to the benevolent instincts of their citizens. There was little lawlessness in the country and everything was kept clean and neat as a pin. The houses all seemed freshly painted and even the milk pails were painted inside and out.

John and Abigail visited the Moravian town of Zest and saw the famous stained-glass windows of Gouda, "reaching from the top to the bottom of a very high church and containing Scripture history." The scenes seemed awkwardly rendered to Abigail but the colors "were beautiful beyond imagination." Their trip was a real tourist jaunt to every historic spot, every shrine and museum that Adams could discover; to Saardam for the famous annual fair where the citizens were turned out in their traditional holiday clothes—bright smocks and starched caps, pantaloons and jackets. There they visited the ship carpenter's shop of Czar Peter, who had made his residence in the town. They walked through miles of galleries past the great Flemish masters, past Vermeers and Der Hoochs, through museums of natural history and "public buildings of distinction." Knowing the history of the country as they did, the past haunted every spot they visited; here William of Orange had met the forces of the Duke of Alba; there Oldenbarneveldt had spoken for liberty; there the burghers of Leyden had compacted to fight tyranny. Abigail noted that the Dutch ladies had fine complexions and, moreover, had "not spoiled them by cosmetics. Rouge is confined to the stage here," she wrote Nabby.[2]

At Amsterdam, Abigail and John visited the Exchange with Mr. Van Staphorst. It was located in a large square where from twelve to two every merchant of the city came to transact business. As many as ten thousand men pushed their way into the Exchange, and Abigail, viewing the scene from a window looking out over the square, thought to herself that the noise that rose from the crowd resembled nothing so much as the sound of swarming bees.

In Helvoet the Adamses were greeted by the ringing of bells and a military guard turned out to honor the representative of the United States and his lady. On the road from Helvoet to Rotterdam they took a lumbering coach driven by "two great, heavy, clumsy, whiffing Dutchmen," one of whom, despite Abigail's protests, took his seat on her bandbox to its imminent peril while the other mounted behind the carriage with a friend, "jabbering and smoking" as they crawled along, "stopping at every village to take a glass of gin." Abigail was indignant but John, experienced in the ways of the Dutch, assured her that there was "no remedy but patience." The Dutch must go at their own pace, puffing their inevitable pipes, stopping to pass the time of day with a friend when the spirit moved them. "The people," Abigail observed a little caustically, "appear well fed, well clothed, and well smoked . . . whether riding or walking or rowing or otherwise employed, a long or a short pipe occupies them all."

At Delft, Abigail bought some tiles and they went to see the marble statue of William I, the liberator of Holland. "On one hand," Abigail noted in describing the monument to Nabby, "is justice; on the other liberty, religion, and prudence; behind him stands fame with her trumpet, reaching forward and balancing herself upon one toe. . . . At the foot of William lies the marble statue of the dog who died for grief at the tomb of his master."[3]

Leyden was the cleanest city Abigail had ever seen. "The streets are wide," she wrote, "the houses all brick, all neat, even to the meanest building." At Leyden they visited the church where the Pilgrims had worshiped "when they fled from hierarchial tyranny and persecution. . . . . I felt a respect and veneration upon entering the doors," Abigail wrote Mary Cranch, "like what the ancients paid to their Druids."

With the Adamses away, Nabby and her husband were left to their own devices. They made happy excursions in the country around London, fishing and picnicking along the banks of the Thames. One night they stopped at an inn so close to the river that they were able to fish out of the windows of their room and catch dozens of silvery little dace. They punted on the river, read poetry to each other, made plans for their life after their return to America, and stole furtive and delicious kisses. When John and Abigail returned from their trip through the Netherlands, Nabby was pregnant.

The Adamses trip across the Channel was "a stormy, boisterous passage of three days, attended with no small danger." Abigail hardly slept a wink for two nights and then rode seventy-five miles from Dover to London, arriving exhausted at Grosvenor Square. There she found a great packet of letters from home and John had to lay down the law to stop her, lightheaded from fatigue as she was, from plunging into them. He sent her sternly off to bed, but she was up early the next morning and read all the letters before breakfast. The news was both good and bad. The boys were well. All of them were now at Harvard, where Tommy had joined Charles and John Quincy. John Quincy and Charles were living in Hollis Hall—John Quincy on the third floor with a "fine view of the Charles to Boston and the extensive fields between"; Charles on the lower floor.

Mary Cranch's only worry about John Quincy was that he studied so hard that his health suffered. Nothing drew him from his books. During the great dedication of the Charleston bridge with the Governor, the Assembly, and thousands of spectators present, with speeches and singing and a general holiday air, John Quincy had remained bent over his books. There his cousins Lucy and Betsy Cranch, who had come up to Cambridge for the festivities, found him with his head buried in Euclid, surrounded, as Lucy put it, with "*learned dirt*—(not to say the *rust* he had *about* and *around* him)"—disheveled, untidy, with a scholarly pallor, his hair uncut, his room a mess. The two girls descended on him and with Charles's help wrestled him out of his soiled gown and jacket, turned up a clean coat among the litter, and prevailed on him to don it. Lucy took her scissors out of her purse and cut his long, rather grimy nails. That left only his hair, sadly in need of a comb and a hair string to catch it off his shoulders. Charles, who watched the assault on his unkempt brother with a broad grin, was a distinct contrast, Lucy wrote, "naturally and habitually neat." John Quincy took his refurbishing by Lucy and Betsy in good spirit. They must come once a quarter, he said, "and perform the like good service for him again."[4]

Under Mary Cranch's supervision Lucy and Betsy had become expert seamstresses, turning out fourteen waistcoats "for the three collegians." The boys had spent the summer vacancy with the Cranches; along with Billy and Lucy they made the little house bulge, but Richard Cranch was delighted with the company. The young people played their musical instruments—the flute, violin, and harpsichord. Charles, with his light, pleasant voice, sang duets, first with Lucy and then with Betsy. "The Indian Philosopher" set to music by Dr. Watts was Richard Cranch's favorite piece. It made him feel twenty years younger, he declared, to hear the children sing it. "Sitting in a row before our chimney board in the parlor drinking tea," Mary wrote her sister, "Mr. Cranch could not help observing . . . what a fine string of young fellows they were, and how much pleasure you would have taken in beholding them."

Other news was less encouraging. Mary Cranch wrote that the state was bankrupt. Her husband could no longer afford to be a representative from Braintree in the Great and General Court. He had to return to farming and watch repairing to support his family and maintain Billy at Harvard. A kind of stupor seemed to possess the state. General Warren had run for Lieutenant Governor and after a campaign in which he had been much abused he had gotten only two votes, which had left him humiliated and indignant. In Mary's view the General's trouble was that he wished for higher office than his talents entitled him to and was embittered because he was not accepted by the voters at his own evaluation. He had turned down so many jobs which he considered beneath him that now it was very difficult to do anything for him. Richard Cranch had tried to get him the office of counselor, talking to many members of the General Court about it and campaigning vigorously for the General, but the latter had missed that office too, and seemed inclined to blame Cranch for his failure. Mercy Warren's somewhat acerbic temper was rubbed raw by her husband's frustrations and "corroded by disappointments of various kinds."[5] Relations were further strained by the fact that the Adams and Cranch boys had been forbidden to associate with the young Warrens because of their reputation for scandalous behavior.

Tristram Dalton and Stephen Higginson in letters to Adams confirmed Mary Cranch's gloomy diagnosis. "Jealousy, pride, and luxury, an unbounded thirst for *baneful* commerce, want of attention to the internal resources of their country . . . with a great disregard to the importance of establishing a fair national character—seems to pervade the continent," Dalton wrote. He deplored, moreover, the vengeful spirit against the Tories. Dalton preferred to let bygones be bygones, but he noted that his friends "Tufts and Cranch of the Senate" had supported restrictive legislation directed against the Tories. The Massachusetts legislature had repealed its navigation act, which Dalton thought a pity since the repeal would invite the importation of "British gewgaws, British manners and customs." Higginson, on the other hand, was delighted at the repeal. The act had been unfair and unworkable; it had encouraged smuggling and evasion. He was in agreement only on the fact that "we appear to be verging fast to a crisis." Some "change of ideas and measures," he wrote

Adams, "must soon happen, either from conviction or from necessity . . .
it will then behoove every man of property and influence to aim at giving
the tide a right direction."[6]

But what this "right direction" might be Higginson failed to say; Adams
read the letters from home with a sinking heart, realizing that serious
rifts were growing between old friends. The Revolution had held all
patriots in a unity of spirit, their attention directed toward a common
enemy, their individual differences subordinated to a single aim. Now
with independence won the ship of state seemed to be coming apart at
the seams. What could it mean? James and Mercy Warren, jealous and resentful, angry with Richard Cranch; Mary clearly offended; even gentle
Eliza Shaw writing sharply of Mercy's "corroded" mind; Dalton had
split with Tufts and Cranch on the treatment of the Tories, Higginson and
Dalton were on opposite sides of the fence; Gerry suspicious of any efforts
to strengthen the general government; Sullivan insisting that it was the
only measure that could save the country. All these were Massachusetts
men. What of the rest of New England and the rest of the country? Was
there similar spirit of wrangling and faction, hostility and localism everywhere? If there was, what hope was there for any stable and orderly kind
of government? What hope, indeed, for the Union?

General Warren wrote in the same vein. Commerce was ruined, "no
debts can be paid or taxes collected. . . . A total change in principles and
manners—interest is the great object, the only pursuit, and riches only respected. Everything seems verging to confusion and anarchy. . . . Our
elections have been much the same this as last year. . . . Few attend the
meetings and hardly one inquired further than who was in last and
vote for him again without the trouble of recurring to principles or tracing
consequences."[7]

As he read the letters Adams became increasingly impatient to escape
from his durance in England. Home was the place for him. There at least
he might find out at first hand what was going on and not have to depend
on conflicting accounts which agreed only that the situation was desperate. When Cotton Tufts wrote that the Veasey land was for sale,
Adams found himself wishing to be home. Veasey's land adjoined his
own. They were on the whole poor, stony acres, but he must have them
nonetheless. "My view," he wrote Tufts, "is to lay fast hold of the town
of Braintree and embrace it with both my arms and all my might. There to
live—there to die—there to lay my bones—and there to plant one of my
sons in the profession of the law and the practice of agriculture like his
father." He thus wanted enough land "to amuse me and employ me as
long as I live, that I may not rust alive." He could certainly use his "little
modicum of means more profitably," he admitted, "but in no way so much
to my taste and humor—or so much for my health and happiness." He
could have bought up the whole town if he had not had to devote the

better part of his life to serving his country. "Now," he added, "I must be content to be poor, and my children too, unless they should have more wisdom than I have had."[8]

The next news from New England seemed to bear out the most somber prognostications. Massachusetts farmers, finding themselves hard pressed by creditors who threatened to bring action against their farms, and indignant over increased taxes, oppressive legal fees, and high prices, began to interfere with the sitting of the courts at Northampton and Worcester. They found a leader in a popular Revolutionary officer, Captain Daniel Shays, and assumed an air of open defiance toward the agencies of government. The thought that came to the mind of everyone familiar with ancient history was that the democratic uprising which must inevitably lead to a dictatorship had in fact started. The bonds of society would be loosened, law would no longer be respected, force would be the only rule, and finally a tyrant, a military dictator, backed doubtless by the Society of the Cincinnati, would rise to restore order and guarantee the security of life and property at the cost of freedom.

These were certainly the thoughts that sprang to the minds of John and Abigail when they received the grim news, but Adams suppressed his anxiety when he wrote Jefferson. He assured the Virginian that he need not be "alarmed at the late turbulence in New England . . . all will be well . . . and this commotion will terminate in additional strength to government."[9]

There was no comfort in subsequent reports from Adams' American correspondents. Samuel Osgood wrote in November that things could hardly be worse. He feared that "the stubborn dignity [of the states] will never permit a federal government to exist." The only hope lay in the fact that there were a few men in every state who "are thinking very seriously in what manner to effect the most easy and natural change of the present form of the federal government to one more energetic; that will at the same time create respect and secure properly life, liberty, and property." It was not uncommon to hear solid and patriotic men speaking of "emperors, kings, stadtholders, governors general, with a Senate or a House of Lords and House of Commons." Many were in favor of abolishing all state governments and for forming an all-powerful central government, but Osgood was confident that "very few will agree in the general principles, much less in the details of such a government." The idea of a special convention called to reform the Articles of Confederation seemed to be daily gaining ground among those most concerned with the critical state of the country. The danger was that men of property would attach themselves to the army, "the final issue of which, it is feared, will be that the army will make the government of the United States." Osgood ended his letter on an ominous note: "Many say already any change will be for the better—and are ready to risk anything to effect it." The finances of the country, so egregiously mismanaged by Congress, could scarcely be in a worse condition.[10]

James Sullivan was, if anything, more pessimistic. The federal government seemed to be daily growing weaker. The "old Whigs" were beginning to talk "very seriously" of a change in the system of government. The "separate sovereignties" were, they felt, "insupportable and quite incompatible with a general government." Congress was raising a small force which Sullivan, like Osgood, considered the beginning of a standing army that would probably first be employed in putting down civil war. "I am sorry to say," he wrote, "that all our fine-spun ideas of democratical governments being founded in the virtue of the people are vanished, and that we find Americans like other people obliged by force only to yield obedience to the laws."[11]

As the reports began to pile up of the desperate state of affairs in America and especially in his native state, Adams grew increasingly touchy and irascible. Mr. Sparhawk, a visitor from Massachusetts who had called at Grosvenor Square, was the unfortunate object of Adams' wrath. Sparhawk provoked the outburst by declaring that "the people of the United States were as much oppressed by taxes as they were in Europe." At this comment Adams exploded. "Give me leave to tell you, sir," he stormed at the unhappy visitor, "that people who hold this language betray a total ignorance of the subject. . . . Pray, are our farmers perishing in the midst of plenty, as in Ireland? Are our fishermen starving? Cannot the laborer find a subsistence?" It was the reckless and greedy merchants who expected to live off the labor of others who were whining and complaining. "Name the article in this country, even to the light of heaven, the air you breathe, and the water you drink, which is not taxed." At this tirade Sparhawk "drew in his horns" and had little more to say.

The gloomy fall, damp and lowering—"all smoke, fog, and darkness"— added to John's and Abigail's depression over the news from America. When, on top of the word of Shays' uprising and the growing paralysis of will that seemed to be infecting the country, Abigail heard that Congress had voted to maintain a regular army, she broke down and wept. "To behold my countrymen who had so nobly fought and bled for freedom, tarnishing their glory, loosing the bonds of society, introducing anarchy, confusion, and despotism, forging domestic chains for posterity," was almost more than she could bear. Had all the sacrifice, all the suffering been in vain, the hopes and dreams of a great democratic republic mere illusions? Were the cynics right—that only force and coercion could suppress the evil propensities in man? It seemed as though the great experiment in free government was to fail before it was properly launched, and every enemy of human freedom would exult in the failure. All those around the world who suffered under harsh and repressive governments, who went to bed every night miserable and hungry and who, looking at America, had dared to hope for a better day, would sink back into the dark night of hopelessness. "The experience of ages and the historical page teach us," Abigail wrote John Quincy, "that a popular tyranny never fails to be followed by arbitrary government of a single person." Caesars and Pompeys would appear if "civil dissensions continue," if honest and faithful leaders were ridiculed and denigrated. But it was not in Abigail or her husband to despair. She would continue to believe in the "wisdom and firmness" of Americans. "I had flattered myself with the hope," she added, "that my children would reap the benefits of an equitable and peaceable government, after the many perils and difficulties which their father had passed through to obtain one." If there was to be disorder and strife, John Quincy and his brothers must be prepared to defend "the rights of mankind . . . in the Senate, and in the field if necessary." "For what have we been contending against the tyranny of Great Britain," she wrote Mary Cranch, "if we are to become the sacrifice of a lawless banditti? Must our glory be thus shorn and our laurels thus blasted? Is it a trifling matter to destroy a government? Will my countrymen justify the maxim of tyrants, that mankind are not made for freedom?"[12]

Her indignation and anxiety spilled over in an angry letter to Jefferson. "The Shaysites were ignorant, wrestless desperadoes, without conscience or principles," she declared, who had "led a deluded multitude to follow their standard under a pretense of grievances which have no existence but in their imaginations. . . . Instead of that laudable spirit which you approve, which makes a people watchful over their liberties and alert in defense of them, these mobbish insurgents are for sapping the foundation and destroying the whole fabric at once." Abigail had little sympathy with the Virginian's response: "I like a little rebellion now and then," he wrote. "It is like a storm in the atmosphere."[13]

Adams for his part was impatient with arguments that the states could not meet their obligations. "I have never heard or read," he wrote Warren, "of sluggards who saw so many fantastical lions in the way as our people appear to have seen since the peace. . . . The picture you draw of the ruin of the country is horrible," he confessed, but he could not bring himself to accept it. Since the beginning of the Revolutionary crisis there had always been those who followed gain and self-interest in preference to their country's welfare. Certainly it was true that Americans "are not and never were Spartans in their contempt of wealth, and I will go farther and say they ought not to be. Such a trait in their character would render them lazy drones, unfit for the agriculture, manufactures, fisheries, and commerce and population of their country; and fit only for war. I am never apprehensive of anarchy because I know there is wisdom and address enough to prevent it." The cure was to restore public confidence by funding the debt and annihilating "all apprehensions of paper knavery."[14]

For some time Adams had been fretting over the growing sentiment both at home and in Europe for governments which consisted of a single legislative body combining the executive, legislative, and judicial functions. In 1778, Turgot, the philosopher and French Minister of Finance, had written Dr. Price criticizing the constitutions of the American states for not uniting all power in a central agency of government. The Americans, Turgot declared, had framed their various state governments "in an unreasonable imitation of the usages of England." Instead of "bringing all the authorities into one, that of the nation, they have established different bodies, a House of Representatives, a Council, a Governor, because England has a House of Commons, a House of Lords, and a King. . . . I see . . . an unreasonable imitation of the usages of England."

Turgot's attack rankled the more as it was supported by Franklin's prestige. The Pennsylvanian, as the epitome of all wisdom, was widely cited for his support of a single-branch legislature in Pennsylvania. The Abbé de Mably had added his voice to the supporters of a single branch of government as being superior to the traditional divisions of executive, legislative, and judicial, even going so far as to state that his advice had been sought in the framing of the respective state constitutions. Now word came from Massachusetts that the constitution of that state, over which Adams had labored so long and which he considered a model of good government, was under attack and that the state itself was convulsed by civil disturbance.

As Adams wrote Jay, "The just complaints of the people of real grievances ought never to be discouraged and even their imaginary grievances may be treated with too great severity. But when a cry is set up for the abolition of debts, equal division of property, and the abolition of senates and governors, it is time for every honest man to consider his situation." Good laws and orderly government alone could protect "lives, liberties, religion, property, and characters." If the laws were "scorned," he wrote feelingly, "in God's name what is ever to be respected? What is there worth living for?"[15]

With these thoughts in mind Adams turned to the task of writing a defense of the constitutions of the various states, a defense that would make clear for all time the true and proper, the scientific, basis of sound government. The work should establish beyond question or cavil the principle of separate and balanced branches by showing how the lessons of history and the writings of the wisest philosophers were in harmony on this point. Adams would answer the charges of Turgot, De Mably, and others; check his fellow citizens of Massachusetts in their mad and destructive course, and point the way for future state constitutions. "It was not to obtain a name as an author or a reputation for literary talents," he later wrote Dr. Price, "that I undertook the laborious work. If such had been my object I certainly should have taken more time to digest and connect it. But it appeared to me that my countrymen were running wild and into danger from a too ardent and inconsiderate pursuit of erroneous opinions of government which have been propagated among them by some of their ill-informed favorites and by various writings which were very popular among them, such as the pamphlet called *Common Sense*, for one example among many others, particularly Mrs. Macaulay's *History*, Mr. Burgh's *Political Disquisitions*, Mr. Turgot's *Letters*. These writings are all excellent in some respect and very useful but extremely mistaken in the true construction of a free government. To accomplish the good I had in view, I thought it would be more useful and effectual to lay facts, principles, examples and reasonings before my countrymen from the writings of others than in my own name."

He withdrew to his upstairs library, barred the door to anyone but Abigail and, surrounding himself with histories, philosophical treatises, and political texts, plunged into his disquisition on the nature of government. He worked with a sense of urgency—the time was short; affairs in America were approaching a critical stage. He read and wrote from early morning to late at night, until his eyes were too inflamed to read and his arm too stiff and sore to write. Then he drafted Nabby as a secretary and pushed on. Abigail worried about his health and fussed and clucked over him like a mother hen, but she knew him too well to entertain any serious hope of slowing him in his headlong pace. "Your father," she wrote John Quincy, "is much engaged in a work that may prove of no small utility to our country. It is an investigation into the different forms of government both ancient and modern—monarchal, aristocratical, democratical, and republican—pointing out their happiness or misery in proportion to their different balances. It appears to be a subject in which America is greatly interested, and upon which her future happiness depends."[16]

The work was pushed to completion in a few short weeks and, as Adams was well aware, had all the imperfections of haste. It was haphazardly organized, or disorganized; it was full of errors and inconsistencies, names were misspelled, dates misplaced, even, in several instances, pages transposed. It was more of an anthology then an original work because large sections were simply quoted from the works of particular philosophers or from standard contemporary histories, some of them hastily and inaccurately translated. The soldier rushing into battle at a critical moment does not stop to check every item of his equipment to see that it is in parade-ground order. Adams conceived of himself as just such a soldier racing to shore up a breach in the defenses of proper government. He was engaged in an emergency operation and he had no time to polish or refine. It did not occur to him that there was anything in the slightest degree reprehensible in copying large portions from various works, sometimes with acknowledgment and sometimes without. There was no vested interest, no personal property in scholarship. Whether a work was directly quoted or paraphrased was simply a matter of convenience; it had nothing to do with any ethic of scholarship. Ideas did not belong to the people who originated them but to all literate men. So he hurried on, not troubling himself about academic canons or scholarly niceties.

The result was a curious jumble, a work that would certainly be sneered at as amateurish and inept by more sophisticated English and Continental scholars. But Adams was not writing for scholars, he was writing for people, for politicians, for students, for everyone interested in a better human society, everyone concerned with the kind of government which would give the greatest scope to human potentiality.

"The arts and sciences in general," he declared in his preface, "during the three or four last centuries have had a regular course of progressive improvement. The inventions in mechanic arts, the discoveries in natural philosophy, navigation, and commerce, and the advancement of civilization and humanity have occasioned changes in the condition of the world and the human character which would have astonished the most refined nations of antiquity." Europe was by such means becoming daily "more and more like one community or single family."[17] The general improvement in social and economic conditions, the spectacular developments in science and technology—"the mechanic arts"—made it all the more "unaccountable that the knowledge of the principles and construction of free governments, in which the happiness of life and even the further progress of improvement in education and society, in knowledge and virtue are so deeply interested, should have remained at a full stand for two or three thousand years." It was Adams' hope to push the science of government a little further forward by his treatise.

Earlier governments had drawn their authority from their supposedly divine origin, he pointed out, but the governments of the United States "have exhibited perhaps the first example of governments erected on the simple principles of nature. . . . . It will never be pretended," Adams wrote, "that any persons employed in that service had interviews with the gods or were in any degree under the inspiration of Heaven, more than those at work upon ships or houses, or laboring in merchandise or agriculture." The governments of the various states "were contrived merely by the use of reason and the senses." The same kind of creative energy went into them as into a painting by West, Copley, or Trumbull, into a poem by Joel Barlow or Timothy Dwight, or into a history by Belknap or Ramsay. Legislation was thought by those who framed the various governments to be no different in kind from the "ordinary arts and sciences," but "only more important." The consequence was "thirteen governments . . . founded on the natural authority of the people alone, without pretense of miracle or mystery . . . designed to spread over the northern part of that whole quarter of the globe." The success of this experiment which "can no longer be called in question," Adams insisted, "is a great point gained in favor of the rights of mankind."

The systems developed by legislators were "experiments made on human life and manners, society and government, comparable to those made by scientists." Unfortunately they could not "be made in a laboratory nor determined in a few hours. The operation once begun," Adams related, "runs over whole quarters of the globe and is not finished in many thousands of years. . . . The institutions now made in America," he added, "will never wear wholly out for thousands of years. It is of the last importance, then, that they should begin right. If they set out wrong, they will never be able to return, unless it be by accident, to the right path." Under such circumstances to choose badly, to go back to some primitive political system in the face of all the lessons of history, would be the worst kind of folly.

To begin with, some form of representation was an essential element in a just society. Even where representation existed it was susceptible to great improvements. Another vital component of a free government was a system of checks and balances. It was only necessary to look at the unhappy history of ancient Greece to realize what dangers awaited a society ignorant of this principle. Thucydides, in his famous account of the Corcyraean rebellion, had observed, "Such things will ever be so long as human nature continues the same." "But," Adams wrote, "if this nervous historian had known a balance of three powers, he would not have pronounced the distemper so incurable, but would have added— so long as parties in cities remain unbalanced. . . .

"Without three orders and an effectual balance between them in every American constitution," he declared, "it must be destined to frequent, unavoidable revolutions; though they are delayed a few years they must come in time." The United States were growing too fast to be held together by a simple government (i.e., a pure monarchy, aristocracy, or democracy), and indeed it would be better for Americans to endure all the turbulence of the Greek city-states than to establish an absolute monarchy among them. A free government, with all its hazards and shortcomings, was superior to a monarchy presided over by the best and wisest king, and every free government must have a solid democratic base in the form of a popular assembly responsive to the people. At the same time there existed a danger in a democratic government that the rich, the wellborn, and the able would acquire undue influence because of their wealth and ability. If there was a single legislature they would dominate it and eventually corrupt it. The cure, Adams argued, was to place these men, whose talents the country needed to utilize and whose ambitions it must check, in a single upper branch of the legislature where their influence would be limited and balanced by a popular lower house.

Adams did not profess to be able to foretell the fate of the monarchies of Europe—whether they would last forever "as the result of a few improvements," or whether still further revolutions were to come. What did seem clear to him was that "democratical branches" would, in time, be introduced into all such governments—popular assemblies representing the mass of the citizens of the state. But this step, desirable as it was, should be aimed at only by "gentle means and by gradual advances, by improvements in general education, and by informing the public mind."

In addition to the need for a legislature which incorporated a democratical and an aristocratical principle in two separate houses, the history of all ages demonstrated another irrefutable truth: "that the people's rights and liberties can never be preserved without a strong executive or, in other words, without separating the executive from the legislative power. If the executive power or any considerable part of it is left in the hands of either an aristocratical or a democratical assembly, it will corrupt the legislature as necessarily as rust corrupts iron, or as arsenic poisons the human body; and when the legislature is corrupted, the people are undone."

The American situation was vastly different from that of Europe. In the United States nineteen-twentieths of the land was divided among the common people. The sovereignty as well as the morality must thus be found "in the whole body of the people." A hereditary king or nobility who failed to follow public opinion would "be tumbled instantly from their places." The people therefore must have "a legal, constitutional, and peaceable mode of changing these rulers whenever they discover improper principles or dispositions in them." In the present stage of development, "and with the present manners, this may be done," Adams observed, "not only without inconvenience but greatly for the happiness and prosperity of the country." If, in the future, the states should "become great nations, rich, powerful and luxurious . . . their own feelings and good sense will dictate to them what to do." What was essential was an executive officer, hereditary or elective, who would have sufficient power to act as a counterbalance to the legislative branch of the government.

In summing up Adams stated emphatically that, since there was "no example . . . in any free government, any more than in those which are not free, of a society without a principal personage, we may fairly conclude that the body politic cannot subsist, any more than the animal body, without a head." Moreover, in every form of government which he had reviewed, there had been a senate or "little council" composed of the ablest and most experienced officers and citizens of the state. There had also been in every instance a larger assembly. "The Americans, then,"

Adams concluded, "whose assemblies are the most adequate, proportional, and equitable representations of the people that are known in the world, will not be thought mistaken in appointing houses of representatives." Similarly, there were everywhere to be observed systems of checks and balances which put a limit to the arbitrary impulses and passions of any one branch.

The mere fact that all the existing European systems had serious and sometimes fatal inadequacies did not for a moment mean that "human nature is incapable of liberty, that no honest equality can be preserved in society," or that there were always forces at work which must eventually reduce governments to despotism, monarchy, oligarchy, or aristocracy. England was proof that such extremes could be avoided, that a government could be properly checked and balanced to the inestimable benefit of the governed.

Having stated his basic postulates, Adams turned to his laboratory—history—for proof. He considered first the governments of "modern democratic republics"—San Marino, Biscay, Switzerland's canons, and the United Provinces of the Low Countries; then the "aristocratic republics"—Bern, Friebourg, Lucerne, Zurich, Bienne, Geneva, Lucca, Genoa, and Venice. Finally there were the modern monarchal republics, such countries as Poland and England. Then came "ancient republics and opinions of philosophers," followed by a conclusion which put forth the central proposition of the book: "that three branches of power have an unalterable foundation in nature; that they exist in every society, natural and artificial." Therefore, if they are not recognized and specifically provided for, the government "will be found to be imperfect, unstable, and soon enslaved." It followed also "that the legislative and executive authorities are naturally distinct; and that liberty and the laws depend entirely on a separation of them in the frame of government; that the legislative power is naturally and necessarily sovereign and supreme over the executive"; and that the executive, to remain independent, must have the constitutional means of protecting itself from the encroachment of the legislative.

Adams realized that it was simple enough to state such radical doctrines but quite something else again to get his message to the people of Europe suffering from arbitrary governments. The channels of communication were in the hands of the supporters of old orders. "Monarchies and aristocracies are in possession," he wrote, "of the voice and influence of every university and academy in Europe. . . . Democratical mixtures in government have lost almost all the advocates they ever had out[side] of England and America." The reason for this was that men of letters needed praise and patronage and they received it from those in power. "Monarchies and aristocracies pay well and applaud liberally. . . . It is no wonder then that democracies and democratical mixtures are annihilated all over Europe, except on a barren rock, a paltry fen, an inaccessible mountain, or an impenetrable forest." It thus fell to America to establish a model for the emancipation of the rest of mankind, to prove that a free government can be just and enduring. The people in America, Adams asserted, "have now the best opportunity and the greatest trust in their hands that Providence ever committed to so small a number since the transgression of the first pair; if they betray their trust, their guilt will merit even greater punishment than other nations have suffered and the indignation of Heaven."

Throughout the book Adams had a good deal to say about equality. It was a cant phrase often used with distressing looseness. People were equal in the eyes of God, in the eyes of the law, in the opportunities open to them. In a healthy society they would be relatively equal in material goods. But in every other way they were manifestly unequal—in size, beauty, talents, fortune. "These sources of inequality which are common to every people," Adams pointed out, "can never be altered by any, because they are founded in the constitution of nature; this natural aristocracy among mankind . . . is a fact essential to be considered in the institution of government. It forms a body of men which contains the greatest collection of virtues and abilities in a free government, is the brightest ornament and glory of the nation, and may always be made the greatest blessing of society if it be judiciously managed in the constitution. But if this be not done, it is always the most dangerous."

If Adams' principles of government held true for the thirteen individual states, what of the states in their federal capacity? Since he felt that Congress could be made an effective agency of the states by simply giving it additional powers, most important among them the right to regulate trade, he was disposed to argue that the system of balanced, equal, and distinct branches did not apply to the confederated government. A single assembly in this instance "was every way adequate to the management of all . . . federal concerns." Congress, indeed, was "not a legislative assembly or a representative assembly, but only a diplomatic assembly like the States-General of the Netherlands, a group of states meeting to resolve certain problems dealing with international affairs, problems of trade and commerce, of debts and foreign treaties."

It was hard, Adams confessed, "to say that more authority in other things is not wanted. Yet," he added, "the subject is of such extreme delicacy and difficulty that the people are much to be applauded for their caution." It was this argument that Jefferson, when he read Adams' work, objected to most strongly. The confederation, the Virginian maintained firmly, was a body containing both legislative and executive functions, and thus by implication subject to the shortcomings of all simple, unicameral bodies where the three powers of government were lodged in one branch.

The fact that Adams did not see the matter in this light reveals how limited his concept of nationhood was, how strongly he was inclined toward the states, especially his own state of Massachusetts. Moreover, as one determined to defend the established order in America against outside criticisms, he did not wish to concede severe structural weaknesses in Congress any more than in the states. If he had extended his principles to a national or federal government, the implication would have been that the present system was entirely inadequate and that the federal government must be reorganized along the line of the state governments. Adams was not willing to go so far. To do so would be to make his work, by inference, as much an attack on Congress as a defense of the state constitutions.

Immersed in the book, John sent Abigail and the Smiths off to Bath for Christmas while he stuck to his desk. Abigail and Nabby were charmed with the winter countryside. It reminded them of New England—"the stone walls, the hills, and the towns bearing the same names"[18]—but Abigail worried about John left alone in the drafty house at Grosvenor Square. Although he professed to find his "state of philosophic solitude . . . very tolerable," Abigail renewed by mail her parting injunctions—he must wear his flannel underclothes and be sure that the fire in the library did not die down and the cold creep about him unperceived. He reassured her; writing on Christmas Day, he promised that if "an additional quantity of bedclothes will not answer the purpose of warming me, I will take a virgin to bed with me. Ay, a virgin.' 'What? Oh awful! What do I read?'" (this Abigail's imagined response). But she need not fear that her middle-aged lover had taken up with the sprightly chambermaid. His virgin was simply the name of a stone bottle, filled with boiling water, wrapped in flannel and laid at a man's feet in bed. "An old man, you see, may comfort himself with such a virgin," he wrote, "as much as David did with Abishay, and not give even the least jealousy to his wife, the smallest grief to his children or any scandal to the world."[19]

A little American colony wintering at Bath received Abigail and the two young people cordially. They enjoyed the local dish, small beer, bread, milk and fish and were squired about by John's cousin, John Boylston ("my gallant," Abigail called him), who, taking a great fancy to them, invited them to the concert, to dinner, and to breakfast and entertained them with "elegance and hospitality." "We have been to three balls, one concert, one play, two private parties," at one of which, a musical evening, there had been a number of "lords and ladies," Abigail informed John. Moreover, if he had his virgin, Abigail had an abbé (another type of heating device) to keep her warm.[20] In the midst of their "amusement and dissipation," Count Zenobia, a Venetian nobleman, joined the little group of Americans. Bath, Abigail wrote Mary Cranch, was a resort "not only for the infirm but for the gay, the indolent, the curious, the gambler, the fortune hunter," and the lady of easy virtue. The gaiety and wild pursuit of pleasure made Abigail ask herself the classic question, "What is the chief end of man?" It was a "subject," she reflected, "well worth the investigation of every rational being. What . . . is life or its enjoyments without settled principle, laudable purpose, mental exertions and internal comfort, that sunshine of the soul; and how are these to be acquired in the hurry and tumult of the world?" Certainly they were not much in evidence at Bath among the frantic search for diversion.[21] Abigail was soon tired of the constant round of entertainment. "I do not wonder," she wrote John, "that you preferred building up republics and establishing governments."[22]

Early in January 1787, John sent off an untidy manuscript of the first volume of his *Defence* to the printer and then started in on the second volume. When the printed books finally arrived after a period of anxious waiting, Adams found that careless typesetting had compounded his own errors of haste. But there was nothing to be done at this point but to make the best of it. He sent off copies to Jefferson and Lafayette, to friends in America—Cotton Tufts, President Willard of Harvard, Professor Williams, the professor of mathematics, to Tristram Dalton, Richard Cranch, John Thaxter, General Warren, Samuel Adams, and Dana; one to each of the boys, and thirty volumes to go to a Boston bookseller chosen by Cotton Tufts.

John asked Abigail (with whom he had discussed the principles of government which he had put forth in the book and who had read the bulky manuscript) how she thought the *Defence* would be received in America. She replied with her usual candor and prescience that Americans would think that he was for setting up a king. That was the trouble, John admitted; the fact that he believed that the governors of every state should have essentially "the same authority which the British King has, under the British constitutions," and be balanced by the other two branches, would be taken by superficial readers as an argument for monarchy.[23]

Like every author, Adams, having scattered his books abroad, waited impatiently for the world's reaction. Lafayette wrote a gracious note: "There is in this book of yours much to learn, and much to think. . . . I . . . cannot sufficiently [express] to you how much pleasure and improvement I have found in it," and several months later, after he had received the second volume, he added, "My dear sir, you have made an excellent work—I confess I am the less unprejudiced as I love the author, and his principles are conformable to mine. But independent of thee, I am your book's warm admirer and constant reader."[24]

Cotton Tufts reported that the book was read by "gentlemen of all learned professions here. It came to America at a very critical moment just before the meeting of the grand convention at Philadelphia for revising and amending the confederation, when the subject matter of your book will naturally be much talked of and attended to by many of the greatest statesmen from all parts of the United States." Tufts had talked to many men "of the first rank for learning and abilities" who were unanimous in their opinion that Adams had supported his "system of the balance in the most masterly manner. . . . . The literati," the doctor continued, "are amazed at the vastness of your reading on the subject of legislation and government, from which you have been enabled so fully to bring your theory to the test of historical facts." Benjamin Rush had sent word that editions of the *Defence* were being published in Philadelphia and New York, and Rush wrote to Adams: "I owe more than I can express to you for your excellent volumes upon government. They shall be the almanac of my boys upon the greatest subject of political happiness. . . . I am not more satisfied of the truth of any one proposition in Euclid than I am of the truth of your leading propositions in government. Go on, my dear friend, in removing the rubbish of ignorance and prejudice from the minds of your fellow citizens."[25] Joel Barlow, sending Adams some copies of his *Vision of Columbus* to dispose of in London, gave it as his opinion that "no book . . . was ever received with more gratitude or read with greater avidity." It would have a long life and would do "infinite service in the United States, by correcting thousands of erroneous sentiments which have arisen from our inexperience."[26]

Jefferson wrote: "I have read your book with infinite satisfaction and improvement. Its learning and its good sense will, I hope, make it an institute for our politicians, old as well as young." As we have noted, Jefferson entered a *caveat* to Adams' opinion that Congress was a diplomatic, not a legislative body, and Jay, applauding the book's "many useful lessons," also objected to his characterization of Congress. "I consider the work as a valuable one, and one that will tend greatly to recommend and establish those principles of government on which alone the United States can erect any political structure worth the trouble of erecting."[27]

Despite such assurances John continued to anticipate an unfavorable reception for his book in the United States. Writing to Jefferson to thank him for his praise of the *Defence*, Adams repeated his wife's forecast. "The approbation you express in general of my poor volume is a vast consolation to me," he wrote. "It is a hazardous enterprise and will be an unpopular work in America for a long time. . . . But as I have made it early in life and all along a rule to conceal nothing from the people which appeared to me material for their happiness and prosperity, however unpopular it might be at the time with particular parties, I am determined not now to begin to flatter popular prejudices and party passions however they may be countenanced by great authorities." As to Jefferson's criticism of his view of Congress as a diplomatic rather than a legislative body, Adams would "wish to have it considered as a problem rather for consideration than as an opinion; and as a problem too, relative to the confederation as it now stands rather than to any other plan that may be in contemplation of the states. It is a most difficult topic, and no man at a distance can judge of it so well as those in America."[28]

Adams' attitude toward scholarly work was expressed in a reply to Jefferson's suggestion that he follow the *Defence* by a work on hereditary aristocracy. He trusted that he would never again "publish so hasty a production as this." An adequate book on the role of the aristocracy in history would be "too extensive and splendid for my means and forces. . . . It would," he continued, "require many books which I have not, and a more critical knowledge of both ancient and modern languages than at my age a man can aspire to." In America he could not find the books he would need "for searching any questions of this kind," so he must give up any idea of continuing his historical investigations after he returned to the United States.[29]

As for the British journals, the Scottish reviewers acclaimed the *Defence* and a few of the most liberal English magazines, but from a majority Adams received rough handling; one especially virulent review was rumored to be the work of poor, embittered Silas Deane. The writer denounced Adams' "ostentatious display of learning," his "embarrassed affection of elocution," his errors and his omissions. "Had the book been written by a youth with a view to obtain some academical prize we should have said that it afforded indications of an active mind that gave hope of future acquirements, but that the young man . . . had carelessly adopted some confused notions of government and hastily skimmed the surface without having taken time to investigate particulars." The book could "neither inform or entertain the philosopher or the man of letters." When Abigail read the review she fretted so over it that she lost a good deal of her precious sleep.[30]

The influence of the *Defence* in America was considerable. By the standards of its day it was a best seller, appearing in a number of editions, widely read and hotly debated. It became a source book for Adams' adherents and his enemies, who quoted from it to prove, alternately, that Adams was a democrat or a monarchist. The *Defence* enjoyed an inevitable pre-eminence by virtue of the fact that for a good many years it had the field to itself. It was the first extensive examination by an American of the nature of government. Since the United States had made and indeed was still in the process of making the most radical innovations in government since ancient times, the reflections of one of its principal constitution-makers were bound to command attention. Adams' countrymen, if they did not interpret the book willfully and wrongheadedly as an attack on republican government, were proud that an American had written such an impressive work, a book so full of what at least seemed like scholarship, so eloquent in defense of the principles of government that most Americans subscribed to.

Because of the prestige of the author and the awesome array of authorities quoted, the *Defence* attained at once the stature of a kind of reference work, a source book on government. The tide in many of the states had been running in the direction of "simple democracy," of unicameral legislatures and weak or nonexistent executives. Everywhere strident voices were being raised in denunciation of law and lawyers, of balanced constitutions and strong executive power. The *Defence* was a massive rock in the path of those who championed "simplified" government. Storm at it as they might, its sheer bulk made it a stumbling block to zealous radicals. There it stood, vast and disorderly, crude and roughhewn, pre-empting the new field of American political science. Attacked by democratic editors and pamphleteers, it had no serious rival. Indeed it might claim to have in a large degree fulfilled the role that his author had destined it for. "The seditions in Massachusetts induced your pappa," Abigail had written John Quincy soon after the book's publication, "to give to the world a book which at first he designed only for a few friends. He thought it was a critical moment and that it might prove useful to his countrymen and tend to convince them that a salutary restraint is the vital principle of liberty, and that those who from a turbulent, restless disposition endeavor to throw off every species of coercion are the real enemies of freedom and forge chains for themselves and posterity."[31] There is no question that Adams' work was a major influence in holding the states steady on the course of conservative, three-branch government and in counteracting tendencies to excessive democracy in governmental forms.

Some historians have argued that the New Englander's book appeared just in time to sway the delegates to the federal convention toward a national government of three balanced, independent branches, but it seems unlikely in view of the fact that Adams supported Congress as a diplomatic rather than a legislative body and nowhere suggested that the Articles of Confederation be replaced by a constitution modeled along lines which he considered essential for state government.

The second volume, dealing primarily with the Italian city-states, caused Adams much labor. He exhausted the resources of the London booksellers searching for Italian histories, works "very high-priced and very scarce," a search which before he was through cost him over eight hundred dollars. He taught himself Italian in the process and worked so long at his desk in the library that Abigail feared for his health. But he stuck to a strict regimen of work and exercise and seemed to thrive on it. Each day he took a brisk walk through the London streets, observing everything about him—the people, the houses, the parks, all the multiform and various sights and scenes of the city. A favorite walk was out Edge-ware Road to a large dairy surrounded by lush, heavily manured meadows. On each side of the road were huge mounds of manure which he examined carefully, noting that they were "composed of straw and dung from the stables and streets of London; mud, clay, or marl dug out of the ditch along the hedges; and turf, sward, cut up with spades, hoes, and shovels in the road." The piles were shoveled over and rotated in order to mix them more effectively. It was good manure, Adams noted in his diary, "but . . . not equal to mine which I composed in similar heaps upon my own farm."

LII

WHEN Abigail returned from Bath with a now visibly pregnant Nabby she found another treasure of letters. Mary Cranch wrote that John Quincy and Billy Cranch had been opponents "in a forensic disputation" before an audience of some four hundred on the question "whether inequality among the citizens is necessary for the preservation of the liberty of the whole." John Quincy had taken the affirmative and Billy the negative; they had argued and rebutted and, although they had been scarcely audible with stage fright, they both performed well, in Mary's opinion.[1]

Mary had been shopping in Boston for the three boys, who were hard on their clothes. Tommy, suddenly conscious of styles, had rebelled against wearing his father's old made-over coat any longer; and John Quincy must have a warm winter waistcoat. The three boys had come back to Braintree to spend the fall vacancy with the Cranches. Quartered in the same small bedroom, they romped and roughhoused until the little house shook and Mary had to call them to order. Billy and Charles were early risers and they tumbled John Quincy out of his bed, depriving him of his cherished morning nap. Mary could hardly work her way through piles of mending and darning—it seemed there was no end of frayed collars and cuffs to be turned, socks to be darned, and knees and elbows to be patched.

The Scottish songs that Abigail had sent had made the vacation much the merrier. The boys with their flutes, violin, and harpsichord joined Lucy and Betsy in learning the tunes and playing them for the family. All of them had had a gay social time and John Quincy appeared "quite a gallant among the ladies." But it was Charles, of course, who was irresistible. "Cousin Charles," Mary wrote, "is a lovely creature. He is so amiable and so attentive that he will be loved wherever he sets his foot."[2]

Charles had lost his heart to a young lady at Haverhill. He rhapsodized constantly over her—"Did you ever see such *heavenly* eyebrows, and she is as amiable as she is pretty"—and displayed a lock of her hair, but Mary was not alarmed. She had seen many such locks from other young ladies who had come and gone in Charles's affections. "As to honest Tom," his aunt wrote, "he does not think that the ladies need so much attention." He did not intend to marry; he much preferred hunting to courting. In a moment of confidence he had told his aunt that there were so many temptations to go astray at Harvard that if he had forty sons he would not risk one of them at Harvard. To this his aunt replied severely that the world, like Harvard, was full of temptations; he must learn to overcome them, for he certainly could not spend his life running away from them.

The only real complaint Mary had about the boys was that John Quincy studied too hard. He looked pale and drawn and was plagued by splitting headaches. At Mary Cranch's prompting Dr. Tufts had had a serious talk with him. His diet was bad and he got no exercise. Both his mind and body would suffer, the doctor warned him, if he drove himself so hard.[3]

Abigail showed a mother's natural concern at the news of her son's poor health. "Light food," she reminded him, "is necessary for a student if as usual your stomach abounds with acid." The best antidote for an acid stomach was "lime water mixed with milk." He should take a pound of stone lime, pour over it a gallon of boiling water, let it stand till clear, then pour it off and bottle it and take a large cupful mixed with milk. She could see him smiling at her remedy and dismissing it as just a mother's fussiness but he had better think twice because a sour stomach could manifest itself in all kinds of complaints. To prevail on him to take her prescription seriously she sent him a handsome piece of satin for breeches, fashionable cloth for a coat, and a set of "very tasty" buttons.[4]

Aside from his carelessness about his health, Mary wrote, John Quincy was in every way admirable. His classmates loved him and were delighted by his daring satires of the President with his "supercilious frown," and of the tutors, so full of self-importance. The President, in John Quincy's view, demanded respect from the students "as an highwayman . . . demands your purse."[5]

John Quincy confessed (or boasted) to his mother that he did nothing but study. "As for public affairs," he wrote, "I have a great aversion even to thinking of them, and as near as we are to Boston, I should know nothing of them if riots, insurrections, and anarchy were not at this time the only topics of conversation. . . . . The people," he added, "are said to be discontented and to complain of taxation, of the Court of Common Pleas, of the Senate, of the salaries of public officers, and of debts, public and private; all of these are, they think, intolerable grievances and they wish to abolish them."

He felt confident that in two or three months "the public tranquillity will be perfectly restored," but it was his opinion that "the present form of government will not continue long, for while the idle and extravagant and consequently the poor complain of its being oppressive, the men of property and consideration think the constitution gives too much liberty to the unprincipled citizen, to the prejudice of the honest and industrious." These men of property had concluded that a "pure democracy" (which they considered the Massachusetts constitution to be) was far better in theory than in practice. John Quincy had feared that, having been educated in Europe, he would not be enough of a republican to please his countrymen, but he had found, on the contrary, that he was "the best republican here" and that in disputes with his classmates he was constantly defending republican government while they argued the advantages of an aristocracy or a monarchy.[6]

College was dismissed three weeks early for the winter holidays because the roads were so bad that wood could not be transported to Cambridge to keep the scholars warm. John Quincy, remembering the noisy exuberance of the Cranch household, decided to remain in Cambridge. He and a friend took a room with Professor Wigglesworth and John Quincy enjoyed the company of the professor's daughter, Peggy, who was unaffected, bright, and appealing.[7]

Shays' uprising had reached into Braintree. Although the town was securely in the hands of the solid and respectable citizens, there was a small Shays' faction which held a town meeting to try to have Ebenezer Thayer recalled from the General Court. The effort was unsuccessful and the Braintree militia was alerted to march in pursuit of the rebels if needed. Such news increased Abigail's apprehensions. "The more quarrelsome and turbulent you grow," she wrote Eliza, "the more anxious I am to be with you; not that I think it pleasant fishing in troubled waters but because imagination paints higher than reality, and the danger apprehended is always worse than that which is experienced. In short I have seen my countrymen armed one against the other and the divided house falling to the ground."[8]

Abigail sent Eliza "a little chamber lamp, which with a small quantity of oil burns the whole night," and a piece of silk. "I was deliberating some time," she wrote, "whether it should be virgin white or sky blue. Upon the whole I concluded that you had more pretentions to the skys than to the appellation annexed to the white, so I bought the blue, which is vastly the present taste. I hope it will meet your approbation," she added, "as I have already fancied how well it will become you and how pretty you will look in it." It should be worn without trimming but with a "very dressy apron," decorated with lace and white ribbon with appliquéd flowers.

As Abigail wrote Nabby sat by the table trimming a white muslin slip with lace around the neck and sleeves, "looking as sober as a deaconess. . . . . She would grumble a little if she knew I had been writing of her," Abigail added. She herself would soon be made a grandmother by her daughter, but she assured her sister, "I do not feel so ancient as that event will make me."[9]

Reading the letters from home, Adams grew more than ever determined to return to the United States. He wrote Jay to that effect, declaring that he would not accept a renewal of his commission to the Court of St. James even if Congress were inclined to make it. Nor would he accept a commission to any other European court. He wanted to come home and he was determined to do so. In case his official letter to the Secretary of State might leave any doubt about the matter, he wrote a personal note to Jay repeating his "ultimate determination to revisit my country, this time twelve months." He indeed wished his friend "to promote, in every way in your power, an arrangement as early as possible by which I may be permitted to return with decorum." At the same time he felt misgivings at the prospect of a return to his own country after a ten-year absence. "For a man," he wrote Jefferson, "who has been thirty years rolling like a stone never three years in the same place, it is no very pleasant speculation to cross the seas with a family, in a state of uncertainty what is to be his fate; what reception he shall meet at home; whether he shall set down in private life to his plow or push into turbulent scenes of sedition and tumult; whether be sent to Congress or a convention or God knows what." If it lay in his power to decide he would "take a vow to retire to my little turnip yard and never again quit it." But then again perhaps he wouldn't. He had been swearing off politics for so many years that his vows no longer carried much conviction, even for himself. Certainly he was not "at home" in England and would not be sorry to leave. His only regret, he told Jefferson, would be "the interruption of that intimate correspondence with you, which is one of the most agreeable events in my life."[10]

Beyond the routine duties of his office there was little diplomatic business to command Adams' attention. He worked long hours on the second and third volumes of the *Defence* and wrote dutifully to Jay: "Parliament opened with uncommon gloom and has been sitting in mournful silence." The members had accepted a French treaty "to appease France and amuse the people," but "a dead taciturnity prevails about America," he noted. The maintenance of the frontier posts in America was estimated to cost the government many times the profit that was made by British merchants engaged in the fur trade. "A life so useless to the public and so insipid to myself," he added, "has become a burden to me as well as to my countrymen."[11] He was pleased and reassured by Jay's account of the coming convention, which was to meet at Philadelphia to revamp the Articles of Confederation. The convention, he noted, was "to consist of members of such ability, weight, and experience that the result must be beneficial to the United States." The fact that the individual states were making determined efforts to resolve controversies between themselves showed that the Union had great strength in the minds of the people. "It is, indeed," he continued, "an object of such magnitude that great sacrifices ought to be made to its preservation. The consequences of a division of the continent cannot be foreseen fully perhaps, by any man; but the most shortsighted must perceive such manifest danger, both from foreign powers and from one another, as cannot be looked upon without terror."[12]

Spring came early after a mild winter. In March the trees had already budded and burst into bloom. "The verdure is equal to June with us," Abigail wrote her uncle Isaac Smith. The spring air, once one left the city, was soft and clear. The talk of English fogs was in fact much overdone, and in Abigail's view, "if the manners of the people were as pure as their air, no one would have reason to complain."[13] But spring had a deeper significance than usual for John and Abigail. New life was stirring in their daughter's womb, and at the end of April she gave birth to a fine baby boy, William, christened at home by Dr. Price, who joined the family and a few close friends in supping and drinking "the young hero's health and that of our country." To be grandparents was somewhat of a shock. It was too much for Abigail in any event. She took to her bed shortly after the christening and to her distress missed seven out of twelve lectures on science to which she had subscribed. She had heard the first five. It was, she wrote Lucy Cranch, "like going into a beautiful country which we never saw before, a country to which few females are permitted to visit or inspect." As in America, such subjects had been confined largely within college walls. The lectures had presented "an assemblage of ideas entirely new . . . experiments upon electricity, magnetism, hydrostatics . . . pneumatics, all of which are connected with and are subservient to the accommodation of common life." While it was doubtless true, as Milton had said, that "the study of household good . . . is . . . the peculiar province of the female character, yet surely as rational beings [women's] reason may properly receive the highest possible cultivation." If this were done, husband, children, and nation would all receive the benefits. Certainly no one would want to argue that a wife and mother would become "less capable or willing to superintend the domestic economy of her family for having wandered beyond the limits of the dressing room and the kitchen," to which, Abigail noted, "even some men of sense have been illiberal enough to wish us confined."

Since men of the present age allowed "more freedom of thought and action in politics, in philosophy, and in religion, it is to be hoped," Abigail wrote, "that the liberality of their sentiments will extend to the cultivation and improvement of the female mind, which stands much in need of motives and incentives to draw it from the present pernicious modes of fashionable levities and polite accomplishments." Such "rational

. . . improvements in the education of women" would lead inevitably to richer lives, lives elevated by "settled principles, laudable purposes, and mental exertions." Despite her strictures on fashion, Abigail sent her niece a pair of sandals, flimsy, frivolous things in the very latest Paris style.[14]

The baby William was a delight and Abigail was most impressed by the efficiency of the English nanny who superintended every detail of his care with unimpeachable authority and awesome skill. For the infant's health she gave him every day a bath in cold water, sponging the squalling little morsel with strong, practiced hands.

With the end of his mission in sight, it turned out that Adams' trials were not yet over. In May an urgent message arrived from the Dutch bankers, the Messrs. Willink. They had warned him earlier that there were insufficient funds in their hands to pay the interest on the American loan, which was due in June. He had instructed them to try to secure a new loan and now they wrote that they had succeeded with much difficulty in securing a loan for a million guilders at eight per cent, but that he must come at once to sign the obligations so that the loan could pass and the interest be paid when it fell due.

John found a temporary secretary and congenial traveling companion in an amusing young American named John Brown Cutting and the two men set off hastily for Amsterdam. The packet from Harwich that carried them to Holland had aboard an assortment of entertaining characters. Two ample Dutch matrons with "one goodly child and two fine bundles of fresh asparagus"; the tutoress to the children of the Stadtholder, Prince of Orange; a "German woman of uncommon corpulency and scarlet features—mincing like a new-made countess, breathing like a porpoise and prating like a magpie; . . . an impertinent and fancy Englishwoman, of age and occupation dubious; a very pretty though somewhat excessively rouged English girl; a German merchant and a Dutchman made up the company." Adams got very seasick in the rough crossing and arrived in Holland wan and unshaven. In an ancient carriage lined with ripped and faded crimson damask, with broken windows and warped sides, he and Cutting bumped and jounced their way to Rotterdam, spent the night, and set off next day for The Hague by canal boat crowded in with six "redoubtable Dutchmen who after fumigating us with tobacco for two hours," Cutting wrote Abigail, at length drove them out on deck, half suffocated, to be thoroughly dampened by a sudden shower. At The Hague they were met by Dumas, enjoyed his congenial company, and then pushed on to Amsterdam. The city was in turmoil. The adherents of the Prince of Orange were being hunted down by the Patriots and there was rioting and fighting. Rumors flew about that thirty houses had been rifled by mobs. The Patriot leaders, in control of the city, welcomed Adams as a friend to their cause. The *Defence*, he wrote Abigail, was much applauded. His Dutch friends referred to it as "the breviary of liberty, safety and good order. . . . . A compliment more flattering to me," he added, "than all the ingenuity of my own self-love and vanity could have invented."

Abigail, ill and anxious for news, was delighted with Cutting's vivid description of the crossing. The letter, she wrote, "carried me to Holland, made me sick on board the packet [and] jostled me in the wagon." John's absence was in part compensated for by her pleasure in the infant William, who, she wrote, "perks up his head like a robin."[15]

At Amsterdam there were two thousand bonds to be signed and Adams sat at a desk for two days, scratching his name until his hand could hardly hold the pen. The chore accomplished, he hastened back to London to be with Abigail.[16]

When John returned from Holland he found his wife still in poor health. Perhaps it was the muggy summer heat of the city that kept her indisposed. They decided to take a trip to Plymouth to visit the Cranch family. They could not leave London, however, before Jefferson's daughter, eight-year-old Polly, who was coming to join him in Paris, had arrived. Jefferson had asked Abigail to take charge of the child upon her arrival until he could come and get her or send a servant to bring her to Paris.

Polly Jefferson arrived in late June accompanied by a slave girl, Sally Hemings, little older than Polly herself. Polly hated to leave the ship and the kindhearted Captain who had taken her under his wing during the long voyage. Abigail tried to humor and distract her. "Come, such a big girl! I know your sister well and I have never seen her cry."

"My sister is older and ought to be better," Polly replied between sniffles, "and besides she has her pappa with her." Abigail could not help smiling at the child's apt rejoinder. She showed her a picture of her father, but Polly only sobbed out that she did not recognize it, for she could not even remember what her father looked like. They would go to Sadler's Wells to see the trained bears and dogs, the dancing and the musical programs, Abigail promised, describing these delights in vivid detail. It did no good. "I had rather see Captain Ramsey one moment," Polly answered, "than all the fun in the world." Finally the tears were checked and Abigail sat down to write Jefferson of his daughter's arrival. "Miss Polly sends her duty to you and love to her sister and says she will try to be good and not cry. So she has wiped her eyes and laid down to sleep." It would help, Abigail suggested, if her sister or Jefferson himself could come to get her. She had had almost too much uprooting and strangeness for an eight-year-old.[17]

Next day Polly seemed quite reconciled. Abigail took her out shopping and brought her four frocks of Irish linen, a smart little hat of brown beaver trimmed with feathers, some checked muslin to make her another frock, six pairs of cotton stockings, a comb and case, a hairbrush and a toothbrush; for the little Negro slave, Sally Hemings, whose delicate features and light skin showed very clearly that she had white blood, she bought some calico for short gowns, linen for aprons, three pairs of stockings, and a kerchief.

It was clear that Polly needed a mother desperately and Abigail was delighted to play the part. "So mature an understanding, so womanly a behavior, and so much sensibility . . . are rarely to be met with," Abigail wrote her sister, and to Jefferson she spoke of his daughter as an "amiable, lovely child." John, equally captivated, wrote to his friend, "In my life I never saw a more charming child." "Books are her delight," Abigail noted. She furnished her a little library and Polly read to her "by the hour with great distinctness," commenting "on what she read with great propriety." "I never felt so attached to a child in my life on so short an acquaintance," Abigail wrote Jefferson. "'Tis rare to find one possessed of so strong and lively a sensibility. I hope she will not lose her fine spirits within the walls of a convent, to which I own I have many, perhaps false prejudices."[18]

The arrival of Jefferson's French servant, Petit, who spoke hardly a word of English, brought on a new crisis. "Since I have left all my friends in Virginia to come over the ocean to see Pappa," Polly told Abigail, her small face intent and serious, "I did think he would have taken pains to come here for me, and not sent a man I cannot understand."

"Well, your father does love you very much," Abigail assured her, "but he has been on a long journey and could not come at once for you. The man he has sent, I know well, and will look after you very well. He is kind and attentive." But Polly felt betrayed and Abigail's explanations of her father's dereliction did not comfort her. It made Abigail's heart sink to know that in Paris her father would place her promptly in a convent and there she would have to accommodate herself to another strange world. For the moment Polly simply refused to leave and Abigail, unwilling to force her physically into the Dover carriage with Petit and send her away "almost in a frenzy," renewed her arguments to the child and sent off a hasty letter to Jefferson asking for instructions.

But Abigail found that Petit, with whom she had almost as much trouble communicating as Polly did, had purchased tickets for the Dover stage, so there was nothing for it but to pack the child off. She must go after all. "If I must go, I will," Polly replied, "but I cannot help crying so pray don't ask me to." With that point agreed upon, she went off in tears, John and the servants joining with Abigail in a watery good-by.[19]

LIII

JOHN sent the second volume of the *Defence* to the printers on the eighteenth of July and a few days later he and Abigail set out for a tour through southern and western England. The Colonel had been dispatched on a mission to Portugal, but Nabby and little William came along. They made up quite a party—John and Abigail, Nabby and the baby William, the nurse, Esther Field, (recently married to John Briesler) the footman, the coachman, and a postilion—nine in all.

At Winchester, Abigail took note of the Sieur de Quincy, first Earl of Winchester, whom she believed to be her ancestor since she had seen his coat of arms in her own family. She excused herself for taking an interest in her distinguished ancestry by noting that "the British sometimes twit us of being descended from the refuse of their gaols and from transported convicts. But," she added, "it is well known that the first settlers of New England were no such persons, but worthy conscientious people who fled from religious persecution to a New World and planted themselves amidst savages that they might enjoy their religion unmolested."

"You will smile at my zeal, perhaps, on this occasion," she wrote her sister, "but can it be wondered at that I should wish to trace an ancestor amongst the signers of Magna Charter?" John, proud of his wife's ancestry, was sure the Braintree Quincys were descended from the Earl and set out to follow the line, while Nabby wrote loftily in her journal: "He may be better acquainted with the importance of it than I am. To me it appears quite a matter of small consequence. We can all trace our descent from Adam, and no one can go beyond."[1]

They went to church in the cathedral and Abigail confessed herself far more impressed "with the venerable and majestic appearance of the ancient pile than with the modern, flimsy discourse of the preacher." Braintree would never tolerate such a performance. But then the cathedral was virtually deserted. The congregation was only a handful and those "the lower order of the people."

From Winchester they rolled on to Southampton, a resort town where it had become the fashion recently to go bathing in the ocean. Here John, Abigail, and Nabby "tried the experiment." The ladies had a bath attendant who escorted them to a small dressing room and provided them with an oilcloth cap, a flannel gown, and warm socks. Thus equipped, they ventured out on the hot sand and then into the ocean. They found it delightful. John had not gone swimming since he was a boy in Braintree and then only in the Neponset River. The ocean water was wonderfully exhilarating. There should be bathing places, Abigail decided, at Boston, Braintree, and Weymouth. In town prostitutes were much in evidence; painted and bedizened, they strolled the streets and frequented the public places, openly plying their trade.

Weymouth was ten miles out of the way, but since they had made a pilgrimage to Braintree they could not pass up Weymouth. That town, like Southampton, was a "watering place" where Londoners came to escape the summer heat. They found nothing to detain them and pushed on through Surrey, Hunt, Wiltshire, and Dorset, "famous for beer and butter," and to Axminster, the leading town of Devonshire.

They traveled through a golden land, "fertile as the Garden of Eden," where, as Abigail wrote, "one would imagine that the voice of poverty was rarely heard, and that she was seldom seen but in the abodes of indolence or vice." But, as always in the countries of the Old World, it was far otherwise. "The money earned by the sweat of the brow must go to feed the pampered lord and fatten the greedy bishop." What might look to the casual tourist like charming, picturesque rural dwellings, Abigail saw more truly as "miserable, shattered, thatch-roof cottage[s]" crumbling "to the dust for want of repair," gloomy, sunless, dank abodes, "equally exposed to cold and the inclement season." She had seen the barren interiors with a few wretched sticks of furniture and a pile of rags for beds.

Hunger and poverty were etched on the gaunt, pinched faces of men and women alike. During harvest time women and children worked with the men in the fields. "How they keep body and soul together the remainder of the year," she wrote, "is very hard to tell." The unequal distribution of property must be the root of this misery, because the countryside was thinly settled and there seemed to be more than enough good farm land to maintain the rural population in comfort. "How little cause of complaint," Abigail exclaimed, "have the inhabitants of the United States when they compare their situation, not with despotic monarchies, but with this land of freedom! The ease with which honest industry may acquire property in America, the equal distribution of justice to the poor as well as the rich, and the personal liberty they enjoy—all, all call upon them to support their government and laws, to respect their ruler and gratefully acknowledge their superior blessings."

At Axminster they hunted up John Cranch, brother of Richard Cranch,

Abigail's brother-in-law. Mr. Cranch was a man of middle height with pleasant, regular features, but awkward and uneasy in his manners. He hung his head, refused to look the person he was talking to in the eye and gave the impression that "he had been cramped and cowed in his youth." With Cranch as their guide the Adamses visited the carpet factory where women and children wove the carpets for which the town was famous. The factory itself was an ordinary barnlike building; the carpets were woven to order in two prices, eighteen and twenty-four shillings a yard, depending on the quality. "The colors are most beautiful and the carpets very durable," Abigail noted. From the factory they then went to Cranch's "small, neat cottage" for tea. The cottage walls were hung with prints of many "eminent persons," Hogarth's etchings of marriage *à la mode,* and a portrait of Sir Walter Raleigh. On further acquaintance it became apparent that their host was "a man of reading, and an accurate taste in the fine arts." But it seemed clear to Abigail that he was a restless, unhappy man who aspired to a higher station in life than he held.

John Cranch rode on with the Adamses to Exeter to visit his brother Andrew. The road to that town was mountainous and the view interrupted by hedges and embankments. Cranch startled his traveling companions by pulling down walls and tearing "gates from hinges, bolts and bars, like a Samson," where they impeded the view or their passage down a particular lane. The violence of his actions spoke volumes about the class bitterness which the English social system engendered.

At Exeter they visited with ancient Andrew, the eldest Cranch brother, lame and infirm, and his wife, "a little smart, sprightly, active woman . . . wilted just enough to last to perpetuity."

The next stop was the port of Plymouth, a dockyard for the Royal Navy and the country seat of Lord Edgecombe, whose handsome estate, with a magnificent view of the harbor and the hills of Cornwall, lay at the edge of town. Edgecombe Manor boasted a lawn thirty acres wide and a deer park of three hundred acres. To visit the grounds the Adamses paid twopence each to a gentleman who informed them that he paid His Lordship four hundred guineas a year for the concession of collecting admissions. Abigail was disappointed. There were, she noted, "no grottoes, statuary, sculpture, or temples," and thus no real elegance.

Another Cranch whom they visited along the way was Richard's uncle William, who had lost his mind. He had a man to look after him, was clean and comfortable, "but took no notice, either of the conversation or persons." His unhappy condition tempted Abigail to a little amateur psychologizing. She was convinced that the cause of his breakdown was that he was "possessed of a genius superior to his station, a thirst for knowledge which his circumstances in life permitted him not to pursue . . . formed to adorn a superior rank in life." He was thus a casualty of the rigid caste system of his native country. His nephew Richard, possessing the same kind of "genius," had gone to America, married into one of the first families in the Province, and become a prominent man in his adopted state, a representative in the Great and General Court, a power in his own community.

Kingsbridge was the "chief resort of the numerous Cranch clan." There the fame of the Adamses had preceded them and shortly after their arrival the bells of the town were rung as a salute to the honored American visitors. This was Dissenting country, the stronghold of English Puritanism and independency, and the reception was in dramatic contrast to that accorded Adams and his family in London. In the city he was the odd, awkward, presumptuous little man who represented a disloyal and upstart people. In Kingsbridge he appeared the champion of the noblest principles of English liberty, a friend, a co-religionist, and a relative by marriage. He came as the agent of a new kind of human society in which no man would doff his hat or pull a forelock in deference to a squire or a lord.

As soon as the Adamses were established in the Kingsbridge Inn they began to receive calls from the various branches of the Cranch family, some fifteen visitors in all, whose names made such "a strange jumble" in Abigail's head that she begged John Cranch to provide her with a genealogical table to sort them all out. One was a prosperous shoemaker, "worth five thousand pounds," another a well-to-do grocer, another a farmer in comfortable circumstances. "They are all serious, industrious, good people," Abigail wrote her sister, "amongst whom the greatest family harmony appears to subsist."

Abigail noted especially the distinction between "tradesmen and gentry, as they are termed." In New England the learned professions and many farmers and tradesmen were equal in every way to English "gentry." Indeed, it would be degrading to compare them to the English nobility, many of whom were thoroughly decadent—"totally depraved," in fact, was the way Abigail expressed it. It was in the English middle class "that virtue and morality are yet to be found," she wrote Mary Cranch.

Carrying dozens of messages to Richard Cranch from his Kingsbridge relatives, the Adamses rode on to Oxford where they hired a guide to show them about the colleges. First the Bodleian Library and the picture gallery with the noble brass statue of the Earl of Pembroke; then New College to see the stained-glass windows designed by Sir Joshua Reynolds depicting the four cardinal and three Christian virtues. There was Fortitude, "her head resting on a broken column, her form robust, her look bold and resolute." Faith, bearing a cross, had her eyes fixed on heaven; Justice held her scales and sword; Prudence her mirror. From New College they went on to Queen's and then through the ancient yard to the river.

The next day they went to Blenheim, the estate of the Duke of Marlborough, some ten miles from Oxford. There they saw the high ceiling in the great hall painted by Sir James Thornhill showing Victory crowning the Duke at the battle of Blenheim. The library alone was a hundred and eighty-three feet long, containing over twenty-four thousand volumes, lined with Doric pilasters of marble, the room paneled in dark mahogany and black marble "in the highest finish and taste." The gardens presented a seemingly endless variety of prospects: the river lined with willows, sweeping lawns, cascades, a magnificent grove of oaks, a handsome stone bridge. The Duke's gardener was a sharp-tongued, out-spoken character who answered Adams' questions with somewhat more wit and asperity than John judged suitable.[2]

The Adamses arrived back at Grosvenor Square in the middle of August, glad to be home after a month of uncomfortable inns and bumpy roads. There they found another batch of letters from America. Again the news was mixed. In Massachusetts, Shays' rebellion had been firmly suppressed but the new General Court was made up of an alarming num-ber of "members in favor of the late opposition to government"—men who favored "a general indemnity, the withdrawal of the troops, removal of the Court from Boston, a liberal tender act, abolition of the Court of Common Pleas, payment of the public securities at the going price," and a number of equally radical and unsettling measures. "Notwithstanding the late successful efforts of government," Cotton Tufts wrote, referring to the defeat of Shays, "I think there is the highest probability that a revolu-tion is not far distant." Indeed some prominent politicians who were advocates of a weak government looked forward to the day and thought it could not come too soon.

"The spirit of the day," Tufts noted, "has brought into public life char-acters that in sober times would have been hissed off the stage and been expelled as members unfit to grace the seats of legislators." It seemed to the doctor that every level of government was infested with former Tories, "avowed friends to monarchy and despotism," who now talked democracy. Allied with them were "disappointed Whigs," debtors, and unknown men, "most of them mushrooms that have sprung up on a sudden," tools of the former Tories, "in principle levelers."[3] Eliza Shaw echoed the same senti-ments; she "never knew greater electioneering than has been this year—a new Governor—a new Senate—new representatives. . . . The way to creep into office at this day is to declaim loudly against a republican government—and to extoll paper currency. This will gain whole sheets of votes." Some of the new legislators had been elected from "the lowest of the people."[4] In John Quincy's words "many . . . who have openly es-poused the cause of treason and rebellion are now among the legislators of the country." Hancock, always pandering to the public, had encouraged the move to reduce the salaries of state officials and offered to give the state three hundred pounds. "It is impossible for a free nation," John Quincy wrote his father, "to subsist without parties," but unfortunately clearly defined parties had not formed in Massachusetts. "The democratical branch of our government," he wrote, "is at present quite unrivaled." The other branches were too weak to balance it. The Senate, which had been a bulwark during Shays' rebellion, saving the Commonwealth from complete anarchy, was now the object of popular disfavor and, he added, "the people are . . . generally disposed to abolish the Senate as a useless body."[5]

On the bright side was the news from Jay that the convention at Philadelphia was apparently making good progress in its task of strengthening the national government. "For my own part," he wrote, "I am convinced that a national government as strong as may be compatible with liberty is necessary to give us national security and respectability." He was confident that the work of the convention would have such a character.[6]

The best news of all were the accounts of the graduation of John Quincy and Billy Cranch from Harvard. Each graduating senior, the reader will perhaps recall, was required to furnish food and drink for the guests at commencement. This task fell to Mary Cranch, who spent the week before graduation preparing for the occasion. It was much less expensive to take food to Cambridge than to pay the inflated prices demanded there, so Mary cooked at Braintree everything necessary for the "cold collation"—two shoulders of beef *à la mode,* four boiled bacon hams, and six large tongues. The whole house was permeated with the rich odors that rose from the pots in the kitchen. "They smell finely I assure you," Mary wrote Abigail. In addition to meat there must be porter, cider, punch, and wine. The Cranches, again to avoid the expense of renting articles in Cambridge, had simple tables and benches made in Braintree that could be disassembled and carried on the wagon to Cambridge. The day before commencement Mary baked dozens of biscuits and a huge plum cake made of twenty-eight pounds of flour.

In all the confusion of preparation, John Quincy, who was to give an oration, wandered about nervously crying, "O Lord! O Lord, I hope it will rain hard that all their white wigs may be wet who would not let us have a private commencement," but his heart wasn't in it. He knew he was plugging a lost cause; it never rained at Harvard commencements.

The great day came at last. It seemed as though half the people of Massachusetts had converged on college—parents and relatives of the students, officials of the state, friends of the graduates, and hundreds who were simply out in a holiday mood to enjoy themselves for a few riotous days. The commencement itself, of course, in keeping with the nature of a progressive universe, was the best ever. Adamses were much in evidence. There was a band playing with gusto and three of the flutists were John Quincy and Charles Adams and Billy Cranch. They participated likewise in "a grand musical symphony and chorus."

After the orations in Greek and Hebrew, "the syllogistic dispute," and the dialogue from the tragedy of Tamerlane, John Quincy joined with Nathaniel Freeman and Moses Little in "a conference upon divinity, physic and law." Freeman was John's principal rival for the intellectual and forensic laurels of the class and while Mary assured Abigail that her son had "happily united the scholar, the man of sense and the gentleman," that "he spoke well, and his action was easy," he himself suffered torments over whether he had outstripped his classmate. Freeman's "natural abilities," he wrote his mother later, "are very good . . . his oratorical talents are great, and I should never wish to be considered as his rival or competitor. If however," he added, "we must be viewed in that light, I have not the most distant pretensions to superiority, nor am I conscious of a decided inferiority." But this last was dangerously like pride. "I have already said too much on this subject, and I hope you will forgive these effusions of vanity and attribute them to the desire of convincing you that I have not entirely neglected to improve those advantages which by the kindness of my parents I have enjoyed," he concluded.[7]

With the ordeal at last over John Quincy and Billy Cranch grinned from ear to ear; Mary swore she had never seen two happier faces. In a chorus of congratulations the two friends made their way to their rooms to join in the cold collation and receive more encomiums from a stream of friends and well-wishers who devoured Mary Cranch's plum cake, drank her cider and wine, and praised the young heroes. Uncle Isaac Smith's Negro, Primus, along with the faithful Phebe and her husband George—he resplendent in his "Sabbath day coat and tie, wig full-powered"—served the food and poured the drinks.

Governor Hancock, the Lieutenant Governor and a number of the Senators, the President, professors, and the hungry tutors came to add their congratulations. There was only one unhappy note; Mary had neglected to ask her sister-in-law, Mary Palmer, until the day before the commencement and she and the General had stayed away in a huff. By the time the afternoon was over Mary estimated that they had served meals to over a hundred guests and wine and plum cake to four hundred.

When the company was gone Mary, helped by Eliza Shaw and Phebe and her husband, set about cleaning up and washing the dishes. Eliza observed George "devouring the delicious fragments—now mouthing a sweet crumb of bread, now a fat slice of bacon, now a fine piece of *à la mode* beef and now a spoonful of green peas, lettuce, pickle, etc., cleaning plate by plate," and handing them to Phebe to wash.[8]

Throughout the day there had been frequent mention of the absent parents, John and Abigail. Many guests had inquired after them and a number had commented on John Quincy's resemblance to his mother. Lucy Cranch, pleased and proud of her brother and her cousin, wrote Abigail that John Quincy had "your mouth when he smiled; your eyes when he bid his classmates good-by." (She did not tell her aunt that she had not dared to wear the French sandals to commencement.)

As for the oration, it was widely praised. Cotton Tufts assured John that John Quincy had spoken "in a manly, spirited manner and at the same time with an air of modesty and with great ease," and Mary Cranch, quite swept away by pride and excitement, reported that people had declared that he "excelled in manner everyone who ever spoke" at commencement. But the historian and editor, Jeremy Belknap, perhaps gave John Quincy the best compliment of all when he asked for a copy of the oration to publish in the new *Columbian Magazine.*

An indication of the strength of partisan political feeling could be found in the Boston *Centinel,* a newspaper friendly to the Shaysite faction, which acclaimed Freeman's oration as much superior to that of John Quincy. Indeed, the editor hinted, young Adams would never even have been chosen for the honor if he had not been the son of the present minister to England and the darling of the university administration. This last was a thrust that pierced John Quincy's tender hide. The fact was that his criticisms of the President's airs and pomposity had gotten back to that gentleman and in consequence the officers of the college had no special love for him. Adams himself was delighted with the oration. "It seems to me . . . to be full of manly sense and spirit," he wrote. "By the sentiments and principles in that oration, I hope you will live and die. . . . To Vattel and Burlamaqui, who you say you have read, you must add Grotius and Pufendorf and Heiniecius, and besides this you should have some volume of ethics constantly on your table. Morals, my boys, morals should be, as they are eternal in their nature, the everlasting subject of your pursuit. Socrates and Plato, Cicero and Seneca, Butler and Hutcheson, as well as the prophets, evangelists, and apostles, should be your continual teachers. . . . Preserve your Latin and Greek like the apple of your eye."[9]

With commencement over John Quincy went back to Braintree to spend a month being spoiled by his aunt and recovering the health that he had damaged by unremitting attention to his books before setting out for Newburyport to begin the study of law with Theophilus Parsons.

Cotton Tufts, the faithful steward, carried out Abigail's commissions, disbursed money for the boys at Harvard, bought public securities, superintended the tenants' care of the farms, and notified her when choice parcels of land appeared on the market. In the summer of 1787 he wrote her that the spacious Borland house was for sale. For some time Abigail had thought uneasily of returning to the tiny farmhouse. John's books alone would overflow it, not to mention the chairs, tables, pictures, and other furnishings which they had acquired in their years in Europe. She therefore wrote at once to Tufts, instructing him to offer six hundred dollars for the house.[10] He did so and the house was acquired against the Adamses return.

There was one dark note amid the good news from home. William Smith, Abigail's brother, weakened by drink and dissipation, had died of "black jaundice" in a remote town far from home. He was in his thirties at the time of his death, a strange, unhappy man, obsessed by demons which could not be exorcised by the devotion of his parents or his sisters. Abigail wept when she heard the news, thinking of their happys days as children, of how close they had been, rocked, as Eliza reminded her, in the same cradle, held in the same parental arms.[11]

WHEN Adams got back from the trip through Devon and Cornwall he found that the second volume of his *Defence* had passed through the press and he forwarded a copy to Jefferson, writing that it contained "three long courses of experiments in political philosophy," intended to test Turgot's political principles, and noting, "It has cost me a good deal of trouble and expense to search into Italian rubbish and ruins." . . . . "Enough of pure gold and marble," he wrote, "has been found to reward the pains. . . . I assure you, it is all genuine history." The whole vast subject of confederations remained to be treated, but Adams had "neither head, heart, hands, eyes, books, or time to engage in it," and he would not be content in any event with "such an hasty performance as the two volumes already ventured before the public."[1]

Jefferson, answering, described the ferment in Paris. The Notables, under the leadership of Lafayette, were meeting with the intention of setting some limits to the power of the Crown, and the provincial assemblies were similarly occupied. "Caricatures, placards, bon mots have been indulged in by all ranks of people," Jefferson wrote, "and I know of no well-attested instance of a single punishment." Mobs of twenty and thirty thousand people roamed the streets, collected around the chamber where the Notables deliberated, and dragged home the carriages of those who were thought to favor the popular cause. Troops patrolled the streets to prevent disorders, but crowds hissed and hooted at the Count d'Artois. "The King," Jefferson added, "long in the habit of drowning his cares in wine, plunges deeper and deeper; the Queen cries but sins on," infuriating the mob by appearing in public with her favorite, Madame de Polignac.[2]

Across the Channel, England watched hungrily and prepared for war against a divided and anguished France. Abigail was shocked to hear English acquaintances speak compacently of the anticipated conflict. One lady expressed to Abigail the wish that war might soon break out. "Pray," Abigail asked, "how can you wish such misery to mankind?" "Oh," was the answer, "if there is a war, my brother and several of my friends will be promoted."³

Holland was likewise in a turmoil. The Patriot party had severely limited the powers of the Stadtholder and offended the Princess, sister of the King of Prussia. It was a costly insult; Frederick, to defend family honor, sent a Prussian army under the Duke of Brunswick to occupy the country. The leading Patriots had been proscribed. Dumas lived in daily fear of his life and dozens of Adams' friends were under house arrest. "History does not furnish a more striking instance of abject submission and depression," Abigail wrote John Quincy. The nation that had astonished the world with its bravery and prowess in resisting the whole force and power of Spain was now "humbled to the dust by an imperious and haughty woman . . . for a mere trifling affront."⁴ Adams grieved over the fate of the Dutch Patriots who had been his friends and advocates in Holland and who were now in arrest or scattered about Europe, refugees from the Stadtholderians. Estimable men as they were, they had shown fatal deficiencies as politicians. They had been "too inattentive to the sense of the common people in their own country, too little acquainted with the nature of government, and too confidently dependent on the support of France."⁵

Jefferson had spoken of the lessons to be learned from the fate of Holland and Adams replied, "Lessons, my dear sir, are never wanting. Life and history are full. The loss of paradise, by eating a forbidden apple, has been many thousand years a lesson to mankind; but not much regarded. Moral reflections, wise maxims, religious terrors have little effect upon nations when they contradict a present passion, prejudice, imagination, enthusiasm or caprice." To perceive the lessons was one thing; to prevail upon passionate and imperfect man to heed them was another. If the Duke of Burgundy or the Dauphin of France should demand one of Jefferson's "beautiful and most amiable daughters in marriage," Adams observed sardonically, "all America from Georgia to New Hampshire would find their vanity and pride so agreeably flattered by it that all their sage maxims would give way; and even our sober New England republicans would keep a day of thanksgiving for it in their hearts." As for the lesson that America should never allow an outside power to intervene in its domestic affairs, that too would be kept faithfully until there was an occasion to violate it, "until a domestic difference of a serious nature will break out."

He had long been convinced, Adams wrote, "that neither philosophy, nor religion, nor morality, nor wisdom, nor interest will ever govern nations or parties against their vanity, their pride, their resentment or revenge, or their avarice or ambition." Nothing but force in the form of soundly drawn constitutions and firm laws could restrain men. "In short, my dear friend," he continued, "you and I have been indefatigable laborers through our whole lives for a cause which will be thrown away in the next generation, upon the vanity and foppery of persons of whom we do not know the names perhaps." The coming war would make the United States rich. Riches would breed luxury and dissipation. "Riches, grandeur, and power will have the same effect upon American as it has upon European minds. . . . A Covent Garden rake will never be wise enough to take warning from the claps caught by his companions." When he has become poxed himself he may repent, or on the other hand he may sink even deeper into iniquity. "Pardon this freedom," John concluded. "It is not melancholy but experience, and believe me without reserve your friend, *O tempora—O mores.*"[6]

In September some American seamen were impressed from American vessels in the Thames and Adams protested vigorously to Lord Carmarthen. He continued to write Jay but the volume of his correspondence fell off sharply. There was little to write about. The British ministry showed no sign of yielding on any significant point. The news from the Continent seemed to Adams "the most critical and important . . . of any that has ever happened in our times. Mankind seem impatient," he wrote, "under the yoke of servitude that has been imposed upon them and disposed to compel their governors to make the burden lighter." Jay had written that he planned to have the diplomatic correspondence published. "I shudder," Adams replied, "when I think of your next volume of my dispatches. I shall appear before posterity in a very negligent dress and disordered air. In truth I write too much to write well and have never time to correct anything."

Adams followed the news of the convention at Philadelphia as closely as he could at such a distance from the scene, and dared to have high hopes for it. The convention was composed, he wrote Jay, "of heroes, sages, and demigods to be sure, who want no assistance from me in forming the best possible plan." But the framers might need "underlaborers to make it accepted by the people, or at least make them unanimous and contented with it"; and Adams would be glad to serve in these ranks.[7]

As he looked at the developments in Europe certain things seemed clear. Holland was virtually extinct, a cipher, disgraced and humiliated. France gave not the "least appearance of fortitude or understanding," and must soon go to war or "sink very low." England was the only country that stood to profit from the disordered state of Europe. She, in turn, with the tide running her way, would be increasingly haughty and intractable. The United States would be treated more "cavalierly" than ever. "The philosophical visions of perpetual peace, and the religious reveries of a near approach to the millennium, in which all nations are to turn their weapons of war into implements of husbandry," would soon vanish, Adams wrote Jay. Europe for years to come must at best be in a state of armed truce. Such a distracted scene only made Adams more aware of the blessed fortune of his countrymen. "O fortunate Americans," he exclaimed, "if you did but know your own felicity!" The news of tumults and unrest in the states filled him with apprehension. "If the common people in America lose their integrity," he observed, "they will soon set up tyrants of their own, or court a foreign one. Laws alone, and those political institutions which are the guardians of them, and a sacred administration of justice can preserve honor, virtue, and integrity in the minds of men." Adams feared an alliance between England, Holland, and Prussia against France, in which case America would be obliged to support France because a victorious England would not hesitate to make war on the United States. In order for the United States to "act with dignity in all events" so as "not to be obliged to join in any war without the clearest conviction of the justice of the cause, and her own honor and real interest, it is indispensably necessary," Adams wrote Jay, "that she should act the part in Holland of perfect independence and honest impartiality between the different courts and nations who are now struggling for her friendship, and who are all at present our friends."[8]

When Parliament convened in November, Fox and Pitt made truculent speeches that, in Adams' view, "set every tie that can bind mankind, every principle which ought to be held sacred, at open defiance." Adams found himself, for the moment at least, in the novel and not entirely unpleasant position of being courted by the ministry, but he was not beguiled. "Depend upon it," he wrote Jay, "this will not last; they will aim at recovering back the Western lands, at taking away our fisheries and at the total ruin of our navigation at least." But, he added cautiously, "the state of Europe at large is so confused that there is not one politician in the world that I can hear of who pretends to foresee what turn affairs may take."[9]

Throughout the fall and early winter Adams labored on the third volume of the *Defence*. "It is very easy to flatter the democratical portion of society," Adams wrote, "by making such distinctions (based on their supposed superior virtue) between them and the monarchical and aristocratical; but flattery is as base an artifice and as pernicious a vice when offered to the people as when given to others. There is no reason to believe one honester or wiser than the other; they are all of the same clay; their minds and bodies are alike. The two latter have knowledge and sagacity, derived from education, and more advantages for acquiring wisdom and virtue. As to usurping others' rights, they are all three equally guilty when unlimited in power."

The two main classes of society were "the gentlemen and the simplemen." The simplemen, or common men, were the workers and artisans, farmers and merchants "who pursue their occupations and industry without any knowledge in liberal arts and sciences." The gentlemen, on the other hand, were "all those who have received a liberal education, an ordinary degree of erudition in liberal arts and sciences." A simple, unchecked democracy was perhaps the worst of all governments because the many would pillage all those who had more of the world's goods than themselves. With an elective executive there was, moreover, the danger that turmoil and faction would rend the fabric of society. If such was the case, it were far better that "first magistrates and senators . . . be made hereditary at once than that the people should be universally debauched and bribed to go to loggerheads and fly to arms regularly every year." If it was necessary to have a hereditary executive to prevent having an absolute one, it was a cheap price to pay.

If it is understandable how Adams' attitude toward monarchy might have troubled his contemporaries who were preternaturally sensitive on the subject, it is harder to understand why it should have troubled later historians. Adams was never in any sense anti-democratic, except as contrasted with the more doctrinaire radicals of his day. He believed that a strong executive was essential to a stable government and that such an executive, embodying the monarchical principle, might possibly at some future date become hereditary or for life. As such he would champion the cause of the mass of the people against the usurping tendencies of an aristocracy of wealth or birth, should wealth enshroud itself in aristocratic forms. Beyond that, he changed his mind and thought one thing one day and another the next. He believed that all such questions should be examined and discussed, weighed and debated in a free and informed spirit. In his own mind he alternately took one side or the other. Principles were immutable but the applications of them might be scrutinized endlessly, held up to the light of history, turned about, juggled, played with. Adams had the true intellectual's zest for ideas, for the play of the mind, darting like a fish through the crystal waters of theory. Not an academic, wedded to a maxim, or a politician, wary of being misquoted and misunderstood, he was not obsessed with the need for consistency. He was a searcher and a seeker. So he was properly indignant when he was accused of wishing to rivet a monarchy on the United States, or of having deserted his Revolutionary principles. Nothing of the kind. It was he who had been, in the larger things, deeply consistent; it was his opponents who had either not listened carefully, willfully misunderstood or, what was as often the case, changed their views. He had written earlier to Lafayette that he, Adams, had "the honor and the consolation to be a republican on principle." It was the best form of government "of which human nature is capable." Almost everything that was "estimable in life," he noted, "has originated . . . under such governments. The two republican towns, Athens and Rome, have done more honor to our species than all the rest of it." But, he added, "I am not an enthusiast who wishes to overturn empires and monarchies for the sake of introducing republican forms of government—and therefore I am not king killer, king hater, or king despiser." There were, in fact, three monarchs in Europe whom he considered models of "human wisdom and beneficence"—the King of France, the Emperor of Germany, and the King of Prussia."[10]

Moreover, while he realized that the United States would not consider a limited, constitutional monarchy, Adams was convinced that there was nothing about such a form of government that was inherently hostile to the democratic principle. It was his countrymen who were the dogmatists; for them a king was inseparable from a despot and thus the natural enemy of democracy.

The federal constitution reached Adams as he was finishing the third volume of the *Defence* and, suppressing certain misgivings about that document, he ended the book with a flourish. "It is now in our power," he wrote, "to bring this work to a conclusion with unexpected dignity." The new frame of government with its plan for amendment, "and the deliberate union of so great and various a people in such a plan, is without all partiality or prejudice, if not the greatest exertion of human understanding, the greatest single effort of national deliberation that the world has ever seen."

Adams' first reaction to the constitution was by no means entirely favorable. Jefferson had written, "There are things in it which stagger all my dispositions to subscribe to what such an assembly has proposed." The House of Representatives would not, he thought, "be adequate to the management of affairs, either foreign or federal," and the President seemed to Jefferson "a bad edition of a Polish King." Since there was no limit on the number of terms he might serve, it was reasonable to suppose that he would be re-elected for life. France and England would both strive to have "a Galloman or Angloman" as President, and the chief executive with the army under his command would soon make himself dictator. Jefferson's main regret was that the President had not been limited to a four-year term of office. Indeed, he would have preferred a government that consisted simply of "three or four new articles to be added to the good, old and venerable fabric" of the Articles of Confederation.[11]

Like Jefferson, Adams found parts of the new frame of government "to which," as he wrote in reply to Jefferson's comments, "I find it difficult to reconcile myself." But while Jefferson feared the powers of the executive, Adams feared those of the Senate. "We agree perfectly," he noted, "that the many should have a full, fair, and perfect representation. You are apprehensive of monarchy, I of aristocracy. I would therefore have given more power to the president and less to the Senate." It seemed to Adams a bad principle to give the Senate the right to approve executive appointments. "Faction and distraction" would be the inevitable result. Whereas Jefferson was apprehensive that the President, once chosen, would be chosen again and again, in effect for life, Adams welcomed this provision as giving the government greater stability and preventing the commotions and intrigues that would be inevitable with frequent changes of office.[12]

Nabby wrote John Quincy that her father did "not wholly approve of the [new form of government] which has been offered—but he thinks that the people had better adopt it as it is—and then appoint a new convention to make such alterations as may prove necessary." He regretted that the framers had not given the President a greater degree of independence and wished that "they had made provision for a privy council—either of his own appointment or chosen by the Senate. . . . If the system at present under consideration is not adopted," she added, "I am of the opinion that he will assist at a future convention and have a principal hand in . . . framing one which may be adopted."[13]

Adams himself, replying to Cotton Tufts' criticisms of the constitution, conceded that there were "reasonable difficulties and objections." But, he added, "is there not danger that a new convention at this time would increase the difficulties and reasonable exceptions rather than remove any of them?" He wished with all his heart for "a Declaration of Rights," although he was conscious of the difficulties of framing one on which all the states could agree. "The press, conscience, and juries I wish better secured," he noted. "But is it not better to accept this plan and amend it hereafter? After ten years' absence from his country a man should be modest, but as at present instructed I think I should vote for it as it is, and promote a convention after some time to amend it."[14]

The more he thought about it, the more the constitution seemed to Adams to be an admirable document. "The public mind," he wrote Jay, "cannot be occupied about a nobler object than the proposed plan of government. It appears to be admirably calculated to cement all America in affection and interest, as one great nation. A result of accommodation and compromise cannot be supposed perfectly to coincide with everyone's ideas of perfection. But, as all the great principles necessary to order, liberty, and safety are respected in it, and provision is made for corrections and amendments as they may be found necessary, I confess I hope to hear of its adoption by all the states."[15]

Writing to Brand-Hollis, Adams defended the new government warmly. He could not guarantee its permanence, of course. "Such," he declared, "is the melancholy lot of humanity that I cannot pretend to promise immortality to liberty or to virtue in any nation or country of great numbers and large extent for any constitution of government within human contrivance." But the new constitution seemed clearly a vast improvement over anything that had gone before. Brand-Hollis had objected to the name and the powers of the President, but Adams replied, "I am not solicitous about the name and power of the first magistrate, provided he have the whole executive power. . . . You and I hold that nations are the creators, the masters, the sovereigns of kings. That the people have a right . . . to pull down a bad government and erect a good one. We believe too that the people are capable of this. How can we suppose them so ignorant and superstitious as to be imposed on and ruined by a word?" It was absurd, too, to blame poor George III for English policy. "For God's sake, sir," Adams burst out, "instead of finding fault with your King find fault with your people and your representatives and make them do their duty."[16]

Nabby, writing to her brother, remarked that the American colony in London appeared "much gratified with our constitution," adding, "The accounts from America are favorable for its reception and adoption by the states, which give their friends on this side of the water much pleasure. Many persons say here that they have followed my father's plan and taken his book for their model."[17]

Shortly after the turn of the year Jefferson, alarmed over the state of Continental finances, wrote Adams an apprehensive letter. The Dutch bankers had notified him that they had no money left in the American loan to meet further drafts. Payment of interest on the Dutch and French loans would exhaust their funds. Jefferson indeed had not money enough at his command to pay the French officers who had served in the Continental Army and who were becoming increasingly vociferous in their demands. It seemed as though once again American credit was on the brink of disaster. It would be particularly unfortunate, with the new government soon to be put into effect, if it should be launched amid the default of its obligations and the collapse of its credit abroad. Would Adams, Jefferson asked, undertake to open one more loan to tide the country over until the new government got well established?

Adams, convinced that the crisis had been induced by the manipulations of the Dutch investors, wrote back indignantly that Jefferson should press Willink and Van Staphorst for some accounting. There should be enough money coming in from the sale of the bonds that he had signed less than a year ago to support American credit. This latest alarm, he felt, was simply an effort to extract a new loan at a higher rate of interest. He was informed on good authority that Dutch bankers had been buying large amounts of American paper currency in Europe on a speculative basis. Now they wished to use Congress' need for money to meet the interest payments on its foreign debt to exact a payment of interest on the domestic paper in private hands. In short, it was a kind of blackmail as he saw it. If the interest were paid on the domestic bonds in Europe rather than in America, the bondholders would see that the balance of Adams' earlier loan was filled and then deduct it from the interest due.

The precedent was a dangerous one and Adams advised his friend to get counsel from the Treasury Board before taking any action. He was certain that if Jefferson refused to be "dunned and teased," and called the Dutchmen's bluff, they would give way. "Depend upon it," he wrote, "the Amsterdamers love money too well to execute their threats. They expect too much by American credit to destroy it."

His departure now set, Adams offered his friend a few reflections on the state of affairs in Europe. The whole Continent, he wrote, "resounds with projects for reviving states and assemblies . . . and France is taking the lead. How such assemblies will mix with simple monarchies is the question. The fermentation must terminate in improvements of various kinds. Superstition, bigotry, ignorance, imposture, tyranny, and misery must be lessened somewhat. . . . Corrections and reformations and improvements are much wanted in all the institutions in Europe ecclesiastical and civil; but how or when they will be made is not easy to guess." Republics, he thought, would not soon work; the effort to establish them would bring confusion and carnage which must again end in despotism because the common people of Europe were not yet ready for self-government, not sufficiently educated or self-disciplined. "I shall soon be out of the noise of all these speculations in Europe," he added, "leaving behind me however the most fervent good wishes for the safety and prosperity of all who have the cause of humanity, equity, equality, and liberty at heart . . . as we say at sea, huzza for the New World and farewell to the old one!"[18]

With the end of his mission in sight, there was an additional complication and embarrassment. Congress, which had sent Adams a letter giving him permission to return to the United States, had failed to address formal letters of recall to their high mightinesses of the States-General in Holland and to the British court. Adams, therefore, could not under diplomatic protocol pay his respects and be properly dismissed by the courts to which he was accredited. It seemed to him a final humiliation when his letter to the States-General requesting his dismissal came back with a note to the effect that this could not be accomplished without direct communications from Congress. "There is no alernative now left for me," he wrote Jay; "home I must go, and leave all Europe to conjecture that I have given offense in Holland and in England, that I have misbehaved abroad, though my conduct has been approved at home. . . . To a man who has taken the utmost pains to do his duty, and to fulfill every obligation to the smallest punctilio, nothing can be more disagreeable than such disappointments, especially as in all my letters I have so expressly and repeatedly requested regular letters of recall."[19]

On further reflection, however, Adams decided to go to The Hague and request his dismissal in person. Before leaving he presented himself to the King in an atmosphere far different than that of their encounter three years earlier. For Adams there had been nothing but frustration and disappointment. The King, like his ministers, felt impatience at the weakness and vacillation of the American government. Where before the air had been charged with emotion, there was now simply correctness and formality. Adams entered, bowed the prescribed number of times, and read in an uninflected voice his brief address. Since the period of his mission was expiring, he wished to repeat in behalf of his country "their assurances of their friendly dispositions, and their continued desire of a liberal intercourse of commerce and good offices with Your Majesty's subjects and states." This and thanks "for the protection and civilities" he had received at His Majesty's court, and best wishes to the "royal family, subjects, and dominions."

The King replied, "Mr. Adams, you may with great truth assure the United States that whenever they shall fulfill the treaty on their part I, on my part, will fulfill it in all its particulars. As to yourself, I am sure I wish you a safe and pleasant voyage and much comfort with your family and friends." Having concluded the formal part of the audience, the King, who liked Adams, graciously engaged him in conversation about his family, their activities, and their health.

Jefferson, meanwhile, found himself "dunned and teased" to the point of despair. No financier, he felt quite out of his depth in trying to deal with the Dutch bankers. The fact was that Adams' advice had not worked. Willink and Van Staphorst seemed as alarmed as Jefferson over the state of American credit. Hearing from Abigail that her husband had left for The Hague, Jefferson decided to intercept Adams there and try to prevail on him to accompany him to Amsterdam. "I was sensible how important it was to have the benefit of [Mr. Adams'] interference," Jefferson wrote to Jay, "in a department which had been his peculiarly from the beginning, and with all the details of which he was as intimately acquainted as I was so little." Together they might be a match for the Dutchmen.

At The Hague, John had scarcely taken leave "of all parties," the Prince and Princess, their high mightinesses, Secretary Fagel and the Grand Pensionary, and "been feasted at court and all that," when Jefferson arrived to bear him off to Amsterdam to haggle with Willink and Van Staphorst. He would be delayed for days and Abigail, who had told Jefferson where he was, "must blame yourself for it, altogether."[20]

With Adams in command, so to speak, the two Americans stood fast against the blackmail. Willink and Van Staphorst, seeing that they were intractable, gave way at last. Encouraged by this victory, Adams and Jefferson decided to try to negotiate a new loan that would take care of the interest payments on the American loans through 1790, when presumably the new government would be solidly established and American finances in good order—"thus to place the government at its ease, and her credit in security during that trying period," as Jefferson expressed it to Jay.[21] A million florins, they estimated, would tide over American credit. Willink and Van Staphorst agreed to undertake the loan; Adams executed bonds for the sum which would remain unissued until Congress ratified the loan, bade Jefferson an affectionate farewell, and hurried back to London to join Abigail in preparations for the trip home.

Abigail had made good use of her time. Despite a nagging cold and sore throat, she had moved to the Bath Hotel to allow packers to crate the books and personal belongings at Grosvenor Square. She had also dispatched elaborate instructions to Cotton Tufts about the new house which he had bought for them. She wanted it painted within and without. The first-floor east room should be painted a "French gray," with a red-figured wallpaper since the furniture that they would bring from England for that room would be upholstered in red. In the room above the furniture would be green and it would be best "to have the paper conformable to it." In the downstairs sitting room with the mahogany paneling she hardly knew what to say. It was a dark room and therefore it might be better to paint it a light color. But she intended to have two windows cut through onto the garden and these would perhaps dispel the gloom, so that if the mahogany was not scarred or scratched it would be better to leave it as it was. She wished to know whether the chimneys in the house had iron backs to throw the heat and whether the locks for the doors were brass. The rest of the repairs and renovations she left to the judgment of the doctor, but he must be careful to get a painter with a good color sense and the ability to mix colors. She remembered one painful experience where she had had to have one room painted over three times before the painter got the color that she had specified. The addition of a library for John's books would have to wait until the boys' schooling was finished.

For herself, Abigail wrote, she looked forward to a life of making butter and cheese, raising poultry and looking after her garden. "Mr. Adams," she added, "means to retire to Braintree as a private man. Nor need anyone fear that he will become a competitor with them for offices. He has always dealt too openly and candidly with his countrymen to be popular and whatever democrats or aristocrats may assert with regard to his monarchial principles, he says they may be assured that he will never hide or conceal a sentiment of heart from the people which he thinks for their interest or happiness to be acquainted with, though he should forfeit by it the highest offices in the United States."

John and Abigail were to sail from Cowes with Captain Callahan on the *Lucretia*, bound for Boston, while Nabby and little William took a vessel sailing directly to New York. It was a cruel wrench for Abigail to leave

Nabby and the baby. Her daughter had gone off with a sore throat and William was teething, so that Abigail felt anxious and uneasy about them.

They left London—John and Abigail and John and Esther Briesler, Esther seven months' pregnant—at the end of March and made their way by coach to Bath and then Falmouth. At Cowes they put up at the Fountain Inn where Abigail was so cramped and confined in their little room that she could not sleep and asked for larger quarters. The change was a happy one. The new room gave "a fine view of the harbor, vessels . . . and surrounding hills," but both she and John grew restless and impatient waiting for Callahan and the *Lucretia*. Abigail found that she missed the baby acutely. "How is my dear sweet boy?" she wrote Nabby. "I think of him by day and dream of him by night. Oh, what a relief would his sportive little pranks have been to me in the tedious hours of waiting—waiting for winds, for captain, for vessel." The little bit of sewing and the few books Abigail had brought with her were soon exhausted. She and John visited the country about Cowes and the ruins of Carlsbrook Castle at Newport where Charles I was imprisoned during the Civil War. There they met a Mr. Sharp, "enthusiastic in favor of America," who insisted on bearing them off to meet his ninety-year-old father and beautiful but affected daughters.[22]

Finally, on the twentieth of April, Callahan arrived and John and Abigail embarked with the Brieslers; they were scarcely at sea before the wind shifted and drove them into Portland Harbor where they lay for another maddening eight days. Whenever Abigail was inclined to feel sorry for herself she thought of Esther, uncomfortably pregnant and "distressingly seasick, and I am then silent."

When the wind changed at last and the *Lucretia* made her escape from the Channel, Abigail was more certain than ever that she would never be persuaded to cross the ocean again. "Indeed," she wrote, "I have seen enough of the world, small as [it] has been, and shall be content to learn what is further to be known from the page of history. I do not think," she added, "the four years I have passed abroad the pleasantest part of my life. 'Tis domestic happiness and rural felicity in the bosom of my native land that has charms for me. Yet I do not regret that I made this excursion since it has only more attached me to America."

Esther Briesler's child was born at sea, "a poor little starvling but with special lungs." Briesler, who had been counted on to act as nurse, was so seasick that he had to be nursed himself most of the trip. Abigail, fortunately, suffered less from seasickness than on the trip to England, but she got precious little sleep and felt numb and weak much of the time. The ship was clean, the passengers agreeable, the Captain skillful, yet she found herself "almost exhausted and my patience wearied out," afflicted by painful sores on her fingers. John, on the other hand, seemed to thrive, chatting with the sailors, quizzing the Captain, poking into every corner of the *Lucretia*.

The apparently endless voyage gave Adams much time to consider his return to his native land after an absence of ten years. A vast amount had transpired in his absence. The Revolution had been fought and won; Congress had found it more difficult to govern a nation at peace than one at war. The solidarity that had been created between the states and between the citizens of respective states by their devotion to a common task was breaking up. Particular interests were taking precedence over general interests. Released from external pressure, states were wrangling with states and neighbors with each other. It was far from certain that the constitution would be ratified. The last word before leaving London was that only six states had accepted the new frame of government; New York had refused even to call a ratifying convention. There were thus pro- and anti-constitutionalists, Southern interests and Northern interests, seacoast and interior, merchants versus farmers, anti-British and pro-British, anti- and pro-French. Luxury and indulgence were becoming more and more evident. People thought more of their purses than of their liberties, more of their bellies than the good of their country.

If all of this was disappointing, to Adams at least it was not surprising. History was full of examples of the propensity of mankind for folly and dissension. Americans were part of the human race, more blessed by circumstances, more honest, more devoted to the principles of good government than the common run, but certainly not incorruptible, not without the impulse toward vanity and self-indulgence that was an apparently unalterable aspect of the human condition.

Just the word that Adams himself was returning to Massachusetts had "set the tools of the present administration spitting like so many cats," Mary Cranch had written. He would return to receive not praise and adulation, not gratitude for his services and sacrifices, for his ten-year exile —much of it an exile from all that was dearest to him—but rather to be the butt of partisan attacks, to be whispered about as a champion of monarchy, to find old friends grown cold, adherents of social and political ideas that seemed to him dangerous and destructive. Walking interminably about the deck of the *Lucretia*, John tried to summon up his philosophy, to arm himself against the indifference or hostility of an insensitive and ungrateful world. Braintree would be changed and Boston too. Old faces, loved faces, would be gone. Eight members of the family and many of the close circle of friends had died since Abigail's absence. There would be new faces—alert, ambitious, aggressive men of doubtful principles and persuasive tongues, who battened on confusion and unrest like evil birds on carrion. The shape of Boston would be changed, and the hearts and minds, the loyalties and the alliances of many would have changed. But there would be among this disconcerting flux certain enduring things. The rough, granitic shape of Penn's Hill, looking out over the bay; the long, long line of the Blue Hills, the sluggish Neponset, the salt flats on the seaside of the town, the farm itself, the winelike air, the pungent heat of midsummer, the loam of the pasture, the delicious taste of Seckel pears, the intoxicating smell of windfall apples, the stone fences that bisected the fields about Braintree, the whir of a partridge rising from the dusty underbrush along the road.

But whatever it was he would be ready, he trusted, armed with his philosophy which allowed him to hold no illusions about the nature of man; loving man in the particular as well as in the general, but more in the particular as his Virginian friend loved them more in the general. He knew them, and still he dared to hope and dream for them, to labor for them, to abuse them, to puzzle over them, to weep and laugh over them. His impatience to be home grew with each league of the ocean that flowed beneath the *Lucretia's* keel.

LV

JOHN HANCOCK, who must have viewed Adam's return with mixed feelings since he had to a degree bartered his support of the new constitution for the assurance that he would be put forward as Vice-President, left a gracious note of welcome with the pilot at the lighthouse. As soon as the *Lucretia* entered the harbor the pilot was to hoist a signal which would alert the Castle to give a proper salute as the vessel passed by. Everything went off without a hitch. At the appearance of the ship the cannon in the fort fired a deafening volley and the Governor's coach set out for the Long Wharf to carry the Adams entourage to the Hancock mansion, where Hancock declared grandly, "I wish you to tarry till you have fixed upon your place of abode."[1] It was possibly at the instigation of Hancock that Adams had been elected delegate from Massachusetts to the Congress of the United States even before his arrival.

Hancock was concerned lest the growing opposition to his own administration coalesce around the new arrival, who had the advantage of having been free of involvement in local politics. Adams would certainly be less of a threat to Hancock's dominance in New York than in Braintree. But if such thoughts were in the back of Hancock's mind he gave no evidence of them. He and his wife, Dorothy Quincy, were all charm and affability. He would escort the Adamses to Braintree in style, Hancock insisted, attended by a squadron of light cavalry. The town of Braintree would turn out and welcome them at the Milton bridge. But Adams vetoed the plan. He wanted no show or parade to feed his vanity or to stimulate his critics. First he, and then Abigail, slipped out of Boston and traveled to the Cranches at Milton to wait for their furniture to be unloaded.

When Abigail rode over to Braintree she was dismayed at the state of the house. The repairs were incomplete and the house itself, which she had remembered as a mansion, after their quarters at Auteuil and Grosvenor Square, looked "like a wren's house." "Be sure you wear no feathers and let Col. Smith come without heels to his shoes, or he will not be able to walk upright," she wrote Nabby, referring to the low ceilings. Carpenters, masons, and hired hands swarmed about under Adams' direction, adding to Abigail's feeling of confusion and disorder. The furniture had been badly packed and it was so chipped and scarred that Abigail was sorry she had ever brought it across the ocean. "The shocking state of the house," she wrote Nabby, "has obliged me to open [the furniture] in the garret." John, with a thousand pressing things to be done and no decent barn, went off and bought six cows and presented them to his wife. Abigail had to smile through her exasperation. It was so typical of his impulsiveness; like a small boy, he could not wait, he must be Farmer Adams at once; and she the dairymaid.

But the birds sang sweetly as only American birds could sing, more so than French nightingales or English larks, and the soil burst with summer life. So there was in all the work and bustle great joy in being home once more with sisters, nieces and nephews, and above all her boys, now tall men looking down from their superior heights at their parents. From every side Abigail heard what comes so welcome to a mother's ears, praise of John Quincy for his industry, his brilliance, and his excellent character. Tom, with "a spice of fun in his composition," was the cutup of the family. "Charles," Abigail wrote her daughter, "wins the heart as usual and is the most of a gentleman of them all."[2]

Soon after their return an impulse carried John on his short, stubby legs up the sides of Penn's Hill to the scene of ocean and sky and islands. It was always with a sense of expectancy that he mounted toward the summit of the hill although he knew every line, every fold of coast, every league of ocean. Always familiar, it was always new. Years ago he had raced to its crest countless times. Now he was an old man, corpulent, palsied, short of breath, his legs lumpy and blue-veined, his eyesight dimmed. But his spirit still rose as he climbed, stopping briefly to catch his breath, until he stood on the top, a sturdy, solitary figure, nudged and tugged at by the wind, gray and square like the granite outcroppings on the hill. In his years of exile abroad he had seen it in his mind's eye a thousand times and he would never get enough of it. Lashed with rain or covered with snow, bathed in the indolent amber light of a summer afternoon, or cold and gray with a kind of heartbreaking sadness, the tragic landscape of late fall—in these guises and many more, changing and unchanging, he knew and loved it. It was certainly of a piece with his New England, thrusting up, hard and granitic, unyielding, infertile. The crops of hay and grain coaxed from its flinty soil were scarcely worth the trouble to horse or plowman or harvester of treading its steep sides. It was more pride than wise husbandry that kept him at it; scattering manure and seaweed among the rocks and boulders to reap a few bushels of oats or a cartload of hay.

Nabby, newly arrived in New York, found as many brides had before and since that her mother-in-law was a rather overbearing lady who thought it quite within her province to tell Nabby how to care for young William, who put her teeth on edge by her constant stream of criticism and advice. Her numerous brothers- and sisters-in-law were not very much more to her liking. With their New York airs they were too inclined to patronize and they showed the same tendency as their mother to tell Nabby and the Colonel how to run their affairs. In such a setting Nabby saw her husband with new eyes. He was less the dashing soldier than the spoiled and pampered younger son in a large and domineering family in which she felt like an interloper. She was also disturbed by his apparent inclination to bask in the admiration of his family, his avowed intention of seeking appointment to public office, and his grandiose plans for making his fortune through speculations in land. With Abigail's whitlows too painful for her to write, John reassured his daughter as best he could. Above all she must show her mother-in-law "dutiful filial respect, affection, and attention."[3]

In addition to the confusion and disorder at the house Abigail had to bear with John's moping and moodiness. He suddenly lapsed into one of his spells of self-pity and pessimism. He had left America ten years earlier in the prime of life; now he was an old man in his middle fifties, broken in health, without any future or any prospects. He had not been able to save enough money to provide for his and his wife's comfortable old age, or to launch his sons in a highly competitive world. There had been talk of his being Governor of Massachusetts but Hancock was apparently well entrenched in that office. Now there were rumors that Jay would be proposed as Vice-President. It seemed to him, he observed darkly, that he did "not stand very high in the esteem, admiration, or respect of his country, or any part of it." In his long absence he had "got quite out of circulation." "The public judgment, the public heart, and the public voice," he wrote Nabby, speaking of himself in the third person, "seem to have decreed to others every public office that he can accept of with consistency or honor or reputation; and no alternative [is] left at home, or to go again abroad." He had spoken of wishing only to return to the life of a farmer in Braintree, but now that such a future faced him it seemed less attractive than he had imagined.[4]

Abigail did her best to brace his spirits, and Nabby wrote firmly, "I do not quite agree with you in opinion. It is true that a very long absence may have erased from the minds of many your services; but it will not take a long time to renew the remembrances of them, and you will, my dear sir, soon find them not obliterated." It was Nabby's opinion, based on "the general voice" in New York, that her father would be either Governor of Massachusetts or Vice-President to Washington. New York had finally adopted the constitution by a margin of three votes after a long and bitter struggle.[5]

Adams also got a boost from Benjamin Rush, who wrote an affectionate letter telling of his delight at having the Adamses back in America. "I owe more than I can express to you," he declared, "for your excellent volume upon government. They shall be the Alcoran of my boys upon the great subject of political happiness. You have laid the world and posterity under great obligations by your researches. I am not more satisfied of the truth of any one proposition in Euclid than I am of the truth of your leading propositions in government." Rush was convinced that, as he put it, "we live in an important era and in a *new* country. . . . America has ever appeared to me to be the theater in which human nature will receive its greatest civil, literary, and religious honor. *Now* is the time to sow the seeds of each of them." Adams was to have a "material hand" in this reformation. "Your labors for your country," the doctor observed, "are only *beginning*." He himself hoped to see Adams Vice-President. Certainly Pennsylvania would support him, especially if in return the Southern and the New England states would support Philadelphia as the seat of the new government. "This," he added, "must be the compensation for their placing a citizen of Virginia in the President's chair and a citizen of New England in the chair of the senate."[6]

While Adams rejected the idea of such a bargain, he was encouraged by Rush's letter. Ezra Stiles, President of Yale, writing to inform him that he had been awarded an honorary degree from that institution, added his opinion that Adams was the natural choice for the second office in the land. From Virginia, Arthur Lee, strongly opposed to the federal constitution, nonetheless wrote that his state would find Mr. Adams most acceptable as Vice-President. "Should Mr. Hancock not interfere," he noted, "your election will be certain. I shall very much rejoice in it."[7] Nabby wrote again to report that she had heard Richard Henry Lee say that the vice-presidency or the chief justiceship of the Supreme Court must go to Adams, though Jay was also being mentioned as a candidate for both offices.

David Ramsay, replying to an inquiry from John Eliot, wrote, "You ask who will be Vice-President. I think John Adams deserves any place he chooses after that of the President, which ought assuredly to be given to General Washington. I would suppose," he added, "that either the place of senator or of chief justice would be his choice in preference to that of a Vice-President." Hancock would certainly not have the votes of the Carolina electors.[8]

But everything was uncertain. Hancock was an enemy certainly. That became clearer with every passing day. George Clinton, the leader of the Anti-Federalists in New York, was also spoken of as a candidate for the vice-presidency. The wrangle over the location of the new capital went on endlessly with intrigues and counterintrigues. "The maxim of the present time," Nabby wrote from her vantage point at New York, "is 'If you can be of service to me in promoting my views, I will give you my assistance in yours.'"[9] In such circumstances it was impossible to predict the outcome of anything. Congress still puttered away, futile but unwilling to surrender entirely, and no one could say when, much less where, the new government would be established. The price of moving it to Philadelphia might be support of Jay for Vice-President. Adams was restless and impatient. He talked of returning to the bar or, half facetiously, of entering into the China trade. He could not hope to support himself and complete the education of his sons simply by farming.

Abigail spent more than her quota of sleepless nights worrying about John's frame of mind and about their financial situation. The renovations to the house, of course, were far more expensive than they had anticipated and both of them watched their little supply of capital dwindling rapidly. Still they were cramped. There was no adequate kitchen, no library, and no dairy for the precious cows. Esther Briesler was sick, and to complicate matters further Nabby was expecting her second child in November. Abigail wanted her at Braintree but it seemed inadvisable for her to try making the trip with the weather so hot and the roads so bad. Abigail thus decided she must go to Jamaica, New York, to help out during Nabby's confinement.

Adams received all kinds of advice from his supporters. He should, some of them argued, take his seat in Congress as soon as it convened as a delegate from Massachusetts. He might then allow his friends to make him President of that virtually defunct body. This would attract attention to him, underline his availability, and allow him to do a little judicious politicking. He must go on to New York in any event to recruit backers and make clear his stand on the principles of the new government. Others advised him to lie low in Braintree until it was clear how the wind was blowing. He himself longed to go to New York with Abigail to see Nabby and visit with old friends. "But as long as this political squall shall last," he wrote Nabby in response to her invitation to visit them, "I can scarcely lie asleep or sit still without censure, much less ride journeys on visits to my friends."

As for the suggestions that he should take his seat briefly in Congress to rally support, he assured his daughter that if his success depended on such expedients "I will never have any other than private employments while I live. I am willing to serve the public on manly conditions," he added, "but not on childish ones; on honorable principles, not mean ones."[10]

It was also suggested to John that he serve as Senator from Massachusetts in the new government, but he declined emphatically. "I have long revolved in an anxious mind," he wrote Theophilus Parsons after a meeting in which the Newburyport lawyer had pressed Adams to accept the appointment as Senator, "on the duties of the man and the citizen; and, without entering into details at present, the result of my reflections on the place of a Senator in the new government is an unchangeable determination to refuse it."[11]

Benjamin Lincoln was a frequent visitor and the Braintree militia held a review for Lincoln and Governor Hancock on Adams' farm, firing blank charges, attacking and withdrawing, and in the process knocking down the fences. "I wish," Adams wrote Colonel Smith, "that Governor Hancock and General Lincoln would not erect their military reputations upon the ruins of my stone walls."[12] The three men eyed each other warily; all had political ambitions that conflicted at certain crucial points.

With his mother in Jamaica, John Quincy came back to Braintree to stay with his father and try to recuperate from a severe attack of nerves which had made him miserable after his return to Newburyport. Father and son spent much time together walking through the Blue Hills, discussing law and politics beside the fireplace, pitching manure in the barnyard, or sitting in the living room reading.

Richard Cranch was Adams' most frequent companion, and John visited his mother regularly, but for the rest he was rather a recluse, enjoying the opportunity, for the first time in years, to read and write undistracted by official duties and responsibilities. John Quincy was even more of a hermit, his aunt wrote Abigail. Holed up in his father's study, he read morning and night. "When we turn [in]to books he will visit us," Mary Cranch noted wryly.

State politicians beat a path to his door but Adams was, at least for him, reserved and discreet. He especially enjoyed the visit of General Knox, who put to rest some of his anxieties about the Society of the Cincinnati. Adams, of course, did not know that General Knox came as an emissary of Hamilton to sound him out and try to deflect him from the vice-presidency by hinting that he was too big a man in his own right to hold a position subordinate to Washington; he was too forthright and outspoken to harmonize with the strong-willed General, Knox suggested. Adams was polite but firm. He would not actively seek the vice-presidency but he showed plainly that he felt he deserved the honor and would do nothing to discourage his supporters. Knox carried back to Hamilton the word that Adams had no intention of withdrawing from the competition for the office.

Hamilton was already the nominal head of the Federalist group. Political management and intrigue came naturally to him. He wanted someone as Vice-President who would be more pliant than the man from Braintree and he cast about to find an acceptable alternative. It is not good politics to advance the cause of a potential rival, and Hamilton was shrewd

enough to know that he could not lead Adams about. When his inquiries
convinced him that Adams could not be by-passed without alienating the
majority of New England Federalists, he gave way reluctantly, writing
to Madison that he was backing Adams, though "not without apprehensions on the score we talked about."[13] To Theodore Sedgwick, one of the
leaders of Massachusetts Federalism, he wrote, "On the question between
Mr. H[ancock] and Mr. A., Mr. King will probably have informed you
that I have upon the whole concluded that the latter ought to be supported. My measures will be taken accordingly. I had but one scruple,
but after mature consideration, I have relinquished it. Mr. A., to a sound
understanding, has always appeared to me to add an ardent love for the
public good, and his further knowledge of the world seems to have corrected those jealousies which he is represented to have once been influenced by. I trust nothing of the kind suggested in my former letter will
disturb the harmony of the administration."[14]

With Hamilton's support Adams' election to the vice-presidency was
assured. Indeed, it might well have been insured even if Hamilton had
opposed it. But John continued to watch anxiously for portents. By the
end of November the returns were in from the state congressional elections. Except for one Grout who had been involved in the Shaysite rebellion, the Massachusetts delegation seemed comfortably Federal.
Adams' friend Tristram Dalton had been elected Senator along with
Caleb Strong. It remained only to await the outcome of the presidential
election. "My mind has balanced all circumstances," John wrote Abigail at
New York, "and all are reducible to two articles—vanity and comfort. . . .
If they mortify my vanity, they give me comfort. They connot deprive me
of comfort without gratifying my vanity."[15] Between voting for the presidential electors in December and the tabulation of the vote and the meeting of the electoral college, tedious months passed. Adams, impatient as
always, passed the time as best he could in Abigail's absence.

Hamilton, if he must accept Adams as Vice-President, was determined
to whittle away his electoral vote so that the New Englander's apparent
popularity and thus his political strength would be diminished. Under the
inept provisions of the new constitution, in order to prevent a tie between
the presidential and vice-presidential candidates, it was necessary that
at least one elector should throw his vote from Adams to some other
candidate for the vice-presidency. As soon as the returns were in for the
presidential electors in the various states, Hamilton launched his campaign
to undermine Adams. He wrote to electors in various states and made
the suggestion to each that they divert several votes from Adams to other
candidates, thus assuring that first place should go to Washington. He
proposed that three should be thrown from Adams in New Jersey and two
in Connecticut. He wrote James Wilson in Pennsylvania suggesting that
the electors of that state drop three or four Adams votes, adding, "For

God's sake let not our zeal for a secondary object [Adams' election to the vice-presidency] defeat or endanger a first." To arm against any Anti-Federalist plots, it might indeed be necessary to deflect enough votes from Adams to imperil his chances for the vice-presidency; "but," Hamilton added, "if risk is to be run on one side or the other can we hesitate where it ought to be preferred?"[16]

Abigail got to Jamaica after the birth of the baby. Nabby, expecting a protracted labor, had told no one that she felt badly and found herself suddenly about to produce the baby. Mrs. Smith had scarcely time to attend; it was too late to summon a doctor and Nabby's Negro maid had to do service as a midwife. "Happily," Abigail wrote to Mary Cranch, "she had on some former occasions assisted some of her own color, but all were terribly frightened." The new baby was a raw, red little morsel and Abigail's chief interest was William, "the very image of his mamma at the same age . . . the merest little trunchion that you ever saw, very pleasant and good-humored." Abigail liked her numerous in-laws. Mrs. Smith was a tall, handsome woman, "charming as far as I have been able to form an acquaintance with her." The Colonel's sister Peggy, "agreeable rather than handsome," totally without affectation; Belinda, not pretty but with "that interesting countenance and openness of manners that interests you at first sight"; Charity, the loveliest of the family although disfigured by the loss of an eye, with "a taste for drawing, for music, etc."; and Sally, only seventeen, with "a fine figure and a pretty face, unaffected and artless in her manners"—all were very pleasing. The Colonel's brothers, the three Js—John, James, and Justus—were gay and charming, and like the Colonel thoroughly spoiled. Abigail was kept busy looking after Nabby and the new baby, John Adams Smith, and playing with William, but she was impatient to be home. She knew that John was going through a kind of purgatory waiting for the outcome of the election. "I think of my poor dear and pity him," she wrote her sister.[17]

To John himself she confided, "I think every separation more painful as I increase in years." She trusted he missed her "vital heat" during the winter nights. He must make up the deficiency with the green baize gown, "and if that will not answer, with the bearskin." Abigail fretted about the sow, wondered if the steer had been properly slaughtered and butchered and hung in the cellar. Briesler must be constantly on guard against the invasions of mice and rats; the cider should be drawn off and bottled before it began to turn to vinegar; and her pears and apples picked over and repacked in straw in the cold cellar so that the rotten ones would not infect the lot. If she was not back by Christmas he might kill a pig and have roast pork for Christmas dinner, then hang up the legs to smoke for bacon.[18]

Hamilton had shown Colonel Smith a letter from James Madison, she wrote John, in which the Virginian had written: "We consider your reasons conclusive; the gentleman you have named [Adams] will certainly have all our votes and interest for Vice-President." If the New Englander had been inclined to suspect Hamilton, this incident removed all doubts in his mind of the New Yorker's good will toward him.

Without Abigail to restrain him, John bought fifteen heifers to augment his dairy herd. "Mr. Adams will cover his farms with living creatures," Mary Cranch wrote Abigail, if something did not soon distract him.[19]

John Jay came to Jamaica to see Abigail and was his usual courteous and affable self. Seeing the chubby, rosy William, he declared, "Well, here is Grandpa over again!" And indeed there was an engaging likeness between the stout infant and his thickset grandfather.[20] With Nabby back on her feet and in good health and spirits, Abigail hurried back to Braintree shortly after the first of the year to be with her husband.

Word finally reached Adams early in March that he had been elected Vice-President. There were sixty-nine votes for Washington and half as many—thirty-four—for Adams. To John, lacking any notion of Hamilton's intrigues, it seemed like a direct rebuff, almost an insult, and for a few days he thought of resigning. "Is not my election to this office, in the scurvy manner in which it was done, a curse rather than a blessing?" he wrote Rush. "Is this justice? Is there common sense or decency in this business? Is it not an indelible stain on our country, countrymen, and constitution? I assure you I think so." Nothing but his "apprehension of the great mischief and the final failure of the government from my refusal and assigning my reasons for it prevented me from spurning it."[21]

Although the unofficial word of his election was received by Adams in March, official notification must wait on the convening of Congress at New York and the formal opening and counting of the ballots by the President of the Senate. Adams used the interim to prepare for his journey to the capital. It was decided that Abigail, who still felt the strain of her trip to Jamaica and back, had had enough traveling for one winter. She would remain in Braintree while John kept bachelor quarters in New York, taking John and Esther Briesler with him. Abigail had her hands full equipping him for his new office. He had to have several new suits, new silk stockings, a new wig, and a dozen other things so that he could cut a good figure in sophisticated New York.

On the sixth of April, Congress convened, the electoral votes were opened and recorded, and messengers were dispatched with official notification to Washington and Adams. Sylvanus Bourne brought word to Braintree on the twelfth of April. Adams had been packed and ready to go for a week and next day he left Braintree for Boston escorted by a troop of light horse.

He departed reluctantly. The months since his return from England, he wrote Mercy Warren, had been "the sweetest morsel of my life, and

I despair of ever tasting such another."[22] He could not get enough of it, of the farm, the fields and pasture and hills. He was a devout worshiper, an inebriate of "the mountain, the meadow, and the stream," who reveled in his dissipations. It was certainly not New England prudence that set him to clearing new pastures, building fences and dairy houses, planting apple trees, buying pigs and cows, turning everything upside down in a kind of frenzy while Abigail watched, dismayed and yet unable to resist his enthusiasm. He had known very well that the chances were all in favor of his being drawn away to some office in the new government, in all probability the second office in the nation, but that did not deter him. There was a streak of perversity in him that led him constantly to deny his own ambitions. He could prove to himself that he was quite content to live the life of a Braintree farmer by the fury with which he hurled himself into the affairs of the farm. Certainly no one, seeing him everywhere at once, directing hired hands and day laborers, carpenters and painters, joining in himself to pick apples or work the cider press, could charge him with sitting back and waiting to be elected Vice-President. But that was not the point of it all. It was simply self-indulgence. He loved it. These were his passions—his family, politics, and the farm. He wished to add acres and acres, to clear and build, to breed his stock and widen his fields until they surrounded Braintree.

As he entered Boston the church bells were rung, and he saw with mingled feelings the streets crowded with Bostonians, cheering and waving their hats and shouting the name of John Adams. There was a holiday atmosphere as he rode down King Street through rows of his fellow citizens whose faces glowed with excitement and affection. It fed his vanity most woefully. Men being what they were, they might some other day be shouting imprecations and threats, shaking fists instead of waving hats. Yet all the same it was enormously gratifying. It was a balm for old slights and wounds, an armor against self-doubt.

The Roxbury Light Horse conducted him to the Governor's mansion and there Hancock, completely master of himself and of the small arts of politics, received his friend and rival with his usual urbanity. They were a sharp contrast: Adams short, awkward, intense, his face betraying his feelings; Hancock thin and elegant, a politician to his bones, to whom power was more precious than principle. Yet Adams had the prize that Hancock had coveted, that he had, indeed, been virtually promised in return for his support of the federal constitution.

The Governor had spread a handsome feast for local dignitaries, the members of the General Court, and the city officials, but Adams noted that many of his Boston friends, political enemies of the Governor, were conspicuously absent. They could not bring themselves to accept the Governor's hospitality, even to honor a friend.

After lunch Adams and his little party set off on the Connecticut road, saluted by thirteen volleys of musket fire. In every town and village he passed through, the inhabitants turned out to wave and cheer. At Hartford he was presented with a beautiful coat of local manufacture with handsome silver buttons. At New Haven he received the freedom of the city, and when he crossed the state line into New York he was met by the Westchester Light Horse, handsomely turned out, and conducted to King's Bridge at the north end of Manhattan where he was met by an official reception committee made up of heads of the departments of the new government, officers of the army, "a great number of members of Congress . . . and private citizens" in carriages and on horseback, "who conducted him through a multitude of people" to the house of John Jay in lower Manhattan. There he had an affectionate reunion with his old friend and received a constant stream of visitors, "Feds and Antis," as he wrote William Tudor with obvious gratification; "Governor Clinton and his friends and Judge Yates and his advocates, corporations, clergy, judges, chancellor, etc., have emulated each other in their testimonials of respect and affection for me."

Washington had not arrived yet, but the city was in a bustle of preparation for him. The taverns and inns and private houses were packed with visitors from all over the country who had come to see the inauguration of the President. Adams was conducted to the Senate by Tristram Dalton and Oliver Ellsworth to be sworn in as Vice-President. John Langdon, President of the Senate *pro tempore,* met him at the door of the chamber and extended the formal greeting of that body: "Sir, I have it in charge from the Senate to introduce you to the chair of this House; and also to congratulate you on your appointment to the office of Vice-President of the United States of America." Adams was then conducted to his seat where he unfolded two sheets of paper and addressed the Senators:

Chosen by the suffrages of his fellow citizens, he thought it his duty cheerfully and readily to accept. "Unaccustomed," he declared, "to refuse any public service, however dangerous to my reputation or disproportioned to my talents, it would have been inconsistent to have adopted another maxim of conduct at this time, when the prosperity of the country and the liberties of the people require, perhaps as much as ever, the attention of those who possess any share of the public confidence."

He had a gracious word to say about his emotions at seeing in the Senate "so many of those virtuous characters of whose virtuous exertions I have so often been a witness; from whose countenances and examples I have ever derived encouragement and animation; whose disinterested friendship has supported me in many intricate conjunctures of public affairs at home and abroad; those celebrated defenders of the liberties of this country, whom menaces could not intimidate, corruption seduce, nor flattery allure; those intrepid asserters of the rights of mankind whose philosophy and policy have enlightened the world in twenty years more than it was ever enlightened in many centuries by ancient schools or modern universities."

The United States had indeed been fortunate in the formation of a national constitution which could offer a fair prospect of a strong and consistent government with a legislative body chosen by the respective states, and a chief executive "whose portrait," Adams declared, "I shall not presume to draw," because by so doing it would be impossible "to increase the confidence or affection of his country, or make the smallest addition to his glory." Looking through all of history, one could not find another leader "whose commanding talents and virtues, whose over-ruling good fortune have so completely united all hearts and voices in his favor, who enjoyed the esteem and admiration of foreign nations and fellow citizens with equal unanimity." It would be inappropriate for Adams to propose or recommend to such a distinguished and experienced body any particular measures, it was only necessary to apologize for his own shortcomings as a presiding officer. He had been more experienced in debate than in presiding over debate, but he would do his best, he as-sured the Senators, to master his new role, "to behave towards every member . . . with all that consideration, delicacy, and decorum which becomes the dignity of his station and character." If "from inexperience or inadvertency" any improper act or observation should escape him, he begged the indulgence of the members. "A trust of the greatest magnitude is committed to this legislature, and the eyes of the world are upon you," he concluded. "May God Almighty's providence assist you to answer their just expectations."

The speech and the speaker were warmly applauded, although William Maclay, a Pennsylvania democrat, noted sourly in his journal that the address was "heavy" and failed to meet the requirements of the highest order of rhetoric. (Maclay, however, was basically unsympathetic. To him, the constitution was "the vilest of all traps that ever was set to en-snare the freedom of an unsuspecting people.")[23]

With Adams in the chair one of the first orders of business was to determine the proper protocol in sending and receiving messengers from the House of Representatives. The issue was decided with a minimum of debate. The Secretary of the Senate would take bills to the House, would bow once on entering the chamber, again on delivering it to the Speaker, and twice more on withdrawing. A bill from the House should be brought by two members who were to repeat the ritual bows, with the Senate standing until the message was delivered and the members retired. But in joint committee the more democratically inclined House rejected the bows and the Senate acquiesced.

On the twenty-third of April, President Washington reached New York. He was met on the Jersey shore by a magnificent barge manned by thirteen master pilots in white uniforms and filled with welcoming dignitaries —the Governor of New York, committees of both houses of Congress, and the principal officers of government. Washington was received on board to the accompaniment of repeated volleys and the barge, propelled by "a propitious gale," moved rapidly across the bay, "the very water," Elias Boudinot wrote, "seeming to rejoice in bearing the precious burden over its placid bosom."

The whole East River was filled with boats and one vessel after another, brilliantly decorated, swung in behind the official barge. Off Bedloe's Island a large sloop came up on the starboard bow and twenty ladies and gentlemen sang "an elegant ode, prepared for the purpose, to the tune of 'God Save the King.'" Their place was then taken by another boat which offered a different ode, sung in parts by a male choir. It was a dazzling scene with one new glory after another; even the fish joined in the celebration, porpoises "playing amongst us," Boudinot noted, "as if they had risen up to know the cause of all this happiness." The New York shore was crowded with tens of thousands of people packed almost as far as the eye could see, "heads standing as thick as ears of corn before the harvest."

As the barge passed the Spanish warship *Galveston*, which many people had noted indignantly displayed no bunting, her Captain gave a command and she broke out twenty-eight flags of all nations and fired a salute of thirteen guns. At the steps of Murray's Wharf where the barge was to land, many of the General's old officers were waiting with the reception committee. The steps themselves were covered with carpeting and the rails hung with crimson cloth. The noise of gun and cannon salutes, the cheers and cries, the music of a dozen bands beat and billowed over the harbor and the city, a great, endless, exuberant outpouring of pride and love.

The General's guard could hardly force a path through the crowd to the line of parade where the procession had formed to escort Washington to the presidential mansion on Franklin Square. The streets were packed with people and every window along the way was filled with spectators. Fenno, the newspaper editor, heard old people remark that they could now die contented; they had clung to life for no other purpose than to get a glimpse of the savior of their country.

In the evening Governor Clinton gave a state dinner for the official welcoming party and the whole city was illuminated with candles and torches. The next day Adams and the Senators paid their respects. ("The President," Adams wrote Abigail with obvious pleasure, "has received me with great cordiality of affection and confidence, and everything has gone very agreeably.")[24] Then all assembled to wrangle about how he should be addressed. In the course of the discussions Adams addressed the Senate on the desirability of calling the Speaker of the House "honorable." Indeed, he lectured the members until someone called, rather pointedly, for the question and it was passed in the negative.

William Maclay, frontier lawyer and surveyor, put himself forward at once as a spokesman for democratic simplicity. Maclay was a huge man, well over six feet, with a broad, ruddy face, the classic small-town politician operating on a larger stage. He had a sharp humor, a deep suspicion of show or pretense, and a rough, quick tongue which the Vice-President soon felt. When the motion to call the Speaker of the House "honorable" was defeated, Maclay, girding himself to do battle against Adams, noted, "From this omen, I think our President [Adams] may go and dream about titles, for he will get none." Maclay had no patience with all this solemn-faced debate about forms. "25th April, Saturday," he wrote in his journal, "Attended the House, ceremonies, endless ceremonies, the whole business of the day."

Again Adams embarked with the greatest seriousness on another question of protocol. He, Adams, was Vice-President of the United States, and thus subordinate to the President. But he was President of the Senate. Now when President Washington came to address the Senate what was he to do? "Gentlemen, I feel great difficulty, how to act. I am possessed of two separate powers—the one in *esse*, the other in *passe* . . . when the President comes into the Senate, what shall I be? I wish, gentlemen, to think what I shall be."

Maclay could hardly suppress a rude guffaw. What would he be, indeed, and who cared? Ellsworth rose to reflect aloud upon the problem and concluded nothing. So the discussions went: where to erect a platform for the ceremony, who was to administer the oath, where various officials were to stand and sit, how many bows, how many handshakes? Maclay had a characteristic American contempt for all formalities. "Sorry I am to say it," he wrote, "but no people in the Union dwell more on trivial distinctions and matters of mere form [than the gentlemen of New England]. They really seem to show a readiness to stand on punctilio and ceremony. . . . It is certainly true that people little used with company are more apt to take offense and are less easy than men much versant in public life. They are an unmixed people in New England, and used only to see neighbors like themselves. . . . Should they go abroad . . . believing that good manners consist entirely in punctilios, they only add a few more stiffened airs to their deportment, excluding good humor, affability of conversation, and accommodation of temper and sentiment, as qualities too vulgar for a gentleman."[25]

To Maclay's surprise he found that Adams' chief ally in the Senate was Richard Henry Lee, reputed to be a stout Anti-Federalist, who suddenly appeared as sponsor of "a most expensive and enormous machinery of a federal judiciary—pompous titles, strong efforts after religious distinctions, coercive laws for taking . . . oaths, etc. etc."

L V I

Aᴘʀɪʟ 30 was the day set for the inauguration. Congress assembled
at ten to await the appearance of the General. As soon as he had
called the Senate to order Adams rose and declared: "Gentlemen,
I wish for the direction of the Senate. The President will, I suppose, address the Congress. How shall I behave? How shall I receive it? Shall
it be standing or sitting?" Mr. Lee, Maclay noted wryly, "began with the
House of Commons, as is usual with him, then the House of Lords; then
the King, and then back again. The result of his information was that the
Lords sat and the Commons stood on the delivery of the King's speech."
Ralph Izard followed Lee and, after making a good deal of his vast experience in observing the deliberations of Parliament, pointed out
that the Commons stood because there were no seats for them in the
House of Lords when the King addressed the joint bodies. Charles Carroll, the aristocratic Maryland Senator, declared he thought it of no consequence how it was done in Great Britain.

In the midst of the discussion the Secretary of the Senate, Samuel
Otis, whispered to Adams that the Clerk of the House was at the door
with a message. How was he to be received? Richard Henry Lee was up
again to give the procedure in the House of Commons. Izard reinforced
him and Ellsworth urged that the Clerk be received promptly, one way or
another. Meanwhile the rumor penetrated the chamber that the Speaker
of the House and the Representatives were waiting at the door for the
Senate to decide how to receive them. The result was complete confusion.
Senators left their chairs, everyone talked at once, and Adams hammered
in vain for order. At last order was restored and the Speaker and Representatives were gotten in pell-mell and given seats to await the appearance of the President. With Congress assembled Lee, Izard, and Dalton
were dispatched to fetch the President. It was an hour before Washington
appeared with his escort. He entered the hall dressed in a dark brown
suit with silver buttons, white stockings, black shoes with square silver
buckles, and a sword. Adams met him and conducted him to the presi-

dential chair. With Washington seated, the Vice-President rose and informed him that he should now take the oath of office. Then, embarrassed and ill at ease, Adams stood for a painfully long moment trying to recollect the rest of the little speech he had prepared. The words refused to come. Finally, as the silence grew almost unbearable, he bowed and, indicating to Washington that he should rise, conducted him out of the center windows of the hall onto the exterior gallery followed by the members of Congress. There the oath was administered by Chancellor Livingston, the Chief Justice of the New York judiciary.

At the conclusion of the brief ceremony the crowd raised three delirious cheers, the President bowed formally, and the cheers resounded once more. Then Washington, with Adams at his side, returned to the hall and the Senators and Representatives took their seats. When the chamber was in order and the General rose to deliver his inaugural address, his auditors rose likewise and stood respectfully while he spoke. Washington's face was grave and sad, and his hands shook so that at times he had trouble reading his speech. His voice was low and tremulous and those in the rear of the crowded room could hardly hear him, but all were aware that they were participants in one of their country's most touching and dramatic moments. The man who had led them to independence as a nation, through all the travail and agony of revolution, now stood before them, ready to lead them once more as the elected executive of a republic. Many (Adams among them), remembering all that had gone before and seeing the stern, proud man so moved, wept unashamedly.

From the hall the members of Congress formed in procession to walk to St. Paul's Church where prayers were said by the Episcopal Bishop of New York for the peace and good order of the new government. The New York militia in full dress lined the street from Federal Hall to the church.

Reconvening, the Senators appointed a committee to reply to—as Adams put it—the President's "most gracious speech," and adjourned to join in the celebrations, see the fireworks and the remarkable illuminated, transparent paintings hung outside the houses of the French and Spanish ministers.

The next morning when the minutes were read, Maclay noted the offensive phrase, "his most gracious speech." He was on his feet at once to protest: "Mr. President, we have lately had a hard struggle for our liberty against kingly authority," he declared. "The minds of men are still heated. Everything related to that species of government is odious to the people." The words suggested were those which were used by Parliament in referring to the King's speeches. "I know they will give offense," Maclay stated. "I consider them as improper. I therefore move that they be struck out."

It was disconcerting to Adams to be gainsaid by this unknown frontier politician. His face showed his displeasure very plainly as he replied. It seemed to him absurd and captious to object to anything simply on the ground of "its being taken from the practice of that government under which we have lived so long and so happily, formerly. . . . He was for a dignified and respectable government, and as far as he knew the sentiments of the people, they thought as he did."

Maclay was dogged in his opposition. It was true enough that the American had been happy under the government of Great Britain, but the injustices of that country had brought about such a complete change in the feelings of America toward her "that even the modes of it were now abhorred." The enemies of the constitution had argued that it would soon be turned into a "kingly government" and they would not fail to denounce such a phrase "as the first step of the ladder to the ascent to royalty."

Adams stood up again. The phrase to which the Senator from Pennsylvania objected was his own; he had suggested it to the Secretary. Maclay got up once more. He was aware that the chair had suggested the phrase, but with all due respect that did not make it right or compel the members to accept it. Adams, in his irritation, had remained standing during Maclay's reply. He now got hold of himself and answered his huge opponent. "I have been long abroad, sir, and I do not know how the tempers of the people might be now."

George Read of Delaware supported the paragraph as it stood in the minutes. It seemed farfetched to object to it simply because the speeches of the British King were styled "most gracious." If Americans were going to object to words "because they had been used in the same sense in Britain, we should soon be at a loss to do business." That might be, Maclay replied, but "at present there is no loss for words. The words 'speech' or 'address,' without any addition, will suit us well enough."

On the question the vote was in favor of striking out the words. Maclay had won. After adjournment Adams took him aside to explain to him how much efficient government and respect for authority rested upon a proper regard for forms and ceremonies. It was all twaddle to the Pennsylvanian. He would yield to no man in his respect for the President, or for Adams himself, whom he had long admired. He considered himself a firm friend to orderly government, but his sense of duty and his consciousness of how his constituents would react to such suggestions had prompted him to speak out. It was the student of government, the theorist and intellectual, confronting the practical politician. All Adams' arguments were unavailing against Maclay's sense of the appropriate and expedient. Theory must fall to the ground in the face of good sense. "He got upon the subject of checks to government and the balances of power," Maclay recounted dryly. "His tale was long—he seemed to expect some answer. I caught at the last word and said, undoubtedly without a balance there could be no equilibrium, and so left him hanging in geometry."

Adams' lack of restraint in his position as presiding officer had already caused some annoyance, and Maclay reported that next day, coming into the hall before the Senate convened, he encountered William Patterson of New Jersey and John Langdon, who congratulated him on his stand. The Vice-President, Patterson said, "made himself too busy." It was not his job to lead the Senate but to preside over it. Robert Morris added that the New Englander had been made Vice-President to keep him quiet, but it seemed that the experiment had failed, and Maclay, puzzling over Adams' politics, wrote: "He is Anti-Federal but of a very different turn from the general cast."[1]

Adams' little lectures to the Senate showed his insensitivity to the temper of his audience. The Senators plainly resented them, and his closest friends were embarrassed by his abuse of his position as presiding officer. His own attitude toward the Senate was evident in a letter to William Tudor in which he declared that the weaknesses "of ignorance will continue to hurt this country more than all other causes." The trumpeters of unchecked and unlimited democracy had "sown the seeds of nonsense that will require time and labor to eradicate. The sentiments that I still continue to hear every day," he wrote, "even from men of education, reading, age, and travel, upon the subject of government appear to me as extravagant as the drivelings of idiotism or the ravings of delirium." While the Senate was "a wise, mild, and noble body of men," only a few were lawyers. ("I will own to you," he wrote Tudor, "I never knew a great statesman in my sense of the word who was not a lawyer.") Most of the members showed "a total inattention to everything in human nature by which mankind ever were or ever will be governed." Only Oliver Ellsworth seemed to Adams to be invariably right, "and what crowns all," he added, "is he is not afraid to think or speak."[2]

In the matter of the reply to the President's speech the members split on the question of whether there should be a reference to the "anarchy and confusion" from which the states had been rescued by the ratification of the new government. There were enough friends of the confederation present to rule out the phrase, and while the committee reworded the letter Adams took the occasion to raise the question of how the President should communicate with the Senate. If he came in person, Adams pointed out, there must be a seat for him which in England was called a throne. Otherwise he might dispatch a minister of state or an aide. Being answered by blank looks, he added a little uncomfortably, "I throw these things out for gentlemen to think of." Richard Henry Lee was all for having a chair with a canopy over it to seat the President on his visits. Thus, as Maclay put it, "the time was trifled until near eight o'clock." When the committee returned with the letter it still contained a phrase that Maclay objected to—it spoke of the "dignity and splendor" of the government, whereas in his view "respectability" was a far better, more republican word. "Splendor, when applied to government," Maclay argued, "brought into my mind, instead of the highest perfection, all the faulty finery, brilliant scenes, and expensive trappings of royal government . . . quite the reverse of . . . firm and prudent councils, frugality, and economy." This time Maclay was defeated. It seemed to the Pennsylvania Senator that in announcing the vote and declaring in ringing tones that he "hoped the government would be supported with *dignity* and *splendor*," the Vice-President was aiming at Maclay and deriving some comfort for his previous defeat, "but it may be I was mistaken," Maclay added. The letter, assuring the President that the Senate would "pursue that enlarged and liberal policy" to which he had called them, was approved and turned over to the Secretary to be prepared for the Vice-President's signature.

The next day the debate swung once more to the subject of titles. "Mr. Lee led the business," Maclay noted. "He took his old ground—all the world, civilized and savage, called for titles. There must be something in human nature that occasioned this general consent; therefore he conceived it was right." Ellsworth, with his notes stuffed into his hat, and glancing surreptitiously at them from time to time, traced the history of titles from the time of Saul to the present moment; then Maclay took the floor to oppose all such trumpery as smacking of superstition and monarchy. The appellation of President, he pointed out, was a common one. There were all kinds of presidents. Yes, Adams put in, there were presidents of fire companies and cricket clubs. "At sundry other times," Maclay noted disapprovingly, "he interfered in a like manner."

Some proposed "Excellency" for the President, others "Highness," and still others "Elective Highness," but Maclay stubbornly rebutted all such suggestions. "It was degrading our President," he insisted, "to place him on a par with any princes of any blood in Europe." "This whole silly business," he noted later in his journal, "is the work of Mr. Adams and Mr. Lee," the one with his "frigid friends" from the North, the other with his "hot and burning" Southern adherents. By his opposition, Maclay felt, he had forfeited all favor with "the court, for a *court* our house seems determined on, and to run into all the fooleries, fopperies, and pomp of royal etiquette."

When the report of the committee to recommend a title for the President was brought in, it was worse than Maclay had feared—"His Highness, the President of the United States of America, and Protector of the Rights of the Same." This certainly went too far. Maclay found new supporters: "Friends seemed to rise in succession." There was a motion to postpone, and Adams looked increasingly anxious and put out. Finally when Izard rose to add his voice to those favoring postponement, the Vice-President's displeasure was plain. He interrupted the Carolinian, reprimanded him "with asperity" for being out of order, and went on to speak at great length "on his favorite topic of titles . . . of the immense advantage, of the absolute necessity of them."

"Gentlemen," he said, looking at the Senators with the stern and reproachful gaze of a schoolmaster, "I must tell you that it is *you* and the *President* that have the making of titles. Suppose the President to have the appointment of Mr. Jefferson at the court of France. Mr. Jefferson is, in virtue of that appointment, the most illustrious, the most powerful, and what not. But the President himself must be something that includes all the dignities of the diplomatic corps, and something greater still. What will the common people of foreign countries—what will the sailors and soldiers say, 'George Washington, President of the United States'? They will despise him. This is all nonsense to the philosopher; but so is all government whatever."[3]

Maclay answered Adams. The constitution clearly said that the chief executive should be called "the President of the United States and the Senate had no authority to change the title." At the end of Maclay's remarks the question was put and carried for a postponement. Adams had to take what comfort he could in the fact that the ladies at the ball in honor of Washington rejected "the President" and drank their toast to "His Highness." Perhaps they would settle the dispute. His campaign for proper titles had brought only ridicule. "A man must take so much pains to carry little points that seem of no importance," he wrote a friend, "that he is despised for a fool by many and not thought very wise by any."[4]

Adams believed, as he put it, "in the efficacy of pageantry." Pageantry could of course be applied to both good and bad purposes. But this was no argument against it. "Religion and government," he pointed out, "have both been used as pageantry. Signs do not necessarily imply abuse. . . . If government cannot be had nor laws obeyed without some parade, as I fully believe, we must have some parade or no laws." The clergy of New England wore their bands and painted their gates red. The Americans had had their liberty poles and liberty trees, their magic signs and symbolic numbers; "they erected gravestones and monuments to the dead, used handsome plate and silver at their communion table, marched in funeral processions. . . . In short," he concluded, "in the meanest family on earth you will find these little distinctions, marks, signs, and decencies which are the result of nature, feeling, reason which are policy and government in their places as much as crowns and tiaras, ceremonies, titles, etc., in theirs."

This was a matter on which Adams felt strongly. In order to have a stable and orderly government it was necessary that there should be proper respect for its officers. The popular mind needed forms and symbols to signify status and dignity, to create intangible but nonetheless important lines and boundaries, to represent a proper deference to legitimate authority. A great and powerful nation must invest its leaders with titles appropriate to their station. "Excellency" might do for the title of Governor of Massachusetts or Rhode Island, but even the ambassadorial address, "Most Illustrious and Most Excellent," would "not suffice for the head of a great and independent nation. . . . . A royal or at least a princely title will be found indispensably necessary," he wrote Tudor, "to maintain the reputation, authority, and dignity of the President. His Highness or, if you will, His Most Benign Highness is the correct title that will comport with his constitutional prerogatives and support his state in the minds of our own people or foreigners." The multitude and the liberal theorists thought all such things were mere trifles, but Adams was convinced "that governments cannot be raised nor supported without them . . . both multitude and philosophers are absolutely governed by them."[5]

Adams' defense of titles in a series of letters to Rush and Tudor led the Pennsylvania physician to hint that the Vice-President inclined toward monarchy and had abandoned the principles which he espoused at the onset of the Revolution. "I . . . am as much a republican as I was in 1775," Adams replied warmly. "I do not consider hereditary monarchy or aristocracy as 'rebellion against nature'; on the contrary I esteem them both institutions of admirable wisdom and exemplary virtue in a certain stage of society in a great nation, the only institutions that can possibly preserve the laws and liberties of the people—and I am clear that America must resort to them as an asylum against discord, seditions, and civil war, and that at no very distant period of time—I shall not live to see it but you may. I think it therefore impolitic to cherish prejudices against institutions which must be kept in view as the hope of our posterity, [though] I am by no means for attempting any such thing at present. . . . Our country is not ripe for it in many respects and it is not yet necessary but our ship must ultimately land on that shore or be cast away." Despite Adams' disclaimer, the implication seemed plain enough to Rush—Adams favored a limited constitutional monarchy on the English model but felt that it was inexpedient to press for it at present. He charged his friend right out with being, as the vulgar rumor had it, a champion of monarchy.

But Adams was not willing, however he might have expressed himself, to be tagged with such a label. He tried at some length to explain his position. First of all it was absurd to equate limited monarchy with either tyranny or the absence of democracy. "I deny," he wrote, "that there is or ever was in Europe a more free republic than England, or that any liberty on earth ever equaled English liberty, notwithstanding the defects in their constitution." The idea "of admitting absolute monarchy into this country, either in this or the next century, strikes me with horror. A little wisdom at present may preserve a free government in

America, I hope forever—certainly for many centuries." Hereditary monarchy and hereditary aristocracy ought not to be introduced into America. The members of the three balanced branches ought to be elected by the people until such time as "intrigue and corruption, faction and sedition" should appear "to such a degree as to render hereditary institutions a remedy against a greater evil." This day might not come "for many centuries" or, indeed, ever.

But it was Adams' opinion that the United States "never shall have either government or tranquillity or liberty until some rule to precedency is adopted, and some titles settled. I totally deny that there is anything in reason or religion against titles proportioned to ranks and truth, and I affirm that they are indispensably necessary to give dignity and energy to government—and on this ground alone I am an advocate for them. In my private character, I despise them as much at least as any Quaker or philosopher on earth." The chief executive must be called "His Majesty, the President. . . . . This," Adams concluded, "is my opinion, and I scorn to be hypocrite enough to disguise it. Miracles will not be wrought for us. We don't deserve them. If we will have government, we must use the human and natural means."[6]

Adams scoffed at Rush's disdain for titles. "I doubt not your veracity," he wrote, "but I believe you deceive yourself and have not yet examined your own heart and recollected the feelings of every day and hour." What would Rush feel if his children, instead of calling him "Sir or Father or Pappa," should accost him with the title of "Ben"? Or if his servant appeared and hailed him by the same familiar appellation? If Adams had time he would write a drama about a Quaker and his wife and ten children and four servants. "They should all live in the same room, dine, breakfast, and sup at the same table. They should promiscuously call each other by their names without titles and live without form." The result could be readily predicted. "The sons would soon be married to the female servants and the daughters to the male. Both children and servants would soon kick and cuff the old man and woman.

"'Poh, Poh, Poh!' say you," Adams continued. "'All this is vulgar and beneath the dignity of a legislator.' Give me leave to say nothing in human life is beneath the dignity of a magistrate to consider. The principles of government are to be seen in every scene of human life. There is no person and no society to whom form and titles are indifferent . . . in the course of fifty years' experience, in various stages of life, among all classes of people and in several different nations I have never yet met with one man, woman, or child," Adams concluded, "who was destitute of a passion for a title. Let us consider, my friend, more reverently and therefore more truly, the constitution of human nature and the invariable progress of human life and manners." Titles contributed to the stability of government and the order of society.[7]

Yet continued reflection and the stability of the new government made Adams far less inclined to anticipate a constitutional monarchy in the United States. A year after his first exchange with Rush on the subject of titles, he wrote, "My friend Dr. Rush will excuse me if I caution him against a fraudulent use of the words 'monarchy' and 'republic.' I am a mortal and irreconcilable enemy to monarchy. I am no friend to hereditary limited monarchy in America. This I know can never be admitted without an hereditary senate to control it, and an hereditary nobility or senate in America I know to be unattainable and impracticable. I should scarcely be for it if it were. Do not therefore, my friend, misunderstand me and misrepresent me to posterity. . . . I am for having all three branches elected at stated periods: and these elections I hope will continue until the people shall be convinced that fortune, providence, or chance, call it what you will, is better than election."[8]

He was equally emphatic in his reply to his friend's praise of "practical" education. Rush, in the true enlightenment spirit, believed that any ills in the arrangements of government might be cured by universal education, from which, incidentally, he would banish the classics as vestiges of a class education which was hostile to the spirit of republicanism. Education would so enlighten the governors that they would rule wisely and well. Adams replied with a kind of epistolary snort. Education, rather than correcting errors in an unbalanced government, would augment them because it would produce "a greater number of able and ambitious men who would not only understand the better how to worry one another with greater art and dexterity," but who would be, if anything, more inflexible and doctrinaire in pursuit of what they conceived to be the proper principles. As for banishing the classics "to improve republican ideas," he would as soon think of closing his shutters to see more clearly.[9]

In the Senate, Adams continued in his attempt to educate Maclay on the subject of titles. If government was a science it was imperative to observe its rules. If researches in the history of nations showed that all had used titles, it followed that titles were necessary to the maintenance of authority and good order. Coming into the Senate chamber shortly after ten one morning, Maclay found the Vice-President in the chair, reading a newspaper. Adams came and sat beside the Pennsylvanian, finished reading his newspaper, and then engaged him in conversation. The citizens of the Quaker state, he declared, were "the best republicans in the Union." They had ratified the constitution by a large majority and seemed determined to support it. Maclay, anticipating what was coming—the now familiar argument that the government could not be supported except with titles and ceremonies—replied that his constituents certainly had the "virtues of plainness, industry, and frugality" and, while they were good Federalists, they abhorred "the pomp and splendid expense of government, especially of everything which bordered on royalty."[10]

While the Senate, as a whole, shared Adams' point of view and rumor had it that the General himself was of a like mind on the matter, the House of Representatives proved irreconcilable—so bare and unadorned "President" it must be. Pleased with their triumph, Maclay and his fellow Pennsylvanian Congressmen took to addressing each other with mock ceremony as "Your Highness of the House" and "Your Highness of the Senate," and bestowed on Adams the title "His Rotundity." As Maclay put it complacently, "I have by plowing with the heifer of the other House completely defeated them [the advocates of titles in the Senate]."[11]

Yet Adams persisted in lecturing the Senate. On the fourteenth of May, when that body was discussing the organization of joint committees of the House and Senate, "the President [Adams] made us his speech for the day," Maclay noted dryly. The burden of it was that "parliamentary customs, when found convenient, should be followed as good examples." Maclay was pleased to remark the qualification and he observed also that the Vice-President was slowly abandoning some of the formalities in the conduct of the Senate's business which he had at first insisted upon. A sign that Adams was yielding to a more informal atmosphere was noted in the fact that he began to come to the Senate without his sword.

On Monday, May 18, the Senate went in a body to the President's mansion to deliver its reply to his address. Adams, who led the way into Washington's presence, followed by the Senators, bowed and began to read the reply. The slight tremor of the hands from which he had suffered for years had recently grown worse and this plus nervousness made his hand shake so much that, although he tried to steady it by resting it against his hat held in his other hand, he could read only haltingly and with difficulty. After the first page he gained more control of himself and read the balance in his high Yankee twang.

Washington, in turn, drew his answer out of his pocket. His spectacles were in his jacket pocket, his hat in his left hand, the paper in his right. In Maclay's words: "He had too many objects for his hands." He put his hat under his arm, took his spectacles from their case and then was left with the case which, after looking around uncertainly, he laid on the mantelpiece. Then, adjusting his glasses with some difficulty, shifting about the hat and the paper, "rather like a juggler," he read the reply with tolerable exactness and without much emotion, his voice made rather "hollow and indistinct" by his false teeth. The practical Maclay could not refrain from observing that much time and embarrassment would have been saved if the General had received the Senators with his glasses already on. The ceremony over, Adams declined the invitation of the President to be seated, bowed, and led his flock out of the chamber.

It was perhaps his clash with Maclay and his defeat that led Adams to reply rather cautiously to Washington's request for advice on the social life of the President—should he, for instance, accept private invitations; should he entertain, and whom and under what circumstances? Adams' response was a moderate one. The President must obviously have certain functions for the accommodation of representatives of foreign powers and of distinguished Americans, state governors and members of the government itself. Rather than announcing some policy which might invite criticism it would be better, he suggested, to simply put into operation what seemed to be the most sensible and effective practice. After replying in detail to the President's queries, Adams added: "These observations are submitted, after all, with diffidence, conscious that my long residence abroad may have impressed me with views of things incompatible with the present temper and feelings of our fellow citizens."

Adams was disturbed, for his part, at what seemed the localism and inexpertness of the New England members of Congress. Each followed the narrow views of his own particular constituents and, in consequence, the general good of the region was neglected. "I see New England outgeneraled in so many instances," he wrote Tudor, "that I begin to be ashamed that I was born there." The states seemed determined to set themselves above the national government. "For fear John Adams should be distinguished above John Hancock," Adams declared, "there is reason to apprehend . . . Massachusetts will revolt."[12]

In the House a memorial from the Quakers on the subject of the abolition of slavery stirred up such bitterness, such "base invective, indecorous language," with "three or four up at a time, manifesting signs of passion," that many of the members, Maclay noted, "do not hesitate to declare that the Union must fall to pieces at the rate we go on. Indeed," he added, "many seem to wish it." Adams was equally disturbed by the petition of "Franklin and his Quakers." It could have no other effect than to embitter the Southern members and make the Union more insecure.[13]

Soon after his arrival in the city, rumors about the manner of his election began to reach Adams' ears. "There was a dark and base intrigue," he wrote Rush, "which originated in New York and [I] am not at a loss to guess the men or their motives. I know very well how to make these men repent of their rashness."[14] Yet Adams failed at first to connect Hamilton with the plot. He prevailed on the New Yorker to take Charles on as his law apprentice and applauded the skill with which he pushed his financial program through Congress. He had, Adams wrote Henry Marchant, "raised himself deservedly a great reputation. No man except

General Washington ever had so fair an opportunity to bring himself before the people in so advantageous a light," he added.

When he first received hints that Hamilton had been behind the maneuver to rob him of electoral votes, Adams expressed irritation but took the line that the New Yorker, in trying to ensure Washington's election, had simply gone too far. "Our Secretary," he wrote John Trumbull, "has . . . I think, good abilities and certainly great industry. He has high-minded ambition and great penetration." His only failing was a "disposition to intrigue," and nothing was more dangerous or could be "more certainly destructive . . . than the spirit of intrigue. Throwing away votes is betraying a trust, it is breach of honor, it is a perjury. . . . If a repetition takes place I will drag out to public infamy both dupers and dupes, let who will be among the number."[15]

Aᴅᴀᴍs had not been in New York long before he received what was to be one of the most trying burdens of his years of officeholding—letters petitioning for jobs. The applications came in floods, not the petitions of sycophants and leeches, but the often desperate pleas of men who had been in many instances among the Revolutionary leaders in their respective states, men of education and substance—lawyers, doctors, merchants, ex-Continental officers. There simply were not enough positions to go around. An overwhelmingly agricultural country, boasting only a half dozen cities, had produced a surplus of upper-middle-class professional and businessmen, many of whom, intelligent, well trained, and able, deserving of their country's gratitude for services rendered, simply could not make ends meet, lapsed ever deeper into debt, saw ruin facing them and poverty and disgrace in store for their families. Adams, who felt the precariousness of his own financial situation, suffered acutely over such appeals, especially those from old friends whom he knew deserved well of the nation.

One of the first applications came from his old friend Mercy Warren. "Though none of my family are soliciting," she wrote primly, "at least I am persuaded you will not forget them at a time when you have it so much in your power to oblige without injustice to yourself, your family, or your country." It would only be an act of disinterested patriotism to appoint General Warren to some office commensurate with his unusual abilities. The General's enemies, not satisfied with attacking him, had tried to get at him through his son. "Ill treated, maligned, and persecuted in a most unjust and singular manner," General Warren could nonetheless, Mercy felt sure, depend upon the support of Mr. Adams. Rumors had associated the General with the Shaysite faction, and she attempted to exonerate her husband of any complicity with "the ignorant and miserable insurgents of . . . Massachusetts." It was a difficult letter for Mercy to write. There had already been some coolness between the Warren and the Adams families over the relations of their sons. This had been augmented by the bitterly partisan feelings engendered by Shays' rebellion. Adams was troubled and annoyed by Mercy's request. He wrote an answering letter which implied that she had not been candid in describing her husband's political views. He had, Adams declared, been "extremely mortified" on arriving in America to hear everywhere of the "unpopularity of my friend Warren and his family." Allowing for exaggeration and misrepresentation, it still seemed clear that the General "did differ for a time from all his friends and did countenance measures that appear to me, as they did to those friends, extremely pernicious." Beyond that he had no patronage to dispense, and if he had, neither his children nor hers would be sure of it. If she wished a post for her husband or her sons she should apply in writing to the President. If Warren was abused by the popular voice he, Adams, was no stranger to its fickle humors. "I have long contemplated in many very solemn hours," he observed, "that injustice, ingratitude, and abuse experienced by myself, and it would be no surprise to me if my latter end should be as melancholy an instance of popular mutability as the annals of anarchy ever exhibited to the world."[1]

General Lincoln, suppressor of Shays' rebellion, and one of the foremost men in the state, asked for any job that might be suitable. Samuel Otis wished to be Secretary of the Senate. All told sad stories of the losses occasioned by war and inflation and by the failure of the United States to redeem its public securities. John Bayard solicited the job of collector of customs for the state of Pennsylvania. Adams' old companion, Robert Treat Paine, another of the Revolutionary stalwarts, would like a federal judgeship; Sharp Delaney wished to be collector of the port of Philadelphia. Judge Sullivan, concerned about launching his six children in life, solicited Adams' backing for a judicial appointment. James Greenleaf, a cousin, wished the post of American consul at The Hague. James Lovell wanted to be appointed collector of the port of Boston. For every job in the new government there were a half dozen well-qualified applicants, men who had made great sacrifices and performed great services for the Revolution, men of proved ability and unquestioned merit.[2]

Even Adams' "brother" and closest friend, Richard Cranch, was a candidate for some government office. He had two daughters and a son to provide for. The farm brought in little and watch repairing less. Samuel Tufts, Dr. Tufts' brother, applied for a government job and Henry Marchant of Rhode Island was another of Adams' old friends who wished for an appointment to the federal judiciary. Marchant recalled their association in Congress years before. Things had gone badly for him. He had invested all his capital in Continental bonds and Massachusetts securities, but they remained unhonored and business was so uncertain and precarious that he was hard put to it to feed and clothe

Courtesy of Frick Art Reference Library

PLATE 17

Thomas Jefferson by Mather Brown. This portrait of Jefferson was painted by Brown at Adams' behest. He wished to have a portrait of his friend, and Jefferson sat for Brown during his visit to England in 1786.

Courtesy of Mrs. Arthur Ad

PLATE 18

Abigail Adams (Mrs. William Stephens Smith—"Nabby") by George Hall. This is a copy of the original by Copley which was destroyed in a fire.

Courtesy Mrs. Robert Homan

William Stephens Smith—"a man of an independent spirit, high and strict sentiments of honor, much the gentleman in his manners and address," Abigail wrote of him—was painted by Mather Brown in London at the same time that Brown painted portraits of the other members of the Adams family—Abigail, John, and Nabby.

Photograph by George M. Cushing

PLATE 20

The Adams Mansion, Quincy, bought by Dr. Cotton Tufts for John and Abigail Adams while they were in England

Courtesy of the New York Historical Society, New York City

PLATE 21

Richmond Hill, where the Adamses lived while the seat of the federal government was in New York. To Abigail it was "one of the most deightful spots...in this country....Perfectly romantic."

The Historical Society of Pennsylvania

PLATE 22

Bush Hill, the Hamilton estate near Philadelphia, where John and Abigail moved during the winter of 1791 to find the paint still wet on the walls.

Wm Strickland. Del.

The Historical Society of Pennsylvania

PLATE 23

The Executive Mansion in Philadelphia. The Washingtons took their furniture with them, and Adams moved into the sparsely-furnished house in March 1797 to await Abigail's arrival from Quincy.

Courtesy of the Museum of Fine Arts, Boston

PLATE 24

John Quincy Adams by John Singleton Copley, painted in 1795. Copley sent the portrait to Abigail who was understandably charmed with it. Her friends declared it "as fine a portrait as was ever taken," and Abigail felt that it caught perfectly "the expression, the animation, the true character" of her son.

his large family. Captain Lyde, of the ship *Active,* which had carried Abigail and Nabby to London, wrote soliciting an appointment as a naval officer.

Among the other applications for government jobs was one from Ebenezer Storer, the second husband of Hannah Quincy, who had caused Adams so much heartache many years ago. Storer wrote pathetically of his family's improvidence and need; the letter, Adams confessed, caused him "many anxious reflections and . . . many melancholy hours." The thought of the charming coquette, now an elderly woman living in want and worry with a husband who could not provide adequately for her, made him reflect upon the strange turns of life.[3] There were, moreover, wheels within wheels. Dana suggested that Theophilus Parsons wished John Lowell to be appointed district judge in Massachusetts and hoped, in consequence, to have Lowell's support for the office of Attorney General of the United States. Dana, for his part, would prefer to have Lowell appointed to the state Supreme Court so that the way might be cleared for Dana to be district judge, since his health was so bad that he could not carry out the duties of the Superior Bench.[4] There was much intriguing over the rumored appointment of Cushing, then Chief Justice of the Massachusetts Court, as an associate of the United States Supreme Court. The Hancock faction, so the story went, wished Cushing appointed to the Supreme Court so that the Governor could appoint one of his tools to the bench—"the great barrier . . . against popular frenzy and the influence of popular demagogues," Stephen Higginson called it. The Federalist judges let it be known that in such a case they would resign and the state judiciary would be taken over by the radical adherents of Hancock and Samuel Adams.[5]

Adams was consulted by Washington on the matter of the appointment of the justices to the Supreme Court, but he found the whole matter as onerous as did his superior. He was especially reluctant to intrude his views on the President, since it was evident to him that he was to be the scapegoat for all of Washington's unpopular decisions. His exertions for General Lincoln had "torn open an hornets' nest at Boston," he wrote Lowell, and he had little inclination to stir up more factionalism and bitterness.[6] But he was very well pleased with the Supreme Court and spoke of the justices as "an assemblage of the greatest talents and abilities . . . which any country can boast of, gentlemen . . . who will prove durable pillars in support of our government."[7]

The competition for government jobs depressed and saddened Adams immeasurably. He wrote to both John Quincy and Tommy, reminding them that a man's independence was the most valuable thing in life. Especially, they must "make it a rule never to become dependent on public employment for subsistence." Let them "have a trade, a profession, a farm, a shop, something whereby [they] can honestly live."

From Braintree, Abigail reported on the state of the farm. The stone wall between the Bass place and the Adams farm had been finished. John's brother had cleared the side hill of stones, gathered up "the overplus manure," and spread it on the field sown in barley. The stock that John had so recklessly acquired now had to be disposed of. There was the hint of a reproach in Abigail's recital of the difficulties she had encountered on this account. Dr. Tufts had taken three heifers and ten sheep in return for a promise to pay the boys' quarter bill at Harvard. Abigail had offered John's brother twenty of the sheep, in return for whose keeping he should have half the lambs and wool. Abigail worried so that she could not sleep. The cows had not calved and "really everything seems to have gone awry, veal has got to twopence per pound." Briesler's second child had been born the day John set out for New York.[8] The season was so backward that scarcely a tree had leaved. Only the lilac bloomed in the yard and perfumed the spring air. Abigail had planted the asparagus beds and manured the little plots of grass before the front door.

Meanwhile John decided he could not make out without his wife. He must have her with him. He was too old and set in his ways to live a wifeless life. He wrote in May, urging her to come on to New York posthaste. She might leave Tom in college, but she should bring Charles with her. As to the place, let his brother farm it on shares. She could borrow money for the trip and if she could not borrow it, he wrote, she must sell the precious horses, oxen, sheep, cows, "any and everything rather than delay. If no one will take the place," he continued, "leave it to the birds of the air and beasts of the field, but at all events break up that establishment and that household."[9]

For Abigail there was a kind of perverse comfort in thinking of John, perched at the Jays', awaiting her arrival so impatiently. She knew him so well—all his dear crotchets and creature comforts. He missed his own bed and pillows, his hot coffee with too much sugar in it, the familiar shape of his own bed warmer. "How many of these little matters," she wrote, "make up a large portion of our happiness and content." The more heavily public cares and duties weighed on one and the older one got, "the more necessary these alleviations." Perhaps the temporary absence of them would make them the sweeter when they were once again part of the pleasant routine of daily life.[10]

Adams' handwriting showed that his palsy had progressed quite far. It troubled Abigail to observe the tremulous letters. She prescribed an ounce of glover salts and half an ounce of manna with an ounce of antimonial wine, thirty drops, three times a day.[11]

Congress had not voted a salary for the Vice-President or indeed an allowance of any kind and Adams found himself virtually without funds and in a position of increasing financial stringency. In a mood of black pessimism, he talked of resigning and wrote Abigail not to join him until he had some assurance of a decent salary. In his anxiety and embarrassment he was more punctual in prayer which, he wrote his wife, "disposes me to bear with more composure some disagreeable circumstances that attend my situation." He would like Abigail to send on Hume, Johnson, Priestley, Livy, Tacitus, Cicero, Plutarch, Blackstone, DeLolme, the "Collection of the American Constitutions . . . and such other books as may be most amusing and useful."[12]

The major task of Congress was to impose taxes and raise a revenue that would pay the cost of government and make it possible to retire the domestic and the foreign debt. For this purpose a tariff bill was hammered out in the House, primarily by James Madison, which among other provisions imposed a duty of six cents a gallon on molasses, New England's principal article of import. The New England Congressmen were resentful but Adams was determined that if the tariff could not be lowered the New Englanders "must grin (as is commonly said) and bear it. We must not grumble as yet."[13] The states had very different economies. What helped one hindered its neighbor and vice versa. It was soon evident that there were many serious conflicts of interest which must be reconciled if the new government was to have the wholehearted support of the respective states and, even more, of the sections. There was a sharp split on the tariff issue between the Northern and Southern states. The "Eastern" members set about, through tough bargaining, to get the duty on molasses reduced. They spread the word about that if the tariff remained at six cents they would join with every member who objected to a duty on any particular article and promise him support in return for his opposition to the molasses duty. The result was a compromise—the duty was lowered to five cents on condition that the New Englanders support the general schedule of duties. But the Yankees were not satisfied until they had forced down the duty on molasses to four cents. "The New Englanders beat this ground," Maclay noted, "even to the hook that caught the fish that went to buy the molasses."

Adams' partisanship and direct involvement in the particular issues before the Senate was resented by more than one member. After the four per cent duty on molasses had been approved, he ruled that the matter of a three-cent impost could be argued. To the Pennsylvanians and the Southerners it seemed that Adams was using his position as presiding officer to further the interests of his section, and Maclay was convinced that the acquiescence of the New England members to the four-cent duty was simply an effort to prevent "their darling President" from being embarrassed.

Pennsylvania, which produced loaf sugar, wanted a tariff on that but Lee waxed eloquent on the inferior quality of American loaf sugar, declaring that he had broken a silver spoon trying to dissolve some of it in his teacup. The Senate divided equally and Adams cast the deciding vote in favor of the duty. Likewise on the question of a tax on salt, which the Southerners wished to see highly taxed and which Maclay opposed as a spokesman for the interior country, Adams again voted to break a tie and defeat the projected tax which, it was argued by its opponents, would fall most heavily on the small farmer.

Day after day the Senators bent to their task of trying to fashion a tariff bill. There was a brief diversion on the fourth of June, when the question arose of whether the Senators should be titled "Honorable" in the minutes. To Maclay's astonishment Adams spoke strongly against the motion on the ground that the title "Honorable" was a colonial appellation and would be a disgrace to Congress.

"Up now rose Grayson, of Virginia," Maclay noted, "and gave us volley after volley against all kinds of titles whatever. Louder and louder did he inveigh against them. Lee looked like madness. Carroll and myself exchanged looks and laughs of congratulation. Even the President himself [Adams] seemed stuck in a heap. . . . Grayson mentioned the *Doge of Venice* in his harangue, as he was mentioning all the great names in the world."

"Pray, do you know *his title?*" Adams interjected.

"No," Grayson replied, "*I am not very well acquainted with him.*"[14]

The Senators also grew warm on the subject of the tariffs, those in one state accusing the others of bias and self-interest. Robert Morris had pledged himself to silence on the subject, but when Pennsylvania was attacked his fellow Senator observed his nostrils widen and his "nose flatten like the head of a viper."

As always when he was separated from Abigail, Adams grew touchy and irascible. It showed in his impatience, his interruption of debates, and his growing pessimism. Meeting Langdon, Charles Carroll, and Maclay in the Senate chamber before the time for convening, he expressed his doubts. "If our new government does well," he declared, "I shall be more surprised than ever I was in my life."

Carroll replied that he had high hopes; certainly it was powerful enough. "From whence then," Adams asked, "did the power arise? It cannot have energy. It has neither rewards nor punishments."

"But the people of America are enlightened," Carroll answered. "Information and knowledge would be the support of it."

"Information and knowledge are not the sources of obedience," Adams replied. "Ignorance was a much better source."

When the impost bill, after weeks of tedious wrangling, deals and counterdeals, concessions and compromises, seemed finally about to be approved by the Senate, Pierce Butler of South Carolina took his seat. That this hotheaded Southerner was to prove a cross to the President of the Senate was soon evident. He at once "flamed like a meteor," charged Congress with trying to oppress the South, and demanded that instead of laws to protect American trade and manufactures the United States should do all it could to encourage "foreigners of every kind to come and take away our produce." Incited by Butler's intemperate language, the discussion raged "with less order, less sense, and less decency" than any question yet debated in that chamber, while Adams, red with indignation, presided as best he could.

The next day Butler continued his tirade, threatening a dissolution of the Union "as sure as God was in the firmament" if the impost was passed, and yet, ever and anon, declaring how clear of local views, how candid and dispassionate he was. . . . . He degenerated into mere declamation," Maclay noted. "His state would live free, or die glorious, etc., etc."

Adams kept his temper with obvious difficulty. He had a strong feeling for the dignity of the Senate and he feared that the Carolinian's extreme language would undermine decency and good order. He stood Butler's antics as patiently as he could but on the twelfth of June, when a bill was reported in for the establishment of a judiciary and the Southerner once again delivered a "flaming" speech, Adams sharply ruled him out of order.

Maclay noted that as the debate on the judiciary moved on to the question of the jurisdiction of the Supreme Court over consuls and ambassadors of foreign nations, Adams grew increasingly fidgety. From "eagerness or restlessness," Maclay could not tell which, the Vice-President shifted repeatedly in his chair and finally, unable to contain himself any longer, "up he got," the Pennsylvanian observed, "to tell us all about ambassadors, other ministers, and consuls; and what he did with His Majesty here, and His Majesty there; and how he got an answer in this case, and how he never got an answer in that; and how he had, with Mr. Jefferson, appointed Mr. Barclay to the Emperor of Morocco—and how the Parlement of Bordeaux mistook the matter, and dismissed Mr. Barclay from an arrest, etc., etc." He seemed to enjoy his role of preceptor so much that even Maclay could not begrudge him his hour upon the stage.[15]

Outside of the Senate chamber Adams was dismayed by the tendency which he observed to downgrade the national government. He was especially put out with Hancock for an address to the Massachusetts legislature which was full of cant about equality and state sovereignty. The Governor, Adams wrote General Lincoln, had gone out of his way to terrify the people with "the phantoms of monarchy and despotism . . . in truth Mr. H himself is a limited monarchy, the constitution of Massachusetts is a limited monarchy, so is the constitution of the United States, both have monarchal powers; and the real defects of both are that they have not enough to make the first magistrate an independent and effectual balance to the other branches. . . . The idea of an equal distribution of intelligence and property is as extravagant as any that was ever avowed by the maddest of the insurgents."

If Hancock meant what he said, he had in Adams' view "made the most insidious attack on the new constitution that has yet appeared." With Hancock expressing such sentiments, with Rhode Island remaining aloof from the Union, with Governor Clinton in New York and Patrick Henry in Virginia avowed enemies to the government, Adams felt that its future was most uncertain. He did not mean to suggest that these men themselves would attempt "to disturb the peace of our Israel"; yet they were rallying points for dissidents and malcontents. Their pronouncements gave heart to the Anti-Federalists and prevented that spirit of concord which would be most conducive to the stability of the federal establishment.[16]

It seemed clear enough to Adams that the national government must be superior to the states. Talk as they might about a sovereignty divided between states and national government, the national government must be supreme. But there were many of his compatriots who felt differently, who believed that state and federal governments were equals, or indeed that ultimately the states were the true and final locus of power. "The state governments," Adams wrote Jonathan Sargeant, "have so much power as to make the whole a composition of thirteen omnipotences against one omnipotence. . . . Seats in the new government are considered still as steps towards promotion at home." Until service for the nation was more highly regarded than for the states the national government would be in danger. "Despondency is not one of my characteristics," he wrote Sargeant; "on the contrary the world in general suppose me too much inclined to be sanguine"; but his role as presiding officer was in truth a crown of thorns. The spirit of particularism, the lack of understanding of the principles of good government, the evidences of personal rancor among the members of the Senate—all these were sore trials. Only New England seemed willing to make sacrifices for the larger good of all the states and she was inclined to go too far—"she mortifies herself and all her friends in complaisance to Southern pride."[17]

To William Tudor, Adams wrote posing the question of how the new government could win solid support and loyalty: "If the national government is to be but a ladder on which to mount into higher regions at home, you will say that this government will soon die the death of the late righteous Congress, and the new constitution expire like the old Confederation." The members of Congress, he pointed out, "live at uncomfortable lodgings instead of their own houses; alone instead of in the society of their families and friends; at a great distance from their estates and business. Professions, faculties, property, families, all going to ruin at home." It seemed to him that zeal and patriotism were on the decline and "one universal and ungovernable rage for the loaves and fishes" governed men's actions. On the other hand, much of the disagreement over principles of government was a matter of terminology. As Adams wrote Tudor, "Our fellow citizens will never think alike nor act aright until they are habitually taught to use the same words in the same sense. Nations are governed by words as well as by actions; by sounds as well as sights."[18]

To Tudor's suggestion that the division in the country was so sharp that it would be better to separate into two nations, one north and the other south, Adams replied: "I cannot reconcile myself to the idea of a division of this continent even fifty years hence. Great sacrifices ought to be made to Union, and a habit of obedience to a well-ordered and judiciously limited government formed at this early period. A dissolution of the Union involves consequences of so terrible a kind that I think we ought to consent to a unity of executive authority at least, if not even to a consolidation of all power in one national government rather than separate." But first there must be a fair trial of the present system.[19]

If he did not discern it at first Adams soon became aware that the vice-presidency was a remarkably limited and inconsequential post. He had not, he wrote James Lovell, "the smallest degree of power to do any good either in the executive, legislative, judicial departments. A mere Doge of Venice . . . 'head of wood,' a mere mechanical tool to wind up the clock." The moment the nation introduced a proper balance into the constitution, "they will cut off [my] head," he observed, "and I myself should be ambitious of the honor of wielding the ax."[20]

"My office," he wrote John Quincy, "requires rather severe duty, and it is a kind of duty which, if I do not flatter myself too much, is not quite adapted to my character—I mean it is too inactive and mechanical." He was often inclined to leave the woolsack to join in debate. "It sometimes happens that I . . . think I could throw a little light upon a subject . . . but it cannot be done, I am content."[21]

Abigail, meanwhile, set out from Braintree. It galled her thrifty soul to have to sell the oxen at half their worth, but she arranged for tenants to take over the farm, paid her debts, supervised the crating of the furniture to go by boat to New York, and left Braintree in the middle of June to join John. Esther Briesler was sick so Abigail took Polly Tailor, a local girl, as her maid and, accompanied by Charles and Louisa Smith, the daughter of her dead brother, traveled through Wrentham and Attleboro to Providence, Rhode Island. From there the party took a packet to New York. The trip was five days, the Sound was rough, and Abigail, desperately seasick, resolved once more "never again to embark upon the water. . . . Want of rest, seasickness, and terror," she wrote her sister, "all contributed to fatigue me, and I felt upon my arrival quite tame and spiritless."

When the packet at last tied up to the wharf at New York, Abigail sent a message to John at the Senate chamber announcing their arrival and Samuel Otis, Secretary of the Senate, soon appeared in a carriage and bore the party off to the house at Richmond Hill which was to be their home.

They drove out of the city, up a long, sloping hill, in at a gate, then through a winding, tree-lined drive which, as Abigail put it, looked "wild and rural as uncultivated nature." The house was run down and much in need of repair but Abigail took to it at once. The second-floor hall, with a wide glass door opening onto a porch, was a light and pleasant space that Abigail made into an upstairs drawing room. Sitting there writing letters or sewing, she could look out over a charming view. "In front of the house," she wrote her sister, "the noble Hudson rolls, his majestic waves bearing upon his bosom innumerable small vessels which are constantly [carrying] the rich products of the neighboring soil to the busy hand of a more extensive commerce. Beyond the Hudson rises to our view the fertile country of the Jerseys, covered with a golden harvest and pouring forth plenty like the cornucopia of Ceres. On the right hand an extensive plain presents us with a view of fields covered with verdure and pastures full of cattle; on the left, the city opens upon us, intercepted only by clumps of trees and some rising ground. . . . If my days of fancy and romance were not past, I could find here an ample field for indulgence."

In the back of the house was a large garden with hawthorn hedges, thick with bees, bordering a broad gravel walk. The birds around Richmond Hill were a special delight to Abigail. A "lovely variety" serenaded her every morning—larks, thrushes, and robins, as well as partridges, woodcocks, and pigeons. She could see that the latter made the Colonel itch to take up his fowling piece, but she sternly forbade him to do any shooting among her flock. Nabby and the Colonel had already moved in with the children and Abigail found the house was "so well arranged that beds and a few other articles seem only necessary towards keeping house with comfort," as she wrote Mary Cranch. She had hardly time to change her clothes before a stream of visitors began to arrive to pay their respects: Governor Clinton's wife and daughter, the Countess de Bréhan, a French lady painter whom Abigail had met in Paris, "Mrs. Knox and twenty-five other ladies, many of the Senators, all their ladies, all the foreign ministers and some of the representatives."

The day following her arrival Abigail went with Nabby to pay her respects to the President and Mrs. Washington. "*His Majesty*," Abigail wrote in deference to her husband's campaign to title him, "was ill and confined to his room," but she was delighted with the first lady, who had a charming ease of manner devoid of all affectation ("dignified and feminine, not the tincture of hauteur about her.") She dressed plainly but richly, had snowy white hair and beautiful teeth, and, although slightly shorter than Abigail herself and inclined to plumpness, had "a much better figure." The two ladies took to each other at once. Martha Washington was delighted with her visitor's wit and intelligence and perhaps most of all with her direct and open manner.[22]

When Abigail met Washington several days later she was as pleased with him as with his wife. She found him "a singular example of modesty and diffidence," possessed of "a dignity which forbids familiarity mixed up with an easy affability which creates love and reverence." His fever had ended in an abscess and he received Abigail in his bedroom propped up on pillows.

As soon as Washington had fully recovered, Abigail and John went to the President's for dinner. The Clintons, the Jays, the Langdons, the Daltons, and Maclay and Bassett made up the company. The President and his lady sat facing each other at the middle of a long table. The table was handsomely set with an elaborate centerpiece of artificial flowers. Beside the footmen there were liveried waiters and a sumptuous spread. The first course was soup; next came roasted and boiled fish of several kinds; then meat—game birds, chickens, ducks, and geese. For dessert there were apple pies, puddings, and cakes; ice cream and jellies; and finally fruit—watermelons, muskmelons, apples, peaches, and nuts.

Neither the President nor the Vice-President had any small talk and their ladies were scarcely more loquacious, so that the meal was consumed in silence. When dinner was finally finished and the table cleared, the President took a glass of wine and with great formality drank the health of every guest. While Maclay watched, half impressed and half contemptuous, each guest followed suit; "and such a buzz of health, sir, and health, madam, and thank you, sir, and thank you, madam, never had I heard before," the Pennsylvanian noted, adding wryly, "Indeed, I was like to have been thrown out in the hurry; but I got a little wine in my glass and passed the ceremony."

After this ritual there was another long silence and then Martha Washington withdrew with the ladies and the men were left to their port, nuts, and cigars. The President made a brave effort with a story of a clergyman who lost his hat and wig crossing a river called the Brunks. It was certainly not a very funny story, but at its conclusion Washington smiled and the company laughed heartily, pleased and flattered at the General's attention. Despite his reserve, Washington seemed ill at ease. He played with a fork after the cloth had been removed, turning it in his strong broad fingers and tapping it against the edge of the table in a distracted, pensive way. There were a few more minutes of silence and then the President rose and led the men upstairs for coffee.[23]

On the social side both John and Abigail found the burdens of his office heavy. Abigail received a stream of visitors and returned dozens of calls.

The General and his wife had set Friday evening as the time of the presidential levee and Abigail usually went with Nabby and Charles. It was all done with some style. The doormen announced the guests, they were greeted by one of the President's personal aides and passed on to Mrs. Washington, to whom they curtsied, and then were seated. The President spoke to the ladies "with a grace, dignity, and ease," Abigail noted, "that leaves royal George far behind him." The guests ate ice cream and drank lemonade, exchanged greetings with friends, made polite conversation and then withdrew.

Abigail busied herself entertaining all the Senators who had wives and families with them, then the single Senators, and then the Congressmen and "public ministers." Even the practiced efficiency of Briesler was strained to the utmost. "I can no more do without Briesler," Abigail wrote her sister, "than a coach could go without wheels or horse to draw it." The city was swelteringly hot. She could not find a cook in the city who was not a chronic drunkard, and the Negro servants were shiftless and poorly trained. In the midst of it all—heat, servant problems, endless visitors, and visits—Nabby's children, little John and William, came down with whooping cough, hacking and spewing, and Charles and Polly Tailor got dysentery, so that Abigail had to do double duty as nurse and hostess.

The one serious inhibition of their social life was the paltry salary that Congress had voted for the Vice-President. Adams took it as a personal rebuke. He had hardly half the President's salary, yet he had almost as much entertaining to do. As he put it with rather more restraint than usual, his pay was "a curiosity," and he blamed the Massachusetts Representatives for his niggardly stipend. They seldom acted in harmony or with decision. They had no set policy, no course they held to. Indeed the opposition to an adequate salary for the Vice-President had originated in Massachusetts. "Man may drudge forever for Massachusetts and die a beggar, nay, what is worse, die in disgrace. God forgive them!" he exclaimed angrily to Tudor.[24] "I must be pinched and strengthened till I die," he complained to John Quincy, "and you must have to toil and drudge as I have done."[25]

Finding a congenial church turned out to be a problem. The sermons in the Congregational churches of New York were not to John's or Abigail's liking. Most of them were delivered without notes (and showed the effects) by preachers who were old-fashioned predestinarians "whose noise and vehemence is to compensate for every other deficiency," illiberal, rigid men, priestly despots with "that solemn phiz and gait which looks so like mummery that instead of reverence they create disgust." Listening to sermons "that I cannot possibly believe," Abigail wrote Mary Cranch, "is really doing penance." The ministers' idea of eloquence consisted, Abigail noted caustically, "in foaming, loud speaking, working themselves up in such an enthusiasm as to cry, but which has no other effect upon me than to raise my pity." She longed to hear "liberal good sense . . . true piety without enthusiasm, devotion without grimace, and religion upon a rational system." The theological atmosphere of St. Paul's, the Episcopal church, was far more to her liking even though the forms of the service were alien to her.[26]

With Abigail at Richmond Hill and the Senate proceeding at least for the moment on a course of moderate Federalism, Adams' spirits rose. He was ashamed of his glooms, he wrote Cushing. "My present office is as agreeable to me as any public office ever can be: and my situation as pleasing as any on earth, excepting Braintree." Yet he suffered from the long hours of sitting and the close attention that he had to give to debates and discussions; his old affliction, a pain in the chest which he had first experienced years before in Congress, now returned to trouble him.

LVIII

THE Fourth of July 1789 was celebrated in the capital with "much pomp." There were parades, speeches, and fireworks. The Society of the Cincinnati, no longer so menacing as they had once seemed, assembled at St. Paul's Church where Colonel Alexander Hamilton delivered an eloquent tribute to General Nathanael Greene.

With the judiciary bill passed, the next serious bone of contention in the Senate was a bill to establish the "great departments"—Treasury, Foreign Affairs, and War. Maclay at once took alarm. He could see no need for such legislation. The President could just as well propose men as the heads of various offices, and "if the Senate agreed to the necessity of the office and the man, they would concur." The whole idea seemed to him and his allies to be simply another effort to exalt the powers of the President at the expense of Congress. Moreover Maclay was opposed to allowing the President to remove the officials that he had appointed "at will." If he must, by the constitution, have the concurrence of the Senate in appointment, he must equally have its concurrence in removal. Without such power, the presidential appointee, liable to be removed, would be inclined to "abject servility," and the President himself to despotism and tyranny.

Maclay was followed by Ellsworth who, wearing a green silk shade to protect his inflamed eyes, argued eloquently in behalf of the constitutional right of the President to remove those officers he had appointed without the concurrence of the Senate. But Ellsworth was followed by Pierce Butler, who feared the "power of removal would be unhinging the equilibrium of power in the constitution," and by Izard and Lee, who spoke against the motion, Lee at some length. The next day Charles Carroll took up the cudgels in its favor. The great danger in the government was not, he maintained, from the power of the executive but from "the *atrocious assumption of power in the states.*" Senate control over removal would be a serious infringement of the President's already inadequate powers. He was supported by Ellsworth in the same spirit. The executive power must be strengthened. America had not objected in 1775 to the powers of the King but to the powers of Parliament. The area of presidential action must not be intruded upon. Once started, there would be no stopping place and the legislative would in time devour the executive branch.

So much for the debates. Maclay observed much "caballing and meeting of members in knots." He came upon Ellsworth, Fisher Ames, and Morris with their heads together on the stairs outside the chamber; a few minutes later he saw Ellsworth, Carroll, and Strong conferring. He noted "a general hunt and bustle among the members," and the thought came to him that debate on the floor of the Senate would no longer be the primary means of determining controversial issues. More important would be the backstage bargains and agreements. Once these had been concluded the most eloquent orations would be useless. As he watched the conferences and consultations Maclay concluded that party lines were forming more and more clearly between those of the "court party," bent on supporting the power of the chief executive, and those who, like himself, were suspicious of that office and determined to throw their weight into the legislative side of the scale.

In all this maneuvering Adams played a leading role. It seemed clear enough to him that the future stability of the government was at stake. Here was the first bold indication, far more important than titles, of the Senate's disposition to limit the President's powers and extend its own. If this fight was lost it would be hard to rally on another defensible line.[1] So he hurried here and there, to this group and that, arguing and exhorting. He encountered Richard Henry Lee and drove at him head on. He had made careful notes of Lee's arguments and undertook to refute his main points. Lee defended himself ably and the voices of the two old friends grew loud and strident as they talked. When the Senate was convened and the debates resumed, Lee took up the cause of the Senate again, but halfheartedly as though his clash with the Vice-President had disconcerted him. As debate continued, Dalton, on whom Adams had exercised all his powers of persuasion, got up and recanted. He had been convinced of the error of his ways, he declared; he would support the right of the President to remove his own appointees. Izard was up at once to suggest rather peremptorily that Dalton had yielded to pressure more than to persuasion, and Morris, his face red with anger, jumped up to defend Dalton and rebuke Izard for his remarks. Richard Bassett of Delaware followed Dalton into the camp of the Federalists and Maclay observed resignedly, "We now saw how it would go; and I could not help admiring the frugality of the court party in procuring recantations or votes."[2]

When the question was at last called for, Patterson and Elmer of New Jersey supported the unqualified power of removal, John Henry and

Charles Carroll of Maryland, Dalton and Strong of Massachusetts, Bassett and Read of Delaware, Morris of Pennsylvania voted with them. Opposed were all the Senators south of the Mason-Dixon line—Butler, Izard, Few, Gunn, Grayson, and Lee, plus Maclay, Johnson of Connecticut, and the two Senators from New Hampshire, Langdon and Wingate. According to Adams' calculations, the Federalists had the votes to block their opponents, but there was still some uncertainty. When the roll call was completed the vote stood ten to ten and Adams' relief and triumph were all too apparent. With the vote tied, he could once more cast the deciding ballot. Without even going through the formality of declaring the division and giving his vote, he called out in a voice high with excitement, "It is not a vote!"

Grayson of Virginia, angry and disappointed, stood up and declared that the day predicted by Patrick Henry had come to pass. "Consolidation," he announced dramatically, "is the object of the new government; and the first attempt will be to destroy the Senate, as they are the representatives of the state legislature."

Adams derived special satisfaction from his tie-breaking vote. To him the issue was the most important that had yet faced the Senate. The preservation of the President's powers was essential. The maintenance of the government in good order and in balance required it.

At the end of August, Washington sent word to the Senate that he wished to consult with it on the subject of certain treaties with the Southern Indians. This would be an important occasion—the President's first effort to "advise and consent" with the upper house. It was decided that Adams, as President of the Senate, should surrender his seat to Washington; that the latter should preside; that assent should be indicated by voice at the instance of the President of Senate, ay or no. On the twenty-second of August, Washington appeared in the Senate chamber accompanied by General Knox, the Secretary of War. Adams conducted the President to his chair, Knox was placed on his left, and Adams took his seat with the Senators. The Secretary of War then handed the President a rather bulky document. The President in turn handed it to Adams, who began to read it rather hurriedly. Carriages rumbling by on the cobblestoned street outside made such a racket that much was inaudible. The first part was the proposed treaty, the second, seven questions on which the Senate's advice was solicited. Adams read off the first question and asked the members' pleasure. Robert Morris rose to request that the papers be read once more: the passing carriages had prevented him from hearing the first reading. Once more Adams read the treaty. When he had finished he repeated the first question and asked, "Do you advise and consent?"

There was an uncomfortable silence, which Adams took for acquiescence. "As many as——" he began, but at this point his nemesis, Maclay,
big as a bear and stiff with rheumatism, hoisted himself to his feet. "Mr.
President," he said, "the business is new to the Senate. It is of importance.
It is our duty to inform ourselves as well as possible on the subject. I therefore call for the reading of the treaties and other documents alluded to
in the paper before us."

Washington's irritation was plainly indicated by his expression. General
Knox shuffled through the documents before him and produced some
miscellaneous papers relating to the treaty, but Lee asked for a particular
document that the Secretary could not find. An air of uneasiness and,
indeed, of embarrassment was evident in the room. The first article of
the treaty concerned the Cherokees. It was moved that it be postponed
until an agent who had just come from that nation could be consulted. The
Senators from Georgia then proposed that the article involving their
neighbors, the Creeks, be likewise postponed.

All this, in Maclay's view, was no way to conduct the business. It was
too complicated to be acted upon in such hasty fashion. The documents
should be submitted to the Senate and referred to a committee for its
recommendations. There could be no free discussion with the magnificent
presence sitting there to "overawe the timid and neutral part of the
Senate."

"When I consider the newness and importance of the subject," he
declared, ". . . that General Lincoln, the first named of the commissioners, would not be here for a week; the deep interest Georgia had in
this affair, I could not think it improper that the Senators from that state
should be indulged in a postponement." He so moved. There was confused discussion of the question and the motion for postponement was
put and carried. Robert Morris proposed referral to a committee. Pierce
Butler opposed a committee and Maclay supported the principle. When
Maclay sat down Washington jumped up, dark as thunder, and declared:
"This defeats every purpose of my coming here." He had brought the
Secretary of War with him to explain the terms of the treaty and the
logic behind its drafting. The action of the Senate meant interruption and
delay. As he talked, the President mastered his temper and ended on a
conciliatory note. He would make no objection to postponement if the
Senate felt it necessary. There was another uncomfortable pause which
the President finally terminated by bowing stiffly and withdrawing, still,
Maclay fancied, "with a discontented air."[3]

The next day the President had full possession of himself. He seemed
"placid and serene and manifested a spirit of accommodation." The debate
on the questions was long and often tedious but he endured stoically and
finally carried away the substance of what he wished for.

While Adams sat as President of the Senate, his friends began to puff him as Washington's successor. Caleb Strong expressed his opinion that as soon as Washington saw the ship of state launched on a safe course he would turn over the helm to Adams. Benjamin Rush, even while he argued with his friend over titles, put Adams' name forward at every opportunity as the next President. In doing so Rush was not entirely disinterested; he hoped for the Vice-President's support in having the capital of the new government seated in Philadelphia, although Adams stated emphatically that he would not involve himself in the politics of the issue.

Adams himself professed to take no notice of such talk. Speaking of himself in the third person, he wrote Tudor, "He will have as much weight [in the government] as he ought, and he would not have more if it were offered him. He flatters himself [that] he knows his stops pretty well at fifty-three or -four years of age."

The talk of Adams as Washington's successor and the general assumption that, as Vice-President, he was heir to the presidency made him vulnerable to attack. This was especially true since Washington was still unassailable, protected by the armor of his fame. Every disgruntled and suspicious Anti-Federalist thus turned his fire on the Vice-President. When he voted to uphold the unconditional power of the President to remove his own appointees, he was accused of trying to augment his own inheritance, and a poet who called himself "Republican" aimed some poisoned barbs at him in the pages of the *Massachusetts Centinel*:

> Be grateful then, YE CHOSEN! mod'rate wise,
> Nor stretch your claims to such preposterous size,
> Lest your too partial country—wiser grown—
> Shou'd on your native dunghills set you down.
> Ape not the fashions of the foreign great,
> Nor make your betters at your *levees* wait—
> Resign your awkward pomp, parade and pride,
> And lay that useless *etiquette* aside;
> The unthinking laugh, but all the thinking hate
> Such vile, abortive mimickry of State;
> Those idle lackeys, saunt'ring at your door,
> But ill become *poor servants* of the POOR.

The poet exhorted the "faithful guardians" of the country's welfare to quell "the lawless lust of POW'R in embryo . . . /The germ of mischief, the first spawn of hell;/Resist the VICE [Adams]—and that contagious pride/To that o'erweening VICE—so near all'y'd."

These were bitter words, written in a bitter spirit, and Adams, characterized as "the first spawn of hell," greedy for power and wealth, smarted at the attack. Both he and Abigail suspected Mercy Warren at first but it turned out that the author was Ned Church, brother of Benjamin Church, the traitor. "Poor devil, I pity him," Adams wrote Dr. Tufts. Yet the connoisseur in him forced him to confess it was "good verse and will do me honor. So I'll enjoy it," he added defiantly.[4]

As Abigail pointed out to her sister, the Vice-President lived in comparative simplicity. It was the President, not Adams, who had "idle lackeys" at the door, "so that under a hypocritical mask [the poet] attacks one and holds the other impiously up and styles him a savior and God."[5]

While Adams confessed to James Lovell that he was not likely to forget "there is only the breath of one mortal between me and [the presidency]," he pointed out that if he had been concerned with improving his own chances of inheriting the office he would have voted to surrender the power of removal since that was the popular course. "There is not," he added, "to be serious, the smallest prospect that I shall ever reach that goal. Our beloved chief is very little older than his second . . . and is a much stronger man than I am." Washington would certainly outlive Adams and the people would be called upon to choose a new Vice-President before they chose a new President. "I know very well," he stated, "that I am not possessed of the confidence and affection of my fellow citizens to the degree that he is. I am not of Caesar's mind. The second place in Rome is high enough for me, although I have a spirit that will not give up its right or relinquish its place." Then the inevitable and defiant assertion: "Whatever the world, or even my friends, or even you who know me so well, may think of me, I am not an ambitious man." He only wished what was his due; that, and to preserve his reputation untarnished to posterity. But he made it clear at the same time that he would serve as Vice-President to no other than Washington.[6]

As to Washington's successor, Jay, Jefferson, and Madison were all possibilities but, Adams added, "I know well that I would carry an election against either of them in spite of intrigues and maneuvers." Yet if he, upon Washington's death or retirement, should enter the lists against any or all of them, he would inevitably be made head of a party. "I will never be in this situation," he wrote. "If circumstances should force it upon me, I will at all events quit the country if I spend the rest of my days in a garret at Amsterdam. . . . In private life I am very sure I should enjoy a green old age contented and healthy, and leave my family prosperous and happy. If that office [the presidency] should ever fall upon me from my sins, I see nothing but vexation, disease, and death for myself, and nothing but poverty, pride, and a humiliating fall for my children." It would make for greater order and stability if a successor to Washington were more or less tacitly agreed upon and the choice made public so that there would be no rivalry and contention.[7]

When the first session of Congress approached the time set for adjourn-ment both Senate and House found themselves engaged in a bitter and extended struggle over the location of the capital. The contest was be-tween the New Yorkers and the Pennsylvanians and the Congressmen from those states were tireless in their efforts to rally support. In the Senate the debates grew increasingly hot. Suddenly the Virginians, taking advantage of the stalemate, began to push for a capital on the Potomac. Virginia would contribute one hundred thousand dollars toward the cost of erecting federal buildings. Pennsylvania was indicted for having self-ish aims and Maclay and Morris were accused of trying to put the good of their state ahead of the good of the Union. A week of wrangling brought no agreement and the Senate adjourned the twenty-ninth of September with the issue unresolved.

His duties as presiding officer had been a severe physical strain on Adams and the end of the first session of Congress found him drained and weary. He fell into one of his dark moods from which Abigail with all her attentions and little stratagems could not draw him. Things had not gone as he had hoped. The Federalist majority was narrow and uncertain. He felt that constant vigilance was required to prevent a disastrous swing to the enemies of the government. The constitution, God knew, was vague enough, subject to different interpretations, obscure and, on certain criti-cal points, maddeningly evasive. Everything was open. There was no single precedent, however small or casually established, that might not have vast implications for the future course of the new nation: a com-mittee appointed or not appointed, a messenger from the House received or not received, the form of reply to a presidential query. If for most of the Senators these were minor matters, too insignificant to quibble about, they were to Adams full of significance and of potential dangers. The affairs of men were governed by chance and by reason. The more that was left to chance, to accident, to inadvertence, the greater the risk. The fortuitous could not be excluded but its power to damage and disrupt could be diminished by careful plans, by taking thought of the conse-quences of every act, every precedent, and imparting, bit by bit, detail by detail, the desired shape to the infant government. Posterity would have no patience with carelessness, haste, indifference, or stupidity. It was all very well for a Maclay or even a Lee to inveigh against the terrors of a powerful centralized government. Their declamations filled them with a sense of republican virtue and cost them very little. It was always easier and usually safer to be against something than for something. But it was the terrible vulnerability of the new government that obsessed Adams; so tender, so exposed to the greed, the indifference, the vanity, and the ambition of men, it must be nourished and protected. This, Adams felt, was his proper role but he was constantly frustrated by the character of his office. He was asked to be a spectator of events that he felt were crucial to the future of the nation when every nerve urged him to interpose, to expostulate, explain and exhort, above all to teach, to point out the proper path. As we have seen, he yielded to such impulses far oftener than he should, but far less often than he was inclined to. Self-restraint had never been a dominant trait; his office was in consequence a kind of purgatory for him.

He was deeply troubled by the "division of sentiment" about everything—some inclining to the French, some to the English; one party to the South and another to the North; one set advocates for the interest of agriculture, another for those of commerce, a third for those of manufacture—every party pushing their own principles too far, and opposing others too much. "How few minds," he wrote, "look through the mighty all with a steady eye, and consider all its relations and dependencies! How few aim at the good of the whole without aiming too much at the prosperity of parts?"[8] But impatient as he became at times, Adams reminded himself that "the scene is new and the actors are inexperienced." Much was gained by the debates, tedious and excessively long as they appeared to be.[9]

His anxieties were augmented by the rising tide of partisan political feeling which he observed everywhere: Hancock, Samuel Adams, Gerry, James Sullivan, Warren, and a dozen others in his home state; Livingston and his coterie in New York, still sore from their defeat on the issue of ratification; Maclay and the radicals of Pennsylvania who had threatened to ignore the constitution entirely; and to the southward an almost unbroken phalanx of Congressmen and Senators who viewed the federal government with suspicion or open hostility. The opposition press had already begun to spew its venom and Adams was its principal object. It was enough to put his faith in republican government to the severest of tests.

Yet in all the delays and discouragements an extraordinary thing was happening. The first self-governing republic in history, established at one instant so to speak, was taking its initial faltering steps. The question that was being put to the test was the extraordinarily complicated one of whether a nation without any tradition of centralized administration, without a common social structure and a unified economy, could govern itself as a democratic republic, could find its own way into the future without the support of custom or precedent. It was a desperate enterprise which, when later generations looked back upon it, seemed quite orderly and more or less inevitable, as the past almost invariably does. But it did not seem so to the men who labored to make the rather vague blueprint of the federal constitution a reality. As Adams put it in a letter to Dr. Price: "The difficulty of bringing millions to agree in any measure to act by any rule can never be conceived by him who has not tried it. It

is incredible how small is the number in any nation of those who comprehend any system of a constitution or administration—and those few it is
impossible to unite. I am a sincere inquirer after truth, but I find very
few who discover the same truths."[10]

Adams, seeing more deeply than most into the contradictions and
ambiguities of man's common life, felt the burden of doubt and anxiety
far more keenly. Who could see how it would all come out? Who dared to
nod or grow faint, to compromise or vacillate, to make purely political decisions on issues that involved the basic and immutable principles of
government? The strain showed; John was moody and distracted, almost
snappish to Abigail, impatient with the children and the interruptions of
the crowded household. He must get away for a time; Braintree drew him
like a lodestone.

A few days before his departure he and Abigail joined the Washingtons
on an expedition to Long Island to visit the famous Prince gardens. It
was a beautiful fall day. The President was almost loquacious and Martha
and Abigail chatted away like old friends. They had much in common in
their preoccupation with their grandchildren. Mrs. Washington was, as
Abigail put it, "dotingly fond" of her Custis offspring. "We live upon
terms of much friendship," Abigail wrote her sister, "and visit each other
often."[11]

Two days later Adams set off for Boston with Tristram Dalton as a
traveling companion. Abigail had planned to accompany him, but the
thought of the stripped house at Braintree and the probable effect of
the long cold trip on her rheumatism deterred her and she decided to
stay at Richmond Hill. The trip was uneventful. "We have met with
nothing but rocks in the road to molest us," he wrote Abigail. "These have
jolted us very rudely but salubriously."[12]

Adams arrived in Boston a few days before the President, who was
making a tour of New England, and joined the city and state officials,
the militia, three bands, and the citizens of Boston who turned out to
greet the General. Only Governor Hancock was absent, kept home by one
of his frequent political indispositions—gout was the official complaint
this time. Many in the crowd waited more than six hours in a cold, soaking
rain and half of Boston came down with what was called "the Washington
cold."[13]

John Adams, accompanied by Samuel, joined the President in the line
of march and the three men sat together at the brief church service in the
Stone Chapel; later, at Faneuil Hall for the official ceremonies, the General sat between the two Adamses. John was delighted by the remark
of one member of the audience which was repeated to him: "Behold,
three men who can make a revolution when they please." "There,"
another was reported as saying, "are the three genuine pivots of the
Revolution." The last was a tribute which Adams felt was not entirely

unmerited. It certainly was an extraordinary spectacle: the two short, round New Englanders flanking the tall, massive Virginian. Washington was, Adams noted, "in character and consequently charming to all." He looked the perfect republican hero, the father of his country, benign, monumental, a figure of enormous assurance, of classic nobility. Elevated before his fellow citizens of Boston, warmed and exalted by the presidential nimbus, Adams tasted for a moment the wine of glory without the sour dregs of partisan bitterness. If America should preserve such an image of its heroes for the view of posterity, all the struggle and travail would have been worth while.[14]

With all this, that implacable temper which ever possessed John Adams made him turn a cold and hostile face toward Hancock. The Governor was the kind of politician that Adams could not endure—the weather vane, the shrewd opportunist, the demagogue who courted popular favor with unquenchable ardor and perennial success. When Hancock invited the President to dine, he included Adams. But the Vice-President felt that the Governor's rather informal, last-minute invitation violated protocol. Although he accepted, he failed to appear and subsequently, when he encountered the Governor, offered no apology or explanation for his absence. It was petty of him, certainly, and it underlined what were his most conspicuous shortcomings as a practical politician—his stiffness, inflexibility, and self-righteousness. In his defense it could only be said that he looked on his former friend as a traitor to the principles of good government, as a man who had used his influence against him in a dozen small ways, whose minions harassed and abused him, Adams felt sure, with their master's encouragement. Under such circumstances it might be very well for Hancock to smile, to shake his hand warmly, to chat agreeably about old times and remote battles when they had fought shoulder to shoulder in the cause of liberty, that was Hancock's forte; Adams could not dissemble. His face would betray him if his words did not. He was all of one piece straight through with no veneer of affability, no artifice, no power to disguise his feelings. [15]

The visit to Boston was all too short. Many old friends and present political allies had to be seen if they were not to feel neglected and, in consequence, resentful, so that it was more than a week before he could make good his escape to Braintree to see his mother and brother, the Cranches, the Palmers, and a dozen others. Indeed, Mary Cranch complained to Abigail that he was so busy picking books out of his library to send to New York that he hardly had time for his relatives and close friends. In addition Abigail had loaded him with a dozen commissions. She wanted some of the cheese that his mother had made, all the butter he could get, "some of the russet apples, the pears," bacon, tongue, several dozen hams, and thirty or forty dozen eggs. Charles wanted half a dozen barrels of cider. The food to be bought in New York was hardly fit to eat.

Adams stayed with his mother and brother: "We live like princes in great luxury—you know my mother!" he wrote Abigail. The farm was in poor condition and he spent much time giving directions for its rehabilitation and doctoring his horse, whose lame leg delayed his departure for New York.[16]

Abigail had her hands full at Richmond Hill. The baby, John Adams Smith, had the smallpox. Louisa had been inoculated from him. The coachman was immobilized by pleurisy and alcohol. Colonel Smith had gone off grouse shooting on Long Island, and Abigail got what comfort she could from visiting with Martha Washington and playing with "Master William Magpie," her older grandson. Martha told Abigail she had a present for Mr. Adams when he returned. It was of no great value, but she piqued Abigail's curiosity by refusing to tell her what it was. "I told her I would be jealous but it did not provoke her to show it to me," she wrote her sister.[17]

LIX

B
Y THE end of December, Adams was back at Richmond Hill with Tommy—"very thin, pale and sallow" from close attention to his studies. The New Yorkers celebrated New Year's in the old Dutch tradition. The stores were closed and the churches open, and the day devoted "to the social purpose of visiting and receiving visits." A New Year's cooky was served with cherry bounce, and Abigail found two of her servants "not altogether qualified for business." When she remonstrated with them they replied cheerfully that "it was New Year and everybody was joyous then." Adams visited the President to pay his respects and then returned home to receive friends. In the evening he and Abigail went to Mrs. Washington's "public day"; when the President discovered a lady already stationed in Abigail's position at Martha's right hand, he displaced her with such exquisite tact that she withdrew pleased and flattered. Abigail could not help being impressed once more with the General's "happy . . . faculty of appearing to accommodate and yet carrying his point. . . . He is polite with dignity, affable without familiarity, distant without haughtiness, grave without austerity, modest, wise, and good," Abigail wrote her sister in a lyrical outburst. "These are traits in his character," she added, "which peculiarly fit him for the exalted station he holds, and God grant that he may hold it with the same applause and universal satisfaction for many years, as it is my firm opinion that no other man could rule over this great people and consolidate them into one mighty empire but he who is set over us."[1]

Early in 1790 news reached the United States of the outbreak of the French Revolution, the storming of the Bastille, and the drafting of a new constitution by the Estates. Americans almost without exception hailed the news as marking the onset of another great struggle for liberty, this time by the allies who had supported them so faithfully in their own uprising. But Adams from the first moment viewed it with misgivings. "The French Revolution will, I hope," he wrote his friend Van der Kemp, "produce effects in favor of liberty, equity, and humanity as extensive as this whole globe and as lasting as all time." At the same time he could not forbear to point out "that the form of government they have adopted" could be "nothing more than a transient experiment. An obstinate adherence to it" would involve France "in great and lasting calamities." A single assembly would be dominated by demagogues and the result would be repeated upheavals and disorder—a succession of bloody contentions.[2]

"I have learned by awful experience to rejoice with trembling," he wrote his English friend, Dr. Price. "I know that Encyclopedists and Economists, Diderot and D'Alembert, Voltaire and Rousseau have contributed to this great event more than Sidney, Locke, or Hoadley, perhaps more than the American Revolution; and I own to you I know not what to make of a republic of thirty million atheists. The constitution is but an experiment, and must and will be altered." He was by experience well aware that in revolutions "the most fiery spirits and flighty geniuses frequently obtain more influence than men of sense and judgment; and the weakest man may carry foolish measures in opposition to wise ones proposed by the ablest. France is in great danger from this quarter." Change was certainly long overdue in Europe.[3] "Abuses in religion and government," Adams noted, "are so numerous and oppressive to the people that a reformation must take place or a general decline. The armies of monks, soldiers, and courtiers were become so numerous and costly that the labor of the rest was not enough to maintain them. Either reformation or depopulation must come." For himself Adams was satisfied that there would be no order or stability until there was a balance between the legislative, executive, and judicial branches.[4] The French, Adams insisted, must become his disciples, the adherents of balanced government, "or they will have no equal laws, no personal liberty, no property, no lives." "I hereby promise and assure you," he wrote Brand-Hollis, an uncritical admirer of the French Revolution, "that you will live to see that I am precisely right."[5]

The second session of Congress mustered a quorum on the sixth of January, appointed a chaplain, and prepared to receive the address of the President. The maneuverings and intrigues over the permanent seat of the government began at once, with no better prospect of resolution than before. The morning of the eighth was spent by the Senate "in hauling chairs and removing tables" in preparation for the joint session to hear the President's message. The Senate was grouped on the right side of the chamber, the House on the left, Washington's official family and the heads of departments in the center. The President read his speech with far greater clarity and assurance than he had shown in the first session, and at its conclusion it was referred to a committee, as Pierce Butler thought, with too much haste. The South Carolinian rose to say so and was called to order sharply by Adams. This was the kind of disrespectful and intemperate action with which he had no patience. Butler had more than his share of the classic Southern choler; he lashed out at the Vice-President and Adams gaveled him to his seat. In Carolina such treatment was proper ground for a duel. Although Adams, after adjournment, told Butler he had meant him no offense, Butler was not satisfied. Adams should have apologized formally from the chair. He dashed off an indignant note protesting the "impropriety" of the Vice-President's remarks. "The strong desire I have of promoting and preserving harmony in that branch of the legislature induces me to take no further notice of it at this time." But, he added threateningly, "if anything similar to it takes place again I shall in justification of my own feelings . . . be under a necessity of personally resenting it"—in other words, of challenging Adams to a duel.[6]

The reply to the President's address, drafted by Izard, was to Maclay "the most servile echo I ever heard. . . . . As a republican," he was "opposed to the whole business of echoing speeches. It was a stale ministerial trick in Britain to get the House of Parliament to chime in with the speech, and then consider them as pledged to support any measure which could be grafted on the speech." Despite Maclay's objections, the Senate resolved to go in a body to deliver their reply to the President.

Rumors circulated that the newly appointed Secretary of the Treasury, Alexander Hamilton, would recommend the funding of all the debts, foreign and domestic. Included was a plan for the national government to take over the debts of the states and pay these off as well—the controversial assumption of state debts. Word of Hamilton's financial plan caused a rapid rise in the value of public securities and Maclay noted, "A committee of speculators in certificates would not have formed it more for their advantage. It has occasioned many serious faces. I feel so struck of an heap, I can make no remark on the matter."[7] Adams, of course, took quite a different view. "It is rapture," he declared, "to see a returning disposition to respect treaties, to pay debts, and to do justice by holding property sacred and obeying the commandment, 'Thou shalt not steal.'" "The national debt," he wrote Stephen Higginson, "I have long thought must be the instrument for establishing a national government and have the pleasure now to see that the President, his ministers, and a majority in the House are of the same opinion." The enemies of the national government, Adams noted, saw that the assumption of the state debts was "the pivot upon which the general government will turn," and in consequence were doing their best to defeat it.[8]

Their attitude was expressed, typically, by Maclay, who wrote that "Hamilton, at the head of the speculators, with all the courtiers, are on one side. These I call the party who are actuated by interest. The opposition are governed by principle." For the whole month of January the funding issue preoccupied Congress as the House debated the plan from day to day with increasing warmth. Hamilton, in a swivet about the fate of his bill, hung about the chamber and, according to Maclay, "spent most of his time in running from place to place among its members."[9]

James Madison, to Adams' indignation, led the fight for an amended bill containing a complicated and cumbersome scheme to provide a fair return to the original purchasers rather than an undue profit for the speculators. As week after week passed, Congress seemed exhausted with the subject; yet neither side was willing to give way or to call for the question. Maclay thought he observed "a kind of spirit of uncertainty hover over the Representative body"—a want of confidence either in the Secretary's scheme or in Madison's alternative. "Like a flight of land fowl at sea, they seem to be bewildered and wish for a resting place, but distrust every object that offers." Madison, worn out by the long fight, was peevish and irritable; everything hung on dead center.

Madison's determined campaign for his own version of the funding bill, a campaign pushed, Maclay thought, more through vanity than anything else, divided and demoralized the opponents of the bill. Early in March, Maclay noted a "rendezvousing of the crew of the Hamilton galley" with "all hands pressed to quarters," indicating that the funding bill was at last to be voted on. Two Congressmen were carried in to vote, one lame and the other sick. Another member was intercepted as he was leaving the chamber on an urgent call. Thus mustered and dragooned, Hamilton's "crew" carried the first three portions of the Secretary's financial plan and then voted, 29 to 27, to recommit the assumption of state debts.

The second session was, in its own way, as trying as the first. Since the critical business lay with the House, the Senate was frequently adjourned; even when in session, the issues debated generally were not of a nature to excite much warmth. But if attendance was less arduous, a certain feeling of slackness, an air of inattention and uncertainty made Adams uneasy. Adams' friend, John Trumbull, who kept in close touch with the progress of the new government, wrote him that he had heard the Southerners in the Senate resented Adams because he was a self-made man of humble origins who had risen above them by his talents. His enemies were also assiduous in spreading the story that he had abandoned his republican principles and in criticizing him for participating in the discussions of the Senate. He could, they argued, "on no occasion with propriety offer his sentiments at large, except when he is requested to give information . . . or when in the case of an equi-vote he states his reasons on giving his casting voice."

His interjections were the more resented since his greatest gifts as a public speaker were "force of argument and strength of language, approaching to sarcasm, and expressive of some degree of contempt for the opinions and reasonings of his adversaries." The consequence was that when he entered discussions in the Senate he more often offended than convinced those on the opposite side of the question and in doing so compromised the cause he was trying to advance. Even the Senators whose views he was supporting resented the implication that they were not effective advocates of their own position. Having said this much, Trumbull trusted to the strength of their friendship to give Adams a lecture on the proper exercise of his office. "He who mingles in debate," he reminded him, "subjects himself to frequent retorts from his opposers, places himself on the same ground with his inferiors in rank, appears too much like the leader of a party, and renders it more difficult for him to support the dignity of the chair and preserve order and regularity in the debate."[10]

Adams replied with a rather studied air of reasonableness to Trumbull's letter. He was pleased with his "friendly cautions," he declared, though as to enemies "I assure you I have none." His greatest crime in the eyes of many was that he was a New Englander. To this he pled guilty. As for "the eternal clamors about my birth," it was enough for him that his father had been "an honest man, a lover of his country, and an independent spirit." The example of his father had contributed, he continued, "to support me among groaning billows, yawning gulfs, and burning fevers. . . . My mother was a Boylston, one of the richest families in the Massachusetts for above an hundred years," and far from obscure. It was ironic that he should be on the one hand abused for the obscurity of his birth and the smallness of his fortune, and at the same time denounced for telling people that they have prejudices in favor of birth and fortune.

As for the accusation that he was devoted to "the splendor of monarchical courts," he was indifferent to it. He had played the game fairly enough. His views were recorded "at great length" in three, "perhaps ponderous" volumes. His opinions had not changed and if his countrymen disapproved them they were quite free to reject their author but he would not equivocate or dissemble.

Clearly the charge that galled him most was that of interference in the debates of the Senate. He had only spoken at length once, upon request, and on that occasion given his views on the President's powers of removal. Sometimes he had asked questions to clarify points under discussion but, he added firmly, "I have no desire ever to open my mouth again upon any question." It was true that sometimes among friends or guests at his own table he was carried away and expressed himself sharply. Abigail frequently rebuked him for allowing his tongue to run too loosely. Yet he would be less than candid not to admit that he, too, had heard some such grumblings; Gerry had carried tales to him. The truth was that his office was "too inactive and insignificant" for his taste and he wished himself out of it.[11]

The charge that he had deserted his republican principles was false. His principles of government, he wrote Trumbull, were the same as they had been previously. He had from his first rough draft of a balanced government, written in 1776, held to that principle. The constitutions of New York and Massachusetts had incorporated such a system of balance, as had the federal constitution. "To that consistency and constancy," America was indebted for peace and orderly government. Without it she would probably have been involved in a civil war, and if his advice had been more closely followed the country would have avoided "her breaches of faith, her violations of property, her anarchy and her disorder." Sam Adams, Richard Henry Lee, Patrick Henry, and many others, adherents of the false notions of the author of *Common Sense*, were "so erroneous in their principles of government as to be now growing unpopular." But John Adams, independent of both right and left, remained "an eyesore" to both camps. Hence the attacks on his birth, his principles, and his presumed ambition.

Then his final vindication. He could not dissemble, could not "act a low cunning . . . a dirty craft . . . a vile hypocrisy. . . . John Adams has done services for North America of which no man is ignorant and which cannot be forgotten." If anyone was inclined to demean him it was his fellow New Englanders. Even the Southerners did him more justice.[12]

Trumbull replied that there were "very few persons" to whom he "would have written with equal freedom." It was true that he had heard slanders against Adams in his own region. "The people of New England," he wrote, "are true republicans and have the strongest feelings of personal independence and universal equality." When New Englanders had reluctantly raised someone to power, they wished to remind him constantly that he was there by virtue of their favor rather than his own merit. "We hate to see great men and endeavor to *belittle* them as much as possible," Trumbull noted. "The V.P. must therefore expect to find his merits and services deprecated among us, but may always be sure of our suffrages. We dislike an office of such high rank, but if there must be such a one, we are satisfied with the person who holds it. Indeed so strong are our ideas of republican equality that were the world peopled only by a certain party of New Englanders with their present feelings, they would be disgusted at the splendor of omnipotence and would wish to limit Almighty Power and establish a democracy in heaven." Since New Englanders all thought themselves as good as the next man, Trumbull remarked, "we have Presidents not out of their leading strings and Vice-Presidents by the dozen in embryo."[13]

That Adams brooded over his exchange of letters with Trumbull is suggested by a letter to his friend expressing the fear that his personal unpopularity might damage the government and suggesting that he had better resign. The proposal was made more in pique than in humility but Adams supported it by the semblance of an argument. He might, he pointed out, succeed to the presidency at any time if Washington died or, what was even less likely, the General might withdraw and Adams fall heir to the office. In such instances his lack of popular support might seriously weaken the government.

The suggestion alarmed Trumbull. Knowing, as Adams of course did, that New England had no one to push forward as a substitute and that the succession might thus fall to Jay, Madison, or Jefferson, Trumbull hastened to assure him that the New England Federalists were solidly behind him. Jefferson was little known in New England. Madison was well thought of but his persistent opposition to the funding plan had cost him much support; he had never, in any event, been seriously proposed for the office of Vice-President. Jay was indeed the only man who had the confidence of the Northern states, "but no party could be formed against you in his favor among us," Trumbull assured Adams. The government could not be in any way endangered by Adams' continuance in it, but the greatest confusion and uncertainty would arise from his resignation. The best antidote to his unpopularity would be to abandon his campaign for more forms and pageantry in the government. It was far better to have too little pageantry than too much. Then to soften the sting of his criticisms, Trumbull added, "I never had any other master in politics but yourself, and am too old to begin in a new school."[14] The letter smoothed the Vice-President's ruffled feathers. He made no more references to an intention to resign. He was notably more circumspect in the exercise of his duties as presiding officer of the Senate, and at least for the moment he had little to say on the subject of pageantry in government.

He continued, however, to be disturbed over the violence of partisan feelings stirred up by the coming elections to the Senate and House. He did not see how government could survive such recurrent shocks. Party and faction were bred by frequent elections. "The tendency of this to civil war is rapid," he wrote a friend, adding, "I confess . . . I can think of no remedy but another *convention*. When bribery, corruption, intrigue, maneuver, violence, force shall render elections too troublesome and too dangerous, another convention must be called, [which] may prolong the period of Senators from six years to twelve or twenty or thirty or forty or for life, or if necessary propose the establishment of hereditary Senators." This could be done by giving the states a number of Senators based on their size and population and by letting the states elect them or the President appoint them "to hold their places for life descendable to their eldest male heirs." If the election of the President should likewise become a scene of bloodshed and riot, Adams could conceive of "no other method to preserve liberty but to have a national convention called for the express purpose of electing an hereditary President." The House should be left as it was, an effective balance for the other branches.[15]

Taking up once more the question of the assumption of state debts, the House was soon bogged down in a prolix debate that retraced now familiar ground with growing acrimony. "The business before them is a Herculean labor," Abigail wrote Dr. Tufts. "The members of different states think so widely from each other that it is difficult to accommodate their interests to each other. What one member esteems the pillar, the bulwark of the constitution, another considers as the ruin of his state." One bright spot was the return to political sanity of Gerry, who performed great tasks on behalf of assumption. "The national debt is a subject of such vast weight and importance as requires the wisest heads and honestest hearts to adjust with any degree of satisfaction," she concluded.[16]

Politics made such inroads upon the Senate that even the death of Franklin became a partisan issue. Charles Carroll made a motion that the Senate should wear crepe a month in respect for the Pennsylvanian's memory. But he was at once opposed by Ellsworth, who placed himself at the head of the anti-Franklin group. Carroll, beset on all sides, withdrew his motion. Listening to the exchange, Adams was inspired to compose a "dialogue of the dead" between the shades of Charlemagne, Frederick the Great, Rousseau, and James Otis, a dialogue occasioned by the appearance of Franklin in the Elysian Fields.

"Have you seen Franklin since he passed over the river Styx?" Rousseau asked Otis, and Otis replied sharply that he had not and had little curiosity to see him. "The frivolity and foppery of science" had little charm for him. It was the realm of morality, of political man, "the policy and divinity of the universe, the intellectual and moral," he declared, that had ever been his concern.

"But had not Franklin a genius for morals?" Frederick the Great interjected.

"He told some very pretty moral tales from the head," Otis conceded, but they were shallow and without heart; they had never appealed to him.

Frederick readily agreed with Otis that Franklin was no politician. The Pennsylvanian's philosophy was primarily "hypothetical and conjectural." He had not thought it worth a reference in his history of the times. But to Otis, Frederick freely paid homage. He felt, he confessed, "small and humble" in Otis' presence. With all his great campaigns he had sown only war and devastation. If results were to be the measure of greatness, Frederick declared, Otis had a strong claim to be "the greatest statesman that ever lived." Boston, by the same token, had contributed more than imperial Rome or republican Rome and Harvard College more than "the school of Cujasius and all the doctors of the Sorbonne."

Charlemagne joined in Frederick's encomium but Otis waved the tributes aside. He had lived and acted in a critical moment of history. But he had simply been the instrument of Providence "to split a very hard knot." Rousseau, too, Otis said graciously, had played his part.

At this unexpected compliment, Rousseau protested that he had done little more than propagate the principles of Locke. It was Otis who had turned theory into action, who had initiated "a vast system of policy which has set the reason and the passions of men at work to promote [Rousseau's] principles."

Rousseau's mistake, Otis replied, was "never to have considered the history of the human heart or the history of the world."

Rousseau admitted his error. He had not given sufficient weight to human passions. But there was more to it than that, Otis insisted. Rousseau's most dangerous error was to reject a future state, "to deny or doubt the moral government of the world and the existence of an all-perfect intelligence." Palestine and Jerusalem, in Otis' view, deserved more honor than even Boston and Cambridge, for they had given the world the greatest teaching of all: "Thou shalt love the Supreme with all thy heart and thy neighbor as thyself." This was the "maxim of eternal philosophy . . . the sublime principle of right order and happiness in the universe."[17]

Dwelling themselves in heaven, Rousseau and Frederick could hardly deny its reality. Otis was right. They had, by their doctrines of skepticism, seriously misled mankind.

It was significant that the newly arrived Franklin never even got into the discussion occasioned by his death. He clearly did not belong in such distinguished company.

LX

THE SPRING of 1790 in New York was bitterly cold and damp. Abigail was brought low by her rheumatism and a raging fever. Richmond Hill was shrouded in snow and more like a hospital than a dwelling house. Its six fireplaces had to be fed constantly to keep the house even tolerably warm. Colonel Smith had a bilious attack, Charles a fever, the housekeeper St. Anthony's fire (a painful inflammation of the skin), and another servant the pleurisy. Even in sickness Abigail was plagued by servant problems. Polly Tailor drove away her subordinates with her autocratic, waspish ways; all the decently trained Negro servants were slaves whom Abigail was unwilling to hire from their masters; and most of the whites were recently arrived immigrants, without experience as domestics, usually stupid and lazy and invariably addicted to the bottle. Abigail wrote in desperation to Mary Cranch to send her on a reliable woman. She was willing to pay three dollars a month and give her the smallpox. She also sent for Briesler's sister, Betsy, and prepared to pack Polly off in the hope that she might thereby at last have some peace in the household. She would, in addition, take "any middle-aged woman of a reputable character who understands pastry."[1]

Only Adams escaped the general illness. The President was stricken by a severe attack of influenza and for two or three days his life was in danger. They were days of severe trial for Adams. The death of Washington would be a terrible disaster for the country. Abigail spoke for her husband as well as for herself when she wrote her sister of the President's ill-health: "It appears to me that the union of the states and consequently the permanency of the government depend under Providence upon his life. At this early day when neither our finances are arranged nor our government sufficiently cemented to promise duration, his death would, I fear, have had the most disastrous consequences." The enormous prestige of Washington held the country together. Adams knew very well that he had no such power. Were the President to die, his successor would in all likelihood simply preside over the disintegration of the Union.

Adams' apprehensions were felt by many others. When Maclay called by to get information about the President's condition, he found a room half filled with Senators, Congressmen, and friends of Washington; he observed tersely, "Every eye full of tears. His life is despaired of."[2] But the crisis passed, mercifully, and the President's powerful physique helped him throw off the effects of his illness in a few weeks.

When the Senate took up the question of the salary proper for an ambassador, Adams was requested to give his views. He did so at length, discussing the etiquette, the forms and ceremonies that a United States ambassador must conform to, and the expense involved, stating that three thousand pounds a year sterling was the minimum salary for such an office. The matter was referred to a committee of which, to Adams' chagrin, Maclay was a member. In committee Maclay, as he put it, "bore most pointed testimony against all this kind of gentry, ministers, ambassadors, chargé d'affaires, etc." He wished "no political connection whatever with any other country whatever." Commercial intercourse could be regulated by consuls who would take their pay in favors and thus cost the United States nothing.[3]

In the debate which followed the committee report Adams found Ellsworth advocating a reduction in the salary of ambassadors from nine thousand to six thousand dollars a year. Some of the ambassadors had been able to make out on the less sum, he declared. Adams jumped up to state that he did not believe any minister could subsist on such a meager sum. "He had kept the accounts with his own hand at Paris, and they amounted to about three thousand guineas yearly." He said a good deal in support of his plea for more generous pay for American diplomats; when he had finished, Ellsworth sprang the trap. Taking a small piece of paper out of his pocket, he offered it in evidence: it was an abstract of Adams' accounts while he was minister plenipotentiary in Paris and it showed that his expenses averaged six thousand dollars per annum.[4] The discussion seemed to Maclay to be often nothing but "snip-snap and contradiction." The South Carolinians, Butler and Izard, were almost invariably hotheaded and extreme—"illiberal" and "ungentlemanly," he called them. "Izard flamed and Butler bounced, and both seemed to rage with madness," Maclay noted.[5]

Contention over the location of the permanent seat of government reached a kind of apogee on June 8. The whole day was spent in excited charges and countercharges, maneuvers and countermaneuvers. Izard. and Butler went out and brought a bed for an ill member, William Johnson, to lie in and had him borne in on a litter to vote for a postponement of the question. The Potomac was proposed and defeated, and then in succession Baltimore and Wilmington. Adams struggled vainly to keep order, but grew so excited himself that he only added to the confusion.

Finally a vote to adjourn was carried and the uproar terminated with the issue unresolved.

When debate was resumed Morris informed Maclay that Hamilton had offered to support the permanent seat of Congress at Germantown or the falls of the Delaware in return for support from the Pennsylvanians for the assumption of the state debts. He needed one more vote in the Senate and five in the House. Morris agreed to confer with his colleagues. But Philadelphia must be the temporary capital. Before they could bargain further, word came from the Secretary of the Treasury that he could not think of negotiating about the temporary residence. That meant, Morris concluded at once, that Hamilton was now negotiating with the Maryland delegates for Baltimore as the capital in return for *their* support. After two more days of aimless discussion word came that Jefferson was prepared to support a compromise whereby Philadelphia would be the capital for fifteen years after which time the government would be shifted to Georgetown on the Potomac.

Soon after the circulation of this rumor the time of temporary residence—ten years—was voted on and passed. Next came the choice of Baltimore as the site—this lost. Then a motion by Butler to stay two years in New York—a thirteen to thirteen vote; Adams cast the deciding ballot against, sweetening it by "lavish praise" for the good people of New York. But the New Yorkers remained unreconciled. When a motion was made to designate Philadelphia as the temporary capital and build a permanent home on the Potomac for the new government, Adams' friend Rufus King "sobbed, wiped his eyes, scolded and railed and accused, first everybody and then nobody, of bargaining—contracting—arrangements and engagements that would dissolve the Union." Adams finally gaveled him to order. King begged the Senate's pardon and then resumed his tirade. Butler replied and "talk followed talk" until there were cries to adjourn, countered by calls for the question. It was called for and carried, fourteen to twelve. After another week of acrimonious debate, in the course of which the friends and enemies of the funding bill accused each other of destroying the Union, the Secretary's measure passed by the same vote, fourteen to twelve.

Adams was triumphant. It would be hard to leave the charming house at Richmond Hill, but it was a small price to pay for having at last established the finances of the country on a sound basis. It may well have been that speculators profited unduly from the assumption of state debts and payment of public certificates, but that was of very little moment against the larger considerations. It would have been the most egregious folly to leave the country to drag along in perpetual insolvency simply to frustrate the speculators. Better bills could doubtless have been drafted, but it was the conviction of those in and outside the government who were most knowledgeable in matters of finance that some such enactment was essential to the economic health of the country, to its credit and reputation at home and abroad.

Exhausted by the effort required to resolve its two most troublesome problems—the seat of the new government and assumption—Congress adjourned early in August. They would convene for their third session, despite Rufus King's lamentations, at Philadelphia.

Adams looked back on the session with mixed feelings. Much had been accomplished to be sure but at the cost of sharper divisions and more bitter feeling in both houses of Congress. What was most painful of all was the malice of former friends. Boston bubbled with Anti-Federalist venom and much of it was brewed by men whom Adams had considered his friends. James Sullivan had become one of the principal hatchet men of the Hancock faction. "Is Sullivan the . . . snake that lifts up his head and bites, then squirms about and sneaks into the grass?" Abigail asked John Quincy. Adams wrote to warn his son against the judge as "a savage . . . a false and faithless character," the author of "paltry scribbles," a man bent on treachery and deceit.[6]

The divisions of party and faction were also deepened, Adams observed, by the emotions engendered by the French Revolution. Many Americans insisted on making a false and misleading analogy between the principles of the French Revolution and those of the American. Such a superficial view could only cause trouble and confusion. With Congress adjourned and time on his hands, Adams began to write a series of essays, *Discourses on Davila,* which were published by the Federalist editor, John Fenno, in the *Pennsylvania Gazette.* Henrico Caterino Davila had been an Italian historian involved in the French civil wars of the sixteenth century. Adams' *Discourses* were in the form of an extended commentary on Davila's work. Large portions of the Italian's history were reprinted, interlarded with Adams' observations. The purpose of the *Discourses* was fourfold. Adams wished to make a comparison between the civil wars and the French Revolution, especially making the point that the French Revolution was doomed, like its predecessor, to end in disaster unless it was based on a balanced government. He wished by this lesson to remind Americans that the peace and security of their own nation depended upon maintaining or if necessary improving the balance that the framers of the federal constitution had established between the three branches of government and the two houses of the legislature. He hoped at the same time to refute the popular dogmas that men were on the one hand equal and, on the other, perfectible. Finally, he sought to justify his insistence on titles, forms, and formalities. To do this he began the *Discourses* with an analysis of the "springs of human action"— that is to say, of motivation.

At the heart of man's nature was the *"passion for distinction . . . a* desire to be observed, considered, esteemed, praised, beloved, and admired by his fellows." This was the most basic need, "the keenest disposition" of the heart. It was evident in every level of society: "Wherever men, women, or children are to be found, whether they be old or young, rich or poor, high or low, wise or foolish, ignorant or learned, every individual is seen to be strongly actuated by a desire to be seen, heard, talked of, approved of, and respected by the people about him and within his knowledge." What Adams was speaking of was the desire for status and acceptance, a quality "that lies at the foundation of our whole moral system in this world, and may be connected essentially with our destination in a future state." This was the motive behind the acquisition of wealth. "The poor man's conscience is clear; yet he is ashamed. His character is irreproachable; yet he is neglected and despised. He feels himself out of the sight of others, groping in the dark. Mankind takes no notice of him." And this was unendurable. He must have some who valued and esteemed him, some point on which he stood superior, at least in his own eyes, to his fellows. The need extended not only to "the poorest mechanic, but [to] the man who lives upon common charity, nay, the common beggars in the streets," the lowest orders of society. To support his argument Adams repeated a story of terrible poignance, the story of the starving man who fed the scraps of food he had to his dog and, when he was asked why he did not kill or sell the animal, replied, "Who will love me then?" "There," he wrote, "is a key to the human heart, to the history of human life and manners, and to the rise and fall of empires. To feel ourselves unheeded chills the most pleasing hope, damps the most fond desire, checks the most agreeable wish, disappoints the most ardent expectations of human nature." It was true that "a sense of duty, a love of truth, a desire to alleviate the anxieties of ignorance may, no doubt, have an influence on some minds. But the universal object and idol of men of letters is *reputation*. . . . In a city or a village little employments and trifling distinctions," he argued, "are contended for with equal eagerness as honors and offices in commonwealths and kingdoms." In short, "avarice and ambition, vanity and pride, jealousy and envy, hatred and revenge, as well as the love of knowledge and desire of fame, are very often nothing more than various modifications of that desire of the attention, consideration, and congratulations of our fellow men which is the great spring of social activity." All men compared themselves with others and from such comparisons, from the desire to excel and to achieve superiority, came most of the great advances of the race. Thus Nature could say, "I have given you reason, conscience, and benevolence; and thereby made you accountable for your actions and capable of virtue, in which you will find your highest felicity." But Nature was not willing to let it go at that; she had also added "a passion for the notice and regard of . . . fellow mortals." It was the proper role of human arrangements to regulate this passion, not to eradicate it. It was "of the highest importance to education, to life, and to society, not only that they should not be destroyed, but that they should be gratified and encouraged, and arranged on the side of virtue."

Another basic need was to find a vicarious satisfaction in the eminence of one great figure whose splendor offered compensation to the mass of people for the simplicity and bareness of their own lives. Thus in monarchies the throne was surrounded by pageantry, by opulence and symbols of wealth and power. In a republican government these instinctive feelings would focus on a president, but if he was challenged by another political leader the country would split into bitter factions, each with its own rival hero. This would bring on the most dangerous divisions. "Where there are rivals for the first place," he wrote, "the national attention and passions are divided and thwart each other; the collision enkindles fires; the conflicting passions interest all ranks; they produce slanders and libels first, mobs and seditions next, and civil war with all her hissing snakes, burning torches, and haggard horrors at last."

As applied to France, the lesson was clear. If the National Assembly tried to impose an arbitrary equality upon all the citizens of the country it would open a Pandora's box of anarchy and sedition; it would be attempting to choke off one of the most basic human instincts and the result could not help but be catastrophic.

The heralds of the new age had proclaimed the new doctrines: "The world grows more enlightened; knowledge is more equally diffused. Newspapers, magazines, and circulating libraries have made mankind wiser. Titles and distinctions, ranks and order, parade and ceremony, are all going out of fashion." There was truth in such a statement, certainly. If attention was given "to the reformation of abuses, the rectification of errors, and the dissipation of pernicious prejudices," much could be gained. But it was also possible that from these new developments, seemingly so full of promise, false conclusions could be drawn which might in time, as their perverted logic was unraveled, "make mankind wish for the age of dragons, giants, and fairies. If all decorum, discipline, and subordination are to be destroyed, and universal Pyrrhonism, anarchy, and insecurity of property are to be introduced, nations will soon wish their books in ashes, seek for darkness and ignorance, superstition and fanaticism, as blessings and follow the standard of the first mad despot who, with the enthusiasm of another Mahomet, will endeavor to obtain them."

It was important to point out to the apostles of the new age that education and the diffusion of knowledge would not alone bring in the millennium. The progress of science, arts, and letters had not as yet visibly diminished the passions of the human heart. If one doubted it he need only go to the citadels of learning and enlightenment. Was there now less desperate contention than formerly in the Royal Society of London for the chair of Sir Isaac Newton, or than there was for the post of honor in a village agricultural society? How do you, he asked his readers, find the learned men of Paris—"united, friendly, harmonious, meek, humble, modest, charitable? prompt to mutual forbearance? unassuming? ready to acknowledge superior merit? zealous to encourage the first symptoms of genius? Ask Voltaire and Rousseau, Marmontel and De Mably." The fact was that "bad men increase in knowledge as fast as good men; and science, arts, taste, sense, and letters are employed for the purposes of injustice and tyranny as well as those of law and liberty; for corruption as well as virtue."

The power to do good was, conversely, the power to do evil as well. On this rock the ship piloted by the enthusiastic champions of enlightenment must surely flounder if they did not alter their course and reform their principles of navigation. Adams directed his exhortations to all Frenchmen. "Act and think like yourselves!" he exhorted. "Confessing human nature, be magnanimous and wise. Acknowledging and boasting yourselves to be men, avow the feelings of men. The affectation of being exempted from human passions is inhuman. The grave pretension to such singularity is solemn hypocrisy. Both are unworthy of your frank and generous natures. Consider that government is intended to set bounds to passions which nature has not limited."

The world truly was in turmoil. Honor, faith, and loyalty were denounced as superstition, prejudice, and servility. "What is loose," the prophets of the new order declared, "must be shaken; whatever is corrupted must be lopped away; whatever is not built on the broad basis of public utility must be thrown to the ground. Obscure murmurs gather and swell into a tempest; the spirit of inquiry, like a severe and searching wind, penetrates every part of the great body politic; and whatever is unsound, whatever is infirm, shrinks at the visitation. Liberty, led by philosophy, diffuses her blessings to every class of men, and even extends a smile of hope and promise to the poor African, the victim of hard, impenetrable avarice. Man as man becomes an object of respect. . . . What some centuries ago it was daring to think and dangerous to express is now realized and carried into effect." Men's dreams and visions were about to be given the forms of reality. All well and good. No one more than Adams would exult in the coming of a new day. But there were, unfortunately, certain old truths which must be respected if tragedy rather than success was not to be the eventual outcome. Americans and Frenchmen would do well to remember, for instance, that "the perfectibility of man is only human and terrestrial perfectibility. Cold will still freeze, and fire will never cease to burn; disease and vice will continue to disorder, and death to terrify mankind." These were the hard facts of the human condition. Whatever was done, if it was to be true and enduring, it must be based upon such facts. Otherwise there was a strong possibility that "the government of nations may fall into the hands of men who teach the most disconsolate of all creeds, that men are but fireflies" and that there is no Father in heaven. "Is this the way to make man as man an object of respect? Or is it to make murder itself as indifferent as shooting a plover? . . . If such a case should happen, would not . . . the most credulous of all believers [in the new faith of man] have reason to pray to his eternal nature or his almighty chance . . . *give us again the gods of the Greeks; give us again the more intelligible as well as more comfortable systems of Athanasius and Calvin; nay, give us again our popes and hierarchies, Benedictines and Jesuits, with all their superstition and fanaticism, impostures and tyranny?*"

Instead of spreading cant about equality or quoting Machiavelli's illiberal strictures against illustrious families, Americans would do much better to face squarely the inevitable inequalities in society and turn them to good account in fashioning a stable, orderly government of free men. Sometimes the well to do had "propagated an opinion that God hates the poor and that poverty and misery on earth are inflicted by Providence in its wrath and displeasure." Such a doctrine, Adams wrote, "is surely as shallow and as execrable" as Machiavelli's and should be as promptly discarded "as a reproach to human understanding and a disgrace to human nature. Let the rich and the poor," he wrote, "unite in the hands of mutual affection, be mutually sensible of each other's ignorance, weakness, and error," and try to support a government which would insure justice for both. People had said that it was extremely difficult to preserve a balance in government, but this was "no more than to say that it is extremely difficult to preserve liberty." History bore abundant testimony to this fact. One island (England) and one continent (America) were the only places on earth where true liberty reigned. Only the intelligence and virtue of the people themselves could preserve it in America or in England. "A balance, with all its difficulty, must be preserved or liberty is lost forever."

Adams had more to say on the subject, but he had misjudged his audience. His compatriots were not ready to be lectured to. The articles as they appeared in Fenno's *Gazette* stirred up a storm. The idols of the day were "equality" and the French Revolution. Adams had undertaken to attack both, and thereby make himself fair game for the Anti-Federal editors. He was at once roundly denounced as an enemy to the rights of man and the dearest principles of liberty, as a monarchist, an opponent of republican government, a champion of aristocratic mummery and show. The Revolutionary statesman, so the arguments ran, had been converted into a reactionary politician by his long sojourn among European kings and nobles. Indeed, Fenno found himself under such heavy assault that he decided to stop publication of the *Discourses*. He notified the Vice-President and Adams brought the essays to an abrupt terminarion. For an active politician to undertake an exploration of a complex subject on which the public entertains strong if misguided notions is a perilous venture at best. Adams had done little more than deliver into the hands of his enemies an inexhaustible armory of weapons to be used against him. There were problems enough in practical politics without getting involved in theoretical wrangles over the nature of man.

Adams was dismayed at the furor that the *Discourses* aroused. He had spoken nothing, he protested, but such truths as were revealed in Scripture. The whole experience activated his paranoia once again. Brooding about his countrymen's lack of appreciation for his services, he broke out indignantly to Rush: "The history of our Revolution will be one continued lie from one end to the other. The essence of the whole will be *that Dr. Franklin's electrical rod smote the earth and out sprung General Washington. That Franklin electrized him with his rod—and henceforward these two conducted all the policy, negotiation, legislation and war.* These lines contain the whole fable, plot, and catastrophe. If this letter should be preserved and read a hundred years hence, the reader will say, 'The envy of . . . JA could not bear to think of the truth.' He ventured to scribble to Rush, as envious as himself, blasphemy that he dared not speak when he lived." But nations must adore someone and they could adore only one man at a time. It was thus fortunate that Americans adored a Washington, a man of "virtue so exquisite and wisdom so consummate." The presidency should not be thought of as a prize awarded by historical justice to the individual who had made the greatest sacrifices or endured the greatest hardships. What must be first consulted was the well-being of the nation. Here Washington was clearly the man.

LXI

J OHN QUINCY, struggling to get a start as a lawyer, found the going very hard indeed. He had enough of his father's temperament to suffer periods of profound, almost morbid discouragement. But he could not resist teasing his mother. Abigail had thought a little wistfully of Nancy Quincy's comfortable fortune. Life was so difficult for a young lawyer that a well-dowered bride, heir to a small fortune, could be an enormous asset. Thinking so, she had been indiscreet enough to let her plot show. John Quincy had seen at once through her transparently casual reflections about Nancy's accomplishments. But the girl had frustrated her schemes by marrying Mr. Packard; "thus," John Quincy wrote, "you will perceive your *darling* project for the advancement of your son blasted even before the bud." It was just as well, for he had no intention of being "indebted to his wife for his property." Abigail denied the charge. She had loved Nancy for her "native good humor and honesty of heart" but had never really projected such a match.[1]

Adams had his son much on his mind. He recalled the early days of his own career as a lawyer, "the mortification, humiliation, and ennui," the "want of business for days, weeks, months, if not years together." Boston was divided into political parties and factions. John Quincy might be made much of if he would join either party, but his father advised him to "admire neither party—despise neither party. Treat both sides with civility and respect but be the devotee of neither. Be always on the side of truth, justice, honor, virtue, and public spirit."

He should also keep up his classical studies, especially his Latin. They would improve his mind and keep him from brooding about his lack of legal business. He should begin with Livy. "Take your book, your dictionary, your grammar, your sheet of paper, and pen and ink," Adams wrote. "Begin at the beginning and read the work through—put down in writing every word with its meaning. . . . You will find it the most delightful employment you ever engaged in. When you have finished the 35th book you will say that you have learned more wisdom from it than from five

hundred volumes of the trash that is commonly read." When he had
finished Livy, he should go through Cicero in the same way, and then
Polybius, Plutarch, and Sallust, "sources of wisdom as well as Roman history." Above all, Adams concluded, "keep up your spirits and take care
of your health."[2]

John Quincy's first case was against Harrison Gray Otis, a few years
his senior and already an outstanding member of the Boston legal fraternity. He had botched it terribly, and was ready to abandon the law
forthwith and go to digging ditches. But his father offered him consolation. Not only had he made a sorry mess of his first case, many years
ago, but so had the greatest lawyer of them all—Cicero. He sent along
the story of Reynard the Fox and reminded John Quincy that La Fon-
taine's fables went very well with juries to make a legal point. As for his
painful embarrassment before the jury and courtroom, that, too, was
understandable and in fact proper. "The audience," he observed, "have a
right to be respected and venerated." To have too casual and offhand a
manner, to be too relaxed and free was apt to be the mark of a vain and
vulgar man.[3]

Adams' letters to John Quincy were full of affection: "God preserve
and keep you, my dear son," he wrote. "Preserve, my son, at every risk
and every loss, even to extreme poverty and obscurity, your honor and
integrity, your generosity and benevolence, your enlarged views and
liberal philanthropy. Candor and honor are of more importance in your
profession even than eloquence, learning, or genius. You will be miserable
without them whatever might be your success."[4]

John Quincy was a boarder in the household of Dr. Thomas Welsh,
a leading Boston physician and the husband of Abigail's first cousin.
Adams wrote Welsh that unless a father's partiality had deceived him
"John is as great a scholar as this country has produced at his age." He
was, he declared, glad that his son had not been successful at first. This
would encourage him to read and study so that when business finally
came his way he would be properly educated in the broadest reaches of
law and politics. "Whether his reputation spreads this year, or two or
three years hence," he declared, "is indifferent to me, provided his anxiety
does not injure his health." He had in his day seen "too many flashing
insects . . . glitter and glare for a moment and then disappear."[5]

Nabby's situation was much on Abigail's mind. The Colonel, affable
as he was, showed more and more clearly that he was not too well equipped
to deal with the colder realities of life. He could sire children certainly—three in a little more than four years—but he could find no job
better than that of a county marshal, whose pay would but "poorly feed
a family." The Smiths had moved from Richmond Hill to a small, hot
house where Nabby spent the last months of her third confinement.

Abigail's sister, Eliza Shaw, only a few years younger than Abigail, produced a nine-pound baby girl in March and named the baby Abigail Adams Shaw. "If some good angel would permit me to look into futurity," she wrote, "and I could behold my daughter like my sister, virtuous and good, adorning every station she may be called to," she would be supremely happy.[6]

Besides superintending the household, Abigail spent much of her time reading and writing letters. If she could not oversee the Adams farms in person, she must do so through a stream of instructions directed to the patient Dr. Tufts. Writing as much as she did, she was attracted by Noah Webster's new simplified "Americanized" system of spelling. Webster discarded any number of superfluous letters—the u's in "labour," "honour," and "candour," for example—and recommended that "thought" be spelled "thot," through "thru," and so on. To Abigail, an indifferent speller at best, the new system had a strong practical appeal.

Life at Richmond Hill was enlivened by the arrival of Thomas Boylston, recently graduated from Harvard. Tom's cheerfulness and high spirits were a tonic to his parents. After long discussions it was decided to apprentice him to a Philadelphia lawyer when the family moved to that city for the next session of Congress. Tom was a delighted spectator when his mother entertained a number of Creek Indians who had come to powwow and sign a treaty with the Great White Father. The savages in all their finery were lodged at a nearby inn and they made frequent visits to Richmond Hill where Abigail received them like royalty. They seemed as delighted as children with the tea and cakes she served, and their hostess in turn was charmed by her guests. With their impassive faces, their straight muscular bodies and simple dignity, they compared most favorably with some specimens of European royalty, she reflected. They had an odor redolent of the woods, a rank animal smell, disturbingly pungent. The Indians were accompanied by the great half-breed Creek chieftain, McGillvery, a "graceful and solid, intelligent" man who dressed like a white man and spoke perfect English.[7] Abigail invited the Creek king, Mico Maco, to dinner and after he had eaten in a very slow and grave manner he gave her an Indian name. Taking her hand, he bowed his head and kneeled, saying, "Mammea, Mammea," as nearly as she could make out.

When the treaty had been signed and the accompanying gifts distributed, the Indians built a great bonfire near the inn and spent most of the night "dancing around it like so many spirits, whooping, singing, yelling, and expressing their satisfaction in true savage style." The Adams family and servants, collected at the windows, watched with fascination.

On the first of September, Abigail saw Martha Washington off for Mount Vernon with a pang of regret. "We have lived in habits of intimacy and friendship," she wrote Mary Cranch. When it came time for the parting Martha put her arms around Abigail affectionately and said, "God bless you, my dear madam, we shall meet again at Philadelphia." Both ladies were close to tears as the barge carrying the President's party to the Jersey shore pulled away from the pier and out into the river.[8]

At the end of the summer Adams traveled to the "beloved city" of Philadelphia to find quarters for the family. It was more than a house-hunting expedition—it was a kind of pilgrimage. John visited Liberty Hall and saw Rush and others of his old Philadelphia friends and, sentimental man that he was, he was overcome by his emotions. Here not long ago he and his fellow patriots had moved the fulcrum that had set the world in revolutionary motion. In the gracious brick building of the old State House a few dozen men had, like heroes of ancient times, shifted the course of history and, like David and his four hundred, raised up a great nation. He was moved to write a nostalgic letter to Samuel Adams that contained a hint of the danger of his friend's political heresies. "What, my old friend, is this world about to become?" he asked. "Is the millennium commencing? . . . Your Boston town meetings and our Harvard College have set the universe in motion. Everything will be pulled down. So much seems certain. But what will be built up? Are there any principles of political architecture? What are they? Were Voltaire and Rousseau masters of them? Are their disciples acquainted with them? Locke taught them principles of liberty; but I doubt very much whether they have not yet to learn the principles of government."[9]

It particularly distressed John to see his cousin in the ranks of the disaffected. He resolved to make one last effort to recall him to good principles. Samuel, as Adams pointed out to him, placed extravagant hopes "in the universal or at least general prevalence of knowledge and benevolence. . . . . I agree with you," he wrote, "that knowledge and benevolence ought to be promoted as much as possible, but despair of ever seeing them sufficiently general for the security of society. I am for seeking institutions which may supply in some degree the defects. If there were no ignorance, error, or vice," he continued, "there would be neither principles nor systems of civil or political government." He agreed entirely with his cousin "that all good government is and must be republican." The trouble was that there was no word that was more vaguely or inaccurately used. Whenever he used it he meant a government "in which the people have collectively or by representation an essential share in the sovereignty." But Samuel Adams took him up on this point. Where Adams said "share," his cousin replied, "is not the *whole* sovereignty . . . essentially in the people?" By "the people" John meant the mass of the people. The natural aristocracy of talent and ability had its own special interest to defend, and the executive power mediated between the two. The majority of men in all ages had preferred "ease, slumber, and good cheer to liberty when they have been in competition." It was therefore useless "to depend alone upon the love of liberty in the soul of man for its preservation. Some political institutions must be prepared to assist this love against its enemies."

The only protection against the aristocratical spirit was "to put these families into a hole by themselves and set two watches upon them: a superior to them all on one side [the chief executives], and the people on the other [in a popular branch of the legislature]." He warned his friend, finally, against selfish and ambitious men in his own state who devoted their talents to exciting "a party spirit and a mobbish spirit, instead of a spirit of liberty," and who in doing so threatened to bring on another Wat Tyler's rebellion. They used violent and bitter language and attacked those with whom they disagreed in scurrilous terms. They made "wellborn" into an epithet full of jealousy and malice which they hurled at their enemies. Actually there was not more "family pride on one side than of vulgar malignity and popular envy on the other. . . . Let us do justice to the people and to the nobles," Adams concluded; "for nobles there are, as I have before proved, in Boston as well as in Madrid."

Adams yearned for "sweet communion" with his old friend. "I do not believe," he wrote, "that we who have preserved for more than thirty years an uninterrupted friendship, and have so long thought and acted harmoniously together in the worst of times, are now so far asunder in sentiment as some people pretend."[10]

When John returned from Philadelphia, Abigail began once more the weary task of preparing to move, supervising the crating and packing of clothes and furniture. "I feel low-spirited and heartless," she wrote her sister Mary. She was going "among a new set of company, to form new acquaintances, to make and receive a hundred ceremonious visits," and endure the endless round of official social life. Bitterest of all, she must leave Nabby and the children. Her health was bad, rheumatism gnawed at her joints, and she dreaded the jolting coach trip to Philadelphia. Charles would board with Nabby and the Colonel, who could use the money, and continue his law studies in New York; Thomas was to come with them to Philadelphia to serve his apprenticeship as a lawyer.[11]

When they were all packed and ready to set off for Philadelphia, Abigail came down with a fever. After the first violent seizure she took an emetic which relieved her a little, but the next day she had another "shaking fit" followed by a high temperature which made her delirious and for five days and nights she was racked by intermitting fevers which deprived her of sleep and left her too exhausted to move. Her condition was certainly not improved by her doctor, who gave her repeated emetics, James' powders, and then the bark. Nabby nursed her mother until she was able to be up and around. Abigail, once she could get out to take the air, made a surprisingly rapid recovery. But it was early November before

John and Abigail were able to set out for Philadelphia, taking with them Nabby's second child, John Adams Smith, a bright, engaging infant who prattled in his lisping way about the "fosses" who drew the coach, about his brother William, and his "other pappa," the Colonel.

Bush Hill was a handsome house about two miles from the city, standing on an elevation which gave a fine view of the Schuylkill River, but Abigail was not readily reconciled; she had left the "grand and sublime" at Richmond Hill, and the Schuylkill was no more to be compared with the Hudson than she with Hercules. Although the British troops had cut down most of the trees on the place there was a fine pine grove in the rear of the house and a wide expanse of lawn before it on which a shepherd, to the delight of little Johnny, grazed a herd of sheep. The Adamses arrived at the house just as Briesler with several handy men was carrying in the furniture, which had been shipped by boat. The painters were painting the walls a soft green and the paint was still wet. There was no wood in the house to make fires and they had no choice but to go to the City Tavern for the night.

The next morning Abigail took command of a scene of confusion and disorder. Boxes, barrels, chairs, tables, and trunks were scattered about. The first thing was to heat the house, which was damp as a tomb, the next to get up the beds. By nightfall the furniture was moved in and at least tentatively arranged. The next day, Sunday, Thomas came down with a severe attack of rheumatism. On Monday, Louisa became ill and Abigail gave her an emetic. On Tuesday, Esther Briesler was brought down by a sharp pain in her stomach and, on Thursday, Polly was "seized" with a violent "pleuritic fever." Although she was bled twice and blistered, she continued very poorly (indeed it is a wonder the treatment did not kill her at once). In addition to a houseful of affliction, every day between eleven in the morning and three in the afternoon a procession of visitors arrived to pay their respects to the Vice-President and his lady. Abigail was driven out of her wits. Besides running what was in effect a hospital she must appear the gracious hostess to dozens of callers who sat themselves down in rooms where the paint on the walls was not yet entirely dry. Only snow and sleet, by keeping the visitors at home, gave her some respite. She was glad to see among many strangers Mrs. Bingham, whose company she had enjoyed in Paris and London, "more amiable and beautiful than ever."[12]

Adams, like most men under similar circumstances, felt useless and neglected. There was nothing he could do but suffer, with as much fortitude as possible, the discomforts and inconveniences that came from living in a makeshift hospital. He was distressed over Tommy's prolonged and painful illness and Abigail's exhausting regimen. She lost weight, which, as she confessed, she could well afford, but she looked drawn and wan and John, who knew how delicate her health was, how frequent her headaches and sleepless nights, was full of apprehension.[13]

To add to their worries they got word that Colonel Smith had sailed for England on some business venture, leaving Nabby to shift for herself. Charles, summoned from New York, arrived early in December and was a patient and attentive nurse for his brother and a comfort to his mother.

Abigail continued to be plagued by the problem of finding a decent cook. Cooks, she had discovered, were in general "a vile low tribe." She had had seven in eighteen months and there had been "in the whole number not a virtuous woman . . . most of them drunkards." Shortly after her arrival at Bush Hill she employed one from Philadelphia who came to her well recommended and appeared to be "very capable of her business"; but three days after she had taken over her duties she "got so drunk that she was carried to bed, and so indecent that footman, coachman, and all were driven out of the house."[14]

John Quincy came down from Boston to visit for the holidays. Of the children, only Nabby was absent, but it was hardly a joyful Christmas. Thomas was still too weak to do much more than sit and read or move slowly about the house. John Quincy was thin and strained and gloomy. His painfully slow progress in his profession depressed him and made him poor company. Even the ebullient Charles seemed subdued and ill at ease. Still it was a comfort to their parents to have them together once more. Abigail fussed over them and stuffed them with good food and their father gave them a vast amount of good advice and reassurance. Life was difficult at best, full of defeats and frustration; success was a fickle and elusive goddess; hardships and disappointments helped to form character; and much more.

Abigail, though she missed her New York friends and above all Nabby and little William, found compensations in Philadelphia. Ann Bingham's aunt, Mrs. Samuel Powel, "friendly, affable . . . sprightly, full of conversation," became a close friend, and Mrs. John Allen with her three beautiful daughters—"the three Graces"—was a frequent visitor to Bush Hill. Abigail and Martha Washington renewed the friendship they had started in New York and found much pleasure in each other's company. The President himself, with the finances of the country provided for and the new Congress substantially Federal, was more genial and relaxed than he had been during the first two sessions. At a dinner at the Washingtons' residence late in February, Abigail noted that he was "more than usually social." He asked affectionately after Nabby and the children and picked some sugar plums from a cake on the dining-room table for Abigail to take home to young Johnny.

While John went dutifully to his drudgery in the Senate, Abigail supervised the household, sending Briesler off to Market Street to shop for the day's food; directing and admonishing the latest cook with a kind of temperate hopefulness, knowing in her heart that in all likelihood she would have to be packed off shortly, drunk and shrieking obscenities; and waiting on Esther Briesler, who was more of a charge than a help with her succession of sicknesses and complaints. But she found time to play with Johnny, to train and instruct him. Isaac Watts' *Moral Songs for Children* were especially suited to inculcate just moral sentiments in the young. They taught "brotherly love, sisterly affection, and filial respect and reverence" and were consequently far superior to "Jack and Jill" and "little Jack Horner" which Johnny lisped out so engagingly. The fact was the infant ruled the household. After dinner every evening he played the tyrant with his grandfather and commanded Adams as his "foss" to drag him about the living room on a chair, "which is generally done," Abigail wrote Nabby, "for half an hour, to the derangement of my carpet and the amusement of his grandpapa."

Yet there was an odd precocity and a streak of the perverse in the child that troubled his grandmother. Though he was obedient and well behaved, he came out from time to time with little phrases and gestures which Abigail feared he must have acquired from the servants, or more particularly from the cooks.[15]

As her patients' health improved, Abigail went more about. Indeed, she wrote Nabby, she would spend "a very dissipated winter" if she accepted half the invitations she received, especially those to teas and card parties. She went to one of the famous Philadelphia dancing assemblies with John, the President and his lady, and the Cabinet officers. The dancing was excellent, but she was critical of the general tone, the etiquette, and the decorations of the room. The ban on the theater had recently been lifted and the actors came to inform John and Abigail that a box had been reserved for them whenever they wished to go. Adams replied that they would attend when the President did. This, since Washington loved the theater, turned out to be very soon. A few days later the two families went in a party to see *The School for Scandal*, "upon the whole . . . very well performed."[16]

Adams, without real scope for his abilities, fell into the way of thinking of himself as an old man whose friends and enemies were dying off at an alarming rate. "My generation," he wrote a friend, "is going off the stage and another rushing on with its opinions, moral, metaphysical, political, and civil, which I comprehend not." Things were undergoing such a revolution in Europe that another century might see governments there "which were not only opposed to Christianity but to any form of religious expression." Another age, incredible as it might seem, could once again see Christians martyred for their faith, if the logic contained in the French Revolution was carried to its conclusion.[17]

Congress convened for its third session on the sixth of December. In the Senate there were two new faces—Philemon Dickinson replacing William Patterson, who had resigned to be Governor of New Jersey, and James Monroe of Virginia, who appeared to take the place of William Grayson.

Congress sat in the courthouse at the corner of Chestnut and Sixth streets, the House of Representatives on the first floor, and the Senate on the second. Due in large measure to Adams' insistence on decent and orderly procedure, the latter body proceeded with far more decorum than its sister branch downstairs. Adams, the apostle of pageantry, sat in a "very plain chair" behind a small mahogany table with a green silk skirt. If a Senator whispered while another was talking, Adams would rap sharply with his silver pencil case on the table to call the member to order. An informal atmosphere prevailed below where the Representatives wore their hats, read the newspapers during debates, or whispered to the neighbors.

President Washington, two days after Congress convened, delivered his address to a joint session of both houses. He "read his speech well enough, or at least tolerably," Maclay noted, but in such a low voice that after he had left the chamber Adams read it again to be sure that the members of both houses had heard and understood it.

The next day, during a recess in the Senate's deliberations, as a half dozen Senators were warming themselves at the big fireplace at the end of the room, the talk turned to the French Revolution. Maclay could not resist the opportunity to tease Adams. The National Assembly, he declared, "had attacked royalty, nobility, hierarchy, and the Bastille, all together, and seemed likely to demolish the whole." Adams rose at once to the bait. It was impossible to destroy nobility, he said, his face flushed and earnest, it was founded in nature. History was full of examples of efforts to destroy this or that aristocratic group, only to have them reappear in another guise. The discussion grew quite warm until Maclay interjected to ask whether the solution to the problem of aristocracy might not be to follow the Indian practice of matriarchial ranking. Smiles and laughter relieved the tension and the Senators drifted back to their seats; but, Maclay noted, "Adams . . . either never was cured, or is relapsed into his nobilimania."

The next day, ironically enough, the Senate received from the French National Assembly a packet of eulogiums delivered by members of that body upon the death of Benjamin Franklin. It fell to Adams, as presiding officer, to read these Gallic effusions to the Senators. He did it with rather poor grace; he could not forbear to call the members' attention to the long list of titles appended to Franklin's name. It was odd to see such a display of honorary doctorates, etc., by a people who professed to have abolished titles, he said in a voice heavy with sarcasm. Having read through the material with what seemed to Maclay at least "coldness and apathy," he announced that he would send it on to the House of Representatives for their perusal. Although the National Assembly was full of fraternal feelings for Congress, Maclay noted, "we, cold as clay, care not a fig about them, Franklin, or freedom."

In contrast to the first two sessions, affairs in Congress went on with a happy absence of partisan feeling. North Carolina and Virginia discovered a tendency to be contentious, Abigail noted in a letter to Nabby, adding, "but, after all, the bluster will scarcely produce a mouse."[18] The Senate, having approved a national bank for twenty years on Hamilton's plan, turned its attention to the protest of the National Assembly over the failure of Congress to give preferential treatment to the ships and goods of France. The Senate seemed determined to make no discrimination in favor of any nation, and the friends of France were convinced that its purpose was to alienate that country and return America "to the fish (or flesh) pots of British dependence."[19]

Jefferson urged war upon the Barbary pirates and the President called for soldiers to protect the frontier. All this increased the anxiety of the Anti-Federalists. From the beginning they had feared that the national government would add bit by bit to its powers until freedom was extinguished. The talk of an army and a navy confirmed their fears. "It seems," Maclay broke out bitterly, "we must soon forgo our republican innocence and, like all other nations, set apart a portion of our citizens for the purpose of inflicting misery on our fellow mortals." Equally serious was the fact that for every man so "set off" some woman remained unmatched and heaven alone knew how many children failed, in consequence, to be born. The money spent for armies and navies led inevitably to war and suffering; it would be far better to use it to alleviate the suffering of mankind, in Maclay's view.[20]

Adams, practicing the restraint that his friend Trumbull had urged upon him, felt his office more irksome than ever. It was, he wrote Trumbull, "though laborious . . . wholly insignificant" and he was "so stupidly pinched and betrayed" by his fellow New Englanders that he wished himself back at the bar, old as he was. "My own situation is almost the only one in the world," he wrote, "in which firmness and patience are useless."[21] But at the same time he was greatly encouraged at the general progress of government. Congress, he wrote William Tudor, had done more in two years than he had dared to hope, "and in two years more if I can keep my machine going so long," he continued, "I may see it so established as to receive my quietus with comfort."[22]

On the twelfth of February an excise bill was passed and Maclay wrote in his journal, "Our government cannot stand." This, in the opinion of the Anti-Federalists, was the most oppressive measure of all. The long arm of the federal government, by the provisions of the bill, would reach into every town and village, every remote farm, to exact an unjust and burdensome tax on, among other things, the distilling of whiskey, which was both the poor man's beverage and his medium of exchange. A host of revenue officers, like the hated minions of the English King, would scour the land and pluck up the last vestige of freedom. "War and bloodshed" would be the consequence. Hamilton had made Congress his tool and by schemes and intrigues was carrying everything before him. So thought the Anti-Federalists.

As the end of the session approached both Senate and House were scenes of confusion. A dozen bills made their appearance at the eleventh hour. "What with the exits and the entrances of our Otis [Secretary of the Senate], the drawings and withdrawings of Beckley and Lear, [Clerk of the House and Secretary to the President], etc., and the consequent running of doorkeepers, opening and slamming of doors, the House seemed in a continual hurricane," Maclay noted. So much unfinished business remained that the Senate had to meet in night session by candlelight to conclude its deliberations. It went into joint session with the House and amid the noise and disorder Maclay found his efforts to speak up for the French treaty "was like letting off a popgun in a thunderstorm."[23] Adams tried repeatedly to gavel the chamber to order, but it was fitfully maintained. Bills were proposed and voted upon that half the Senators and Representatives had not read, let alone deliberated on.

The winter had been severe and the spring was unpredictable. In the middle of March the temperature soared to eighty degrees and Abigail threw open all the windows in the house and ate ice to keep cool. The following day it snowed and there was a bitter northwest wind.

As soon as Congress adjourned and the weather permitted, John and Abigail made plans to leave for Braintree. Charles had returned to his law studies in New York and John Quincy to Boston, but Thomas was still pale and weak and Abigail was determined to carry him home and nurse him back to good health. She wrote to Mary Cranch asking her to round up some odds and ends of furniture for the house, to get Pratt to make two kitchen tables and a collapsible bed, to buy a dozen yards of tow cloth and some kitchen utensils, a milk pan, broom, brush, teakettle, chafing dish, flatirons, skillets, and pots. She wished the house cleaned and aired, the oilcloth put down on the floors, and Phebe and George, the Negro couple, employed to cook and tend the yard.[24]

Early in July, leaving Bush Hill in care of Briesler and his family, John and Abigail set out for Braintree with their unwieldy entourage. "A very clever black boy of fifteen" indentured to the age of twenty-one, the coachman, Thomas, young Johnny, and Louisa Smith made up the company. Providing beds in the almost empty house for such a number was no small undertaking. In addition to several old bedsteads and the folding bed built by Pratt, Abigail wrote Mary, two mattresses were needed for the coachman and the Negro boy. The couple that Mary Cranch was to employ must bring their beds with them.

The Adamses stopped off in New York for a happy reunion with Nabby and the children and then pushed on, impatient to get home. Up through the Connecticut Valley, rich with summer foliage, into the familiar landscape of New England, they bumped over roads still scarred with spring ruts. Abigail was a poor traveler but she cheerfully bore the inconveniences—the jarring, lurching coach, the crowded, untidy inns, the indifferent food—because along with her husband and son she was going back to family and friends, places and people well known and well loved. The summer lay ahead at Braintree, a summer without court calls and state dinners, without strange servants to contend with, without the strain of political maneuverings and stratagems. The journey was a tonic to John. He grew more cheerful and lively with every passing mile.

At last, hot and tired, they arrived in Braintree. The house with oilcloth on the floors and the few scattered pieces of furniture had a cool austerity about it that was most pleasant. Housekeeping was simple and in such a Spartan setting there was time for visits and talk and reading. Eliza Shaw made the trip from Haverhill to Braintree, proud as punch of her baby Abigail, and Mary Cranch visited almost daily. As the wife of the Vice-President of the United States, Abigail was a great lady and old friends, visiting, sat a little uneasily in the sparsely furnished living room, wary of "airs" or signs of hauteur in Abigail Adams of Weymouth and Braintree. But after their hostess had heard with almost perfect equanimity the first half dozen greetings that started off, "I'm sure now that you have been going to fine balls and parties in New York and Philadelphia, the simple folks hereabouts will seem pretty dull to you," and replied with warm assurances of the pre-eminent place of Braintree in her heart, things were as they had been before, plain-spoken, friendly, and unaffected.

THE friendship of Adams and Jefferson was placed under a heavy strain by an incident that followed the publication of the *Discourses.* The first part of Thomas Paine's *Rights of Man,* written as an answer to Burke's attack on the French Revolution, was published in England in the early spring of 1791. John Beckley, the Virginia democrat who was clerk of the House, obtained a copy of the pamphlet with the idea of having it published in the United States. Before sending it to a printer Beckley loaned the work to Madison, who in turn passed it on to Jefferson with a request to forward it to the printer when he was through with it. In sending it on to the printer, Jefferson added a note to explain why the *Rights* was coming from him and, "to take off a little of the dryness of the note" as he explained subsequently, remarked that he was glad to learn that "something was at length to be publicly said against the political heresies which had of late sprung up among us, not doubting but that our citizens would rally again around the standard of *Common Sense.*"[1]

A week or so later the Philadelphia printer produced an edition of *Rights of Man* with Jefferson's letter printed as a foreword. The political heresies to which Jefferson had referred were the *Discourses,* and this was generally understood by those who read the pamphlet. The enemies of Adams were delighted. They had found a champion. Adams was hurt and indignant at what looked like a deliberate attack upon him by a man whom he had considered one of his closest friends. The Anti-Federalists, with no intention of letting the incident die a natural death, puffed up Paine's essay and Jefferson's letter as complete refutation of the aristocratic and monarchial principles of the "Duke of Braintree," as one Anti-Federalist editor had titled Adams. It was certainly true that the *Rights of Man* with its classically optimistic, liberal, Utopian outlook, with its faith in reason and its doctrinaire devotion to the principles of the French Revolution, was in direct opposition to Adams' own political and moral philosophy.

Jefferson, reporting to Washington, testified to his embarrassment over the episode. "Paine's answer to Burke's pamphlet," he noted, "begins to produce squibs in our public papers." One reply to Paine, Jefferson suspected, was by Adams himself. "I am afraid the indiscretion of a printer has committed me with my friend, Mr. Adams, for whom, as one of the most honest and disinterested men alive, I have a cordial esteem, increased by long habits of concurrence in opinion in the days of his republicanism; and even since his apostasy to hereditary monarchy and nobility, though we differ, we differ as friends should do." Adams would be offended and assume that Jefferson intended to injure him "in the public eye." Nonetheless, Jefferson associated himself unreservedly with the sentiments of "this popular and republican pamphlet" [Paine's], which "at a single stroke" would "wipe out all the unconstitutional doctrines which their bellwether Davila has been preaching for a twelve-month."[2]

Republican editors everywhere took up Jefferson's charge. The New Haven *Gazette*, "an unprincipled libeler," accused Adams of being an enemy to freedom and to republican institutions, and papers in New York, Boston, and Philadelphia followed suit.

Even Samuel Adams entered the fray in a speech before a joint session of both houses of the Great and General Court in which he quite pointedly denounced those who argued for "hereditary powers" in government. It seemed to Adams that his enemies everywhere had been inspired by Paine's pamphlet and its endorsement by the Secretary of State to hunt him down "like a hare, if they could," and destroy him politically.

Adams considered replying to Paine, whose doctrines seemed to him a dangerous poison that must not be allowed to contaminate the blood stream of a republican nation, but he was conscious that it would be inappropriate for the Vice-President of the United States to appear to be taking up the gage thrown down by the Secretary of State. As he feared and abhorred faction, he must do nothing that would encourage it regardless of how Jefferson might conduct himself. The solution was to leave the counterattack to John Quincy. The son would take up his pen in defense of the father. Under the *nom de plume* of "Publicola," John Quincy began a series of articles defending *Davila* and detailing the fallacies contained in Paine's treatise. The strategy failed, at least to a degree, because the articles, which appeared in the *Columbian Centinel* of Boston and were widely reprinted, were attributed to the elder Adams and served to give fresh impetus to the hot newspaper and pamphlet warfare.

Jefferson, dismayed at the continuing furor, sat down after his return from a "botanizing expedition" to New York to express to Adams his regret over the episode. He was prompted by the rumor that Adams himself was Publicola. "I have a dozen times taken up my pen to write you,

and as often laid it down again, suspended between opposing considerations," he began. He had finally decided to tell Adams the whole story,
since "our names [have been] thrown on the public stage as public
antagonists." Certainly they had differed in their ideas as to the best form
of government, but they had respected "the purity of each other's motives" and confined "our difference of opinion to private conversation.
And I can declare with truth," Jefferson continued, "in the presence of
the Almighty that nothing was further from my intention or expectation
than to have had either my own or your name brought before the public
on this occasion." Yet he could not forbear an implied reproach. He had
been accused of being one of the republican writers who had replied to
Publicola, but, he wrote, "I never did in my life . . . have a sentence of
mine inserted in a newspaper without putting my name to it; and I
believe I never shall."[3]

Adams replied at once, expressing his "great pleasure" at Jefferson's
friendly letter. He accepted the Virginian's account without hesitation;
but the printer's indiscretion, he wrote, had "sown the seeds of more
evils than he can ever atone for." It had given color to "the false interpretation of my writings as favoring the introduction of hereditary monarchy
and aristocracy into this country."

Having said this much, Adams went on to correct Jefferson's assumption that he was the author of the Publicola papers. "I neither wrote nor
corrected Publicola," he stated. The writer "followed his own judgment,
information, and discretion without any assistance from me." To
Jefferson's statement that they differed in their ideas about the best form
of government, Adams replied: "I do not know this. I know not what
your idea is of the best form of government. You and I have never had a
serious conversation together that I can recollect concerning the nature
of government. The very transient hints that have ever passed between us
have been jocular and superficial, without ever coming to any explanation." If Jefferson assumed that Adams had ever had a desire to introduce
a government of "Kings, Lords, and Commons" into the United States he
was "wholly mistaken. . . . . There is not such a thought expressed or inti-
mated in any public or private letter of mine, and I may safely challenge all mankind to produce such a passage and quote the chapter and
verse."

Few of the people who professed to say that he was a monarchist and
champion of aristocracy had ever bothered to read his writings. "Of the
few who have taken the pains to read them," he added, "some have misunderstood them and others have willfully misrepresented them, and
these misunderstandings and misrepresentations have been made the
pretense for overwhelming me with floods and whirlwinds of tempestuous
abuse, unexampled in the history of this country." The Pennsylvania
radicals, the Shaysite faction of Massachusetts, and the Anti-Federalists

had joined forces to replace Adams with John Hancock. "The Janizaries of this goodly combination, among whom are three or four who hesitate at no falsehood," he continued, "have written all the impudence and impertinence which have appeared in the Boston papers upon this memorable occasion.

"I thank you, sir, very sincerely for writing me," Adams concluded. ". . . It was high time that you and I should come to an explanation with each other. The friendship that has subsisted for fifteen years between us without the smallest interruption, and until this occasion without the slightest suspicion, ever has been and still is very dear to my heart. There is no office which I would not resign rather than give a just occasion to one friend to forsake me. Your motives for writing to me I have not a doubt were the most pure and the most friendly."[4]

The letters were characteristic of their writers. Jefferson's was precise and factual and a little formal. Adams' was rambling and emotional, marked as always by a sense of outraged virtue, by a thin-skinned vulnerability that made him suffer acutely from every barb discharged at him. One thing was clear enough: Adams flatly rejected the accusation that he was a monarchist. Always candid, unwilling to trim or modify his opinions to curry favor with any group or win popular support, he would never have so explicitly denied his "design or desire" to introduce a monarchy into the United States if he had believed that such a system was necessary for the good order and stability of the country. He had, to be sure, in letters to Rush and in conversation, expressed the opinion that if popular elections grew riotous and disorderly it might be necessary in order to preserve liberty to adopt an executive and perhaps a Senate elected for life. But this was simply conjecture and speculation, not a program. The important thing, as Adams never tired of saying, was that there should be a strong executive embodying the *monarchial principle* in a republican government.

At the same time the fact that so many people, Jefferson among them, misunderstood Adams suggests that in the climate of opinion of the time, with the mass of Americans hypersensitive to any reflection on democratic and republican principles, it was almost impossible to speak in an objective or, as Adams would have put it, a "scientific" way about the positive aspects of a limited constitutional monarchy without being accused of wishing to rivet chains on the American people. It was as though in twentieth-century America a prominent politician were to attempt to carry on a public debate about the advantages, let us say, of moderate socialism. Even though our government and our economy are today quite highly "socialized," to say so openly and to talk about the desirability of extending this socialization would be to expose the advocate to a storm of denunciation as an enemy of his country, a person of authoritarian leanings and friend of Russian communism. This was the case in 1790 as in 1960, but Adams with his stubborn honesty refused to learn the lesson that a democracy demands orthodoxy from its political leaders even at the cost of truth.

Jefferson, as stiff in his own way as Adams, was unwilling to let the matter rest there. He must justify himself and show Adams that his note to the printer of *The Rights of Man* had had no effect on public sentiment. "It was," he insisted, "unnoticed." It was rather the warm response of Publicola which had raised the issue to the level of a national controversy. "I am certain," he wrote, "not a word on the subject would ever have been said had not a writer, under the name of Publicola, at length undertaken to attack Mr. Paine's principles, which were the principles of the citizens of the U.S. . . . To Publicola then, and not in the least degree to my note, this whole contest is to be ascribed and all its consequences." Jefferson's reference to "political heresies" was not directed at Adams at all and would never have been so interpreted had it not been for Publicola's defense, the Secretary of State insisted. Either Jefferson's memory was short or he was less than candid, for in his letter to Washington apropos of the publication of Paine's pamphlet Jefferson had specifically said that he had Davila in mind when he wrote the unfortunate note.[5]

Adams must have felt the letter to be disingenuous. His own letter, fervent as it had been, had ended with an affectionate assurance of friendship. Jefferson, by insisting on freeing himself of any blame and placing it instead upon the partisans of Adams, more especially on Adams' son, whom Jefferson may well have suspected to be the author, poured salt in the wound. Adams did not reply and when he wrote again several years later it was in a friendly spirit. But the rupture had been made nonetheless. From here on the two men drifted further and further apart, until they came to see each other as enemies, opposed in every important political principle, each threatening the very existence of republican government.

Despite his experience with the *Discourse*, Adams was only temporarily suppressed. If his "friends and . . . enemies" concurred "in forbidding me to publish any of my speculations," he would still write freely to his friends. "A society can no more subsist without gentlemen than an army without officers. So says Harrington; so says history; so says experience; so says reason. Out of a body of gentlemen," he declared to Trumbull, "somehow or other formed, are to be drawn officers to command your armies for national defense; magistrates to execute the laws and distribute justice; legislators to enact laws; physicians to preserve or restore health; clergymen to preach the moral science, etc." This was the group that put service to their country above gain, and every society needed such a group.[6]

As the summer drew to a close John and Abigail bethought themselves of their return to Philadelphia. Bush Hill, both decided, was too far from the city. They must have a house in Philadelphia. Adams wrote to Tench Coxe, Undersecretary of the Treasury, asking him to try to find them suitable quarters. The best Coxe could do was a comfortable house at the corner of Fourth and Arch Street at the exorbitant rent of nine hundred dollars a year.

In September the Adamses set out on the long trek to Philadelphia, accompanied by Thomas, Louisa, and in place of the shrewish Polly Tailor, a new maid named Katy. John and Abigail left Braintree reluctantly and with deep misgivings. Richard Cranch was dangerously ill and Billy Shaw had smashed his leg in a carriage accident. Both of Abigail's sisters were distressed and anxious, and between her concern for them and her worry over John Quincy, who had been suffering from nervous headaches and studying so hard that his eyes were sore and inflamed, Abigail lost her usual self-possession and forgot a dozen small details in closing the house. They were hardly an hour on the road before she remembered that she had made no provision to have the cider and potatoes put in the cellar after it had been banked with marsh hay and seaweed to keep out the frost.

On the last lap of the trip southward Adams' "Dutch" complaint came on him with a savagery that left him weak and shaken. When Congress convened on October 24 he had barely strength enough to attend, returning home each evening exhausted by his duties as presiding officer. With John in precarious health, Abigail had hoped to curtail her social activities but found that she must set aside one "public evening" a week (Monday) for "those strangers who are daily brought to this place either by business or curiosity" as well as for the members of Congress. Wednesday evening was allotted for having company to dinner, sixteen or eighteen persons, "which," Abigail noted indignantly, "are as many as we can accommodate at once in our thousand-dollar house." "It is much of an Egyptian task," she wrote John Quincy, "and falls sometimes much heavier upon me than my state of health will bear." Fortune smiled on her domestic arrangements and she at last acquired a reliable cook whom she described almost lyrically to Mary Cranch as "a clever, sober, honest, and neat black woman."[7]

With Richard Cranch so ill, Abigail had Mary much on her mind. She wrote Dr. Tufts to send her five cords of wood "on my account," adding, "Do not let her know from what quarter it comes." Mary was sensitive to receiving anything that seemed like charity from Abigail. She also charged the doctor with sending on beef, a cask of tongues, and six barrels of cider to sustain them through a Philadelphia winter.[8]

Colonel Smith returned from his voyage to England with the suggestion that he be appointed to reside at the Court of St. James to settle the disputed points of the Treaty of Paris, "as a primary essential to establish such commercial regulations as the interests of the two countries require." He had made the acquaintance of Lord Grenville and George Hammond and he had been assured that he would be most acceptable to the English ministry.[9] When the appointment went to William Short, Smith found some wealthy New Yorkers to back him in a scheme to sell American land to English investors. The plan called for him to spend several years in England as agent of his principals, and he prepared to sail and take Nabby with him. Nabby, in consequence, set out for Philadelphia with the children, William, John, and the new baby, Thomas Hollis, to make a farewell visit to her parents. Before she arrived in the city her mother became seriously ill. Abigail suffered from a severe attack of rheumatism, from the intermitting fever, from splitting headaches, from such an inflammation of her eyes that she could not bear to have a light in her room or even endure the flames from the fireplace. Nabby took over at once as nurse and Esther Briesler, happily revived, helped to care for the mistress who had recently tended her. Mrs. Samuel Otis, Mrs. Dalton, and Louisa all took turns nursing her.

Although faithfully attended by Dr. Rush, Abigail seemed unable to throw off the fever's debilitating effects. Nabby was convinced that Dr. Rush's bleedings and blisterings simply prolonged her mother's illness. She saw how pale and weak Abigail was and she urged her father to find a physician who was less radical in his treatment. She felt sure that if her mother were simply left alone she would have a much better chance of regaining her strength and health. Nabby's arguments disturbed John. He too had observed the effects of the bleedings and purges, and seen his wife too weak to stand or walk about afterward; still he hesitated to enter the lists as a layman against his learned friend who burst into the house, so confident and cheerful, attending his patient with so much obvious devotion. He finally decided that his wife's health was more important than his friendship with her physician. With her permission he would try another doctor, perhaps Philip Physic, who had so many miraculous cures to his credit. But Abigail would not hear of it. She was, as John wrote Nabby after her return to New York, "perfectly satisfied." Rush's "anxiety to do everything in his power" to cure her had been "most apparent." Clearly Abigail had come to depend on the encouragement she drew from her doctor's ebullient and optimistic nature.[10]

For a person as active as Abigail, her confinement to her bed and chair was especially burdensome. Prevented from reading or writing, her thoughts turned constantly to Braintree. She fretted about the houses and farms and yearned to be back. There she could recover her health amid familiar surroundings. As soon as she could hold a pen she wrote Mary Cranch asking her to prepare the house for their return. She wished the entry hall and the stairs painted, and commissioned Dr. Tufts to buy her a barrel of brown sugar.

Adams, with Abigail in bad health and himself bored and frustrated by the tedium of the Senate routine, fell into one of his dark moods. Even Nabby and the children, William, little John, and the new baby, Thomas Hollis, could not draw him out of it. The bitterness of feeling unleashed by the Paine pamphlet and Publicola's reply left him deeply depressed. It seemed to be his fate to be an agent of rancor and partisanship. His only concern was with the good of his country, with the preservation of liberty, property, and order, with the strengthening of the nation moral fiber. He saw its perils with a terrible prescience; he felt pain as sharp as nausea over every new wrangle or contention that threatened its unity. For this he was denounced daily as an enemy to the principles of freedom in whose service he had expended the best part of his life; for this he drew upon himself all the accumulated anxieties and hostilities that dared not play about the head of the sacred Washington. Adams' vulnerability was somehow in inverse ratio to the President's invulnerability. He must be, like one of Franklin's rods, the figure that attracted all the democratic lightning. He must outrage his nature and mortify his proud, vain spirit by bowing his head and bearing the storm of obloquy. He had been born to suffer; it made little difference where he was at the time. As he voiced his complaints to Brand-Hollis: "My office is too great a restraint upon such a Son of Liberty. Such sedentary confinement for so many hours every day for six or seven months together is too much for a man habituated for a long course of years to long voyages and immense journeys. . . . Such long continued attention to debates and business is not very charming to a man accustomed to the conversation and amusements of Paris, of London, and The Hague."[11]

In the Senate there was a deceptive spirit of affability. The news of General St. Clair's disastrous defeat by the Miami Indians under Little Turtle was the only cloud apparent on the horizon. It stirred the Senate to initiate an investigation of St. Clair's conduct ("poor, gouty, infirm General," Abigail called him) and to increase the regular army to five thousand men. This in turn required an increased expenditure of five hundred thousand dollars and an increase in the tariff schedules to cover the new appropriation. There was general agreement that the number of representatives in the House should be increased, but a hot dispute developed over the question of whether Negro slaves should be counted as a basis for representation. The split was along sectional lines, of course, with Rufus King referring caustically to "the Negro Representatives" who would doubtless appear if the blacks were included in the population totals for the Southern states. The views of the Adamses were expressed by Abigail's comment, in a letter to her sister, "that the black cattle in the Northern states might as well claim to be represented."

The Senate differed with the House on the ratio of representation, the House standing for a ratio of one to thirty thousand and the Senate for one to thirty-three. On this issue the Senate triumphed, but on the question of the proper emblem for coins turned out by the newly established mint, the House successfully opposed the head of Washington and substituted the figure of Liberty.

Although the Senate proceeded harmoniously enough, trouble was brewing in several quarters. The growing friction between Yankees and Southerners was temporarily concealed by the Federalist-Anti-Federalist clash. Hamilton, as the principal shaper of Federalist policy, came under heavy fire, especially from the Congressmen south of Mason's and Dixon's line; thus Adams enjoyed a respite. Madison and Jefferson had brought a republican poet, Philip Freneau, to Philadelphia to establish an opposition newspaper, the *National Gazette*. Freneau had passed rapidly from philosophical disquisitions on republican government to outright attacks on the Washington administration, directing his attention especially to the Secretary of the Treasury. His patron, Jefferson, wrote bitterly to Lafayette of the "stock jobbers and king jobbers" who had secured seats in Congress and were trying to make the American constitution a replica of the British.[12]

Hamilton, for his part, at about the same time reached the conclusion "that Mr. Madison, co-operating with Mr. Jefferson, is at the head of a faction decidedly hostile to me and my administration; and actuated by views, in my judgment, subversive of the principles of good government and dangerous to the union, peace, and happiness of the country."[13]

"The rage of speculation" further poisoned the atmosphere. In April the bubble burst and dozens of prominent families were ruined. "Terrible is the distress in New York," Abigail wrote, "from the failure of many of the richest people there." The opposition to Hamilton's "well-built systems" grew daily. Led by Madison and Jefferson, it sought to "give a fatal stab to the funding system." The good order and good humor in the Federalist-dominated Senate contrasted sharply with the strife and contention in the House. "I firmly believe," Abigail wrote her sister, "if I live ten years longer, I shall see a division of the Southern and Northern states, unless more candor and less intrigue, of which I have no hopes, should prevail."[14]

It was the end of April before Abigail felt strong enough to undertake the long trip to Boston. She had packed off most of her belongings and the furnishings of the house to Braintree in the brig *Isabella*, since it had been decided that she could not risk another winter in Philadelphia and John must keep bachelor quarters on his return. Adams secured permission from the Senate to leave his chair before the end of the session to accompany Abigail, and Richard Henry Lee was elected President of the Senate *pro tempore* in his absence.

John and Abigail set off at once for Braintree. They stopped briefly in New York and found the city in a turmoil over the wave of business failures. Many of Abigail's close friends, "whose affluence," as she wrote her sister, "was great and well founded when I lived here . . . are now in ruinous circumstances. . . . Such is the wheel of fortune."[15] From New York they hastened on to Braintree. As always, they were glad to be home. The only thing that had changed about the town was its name. The south parish had split off, retaining the name of Braintree, and the north parish had been named Quincy after Colonel John Quincy, Abigail's grandfather. Richard Cranch had recovered from his illness and Mary spent much time pampering her sister. Neighbors and relatives came with their good wishes for her rapid and complete recovery, and with tokens of their affection for "the Duchess of Braintree"—an apple or cranberry pie, a sweet-fleshed halibut, a bottle of homemade wine.

Adams, for his part, busied himself with the farm, supervised the carting of seaweed to fertilize the fields, directed the removal of rocks heaved up by the frost, painted the apple trees with tar to discourage tent caterpillars, and to Abigail's despair plotted to buy more land when he could not find tenants for what he had. He spent much time in his library putting his voluminous papers in order, reading over his correspondence, preparing the brief for Adams versus posterity. In the evening he took up his old delight, reading the classical authors—Horace and Livy, Cicero, Virgil, Thucydides and Tacitus. He spent hours with Richard Cranch talking on and on, expounding his theories of government and of the nature of man, indulging or perhaps overindulging his impulse to self-pity, to see himself as one despised and rejected, unloved, a prophet without honor. Then, with the inevitable self-mockery, he would deride his vanity and hunger for acclaim.

Almost daily Prince saddled Cleopatra and Adams rode through the Blue Hills behind the town where he had roamed and hunted as a boy. But the principal pleasure of the summer for him lay in the proximity of John Quincy at Boston. John rode sometimes to the city to visit his son's law office, but more often John Quincy traveled to Quincy to enjoy Abigail's good food. One way and another he and his father were often together. John did his best to raise his son's spirits, depressed by his inability to make his living as a lawyer. They read and argued cases, discussed torts and replevins, trespass and assault. The senior Adams had preserved many of his notes on cases that he had argued twenty-five or thirty years before and he reviewed them with John Quincy, spicing his instruction with hundreds of amusing incidents that showed the vice, folly, or wit of men entangled in the meshes of the law.

During the summer he left off wearing his wig. It was becoming the republican mode to go about wigless, but it was more a matter of comfort than style with Adams. The weather was unusually warm at Quincy and the wig was hot and itchy. Without it his appearance was so different that some of his friends failed to recognize him. Now, for a fact, he looked like Farmer John.[16]

THE election of 1792, the second presidential election, would take place in November. Its approach added fresh fuel to the struggle for control of the administration that was being waged more and more openly between Hamilton and Jefferson. Freneau, who had perhaps gone further in his attacks on the administration than Madison and Jefferson had envisioned, was accused by Hamilton of being a paid hireling of the Anti-Federalist faction. Freneau denied the charge and Jefferson wrote a long letter to Washington declaring his innocence of any complicity. Washington replied by urging his two Secretaries to compose their differences for the sake of their country, but since each suspected the other of a plot to subvert the government of the new nation, the appeal was futile.

At Quincy, Adams watched uneasily while the struggle grew more bitter throughout the summer. Jefferson was his old and close friend; on the other hand, he admired the financial brilliance of the New Yorker and applauded his skill in providing for the obligations of the United States. While Hamilton's attack on Jefferson drew off some of the Anti-Federalist rancor that had been directed at Adams, it pushed Jefferson forward as champion of all those who for one reason or another opposed the Washington administration and thereby strengthened the Virginian as a potential rival to Adams for the presidential succession.

There was still the question of whether Washington would consent to run for another term. Adams devoutly hoped that he would, but if Washington refused another term the Vice-President had no intention of stepping aside for Jefferson, whose political principles seemed to him to grow daily more dangerous and extreme. The violence of feeling bred by the dispute between the two Secretaries and Adams' observation of the activities of Massachusetts radicals like Benjamin Austin and Ned Church filled him with anxiety. This was just what political philosophers since Aristotle had warned would be the result of popular elections and what history had repeatedly confirmed. From pamphlet disputes between rival publicists and newspaper editors, the spirit of factionalism would go on to riots and bloodshed. The people, misled by catchwords in the mouths of demagogues, their emotions played upon and their reason clouded, would divide into irreconcilable factions. Already democratic newspaper editors spoke of the President with savage contempt.

Word reached Adams from a number of states that the "Antis" were making an all-out effort to overturn the Federalist majority in Congress. His old friend, Elias Boudinot, found himself under heavy fire in New Jersey for his support of funding and assumption; a handbill was widely circulated accusing him of speculating in public securities. In New Hampshire sentiment was strongly Anti and in Massachusetts Fisher Ames was opposed by Austin, described by a Federalist as "a democratic *enragé*, who has long been known as an instigator and patron of faction in this town."[1]

John's cousin, Samuel Adams, worked with Hancock and Warren to undermine Adams' position in Massachusetts, and word reached him from New York that the Antis there were writing to their corresponding members in every state to urge that Governor Clinton be chosen Vice-President at the coming election.

Charles, trying to find an office and get himself established as a lawyer at New York, kept his father informed of political developments in that state, and Thomas, boarding with a most congenial Quaker family, wrote regularly about the Pennsylvania scene. In the latter state the Federalists and the Antis had chosen different methods for selecting representatives to Congress. The word that reached Adams of plot and counterplot, of maneuverings and alliances, depressed him. The second session was to convene November 5, but Adams let it be known that he did not intend to come to Philadelphia until after the electors had chosen the President and Vice-President. He had no intention of appearing on the scene like a man hungry for office. His depression over political developments was deepened by the slowness with which Abigail responded to the curative effects of Quincy, and by his own ailments. The tremor of his hands was an increasing affliction, his eyes gave him trouble, and he suffered from infected teeth.

When word reached Hamilton and the other Federalist party managers that Adams intended to play the part of a bashful candidate and remain at his farm, they began a campaign to prevail on him to come to Philadelphia by the end of October. If Hamilton had no special liking for Adams, he hated Clinton. To try to push another Federalist for Vice-President was clearly impractical. Moreover Hamilton no longer feared Adams as a possible rival for leadership of the Federalists. The Secretary's dazzling success in placing the finances of the country on a sound footing had made him the unquestioned leader of his party. Hamilton thus wrote to Adams early in September that he had "learnt with pain that you may not probably be here till late in the session." Adams' enemies would seize on his absence to boom Clinton, arguing that the Duke of Braintree was too aloof or too vain to appear but, like Achilles, preferred to skulk in his tent, awaiting the outcome of the battle. Even if Adams was "very indifferent personally to the event of a certain election," he must have a deep concern for the cause of good government. "The difference in that view," Hamilton wrote, "is in my conception immense between the success of Mr. Clinton or yourself; and some sacrifices of feeling are to be made." Then Hamilton played the notes that he knew Adams could least resist: courage and duty. "Permit me to say," he added, "it best suits the firmness and elevation of your character to meet all events, whether suspicious or otherwise, on the ground where station and duty call you." To remain in Quincy would "give the ill disposed the triumph of supposing that an anticipation of want of success had kept you from your post." Moreover it was not only Hamilton's desire but the "universal wish" of all Adams' friends that he come to Philadelphia as soon as possible.[2] Samuel Otis, Secretary of the Senate, wrote also at Hamilton's prompting, "With your other friends, I very much regret your absence; it gives your enemy a handle."

When Adams still lingered on at Quincy, Hamilton prompted Thomas Boylston to write his father that his absence was being used by his enemies to "injure your cause." The word had been circulated that he would not leave Quincy until after the election and then only if he was re-elected. If he failed of election, the rumor went, he would not even put in an appearance to finish out his term as presiding officer of the Senate. The picture thus passed about was that of a bad loser who refused to play the game unless he was assured of winning. The Southerners had been especially busy derogating Adams and pushing Clinton as his successor. "The friends and advocates of the present state of things feel themselves extremely alarmed," his son wrote. He was needed in his post as President of the Senate "to counteract the progress of dangerous measures." Kentucky, recently admitted as a state, would undoubtedly cast two Anti-Federal votes in the electoral college.[3]

But Adams, despite such persuasions, remained in Quincy. The state of Abigail's health and his own ailments made him especially reluctant to depart. The news that continued to reach him of Clinton's growing strength deepened his gloom. It would be a sad climax to a career of service to be replaced in the second office of the land by a demagogic state politician whose claim to the gratitude of his countrymen was not to be mentioned in the same breath with that of Adams. To those who importuned him, he offered as excuse for remaining at Quincy the fact that he had not entirely recovered from the "brake-bone fever," and referred to "considerations of delicacy" which prevented his attendance in the Senate at the opening session.[4] "The considerations of delicacy" may have been the inflamed condition of his mouth and gums. He apparently had a form of pyorrhea which resulted in the loss of a number of his teeth during the summer. (Washington, who had lost his teeth, wore false ones made for him by Gilbert Stuart; pieces of ivory set in wood, clumsy and painful. Instead of suction, the teeth were held in place by a spring which pushed the upper and lower plates apart. Washington's jaws, clamped grimly on this primitive contrivance, helped to give his face the set expression characteristic of the Stuart portraits.) Adams was unwilling to subject himself to such torture and as a consequence the loss of his teeth changed the contours of his face and altered his voice so that he spoke with the muffled, slightly lisping sound of the toothless. The "considerations" may equally well have been Abigail's change of life, which made her acutely nervous and susceptible to fits of despondency.

Furthermore Adams' eyes were too sore to permit him to do much more than read the newspapers and he had no inclination to write. He spent much of his time with Abigail and gave the rest of his attention to the farm. The news of the arrest of Louis XVI, which reached America in the early fall, was for Adams "to the last degree disgusting," and a predictable result of the mad course on which the Revolution had plunged. What was most troubling, he wrote Rufus King, was "that there should have been in America from the beginning so blind, undistinguishing, and enthusiastic an admiration of everything that has been done by that light, airy, and transported people."[5]

It was the end of November before Adams said a sad and reluctant farewell to Abigail and started off through snow and cold rain for the seat of government. On the way to Springfield, Adams fell in with a traveler who, not knowing his identity, regaled him with a long account of the maneuvers in Philadelphia and New York for and against the Vice-President. "The Vice-President had been, as all acknowledged," the man told Adams, "a great friend of his country, but he had given offense to his fellow citizens in Massachusetts by writing something in favor of hereditary descent; that he had been long in Europe and got tainted." Adams laughed at this analysis of his political theories and replied, "It [is] hard if a man [cannot] go to Europe without being tainted. . . . If Mr. Adams had been sent to Europe upon their business by the people, and had done it, and in doing it had necessarily got tainted . . . the people ought to pay him for the damage the taint had done him, or find some means to wash it out and cleanse him."

In Hartford where he was marooned by a heavy snowstorm, he was told that Governor Hancock had visited the town recently and given a dinner for the leading citizens. In the course of the dinner a guest had inquired about Adams; Hancock reportedly had replied that he had not spoken to the Vice-President this year, since he, Hancock, was not one of the wellborn. The Massachusetts Governor had been seen in Hartford, however, for what he was: "a mere rich man, prodigal of his wealth to obtain an empty bubble of popularity." The Hartford Federalists wined and dined John and assured him that he would get the unanimous votes of Vermont, New Hampshire, Connecticut, and Rhode Island. But Adams, knowing how fickle the temper of men could be, was prepared for a unanimous vote against him. Indeed, with his impulse to morbidity and pessimism, he had virtually conceded the election to Clinton and in anticipation was already allowing himself some feeling of self-pity.

When the snow continued to fall Adams decided to leave his chaise at the Bull Tavern to be returned to Boston, and his horses to be sent on to Philadelphia when the roads were cleared; he himself continued his journey by the mail stage. He arrived at New York with a sore throat and spent four days "nursing" his cold in the heart of enemy territory. He found Charles, who had been admitted to the bar in August, established in an office in Hanover Street and very pleased at winning the first case that he had argued before a jury. It was an affectionate reunion. Charles loved and admired his father and John, in turn, was reassured to see his son hard at work and with good prospects of a successful career as a lawyer. Charles's law library, John noted, was too skimpy. He made a mental note to send him money to buy more books and jotted down a list of the works essential to a young lawyer. Before he left New York it occurred to John that the horses he had abandoned in Hartford might be sold and the money applied to augment his son's law library. Charles, who kept himself informed on political developments in the state, told his father that the Anti-Federalist plan was for Clinton to be Vice-President as well as Governor of New York. By holding both offices at the same time, he would illustrate dramatically that the Federal government was simply the creature of the states. Pierpont Edwards, Alexander James Dallas, and several of the Livingstons were deep in the plot. Adams professed to be indifferent to the outcome. However it might turn out, he wrote Abigail, "I hope I shall not be obliged to lie alone next winter."[6]

The defection to Republican ranks that most distressed Adams was that of his friend Benjamin Rush, who had so fallen under the influence of Jefferson and his adherents that he joined the movement to replace Adams by Clinton, writing to Aaron Burr, the astute party manager in New York, "It is time to *speak out*—or we are undone."[7] John Beckley, clerk of the House and errand boy for Jefferson and Madison, returned from a visit to New York with word that Colonel Burr "would cheerfully support the measure of removing Mr. A[dams] and lend every aid in his power to C[linton]'s election."[8]

At Philadelphia, Adams found temporary lodgings with the Otises.

The support of Clinton as his opponent for the vice-presidency, his friends assured him, was directed less at Adams personally than at Hamilton and the Federalists. "Both parties," he wrote Abigail, "were of opinion the question was no less than whether the government should stand or fall. In this probably they were both too sanguine," he added. The fact was, nonetheless, that if Clinton was chosen the administration would be so changed that the government might be dissolved much sooner.

Adams, surveying the situation from the vantage point of Philadelphia, decided that if he failed to be re-elected it would be primarily because electors threw away votes to other candidates for reasons that had little to do with Federalism and Anti-Federalism. "These follies," he wrote Abigail, "will be occasioned by causes much more ancient than the federal government or my writings. I mean jealousies of South versus North and dubitations about federal towns and foreign debts."[9]

Meanwhile the French Revolution loomed larger and larger as an issue separating Federalists and Republicans, as the Anti-Federalists were beginning to be called. Every new atrocity served, it seemed, to deepen the affection of the Republicans for their country's former ally. Francophiles built miniature guillotines and dropped the blades suggestively at fraternal feasts; the heads of American aristocrats would soon roll as French heads had rolled. The Anti-Federalists sang the "*Ça ira*" and breathed fire and damnation to all enemies of revolution and democracy. "The liberty of the whole earth was depending on the issue of the contest," Jefferson declaimed, speaking of the French Revolution; ". . . rather than it should have failed, I would have seen half the earth desolated; were there but an Adam and Eve left in every country, and left free, it would be better than as it now is." To the Virginian, "the form our own government was to take depended . . . on the events of France." "The tassels and baubles of monarchy" were now being discarded by a people awakened to the true principles of republicanism by the zeal of the French patriots.[10]

Such talk, to Adams, was madness. To applaud bloodshed, violence, and anarchy was to loosen the bonds of society and endanger everything that had been built so laboriously and at such cost. "A few years," he wrote John Quincy, "will show whether the French Republic will last longer than the English one in the last century. I think there will be a general revolution in religion and government all over Europe. How many centuries will be employed in civil distractions and what new forms of things will rise up I pretend not to foresee or conjecture." His fear was the reverse of Jefferson's—that the example of the French would "produce anarchy among us."[11]

As part of the Republican campaign, word was spread among the Virginia Federalists that Adams was the only member of the administration who opposed Washington. Washington, hearing the story, denounced it as a lie. The Vice-President had always supported him loyally. Judge Cushing reported to Adams that he had dined with Patrick Henry and listened to him criticize Adams' writings in a way that made it very clear to the Massachusetts jurist that Henry had not read them.

"Have you read these volumes?" Cushing asked dryly.

"No."

"Well, I recommend them to your perusal."

"No, I am too old to read so extensive a work. But," Henry said, with a sweeping gesture indicating several young men at the dinner table, "they have read it and given me an account of it."

One of the young men thus appealed to confirmed that he had read the *Defence*, or part of it at least, and despised and abhorred it. At this Arthur Lee, who had been a silent auditor, spoke up. "They must have been boys then," he declared, "for it was the work of the greatest genius that had ever written in this country."

Adams found another defender in John Trumbull, who listened patiently while William Giles expatiated on the monarchal principles of the *Defence* and the *Discourses*. Finally Trumbull interrupted to inquire if he could ask a single question. Giles nodded. "Pray, Mr. Giles," Trumbull said, "have you ever read those volumes of Mr. Adams'?" Giles, taken by surprise, hesitated, blushed, stammered, and at last admitted that he had not. But he had seen accounts of them in the newspapers and read extracts.

"Then," said Trumbull, "I insist upon it, Giles, you have no right to give your opinion of those books. The first two volumes are fact and authorities. The last is reasoning upon them—you can therefore have no idea of the work without reading all three."

At this sally Nancy Allen, the attractive daughter of James Allen, turned to the discomfited Virginian and said, "I hope, Mr. Giles, that all your opinions are not taken up with so much levity and upon so little foundation!"[12] Another story was balm to Adams' bruised spirit. Gilbert Livingston, a Clinton supporter, had been heard to say apropos of the news from France: "Nothing mortified me so much [in] the misconduct in France and America too, as to see that the fools are all playing the game into the hands of that Mr. John Adams." A friend of Adams who was present replied: "Mr. Adams reads the Scriptures and there he finds that man is as stupid as the wild ass's colt. He believes what he reads and infers his necessary consequences from it, that is all. Mr. Adams is not to blame. He did not write the Scriptures. He only reads and believes."[13]

John missed Abigail acutely. "You must come to me another year," he wrote, "or I will come to you." He maintained stoutly that he was ready for any outcome in the election. "I am of the cat kind and fall upon my feet, throw me as they will," he declared. The New York and Virginia Anti-Federalists were joined by a strong faction in Pennsylvania; together they mustered up fifty votes for Clinton, including all of the electoral votes of New York, Virginia, North Carolina, and Georgia. Adams had seventy-seven—all of New England, the Middle States, and South Carolina.

Although they failed in their efforts to defeat Adams, the Anti-Federalists made conspicuous gains in the Congress that would be seated in the fall of 1793 and they were confident that the tide was running in their direction. Jefferson seemed more clearly than ever the center of resistance to the Washington administration. Pierpont Edwards, the Clintonian from New York, arrived in the city and "was seen in close consultation at his lodgings with Mr. Jefferson. . . . I am really astonished," John wrote Abigail, "at the blind spirit of party which has seized on the whole soul of this Jefferson. There is not a Jacobin in France more devoted to faction."[14]

Adams' own militant spirit was thoroughly aroused. The Federalists, he insisted, must let "nothing pass unanswered; reasoning must be answered by reasoning; wit by wit, humor by humor; satire by satire; burlesque by burlesque and even buffoonery by buffoonery." The mass of people seemed to be carried away "with every wind of doctrine and every political lie." The only recourse of the Federalists was to meet all attacks with vigorous countermeasures.[15]

Living a bachelor life, Adams enjoyed his freedom from the social responsibilities of his office. For the first time since his election he was able to live within his income. He dined only with old frends or with new members of the Senate, and continued to try to steer a middle course through the shoals and whirlpools of party politics. "When, where, ah, where, my son, will these things end?" he inquired of John Quincy. If there was ever a man who had excuse to plunge into partisan politics, he was the man. He was determined never to involve Massachusetts in such rancorous disputes as had split Pennsylvania into rival camps. Yet he suffered none the less acutely for his resolve. "The persecutions against me, set on foot in Boston by the little passions of little minds," he wrote, "is the most unprovoked, the most destitute not only of grounds but of pretexts that ever happened in this world."

Congress gave ample evidence of the increased spirit of partisanship. Under the guidance of William Branch Giles and James Madison in the House, and with the behind-the-scenes direction of the Secretary of State, the Anti-Federalists launched an all-out attack on Hamilton. The purpose was to discredit the administration, cripple the Treasury Department, and impeach the Secretary. "Hamilton," John wrote Abigail, "will find no more mercy than is due from a generous nation to a faithful servant. But I presume," he added, "his character will shine the brighter." The real issue that hung in the balance was not so much the fate of the Secretary of the Treasury as the effort of the legislative branch to dominate the executive.

The attack on Hamilton was too plainly the work of malice to succeed. The extremism of the Republicans brought a reaction in Hamilton's favor. The most votes received by any of the resolutions of censure directed against him were fifteen as against thirty-three in his support.

Even more important than the fate of the Treasurer were the events transpiring in Europe. "Danton, Robespierre, Marat, etc., are furies," Adams wrote his wife. "Dragons' teeth have been sown in France and come up as monsters." The United States had its "Robespierres and Marats whose wills are good to do mischief but the flesh is weak. They cannot yet persuade the people to follow them." As the Republican newspapers became more virulent, Washington was more and more their target. "The hell hounds are now in full cry in the newspapers against the President, whom they treat as ill as ever they did me," Adams noted. The same "insolent and impudent Irishman," James Callender, who had attacked Adams, now turned his fire on the General and Washington writhed under the lash. Adams saw him white with anger and was concerned that the abuse might be "carried to a point that he will not bear. He has not been used to such threshing and his skin is thinner than mine," he observed to Abigail.[16]

Amid the tension and bitterness that possessed the capital there were a few bright spots. The fall and winter weather had been "the fairest, softest, and finest" that anyone could remember. In February there was heavy snow but the sun gleamed upon it like jewels and the city was fresh and beautiful in its "white robe of innocence," an ironic contrast to the human sin and rancor which it enveloped. Adams enjoyed more than ever the company of old friends like the Daltons and the Otises. He was invited to join "The American Philosophical Society for Promoting Useful Knowledge to be held at Philadelphia" and his warrant as a member was signed by his old adversary, John Dickinson. Jefferson came to escort him to his first meeting and they so far forgot their political differences as to talk in the familiar way of close friends. Dr. Barton read a paper on the origin of the *Apis mellifica*, supporting Jefferson's view that it was imported into America from Europe. But Adams was unconvinced. "There are so many species of hornets, wasps, and bees which we call bumble or humble bees which no man can suppose to have taken pains to import from abroad," he noted, "that I see no reason to suspect that the honey bee, which resembles them so much, might not have been here as early as those species."

The meeting was thinly attended and in no way, Adams thought, superior to his own Academy of Arts and Sciences at Boston, but it was certainly a company of "able men," and he confessed to Abigail that he had been "agreeably entertained." Being with Jefferson made him reflect again on what seemed to him the strange defection of the Virginian to doctrines subversive of the stability and thus of the freedom of his country. Adams might be forgiven if his analysis of the Virginian's motives was an ungenerous one. "I wish somebody would pay his debt of seven thousand pounds to Britain and the debts of all his countrymen [Virginians]," he wrote Abigail, "and then I believe his passions would subside, his reason return, and the whole man and his whole state become good friends of the Union and its government."[17]

Adams' friend and correspondent, the historian Jeremy Belknap, wrote to solicit his support for a new magazine which he was planning to publish. Adams subscribed but met with little success in his effort to peddle the magazine among the Senators. Replying to Belknap's letter, he could not forbear to correct his views of the European crisis. Belknap had joined in the popular clamor against kings, but he was, Adams wrote, "so able an historian that I wish his philosophy to be such as will endure and be no diminution of his authority when the momentary fanaticism of the times shall have subsided." European nations for many years to come must have kings or anarchy, and kings, constitutionally limited, he reminded the New Hampshire historian, were by no means incompatible with republicanism, Tom Paine to the contrary.[18]

Adams looked forward impatiently to the end of the session of Congress. Since that body was clearly more concerned with making trouble than with passing legislation, their adjournment might allow passions to cool. "I live in terror," he wrote Abigail, "lest the state of Europe should force the President to call Congress together in summer. . . . The personal hatred and party animosities which prevail here have left me more in tranquillity than any other person. . . . . I am weary of reading newspapers," he added. "The times are so full of events, the whole drama of the world is such a tragedy, that I am weary of the spectacle. Oh, my sweet little farm—what would I not give to enjoy thee without interruption? But I see no end to my servitude, however the nations of Europe and even of Africa may recover their liberty."[19]

A sign of the times was an article in a Boston newspaper signed Stephen Colonna, charging that the constitution "was adopted by means of artifice, cajoling, deception, and . . . corruption." Unless the President took some Anti-Federalists into his administration the people would pull down the government which so poorly represented them, warned the writer. Colonna, it was reported on good authority, was none other than General Warren.[20]

The news in January of the triumph of the French Revolutionary armies over the Prussians and Austrians brought a new wave of rejoicing among the Republicans. Adams was, as he put it, "enough in the spirit of the times" to be glad that the Austrian and Prussian armies had not succeeded in destroying the French; but to him it was cruel to exult at the imprisonment and humiliation of Louis XVI, to whom Americans owed so much for his support during their own Revolution. It seemed ironic to Adams that he, who had felt the King's displeasure and who had retired from the court without that conventional mark of royal favor—a portrait of His Catholic Majesty—should be one of the very few "to bewail his misfortune." The consequences of the destruction of the French nobility Adams had predicted six years ago in his *Defence*, but the French would not listen. "The vengeance of heaven for their folly has been revealed in more shivering terms than any of my numerous examples," he noted.[21]

In Boston the politically emancipated admirers of the Revolution took to calling each other "Citizen" and "Citizeness" rather than Mr. And Mrs. in imitation of their French comrades; they delighted at the sight of Citizen Hancock and Citizen Samuel Adams joined in fraternal embrace. "We shall see in a few months the new French constitution," Adams wrote, "which may last twelve months but probably not more than six. Robespierre and Marat with their Jacobin supporters I suspect will overthrow the fabric which Condorcet, Paine, and Brissot will erect. Then we shall see what they in their turn will produce." He ended a letter to Abigail with the observation that "Citizen Briesler and Citizen V.P. are very happy together. Since they are equal and on a level it is proper that sometimes one should be named first and sometimes the other. Our countrymen are about to abandon the good old grave solid manners of Englishmen, their ancestors, and adopt all the aping levity and frivolity of the French."[22]

The papers were full of news of a celebration at Boston in honor of the masters of the Terror. A tax of three dollars a head was imposed to pay for a great "Civic Feast" in honor of the French comrades, and the Boston Federalists were afraid not to pay it for fear of being denounced as aristocrats. The democratical distemper was worse than the smallpox, and Adams was pleased at the news that John Quincy had dared to decry this infatuation within the sacred walls of Faneuil Hall.[23]

At the end of February, Colonel Smith and Nabby returned from Europe. The Colonel exuded confidence and prosperity. He and Nabby had been taken up in fashionable circles in both France and England. He had been spectacularly successful in disposing of American land to foreign investors, and he scattered money about in an obvious effort to impress his father-in-law and anyone else within range. He was expansive and boastful, dropping names right and left, from British lords to French Jacobins. He had, he reported to Adams, seen the *Defence* and the *Discourses* "upon the table of every member of the committee for framing a constitution of government for France except Tom Paine, and he [was] so conceited as to disdain to have anything to do with books." John discovered in his son-in-law some evidence of sympathy for the Revolution and he was clearly put out by the Colonel's brag and bluster. But he was so delighted to have the family back, to see Nabby happy and proud of her dashing and successful husband and both relieved of their straitened financial circumstances that he suppressed his misgivings. He decided that the Colonel, although he had "too little knowledge of the world; too little penetration; too little discretion," was "very clever and agreeable," and even found himself wishing his own sons had a little more of the Colonel's enterprise. He contented himself with warning Smith against his "disposition to boasting. Tell not of your prosperity," he advised, "because it will make two men mad to one man glad; nor tell of your adversity, for it will make two men glad to one sad."[24]

LXIV

ABIGAIL, well attended by Betsy and Louisa Smith and fussed over by devoted Polly Tailor, nonetheless missed her husband acutely. John had put aside a pile of books to take on his trip to Philadelphia and then gone off without them. The sight of the forgotten books conveyed a sharp sense of her deprivation. "With your books about me," she wrote, "I have felt dismal and lonely." On his trips he usually read himself to sleep. What would he find to read in wayside taverns? She worried about his sheets and blankets. Briesler had strict instructions to start a fire in the bedroom each night before his master retired, to air the sheets and see that Mr. Adams had enough blankets. In her anxiety Abigail even brought herself to doubt that faithful servant's discharge of his duties. "I did not think I should have felt so lonely," she wrote poignantly. "It seems so still all day as if half the family were gone."[1]

The routines of farm life kept her well occupied however. The storm that stranded Adams in Hartford shrouded Quincy in a blanket of snow. But the sheep were cozy in their new shed and the horses bedded down with plenty of hay. The hired man used the sleigh to cart seaweed; he cut timber for the projected corn crib and hauled it out of the woods with the new yoke of oxen that Abigail had bought for fifty-eight dollars, *"right handsome cattle,"* she wrote proudly, "kind and smart in very good flesh." She watched for her weekly letter from Philadelphia with the eagerness of a bride, and returned John thanks for his epistolarian faithfulness, particularly the letter "in which you say you are not less anxious to see me than when separated twenty years ago. Years subdue the ardor of passion," she wrote, "but in lieu thereof a friendship and affection, deep rooted, subsists which defies the ravages of time, and will survive whilst the flame exists. Our attachments . . . increase, I believe, with our years."[2]

John was equally dependent on her letters—at least one a week and as many more as she pleased. He took advantage of every extra opportunity beside the weekly post to send off another "love letter" as he put it, although they invariably contained more politics than love. When John reported that a Federalist friend, lamenting her absence, proposed making her "Autocratrix of the United States," Abigail responded with a sly dig: "Tell [him] I do not know what he means by abusing me so," she wrote. "I was always for equality as my husband can witness."[3]

Like her husband, Abigail was dismayed by the virulence of party feeling. "Such," she wrote, "is the spirit of a party who are mad with the cry of liberty and equality." The irony or absurdity was that the Bostonians had "no clergy to level, no nobility to annihilate; all are entitled to the same natural liberty, have equally the protection of the laws, and property is in the hands of so numerous a body of the people that they cannot strike at that without striking at a majority of the people." The truth was that, although they had "no real cause of complaint," they acted as if bereft of reason, attacking "the President in an open and insolent manner," abusing him for his receptions, for his birthday parties, and for refusing to "mix in society." The unanimous electoral vote had given Washington delusions of grandeur, the Anti-Federalists declared. He had become "self-important and supercilious," swollen with the illusion that the safety of government rested on him alone.

Behaving irrationally and intemperately, Abigail noted, the Jacobins continued to denounce John, "the only man who had the courage to point out to them the nature and disposition of the human heart, to tell them the consequences resulting from a government not properly balanced and proving his doctrine by a laborious research into government both ancient and modern."[4]

At the end of February, Abigail, after two months of good health, was stricken once more with the intermitting fever. When John heard of it he made plans to dash back to her bedside. Congress was about to adjourn, so he set off with Briesler, stopping briefly in New York to assure himself that all was well with Charles, and then hurrying on over icy roads. After a "jolting journey of nine or ten days in bad roads" Adams reached Quincy to find Abigail very weak but mending after almost six weeks in bed. Another trying separation was over. Together they picked up the threads of their common life. John settled comfortably into the cycle of the farm. There was spring plowing to be done, the fields to be fertilized with seaweed and manure, the new lambs to be cared for, the frost-heaved stones to be carted off, the farm to be prepared for its burden of growing things, laid open to the vernal sun. Like the fallow ground, John and Abigail had their own renewal and refreshment in each other, in the farm, and in the house which every year they settled more into, marked more with the shape of their own lives, changed and molded and made more thoroughly and unmistakably their own, so that in a sense they would live on in it as long as its walls stood.

Adams had hardly left Philadelphia before news arrived which injected a new set of issues into the political scene. Dispatches from Gouverneur Morris told of the execution of Louis XVI and his Queen, the declaration of war by France against Britain and Holland, and the dispatch of a volatile Frenchman, Edmond Charles Genet, as minister of the French Republic to its sister republic and recent ally, the United States. All this was dramatic and unsettling enough; more serious were its implications for American policy. The French made it apparent that they expected the United States to fulfill its obligations under the Treaty of 1778, by whose terms each nation was pledged to come to the support of the other in case of war. The loophole for America was the fact that the treaty specified aid only in the case of defensive war and France had clearly declared war on Britain.

Washington, proceeding to chart his course in his usual deliberate way, consulted Jefferson and Hamilton. Both men were agreed on the necessity for formal American neutrality but they differed on the proper grounds for neutrality and on the degree of help that might be afforded the French under the guise of neutrality. Jefferson wished to have Genet received as minister of the Revolutionary government, while Hamilton argued that to do so would be to give recognition to a government with a very uncertain future and bind the United States to observe its treaty agreements with France. The two men also differed on the question of where the power lay to declare American neutrality. Jefferson insisted it was the responsibility of Congress and Hamilton was equally sure that it was an executive right.

While the controversy raged in the Cabinet, Tench Coxe, Hamilton's assistant in the Treasury Department, wrote Adams to try to secure his support for the Secretary's stand. Adams replied cautiously. He was unwilling to be quoted as to his own views on the reception of Genet. The decision was the President's and no one else's. "I have no constitutional vote in it," he wrote Coxe; "I therefore protest against taking any side in it or having my name or opinion quoted about it." His own impulse was to delay the whole matter of recognition. The United States' treaties with Holland, Prussia, and England should be carefully reviewed. America had other obligations beside those to France. It was certainly true that delay in receiving Genet would cause a strong reaction. On the other hand, the President must consider whether "we are to go to war with Germany, Prussia, Holland, England, Spain, Portugal, and Italy added to Louis XVII and his Regent, Monsieur Egalité, or [whether] the Mountain or Mr. Paine or Condorcet would have us?" Where was American trade to go in such a case? "A neutrality, absolute, total neutrality, is our only hope," he concluded. As for the treaty obligations, all treaties were made on the assumption "that the state of things in both nations will remain nearly the same and the interests of both parties not essentially changed: not that one party will turn the world upside down. Any total change of interests made by the act of God or by the act of one of the parties," he wrote, "will discharge the other from all moral obligation to fulfill the treaty."

It was a matter, in Adams' view, of expediency rather than moral obligation. "It is to me," he noted, "more a question of fear. Are we afraid to offend the Mountain? I own I am: but at the same time I confess I am afraid to offend Louis XVII and his friends and allies." The soundest policy therefore was caution and delay.[5]

Throughout the spring and summer Adams watched with a curious sense of detachment as the crisis over "Citizen Genet" swept to its climax. Adams had known the Genet family in France. He had, indeed, counted the elder Genet as his friend and taken notice of the lively and enthusiastic boy who loved to participate in adult discussions. He therefore observed with mixed feelings the activities of the French ambassador, who busied himself commissioning privateers to prey on British shipping and making plans to raise an army under the command of the faded Western hero, George Rogers Clark. While Jefferson greeted Genet warmly and assured him that the vast majority of Americans were supporters of the Revolution, Hamilton made the British minister, George Hammond, privy to many confidential matters which should never have come to his ears.

Misled by the wild acclaim with which rabid Republicans greeted him on his triumphal tour through the states, Genet demanded that the President call Congress into session so that the representatives of the people could judge between Washington and himself. By implication it was a call to revolutionary action, or at the very least to a rejection of Washington's stated policy, and it brought a prompt reaction. By August the Cabinet had voted unanimously to demand his recall and Republicans who had hailed him so enthusiastically a few weeks before made frantic efforts to dissociate themselves from the bewildered young man. Jefferson, as disillusioned as his countrymen, described Genet as "hotheaded, all imagination, no judgment, passionate, disrespectful, and even indecent towards the President."[6]

Adams kept in touch with affairs in Philadelphia largely through Tench Coxe, who wrote him long, informative letters, solicited his opinion on different issues, and performed various chores such as trying to find a suitable house for him to rent on his return to the capital.

In March, Adams' English publisher, Stockdale, wrote to ask if he might publish *Publicola*, which in England had been attributed to Adams and highly praised by the Speaker of the House of Commons, by Pitt himself and other "gentlemen of the first abilities." The Attorney General, indeed, had assured Stockdale that "it was the ablest work of its kind he had ever read." In addition Stockdale wished to publish a new and corrected edition of the *Defence*.[7]

Adams disclaimed authorship of *Publicola* and suggested to Stockdale

that he seek further information from John Quincy. As for a new edition
of the *Defence*, "neglected and insulted" as the work had been, it must
"be transmitted to posterity exactly as it is . . . without any corrections,
additions or subtractions, except literary or grammatical ones." Stockdale
wished to reproduce a portrait of Adams by Copley as a frontispiece for
the new edition and Adams consented to this, adding, "I own I should be
much mortified to see such a bijou affixed to those republican volumes.
. . . . Mankind will in time," he noted, "discover that unbridled majorities
are as tyrannical and cruel as unlimited despots. . . . The King of France
and a Duke de la Rochefoucauld were destined to die martyrs to a miserable crudity of Ben Franklin"—Franklin's passion for single-branch
legislatures.[8]

Summer and fall sped past much too quickly. Abigail's health forbade
her risking the trip and the Philadelphia winter. In November, Adams
set off with Briesler for the first session of the Third Congress,
scheduled to convene early in December. By the time he left Quincy the
Republican tide had clearly ebbed, at least for the moment. Genet was in
disgrace and his adherents subdued. Adams stopped in New York to visit
Nabby and the children. "Charles," he wrote Abigail, "is well, fat, and
handsome, and persists in the line of conduct which we so much approved. His business increases and he will do very well."[9]

In Philadelphia the mood was much changed over the previous fall.
Although the Republicans had a majority in the House and had increased
their representation in the Senate, the war between France and its numerous enemies had created a general atmosphere of uncertainty. Things
were in confusion in France as the Jacobins overthrew the Girondists, as
Marat was assassinated by Charlotte Corday and Robespierre gradually
came to exert his sinister influence through the furthest reaches of the
government. As Adams put it in a letter to his Dutch friend, Van der
Kemp, we do not "hear of so much justice from French, English, or
Spaniards as to make us fall in love with either."[10]

Congress assembled on the second of December. Adams took the chair
and administered the oath of office to three Senators—Pierce Butler,
back again from South Carolina, Albert Gallatin, the Pennsylvania Republican, and Alexander Martin, a North Carolina democrat. Stephen
Mix Mitchell from Connecticut appeared to take the place of Roger
Sherman, who had died, and Mitchell was also sworn in by Adams.

The following day both houses assembled in the Senate chamber to
hear the President's address; and he, with his instinct for conciliation,
placed the blame for Genet's behavior on the minister rather than his
government and scrupulously included an account of the depredations of
the British as well as of the French on American commerce. He explained
and defended his Proclamation of Neutrality and spoke firmly of the need

to restrain American citizens from imperiling the policy of neutrality by involving themselves with the belligerent powers. The jurisdiction of the federal courts should be extended to cover such cases, he suggested. The Senate in reply gave the measure its "hearty approbation" and declared the address to be "well timed and wise, manifesting a watchful solicitude for the welfare of the nation."

Although the Senate endorsed the President's actions, Adams knew that there were many members of the House "who gnash their teeth with rage which they dare not own as yet." If the President had made any mistake at all it was, in Adams' view, by inclining too much to the French side. But he had not inclined far enough to suit Freneau and the Anti-Federalist newspapers, and he would soon find "many bitter and desperate enemies . . . in consequence of his own judgment against Genet."[11]

Benjamin Franklin Bache, Franklin's grandson and editor of the Republican Philadelphia *Aurora*, promptly attacked the President as a modern-day Cosimo de' Medici, and Freneau compared Washington to the tyrant Sylla and to imperial Caesar. He was once again denounced "for his drawing rooms, levees, declining of invitations to dinners and tea parties, his birthday odes, visits, compliments, etc.," Adams wrote in a letter to Abigail, adding, "I have held the office of Libelee General long enough. The burden of it ought to be participated and equalized, according to modern republican principles." Nonetheless the abuse of the President distressed him. "The Anti-Federalists and the Frenchified zealots have nothing now to do that I can conceive of but to ruin his character, destroy his peace, and injure his health." But he was reassured to observe that Washington "supports all their attacks with great firmness and his health appears to be very good."[12]

In the Vice-President's opinion, the new Congressmen were "not quite so good as the old ones. The funding system, the bank, and all public creditors are struck at but without success. The spirit of party is very subtle although very violent. But I trust it will be defeated." It seemed to Adams that everything his books had predicted seven years ago had come to pass in France and would come to pass in America if the latter persisted in following such a path.

John Taylor, the farmer-philosopher from Virginia, was one of the new Senators. Adams was pleased with a pamphlet by Taylor attacking banks as instruments of the devil, but the rest of the essay, which John forwarded to Abigail, was in his opinion "an ill-natured, wrong-headed, and low-lived thing."[13]

The Genet affair continued to hang fire. Although Washington had presented the correspondence of the intemperate young diplomat to the Senate, and the Cabinet had voted for his recall, he still lingered on, clearly in eclipse but not yet summoned home. John Quincy, under the pen name of "Columbus," began a series of articles directed at Genet's conduct as minister. It was a sign of the times that he could not find a newspaper in Boston to publish the pieces. Finally Noah Webster in New York accepted them; published serially through the month of December, they hastened the waning of the Frenchman's star. Adams was enormously proud of his son's articles, although he suggested that they might have shown "less indignation."

Washington, still much concerned about the best line to take in the affair, visited Adams soon after his arrival in Philadelphia and the two men discussed the various legal and political problems involved. The next day Adams returned the visit and reviewed the broader issue of America's relations with France. "The President's position, which is highly responsible, is very distressing," John wrote Abigail after his sessions with Washington. The General seemed genuinely perplexed and apprehensive but Adams was, once again, much impressed by "his earnest desire to do right, and his close application to discover it, his deliberate and comprehensive view of our affairs with all the world." The conversation, John observed, "was extremely interesting and equally affectionate."[14]

Tristram Dalton reported to Adams that the President had inquired "of him very particularly concerning the Vice-President's son—his age, his practice, his character, etc., etc., etc." From the questioning Dalton concluded that Washington was considering appointing John Quincy as a federal district attorney. Adams was pleased but inclined to advise John Quincy to refuse the office if it were offered to him. He had loftier ambitions for his eldest son. "Let him read Cicero and Demosthenes," he wrote Abigail.

Adams slipped resignedly into his duties as President of the Senate. "My own is a situation of such complete insignificance," he wrote Abigail, "that I have scarcely the power to do good or evil; yet it is the station the most proper for me," he added, "as my eyes and hands and nerves are almost worn out."[15] He had finally achieved a kind of equilibrium so that "in proportion as dangers threaten the public I grow calm," he wrote. "My country has in its wisdom contrived for me the most insignificant office that was the invention of man . . . or his imagination conceived; and as I can do neither good nor evil, I must be borne away by others and meet the common fate."[16]

Abigail firmly rebutted John's contention that the office he held was a cipher. "Suppose for instance," she argued, "as things are often exemplified by their contraries, a man in that office of unbridled ambition, subtile, intriguing, warped and biased by interested views, joining at this critical crisis his secret influence against the measures of the President, how very soon would this country be involved in all the horrors of a civil war." She was pleased to note that "the only fault" in his "political character" and one which, she confessed, had always "given me some

uneasiness is wearing away"—that is to say, "a certain irritability which
. . . has sometimes thrown you off your guard and shown . . . that a man
is not always a hero."[17]

"Citizen" Genet visited Adams and left his card, and Adams returned
the call. The conversation was cautious enough. Adams asked after
Genet's mother and sisters; they talked briefly of the most recent French
constitution but avoided any mention of the unhappy episodes that had
led to the demand for the French minister's recall. "I perceive some traits
of his countenance," he wrote Abigail, giving an account of the meeting,
"which I knew in 1779." He seemed to Adams "a youth totally destitute of
all experience in popular government, popular assemblies, or conventions
of any kind: very little accustomed to reflect upon his own or his fellow
creatures' hearts; wholly ignorant of the law of nature and nations, the
civil law, and even of the dispatches of ancient ambassadors with which
his nation and language abound." His only attributes, as far as Adams
could see, were "a declamatory style, a flitting, fluttering imagination,
an ardor in his temper, and a civil deportment."[18]

Seeing Genet led Adams to reflect on the folly of the Francophiles.
"The Anti-Federal party," he wrote John Quincy, "by their ox feasts and
their civic feasts, their King-killing toasts, their perpetual insolence and
billingsgate against all the nations and governments of Europe, their everlasting brutal cry of tyranny, despots, and combinations against liberty,
etc., etc., etc., have probably irritated, offended, and provoked all the
crowned heads of Europe at last; and a little more of this indelicacy and
indecency may involve us in a war with all the world." It seemed to him
that the government was in a most critical situation, brought there largely
"by the heat and impatience of the people." Much was to be laid to
"Paine's yellow fever . . . a putrid, malignant, mortal, fatal epidemic.
. . . It is reported this luminary is coming to America," he concluded.
"I had rather two more Genets should arrive."[19]

Decisively defeated in his efforts to engineer the censure of his rival,
Jefferson resigned from the Cabinet at the end of December and, leaving
Madison and Giles to carry on the fight, withdrew to Monticello. His
departure aroused mixed feelings in Adams. "I have so long been in an
habit of thinking well of his abilities and general good dispositions," he
wrote Abigail, "that I cannot but feel some regret at this event." But
Jefferson's "want of candor, his obstinate prejudices both of aversion and
attachment; his real partiality in spite of all his pretensions, and his low
notions about many things have so nearly reconciled me to it that I will
not weep." Nor was he deceived by the Virginian's talk of abandoning
the political arena for the quiet of his plantation. If he was neglected at
Monticello he would soon die of frustration, "for instead of being the
ardent pursuer of science that some think him," he added, "he is indolent

and his soul is poisoned with ambition." The retirement to Monticello was simply to allow his reputation to grow until a clamor was raised for him to succeed Washington as President. "So be it," Adams concluded, "if it is thus ordained. I like the precedent very well because I expect I shall have occasion to follow it." When he was obliged to retire himself he trusted that he would be able to conquer "the foul fiend" ambition and withdraw contentedly to the asylum that he had been preparing for thirty years.[20]

"I am almost tempted to wish he may be chosen Vice-President at the next election," he wrote Abigail, "for there, if he could do no good, he could do no harm. He has talents I know, and integrity I believe; but his mind is now poisoned with passion, prejudice, and faction."[21]

In a letter to John Quincy he continued his speculations on the cause of Jefferson's resignation. Perhaps it was because he was addicted to expensive living and "could not subdue his pride and vanity as I have done, and proportion his style of life to his revenue. . . . Mr. Jefferson has been obliged to lower his note in politics. Paine's principles, when adopted by Genet, were not found so convenient for a Secretary of State. . . . He could not rule the roost in the ministry. He was often in a minority. . . . Ambition is the subtlest beast of the intellectual and moral field. It is wonderfully adroit in concealing itself from its owner, I had almost said from itself. Jefferson thinks by this step to get a reputation of an humble, modest, meek man, wholly without ambition or vanity. He may even have deceived himself into this belief. But if a prospect opens, the world will see and he will feel that he is as ambitious as Oliver Cromwell though no soldier. . . . Numa was called from the forest to be King of Rome. And if Jefferson, after the death or resignation of the President, should be summoned from the familiar society of Egeria, to govern the country forty years in peace and piety, so be it."

After this tortuous examination of the Virginian's motives, a problem that clearly cost him some sleep, he added, "But after all I am not very anxious what were his motives. Though his desertion may be a loss to us of some talent, I am not sorry for it on the whole, because . . . his temper [is] embittered against the constitution and the administration as I think."[22]

It was clear enough that Adams, even if he hesitated to admit it to himself, thought of Jefferson as his rival. He wished and intended to succeed Washington and he watched with apprehension every move of his former friend, analyzed it, and calculated its effect. What he saw plainly disturbed him. Jefferson was a master of political maneuver, subtle, shrewd, tenacious, a politician to his fingertips and politician in the new style, resourceful in developing and exploiting every opportunity presented by the emerging democracy. Complex and many-faceted as the Virginian was, he was a simpler man with a simpler creed than Adams. Viewing the world with a naïve optimism that was shared by the great majority of his countrymen, he had no doubts about man's fallen nature, no sense of the precariousness of the human or the political situation. If the monocrats could be forestalled in their efforts to rivet chains on the American people, if the national government could be confined to a narrowly proscribed role and kept subordinate to the states, all would be well. In any contest for the affections of the people, the man who perceives the terrible ambiguity of life, who sees into the heart of darkness and insists on speaking of what he sees, will lose out to the confident optimist who assures the people that they are good and that their troubles are due, quite simply, to a small group of malign or willful men. So Adams, as he girded himself for the contest that he foresaw, was perhaps already doomed. Certainly he was seriously inhibited by his image of himself as a man above politics, an independent man whose fiercely guarded integrity would not allow him to truck and bargain and scheme for the prize he so much desired. Yet within the rules of the game as he played it, his restless mind was applied without respite to the knottiest political problems and even with one hand tied behind his back, in a manner of speaking, he would prove a tough and wily fighter.

As always, Adams' own feelings oscillated between hope and gloom. On the sixth of January the people of America seemed to him "wise, upright, firm, and steady in spite of little groups of wrong heads in every principal town." But three days later he found the prospects of the country "gloomy," the people full of faction and unreason, "nearly one half the continent . . . in constant opposition to the other." It seemed clear to him from the mad course of the French Revolution that "the eighteenth century, which has been the pride and boast of mankind for its humanity," as he wrote his friend Van der Kemp, "is to end in horrors more horrible than the proscription of Sylla or the massacres of Charles IX."[23]

The routine of the Vice-President's life was a simple and austere one. He had a substantial breakfast, read the daily newspapers, smoked a cigar, and took a brisk walk in the State House yard, "a beautiful thing formed on the English plan." After he returned home from the Senate he spent the evening reading state papers, saw a few friends once or twice a week, and spent much time with Thomas. Besides his weekly letters to Nabby he wrote regularly to John Quincy and often to Charles. Charles was frequently on his mind. He was disturbed by his son's inclination to get married. To saddle himself with a family before he was well started in the law would be disastrous, especially for someone so unstable. Adams hoped, by his frequent letters, to "fix his attention and excite his ambition; in which design," he added, "I flatter myself I shall have success."

Charles had fallen in love with Sally Smith, the Colonel's youngest sister and his own sister-in-law. She was the girl whom Abigail had described five years earlier as having "a fine figure and a pretty face, un-

affected in her manners, modest and composed." Charles was far from
being able as yet to support a wife, and both John and Abigail warned
him sternly against considering matrimony. He was, in effect, forbidden
to see Sally and urged to banish any thought of marrying her. Having
issued the ukase, Adams, after some months, inquired whether his son's
infatuation had subsided. "I shall say that it was my wish to have concealed in my own bosom every chagrin," Charles replied. But now that
his father had probed the wound he was bound to say that he was not
convinced of his own "weakness and error," and if he were to say so it
would be far from the truth. "Were I to declare," he wrote with a touching
candor, "that I did not entertain the same opinion of Sally Smith that I
ever did, I should declare a falsehood."[24]

Thomas Boylston had completed his legal training and been admitted
to the bar during the summer, and Adams went to hear him argue his first
case. It involved a prosecution of the keepers of a brothel and as a result
the court was crowded with interested spectators. Thomas conducted his
defense "at least to his own satisfaction," John observed a little dryly. He
kept a close eye on Thomas in his little circle of Quakers and set him to
reading Clarendon "in order to from a judgment of the duration of the
French Republic, and all other democratical republics." In the evenings
Thomas came to his father's apartment and they discussed Hampden,
Charles I and Cromwell, Essex and Rupert. "I fear," John wrote Abigail,
"he makes too many visits in families where there are young ladies. Time
is spent and nothing learned. Pardon me! disciple of Wollstonecraft!" he
added mischievously. "I never relished conversations with ladies except
with one at a time and alone rather than in company. I liked not to lose
my time." It seemed to him, indeed, that all time was lost that was "not
employed in farming, innocent, healthy, gay, elegant amusement! enchanting employment!"[25]

Charles passed the New York State bar examinations with honor and
was admitted as a barrister. The Reverend William Shaw died suddenly
and left Abigail's sister, Eliza, a widow with three children to provide for.
"I must assist them as much as I can," Adams wrote John Quincy. "They
have deserved it by their kindness to me and mine upon all occasions."[26]

Colonel Smith came to Philadelphia for a fortnight, full of mysterious
plans designed to make his fortune several times over. It was a matter of
some embarrassment to Adams that the pro-French party in New York
managed to employ Colonel Smith, by playing on "his foible vanity," in
framing resolves charging the state's representatives in Congress with
being hostile to France.

Abigail's letters kept John alive; they were "a feast," "a rich treasure,"
and he their miser, he assured her. They gave him "more entertainment

than all the speeches I hear" in the Senate. "There is more good thoughts, fine strokes, and mother wit in them than I hear in the whole week." For him the old adage was true—an ounce of mother wit was worth a pound of clergy—and he rejoiced that John Quincy had "an abundance of not only mother wit, but his mother's wit." It was "one of the most amiable and striking traits in his compositions." Equally, if he had any family pride, it came from the same source, those family-proud Quincys and Nortons. "His pa," he wrote, "renounces and abjures every trace of it." But the mail was unpredictable. Sometimes it took two weeks and on one astonishing occasion a letter from Abigail arrived in five days. How it "could have leaped to this distance in five days I know not," he wrote.

Abigail looked on her letters as a kind of conversation with her absent husband. "I want to sit down and converse with you every evening. I sit here alone," she wrote, "and brood over probabilities and conjectures." She had no intention of letting John's reference to Mary Wollstonecraft pass without rejoinder. He might scoff at feminine pretensions to equality, but he must "confess the truth and own that when you are sick of the ambition, the intrigues, the duplicity, and the treachery of the aspiring part of your own sex it is a comfort and a consolation to retire to the simplicity, the gentleness and tenderness of the female character."[27]

The letters from Quincy that John awaited so impatiently contained among other delights a day-to-day account of the farm. The wells had been very low and there had not been enough water in the river to turn the water wheel at the mill, but "four days and nights of . . . an old-fashioned rain . . . laid our fences in the meadow below the house flat," she wrote. The water was a foot above the bridge and over the top of Mr. Black's wall. A newborn lamb was sick with the mumps and couldn't eat and Abigail had its throat rubbed daily with "goose oil." "The grass is turning up green and today we have a fine rain," she noted. If John intended to go to dairying on a large scale, Abigail would need extra pails, tubs, and stools. In addition she wanted two wheelbarrows for the two farms, two spades, two forks, two shovels, two oxen, two hoes. Money seemed scarcer than ever. She had limited her non-farm purchases to two dollars and fifty cents for a pair of shoes, yet she could hardly make ends meet. She had tarred the trees for six weeks, she wrote, and "the slugs still crawl." The wagon wheels were worn down with carting and there were over a hundred loads of manure to be spread as soon as the plowing was finished.[28]

John was vastly pleased by the intelligence and vigor which Abigail displayed in running the farm. "It is a noble regale to read your letters," he wrote, adding, "Plant the ground which we broke up last fall with corn. Sow barley where we had corn last year. Plant again the lower garden. Potatoes again at the beach meadow."[29] He looked forward to adding ten more cows to the dairy herd come summer. They could be pastured on Penn's Hill until after the spring mowing. Abigail, therefore, was to buy as many yearlings, calves, and two-year-olds as she could to bring the herd to twenty in all. He sent a hundredweight of clover seed and twelve quarts of hard grass by boat to be planted in the meadow lot. "You are so valorous and noble a farmer," he declared, "that I feel little anxious about agriculture. Manure in hills, if you think best: but manure your barley ground well and harrow it well." "The more I am charmed with your bravery and activity in farming," he wrote, "the more I am mortified that my letters in answer to yours are so insignificant and insipid."[30] If the world was as well governed as the Adams farm was by Abigail, the fate of man would be a much happier one.

In addition to her almost daily calendar of farm life, Abigail kept her husband in touch with political developments in Massachusetts. ("What a jumble are my letters—politics, domestic occurrences, farming anecdotes—pray light your segars with them, leave them not to the inspection of futurity," she wrote, knowing better.)[31] The Democratic Club (Abigail called it the Jacobin Club) was busy recruiting members and corresponding with sister clubs in other states, she noted. The death of John Hancock in October had encouraged a number of candidates for governor to come forth. The club intended to put up Bowdoin, Dana, and Gerry at the next election. It was, among other things, militantly atheistic and if it flourished it would do its best to "overturn our religion and all the rest (violence and anarchy) would soon follow."[32]

Sullivan, the Attorney General of the state, had clashed with John Quincy, referring to his *Columbus* papers as "puerile and literary plagiarism," and warning that "even the high station of his sire will not screen him from contempt." Abigail was indignant and denounced Sullivan as a "false and hollow . . . hypocrite." John Quincy was more disturbed to note that some of his friends seemed pleased at the attacks made on him by "Americanus" (Sullivan), but his father drew a moral from it—we are no more secure from the envy of those we consider our friends than from the malice of our enemies.[33] Sullivan seemed intent on seeking the governorship and John Quincy wrote his father that he would be interested to see how he would keep in "with the prophet Samuel." Both, to be sure, were Jacobins; "both Frenchmen, both pretending to be the slavish adorers of our sovereign lords, the people," but Samuel Adams had the greater name and broader backing.[34]

Samuel was Adams' own candidate. "I wish the old fellow was a little more national," he wrote Abigail, "but he cannot do much harm and will not last long. Master Cleverly used to say thirty years ago, 'I pity Mr. Sam Adams, for he was born a rebel.' I hope he will not die one," John added.[35]

Thinking of Samuel filled him with nostalgia for days long past when decisions seemed simple and clear enough. He wished "for the times when old Sam and old John conducted with more wisdom and more success" the affairs of the country. But this, he remarked wryly, "is egotism enough to deserve the guillotine to be sure. . . . . Old scenes and old results" haunted his memory. Although Adams confessed that his cousin's conduct was "not such as I can approve in many things of late years," he hoped that Samuel would win the governorship and could not bring himself to believe "that the people of Massachusetts will forsake him in his last moments. Alas," he added, "his grandeur must be of short duration if it ever commences." If Cushing were elected Governor, Adams would find the political atmosphere much more congenial in his home state and its affairs would be "more prudently conducted," but sentiment was stronger than practical considerations and Adams was delighted when word reached Philadelphia that the old hero had won an overwhelming victory. "I have no apprehension that he will oppose or embarrass the general government more than another," he wrote Abigail;[36] if he had been defeated "it would have been [a triumph] to despots through the world, to have seen Sam Adams forsaken by the people."[37]

The Boston Federalists showed none of Adams' charity for Governor-elect Sam Adams. They protested the election and in effort declared war on his administration. Their action seemed to Adams shortsighted and ill natured, "a very unwarrantable and indecent attempt. . . . . He will forever defeat them," he wrote Abigail, "unless the people lose all sense of justice as well as gratitude. He has more merit than they all, and in my opinion will be as good a Federalist as any of them would be, after being chosen Governor. We shall see as Governor an overzealous Federalist."[38]

Abigail, if anything, took a gloomier view of things than her husband. She was convinced that "the halcyon days of America" were past. "Unless mankind were universally enlightened, which can never be, they are unfit for freedom," she wrote. "Nor do I believe that our Creator designed it for them. If such a boon had been designed for them, all ages and nations from Adam to the present day would not have been one standing, continued, universal proof to the contrary." It seemed clear to her, for the moment at least, that "some were made for rule, others for submission." For her part, her ambition, she wrote John, "will extend no further than reigning in the heart of my husband. That is my throne and there I aspire to be absolute."

The poor, battered furniture that Abigail had brought to Philadelphia to furnish the Bush Hill house their first winter in that city had been stored since her departure. The Quincy house was sparsely furnished in consequence and Abigail wished to have her things back; so Adams undertook to have them crated for shipment on Cheeseman's coastal packet. It was a sad chore. The tables and chairs, scratched and nicked, told the story of their peregrinations. As the furniture was being unloaded at the Quincy town wharf it began to rain, soaking the upholstery and spotting the wood. To Abigail, it seemed the last straw. Were they never to cease their wanderings?

As winter dwindled, Adams' thoughts turned more and more to Quincy and the farm. "The spring opens," he wrote lyrically, "the birds sing, the weather is fine, and all things cheerful but my thoughts about my home and our public prospects. . . . . I am weary of this scene of dullness. We have done nothing and shall do nothing this session which ought to be done. . . . One day spent at home would afford me more inward delight and comfort than a week or a winter in this place."[39]

LXV

On the twelfth of March the Senate debated the question of the Algerine depredations and Adams, on a motion that in his view would have resulted in war, cast the deciding vote on an equal division. "If . . . this country is involved in war," he wrote Abigail, "it shall not be by my fault." Despite such occasional triumphs, his duty as presiding officer of the Senate was a cruel chore.. "It is to be sure a punishment," he complained, "to hear other men talk five hours every day, and not be at liberty to talk at all myself, especially as more than half I hear appears to me very young, inconsiderate, and inexperienced."[1]

The Francophiles in the Senate seized on the rumor that the Duke of York had been captured by the French and carried in a cage to Paris and that the British fleet had surrendered to the French navy. They informed Adams of the great event and requested him to announce it from his chair. Adams was not taken in. It was a trap to "gull the gudgeons," he wrote Abigail, "but I was too old to be taken in, at least by so gross an artifice, the falsehood of which was to me palpable."

Fauchet appeared at the President's ball as Genet's replacement and Washington gave the new emissary the place of honor at his right. In consequence the Spanish minister was deeply offended and the British minister, George Hammond, left the hall in a huff. Adams was pleased with Fauchet, "reserved, cautious, discreet . . . a very different character from Genet." He dined with the former and present minister at Governor Mifflin's and Genet was as lively and gay as if he had enjoyed nothing but success in his American mission, while his successor looked as bland as a Chinee.

The new minister had reason to be pleased; shortly after his arrival he found himself the beneficiary of the highhanded behavior of the British ministry, who had issued an order in council aimed at American merchant shipping in the Caribbean. By its provisions, British warships were authorized to seize any neutral vessels carrying provisions or supplies to the French islands or transporting products of those islands to Europe or continental United States.

Without warning, a British fleet sailed into the Caribbean and scooped up more than two hundred and fifty unsuspecting American ships, half of which were condemned by British Admiralty Courts. It was not difficult to anticipate the reaction. News from Montserrat of the capture of American vessels by English cruisers "has occasioned," Adams wrote, "a more serious alarm than anything before. . . . I doubt whether this people will bear, another whole year, the detention of the posts and the depredations in their trade." In the face of such arrogant acts, Fauchet had only to bide his time.

The seizures of course aroused the fury of the Francophiles. They demanded war at once on the side of their ally, France, against their enemy, England. The wild clamor, so intemperate and ill considered, distressed Adams. The militants were ready to go to war without an army or a navy, with the new government holding grimly to a hazardous existence, and the foreign and domestic debt still unpaid. "Club meets to counteract club," he wrote Abigail, "merchants to undo what merchants or pretended merchants have done, and the public opinion is a chaos, a proteus, anything, everything, and nothing. Yet all sides trumpet and dogmatize about the public opinion." Even the New England men in Congress seemed swayed toward a war that could only be disastrous for their region. Henry Dearborn and William Lyman were reported to be falling under the influence of the Virginians. Lyman, a warm Republican, was a "pupil and correspondent of Sullivan, certainly; probably of Jarvis and Austin," the two leading Jacobins of Boston, and it seemed to Adams that he had "a false, subtle, and malicious countenance."

The people, urged on by the counsels of rash and ambitious men, were every day more clamorous for war. Among them was John's own brother, Peter Boylston. Such was human folly. "I love them too well with all their faults to be glad to see their present rapid rise toward destruction," he wrote Abigail, adding, "All that I have and all that I am cheerfully would I give to prevent it but I see no means." Only disaster would open people's eyes to the truth. "It is some relief against melancholy to laugh," he concluded. But it was little relief at that; the laughter was forced and the old black mood seized him, a lassitude and a weariness of the spirit. To see so much and feel so deeply—these were exhausting gifts. He wished once again, quite sincerely, to be rid of his office, duties, and honors, and back in the seaside hills and fields of Quincy. His frustration broke forth in a letter to Abigail. "I . . . am wearied to death with ennui," he wrote. "Obliged to be punctual by my habits, confined to my seat, as in a prison, to see nothing done, hear nothing said, and to say and do nothing. Oh, that my books were here within a mile or two and my little habitation and pretty little wife above all." It must have been divine punishment for some unperceived vice which condemned him to be separated from Abigail "when we were too young and when we are too old."[2] The majority of the House was certainly for mischief, he noted, "and there is no doubt they represent the people in the Southern states and a large number in the Northern. *Vox populi vox dei*, they say: and so it is sometimes, but it is sometimes the voice of Mahomet, of Caesar, of Catiline, the Pope, and the Devil," he added ruefully.

The British had certainly given ample cause for offense. "What can be done with that mad and unjust nation?" Abigail exclaimed. "If they force us into a war with them George will deserve a second time to lose his head." And Adams agreed that "Britain has done much amiss and deserves all that will fall thereon." No one knew her insolence better than he and Abigail, but he could not forbear to reflect that in that particular quality America was "her very image and superscription . . . as true a gamecock as she and, I warrant you, shall become as great a scourge to mankind."[3]

While the Southerners paid lip service to peace, they voted consistently for every measure that would bring on war and allowed themselves to express sentiments in private very different from their public professions. "Oh, my soul," John exclaimed, "come not into the secrets of such Republicans! . . . The spirit, principles, and system of rational liberty to all nations is my toast; but I see no tendency to anything but anarchy, licentiousness, and despotism. Mankind will not learn wisdom from experience."[4]

The Vice-President read Rousseau to divert himself from the angry cries of "our madmen," the warmongers, yet Rousseau drew his thoughts back constantly to the present moment. He saw in Americans, he wrote Thomas, "the same ardent passion for war" which had characterized Athenians, Romans, and more recently Britons. This disposition would draw the United States into war and a "monstrous debt," the debt would "beget corruption," and the war inflame and excite ambition. Plunging the country into war would almost inevitably involve the United States in civil conflict and a division of the continent under two generals who would become kings.

While he was convinced that the nations of Europe had no chance of introducing liberty into their governments without hereditary executives and hereditary Senates, he insisted to his son, "I have not the least thought or the smallest desire to introduce any such institutions into America." The United States could "live and be happy without them." He was sure that the constitution would last at least for his own lifetime, for it seemed to him the best adapted for the state of American society; furthermore American circumstances would "admit of no other, or at least of very little variation from it."

Rousseau had believed that society found man a god and made him into a brute. Adams believed quite the opposite; "that time, education, government, and religion have changed his brute into a god. So widely we differ. . . . . The state of nature," he continued, "is not so beautiful nor that of society so deformed as he paints them." The very idea of equality was repugnant to Adams, for it ran counter to his most direct experience of the world—its extraordinary multiformity and variety. The Frenchman's determination to free nature from blame for the inequalities that were part of the human condition was "weak and foolish." But Rousseau's formula had found an echo in the Revolutionary theorists of France. The law of God, the law of nature and nations, "the whole science of moral obligation, the doctrine of conscience," the Christian religion, the teachings of Mahomet, Moses, Confucius, Zoroaster—these were simply the "artful devices of aristocrats and subtle politicians" which the Revolution, led by philosophers, would unmask. After centuries of ignorance and superstition men's minds would at last be unshackled. Forty years after Rousseau's book was printed philosophers became the rulers of France and "have been these five years employed in making experiments upon man; hitherto not much to his honor, and not at all for his comfort."

The proper view of man and his relation to his fellows might be simply put, Rousseau or no Rousseau. If A considered himself the work of God —and also considered B as another work of the same God—"reverence for the common Maker, the common Parent will respect B as much as A, and A as much as B." This was the true law of nature, the proper equality of man, and the foundation of all humane society.

The French philosopher had created a system out of nothing and sold it to the eternally gullible theorizers. Against all facts and experience, against knowledge of the sordid and depraved lives of savages, of their starvings, their fears, their diseases, their terrible vulnerability to nature, Rousseau argued their superiority to civilized man, and civilized man, in a comedy of self-denigration, believed him. Adams agreed certainly that there was a difference between men "in a savage and domestic condition," but insisted that the "advantages in point of health, strength, activity, and courage, as well as understanding, is on the side of the citizen in general."[5]

But Adams' philosophical reflections did little to isolate him from the tempest that raged over the actions of the British. Twenty-five years before, Adams had held himself aloof from those aspects of the Revolutionary agitation which, he felt, threatened his treasured integrity and independence. He was no less disposed to do so in the present crisis. Although he considered himself philosophically a Federalist, he observed the maneuverings of the Federalists and the Antis with a critical and to some extent dispassionate eye. He noted with more than a little skepticism that the Federalists, emboldened by the discrediting of Genet and their success in holding off Republican attacks on funding and assumption, were promising or threatening "mighty things." Knowing them perhaps better than they knew themselves, he doubted "their power, their union, their spirit. . . . . They are seeking popularity and loaves and fishes as well as the Antis and find it inconvenient to act a decided part in anything."[6]

News of a great British naval victory in the West Indies delighted the Anglophiles and they in turn made public demonstrations to honor the event; but Adams could "see no cause of joy in all the exultation in either side. I am compelled," he wrote Abigail, "to console myself as well as I can." It seemed to him that the only recourse of a wise man was "in stoicism or Christianity. . . . . *Vive la bagatelle!*" he exclaimed. ". . . I have no other resource in my solicitude, amidst all my gloomy forebodings, of the future miseries of my beloved species. . . . In short I see no end of wars. It is a comfort to reflect that they can do no greater evil to me than to put an end to their lives."[7]

Adams roused himself from his depression to write John Quincy who, suffering from his own glooms, lamented the fact that, although "advanced almost to the age of thirty, I have no political existence, and my ideas of liberty and government are so widely distant from the fashion of the day that they are much more likely to be injurious than beneficial." Moreover after four years of practicing law he remained "obscure and unknown without any expectation of brilliant success, and scarcely with the hope of obtaining with all the industry in the power of man . . . even a decent subsistence."[8]

"You must bustle in the crowd," Adams advised his son, "make speeches in town meetings, and push yourself forward. Meet with the caucuses and join political clubs." John Quincy was inclined to be careless in his dress; he must give attention to little things—"an erect figure, a steady countenance, a neat dress, a genteel air; an oratorical period, a resolute, determined spirit." He must not ask favors of the people but through his ability and influence compel them to ask favors of him. "When you arrive at my age," he concluded, "and look back upon your youth you will see your errors as I do."[9] He should not be satisfied with mediocre success, considering his talents and his opportunities. "If you do not rise to the head not only of your profession but of your country," he wrote sternly, "it will be owing to your own *laziness, slovenliness,* and *obstinacy.*" To Abigail he noted that their eldest son was a man "of great experience and I hope sound philosophy." But he must learn "silence and reserve, prudence, caution—above all to curb his vanity and collect himself, faculties or virtues that his father has often much wanted." That dangerous impetuousness, that pride and irritability which was part of his heritage, he must exorcise or discipline. "I have often thought he has more prudence at twenty-seven," John wrote, "than his father at fifty-eight."[10]

Spurred on by the popular excitement, Congress passed an embargo on all goods in March. The effect, in Adams' view, would be more psycho· logical than practical. It had the immediate result of quieting the clamor, and some of the people, among them "the foolish tradesmen and laborers" who had been "the most noisy and turbulent," were the first to feel its effects. But there were still many belligerent individuals in Congress and out who wished to break American neutrality and who proposed such measures as sequestering all English debts, an act tantamount to declaring war.

Watching the war spirit grow and unable to check it or to speak out against it, Adams declared, made his situation "as disagreeable as any I ever knew. I should have no fear of an honest war," he added, "but a knavish one would fill me with disgust and abhorrence." Writing to John Quincy in a similar vein, he declared that such a war would be "the most cruel war that was ever waged, of the most uncertain object and most incomprehensible issue. We know not who would be our enemies, nor who would be our friends, nor what we could get nor what we might lose." It had been fashionable to charge wars to kings, but it seemed to Adams that *"le peuple souvereign* is as inflammable and as proud, and at the same time less systematic, uniform, and united; so that it is not so easy for them to avoid wars." The administration had labored long and hard to avoid war, "but the *peuple souvereign"* was "continually committing some intemperance of indiscretion or other tending to defeat all our precautions."[11] The very people who were most hot for war were, with splendid illogic, opposed to any increases in the budget to provide for waging it. "But the inconsistencies and absurdities of men are no novelties to me," Adams noted wryly.

Madison suggested that the United States hire the Portuguese navy, and his ally, William B. Giles, declared "navies altogether as very foolish things." Despite the determined opposition of the Virginians, Congress voted to build six frigates to augment the handful of ships that made up the American navy. In April a nonintercourse bill prohibiting all commerce with Great Britain passed the House and was sent to the Senate. It was a tense and dangerous moment. Passage of the bill was almost certain to bring war with England. After feverish maneuvering the Senate split evenly and Adams cast the deciding vote against the bill, again an issue in his mind of either war or peace.

With the nation apparently determined on war, Hamilton and a group of Federalist Senators urged Washington to send a minister plenipotentiary to England for one final effort at negotiation. The President and the other members of the Cabinet were as anxious to avoid war with England and preserve America's neutrality as Hamilton and Adams; in April, Washington proposed to the Senate that Chief Justice Jay be sent to England to make another effort to remove the most serious sources of friction between the two countries.

After three days of warm debate the Senate approved the appointment by a vote of eighteen to eight. The combination of Federalists and moderates overrode the militant Republicans and won the administration at least a few months' respite from the clamor for war. The Francophiles were furious. "You cannot imagine what horror some persons are in, lest peace should continue," John wrote Abigail. "The prospect of peace throws them into distress." The Anti-Federalists attacked Jay for his reputedly "monarchial principles, his indifference to the navigation of the Mississippi, his attachment to England, his aversion to France," all of which allegations were false, in Adams' opinion.

Although Adams had "no very sanguine hopes" of Jay's success, he was pleased with the appointment. He liked and admired the New Yorker and felt sure that he would "give as much satisfaction to the American people as any man." Jay's mission, Adams remarked, "will recommend him to the choice of the people for President as soon as a vacancy shall happen. This will weaken the hopes of the Southern states for Jefferson."[12] And his own as well, though he did not say it.

Early in May, Adams dined with two former members of the French Constituent Assembly, Monsieur Beaumez and the former Bishop of Autun, the shrewd cripple, Talleyrand-Périgord, both of them refugees from the Terror who had fled from France to Britain, been expelled from that country, and found asylum in America. Talleyrand had a dozen schemes for making his fortune, most of them involving speculative ventures in land. He had already made a friend of Hamilton. Although Adams did not warm to the Frenchman, he was aware of the force of his bold and realistic mind. Conscious as he was of the strange quirks and turns of fortune, John could hardly have guessed that the sharp-faced little man who had been cast off the Revolutionary merry-go-round would within a few years be one of the most powerful men in France, the French Minister of Foreign Affairs and an enemy of Adams' own administration. The Frenchman, for his part, professed to be unimpressed by Americans. They seemed a volatile, unstable people, given to emotional proclamations about freedom and liberty, but more concerned with money than with principles. Indeed, he returned to France convinced that his hosts could be bought and sold with impunity, a mistake that would be perhaps the astute statesman's gravest error.

May was "terribly hot and dry for the season," yet the country looked charming, and farmer Adams longed to be back in Quincy. But important issues and important bills were pending and he dared not leave. A new minister must be dispatched to France where Gouverneur Morris had infuriated the French by his haughty contempt for the Revolution. Adams sweltered and pined for home and wrote notes to Abigail during sessions of the Senate, which he had never done before. "We go on as usual," he observed, "Congress resolving one thing and the Democratical Societies resolving the contrary—the President doing what is right and clubs and mobs resolving it to be all wrong." Fauchet had begun to put in an appearance at meetings of the Democratic Clubs where he was featured and lionized. "This must not be carried very far," Adams declared. "These assemblies are very criminal."[13]

To Adams it seemed increasingly clear that the behavior of the Southerners was only to be explained by their determination to avoid paying their British debts. This was the "real object of all the wild projects and mad motions which have been made during the whole session," he wrote Abigail, adding dramatically, "Oh, Liberty! Oh, my country! Oh, debt and oh, Sirs! These debtors are the persons who are continually declaiming against the corruption of Congress. Imprudence! thy front is brass. There will be no end of my tragic Oh's and tragic Ah's," he concluded. Abigail replied, "If the Southern states force us into a war I hope their Negroes will fight our battles and pay these real and haughty aristocrats all the service due to them from the real and true Republicans." Abigail reconciled herself to John's continued absence with the thought of how necessary he was "to the welfare and protection of a country which I love and a people who will *one day* do justice to *your memory.*"[14]

As the session dragged on Adams grew more and more restless. Writing to Abigail for the third time within a week, he closed his letter with the words: "I am, patience almost exhausted, tenderly, tenderly, tenderly yrs." The absence of his weekly letter from her put him in a pet. For the first time in months he had failed to receive the expected epistle, "a delicious letter worth a dozen of mine. . . . Never in my life did I long to see you more." "The world is a riddle," he wrote, "which death, I hope, will unravel." In spite of what he had endured, he had much to be grateful for—"good parents, an excellent wife, and promising children—tolerable health upon the whole and competent fortune. Success, almost without example, in a dreadful revolution, and still hopes of better times."[15]

At the end of May, with the business of Congress hastening to a conclusion, he asked for and obtained leave to withdraw from the Senate. Impatient as he was to be home, he dreaded the trip—the heat, the dust, the crowded carriages, the disheveled inns with their flies, fleas, and bedbugs, the weary jolting, hour after hour, over bumpy roads. He was an old man, as he never tired of saying, nearly sixty, and the trip to Quincy lay before "like a mountain. I am too old and too feeble for these long journeys," he wrote Abigail. "I am at an age when I ought to be at home with my family." In a few weeks he would take her in his arms once more. The thought sustained him.[16]

A few days before he left the city Adams got word from the Secretary of State, Edmund Randolph, that the President had decided to nominate John Quincy as "resident minister" to Holland. The news was compensation for any number of political bruises and lacerations, for months of boredom and anxiety, for a host of personal frustrations and disappointments. He wrote at once to his son, admonishing him to "be secret. Don't open your mouth to any human being on the subject except your mother." He could hardly contain his delight, and having written to give John Quincy the news, he sat down the same day to compose a lengthy letter of advice and admonition. (He did not know that John Quincy, just a few days before, had made a resolution to give up politics.) He must come on to Philadelphia as soon as possible and master all the affairs and interests of the United States; he must read the correspondence of his predecessors, including that of his father; go over the Journals of Congress and talk to the Secretary of State. Beyond this, he must take the President as a model of personal appearance and deportment. "No man alive," he wrote, "is more attentive to these things." He must be "neat and handsome" in his dress, but personally frugal; he should be cautious in his dispatches but make them models of "art and elegance as well as information."

Just before Adams' departure for Quincy, the Senate received a message from the President of the United States, nominating "John Quincy Adams of Massachusetts to be resident minister of the United States at The Hague." As the Vice-President read the words to the Senators he was fully conscious of the drama of the moment, and the Senators, however strongly opposed some of them may have been to the Vice-President's political principles, were touched by his obvious pride and excitement. After perfunctory debate they "unanimously advised and consented" to the appointment, and Adams set out by stage for New York, bursting with the news.[17]

Shortly after Adams left Philadelphia the Neutrality Act passed both houses of Congress. The bill, which reinforced the President's proclamation of the previous year, forbade United States citizens to enlist in the service of a foreign power and prohibited the fitting out of foreign armed vessels in American ports. The measure was designed to meet strong English protests over the activities of French privateers, but it did little to placate the British and increased considerably the bitterness of the French party.

The principal event of the summer was the so-called Whiskey Rebellion among the farmers of western Pennsylvania who, resenting the excise tax on spirituous liquors, refused to pay and proceeded from defiant proclamations to armed resistance. The new crisis fed the fires of faction. If the insurgents were successful in their resistance to the authority of the federal government, the government's days were clearly numbered. There had been similar rumblings in Maryland, the Carolinas, and Georgia, and the Pennsylvania rebels were reported to consider themselves the vanguard of a popular uprising against the "monocrats." They would march on Philadelphia, "accumulating in their course, and swelling over the banks of the Susquehanna like a torrent—irresistible and devouring in its progress."[18]

When Washington's orders to the insurgents to disperse were ignored, the President called on the states for a levy of twelve thousand men. The response was astonishing and reassured Adams and the Federalists. So many volunteers turned out that the administration was hard put to it to accommodate them. Washington placed himself at the head of the hastily assembled force and, with Hamilton as second in command, marched west as far as Harrisburg without turning up a single rebel. Thoughout the month of August, while the country waited anxiously for news of a bloody clash, the federal force, its command devolving on Hamilton, scoured western Pennsylvania and finally turned up some twenty unhappy farmers who were eager to recant their heresies.

Adams was pleased that the national government had acted with so much energy to suppress the challenge to its authority, but the campaign did little or nothing to add to Federalist strength. Indeed, the ablest spokesman for the Federalist cause in the House of Representatives, Fisher Ames, found himself under heavy attack in his home state of Massachusetts, and Adams was much concerned lest he should become a casualty in the approaching congressional elections.

Aside from his attention to local and national politics, Adams' time was occupied with his farm and his library. His plan for converting the three farms into a dairy operation involved broad changes in crop and pasture, the construction of new stalls and feed bins, the purchase of cheese presses, and the mastery of the art of large-scale cheese making.

So occupied, the summer slipped away before he quite knew it was gone. The golden days of late August shaded into a crisp September. The corn was picked and husked and the stalks grew so dry they rattled in the fall winds; pumpkins with their strange pulpy burden of seeds swelled in the fields; the apples ripened—the bittersweet Winesaps, the Golden Delicious, the fragrant Mackintosh for baking, the firm-fleshed apple-green pippins, the Gravensteins which made the best pies and applesauce. They gave the fall its most characteristic aroma, the odor of windfalls, gleaming in the sere grass, the odor of the cider press and the felted brown mass of pulp, skins, and seeds fed to the hogs. Pressing the cider was the pleasantest ritual of farm life. It poured out, a sweet brown liquid, as Minos, the Negro hired hand, sweating and grinning, turned the handles of the press. Abigail had supervised Betsy and Louisa and Polly Tailor in preparing food for the winter—the potatoes, the vegetables, the preserved fruits, the jellies—crabapple, quince, plum, and grape.

The harvests were all in, the winter feed stored, the wood split, seaweed spread on the fields, the great round cheeses wrapped in cloth and laid in neat rows to ripen, the cellar banked with seaweed and salt hay as protection against winter wind and frost, when John set off with Briesler early in November. He found pleasant companions on the Hartford coach and took advantage of every stop to sound the local sentiment for Fisher Ames, delighted to find "a spirit in his favor very different from that of some people of Boston." It showered frequently, but not enough to make the roads miry. At Hartford, Adams visited with old friends, and then, riding on to New Haven, took the packet boat for New York. Nabby and the children were in fine health and spirits and the Colonel looked sleek and bursting with importance. Charles lodged with the Baron von Steuben and prepared for his advancement at the bar to counselor at law.

LXVI

WHEN he arrived at Philadelphia, John found that Samuel Otis had procured lodgings for him across the street from the Bingham mansion. From the window of his upstairs room, Otis pointed out, Adams could see the Beautiful Ann Bingham walking in her garden. In spite of such an attraction, John decided to move. His landlord was an Englishman, an upholsterer by trade, and his rooms were drab and stuffy. At Francis Tavern on Fourth Street he rented a luxurious suite and there found all the company he cared for in the persons of a number of Congressmen who were "virtuous Republicans."

Comfortably lodged as he was at Francis Tavern, he could not help dreading the months of "tedious solitude" that lay ahead of him "amidst the noise, smoke, wealth, luxury, eloquence, learning, wit, and wisdom of this proud city and our venerable Congress! . . . . To me," he added, "one week of domestic felicity and rural amusements would be worth it all."[1]

The Senate had convened November 3 without a quorum. When Adams arrived a week later there were only twelve members present—the two Pennsylvania Senators were still with the army dispatched to suppress the Whiskey Rebels. Pierce Butler and Aaron Butt, the latter newly elected from New York, were among those conspicuously absent and the Senate adjourned from day to day, waiting for a quorum. It was the eighteenth of November, two weeks after the House had formed its own quorum and proceeded to business, before the arrival of Aaron Burr, "as fat as a duck and as ruddy as a roost cock . . . made a Senate." Rumor had it that he had lingered in New York to consummate a speculation that had made him richer by a hundred thousand pounds. It was easy to believe because the Colonel seemed swollen with self-satisfaction, and Adams could not help noting a little enviously, "These simple Republicans are rewarded in this world for their virtues, as well as admired for their talents." Adams observed that the proposed gallery for visitors to the Senate had not been built, "From which neglect," he wrote Abigail, "some conclude that the soi-disant friends of the people are afraid that the Senate will appear to the people better friends than themselves."[2]

Adams was pleased to discover in both houses a disposition to support the government. "An army of 15,000 militia so easily raised from four states only, to go upon such an enterprise," he noted, referring to the suppression of the Whiskey Rebels, "ought to be a terrible phenomenon to Anti-Federal citizens as well as to insolent Britons. Anti-Federalism, Jacobinism and rebellion are drooping their heads very much discouraged," he wrote Abigail.[3] The events of the summer "had rendered unpopular the rant that was in vogue last [session]," Adams declared, adding cautiously, "but as everything has its revolution in these revolving days it may become fashionable again."

Washington took the occasion of the insurrection to proscribe the Democratic Clubs as centers of sedition and resistance to government and requested the Senate and House to follow his lead. The Senate complied with little debate, but in the House Madison argued eloquently that it was unconstitutional for Congress to censure the clubs. Their members were simply exercising their right of free speech; "the censorial power is in the people over the government, and not in the government over the people," he declared dramatically.[4] Adams had no such misgivings. Certainly people had "a right to meet and consider of law, express their opinions and feelings, for the purpose of petitioning the legislature for repeals or amendments." But in his view it was "not lawful to meet and publish censures upon laws and libels upon men or measures." The legality of the meeting depended not upon the nature of the assembly but upon the legality of their conduct. It was therefore "incautious and improvident . . . to acknowledge their legality without exceptions, qualifications, and limitations" as some had done who were no friends to the clubs themselves.[5]

Adams took it for granted "that political clubs must and ought to be lawful in every free country." He had belonged to several in his youth; but they could not be allowed to shake the foundations of the state. The American people must "either dismiss their Congress or . . . restrain their clubs. I don't mean to hang or transport to Botany Bay the members of these societies as the English and Scotch have done; nor to banish, imprison, or hang as the Canton of Berne has done; but to discountenance and discourage their assemblies. . . . Is it not abominable," he asked Abigail, "to see a crew headed by such an ignorant, blundering, thick-skulled Irishman as Blair McClenachen, publishing their manifestoes against the President and both houses of Congress?" The government must be firm but restrained. "The mildness of our government," Adams noted, "is a pleasing, delightful characteristic and although it will probably give encouragement to some disorders and even some daring crimes it is too precious to be relinquished without an absolute necessity."[6]

In Philadelphia the political scene was enlivened by the appearance of a pamphlet by James Callender which Adams characterized as "the most astonishing concentration of Jacobitical malevolence that ever Scottish spite exhibited. I have read it, however, with interest and avidity," he wrote Abigail. "It has little of the wit and none of the humor of Tom Paine, but more than his malice and revenge." Any foul-mouthed and profligate foreign journalist seemed to be sure of an audience in America. "This country," he added, "is to be the asylum of Europe, and Demo-cratical Societies are to raise them to fame, popularity, station, and power." Such immigrants were apparently to be free to spew out their venom against a President and a government whose principles they did not understand and to whose survival they were hostile.

To have labored long and hard to erect an enduring government and then see it torn and defiled by a set of irresponsible scribblers was hard indeed. Even more disturbing was the fact that Jefferson had given the "first passport to these incendiaries" and encouraged them in their rancor and malignity.[7] Nonetheless the ship of state sailed smoothly for the moment. "This session of Congress," Adams wrote Abigail, "is the most innocent I ever knew. There is scarcely animation enough in either house to excite attention. One may sleep in the midst of a debate. I have not yet tried however," he added. "We have done no harm. . . . I know not what to write you, unless I tell you I love you and long to see you—but this will be no news. . . . Three long months before I can see you. Oh! what to do with myself I know not." Without a horse he missed his rides but he took brisk walks through the streets of Philadelphia and out of town toward the Schuylkill River.

Hamilton was expected to resign soon as Secretary of the Treasury and it was assumed that Knox would accompany him. Oliver Wolcott, the Assistant Secretary, was mentioned as the probable successor to the New Yorker and Timothy Pickering had been spoken of as the new Secretary of War.[8] Adams was sorry to see Hamilton leave the Cabinet. He felt that the Secretary had responded to the Whiskey crisis "with dignity, moderation, and decision"; he admired his genius for financial matters and respected his political acumen. As a reward for his services he had been abused and reviled daily by Republican journalists and politicians. But of course it was no more than was to be expected by the servants of democracy. He worried about General Knox too. The Secretary of War was a faithful but limited man whose unquestioned military talents had raised him to higher civil station than his ability qualified him for. He might have a difficult time making his way in the world, and his frivolous and extravagant wife would be no help. Hamilton would do better; "he is younger and has more economy," John noted; he was pleased to hear that the New Yorker had refused "all public employment" and gone resolutely to the New York bar.[9]

To Adams the man most to be pitied was the President. "With his exertions, anxieties, responsibilities for twenty years without fee or reward or children to enjoy his renown, to be the butt of the insolence of Genets and clubs" was "a trial too great for human nature to be exposed to. . . . . Like the starling," he added, "he can't get out of his cage, but Knox says, and I believe it, he is sick, very sick in it. . . . The Southern states continue to give the old gentleman so much trouble that I fear he will resign," Adams confided to Abigail. If that happened and the succession thus devolved on him, he would make Quincy his headquarters and conduct his administration from there. But as yet the resignation was only a rumor.[10]

In the political lull America hung uneasily upon European developments, watching the devastating progress of the Revolutionary army of France and trying to calculate the course of events. Adams confessed that "the denouement, the catastrophe of the whole vast plot is beyond the reach of my comprehension or conjecture." Abigail, in reply, wrote: "I ruminate upon [France] as I lie awake many hours before light. My present thought is that their [France's] virtuous army will give them a government in time in spite of all their conventions, but of what nature it will be, it is hard to say."[11]

Adams had frequent visits from New England Senators and Representatives and he found himself, in consequence, acting as an adviser and strategist. He assumed the role willingly and clearly enjoyed it but it was not enough to keep him out of one of his periodic spells of depression. "The time seems longer to me than ever any time did in America . . . . Ennui . . . now torments me as the blue devils would if I had them, which by the way I never had. . . . Low spirits and the blue devils are not the same." He embarked on the works of the Swedish mystic Swedenborg in an effort to throw off the glooms. The Swede sounded like his kind of intellectual dish—"anything that shows a strong and strange imagination and is neither melancholy nor stark mad," he noted, "is amusing."

Adams was disturbed by the skepticism and anti-religious feeling that was a characteristic of so many Republican leaders. "I fear the atheistical and theistical philosophers lately turned politicians," he wrote Abigail, "will drive the common people into the receptacles of visionaries, enluminees, illumonies, etc., etc., etc.," so that, far from being rational and emancipated, they would be enthusiastical and wildly emotional. The fact was that the common people would have their religion despite the prevailing spirit of skepticism; they would "insist upon the risk of being damned rather than give up the hope of being saved in a future state. The people will have a life to come," he concluded, "and so will I."

Cerrachi, the sculptor, had sent Abigail a present—a marble medallion of Adams' head, "as grave, as sad, as anxious, as severe as the marble is hard and the work fine," he noted, forwarding it to her.[12]

Tormented by loneliness and low spirits, John found that shopping for Christmas books for Abigail only increased his homesickness. He bought, at her request, Lady Craven's *A Journey to Constantinople*, Bennett's *Strictures on Female Education*, and *Letters to a Young Lady;* he made purchases for Charles, Nabby, and the grandchildren, went to church to hear Dr. Ewing preach, then had dinner with Thomas Shippen, a good Philadelphia Federalist, "and his pretty little puppet of a wife." But he failed to exorcise his demons. "I read my eyes out," he complained, "and can't read half enough neither. The more one reads the more one sees we have to read." The weather was too mild for the Christmas season. There was an old adage, "A green Christmas makes a growing churchyard." Cold weather was "necessary to confine or kill the putrid, deleterious vapors which arise from uncultivated fruits and undrained marshes," Adams observed.[13] He had one of his "great colds" and sniffled and wheezed and dosed himself with Abigail's prescriptions.

In January, Charles came on from New York to visit his father. "As fat as a squab," bright and agreeable company, there was a shadow of sadness on his handsome face that told the story of his frustrated romance with his sister-in-law, Sally Smith.

Abigail once more supplied her husband with the "farm calendar" —"it refreshes me like a cordial," he wrote. The orchard was covered with seaweed; Joy was cutting wood; Hayden, Minos, Arnold, and Bass were digging potatoes—some ninety bushels—and the whole crop not yet in. But the potatoes were small and the work went slowly. Abigail had to scrimp and improvise as usual, send creditors away with promises for money, and borrow from Dr. Tufts to pay the hired hands. The weather was so mild in Quincy that the rosebush under the study window began leafing out in December and clover and grass sprang up in green, moist patches.

In addition to the farm calendar, Abigail sent the usual quota of local political news and town gossip. John Hancock's widow, Dorothy, was engaged to marry "an able-bodied rough sea captain," she wrote disapprovingly, adding: "Frailty, thy name is woman." But John answered in a different spirit: "As Dorothy has hitherto had only a peevish, fretful, feeble child for an husband, I congratulate her opening prospects of advancement in the world, to the arms of a generous, cheerful, good-humored, and able-bodied man."[14]

"It gives me pain to find you so lonesome in the midst of so many amusements," Abigail wrote her husband. He would be more cheerful if he went into society. What he needed was "a wife to hover about you, to bind up your temples, to mix your bark and to pour out your coffee."

But he would prize her the more for feeling the want of her for a time. Master Cleverly, Adams' old teacher and reader in the Episcopal church, she reported, was very much put out at the news that the President had appointed a day of thanksgiving during Lent. "He shakes his head and says 'tis a very arbitrary thing. I suppose," she added, "he cannot help connecting plum pudding, roast turkey, and minced pie. He cannot give thanks upon eggs and fish."[15] She was charmed with the Cerrachi medallion, but she thought it would be more suitable to send it to the Massachusetts Academy of Arts and Sciences. To keep it would suggest vanity.

Abigail mentioned that Bowdoin had explained his defection to the Republicans on the grounds that the Federalists had slighted him. The story provoked an indignant outburst from Adams. "Mr. Bowdoin's morality is the same with that of all . . . men who have more ambition than principle," he wrote in reply. "I have gone through a life of almost three score years, and how few have I found whose principles could hold against their passions, whose honors could contend with their interests." For himself he had never given a vote against his best judgment and his most earnest prayer was that he would never deprive himself "of the power of saying this to my wife and to my God in my last hour! . . . . My forces of mind and body are nearly spent," he continued; "few years remain to me, if any; in public life fewer still. If I could leave my country in greater security I should retire with pleasure. But a great cloud hangs over it yet. I mean a cloud of ignorance, knavery, and folly. Whether a torrent can be stemmed or not is yet uncertain. My hopes, however, are stronger than my fears, and I am determined to be as happy as I can."[16] Reviewing the past years, he reflected that "the adventures of myself and my wife and daughter and sons" were "a kind of romance which, a little embellished with fiction or exaggeration or only poetical ornament, would equal anything in the days of chivalry or knight-errantry."[17]

"The political horizon is serene at present," he noted, "though the Democratical Societies flutter like shot pigeons."[18] But the calm that hung over the capital was deceptive. The political barometer was falling and a storm was on the way. Federalists and Republicans alike waited for Jay's return. The news that he had negotiated a treaty had preceded him. While the supporters of the President and of the policy of neutrality waited anxiously, the Anti-Federalists and Jacobins sharpened their political knives. "A battle royal I expect at its ratification, and snarling enough afterwards," John wrote Abigail.[19] "Let us know what it is first, however, before we oppose or criticize or applaud or approve." Congress was thinly attended but Adams was "chained to the oars" by his duties as presiding officer. If he left before the end of the session he would be accused of "sacrificing my country to a weak attachment for a woman."[20] To while away the time he dined at Robert Morris', "whose hospitality is always precious." There he found "a company of venerable old rakes . . . three score years of age, or a little over or a little under, fat, smoking segars, drinking burgundy and madeira and talking politics till almost eleven o'clock."

As weeks passed without a sign of Jay or his treaty the tension beneath the surface serenity began to reveal itself. A bitter attack on the yet unseen treaty circulated through the city, an indication, Adams noted, "that poor Jay has a fiery ordeal to go through. . . . I am very much afraid of this treaty," he added, "but this is in confidence." The waiting was made more onerous by the weather. In late January the city was blanketed with snow and John's cold confined him to his lodgings. On the coldest night of the year Adams wrote Abigail that only the thought of receiving a letter from her the next day kept him from freezing. "I am tired of reading and writing," he lamented, "my eyes complain; I want exercise; I must have my horse; and I must be at home." When he was sixty he would resign his office unless Abigail would come with him "in a stage wagon and lodge at a tavern in Fourth Street."[21]

At the end of February, Adams decided that he would wait no longer for the treaty. Congress was scheduled to adjourn in March; on the pretense of Abigail's bad health, he asked to be excused on the twentieth of February and set out with Briesler for New York. Abigail had urged him to stay there for a week or so. The brevity of his previous visits had upset Nabby, who felt that her father was slighting her. Now she had a new baby daughter and it was more important than ever that he not hurry through the city. John grumbled but complied. He loved his daughter and doted on the grandchildren, William and John, but the Colonel's boasting and ostentation irritated him, and he had no interest in the round of balls, assemblies, and hunting that made up his son-in-law's style of living. He served out his term in New York with as good a grace as possible, admired the pink, pretty little infant, Caroline Amelia, endured the Colonel's expansiveness as best he could, and spent some happy hours with Charles. Then, having carried out Abigail's orders, he hurried on to Quincy, to her and the farm.

It was a cold, dreary spring in Quincy and the inflammation of Adams' eyes rendered him almost blind. But being home was compensation for everything. The farm was "a gay hobby horse" that took up all his time. "I hope to make my farm shine," he wrote John Quincy, "against your return." The congressional elections went "in general in favor of the federal government," and in Massachusetts the radical Benjamin Austin, "Honestus," was defeated by Coffin Jones. For the moment there was "no news but of marriages, shipbuilding, housebuilding, canal digging, bridge making, etc., etc." John Quincy had taken up his duties at The Hague and began at once to send long, brilliant reports on Dutch and European politics. Washington was very pleased with the dispatches of the young minister and praised them in a letter to the proud father.

With his inflamed eyes hurting him so much that each word was a penance, Adams wrote his son, "I have no language to express to you the pleasure I have received from the satisfaction you have given to the President and Secretary of State. . . . Go on, my dear son, and by a diligent exertion of your genius and abilities continue to deserve well of your father but especially of your country." He apologized for his own letter. Half-blind eyes and a trembling hand made a poor team. It was "painful to the vanity of an old man to acknowledge the decays of nature," but his infirmities had made "a pen as terrible [to him] as a sword to a coward, or . . . a rod to a child."²²

Adams' rural interlude was to be short-lived. Jay's treaty arrived in Philadelphia in early April. The President took a dismayed look at the document and prepared to call the Senate into special session to ratify it. Jay had abandoned by implication two of the principles for which America had contended ever since the outbreak of the American Revolution—the doctrine that free ships made free goods, and that neutrals might trade freely with belligerents in noncontraband goods. Instead he had accepted the "Rule of 1756" which held that trade prohibited in time of peace could not be legalized in time of war. The American emissary had also agreed that private debts were not subject to sequestration, and promised that the United States would not allow its ports to be used as bases for enemy privateers. In return the British promised to give up the frontier posts by June 1796 and to submit to the arbitration of a joint commission the questions of compensation for the seizure of American vessels in the West Indies, the claims of British creditors (whose efforts to collect their money had been frustrated by the states), and of the boundary line between the United States and Canada. There was no mention in the treaty of one of the principal American grievances—the refusal of the British to make any compensation for the slaves carried off when they evacuated New York in 1783—nor did the treaty abjure what was to Americans one of Britain's most arrogant and offensive practices—the impressment of American sailors by the royal navy.

Jay had been instructed that he might negotiate a commercial treaty. The best he could manage was a rather insulting provision which allowed United States ships of less than seventy tons to trade with the British West Indies. In return Jay, in Article XII of the treaty, had promised that molasses, sugar, coffee, cocoa, or cotton from the British Caribbean islands would be carried in American ships only to the United States and that no "tropical produce" would be exported from the country.

The New Yorker's effectiveness as a negotiator had certainly been compromised by Hamilton's assurances to George Hammond, the British minister to the United States, that the administration had no intention of joining the Armed Neutrality, and by James Monroe's perfervid acclaim of the French Revolution in an emotional speech to the National Assembly. The British, sorely pressed by the French, felt that they were fighting not only for their lives but to uphold decency, law, and civilization against a new barbarism which butchered its enemies in the name of the Goddess of Reason. Beleaguered Englishmen were pained and astonished to find their cousins across the ocean espousing a cause whose violence and savagery threatened the very foundations of society. They were thus hardly in a conciliatory mood; at the same time they wished to avoid war with still another adversary. The British ministry, therefore, had made what it considered to be generous concessions. Lord Grenville was convinced that Parliament would not have supported him had he gone any further, and he was forced to defend himself in the House of Commons against the charge of being pro-American.

The Americans, on the other hand, displayed what, it soon became apparent, was to be a national characteristic: an inclination to see everything in terms of black and white. Without experience in the art of diplomacy or any understanding of that tortuous and complex game, they had expected a treaty which would remove all American grievances and many of them were prepared to go to war rather than accept anything less sweeping. As Adams had prophesied, a stormy passage awaited the treaty in the Senate and a far stormier one in the country at large. But Adams was not of course privy to the terms of the negotiation when shortly after Jay's arrival in America he wrote to his friend congratulating him on securing a treaty, presumably on the grounds that any treaty was better than none. "The spirit of peace and neutrality in this country increases and prevails," he added hopefully.[23]

Abigail's health was much improved and she decided to accompany her husband as far as New York to visit Nabby and see the new baby. On the twenty-sixth of May they set out from Quincy by coach "through the finest fields of wheat, rye, barley, oats, and clover, but very indifferent roads." At New York they found that the Colonel's fortunes had recently suffered a severe blow. Several ships in which he had invested heavily had been seized by privateers and he found himself dangerously overextended. The misfortunes cast a cloud over Abigail's visit. Nabby was strained and apprehensive, suddenly aware of the unsubstantial nature of her new prosperity. Leaving Abigail with Nabby, Adams hurried on to Philadelphia.

The Senate assembled on the eighth of June at eleven o'clock and received a message from the President along with the treaty and supporting papers. Three new Senators, all Federalists, were sworn in— James Gunn from Georgia, John Henry from Maryland, and Elijah Paine from Vermont. The next day the Senators received the budget—"a bone to gnaw for the aristocrats as well as the democrats," Adams noted. The Vice-President dined the same day with the General and his family and carried away a warm exchange of messages from Martha and her daughter, Nelly Custis, to Abigail—"the usual inquiries . . . and . . . the usual compliments." Mrs. Washington had inquired after the family and when Adams told her that Johnny Smith was troubled with the ague she diagnosed the source of the distress as worms and prescribed pinkroot as an effective remedy.[24]

The weather was blisteringly hot and three days of soaking rain made the city as humid as a tropical jungle. Letters between Abigail and John urging precautions against the sun crossed each other. John must not go out without an umbrella, and John in turn cautioned Abigail to keep out of the direct rays of the sun.[25]

On the eleventh the Senators launched themselves into the treaty. The first question was the matter of the secrecy which the President had urged upon them. This was earnestly debated and the alignment of the Senate suggested by the vote of twenty to nine to withhold the terms of the treaty from the public. (Pierce Butler, however, defied the ruling by passing along the treaty to Madison, a page at a time.) That night, heartened by the preliminary skirmish, Adams talked at length with Jay who, as he put it, "let me into the history of the treaty and negotiation, explaining his views of its intent and operation. . . . . The treaty," he wrote Abigail, "is of great extent and importance and will not be rejected nor adopted without a thorough examination."[26] There was no hope of getting away from Philadelphia for another ten days.

The Senate met in the morning, adjourned during the heat of midday, and then resumed its discussion of the treaty in the late afternoon. After an initial opposition to the commercial clause contained in Article XII had been by-passed, the debates—"temperate, grave, decent, and wise"— proceeded to their conclusion, delayed only by Aaron Burr's effort to have the treaty rejected in toto.

Adams felt quite useless as he presided over the deliberations. He had learned his lesson of restraint well and kept his own counsel; besides it was soon clear that the Federalists held the necessary two thirds to ratify the treaty. Pierre Adet, the successor to Fauchet, did his best to swing some votes into the Republican column and when his efforts were unavailing wrote his government that Read from South Carolina and Gunn from Georgia had been bribed to support ratification.

Adams went to call on Adet and was pleased to find the Frenchman no lover of political clubs. In France, Adet declared, the government had annihilated all factions. Adams dined with Robert Morris at his great estate, Landsdowne, and spent the evening at Oliver Wolcott's with Rufus King, Ellsworth, and George Cabot. When the talk turned against his old friend Elbridge Gerry, Adams took up his defense warmly. While it was true that he might be "more enlarged . . . and more correct in his views," Adams considered him second in merit to no man in Massachusetts except Samuel Adams.[27] John was Timothy Pickering's guest at his "splendid house," admired the "gravel walks, shrubberies and clumps of trees in the English style," sounded out that crabbed and curious man on the firmness of his Federalism, and came away satisfied he was steady.

On the twenty-fourth of June the Senate, making the best of a bad bargain, ratified the treaty without the twelfth article and two days later the special session adjourned. Adams set out at once for New York and arrived in that sweltering city to find Abigail and the Smith family in good health with the exception of poor Johnny, still in the grip of the ague despite generous doses of pinkroot. The infant, Caroline Amelia, to Nabby's mortification had bright red hair, but she was a fat and happy creature quite unconscious of the defect that so embarrassed her mother. Charles was prospering in business and reputation, and of course there were glowing reports of John Quincy and Thomas, who had accompanied his brother to The Hague.

Abigail, hating to leave the children, especially the ailing Johnny and the new granddaughter, tried to prevail on her husband to tarry in New York, but John was impatient to be back at Quincy and on the last day of June they began the hot, dusty ride north. Adams contracted dysentery on the trip and arrived at the farm weak and ill, to be nursed back to health by an attentive Abigail.

Even before the Jay treaty had been ratified contraband copies were being circulated. On the twenty-ninth of June, less than a week after the Senate had approved it, Benjamin Franklin Bache published an abstract in the *Aurora* and three days later he produced the whole treaty in pamphlet form. Determined to rally public sentiment against the document, he set out for New York and Boston, scattering his pamphlets as he went. Everywhere he sowed them, a storm of popular protest blew up. At New York, Hamilton appeared at a meeting called at City Hall to protest the treaty and tried to get permission to defend it before a hostile crowd. Colonel Smith, acting as chairman, appealed to the audience, who howled Hamilton down. Smith then called for a division and the opponents of the treaty marched off to the Battery where they burned copies of the offending document before the residence of Governor Jay. When the crowd returned carrying a French flag, Hamilton was the target for a shower of stones which drove him from the scene, bleeding from a cut in the head. Adams was acutely embarrassed when word reached him of his son-in-law's role in the episode.

An anti-treaty meeting in Philadelphia included such prominent citizens as Alexander James Dallas and Chief Justice McKean, Stephen Girard, the wealthy merchant, Frederick Muhlenberg, Speaker of the House, and Blair McClenachen, who waved a paper above his head and shouted, "What a damned treaty! I make a motion that every good citizen in this assembly kick this damn treaty to hell!" Impaling the treaty on a pole, the mob marched first to Adet's house and then on to the residence of George Hammond, the British minister, where they smashed the windows and burned the treaty on his doorstep.

In Boston, Samuel Adams and General Warren both joined in the attack, speaking and writing, John felt, in a manner "not only illegal and unconstitutional but indiscreet to a high degree."[28] Fisher Ames, observing the turmoil in the city, was ready to concede that "the Jacobins have been successful in prejudicing the multitude against the treaty. . . . Our federal ship is foundering in a millpond." But Adams, from the calmer perspective of Quincy, felt confident that "the treaty will become the law and be carried into execution," although he deplored the fact that "poor Jay has gone through as fiery an ordeal as I did when I was suspected of a blasphemous doubt of Tom Paine's infallibility in consequence of . . . Jefferson's rashness."[29]

On the issue of the treaty itself Adams never wavered. With all its imperfections, it was far better than nothing or, what was more likely, than war. It was certainly not that he was pro-British: "I wish that misfortune and adversity could soften the temper and humiliate the insolence of John Bull," he wrote Abigail, "but he is not yet sufficiently humbled. If I mistake not, it is to be the destiny of America one day to beat down his pride. But the irksome task will not soon, I hope, be forced upon us."[30] He spoke angrily of British "jealousy, envy, hatred, and revenge covered under pretended contempt." As for George III, "the mad idiot will never recover," he concluded. He was a "blunderer by nature."

Public feeling was further inflamed by a new British order in council which authorized the seizure of all ships carrying grain to French ports. American vessels suffered most severely by the order and there was a fresh wave of resentment and hostility toward the English. Thus the summer dragged by with much uncertainty and apprehension in the Federalist camp. Adams, who at first felt sure that the people would repent of their excesses, had second thoughts; but with his health recovered, with Abigail to humor and divert him, and with the farm neat and "shining," he preserved his equanimity.

The only thing that disturbed the even tenor of life at Quincy was the news that Charles had married Sally Smith. John was furious. For his son to risk everything just at the moment when he appeared at last to have made a start on his career seemed to Adams the wildest folly and indulgence. At the age of twenty-five, without prospects of supporting a wife adequately for years, he had taken on a burden that would almost inevitably drag him down to penury and disaster. The marriage seemed as unfortunate to Abigail as to her husband but she was readier to reconcile herself to the fact than John. After all they had been madly, desperately in love for almost two years and Sally, a year older than Charles, could not wait indefinitely for him to establish himself in the practice of law. He had completed his training, been admitted as a barrister, and made a promising beginning as a lawyer. When Abigail repeated the arguments to John, to be sure with little conviction in her voice, he waved them aside impatiently. He was devoted to Charles and to his happiness, future as well as present. Life was a struggle at best. He had no pity on the man who faltered, whose nerve or resolution failed him. The weak or the unlucky were pressed to the wall, went to wretched, unremembered graves or dragged out forlorn and miserable lives, a burden and sorrow to those who loved them, if they could count any such. Adams had seen too many of his childhood friends, some of his Harvard contemporaries, and a few of his and Abigail's own relatives destroy themselves by early and inopportune marriages. He was haunted by Charles's instability, by a certain veiled, tormented sadness that dwelt just behind the handsome, smiling face and shaded the gray eyes. No good could come of it. It was a hard judgment on his son, but then it was a hard world and easy judgments were poor armor against its bruises and abrasions.

Abigail was touched by her son's happiness—he had never been so happy in his life, he wrote—and there was some truth in Nabby's practical observation that "after all the hair-breadth scapes and imminent dangers, he is at last safe landed."[31] A young man so handsome and so charming was beset by a thousand temptations. Abigail absolved him and gave him the benediction of her love and good wishes; even John, by the time he passed through New York for the first session of the fourth Congress, had thawed. He stayed with Nabby and the Colonel and went looking for Charles, whom he found in a comfortable new house "well stored with book learning," very busy "with three clients about him in very deep and earnest consultation." Sally behaved "prettily in her new sphere," John wrote Abigail. She had shown her father-in-law an elegant bed which, she said, would be his if he would visit them and he was pleased in spite of himself. He went away reassured and ready to believe that Charles might still make a go of it in spite of his recklessness.[32]

In Philadelphia, Adams found a somewhat brighter prospect than he had expected. The effect of the order in council, which had resulted in the seizure of so many American ships carrying wheat to France and which had indeed persuaded Washington not to sign the Jay treaty, had been to a considerable extent counteracted by intercepted dispatches from Fauchet to his government which suggested that Edmund Randolph, Jefferson's successor as Secretary of State, was prepared to serve the interests of France in return for money. (John wrote Abigail, "Your old friend, real or pretended, Randolph, is under a dark cloud and his behavior under it increases its blackness and thickness.") Adams was still convinced that the only acceptable course was to ratify the treaty, distasteful as it might be, rather than face a war for which the United States, despite all its bluster, was totally unprepared. He concluded "upon meeting and conversing with the members of Congress . . . that although there will be noise there will be no serious evil this session." If the treaty was ratified by Britain it would be "supported and executed without any difficulty."

The Senate at last had its gallery and the Senators had a sizable audience when they began their deliberations on December 7. The alignment for and against the treaty remained the same as it had been in June, twenty supporters and ten opposed. "The voice of the people so much vaunted by the ten," he added, "is not in reality in their favor," Adams stated. "A great majority will support the government and the twenty." Jay had resigned from the Supreme Court to serve as Governor of New York State, thus thwarting the schemes of those who wished to impeach him. Washington had appointed John Rutledge of South Carolina to succeed him. Rutledge, however, had led a bitter assault on the Jay treaty in his home state and the Senate refused to confirm his nomination to the chief justiceship. Adams, surprised at the Carolinian's defection, wrote to Abigail that he had "never thought him the greatest man in the world nor had any fixed confidence in his penetration or his constancy or consistency." The temper of the people, especially from Maryland north, seemed more in favor of the treaty than he had dared to hope. Indeed, it appeared to him that "the prospect of peace is brighter now than it has been for several years." The President was in excellent health and his good spirits suggested that he had at last developed some immunity to the barbs of Bache and his fellow editors.[33]

Adams' estimate of the Federalist strength proved, in fact, too optimistic. The South Carolina legislature indicted the treaty because of its failure to contain a provision compensating slaveowners for the slaves carried off by the British. "The vote," Adams wrote indignantly, "is the meanest which has ever been passed; not one of the mobs have been so sordid as to put the whole treaty upon the single point of pay for the Negroes. . . . . S.C., V., and Kentucky, I believe," he added, "will be the only states which will show their teeth and they cannot bite." But he was inclined to agree with Benjamin Goodhue, one of the Massachusetts Representatives, who declared: "The whole history of the government has been one continued labor to roll a stone up a steep hill. It is too fatiguing to be always on the stretch—and government that requires so much pains to support it is not worth preserving." It was the stone of Sisyphus.

The plight of the administration was perhaps indicated by the President's difficulty in finding a Secretary of State to replace Randolph, who as soon as he had retired from office wrote a vindication of himself in which he bitterly attacked Washington for his enmity to France. The President asked at least five men to serve, including Patrick Henry, Charles Cotesworth Pinckney, and Rufus King, before he came at last to the former Assistant Secretary, Timothy Pickering.

Randolph's treachery—Washington at least viewed it as that—and the resignation of Hamilton and Jefferson inclined the President to lean more heavily on Adams. Washington reviewed the Randolph affair in detail and solicited the Vice-President's advice. "The President and Presidentess . . . send their regards to you," John wrote Abigail. "Madam invites you to come next summer to Mount Vernon and visit the federal city."

Congress was wasting much time waiting for the Jay treaty to return from England. "Nothing of any consequence will be done till that arrives and is mauled and abused and then acquiesced in," he noted, adding, "The Democrats continue to pelt us. . . . We go on as we have always done for the first three months of the session, distributing business into the hands of committees, meeting, and adjourning."[34]

LXVII

THE question of the presidential succession was never far from Adams' mind, and word from one of the members of the Cabinet that Washington meant to resign in 1797 at the end of his present term made the subject an obsession with him. When Jay had been appointed to negotiate the treaty with Great Britain, the first thought that struck Adams was that if the New Yorker brought back a popular treaty he would be a formidable candidate for the presidency when Washington retired. Similarly, when Jefferson resigned as Secretary of State to return to Monticello, Adams had analyzed the effect of this move on what he was convinced were Jefferson's presidential ambitions. The unpopularity of the treaty had virtually removed Jay from contention, but Jefferson, as leader of the Republicans, had been strengthened by the resultant uproar. His withdrawal, as Adams anticipated, had increased his stature as the leader of a party. From Monticello he had directed Republican strategy while remaining aloof from the bitter contentions that swirled around the administration. Jefferson would in all probability be Adams' principal rival for the presidency when Washington returned to Mount Vernon.

But Adams of course would not admit, even to himself, that he wanted to be President. According to his system of political ethics the job should seek the man. Even then the man must play out to the end the role of the reluctant candidate, drawn from humble tasks to serve his country. The models were the statesmen of republican Rome who, like Cincinnatus came from their farms to lead an army to victory or carry the nation through a crisis, then returned to the simple life of a private citizen. That was how Adams saw himself—called from relative obscurity by the virtually unanimous voice of his fellow citizens to take the helm of the ship of state. He wrote to Abigail as soon as he heard the report of the President's intention to retire. She must know what the consequences would be; "Either we must enter upon ardors more trying than ever yet experienced; or retire to Quincy, farmers for life." Rumors reached him that certain Southerners were circulating the word to Northern Federalists "both in conversation and in letters" that they would be willing to make a bargain. Since Adams, "although rather inclined to monarchy and somewhat attached to the English," was a moderate Federalist, they would accept him as Vice-President if the Northerners in turn would, for the sake of conciliation, support Jefferson for President. "I most humbly thank you for your kind condescension, Messieurs Transchesapeaks," Adams wrote sardonically.[1]

Of one thing he was quite sure: he would not serve as Vice-President under Jefferson. "I will not be frightened out of the public service," he wrote Abigail, "nor will I be disgraced in it."[2] He would take his "resolutions with cool deliberation . . . watch the course of events with . . . critical attention," and what Providence pointed out as his duty, that path he would follow with "patience and decision." If he had a "reasonable prospect of being able to serve [his country] to her honor and advantage" he would shrink from no danger or hazard. On the other hand, even if he were to be elected President, Jefferson might very well be elected to the second office and in that case it would be "a dangerous crisis in public affairs" to have the President and Vice-President "in opposite boxes." Taking one thing with another, it seemed most likely that he would "make a voluntary retreat," he wrote Abigail, "and spend the rest of my days in a very humble style with you."[3]

Adams' letter, full of speculations about the presidential succession, crossed one from Abigail congratulating him on the New Year and on the fact that they were "one year nearer the end of our journey. . . . 'And not a year, but pilfers as he goes/Some youthful grace, that Age would gladly keep/A tooth or auburn lock.'" It was hardly a welcome reflection to a man who was contemplating the highest and most demanding office in the Republic.[4]

"I feel bold and strong myself," he wrote in answer, "though my hands shake." He was "quite a favorite" with the President. "I am heir apparent, you know, and a succession is soon to take place." But whatever the President's wishes might be, "the French and the demogogues intend," Adams observed dryly, "to set aside the descent. . . . I have a pious and a philosophical resignation to the voice of the people in this case which is the voice of God. . . . I have no very ardent desire," he added, "to be the butt of party malevolence. Having tasted of that cup, I find it bitter, nauseous, and unwholesome."[5]

He was impatient to have Abigail's reaction to the news that Washington was determined to retire and when her weekly letter failed to appear on time he found nothing to his taste. "All day in a bad humor," he wrote, "dirty weather—wet walking—nothing good—nothing right." His first thought was to abuse the post office; his second was: "Perhaps Mam is sick—oh dear! Rheumatisms—oh dear! Fever and ague! Thus peevishly, fretfully and unphilosophically was [the day] passed." To divert himself he read a number of passages in Homer "and smoked I know not how many segars." When the next day still failed to bring the expected letter he "went pesting all day long against the post office." Deprived of his regular letter, he felt "humiliated and mortified, and at the same time irritated," disposed to make "a rash vow never to spend another winter separated from my small family that remains to me."[6]

Abigail, for her part, blamed the delay in receiving certain of John's letters on "that blundering blockhead of a postman." When she heard the news of the President's impending retirement she was dismayed. "My ambition leads me not to be first in Rome," she wrote her husband; "there is not a beam of light nor a shadow of comfort or pleasure in the contemplation of the object. If personal considerations alone were to weigh, I should immediately say retire with the principle." But she must leave the decision to him and to the circumstances, praying that God would guide him in making the proper one. As to his serving as Vice-President to Jefferson, she was as decided on that point as Adams himself: "Resign, retire. I would be second . . . to no man but Washington."[7]

Abigail's principal concern was with her own role as President's wife. She who had always been outspoken would have to school herself to caution and discretion. "I must impose a silence upon myself," she wrote a little wistfully, "when I long to talk." She would have to abandon the warmth and intimacy of a village where she was known and loved for the pageantry and pomp of the great world.[8]

But John reassured her. "I have no concern on your account but for your health. A woman *can* be silent when she will." For himself, he continued to play with the idea of withdrawing from the presidential contest, although there was not in fact the remotest possibility that he would do so. "The question is," he declared, "between living at Philadelphia or at Quincy; between great cares and small cares. I have looked into myself," he added, "and see no meanness or dishonesty there. I see weakness enough but no timidity. . . . I hate speeches, messages, addresses and answers, proclamations, and such affected, studied, contraband things. I hate levees and drawing rooms. I hate to speak to a thousand people to whom I have nothing to say. Yet all this I can do," he concluded.[9] The fact was he was determined to do it.

Abigail, with her sensitivity to her husband's temper, could read between the lines. John had no intention of letting the office of presidency go by default to the man who had once been one of his closest friends and was now his bitterest rival. She was sure that the presidency would be "a most unpleasant seat, full of thorns, briars, thistles, murmuring, fault-finding, calumny, obloquy. . . . But the Hand of Providence ought to be attended to and what is designed, cheerfully submitted to."[10]

With the presidential succession much on his mind, Adams undertook to sound out his rival. He wrote the Virginian an elaborately casual letter, deploring the excesses of the French Revolution. In France, he told Jefferson, "passion, prejudice, interest, necessity has governed and will govern; and a century must roll away before any permanent and quiet system will be established." Then, he hoped, "an amelioration of human affairs" would be the result. "But you and I must look down from the battlements of heaven," he added, "if we are to have the pleasure of seeing it."[11]

Jefferson, in reply, repeated the formula of disavowal. The truth was that at Monticello he had no time to give much thought to politics. Indeed, he wrote, politics was "a subject I never loved and now hate."[12]

Adams had deplored the excesses of the French. Jefferson gave a cautious endorsement of the New Englander's strictures—"I fear the oligarchial executive of the French will not do"—and went on to deliver his own counterthrust: "I am sure, from the honesty of your heart, you join me in detestation of the corruption of the English government, and that no man on earth is more incapable than yourself of seeing that copied among us willingly." He wished "there was an ocean of fire" between England and the United States.[13]

If they were divided on politics, they shared a common passion for farming and Jefferson was assured of a sympathetic reader when he wrote of the effects on his wheat crop of a "hard winter and a backward spring. Our first cutting of clover is not yet begun," he informed Adams. "Strawberries not ripe till within this fortnight, and everything backward in proportion." He was on horseback half the day supervising his plantation and the other half he devoted to his "nail manufactory," counting and measuring nails.[14] Reading as best he could between the polite but noncommittal lines of Jefferson's letters, Adams grew more convinced than ever that Jefferson would be his most formidable rival for the presidency.

One can hardly escape the feeling that in a sense Adams' response to the prospect of succeeding Washington was visceral or chemical. Before he had admitted to himself that he was in the presidential race to the finish, his heart had begun to betray him by sending the blood faster through his veins, by stirring him to a new restlessness and activity. Like an aging athlete suddenly called from a sedentary life to one more contest for honor and fame, he began to tense old sinews and tighten old muscles. His "health and spirits" were better than they had been for years and when he heard of plans to shunt him aside he tightened his mouth into a hard line and vowed: "I will not by any pusillanimous retreat throw this country into the arms of a foreign power, into a certain war and as certain anarchy." The sentence disclosed that the decision, in a sense, had already been irrevocably made. He had begun to think that his services were perhaps indispensable to his country; that the United States must keep out of war and that he, better than Jefferson or Hamilton or Jay, could keep it out of war. It was with a kind of grim satisfaction that he observed that the presidency was "the great object of contentions—the center and main source of all emulation as the learned Dr. Adams teaches in all his writings, and everybody believes him though nobody will own it." Those who professed to consider the office a nugatory one, a figurehead without power or real authority, were clearly prepared to contend as hard for it as those who saw it as an equal and co-ordinate branch of the national government.[15]

Although he could not quite bring himself to involve God in his decision, Adams spoke of his willingness to resign himself to Jupiter's will. "If his will is that . . . any other should be President," he wrote Abigail, "I know that his will also is that I should be a farmer—for he has given me an understanding and a heart which ought not and cannot and will not bow under Jefferson nor Jay nor Hamilton. It would be wicked in me. It would be countenancing tyranny, corruption, and villainy in the people."[16] He had thus passed from doubting whether he should be a candidate at all to the feeling that if he was not elected President it would be because the people of the country would have defrauded him of what was rightfully his.

As the weeks passed he felt more and more the exhilaration of politics. It showed in his letters to Abigail, which took on a jaunty, almost insouciant air. "We have weather as mild as April and streets as dirty as March. . . . Business in Congress as languid, as gaping and yawning as if Morpheus had poured out all his soporifics upon the two houses." Where six months before he had been speaking as a feeble old man whose hours of life were numbered and who wished no more than to spend a few years in rural contentment, he now felt confident that "the forces of nature" were "adequate," that they would "hold out one or two heats," or presidential terms.[17]

Beyond all this he began to stir himself out of a kind of intellectual lassitude that had taken hold of him during the long, tedious years as Vice-President. "I read forever and am determined to sacrifice my eyes like John Milton," he wrote Abigail, "rather than give up the amusement without which I should despair." He even neglected his beloved horseback rides to sate his revived appetite. He read four thick octavo volumes of Tacitus in translation and a large portion of the *Iliad*, besides a constant flow of pamphlets and newspapers. William Cobbett, an Englishman, had taken up cudgels for the Federalists under the pseudonym of Peter Porcupine, and Adams was delighted with his savage thrusts at the Democrats.

But with all this reading, he was not writing enough. "'Search we the spot which mental power contains?'" he quoted to Abigail. "'Go where man gets his living by his brains.'" If he had had to get his living by his brains over the past seven years that organ would be a keener instrument than it was at the moment. But as Vice-President, brains had "not only been useless but even hurtful and pernicious." His had been so long idle that they had grown rusty.

In the middle of February, Adams sat down to make a careful analysis of the probable effect of Washington's retirement. Concern had been expressed about the dangers involved in a transfer of power from the President to his successor, much of it indeed by Adams himself, but looking more coolly at the prospective devolution of authority, he felt sure that there would be "no more danger in the change than there would be in changing a member of the Senate." If Jay or even Jefferson "(and one or the other it certainly will be if the succession should be passed over) should be the man, government will go on as ever," he wrote. "Jefferson could not stir a step in any other system than that which is begun. Jay would not wish it." The votes would be split among the three of them—himself, Jefferson, and Jay. If Jefferson and Jay were President and Vice-President respectively, as was not improbable, he, Adams, would retire without "a murmur of complaint to his farm, forever." If, on the other hand, he should be elected, he and Abigail would serve four more years and then withdraw, "or if by reason of strength and fortitude eight years should be accomplished," that would be the utmost period of service. "Be of good courage therefore," and "tremble not," he advised Abigail. "I see nothing to appall me and I feel no ill forebodings or faint misgivings. I have not the smallest dread of private life, nor of public."[18]

Jay, lest there be any doubt, hinted at his availability in a letter which was widely circulated. Washington still gave no open declaration of his intentions but the conviction grew that he would retire when his term was over. Adams heard reports of Jefferson's views which indicated that the Virginian "in good hands . . . might do very well; yet in such hands as will hold him," he added, "he would endanger too much." He noted uneasily that Patrick Henry and Hamilton were also talked of as presidential candidates and calculated that both might cost him votes. Certainly Hamilton would, and Henry also might draw off some Southern Federalists from Adams.

Certain prominent Federalists tried to sound Adams out, but he was reserved and discreet. Until the President announced his decision he was constrained to give not even a hint of interest in being his successor. Moreover, he assured Abigail, he would never accept the office if the election were thrown into the House of Representatives; he felt strongly that no man should "serve in that high and responsible situation without some foundation of people to stand on. . . . . Indeed," he added, "I feel myself to be a fool to serve here at all."[19]

With all this he could write to John Quincy, just before he left Washington in May, that he was "very indifferent" to the outcome, "really, truly, and sincerely, not affectedly or hypocritically indifferent,"[20] and he doubtless believed it—at the moment.

Deprived of the domestic pleasures and conveniences that were his principal pleasure, the Vice-President passed his time as best he could. He dined with Adet and found there "the virtuous Mr. Gallatin," Alexander James Dallas, Jonathan Dayton, the porcine and rancorous Speaker of the House, and the "virtuous ten"—the Senators who had voted against the ratification of the Jay treaty.[21] He relayed to Abigail a most sensational bit of gossip concerning Dr. Redman—"the smiling, the genteel, the well-bred, the gentlemanlike, the I don't know what"—manager of the Assembly and social arbiter of Philadelphia society. He had committed what in England was called "lady's pillage" of a "very gross kind," so that banishment was the mildest punishment that could befall him.

Charles came from New York with a copy of the treaty with the Algerine pirates and Adams went with him to one of the President's levees. Shining amid "a great circle of ladies and a greater of gentlemen" was Mad Anthony Wayne, lionized for his recent victory over the Indians at Fallen Timbers. The presence of so many of Abigail's friends made John acutely homesick. He must stay on in Philadelphia through the long months of March, April, and May, but he comforted himself with the thought that "the time will be soon gone, and we shall be surprised to know what is become of it. . . . After sixty, the days and hours have additional wings, which they wave and beat with increasing rapidity." He agreed with Dr. Price that "old age was the pleasantest part of life" even though "one knows not what infirmities may come on, what pains, griefs, or sorrows." For his part, he was determined "to make my small remainder as easy as I can, and enjoy the hours as they pass, but do a little good as I have opportunity."[22]

On the tenth of February, Bache's *Aurora* opened the first editorial gun of the coming campaign. Jefferson, the "good patriot, statesman, and philosopher," must inevitably be the choice of the people to succeed the retiring President. As Adams read the editorial he felt his hackles rise. Here was the beginning. In his Vice-Presidential backwater he had almost forgotten the sensations produced by the lash of public excoriation. Now he must stand forth and take the blows as they fell or flee the field. "I am determined to be a silent spectator of the silly and wicked game," he wrote Abigail, "and to enjoy it as a comedy, a farce, or a gymnastic exhibition at Sadler's Wells. . . . I will laugh, let them say what they will." He could foresee the course of the coming months with a kind of agonizing prescience—the rumors and innuendoes, the false charges, the revived cries of monarchist and aristocrat, the personal vilification: "The accursed spirit which actuates a vast body of people, partly Anti-Federalists, partly desperate debtors, and partly Frenchified tools, will murder all good men among us and destroy all the wisdom and virtue of the country." He was, he declared, weary of the game. Then he added in one of his characteristic flashes of self-understanding: "Yet I don't know how I should live out of it. I don't love slight, neglect, contempt, disgrace nor insult more than others," he concluded. "Yet I believe I have firmness of mind enough to bear it like a man, a hero, and a philosopher. I might groan like Achilles and roll from side to side abed sometimes at the ignorance, folly, injustice, and ingratitude of the world, but I should be resigned, and become more easy and cheerful, and enjoy myself and my friend better than I ever did."[23]

One thing that stuck in his craw like a great indigestible lump was the defection of Samuel Adams to the side of the Virginians—"a very mad people," Abigail called them. The Virginia legislature had issued a denunciation of the Jay treaty which included an attack on the Senate and the office of President. When Sam associated himself with the Virginia position Adams felt betrayed. He had persisted in believing, against the arguments of his Federalist friends, that his cousin would prove a faithful supporter of the national government; thus the disillusionment was especially bitter. The Massachusetts Governor's stand, he assured Abigail, was "the fruit of old spite against Washington, Jay, and old England, as well as much weak affectation of popularity." Samuel's pride and vanity were "vastly more extensive than his abilities. He always had a contracted mind," he reminded Abigail, "though a subtle and a bold one. He never was overhonest or overcandid. He will lie a little for his own vanity and more for his party, and as much as a Spartan for his notion of the public good."[24] Though there was more than a little truth in the charges, Adams at once regretted that he had made them. He reflected that his cousin, whatever his latter-day heresies might be, stood second only to James Otis as an architect of the Revolution. The trouble, as he had observed before, was that Sam was a congenital rebel.

The relations of Adams and the President continued as warm as they could be between two men of such impenetrable reserve. "Yesterday," he wrote Abigail, "the President sent his carriage for me to go with the family to the theater. *The Rage* and *The Spoiled Child* were the two pieces. It rained and the house was not full." Adams sensed that the President was a little chagrined at the sparseness of the audience. Washington, he thought, looked "worried and growing old faster than I could wish and his lady complains of infirmities of age and lowness of spirits for the first time."[25]

Adams was secretly much pleased at word that he was being toasted at political meetings. He waved it aside as mere electioneering of no real significance, but he was plainly touched at a toast relayed from Ipswich:

"John Adams: may his virtues, genius, and knowledge long revolve, the first planet from our political sun!" He felt calm and self-possessed, he kept assuring himself. The principles of the Vatican conclave went a long way in most elections. There was an inclination to "concur in the choice of the oldest Cardinal, because he cannot hold the papal chair long. I am so old that they all know they can make me miserable enough to be glad to get out of it as soon as Washington, if not in half the time."[26]

In Congress things went reasonably well. The Senate ratified the Spanish and the Algerine treaties and, while it seemed apparent that the House would denounce the Jay treaty, the general opinion was that they would eventually appropriate the money required to carry it into execution.

But the facts proved quite otherwise. The House fell upon the treaty with unexpected ferocity, "fastened with all their teeth and all their nails," in Adams' words. The members seemed determined to "bite like savages and tear like lions." The Anti-Federalists had apparently decided that their hopes of seizing power lay in destroying the treaty, and everything remained in abeyance while that issue was fought out. There were predictions that a majority would be unfavorable with the most "pernicious and destructive results." Yet Adams could not bring himself to believe "that they will be so desperate and unreasonable. If they should be," he added, "what is to come next I know not. . . . It will be then evident that this constitution cannot stand. . . . If the House of Representatives condemn the treaty and defeat its operation I see nothing but the dissolution of government and immediate war. President, Senate, and House all dissolve and an old Congress revives, debts are all canceled, paper money issued and forced into circulation by the bayonets, and in short heaven and earth set at defiance." But he was determined to keep up his own spirits and he quoted his "whistling shoemaker in Hanover Street" who, with nine children in one room, declared stoutly, "Ise never lays anything to heart."[27]

As the fight grew more bitter in the House, Adams diverted himself with a conceit. He wished for the harp of Amphion, King of Thebes, who had charmed the rocks into a wall for his city by playing upon his lyre. With Amphion's harp, he wrote Abigail, "in my walks in the Cedar Grove, in Rocky Run, and on Penn's Hill, I should play upon my lyre, and the merry rocks would dance after me and reel into walls." For thirty years he had been "singing and whistling among my rocks, and not one would ever move without money." For twenty years he had been "saying if not singing, preaching if not playing, 'from various discords to create/ The music of a well-tuned state;/And the soft, silent harmony that springs/From sacred union and consent of things,' but an uncomplying world" would not heed his discourses. "If I had eloquence, or humor, or irony, or satire, or the harp or lyre of Amphion," he lamented, "how much good could I do to the world; What a mortification to my vanity! What a humiliation to my self-love!"

The rocks in the House of Representatives would not dance to his lyre. They were unmoved by the ideal of a "well-tuned state," they had no concern with the "harmony that springs from sacred union and consent of things." They were for smashing all instruments except "the thorough bass, and then blowing you deaf and dumb." Cacophony, not harmony, was their purpose. But they would not prevail. The treaty would be executed. Even so the noise of battle stirred him, old warrior that he was. If he were in the House he could make some speeches that would "throw some light upon these things." Indeed, if Jefferson became President, he might seek election to the House, palsied and toothless as he was. "I declare," he wrote Abigail, "if I were in that House, I would drive out of it some demons that haunt it. There are false doctrines and false jealousies there at times that it would be easy to exorcise." But he was determined to keep possession of his wits and his emotions. "Be sober. Be calm, oh, my heart," he cautioned himself, "and let your temperance and moderation be known to all men." It required "a great command of one's passions to be serene amidst such indiscretions and irregularities of wise men when we have so much extravagance of the universe."[28]

As the battle over the Jay treaty continued in the House, Adams once more felt misgivings about what lay ahead of him. "There is such rancor of party," he noted, "that the prospect of a change in administration quite cures me of all desire to have a share in it." But in the next breath he declared: "I am not intimidated." He was well aware of the ambiguity of his own feelings and he was very ready to admit that "the heart is deceitful and I do believe as well as suspect that I know not mine. . . . I feel myself fixed as fate."[29]

While the House, led by Giles and Madison, fiddled, the country burned. There were meetings and countermeetings, petitions and counter-petitions. The newspapers flamed with editorials and the dissolution of the government was freely predicted north and south. The talk of disunion troubled Adams. "I sometimes think that I am laboring in vain and spending my life for nought, in a fruitless endeavor to pursue a union that, being detested on both sides, cannot long last," he wrote Abigail. "But I shall preserve a compact which is useful and might be more so," he concluded. The principal obstacle to the preservation of the Union was "the pride of aristocracy" in the Southerners which frustrated every measure that did not serve their section's interest.[30]

Abigail herself suffered so much anxiety "for the peace of the country" that she could not sleep nights or bring herself to write to John. A petition in support of the treaty was signed in Boston by fifteen hundred subscribers. The clergy were uniting in another petition, and Abigail herself helped to get signatures in Quincy to an address protesting the actions of the House of Representatives. Canvassing the town, she found Captain Newcomb drilling the militia on the Quincy common and read him a portion of one of Adams' letters predicting that anarchy and war would follow rejection of the treaty. Newcomb, who had refused other requests to sign, gave way before this combined assault, added his name, and persuaded his company of some forty men to do likewise. Abigail was delighted at her victory.

Boston was most affected by the general stagnation of trade brought on through the uncertainty over the fate of the treaty. Insurance underwriters refused to insure cargoes and merchants discharged their sailors and left ships to ride at anchor in the harbor. At a town meeting the radical Democrats Jarvis, Austin, and Morton were defeated on the issue of the treaty and dozens of Massachusetts communities dispatched petitions to Philadelphia condemning the obstructionist tactics of the Anti-Federalists.[31] "But," Adams remarked dryly, "those who have heretofore pretended that instructions [from the people] were to be implicitly obeyed now declare they will disregard them. . . . . Pegg'd like Ariel in a rifted oak," he wrote Abigail, "we can only sprawl in the air with our arms and legs, like Ariel, and fill the atmosphere with our cries and clamors."

So the struggle moved on to its denouement with Adams among the anxious spectators: "The anarchial warriors are beat out of all their entrenchments by the arguments of the friends of peace and order. . . . But party spirit is blind and deaf—totally destitute of candor," he declared. The popular support that was being rallied behind the treaty obviously disconcerted its opponents. Madison appeared "worried to death, pale, withered, haggard," and Edward Livingston, Burr's lieutenant in the House, looked "like horror." The foreigner, Gallatin, had been exposed in his ignorance, and Varnum, the Massachusetts Representative, who had been "as cross a goat as any from Virginia," was feeling the pressure of his constituents' displeasure.

In March "the birds, in number and variety, began to sing, and the grass to grow green," when the weather suddenly turned bitterly cold and a howling northwest wind ripped the city, tearing off roofs and chimneys, and depriving Adams of his Thursday letter from Abigail. The poor birds who had sung so merrily "before this last gripe of Queen Mab . . . have hard times now," he wrote Abigail. The storm in Congress still raged and if the House continued "frenzical" Adams would be a prisoner in Philadelphia indefinitely. But he comforted himself with the assurance that after venting their spleen the Representatives would "make the best of a bad bargain, and come off thus, as well as they can, by abusing Jay, President and Senate, and treaty, without pretending to annul it." "Hi! ho! Oh dear! I am, most tenderly, J.A.," he concluded.[32]

Abigail kept the farm running smoothly and made her faithful, detailed reports to her husband. The upper parish was still looking for a minister to replace the Reverend Mr. Wibird and she took an active interest in the search. Bass, one of the hired men, had jaundice and was of little use; the price of grain was rising; the spring sun was drawing the frost out of the ground and soon the canker worms would start their assault on the apple trees; the cows had produced six calves, and Cleopatra, John's favorite riding mare, was clearly pregnant; the salt and English hay had been stacked wet and rotted, and creek thatch had to be used for bedding for the horses. Abigail, to get help, was forced to pay fourteen dollars a month. "Things can never go on at this rate," she declared.

Captain Beals wanted an academy at Quincy to educate the youth of the town, but Abigail, straining to make ends meet, fretted about the tax rise that such an undertaking would necessitate. "I fancy," she wrote, "the cash will come harder than the vote."[33] But Adams was delighted: "So! We are to have a Quincy academy! With all my heart—I am willing to pay my quota of the expense."

The Vice-President and his wife provided a kind of counterpoise for each other. When Abigail was inclined to doubt that man was ever made to enjoy the delights of freedom John assured her that a wise and beneficent God would not have foreclosed that possiblility, and when John was tempted to despair of the capacity of Americans for republican government Abigail expressed her faith that Americans had a special "character trait. Though sometimes misled and deceived, they wish to know what is just and right, and to conduct accordingly. In the thirty years of my life, in which I have attentively observed them," she wrote, "I have always found them returning to the right path, as soon as they have had time to weigh, consider, and reflect."[34]

To Abigail's remark that "no man even if he is sixty years of age ought to live more than three months at a time from his family," John had a warm answer: "Oh, that I had a bosom to lean my head upon!" he wrote. "But how dare you hint or lisp a word about 'sixty years of age.' If I were near I would soon convince you that I am not above forty."[35]

April brought another upsetting bit of news, this from Nabby at New York. Colonel Smith, it turned out, had involved himself in a speculative business venture with "a swindler and mountebank," a Frenchman who had defrauded the greedy and gullible Colonel and left him bankrupt. When he heard the unhappy story John burst out indignantly: "It is the decree of fate that I should be connected by two branches with a weak family and I must make the best of it. Nothing can happen from it worse than my fears and long expectations."[36] The simple fact of the matter was that his daughter was married to a pretentious simpleton.

Dining at the President's house the end of March, Adams was left alone with Washington when the ladies and gentlemen withdrew after dinner. For several hours the two men talked on a variety of subjects, but especially "respecting England and France and our American parties." Adams had never heard the President "more frank and open upon politics. . . . . I find his opinions and sentiments are more exactly like mine," he wrote Abigail, "than I ever knew before."[37]

By the middle of April, as the debate on the treaty seemed no nearer a conclusion, Adams grew more and more pessimistic. The merchants of Philadelphia had met and petitioned Congress to honor the country's treaty obligations. Merchants in other seaport towns were raising voices of protest, and party spirit was being fanned everywhere to the highest possible pitch. Adams did not dispute the right of the House to request the executive papers relative to the treaty, or to express an opinion upon its merit, but they could abuse their powers and, in fact, they seemed determined to do so. "I fear we do not deserve all the blessings we have within our reach and that our country must be deformed with divisions, contests, dissensions, and civil wars as well as others," he wrote Abigail. As the mass of the people throughout history had scrambled for power against the other branches of government, so, apparently, was the House determined to "scramble for power against the President and Senate. . . . . May God of His infinite mercy grant that some remedy may be found before it be too late, in the good sense of this people."

When the constitution was first ratified Adams had predicted a life of ten years for it; now it was doubtful if it would survive eight. "The House of Representatives seem determined to dictate to the whole government," he wrote, "and Virginia is equally desirous of dictating to the House, and through the ignorance, weakness, and wickedness of Boston, New York, and Philadelphia she has been but too successful." One of the difficulties, Adams was convinced, lay in the fact that the House contained many able men who should have been in the Senate and who were jealous of that body. As long as the House was popularly elected and the Senate appointed by the state legislators, that problem would continue to plague the legislative branch of the government.[38]

The Anti-Federalists were daily more aware that they had gone too far and that instead of appearing as champions of the people against a wicked and tyrannical government they seemed more like a group of willful and contentious man determined to have their own way at whatever cost. Taking advantage of the changing atmosphere, Fisher Ames, who had been absent because of illness through much of the session, rose, weak and shaky, and delivered the most notable speech of the long debate. The House chamber was packed with spectators, many of them from the Senate, and the Boston orator "was attended to with a silence and interest never before known, and made an impression," in Adams' words, "that terrified the hardiest [of his opponents] and will never be forgotten." Adams sat beside Supreme Court Justice James Iredell of North Carolina, a good Federalist, and the two exchanged whispered exclamations. "My God! how great he is!" the Judge murmured. "He is delightful," Adams replied. A pause, and then Iredell again: "Gracious God! how great he has been!" and Adams responded: "He has been noble."

There was another pause, while they listened quite transported, and once more it was Iredell who broke out: "Bless my stars, I never heard anything so great since I was born!" "It is divine," Adams answered; and so they went on with their "interjections, not to say tears, till the end." Many members of the audience wept unabashedly as Ames described the struggle for independence and nationhood, now imperiled by the stubborn and implacable disposition of a few dozen men. By refusing to accept the treaty and thus procure the evacuation of the frontier posts the House would "light the savage fires . . . [and] bind the victims. . . . The darkness of midnight will glitter with the blaze of your dwellings. You are a father—the blood of your sons shall fatten your cornfield; you are a mother—the war whoop shall wake the sleep of the cradle."

The Anti-Federalists affected to listen with scorn and amusement to the eloquent, impassioned sentences, but to Adams "their visages grimaced horrible ghastly smiles" which betrayed their feelings more eloquently than words. It was an extraordinary drama; John and many others who sat enthralled at Ames' oratory believed that the fate of the Republic hinged on its outcome. Dr. Priestley, who was in the audience, compared the Boston Federalist with Pitt and the finest parliamentary orators.[39]

There is little doubt that Ames' speech broke the spirit of the Anti-Federalists. A few days later they gave way and passed the appropriations required to give effect to the treaty. The battle was over and, if the Federalists could hardly claim a conclusive victory, it was plain enough that their opponents had suffered a sharp defeat. The bitterness of feeling was indicated by the fact that after Frederick Muhlenberg, the chairman of the House, cast the deciding vote in favor of the treaty he was stabbed by his brother-in-law, a fanatical Republican.

With the treaty accepted Adams at once requested leave from his duty in the Senate on the ground that he was not well and that Abigail had been sick, as indeed she had. Before he packed up and departed, he could not forbear to reflect on the events of the past five months. It was mortifying that so much time had been wasted on the simple question of "whether national faith is binding upon a nation." The debates on the treaty had served to demonstrate to the world that Americans had "no national pride—no national sense of honor." With this issue now settled there seemed little doubt that the President would hold to his intention of retiring and the question of his succession would doubtless "occasion as much controversy and animosity as the treaty with Great Britain," John noted glumly.

After a brief and rather depressing visit with Nabby and the Colonel, the latter now thoroughly subdued, and an evening with Charles and Sally, he hurried on to Quincy where a few days after his arrival he wrote John Quincy that he was "so absorbed in the embraces of my family and my rural amusements" that he had already forgotten "all the unpleasant moments of the whole winter." Popular sentiment had shifted dramatically to the Federalists, especially in Boston, but Adams took little comfort in the fact. The people were notoriously mercurial and surely, he wrote, "newspapers are not the vehicles, nor town meetings the theaters of negotiations between nations."[40] But during the summer he would be entirely nonpolitical and put all that away for the healthier preoccupations of a farmer. "Kings and princes will be kings and princes, in spite of experience, and demagogues will be demagogues, and people will be people . . . and mankind are condemned to such a state of humiliation that the best they can do is to set one fool, knave, and madman to watch and bind another fool, knave, and madman," he declared to John Quincy.[41]

LXVIII

THE big undertaking of the summer was the erection of the new barn. It was to be forty-five feet long and proportionately wide, and Adams busied himself with drawings and sketches, supervising the selection and preparation of the beams, the roof frame, and the sidings. The routine of the farm was a restorative; he felt his health improve; even the wretched palsy seemed to loosen its grip on him, his eyes were clearer and his step more sure. Only his hair and teeth could not be rejuvenated.

He had a small company of hired men working under his direction and he labored beside them, mowing, plowing, and superintending Briesler as he prepared the foundation of the new barn. The days were not long enough for all the jobs that needed to be done. He rose often at the first light and "enjoyed 'the charm of earliest birds,' their song . . . never more various, universal, animating or delightful." He struggled with two breeds of enemy worms which attacked his corn, a mouse-colored one that lay at the root and gnawed the stalk; the other "long and slender as a needle, of a bright yellow color," that bored its way into the center of the stalk and pierced its inner life.

The frame of the barn was raised in the middle of July where his father's old barn had once stood and Adams felt a thrill of satisfaction as he looked at the naked timbers "very stately and strong," incised against the range of hills beyond the farm.

Playing the cheerful sensualist, he carried his joys to the long-neglected diary. On July 14 he wrote: "It rains at eleven o'clock. The barley is growing white for the harvest. My men are hilling the corn over the road. A soft fine rain in a clock calm is falling as sweetly as I ever saw in April, May, or June; it distills as gently as we can wish; will beat down the grain as little as possible, refresh the gardens and pastures, revive the corn, make the fruit grow rapidly, and lay the foundation of fine rowen and after feed."[1]

The next day he rode to the lower township with three hands and cut fifty red cedars and with a team of five oxen brought home twenty or more of the long, straight, pungent trees at a time. Not only were they needed for the barn, but he had had them felled from the grove so that they opened a lovely prospect of the distant meadow and the Blue Hills beyond.

John worried over Billings, who was an excellent hand when sober but who suffered periodic lapses when he would spend "a terrible, drunken, distracted week . . . a beast associating with the worst beasts in the neighborhood, running to all the shops and private houses, swilling brandy, wine, and cider in quantities enough to destroy him." When he had slept off his binge Adams sent him out to the cornfield to hoe and watched him, sick and dizzy, lurching from hill to hill, cutting down more stalks than he cultivated.

On Penn's Hill, Adams supervised the thinning of the beautiful stand of trees that had been his refuge since boyhood. Many of them were rotten. He left the white oaks standing and trimmed and pruned them as high as a man could reach. The rattlesnakes had begun to appear on the flat, warm rocks of the hillside, to shed their skins and bask in the sun.

On a hot July afternoon he walked his acres, fecund from careful husbandry, over the hills and across the fields and meadows up to the old plain above the town. He stepped with the easy stride of a man who had walked all his life and with the pride of a proprietor. In spite of the distractions of an active political life, he had added to his farms until, taken together, they covered a considerable stretch of land west and north of Quincy. He had made their thin, stony soil bear rich crops; he had plowed and manured, harrowed, and plowed again, rotated his crops, spread his fields with seaweed, lime, and bone meal. Now the summer sun and rain drew corn and grain—barley and oats and rye—out of the nourishing earth. The corn was already knee high, as good a crop as he had ever seen, he thought, looking for the enemy worms, mouse-colored or bright yellow. A thunderstorm caught him in the middle of his walk and he came home happily enough in the warm, soaking rain, wet through but exultant, enjoying the rain for its own sake and for the sake of his thirsty fields.

For a hundred years the road running past his father's farm had taken a jog around an apple tree that bore on its gnarled limbs enough apples to make two barrels of cider. The Quincy selectmen had decided that the road must be enlarged and the tree must fall, a sacrifice to convenience of travelers. Adams watched it hacked down with a pang for the rough beauty of the tree and the thought of the lost barrels of cider. The fence along the road, part stone and part rail, must also be moved. Adams and Billings debated the new site. Billings split and mortised some posts and he and John carried them to the fence. There they bent their backs till they were ready to crack, the Vice-President and his hired hand, straining and puffing, trying to budge the large stones that must be moved to straighten the road. Adams was determined to sweat the liquor out of Billings' system, and he kept him at the job until the man was ready to call quits—the stones were too heavy for two men to move. They must have four. So Billings broke off, ranting. He was worked too hard, driven and lectured to from morning to night. He was through playing the part of a dumb beast. He would find himself an easier master. Adams heard him out and then took him to Abigail to receive the wages due him. At this point Billings had second thoughts and after some haggling he agreed to stay on at forty-five pounds a year and pledge not to drink hard liquor or cider for the whole time. Adams was pleased. There seemed a prospect of reforming a drunkard and keeping a good hired hand.

Saturday, July 23, contained a typical journal entry: "Rode down to the barley and black-grass at the beach. The barley is better than I hoped. The clover has taken pretty well in general. Parts where the tide has flowed are killed. Weeds very thick round the margin of the salt meadow. . . . Twitch-grass scattering and thin. Billings sober, as composed as ever. . . . James the coachman, enjoying the pleasures of a sportsman, shooting marsh birds instead of mowing."[2]

John read Dr. Watson's *Apology for the Bible* and it promoted the reflection: "The Christian religion is, above all the religions that ever prevailed or existed in ancient or modern times, the religion of wisdom, virtue, equity, and humanity, let the blackguard Paine say what he will; it is resignation to God, it is goodness itself to man." He finished the *Apology* and went on to a life of Petrarch and then to Tully's treatise on moral obligations. He supervised the work on the farm and lent a hand himself here and there as the impulse moved him—with Tirrell, hoeing in the lower field; with one of the Lathrop brothers carting seaweed; or with Bass, adding to the compost according to Adams' special formula: earth, salt hay and seaweed, horse dung and cow dung, interspersed with layers of lime.

Sunday he gave faithfully to the Church, morning and afternoon, and to reading and reflection on the Christian faith. So reflecting, it seemed to him that one of Christianity's greatest virtues was that it brought "the great principle of the law of nature and nations—Love your neighbor as yourself, and do to others as you would have that others should do to you—to the knowledge, belief and veneration of the whole people; children, servants, women, and men are all professors in the science of public and private morality. No other institution for education, no kind of political discipline could diffuse this kind of necessary information so universally among all ranks and descriptions of citizens." If mankind should come someday to live in universal brotherhood it would be because it came finally to accept the great Christian ideals as its own.

So the days, rich in small rural pleasures and satisfactions, ran on, shadowed only by Abigail's poor health. "Of all the summers of my life," John wrote in the diary, "this has been the freest from care, anxiety, and vexation to me. . . . My health has been better, the season fruitful, my farm was [well] conducted." It was doubtless transitory enough. "Alas," he exclaimed, "what may happen to reverse all this?" But it was "folly to anticipate evils, and madness to create imaginary ones."[3]

As fall approached Adams was more than ever preoccupied with the question of the presidential succession. Washington had still given no public word of his intention to withdraw, but Samuel Otis and other visitors from Philadelphia assured Adams that the President's resolution was unshakable. David Howell of Rhode Island stopped at Quincy to see Adams and dropped the hint that Rhode Island would support the man who, in turn, had supported the funding bill. His state would like Hamilton for Vice-President. To this feeler Adams made no reply. He was equally reserved when Theodore Sedgwick, the Boston high-Federalist, rode out to give him an optimistic forecast of the coming state elections for Senators and Representatives, but he was pleased when he received word of a toast to him offered at a political rally at, of all places, New York: "To John Adams, inflexible to preserve, virtuous to pursue, and intelligent to discern the true interests of his country." "God grant they may never be belied, never disproved," he wrote.

In September, soon after the cider had been poured into dozens of sturdy barrels and stored in the cellar, the Boston newspapers carried Washington's Farewell Address to the nation that he had served so well for eight trying years. The work, in large part, of Madison and Hamilton, the address stated the principles of Federalism in eloquent phrases that would resound through succeeding generations. John and Abigail read it with mixed emotions. Their feelings were well expressed by Abigail in a letter to John Quincy. "He resigns the important trusts committed to him," she wrote of the President, "covered with glory and crowned with laurels which will place him in the archives of time with the first of heroes and greatest of benefactors to mankind. . . . Take his character together, and we shall not look upon his like again." He was a pure republican, a firm friend to France and an enemy to the haughty tyrant, Great Britain. At the same time his resignation must give the people of America "a solemn pause." It marked "an epocha in their annals big with the fate of America." The critical question was whether the wise policy of Washington's administration would be continued, or whether a President with very different views of the nature of the federal government and the best interest of the American people would direct the country on a different and perhaps fatal course. The new President "must be armed, as Washington was, by integrity, by firmness, by intrepidity—these must be his shield and his wall of brass—and with religion too, or he will never be able to stand sure and steadfast."[4]

Abigail's sentiments were by no means unanimous, however. The extent of partisan feelings was indicated by Bache's *Aurora*. There Washington was castigated as "the source of all the misfortunes of our country," and his resignation hailed as a cause for universal rejoicing: "Every heart in unison with the freedom and happiness of the people ought to beat high with exultation that the name of Washington from this day ceases to give currency to political iniquity and to legalized corruption."

Washington's Farewell Address was, in the words of Fisher Ames, "a signal, like dropping a hat, for the party racers to start."[5] Scarcely two months were left for the partisans of each faction—Federalists and Republicans—to campaign for their party. No candidates were put forward for the voters to choose between. The constitution provided for electors who, in turn, would select a President. The task of the Federalists was thus to secure the election of men of known and avowed loyalty to the principles of their party who could be relied on to vote for a Federalist President.

There was never any serious question that Adams would be the choice of a great majority of the Federalists. The most likely vice-presidential candidate for the ticket was Thomas Pinckney, widely acclaimed for negotiating a popular treaty with Spain. The only question was whether Jefferson, with Aaron Burr as his running mate, would rally enough support to capture the presidency for the Republicans. As the returns from the voting for electors trickled in that chance seemed reasonably remote. The indications were that the Federalists would be assured of a comfortable majority, with the vote split primarily along sectional lines—the North solidly Federalist, the South strongly Republican.

Campaigning, for the most part, was unorganized and sporadic, confined to newspaper polemics, pamphlets, and political rallies. Adams himself took no part in political activities. His supporters traveled to Quincy to confer with him, but he declined to play the part of an active candidate or even a director of strategy. Rumors came from all quarters: Virginia, as might have been expected, was solidly for Jefferson; Pennsylvania would choose Anti-Federal electors. *The Defence of the Constitutions* and the *Discourses* came under attack once again by Republican editors as blueprints for American monarchy. Adams winced at the blows aimed at John Quincy and Thomas who, one writer sneered, "are no doubt understood to be . . . wellborn and who, following [the Vice-President's] own principles, may, as he hopes, one time become Seigneurs or Lords of this country." Jefferson, on the other hand, had daughters only, so the country was safe from a dynasty if the Virginian were elected President.

While Adams professed indifference to all such "false and glaring absurdities," Abigail made no secret of her resentment. "I feel perhaps too keenly," she wrote her eldest son, "the abuse of party." To be sure, Washington had endured it with only occasional breaks in his stoicism, but the strain had clearly told on him toward the end of his administration; and he, after all, "had the support of the people and their undiminished confidence to the hour of his resignation." John would have no such shield. If he were elected President he would begin his administration as simply the best man available with none of the enormous prestige which had helped to carry his predecessor through stormy political seas. He would inherit all the accumulated resentment and bitterness of the past eight years without that extraordinary moral persuasion which Washington, through his stature as a nearly sacred hero-figure, had been able to exercise. It was small wonder that Abigail quailed when she contemplated what lay ahead.

Adams himself gave a more temperate estimate of the campaign. "Party spirit" was in his view "busy but not fiery." The Republican journalists, "the scribblers," must "have their itching scratched." He wrote John Quincy: "Poor Jefferson is tortured as much as your better acquaintance. If he feels as little," he added, "he will not mind it."[6]

Adet, the French minister, was instructed by his Foreign Minister, Delacroix, to enter the campaign actively on behalf of Jefferson. Early in November he published four proclamations in the form of letters to Secretary of State Pickering, blaming the Federalists for the deterioration of Franco-American relations and threatening various punitive measures by the Directory if the Washington policy were not reversed. Adams was undismayed by the Frenchman's intrusion into the presidential contest. He dismissed his charges as "some electioneering nuts [thrown] among the apes," and guessed shrewdly that they would have the opposite effect from that intended.

Jefferson, despite Adams' suspicions, was a reluctant candidate. Like his rival he took no part in the campaign, writing to Edward Rutledge, "I have no ambition to govern men; no passion which would lead me to delight to ride in a storm." He wished only to be allowed "to plant my corn, peas, etc., in hills or drills as I please . . . while our Eastern friends will be struggling with the storm which is gathering over us; perhaps be shipwrecked in it. This is certainly not a moment to covet the helm."[7]

It was a rather curious reaction from a man who had helped to make a revolution and professed to be an ardent admirer of revolutionary principles, but it was characteristic of an impulse in Jefferson which appeared more than once in his active political life, an impulse to avoid tough and demanding decisions, to rely on time or halfway measures to forestall disaster. The implications were plain enough: the situation of the country was too desperate to become involved. The same sentiment was expressed by Adams' old friend, Benjamin Rush, who was now a more enthusiastic Jeffersonian than Jefferson himself. "In the present situation of our country," Rush wrote his hero, "it would have been impossible for you to have preserved the credit of republican principles or your own character for integrity. . . . The seeds of British systems in everything have at last ripened. What a harvest of political evils is before us!"[8]

In Massachusetts the Jeffersonians put up Samuel Adams as an elector, hoping that the old man's popularity would carry the vote for him and confident that he would vote for Jefferson. Fortunately he was defeated and Adams was spared the bitterness of having his old ally aligned against him.

The Anti-Federalists or Republicans played a thousand variations on the old theme that Adams was the "advocate of hereditary power and distinction" who would impose an oppressive aristocracy upon the American people. Adams' friend, Tench Coxe, embittered at failing to be Hamilton's successor as Secretary of the Treasury, wrote a series of articles for the *Gazette of the United States* in which, professing to be a Federalist, he argued at considerable length that the Vice-President was a firm friend of monarchial government. A Republican handbill proclaimed: "Thomas Jefferson is a firm republican—John Adams is an avowed monarchist."[9]

Pennsylvanians were presented with a slate of Republican electors on a broadside that asked them to vote in favor of "the uniform advocate of equal rights among citizens," rather than "the champion of rank, titles, and hereditary distinctions . . . the warm panegyrist of the British monarchial form of government." "*Thomas Jefferson*," a handbill proclaimed, "first drew the declaration of American independence; he first framed the sacred political sentence that all men are *born* equal. *John Adams* says this is all farce and falsehood; that some men should be born Kings, and some should be born Nobles. Which of these, freemen of Pennsylvania, will you have for your President? . . . Put in your tickets for fifteen good REPUBLICANS, and let the watch word be LIBERTY and INDEPENDENCE!" Some publicists based their preference for Jefferson on the grounds that he was without political ambition while his rival was devoured by that vice and in addition was a trimmer and vacillator, "frigid in council, phlegmatic in determination, and slow in the execution of his resolves."[10]

Among the charges leveled against Adams was the story, published in the *Aurora*, that is was he who had drafted Alexander Hamilton's proposal, submitted to the federal convention, advocating a government consisting of a King, Lords, and Commons. Adams, moreover, in his *Defence* and in the *Discourses* had shown "an *active unfriendliness* to the *essential* and *cardinal* principles" of all American constitutions, state and federal.

He was also charged with "greatly" disapproving "the *funding* and *banking systems*" and being an enemy of Hamilton's financial policy.

"The fact is absolutely true and the importance of it is immense," a writer in the *Aurora* declared.[11]

A few days before the citizens of Pennsylvania were due to cast their ballots for the presidential electors the members of the Republican slate warned them that "attempts are at this moment making to place in the presidential chair a man who has proclaimed to the world his hostility to republican government." John Adams was in nomination for the presidency of the United States, a man who was "the declared advocate of ranks and orders in society . . . the enthusiastic friend of hereditary power. . . . We pronounce with the utmost solemnity that our constitutions will afford no bulwark against encroachment on our rights when administered by men who contend for the power of molding it according to their own sense of expediency." The voters must cast their ballots for the supporters of Jefferson. "Only a man of such enlightened views, such pure patriotism, such unsullied integrity, and such zeal for human happiness" could make America "flourishing, tranquil, and happy. . . . To promote the election of the great Jefferson," the letter concluded, "ought to be the object of every friend to republicanism and his country." Leading the list of electors was Adams' old friend, Thomas McKean, Chief Justice of the Superior Court, and prominent on the roll was his old enemy, William Maclay.[12]

Jefferson, meanwhile, was denounced by the Federalist press as an enemy of the constitution and the leader of a party bent on remodeling the American government along the lines advocated by French theorists. The Virginian was charged with being a revolutionary enthusiast, an atheist and a freethinker, and much was made of his so-called cowardice, when as wartime Governor of Virginia he had retired rather hastily from his post at the rumor of a British invasion.

What counted perhaps more than the heated polemics on both sides were the efforts of John Beckley, Clerk of the House, who was the most enterprising Republican propagandist. Beckley scattered thousands of sample ballots bearing the names of Republican electors throughout Pennsylvania, which he saw as the key state in the election, and reinforced these with a flood of handbills and pamphlets.

Aaron Burr was also assiduous in his promotion of the Republican cause. He spent six weeks campaigning in Connecticut, Rhode Island, Massachusetts, and Vermont, and he was credited with the idea of putting Governor Sam Adams up as a presidential elector for the Boston district. Burr arrived in Boston in October and spent the better part of several days closeted with the Anti-Federalist leaders, Jarvis, Austin, and Eustis.

There was a last-minute flurry of activity in Massachusetts by the Republicans. Handbills denouncing Adams as an aristocrat and monarchist were nailed to gateposts, doors of houses, and posts throughout the county and men were hired to ride through the state, their saddle-bags stuffed with Anti-Federal broadsides.

With a majority of electors apparently of Federalist persuasion, Adams' election seemed almost assured but at the last minute Alexander Hamilton's scheming threw everything into doubt. Hamilton wished a more pliant President than Adams and he once more began his devious maneuvers. In 1789 he had succeeded in depriving Adams of a clear majority of the votes for the vice-presidency, now he would see if he could deprive him of the presidency by the same technique.

Hamilton's plan called for the New England Federalist electors to cast their votes unanimously for Adams and Pinckney while the electors of South Carolina would cast all their votes for Pinckney as Vice-President but throw away a few from Adams. The result would be that Pinckney, with a larger number of votes, would become President and Adams Vice-President. It was at best a reckless gamble that could very well have thrown the election to Hamilton's bitter rival, Jefferson. Hearing of the New Yorker's plot in the nick of time, the New England electors countered by scratching out Pinckney's name, but in South Carolina eight votes went to Pinckney and eight to Jefferson, bringing the latter within three votes of the presidency.

By the sixteenth of November, Samuel Otis, from his vantage point in Philadelphia, had compiled a preliminary count of the electoral vote. It was based primarily on rumors as to the preferences of the electors in various states. "By lies, abuse, and bribery," he wrote Adams, "the disorganizers will carry their ticket through the state [Pennsylvania]." The prediction proved correct, although the intense Republican activity in Pennsylvania gave that state to Jefferson by a margin of only a few hundred votes. In New England and New York, Otis counted fifty-one votes for Adams; he calculated three from Delaware, seven from New Jersey, and perhaps as many as five from Virginia. South Carolina should produce four, Kentucky one, North Carolina two, and Maryland five or six. The total for Adams: seventy-six, a six-vote margin. "I presume further," Otis wrote, "that these 76 contain 7/8ths of the honesty and property, and 4/5ths of the good sense of the nation."[13] The estimate was remarkably close. Otis did not know of Hamilton's intrigue, which cost Adams the four South Carolina votes that Otis had credited him with. With these four votes subtracted, Otis came within one of the actual total for Adams.

LXIX

With the issue of the election still in doubt, Adams set out for Philadelphia the last week in November, leaving Abigail at Quincy. At Hartford he saw for the first time the full text of Adet's bellicose dispatches to the Secretary of State. It was, Adams noted, "an instrument well calculated to reconcile me to private life. It will purify me from all envies of Mr. Jefferson, or Mr. Pinckney, or Mr. Burr, or Mr. anybody who may be chosen President or Vice-President. Although, however, I think the moment a dangerous one, I am not scared. . . . I dread not a war with France or England, if either forces it upon us, but will make no aggression upon either with my free will." What was most disturbing was the thought of how gratified the English would be at this evidence of French belligerency. He feared they would "show us some cunning, insidious kind of kindness upon the occasion. I should dread this kindness as much as French severity," he added, "but will be the dupe of neither." The journey was so cold that it made him regret the "loss of . . . bed and fireside, and especially the companion and delight of both."[1]

Adams spent a day in Eastchester with Nabby and the children. The Colonel was in severe financial straits as the result of collapse of his various speculative ventures and Adams remarked disapprovingly that the crisis in his affairs had not prevented him from spending two days hunting partridges and quail with his brothers. The halcyon days were over, but the Colonel still kept a half dozen horses in his stable and lived as though he had no worry in the world. Such was the way of improvidence. The baby girl, Caroline Amelia, was "as fat and rosy and hearty as a country girl can be," John reported to Abigail. Charles and Sally had produced an infant girl and John went to the city to visit them. The baby was pretty, Charles had a great deal of business, looked and dressed respectably, and kept good company. From Charles's, Adams went on to spend an evening with John Jay, a "very happy" occasion with the two old friends reminiscing about the past and speculating on the outcome of the election. Jay had heard rumors of the plot to throw the presidency to Pinckney although he apparently did not know, or did not care to tell Adams, where the scheme had originated.[2]

John arrived in Philadelphia on the second of December, after a frosty ride of some eighty miles from Elizabethtown, and the next day he dined with the President and John Watts, King of the Cherokees, and a number of chieftains' wives and daughters. Washington, through his reserve, seemed pleased to see Adams again and showed him an angry and abusive letter which he had recently received from Tom Paine. The author of *Common Sense* had concluded his letter: "I must continue to think you treacherous till you give me cause to think otherwise." The epistle appeared to Adams the weakest "of all Paine's productions" and "at the same time the most malicious. . . . He must have been insane to write so," he noted, telling Abigail of the incident.[3] Such were the lengths to which partisan bitterness drove those who succumbed to it.

Philadelphia was in a state of uneasy suspense over the outcome of the election and the prospects of war with France. Adet's activities had definitely brought a reaction, "an antidote to the violence of their passion . . . an antiseptic";[4] and John wrote Abigail: "Americans must be cool and steady if they can. Some of our people may be cured of their extravagant love and shaken in their unlimited confidence." The French character, monarchial or republican, he reminded his wife, was "not the most equitable nor the least assuming of all nations. The fire, impetuosity, and vehemence of their temperament is apt to be violent, immoderate, and extravagant."[5]

Adams was determined to try his best to cling to his own sense of proportion. The more he thought about the possible outcome of the election, the more he was convinced that if Jefferson triumphed the Virginian would not, in fact, deviate from the course followed by Washington. There simply was no other course that made sense and, once in office, Jefferson, an intelligent man, must realize as much.[6] Abigail wrote in a similar spirit: "Though wrong in politics, though formerly an advocate for Tom Paine's *Rights of Man*, and though frequently mistaken in men and measures, I do not think him an insincere or a corruptible man. My friendship for him has ever been unshaken."[7]

As the date for the convening of Congress drew closer, the day when Adams, as presiding officer of the Senate, would open and record the votes of the presidential electors, he was swept by conflicting emotions. He looked deep into his psyche and was both appalled and amused by what he saw there. "I laugh at myself twenty times a day," he wrote Abigail, "for my feelings and meditations and speculations in which I find myself engaged. Vanity suffers, cold feelings of unpopularity, humble reflections, mortifications, humiliations—plans of future life. Eonomy, retrenching of expenses. Farming. Return to the bar. Drawing writs, arguing causes, taking clerks, humiliation of my country under foreign bribes. Measures to counteract them. All this miserable nonsense will come and go like evil into the thoughts of gods and men, approved or unapproved." The new President, "with half the continent upon his back besides all France and England, old Tories and all Jacobins to carry, will have a devilish load," he noted. "He will be very apt to stagger and stumble."

He counted and recounted the prospective votes from the various states. There were reports that he would get all the Northern votes but that Jefferson would get all the Southern. In that case he would be defeated. But other analysts gave him three from Virginia and one from North Carolina. These would be enough, with the solid North, to give him victory. He had moments of wishing that he was out of it all. Indeed, what did he wish? "Let me see!" he exclaimed. "Do I know my own heart? I am not sure." What he dreaded most of all was defeat and then "a foolish, mortifying, humiliating, uncomfortable residence [in Philadelphia] for two tedious months after I shall be known to be skimmed."

He was confident that he could pronounce in the Senate after the votes had been recorded: "Thomas Jefferson to be chosen President of the United States," and that he could do it "with firmness and a good grace." But alone in bed, tossing and turning, missing Abigail's warm and comforting presence, or by his fireside through a long evening, trying with little success to read—it was in those moments that he felt close to despair. The terrible irony of it was that he needed the job. He who had always cherished his independence needed the income from public office. Much as he professed to despise the pittance that he received as Vice-President, if it did not enable him to maintain a handsome establishment in Philadelphia, it at least made it possible for him to live comfortably in Quincy and improve his farm with careful husbandry against the day when he must retire from public life entirely. He could not return to the bar, for all he talked of it. He wrote with increasing difficulty, the loss of his teeth had made speaking difficult, and he had been away from the law for twenty years. These were ugly thoughts. In the face of them it was a curious comfort to anticipate his defeat. "The 16 of Feb will soon come," he wrote Abigail, "and then I will take my leave forever. Then for frugality and independence—poverty and patriotism—love and a carrot bed." He added, "Don't show this stuff."[8]

The night before Congress convened he had the glooms again. The thought of the friends who had deserted him was especially depressing and he poured out his resentment to Abigail. Although he professed indifference he could not suppress his curiosity as to how his old friend McKean, who was one of the presidential electors, had voted. How would Sam Adams have voted if he had been chosen as an elector? Would he have been the only New Englander to cast his vote for Jefferson? Adams could not bring himself to believe it. He had lost a succession of friends through the political battles of the last thirty years, beginning with Jonathan Sewall and Samuel Quincy and extending through Jefferson, Hancock, Richard Henry Lee, Sullivan, James and Mercy Warren, Tench Coxe, Benjamin Rush, and dozens of others whom he had loved and esteemed. Perhaps that was why every new defection was harder to bear.

"Nothing affects me so much," he wrote, "as to see McKean . . . Osgood, and even Sam Adams and such men set up in opposition to me." These were old friends and allies. That they could be prevailed upon to join the ranks of his enemies showed how far party spirit had gone. He found it, he confessed, "very disgusting, very shocking." Among many defections, one friend with Republican leanings remained constant. He was Elbridge Gerry, and Adams, contrasting his loyalty with the "weathercockism" of former Federalist friends, never forgot his support. But such matters aside, he had his nerve back. It had soothed his spirits to pour out all his doubts and anxieties to Abigail. Now he felt "in a very happy temper of mind, perfectly willing to be released from the post of danger, and determined, if called to, to brave it, if its horrors were ten times thicker than they are. I have but a few years of life left," he wrote, "and they cannot be better bestowed than upon that independence of my country in defense of which that life has ever been in jeopardy."[9]

Shortly after the Senate convened and before the electoral college votes had been counted, a committee was appointed to prepare a reply to the President's Farewell Address. It fell to Adams, as President of the Senate, to deliver that body's "most affectionate" response. The occasion was a trying one for Adams as well as Washington. Adams was determined to keep his emotions in check, to be "firm and cool," but his feelings betrayed him. "The Senators say I pronounced it in so affecting a manner," he wrote Abigail later, "that I made them cry. The tears certainly did trickle," and the President had trouble preserving enough composure to get through his brief reply.[10]

By the twelfth of December even Giles was willing to concede the presidency to Adams, adding in his rough way, "The old man will make a good President, too. . . . But we shall have to *check* him a little now and then. That will be all." Adams was pleased when the remarks of the Virginia Anti-Federalist were repeated to him.

Others besides Giles began to speak of Adams' election as assured, and with this assumption he suddenly found a new deference and respect expressed by individuals who had formerly preserved a certain coolness. The "Southern gentlemen" especially, gracious in defeat, "expressed more affection," he noted, "than they ever did before since 1774." The principal uncertainty was still that Pinckney, by some trickery, might become President. Rumors continued to circulate to that effect and some of them associated Hamilton with the "insidious maneuver," but Adams refused to believe that the New Yorker would engage in such an unscrupulous scheme. He himself would prefer "the pilotage of Jefferson" to that of Pinckney or Burr. Indeed the whole system with its opportunities for manipulation and chicane was, he declared, "utterly repugnant to my judgment and wishes." He would rather see Patrick Henry with the whole 138 votes than Pinckney elected by a ruse. "If chance and tricks" were to decide the issue "it had better be decided by French influence for ought I know, or even by English, for either Jefferson or Hamilton had better pretensions and would have made better Presidents than Pinckney."

Despite Adams' skepticism, evidence began to pile up that Hamilton and perhaps Jay were involved in the Pinckney intrigue. It was hard for Adams to accept the fact that Hamilton had been conniving against him. He had admired the New Yorker and defended him on numerous occasions against his detractors, albeit he thought him too ardent in his zeal for Great Britain. But the persistence of the rumors and the gradual accumulation of evidence forced him to take account of the possibility that the reports were true and to analyze their significance. He could believe that both Jay and Hamilton would prefer Pinckney to Jefferson as President and Hamilton doubtless thought he would have more influence with Pinckney than with Adams. "Both of them," he speculated, "might think that if I was out of the way one or the other of them might have a better chance to come in at the next election into one or the other office." Both might also wish for closer relations with England than Adams would approve. Whether or not these stories were true, "they shall make no impression on my friendship for those characters," he wrote Abigail. "I believe that their motives were what they [conceived] for public good." Jay, he was sure, had no active part in the whole scheme. It had apparently been Hamilton's idea and Hamilton had tried to give it effect. Moreover Adams suspected that his Boston friends, Stephen Higginson and George Cabot, had been party to the plot which, if it had followed their design, would have made Pinckney President, Adams Vice-President, and shut Jefferson out entirely. That was the desideratum of many of the New England Federalists. Once again John was ready to concede defeat and to view the "dull prospect" of "nothing but one's plowshare between one and the grave." But the next moment he was overcome by indignation at the shabby plot to rob the nation of one or other of the men whom an overwhelming majority of its citizens intended to have as President. It was treating the election like a bag of tricks in a cheap side show, hoodwinking the yokels by sleight of hand. Only a particular kind of moral opacity, in Adams' view, could lend itself to such a callous perversion of the popular will.

Abigail was incensed at the reports of Hamilton's plot and she reminded her husband that she had often warned him against the New Yorker as a man "ambitious as Julius Caesar, a subtle intriguer. . . . His thirst for fame is insatiable. I have ever kept my eye upon him," she added. For herself she hoped that Jefferson would win out over Pinckney as Vice-President. "You know," she wrote John, "my friendship for that gentleman has lived through his faults and errors—to which I have not been blind."[11]

As more evidence accumulated of Hamilton's double-dealing and the outcome of the election continued uncertain, Adams replied to Abigail's strictures with an entire absence of that equanimity which he had professed only a few weeks earlier. He too knew Hamilton "to be a proud-spirited, conceited, aspiring mortal, always pretending to morality, with as debauched morals as old Franklin, who," he added, "is more his model than anyone I know. As great an hypocrite as any in the U.S., his intrigues in the election I despise. That he has 'talents' I admit, but I dread none of them. I shall take no notice of his puppyhood but retain the same opinion of him I always had and maintain the same conduct towards him that I always did—that is, to keep him at a distance."[12] Abigail's answer was in a similar vein. "Beware of that spare Cassius, has always occurred to me when I have seen that cock sparrow," she wrote. "Oh, I have read his heart in his wicked eyes many a time. The very devil is in them. They are lasciviousness itself, or I have no skill in physiognomy." And then, dismayed at her indiscretion, she added, "Pray burn this letter. Dead men tell no tales."[13]

By the twentieth of December Adams reported, "It is supposed to be certain that Mr. Jefferson cannot be President and a narrow squeak it is, as the boys say, whether he or Pinckney shall be Daddy Vice."[14] Although the final vote was not yet tallied, Adams began calculating the cost of a carriage and horses suitable for the President of the United States and was appalled to find that "a common chariot of the plainest sort" could not be bought for less than six hundred dollars. House rent would also be extravagantly high, and prices in general excessive. The fever of speculation had affected everyone and the numerous business failures seemed only to excite more activity. The get-rich-quick mania was only too apparent. It would lead, Adams feared, to "rolling in luxury upon the property of others." Dishonesty would increase with distress. Already it was observable that "everyone cheats as much as he can." But he and Abigail must make out as best they could and live within their income even though it meant a degree of austerity. He could not forbear to reflect on his folly in seeking the presidency. It was hard to understand how a man who had a fertile farm and "a Narragansett mare that paces, trots, and canters" could aspire to public office. "But I don't know but all men are such fools," he added. When all was said about the pleasures of retirement, it was better for a man to "wear than to rust."[15]

Adams was distressed at the volume of abuse aimed at Washington. It came, to be sure, from a handful of radical newspapers whose editors in several instances were recent arrivals from Ireland and England, but the attacks were vicious and Washington was plainly upset by them. Bache, the master of vituperation, led the pack. "If ever a nation was debauched by a man," he wrote in the *Aurora*, "the American nation has been debauched by Washington. If ever a nation has been deceived by a man, the American nation has been deceived by Washington. Let his conduct, then, be an example to future ages; let it serve to be a warning that no man may be an idol; let the history of the federal government instruct mankind that the mask of patriotism may be worn to conceal the foulest designs against the liberties of the people."[16] Other Republican journalists accused the President of having committed murder and of attempting to betray the Continental Army during the Revolution. One ingenious editor used Adams to derogate Washington, declaring that the country would be fortunate to be governed by "talents and science" rather than the "mysterious influence of a name." "The sting at the retiring hero hurts me," John wrote Abigail. "Science in some of its branches, he may not have been possessed [of] in any eminent degree; but talents of a very superior kind are his. I wish I had as good." In the science of understanding and managing himself and others, of self-control and leadership, the General was gifted as few men in history. "I never shall attain so much of that most necessary and useful science," John concluded ruefully.[17]

Jefferson, a reluctant candidate, was ready to concede by the middle of December. He had also heard of Hamilton's plot but was satisfied that the Eastern states would not suffer themselves to be "made tools for the bringing in of Pinckney instead of Adams." If, as seemed possible, there were a tie between himself and Adams for the electoral vote, throwing the election into the House of Representatives (which in turn might be equally divided), Madison was authorized to request in Jefferson's name that the preference be given to Adams. "He has always been my senior," Jefferson wrote, "from the commencement of our public life, and the expression of the public will being equal, this circumstance ought to give him the preference." In his view the prospects for the nation had not looked so dark since 1793. "Let those come to the helm," he added, "who think they can steer clear of the difficulties. I have no confidence in myself for the undertaking." It was a gracious gesture. Madison waited until it was evident that Adams had won and then published the letter. Its conciliatory tone made a favorable impression, and Adams of course was specially pleased. "It is considered as evidence of his determination to accept [the vice-presidency]," he related to Abigail, "of his friendship for me—and of his modesty and moderation."[18]

On the twenty-eighth of December, Jefferson wrote a letter to Adams congratulating him on his victory. He had never doubted the outcome, he declared, or wished it otherwise. Adams had almost been cheated of the election by the subterfuge of Hamilton, who had been able "to make of your real friends tools to defeat their and your just wishes." For himself he preferred "the society of neighbors, friends, and fellow laborers of the earth" to that of "spies and sycophants." He did not envy Adams his "painful and thankless office"; he only wished he would preserve the nation in peace. If he succeeded in doing so, wrote the Virginian, "the glory will be all your own." Despite the "various little incidents" which had occurred to separate them, he retained for Adams "the solid esteem of the moments when we were working for our independence."[19]

It was typical of Jefferson that he sent the letter unsealed to Madison and left it to his discretion whether or not to send it on to Adams. Despite professed lack of interest in politics, Jefferson was a politician to his fingertips. The letter was not simply an expression of personal warmth and good will; it was a political document. Madison read it over, considered its possible effects, and decided not to deliver it to Adams.

Among the apostates who came to call on Adams when it appeared he had carried the election were Tench Coxe—"what a puppy," Adams wrote Abigail—and Adams' old friend, Benjamin Rush. He welcomed Rush warmly and accepted a copy of his oration on the death of the radical scientist David Rittenhouse. "We must put up with the vagaries of our flighty friend," was the way he expressed it to Abigail, forwarding the address to her.

The doctor overflowed with "so many compliments, so many anecdotes." He was pleased, he declared, at Adams' election. Even though he had opposed him, he felt real affection for him, and so did many who had labored for the Republican cause. He had met Madison in the street that very day, and when he asked Madison if he thought Jefferson would accept the vice-presidency under Adams, Madison had pulled from his pocket the letter from Jefferson urging that in the event of a tie the election be given to Adams in the House, "for Mr. Adams' services have been longer, more constant, and more important than mine." Adams listened to his voluble friend rattle on with amusement and affection. His simple goodness of heart preserved the doctor from any feeling of embarrassment, and Adams could not find it in himself to harbor resentment. It pained him, however, to hear Rush abuse Washington and declare that the United States would rise in the estimation of the world on the day that the President stepped aside. "His old griefs and prejudices still hang about him," he wrote Abigail. The truth was that the Pennsylvanian was incurably naïve in the field of politics and no more responsible than a child for all his outlandish ideas and extravagant opinions.[20]

Adams was also visited by Letombe, the French Consul General, who assured him that it had never been the intention of the Directory that Adet should mix in the election. Adams, in turn, told Letombe that he supported the constitution and the congressional declaration of neutrality but was friendly to the French people and Letombe passed on these assurances to the understandably apprehensive Adet.[21] Subsequently, dining with Robert Liston, the British minister, Adams was at pains to make clear his desire to maintain good relations with that country.

The success of his talk with Liston was indicated by the British minister's opinion that Adams' election might be "considered as favorable to the interests of His Majesty; not because I perceive in Mr. Adams any partiality of sentiment towards Great Britain, but because he detests the principle and dreads the predominance of our enemy, and because the firmness of his character removes all danger of his being *bullied* into measures which he does not approve."[22]

Adet, on the other hand, believed that Adams would be favorable to the French,[23] and Adams himself insisted that the French had misjudged him; "I am more their friend than they are aware of," he declared. He intended, he wrote Abigail, to use the time before his inauguration to "remove many prejudices both at home and abroad."[24]

One of the special treats for the President-practically-elect was dinner at the Binghams' where he was seated beside his hostess. Whether it was the wine or the witchery of her beautiful eyes, he found that he was able to carry on "something like a political conversation with her" and went away convinced that, if not brilliant, Ann Bingham nonetheless had "more ideas on the subject" than he had suspected, "and a correcter judgment."[25]

To Adams the most gratifying expression came from the President's lady. When he attended her Tuesday evening levee she congratulated him "very complaisantly and affectionately" and, he wrote Abigail with obvious gratification, "went further and said more than I expected." His election, she declared, had given her and the President great pleasure. "I doubted," Adams added, "whether their prudence would have ventured so far." However, all the members of the Washington household were not of the President's mind. Kidd, the steward, had campaigned vigorously for Jefferson. If the Virginian was elected he might well keep Kidd on, but if Adams won he would certainly be replaced by Briesler.[26]

On the first day of the New Year Adams sat down to write Abigail. The year that lay ahead was pregnant with troubles, foreseen and unforeseen. Yet he faced it undismayed. With the prize of the presidency apparently in his grasp, he experienced a strange sense of serenity and assurance. The sensation had come to him in all the great crises of his life. Often obsessed with feelings of self-doubt, of hostility and even despair, he found springs of strength and resolution within himself when he most needed them. "I never felt easier in my life," he wrote Abigail. "My path is very plain, and if I am not supported I will resign."[27]

In snowbound Quincy, Abigail had a New Year's wish for her distant husband: "To Him who sits Supreme, let us commit the hour, the day, the year, and fearless view the whole. There needs but thinking right and meaning well, and may this ensure to you the soul's calm sunshine and the heartfelt joy." Her own anxiety was shown by a vivid dream in which she had been riding in her coach, she knew not where, when suddenly she had seen flying through the air toward her a number of large black cannon balls. For a moment she felt a spasm of terror and then the balls burst and fell before they reached her, crumbling to atoms as she continued on her way. At the same time two guns were discharged at her left ear. She saw the flash and heard the report but remained unscathed and pushed resolutely forward.[28]

It was hard to be separated from John at such a time, but their letters bound them by invisible cords stronger than chains. As Abigail waited and watched, Quincy was gripped by the same cold wave that held the capital in its icy clasp. It was colder than she could ever remember; it froze the ink in her pen and chilled the blood in her veins but, she wrote, pleased to turn the metaphor, "not the warmth of my affection for him for whom my heart beats with unabated ardor through all the changes and vicissitudes of life, in the still calm of Peacefield [the name Adams had given to the farm], and the turbulent scenes in which he is about to engage."[29]

With the outcome certain, Adams gave a good deal of thought to the problems that faced his administration. "There is a curious mass of matter in fermentation at this time," he wrote Abigail. The French and the Spanish were pursuing a belligerent course. In addition, "as if it were to irritate every feeling nerve, a land tax must be discussed . . . and the debtor states must be called upon for their balances." The truth was that the nation faced difficult and dangerous times and must draw in its belt and prepare to meet them. "The people of America must wake out of their golden dreams, consider where they are and what they are about," he wrote Abigail. "The foolish idolatry of France and Paine . . . the ignorance in which our people will keep themselves of the true character of the French nation in general and of their present government as well as all their former governments since the Revolution [is] astonishing." It remained for Adams to surmount these difficulties or to be overpowered by them.[30]

Another cloud that lay on the horizon, somewhat larger than a man's hand, was the recall of Monroe. As United States minister to France, the

Virginian had broken every rule of diplomacy by critizing his government's policy and deliberately acting counter to his instructions. As another French zealot, the man had, in Adams' words, made his ministerial quarters in Paris "a school for scandal against his country, its government and governors." Monroe's feeling seemed to be that America could serve no greater cause than to be a tail to the French kite and set out, with the French, to revolutionize the world.

Finally Washington, his patience stretched to the limit, had summoned the recalcitrant diplomat home. The recall predictably enraged the Francophiles and presented them with an issue which Adams predicted "will come up after the 4 of March, and stare at me." When all was said and done, although the coming storm looked "black and thick enough," Adams was confident that he could ride it out. "I have confidence," he wrote Abigail, "in the sense, spirit, and resources of this country, which few other men in the world know so well [or] have so long tried and found solid." Inconveniences and distresses enough awaited the United States, but once wakened from their dreams the American people would prove to be citizens worthy of the best and freest government man had ever known.[31]

One serious problem that faced Adams was the retirement of so many able Federalists from the government. Rather than being encouraged by Adams' victory, they seemed inclined to despair. They lacked the ideological zeal of their opponents, whose enthusiastic and undiscriminating devotion to democratic dogmas and the French Revolution combined with their opposition to the party in power to give them a unity and a drive that the Federalists were sadly lacking. It appeared to Adams that the Federalists were "divided and crumbling to pieces." If there were serious divisions among the Republicans they were obscured by their common dedication to wresting the government from the Federalists.[32]

Madison, no Federalist to be sure, announced his retirement from the House, and Adams noted, "It seems the mode of becoming great is to retire—Madison, I suppose, after a retirement of a few years is to be President or Vice-President—Mr. Cabot, I suppose, after aggrandizing his character in the shade a few years, is to be some great thing too—and Mr. Ames—etc., etc., etc. It is marvelous how a political plant grows in the shade—continued daylight and sunshine show our faults and record them. Our persons, voices, clothes, gait, air, sentiments, etc., all become familiar to every eye and ear and understanding, and they diminish in proportion upon the same principle that no man is a hero to his wife or valet de chambre." All of these gentlemen were right "to run away and hide."[33]

O N THE eighth of February the votes of the state electors were counted and the results became official: Adams seventy-one votes, Jefferson sixty-nine, Pinckney fifty-nine. The result of Hamilton's strategy had been to narrow Adams' margin of victory and make his opponent, Jefferson, Vice-President. "The common saying here," Adams noted, "is that it is an interposition of Providence that has saved me, defeated Pinckney, and disappointed the English party as well as the French."

As President of the Senate, it fell to Adams to announce himself the President-elect. A week later he made an affectionate speech of farewell to the body whose deliberations he had faithfully presided over for eight trying years. After he had conquered his early impulse to involve himself in their deliberations he had lived in harmony with the Senators. Now, "with much anxiety and diffidence," he accepted his election as President. Thus he must reluctantly take leave of the Senate, consoling himself that in his tenure he had "never had the smallest misunderstanding with any member of the Senate." In all "the abstruse questions, difficult conjunctures, dangerous emergencies, and animated debates" upon the great interests of the country, he had been treated in turn with politeness and respect. "Within these walls," he concluded graciously, "for a course of years I have been an admiring witness of a succession of information, eloquence, patriotism, and independence which, as they would have done honor to any Senate in any age, afford a consolatory hope . . . that no council more permanent than this, as a branch of the legislature, will be necessary to defend the rights, liberties, and properties of the people, and to protect the constitution of the United States." The Senate replied with a pointed reference to Adams' "undeviating impartiality." Americans had placed in him "for a long period . . . a steady confidence which has never been betrayed or forfeited." Confident that he would uphold the constitution, the Senators pledged their loyal support to his administration. John, always emotional, was near tears. "I assure you," he wrote Abigail, "it was a tender scene at parting."[1]

Now that the issue was finally settled, the country demonstrated a capacity that was to be one of its happiest qualities as a nation and perhaps its salvation—the ability to bury the bitterness and rancor of the campaign, to forget the dire predictions of national disaster and pick up the ordinary business of life, confident that neither the world nor the Republic was coming to an end. This could be done because among Americans there was a consensus—common traditions and ideals—that lay deeper than the transient passions of party and faction. As long as that remarkable consensus held fast, the nation would somehow endure. Beyond that, it dawned on many who had opposed Adams that in him, providentially, the times had met the man. Once he was President, it was hard to imagine how it could have been otherwise. He was so clearly the one candidate who could represent national unity. Jefferson was too much the prisoner of his passion for the French, too hesitant, too indecisive for the moment. Pinckney was a political accident, Burr an opportunist. Out of the confusion and disorder, the chancy, hit-or-miss nature of democratic politics, the nation had found, as it was to do time and again in its subsequent history, the man best suited for the exigencies of the hour. More than anything else the country needed a President who, like Washington, stood consciously above party and tried patiently, laboriously, and not always successfully to do justice to all factions, to pierce through the ephemeral passions and the partisan enthusiasms, grasping and holding firmly to what was essential—peace for the infant Republic so far as honor would allow it.

The nation came to be conscious of all this, not publicly or self-consciously, but through some kind of interior illumination. It showed itself in dozens of small ways: in spontaneous expressions of affection from the citizens of some distant rural community who suddenly felt a kind of comfort and assurance in that stout, indomitable little man who would do what he thought was right regardless of party, press, the powers and potentates of the earth, or all the hounds of hell that might howl about him; it showed itself in comments from the leaders of the opposition party; in the abashed and awkward gestures of reconciliation from friends who had distrusted his political principles. It was clear that whether he was a monarchist or not weighed little against his special virtues as chief executive of the United States. He was especially pleased at being called an "old fielder" by a Baltimore newspaper. "An old fielder," he explained to Abigail, "is a tough, hardy, laborious little horse that works very hard and lives upon very little. Very useful to his master at small expense."[2] It was certainly evident that the new President would have to live austerely. A decent house would cost twenty-seven hundred dollars a year to rent, and horses were three to five times as high as they had been seven years ago. Everything had doubled or tripled in cost and the consequence was that "all levees and drawing rooms and dinners must be laid aside and I am glad of it." Then there would be the problem of furnishing the presidential mansion. The furniture belonged to Washington and he would take it with him. Adams must provide all the glasses, kitchen utensils, chairs, settees, china, glass and crockery, secretaries, servants, wood, the charities "which are demanded as rights, and the million dittoes." He was appalled when he realized the expenses that were involved, but there was no turning back now. "We must stand our ground as long as we can," he wrote Abigail.[3]

Abigail replied with her usual good sense: "My dearest friend, as you have been called in Providence into the chair of government, you did not accept it without knowing that it had its torments, its trials, its dangers and perplexities. Look steadfastly at them, arm yourself with patience and forbearance and be not dismayed, and may God and the people support you. Having put your hand to the plow, you must not look back." At the same time Abigail was determined to keep up the farm as their "*dernier* resort," their "ark of safety." She was pleased at the rumor that Madison had been appointed minister to France. She had confidence in his integrity if not his principles. Then she added, "My pen runs riot. I forget that it must grow cautious and prudent. I fear I shall make a dull business when such restrictions are laid upon it." Amid the comforts and conveniences of Quincy, she wrote, there was "one pleasure wanting to me—that of folding to my bosom the dear partner of all my joys and sorrows and telling him that I am ever his." Even though Abigail professed to dread being "fastened up hand and foot and tongue to be shot at as our Quincy lads do at the poor geese and turkeys," she was determined to be resolute; she once again found a verse to express her feelings: "Still has my life new wonders seen/Repeated every year,/Behold my days which yet remain,/I trust them to thy care."[4]

John Quincy had written his mother that in the event of his father becoming President he not only would make no solicitation for an office but that he was affronted that she should for a moment think him "so totally regardless or forgetful of the principles which my education had instilled, nor so totally destitute of a *personal* sense of delicacy," as even to be susceptible to such a wish. Abigail was delighted with the letter and sent it on to John, who declared it "the most beautiful thing I ever read," and with a father's pride showed it to Washington. The President replied that while he admired the sentiments of the son he hoped that the father would not withhold a well-deserved promotion because of a nicety of feeling. "I give it as my decided opinion," Washington wrote, "that Mr. Adams is the most valuable public character we have abroad, and that there remains no doubt in my mind that he will prove himself to be the ablest of all our diplomatic corps."[5] The President's letter was all that was required to complete Adams' joy.

Soon after John Quincy's declaration of principle, Abigail received more momentous news. Her eldest son was in love with a young American expatriate, Louisa Catherine Johnson, and wished his parents' permission to marry her. Abigail, who had warned him of the danger of marrying a wife accustomed to European luxury and thus likely to be dissatisfied with the comparatively simple style of life in America, promptly recanted. Not only did she bless the proposed union but, with John's approval, wrote urging him to get married before he left for his new post as minister to Portugal. She knew how much he prized family life and it would keep him from feeling alien in an unfamiliar country. She was ready to take her son's fiancée to her heart. John Quincy must send along a miniature of her prospective daughter-in-law together with a lock of her hair; Abigail would send Louisa one of her and John.[6]

As the day of the inauguration approached Adams was immensely pleased at the evidences of respect and affection that were daily manifest. He was given a large front pew in the new Presbyterian church. Even the *Pennsylvania Chronicle* made gestures of conciliation; and Jarvis, the Boston Anti-Federalist, declared himself reconciled to Adams' election on the grounds that it was impossible for him to do worse than Washington. He was praised for his integrity and independence—praise especially sweet to his ears—and the report was circulated that he had been an enemy of the Jay treaty. Congress, partaking of the spirit of conciliation, voted him fourteen thousand dollars to purchase furniture for the presidential mansion. Jefferson came to visit him the day before the inauguration and gave warm expressions of support. For that great event he bought a new carriage, "simple but elegant enough," liveries for his coachman and footman, and a new suit of gray broadcloth for himself. Briesler helped him dress, resplendent from the handsome sword strapped to his side to the cockaded hat he carried under his arm.

Adams, with his sense of history, felt the significance of the moment. For the first time in the brief life of the new Republic the position of chief executive was changing hands—"the sight of the sun setting full-orbed, and another rising (though less splendid), was a novelty," he wrote Abigail. Once again he found himself more than close to tears. "One thing I know," he wrote Abigail, "that I am a being of too much sensibility to act any part well in such an exhibition." The chamber of the House of Representatives was packed. Adams had had a restless, tossing night. His hands trembled more than usual and he felt for a time that he should hardly get through the ordeal. But the presence of Washington steadied him. The General, with his magnificent presence towering above Adams, was steady and self-possessed; it almost seemed to John as though he were saying, "Ay! I am fairly out and you fairly in! See which of us will be happiest." Adams was not alone in being affected by the occasion. Many of the audience wept unabashedly. "Everybody," he remarked later, "talks of the tears, the full eyes, the streaming eyes, the trickling eyes."[7]

Chief Justice Oliver Ellsworth administered the oath of office in vibrant, ringing tones, and Adams stepped forward to deliver his Inaugural Address. He began with a review of the struggle for independence. When it was first perceived that "no middle course for America remained between unlimited submission to a foreign legislature and a total independence of its claims, men of reflection were less apprehensive of the danger from the formidable power of fleets and armies . . . than from those contests and dissensions which would certainly arise concerning the forms of government to be instituted over the whole and over the parts of this extensive country." But relying on the purity of their intentions, the justice of their cause, and the support of Providence, the people of the colonies went ahead, "broke to pieces the chains" which bound them, and "launched into an ocean of uncertainty."

The confederation had been established "for the temporary preservation of society," but it was evident from the first that it would not be durable and even before the war was over its melancholy consequences were apparent—"universal languor, jealousies and rivalries of states, decline of navigation and commerce, discouragement of necessary manufactures, universal fall in the value of lands and their produce, contempt of public and private faith, loss of consideration and credit with foreign nations, and at length in discontents, animosities, combinations, partial conventions, and insurrection, threatening some great national calamity."

To this crisis the American people had responded with "their usual good sense, presence of mind, resolution, [and] integrity." The federal convention had produced, after careful deliberation, "the present happy constitution of government." From the first Adams had felt it was "better adapted to the genius, character, situation, and relations of this nation and country than any which had ever been proposed or suggested. It was not then, nor has been since, any objection to it in my mind that the executive and Senate were not more permanent." Nor had he ever thought of any changes other than those which the people themselves should feel the need of and Congress in consequence "adopt and ordain."

The operation of the constitution had equaled the most optimistic hopes of its friends. "From an habitual attention to it, satisfaction in its administration, and delight in its effects upon the peace, order, prosperity, and happiness of the nation I have acquired an habitual attachment to it and veneration for it," he declared. "Robes and diamonds" and the slow accumulation of traditions and orders could not be more respectable than the authority that sprang "fresh from the hearts and judgments of an honest and enlightened people. . . . It is their power and majesty that is reflected, and only for their good, in every legitimate government."

But the underpinning of a republic was free and honest elections and Adams warned his audience that the government would be in peril from the moment when a single vote could be influenced "by foreign nations, by flattery or menaces, by fraud or violence, by terror, intrigue, or venality." Then it would be foreign nations "who govern us, and not we, the people, who govern ourselves." (This for Adet and those who had aided and abetted him.)

There was an eloquent tribute to General Washington, whose wise administration of the new government had "merited the gratitude of his fellow citizens, commanded the highest praises of foreign nations, and secured immortal glory with posterity"; and a solemn declaration that Adams would honor the law and letter of the constitution, the "rights, interest, honor, and happiness of all the states in the Union, without preference or regard to a Northern or Southern, an Eastern or Western, position." He wished to reconcile "various political opinions . . . and virtuous men of all parties and denominations"; to support "every rational effort to encourage schools, colleges, universities, academies, and every institution for propagating knowledge, virtue, and religion among all classes of the people, not only for their benign influence on the happiness of life in all its stages and classes and of society in all its forms, but as the only means of preserving our constitution from its natural enemies—the spirit of sophistry, the spirit of party, the spirit of intrigue, the profligacy of corruption, and the pestilence of foreign influence which is the angel of destruction to elective governments." He pledged himself to a policy of "equity and humanity toward the aboriginal nations of America and a disposition to ameliorate their condition," and above all to carry into effect a "system of neutrality and impartiality among the belligerent powers of Europe." He had "personal esteem for the French nation . . . a sincere desire to preserve the friendship which has been so much for the honor and interest of both nations," and an "unshaken confidence in the honor, spirit, and resources of the American people, on which I have so often hazarded my all and never been deceived." With the blessing of God upon the nation and its government he would strive to do his best to support the constitution of the United States and promote the peace and prosperity of his country.

When the address was over there was a storm of applause and Adams made his way out of the chamber and back to his quarters. There Washington visited him, congratulated him on his accession, and wished him a "happy, successful, and honorable" administration. After the General left, Adams occupied himself with anxious speculations about the reception of his speech. Had he been too bold in castigating foreign influence?

Would he be charged with throwing down the gauntlet to the Francophiles? Should he have been so critical of the confederation? Would the
Anti-Federalists declare war on him for his endorsement of Washington's
policies and his uncompromising support of the constitution? Would he
be accused of vanity and egotism for emphasizing his own role in con-
stitution-making? He was charmed and reassured by the report that
Senator Mason of Virginia had said America "should lose nothing by the
change, for he never heard such a speech in public in his life." "All
agree," he wrote Abigail of the inauguration, "that, taken together, it was
the sublimest thing ever exhibited in America."[8]

When word reached him that the Federalist ultras had complained
about the speech as being too "temporizing" and conciliatory toward the
Republicans, Adams was indignant. It was just this spirit of intractability
which would, if not checked, destroy the country. If the Federalists "go
to playing pranks," he wrote Abigail, "I will resign the office and let
Jefferson lead them to peace, wealth, and power if he will." He saw
before him "a scene of ambition," as he expressed it, "beyond all my
former suspicions or imaginations. An emulation which will turn our
government topsy-turvy. . . . At the next election," he added, "England
will set up Jay or Hamilton, and France, Jefferson, and all the corruption
of Poland will be introduced, unless the American spirit will rise and say,
'We will have neither John Bull nor Louis Baboon—Silence.'"[9]

Bache was delighted with the address and hailed it in the *Aurora*
as a model of wisdom and moderation. Its author was "a man of incorruptible integrity," a "friend of France, of peace, an admirer of republicanism, the enemy of party. . . . How characteristic of a patriot!" he
concluded in a kind of ecstasy. Noah Webster, a Federalist editor, saw in
the speech evidence that Adams had been seduced by the Francophiles.
Perhaps most satisfying of all was a brief note from Sam Adams: "I congratulate you as the first citizen of the United States—I may add of the
world. I am, my dear sir, notwithstanding I have been otherwise represented in party papers, your old and unvaried friend, S. Adams."[10]

Bache, having hailed Adams, could not resist a parting shot at Washington:"'Lord, now lettest thou thy servant depart in peace,'" he wrote,
"'for mine eyes have seen thy salvation. . . .' If ever there was a time
that would license the reiteration of the exclamation, that time is now
arrived, for the man [Washington] who is the source of all the misfortunes of our country is this day reduced to a level with his fellow citizens
and is no longer possessed of power to multiply evils upon the United
States. If ever there was a period for rejoicing this is the moment—every
heart, in unison with the freedom and happiness of the people, ought
to beat high with exultation, that the name of Washington from this day
ceases to give a currency to political iniquity and to legalize corruption."
Washington had "cankered the principles of republicanism . . . and

carried his designs against the public liberty so far as to have put in jeopardy its very existence."[11]

Adams was not deceived by the praises that the Republican press showered upon him, by their effusions over his statesmanship, his independence, his eloquence, his democratic simplicity (he had only two horses to his coach, to Washington's six). The fact was that the country was bitterly and deeply divided, and divided, moreover, not on domestic policy but on the question of whether the British or the French were the better friends to America and humanity. Determined as he was to be fair and impartial, to maintain the strictest neutrality, Adams was conscious that he must soon incur the wrath of the extremists in both parties. As one historian has put it succinctly: "The Republicans were for yielding to the demands of the Directory, abrogating the [Jay] treaty, defying England, and forming a close alliance with the Republic of France. The Federalists were for the treaty, a strict neutrality, or, if needs be, a war with France."[12] It was manifestly impossible to satisfy both.

The President's own sympathies were clearly with the British. Much as he resented their insolent and highhanded ways, they were, in his view, far less of a threat to the United States than the ferocious and implacable revolutionaries of France. From that unhappy country came an apparently endless recital of cruelty and violence. The guillotine fell with the regularity of a metronome, decapitating the "enemies of the Revolution," many of them the makers of the Revolution; young women whose crime lay in their birth were roasted alive in the Place Dauphine; priests were hacked to pieces on their altars; boats crowded with aristocrats were sunk with all aboard and toasted as "the national bath." Young men and women were lashed together in "Republican marriage," drowned or smashed by cannon fire, and hurled into open pits. One government followed another; an old terror gave way to a new one, and each new turn of the Revolutionary wheel served only to double the enthusiasm of the American Francophiles. All was justified in the name of "Liberty, Equality, and Fraternity," in the name of the new social order that was to liberate men from the tyranny of kings and nobles. To Adams such behavior was simply confirmation of the fact that man was governed more by his passions than his reason, more by emotion than by rationality. It was especially distressing to him to see such rant and folly possess his beloved Americans. Rancor, violence, bitterness, and vituperation seemed the order of the day. This was his inheritance.

With such a prospect before him, Adams' volatile emotions swung him from the heights of exultation to the deeps of gloom and pessimism. It was not so much the Republicans who depressed and angered him. He had taken their measure and was prepared to fight or beguile them as the occasion required. His primary concern was about his own party, the Federalists. He was aware, in a general way, that most of the members of the Cabinet he had inherited from Washington were strong Hamilton men; but still he assured Elbridge Gerry that "Pickering and all his colleagues are as much attached to me as I desire. I have no jealousies from that quarter."[13] It would doubtless have been better for Adams had he been less trusting, for from the beginning of his administration several of the Cabinet members, Pickering among them, looked to Hamilton as the leader of the party and their guide and adviser.

The President found, as Washington had before him, that he had to struggle with a flood of applications for government jobs. It was an apparently endless, maddening, pitiful tide of requests and supplications—old soldiers, faithful servants of the Revolution, destitute patriots, friends, relatives, friends of friends, anyone who could assert a claim begged, pled for, or in some instances demanded, government positions so that they could keep their families from destitution, educate a deserving son, or make some provision for their declining years. Adams waded conscientiously through the applications—supplications would probably have been a better term—reading and answering them, forwarding the names of those best qualified to the appropriate heads of departments, unhappily aware that he was making ten enemies for every friend.

There was no doubt, however, that Adams had come into a goodly heritage. Washington had made the presidency a strong office and Adams intended to keep it so. He expressed his views forthrightly in a letter to Elbridge Gerry. Gerry had accused Washington of usurping legislative power and of appointing officials in his administration who were too servile. The power of appointment and removal by the President, Adams pointed out in his answer, was "a sacred part of the constitution without which the government could not exist. If executive offices," he continued, "hold their offices independent of the head and can intrigue with members of the Senate and House to assist them in opposing the execution of the laws, the executive authority would be a nose of wax." In actual fact Washington had "appointed many rancorous Anti-Federalists who employed the influence of their offices, and in some instances public money, to promote the opposition to his government."

The government must be able to act with dispatch—"the unity, consistency, promptitude, secrecy, and activity of the whole executive authority are so essential in any republican system," he added, "that without them there can be no peace, order, liberty, or prosperity in society. . . . Instead of the executive encroaching on the legislative," it was Adams' opinion that "the House of Representatives have discovered an incessant hankering after the executive power." The leaders of Congress had "fallen into all the ambition, jealousies, and rivalries which constantly spring up, obstruct the government, and produce anarchy, whenever popular assemblies meddle with executive power."[14] The President made it plain that he would rebuff all such "meddling."

Suddenly engulfed in his new duties, Adams found himself missing Abigail acutely. Not simply her presence, though that was lack enough, but her wise counsel on affairs of state. "I never wanted your advice and assistance more in my life," he wrote. She must come on and join him at whatever cost and inconvenience. She could make the trip in her own coach with Louisa Smith, Mrs. Briesler and her children, and James, who could ride Adams' little mare. He was ragged by a "violent cold and cough" which left him weak and fatigued. He needed her and would have her.

One of Abigail's small vanities had been to have the Quincy coat of arms painted on her carriage door. In the midst of his multitudinous concerns, he thought of this trifling symbol of aristocratic pretension and winced. She must have the arms "totally obliterated. It would be folly," he added, "to excite popular feelings and vulgar insolence for nothing." He could imagine what Bache or Callender would make of it.[15]

It did not help Adams' frame of mind to move into the presidential mansion recently vacated by Washington. The house was a shambles and he longed to hear Abigail's brisk step and her voice directing the servants to bring order out of chaos. The few sticks of "public" furniture, bought by congressional funds and left behind by Washington, were in deplorable condition. "There is not a chair fit to sit in," he lamented, adding, "The beds and bedding are in a woeful pickle." In the interregnum between the Washingtons' departure and the arrival of Adams and his household, the servants had made the house the scene "of the most scandalous drunkenness and disorder . . . that was ever heard of."[16]

The appearance in the midst of the general confusion of a mammoth cheese weighing a hundred and ten pounds, "as big as a chariot wheel," a gift of the state of Rhode Island, seemed the last straw. But perhaps when their money ran out they could live off it. Adams was appalled at the cost of things and, forgetting Abigail's admonition to keep up his spirits, he wrote, "I expect to be obliged to resign in six months because I can't live. I had rather live on potatoes and beef and pork, fresh or salt, of my own growth."[17]

The first real crisis of his administration confronted Adams even before he was well settled in his new office, and of course it concerned France. Word reached Philadelphia in March that the Directory had refused to receive Charles Cotesworth Pinckney, who, when Madison declined the position, was sent to replace Monroe. Not only had Pinckney not been received, he had been jockeyed and insulted and ordered to quit French soil. In addition French frigates had seized American ships in the West Indies.

As soon as Adams heard of Pinckney's rebuff he directed a note to the members of the Cabinet asking for their views on the proper action to be taken by the United States Government. What preparations, he inquired, should be made for war? Should American privateers be released to prey on French shipping? Should the coastal forts be equipped and placed in readiness for attack? Should new frigates be commissioned? Finally, should new negotiations be undertaken and with what instructions?[18] The inquiries contained fourteen questions, the most important of which was the first: should a fresh mission to Paris be undertaken or would such a mission be "too great a humiliation of the American people in their own sense and that of the world?"

Several of the members of the Cabinet, Wolcott among them, referred first to Hamilton for instructions, and the New Yorker told them firmly that they must support further negotiation in order to disarm the suspicion that "the *actual* administration is not much averse from war with France. . . . . How very important to obviate this!" he added. So instructed, the Secretaries made able replies supporting further negotiation and advising on the points to be conceded and those to be insisted on. The general feeling was that an effort should be made to reach an agreement with France comparable to the Jay treaty.

A few days after he had solicited the opinions of his department heads Adams decided to call a special session of the Congress to approve the negotiation with France. On the twenty-fifth of March he issued a presidential proclamation setting May 15 as the date for Congress to convene. He then proceeded to canvass the Secretaries as to the content of his address to both houses. To McHenry he directed a special request for an estimate of the defensive forces needed to protect the United States against invasion and the cost of recruiting and equipping such a force. From Pickering he requested recommendations of "such things as ought to be communicated to Congress concerning the state of the Union." He wished the Secretary not to confine "himself to matters merely within the Department of State but [to] give himself a liberal latitude, both in relation to the other departments and to the illustrations and reasonings in support of his opinions."[19]

Having done this much, he gave his principal attention to the extremely delicate business of selecting a commissioner or commissioners to undertake the mission. General Knox and Elbridge Gerry, among a number of others, wrote suggesting Jefferson as the ideal person to undertake a special mission of conciliation. Adams answered that he had approached the Vice-President but that he had refused, and in Adams' opinion with good reason. It would not have been dignified, he felt on further reflection, to dispatch the Vice-President of the United States on such a precarious diplomatic venture. "The nation must hold itself very cheap," he wrote to Gerry, "that can choose a man one day to hold its second office, and the next send him to Europe to dance attendance at levees and drawing rooms among the common major-generals, simple bishops, earls and barons, but especially among the common trash of ambassadors, envoys, and ministers plenipotentiary."20

When Jefferson declined the mission Adams had asked him to sound out Madison, and the Vice-President consented, reluctantly, to query his fellow Virginian. Several days later at Washington's, Jefferson told Adams that Madison had declined. The President was both embarrassed and relieved. In the interim he had canvassed the Cabinet and gotten from Wolcott the threat of a mass resignation if he pushed Madison for the post. He had been in office scarcely a month and already he felt himself ground between the nether stones of Federalism and Republicanism. It was plain that Jefferson had no intention of reinforcing or co-operating with Adams' administration; he was resolved to preserve his position as party leader intact. It was equally evident that the Federalists were determined to cause Adams almost as much trouble as the Republicans. He must have Abigail. "Leave the place to Jonathan and Polly," he wrote, ". . . to my brother—to anybody or nobody. I care nothing about it. But you I must and will have." He feared for his health. Such constant attention "to business of a very dry, dull, and perplexing nature" was enough to cost a man his life. Even his daily rides were sacrificed to the business of his office. "Don't expose this croaking and groaning however," he warned Abigail. "I should lose all my character for firmness if anyone should read this. Indeed I sometimes suspect," he added, "that I deserve a character for peevishness and fretfulness rather than firmness."21

Abigail had her own anxieties and concerns. The news of the special session cost her many hours of sleep and uneasy speculations about "how the Senate, how the House will conduct. How the people will act. How foreign nations will be affected." Her imagination wandered in "this dark abyss," she complained, "without anyone to converse with who can enlighten me." But she consoled herself with the thought that "the people will judge right if they are left to act for themselves." Her best friend was constantly on her mind. She was distressed to hear of his perplexities and, above all, of his cold. Men could never be depended on to look after themselves. They were like great babies, going out without overshoes, getting their feet wet, sitting in drafts, neglecting to change damp clothes. She could see him in her mind's eye, hacking and coughing, he and Briesler rattling around in the dreary, half-furnished house, and it wrung her heart. "I advised you to take for your cough rhubarb and calomel. Do not omit it . . . take it immediately," she wrote sternly. Billings had been sober long enough to finish the brick wall and it was a beauty—the work of a loving and expert craftsman; she had purchased new plows and tools for the farms, and she would come as soon as she could find satisfactory tenants.²² Meanwhile, she had a delicious local tidbit to relay to John. She had sent the little Negro boy, James, who worked as a household servant, to the Quincy school where simple reading and writing and ciphering were taught to the less able boys in the community. Soon after James had been entered in the school, "Neighbor Faxon" requested a word with Abigail. If James persisted in going to the school, he declared, the school would break up because the other lads would not attend with a Negro.

"Pray, Mr. Faxon," Abigail had asked with disarming blandness, "has the boy misbehaved?"

"Oh no!" it wasn't that, replied the discomfited Faxon. "It was just . . ."

"Well, they don't object to going to church or to dances with James or to playing with him. Why should there be objections to going to school with him?"

Faxon assured her that he, personally, had no objections. It was others who had objected.

"What others?" Abigail asked a little tartly. "If it is the 'others' who object, why didn't they come, then?"

At this Faxon could only look confused and unhappy, and Abigail pressed her advantage. "This, Mr. Faxon," she declared, "is attacking the principle of liberty and equality upon the only grounds upon which it ought to be supported, an equality of rights." James was a freeman as much as any of the young men, and a black face should not bar him from instruction. How else indeed was he to be prepared to make a living?

"Oh, ma'am, you are quite right," Faxon blurted out, anxious only to be out of the house and gone. "I hope you won't take any offense."

"None at all, Mr. Faxon. Only be so good as to send the young men to me. . . . I have not thought it any disgrace to myself to take him into my parlor and teach him both to read and write. Tell them, Mr. Faxon . . . I hope we shall all go to heaven together."

At this final sally, Faxon laughed and made good his escape, and Abigail heard no more of the matter. She wrote proudly of her small triumph. While her husband was contending, or preparing to contend, against the powers and principalities of the great world she had struck a blow for true equality and freedom in her own bailiwick.²³

LXXI

LEST anyone should mistake the intention of the Directory to browbeat and humiliate Adams' administration, that body issued orders
that any American sailors taken from English warships would be
hanged as pirates. That was certainly militant enough. McHenry meanwhile estimated that the minimum force to protect American cities and
commerce must include one corps of artillerists and engineers, one regiment of infantry, two companies of dragoons, three frigates of thirty-two
guns, and six sloops of war of sixteen guns. Even this limited establishment would cost over a million and a half dollars to recruit, equip, and
supply. The frigates and sloops alone would absorb almost a million
dollars.[1]

How would Congress react to requests for such an exorbitant sum?
"The times are critical and dangerous, and I must have you here to assist me," Adams wrote his wife. "I want physic and I want exercise! but
I want your assistance more than either. You must come and leave the
place to the mercy of the winds. . . . I can do nothing without you." She
must assist "with your counsels and console me with your conversation."[2]

McHenry, having given Adams his estimates on the military and naval
establishment, sent him a copy of the "regulations and instructions" of the
army and a detailed account of the existing state of negotiations with
the Southern Indians, the Chickasaws, Creeks, Cherokees, Shawnees,
Choctaws, the state of the coastal fortifications and of the frigates that
were being built at Philadelphia and Boston.[3]

Oliver Wolcott produced a long and ably argued paper on the requirements for the French negotiation. He ended with the conclusion that it
would be expedient to send two more ministers to join Pinckney in Paris,
and suggested John Quincy and Rufus King for the posts. Some intelligent observers felt strongly that at least one of the three commissioners
should be a known friend to the French cause. Adams was pleased with
the Secretary of the Treasury's paper. It suggested he would be well
served.[4] Taken as a whole, the papers of the Cabinet members

were ably and even eloquently argued, and they were all to one effect—
negotiation on the one hand and preparations for war on the other.
McHenry spoke for all the Secretaries when he urged the President to be
mild and conciliatory, "to obviate causes of discontent and restore and
confirm cordial harmony; to discuss and settle amicably the topics of
mutual complaints, and thereby to obtain a revocation of those acts on
the part of France and of her agents in the colonies which have oppressed
our trade and injured our citizens."[5]

While the *Chronicle, Argus,* and *Aurora* continued to laud Adams, he
prepared an address for the special session of Congress which would,
as he put it, acquit him of the crime of receiving the praise of those journals. His principal problem was to settle on the negotiators. Elbridge
Gerry refused to accept Adams' statement that Jefferson was unavailable
and, in any event, an improper person to send on such a mission. He wrote
a rambling, incoherent letter denouncing Washington for encroaching on
the authority of the legislative branch and urging Adams to send Monroe
back to France as minister to that country. But he tempered his judgment
with the admission that if Monroe had indeed befriended Paine after the
latter's bitter attack on the United States he must forfeit the support of
all honest men. Morever he assured Adams that in New England the
President stood "as firm, I believe, as Mount Etna," while reports from
Southern Republicans indicated that he was popular there too. Gerry's
proposal should have told Adams all he needed to know about his friend's
political acumen, but he continued to think so well of his heart that he
overlooked the head.[6]

At the end of April, Abigail set out from Quincy with a little retinue to
join her husband, the President of the United States, in Philadelphia.
Just before she left, John's mother, Susannah Boylston, died peacefully
after several years of bad health. John was saddened by the news. He
had given up hope for his mother's life three years before during a serious
illness. She was "a fruit fully ripe" gone to "a country where there will
be no war or rumor of war, no envy, jealousy, rivalry, or party," and
where, he trusted, he and Abigail would soon join her. "My mother's
countenance and conversation," he wrote Abigail, "was a source of en-
joyment to me that is now dried up forever at Quincy."[7]

Abigail stopped off at Eastchester to spend a day or two with Nabby.
She found her daughter sad and distracted. The Colonel was off on some
new land speculation. There were evidences everywhere of the depressed
state of the family finances. Nabby could not even bring herself to discuss the unhappy situation with her mother. "Such is the folly and madness of speculation and extravagance," Abigail wrote her sister. No blame
was due Nabby. "Educated in different habits, she never enjoyed a life
of dissipation," Abigail added. The boys were fine lads and she wished

they might be under Eliza's tutelage at Hingham rather than under the demoralizing influence of their father.

Charles, on the other hand, was living "prettily but frugally," with a "lovely babe" and "a discreet woman . . . for his wife," quite different from most of her luxury-loving and improvident relatives.[8] At Charles's house in the city Abigail, ensconced like a touring queen, received a constant stream of visitors come to pay their respects to the new first lady.

On Monday, May 8, the party left New York and some twenty miles from the city Abigail was met by John, who handed her into his Presidential carriage, and they rode off, abandoning the others to make their way on to Philadelphia. At Bristol in Bucks County, just over the Pennsylvania line, he had engaged a lavish dinner. Next day they loitered along the banks of the Delaware, talking at one moment like lovers, the next like ministers of state. The spring was soft about them, tender and green, warm, indolent, and inviting, the early flowers precious and exquisite as jewels after the long months of ice and snow; the wide river bearing the detritus of winter on its slow current. The love that flowed between them was such as no young lovers in the heat and impatience of their passion could know; it was a love enriched by time, by a great, crowding host of memories, by the small daily sacrifices of self that made a larger self and a deeper love. When at evening they turned toward the city John felt a renewal of courage and hope. Without Abigail he was only half a man; with her he could face whatever testing was in store for him and the nation.

They arrived in Philadelphia Thursday evening, May 9, to find that under Briesler's direction the house had been put in good order. A few days later Abigail held her first formal reception as the wife of the President—"thirty-two ladies and near as many gentlemen." With Abigail in command of the household, Adams turned back to his speech for the opening of the special session. In preparing the draft he drew primarily from McHenry and Pickering. Many of the phrases and sentences of the Secretary of State were taken over virtually intact and woven into the fabric of the address. After a reference to the peace and harmony of the United States he plunged directly into French refusal to accept a minister who had been directed "faithfully to represent the disposition of the government and people of the United States . . . to remove jealousies and obvious complaints . . . to restore that mutual confidence which had been so unfortunately and injuriously impaired, and to explain the relative interests of both countries and the real sentiments of his own." The Directory had met this conciliatory measure by the flat statement that they would not receive the new minister until the American government had redressed a list of French grievances. Not only had the Directory refused to receive Pinckney; he had been threatened with arrest and harried by agents of the government. All this in defiance of settled and long-standing laws of nations. Peremptory demands and insolent accusations had been substituted for the normal means of diplomatic intercourse. Such behavior, Adams declared, "ought to be repelled with a decision which shall convince France and the world that we are not a degraded people, humiliated under a colonial spirit of fear and a sense of inferiority, fitted to be the miserable instruments of foreign influence, and regardless of national honor, character, and interest."

Having stated the case thus strongly, indeed militantly, Adams repeated his desire to preserve "peace and friendship with all nations." It was this desire which had determined him to try once more to promote and accelerate an accommodation on terms compatible with the rights, duties, interests, and honor of the nation." Accompanying the attempt to secure peace by negotiation must go a determined effort to strengthen the power, especially the naval power, of the country, because it was only by means of a navy that a commercial nation could protect the enterprise of its citizens. The President thus recommended to Congress that it provide for the arming of merchant vessels for their own protection and the enlargement of the naval establishment. At the same time that body would do well to consider "a revision of the laws for organizing, arming, and disciplining the militia, to render the natural and safe defense of the country efficacious." He challenged the Senate, by its support of the administration's policy, to give the lie to the charge that the nation was dangerously divided in its hour of trial. It remained to them to demonstrate that Americans had no intention of "surrendering themselves to the direction of foreign and domestic factions." To the House of Representatives he passed the sobering task of finding new sources of revenue to raise and maintain an augmented army and navy.

Adams delivered the address to both houses in the chamber of the Representatives on the fifteenth of May at twelve o'clock. His manner of speaking, as befitted the occasion, was as calm and deliberate as the words themselves were hot with indignation. The speech fell on the unprepared Republicans like a bombshell. They were the more furious for the eager self-deception by which they had convinced themselves that John Adams was simply Thomas Jefferson in disguise. Jefferson himself was one of the first to dispel the illusion. He had been convinced, when Congress first began to assemble, that the wish of members from all parts of the Union was for "universal peace." But after the President's warlike exhortation, he was fearful that the House and Senate might "raise their tone to that of the executive, and embark in all measures indicative of war and, by taking a threatening posture, provoke hostilities from the opposite party." The Vice-President felt that any preparation for war should be avoided on the grounds that it might further irritate the French.[9] As Abigail put it, "The Antis. want to qualify. They dare not openly countenance the conduct of France, but they want to court and coax her."[10]

Giles likewise recanted his earlier opinion that Adams would make a good chief executive. It was clear that the President was determined to involve the United States in war with France. Benjamin Franklin Bache, rather than admit that he had misjudged his man, declared that Adams had been "fed upon pepperpot these three weeks past in order to bring his nerves to a proper anti-Gallican tone." The Secretaries of the Treasury and State had plainly led the President by the nose and aroused his "cold Northern constitution" to a warlike heat. Adams, Bache charged, was a master of dissimulation who had led the people to believe that he was "under no *extraneous influence*," whereas it was evident that he was simply the creature of the Hamiltonians.[11]

George Cabot, who had shared the fears of many high Federalists that Adams would become a tool of Jefferson and the Francophiles, was delighted with the President's resolute spirit. He expected the speech to "excite the most national feeling of anything that has been published since the French disease infected the country." He added further: "After reading and considering it all Sunday afternoon at my home, a large company of good men all agreed that it was in every particular exactly what they would have wished, and was expressed in a masterly and dignified style."[12] But the Republican press was in full cry. The President was in his dotage, a tool of the British, the unrelenting enemy of the French, of freedom, and of democratic government.[13]

Adams had declared that he was confident that the people of the United States would support their government. Who, Bache asked, was the government? The government was John Adams and Adams was thus in effect saying, "It is not for ME to hesitate . . . I, who have devoted the best part of MY life to gain and uphold its independence. It is not for ME to hesitate. Were the man in his second childhood, this egotism would be excusable. . . . But for the President by three votes to talk in this wise is ridiculous. Were not the crisis of our country so awful it would force a laugh from the most stoical. Because by tricks, by frauds, by finesse he secured the greater number of electoral votes, he plumes himself on being the government! Poor old man, how miserably he deceives himself."[14]

Even the launching of the frigate *United States*, which constituted the greater part of the American navy, occasioned the *Aurora's* scorn. Certainly it would be no threat to the French. Talleyrand had been quoted as saying that France need fear nothing from a nation of debaters who had been trying for three years to build three frigates.

The Senate in reply to Adams' speech expressed its "entire approbation of your conduct in convening it on this momentous occasion," and com mended the President for his "vigilance, firmness, and promptitude." It agreed that "effectual measures of defense" were the best means "to check aggression and prevent war. . . . We learn with sincere concern," the address continued, "that attempts are in operation to alienate the affections of our fellow citizens from their government. Attempts so wicked, wherever they exist, cannot fail to excite our utmost abhorrence." The conduct of the government had been "just and impartial to foreign nations," and the Senators declared themselves "happy in possessing an entire confidence in your abilities and exertions in your station to maintain untarnished the honor, preserve the peace, and support the independence of our country." If all efforts at peaceful negotiations failed, Adams could be assured of the Senate's support in whatever measures were needed to uphold "the dignity, interest, and independence" of the country. It cost Jefferson something, as President of the Senate, to place his neat signature below the reply.

The reply of the House was equally firm ("very handsome," Abigail called it), assuring Adams of "our zealous co-operation in those measures which may appear necessary for our security or peace," and approving "the wisdom, dignity, and moderation which have marked the measures of the supreme executive." But the draft of the reply which a committee submitted to the House had occasioned much more debate than that of the Senate and been approved by a narrower margin (sixty to forty). When the House had accepted the committee's draft, Matthew Lyon, a representative from Vermont, rose to protest against going to deliver the reply to the President. The words "attended by the House" should be struck out and replaced by "attended by such members as may think proper." As a legislator in a free and democratic nation, he wished to have no part in such subservience and mummery. He represented the dignity of eighty thousand citizens of the state of Vermont and he must resist. Let the fancy "gentlemen of blood" and good breeding go. For himself, he did not spring from "the bastards of Oliver Cromwell" or from the witch-hanging Puritans of New England who persecuted the Quakers and despised all joy. The House was in no mood at the moment to support such a contentious and intractable spirit. They voted Lyon down without a dissent and departed to deliver their answer to Adams' speech.

On the whole Adams had every reason to be pleased with his first major presidential effort. At the same time he was of course well aware that his support was highly volatile, and he was disturbed, though not surprised, at the fresh evidences of party spirit that his address had provoked. Particularly galling were the anti-government efforts of a Massachusetts representative, Nathaniel Freeman, Jr., who "appeared a full-blood Jacobin."[15]

On the twenty-sixth of May, Adams placed before the Senate for ratification a treaty with the Barbary pirates. On the last day of the month he submitted the nomination of Charles Cotesworth Pinckney, Francis Dana, and John Marshall as "envoys extraordinary and ministers plenipotentiary to the French Republic . . . to dissipate umbrages, to remove prejudices, to rectify errors and adjust all differences by a treaty between the two powers."

The Senate approved the nominations after some debate and when Dana begged off on the grounds of health Adams turned to Gerry to replace him. He had originally proposed Gerry, but the Cabinet had balked and the President had given way. Throughout the spring Adams had carried on a correspondence with his friend on the subject of Monroe's recall and the charges of English influence in the government. Although Gerry's sympathies were firmly with the French, the mercurial New Englander treasured his friendships with Adams and Jefferson and sought to reconcile the two men. He professed to abhor party and believed that differences could be composed by reasonable argument and debate. Adams in turn held fast to Gerry, partly out of gratitude for his loyalty and in part because he was the only Republican with whom he could still discuss the issues that separated the two factions. Moreover, like Adams, Gerry struggled manfully with his prejudices and Adams honored him for the effort.

Adams had been impatient with Gerry's solicitude for Monroe, whom the President characterized as "dull, heavy, and stupid." The Virginian had forfeited all respect by his behavior in France, by his private correspondence with the enemies of the administration which had appointed him—Bache and Beckley among them—and by his departing address to the Directory, "a base, false, and servile thing." To Gerry's complaint that an anti-Gallican faction existed in America, Adams replied quite as emphatically. It was true that there was a group who opposed the undue influence of France in the United States. Some of these were anti-French because they considered the French "a false, deceitful, treacherous people," others because they hated "atheism, deism, and debauchery," still others because the country teemed with "democrats, sans-culottes, and disorganizers." As to Gerry's suggestion that some Americans hated the French because they were good republicans, Adams waved that aside. The French were not republicans at all. They were no more capable of a republican government "than a snowball can exist a whole week in the streets of Philadelphia under a burning sun."

There were many who believed that the French system, called by whatever name, could not endure and Adams counted himself one of these. There were many others who held, he wrote, that a republican form of government could not last long in the United States. "I am not one of those," he declared. "Though our cities are corrupt our country is not, and I believe our republican plan may last a good while." But it would not, he added, "if French influence as well as English is not resisted." Adams himself knew of only a handful of people—old Parson Wibird, Chief Justice Chew, and Dr. Nisbet of Dickinson College—who professed to believe that "an hereditary King and House of Lords with a good House of Commons the best form of government," and these were old Tories, harmless relics, certainly no danger to the state. If there were dangers they came not from such a quarter but from "the universal avarice and ambition of the people" who seemed to think of nothing but wild speculation and of making money by whatever means; and who, if they were not restrained, would even make of elections "a species of lucrative speculation, and consequently scenes of turbulence, corruption, and confusion of which foreign nations will avail themselves in the future."[16] Having said so much, Adams perhaps assumed that he had completed the conversion of his friend. In any event, over the stout objections of most of the members of his Cabinet and such Federalists as he admitted to his confidence, he sent Gerry's name to the Senate as a replacement for Dana.

Elbridge Gerry accepted the position of minister plenipotentiary with alacrity and in light of the future history of the commission his comments are of interest. "Considering the prevailing prejudice in France of our being a divided people, and the sanction it has received by some of the debates of the last session of Congress," he wrote, "is it not indispensably necessary for the envoys, should they differ on important points . . . to be finally unanimous on those points by the minority yielding to the majority? Without such an agreement may they not encourage an opposition to their measures?"[17]

Adams confirmed Gerry in his opinion that a united front was essential. "There is the utmost necessity," he wrote, "of harmony, complaisance, and condescension among the three envoys, and unanimity is of great importance." He tried to quiet Gerry's concern about the United States appearing to be a divided country. In all countries the people were divided. "There will ever be parties and division in all nations," he wrote; "but our people will support their government. . . . Not to expect divisions in a free country would be an absurdity." Then, still a little uneasy, the President sent off a final letter of admonition. No one could undermine his confidence in Gerry, he wrote. Some, to be sure, had "expressed doubts of your orthodoxy in the science of government," and others "fears of an unaccommodating disposition" and a tendency to "risk great things to secure small ones," but such anxieties had made no impression on Adams. Marshall was "a plain man, very sensible, cautious, guarded, and learned in the law of nations." Pinckney he knew well enough.[18]

The President was satisfied that in sending the mission he was taking the proper step. "If there is reason or justice or decorum in France," he wrote John Quincy, "the measure we have taken is respectful enough to it to draw it all out. But if we are again insulted we must defend ourselves.

. . . I am weary of conjectures. My mind is made up. I believe in a Providence over all—am determined to submit to it alone, in the faithful, steady discharge of my duty. 'All the distant din, the world can keep, rolls o'er my grotto and but soothes my sleep.'"[19]

Adams' other diplomatic arrangements were to alter John Quincy's mission from Portugal to Prussia—"the north of Europe at present is more interesting to us than the south," he explained—and appoint John Quincy's friend, the brilliant young William Vans Murray, to his son's vacant post at The Hague. Denmark, Sweden, and Prussia, because of their position as neutrals, were "naturally more allied by sympathy with us," Adams wrote John Quincy, " . . . and I thought your talents, sagacity, and industry might be more profitably exerted in collecting and transmitting intelligence . . . of those courts and nations than they could be in Lisbon." He should try to discover "the future system of Europe, and how we can best preserve friendship with them all, and be most useful to them all. . . . I wish you," Adams concluded, "to continue your practice of writing freely to me and cautiously to the office of state."[20]

To John Quincy's protests at his father appointing him minister to Prussia, Adams replied peremptorily: "Your reasons will not bear examination. . . . It is the worst founded opinion I ever knew you to conceive. . . . It is a false principle. It is an unjust principle—the sons of the President have the same claim to liberty, equality, and the benefit of the laws with all other citizens. . . . Mr. Washington made it a rule not to appoint his relations. But if Washington had been blessed with sons and those sons had been qualified, I presume to say he never would have observed the rule."[21]

Adams could deny himself much, but to call his adored son home from a career in which he had already distinguished himself was too much. Beside a father's pride there was the practical fact that John Quincy's letters were unequaled sources of information. No minister, ambassador, or special envoy could have given him a recital of European affairs which he would have read with as much confidence and enlightenment.

France was very far from being the only problem with which Adams had to deal. Great Britain continued to provide the Republicans with ammunition by her arrogant and highhanded actions on the seas. She stopped American vessels, seized them where she dared, often on the flimsiest of pretexts, and impressed American sailors by the hundreds. Impressment was an especially sore point and hardly a week passed without word reaching the United States that more seamen who claimed American citizenship had been snatched from the decks of an American vessel.

In addition Spain was busy fomenting trouble on the Southern frontier, plotting to detach portions of United States territory and refusing to evacuate the forts that she had agreed to surrender by the terms of the Pinckney treaty. (As Abigail put it, "The Dons are cutting out work for us, stimulated no doubt by our dear friends the French."[22]) So the lamp burned late in the presidential mansion and Adams was frequently closeted with his Secretaries. A stream of correspondence passed over his desk and he read until his eyes gave out and he could read no more.

When pressed to fulfill the terms of the treaty, the Spanish minister made trifling or impossible conditions. The question of whether the Spanish forts should be demolished or left standing was simple enough, if unimportant; even the question of the property rights of individuals who had lived within the Spanish jurisdiction was susceptible to easy solution, but the stipulation that the forts would not be evacuated until the officers in charge were convinced that the Indians in the vicinity would be pacific was no more than a delaying tactic. The truth was that Spain had made a bad bargain and was trying desperately to retrieve something from it in defiance of the spirit as well as the letter of the treaty.

Pickering was of the opinion that the Spanish procrastinated on the evacuation of the forts in the hope that France and the United States would soon be at war, in which case the Spanish might find an opportunity to abrogate the unfortunate Pinckney treaty, which Godoy had never ceased to regret. On the twelfth of June, Adams requested Congress to pass a law at once making the inhabitants of the region secure in their property and erecting a government in the district of Natchez similar to that which had been established for the Northwest Territory.

WHILE Adams wrestled with matters of state Abigail acted as minister without portfolio. The President discussed almost every important problem with her and, although her advice was usually in support of his own opinions, it helped him to come to a decision on tender matters and to act with resolution once he had decided upon a course of action. She proposed an apt quotation to hearten him when he needed it, to arm him against the barbs of a Bache or Callender. "There is no terror, Jack cuss, in your threats," she quoted from *Julius Caesar,* "For I am arm'd so strong in honesty/That they pass by me as the idle wind,/Which I respect not."[1]

In addition to her advice and moral support Abigail wrote many semi-official letters, especially to friends, underlining or reinforcing some point made by the President; those who knew the influence she exerted upon her husband took pains to try to enlist her support. Elbridge Gerry wrote her a long letter explaining and justifying his opposition to the constitution, confident that she would be his advocate with Adams.

Beside her attention to her husband's health and the running of a large, complicated household, Abigail, by correspondence with Cotton Tufts and her sister, Mary Cranch, managed the Quincy farms. Always a poor sleeper and constantly ailing, she usually rose at five o'clock; the hours between five and eight were invaluable to her. She prayed and read, wrote letters or simply savored the slow rising of light, a time inviolate, full of peace, the silence gently broken by the sounds of the house coming to life, the cook rattling pots in the kitchen, the coachman banging a feed pan in the echoing stable, John stirring in the bedroom, struggling out of the sleep that healed and restored him. Abigail directed Mary Cranch to supervise the curing of the cheese, to get the dill from her table drawer in the parlor and give it to Mrs. Burrel to make the cheese tastier. Her new crepe cap had been left behind and she wished Mary to send her that as well as a piece of canvas from her "bathing machine." Faithful Mary aired the house from time to time, carried out Abigail's commissions, and kept an eye on the farm. Cotton Tufts tended to the business, selling the old bay horse with the heaves for fifty dollars to Elisha Turner, directing the fattening of the four oldest cows for beef, and making sure that the work went forward in good season.

At eight each morning Abigail had breakfast with John and Louisa; then until eleven she did the numerous chores connected with running a house. There were menus to be planned, food ordered, instructions given to Briesler and the cook, a thousand details which she dispatched with brisk efficiency. At eleven o'clock she dressed for the day and next received company from twelve until two or three. Lunch, or more properly dinner, was an elaborate meal with wine and dessert, and afterward she "rode out" until seven, visiting, shopping, or simply taking the air in the countryside around Philadelphia. She often had thirty or forty guests to dinner—the whole Senate on one occasion, and the House in rotation, the Secretaries of the various departments, the foreign ministers and visiting dignitaries.

For Abigail the brightest spot in the soggy, trying month of June was the arrival of a crate addressed to Mr. and Mrs. John Adams from England. When it was opened it disclosed a portrait of John Quincy by Copley. It was one of the painter's happiest efforts. It had Copley's unmistakable lyric touch—the handsome head, proud and graceful, the fine, expressive modeling of the face, the beautiful eyes, wide and intelligent. It pierced Abigail to the heart, a sweet pain for her "dear absent son." Everyone who saw it was charmed. It was impossible to imagine a finer picture, "as fine a portrait as was ever taken," some said. To Abigail it caught to perfection "the expression, the animation, the true character," and she was delighted by the comment that her own features showed plainly in her son's face. Whether it was a gift from John Quincy or from the Copleys was not apparent, but in any event it was the most acceptable present she could possibly have desired or received.[2]

Despite her resolution not to pay attention to newspaper attacks the first lady could not help bursting out from time to time at the "lies, falsehoods, calumny, and bitterness" directed at her husband's administration. The Boston *Independent Chronicle* infuriated her by stating that the President was to receive a salary of a hundred and fourteen thousand dollars for his four-year term; and that John Quincy, only twenty-three years old (he was in fact almost thirty), received a salary of ten thousand dollars a year as minister (his actual stipened was four thousand five hundred.)

"I expected to be vilified and abused with my whole family when I came into this situation," she wrote her sister. The only course to follow was "strictly to adhere to our duty and keep ourselves unprejudiced."[3] "We may truly say, we know not what a day will bring forth. From every side we are in danger. We are in perils by land, and we are in perils by sea, and in perils from false brethren." If it was not for their trust in the Lord Jehovah as the source of everlasting strength, she and her husband would hardly have the courage to face the problems that pressed upon them.[4] There was "no measure of a subtle, secret, insidious nature," she complained, "which is not practicing in every part of the Union to stir up hostilities with the Indians, to make us quarrel with Spain, to insult our independence, and to drive us into war. . . . That the Lord reigneth supreme over all nations is my only consolation."[5]

Washington had established the precedent of a presidential party on the Fourth of July for the members of Congress, the gentlemen of the city, the Governor, and the officers and men of the militia companies. Long tables were spread in the yard to hold the overflow from the house and Abigail was informed that over two hundred pounds of cake and two quarter casks of wine had been consumed annually, besides the rum that went into the wine. She dreaded the occasion, but her weeks of planning bore fruit and she got through the day with "much more ease" than she had expected.[6] The Philadelphia Light Horse appeared, fired a salute, drank the President's health, gave three cheers, and marched off "with perfect decorum and decency." Then came the House in a body, after them the Senate, the Foreign Ministers, and finally the Cabinet members and their ladies.

In June the President was confronted with a most unsavory episode. William Blount, Senator from Tennessee and a reckless land speculator, had plotted with John Chisholm, a former British soldier and Indian agent, to organize a filibustering expedition into Spanish territory with the support of the British. Robert Liston, the British minister, had conferred with Chisholm, given him money for a passage to England and a letter of introduction to Lord Grenville. The ministry turned down Chisholm's scheme, but one of Blount's letters, revealing the whole plan, came into Adams' hands. The fact that Liston had implicated himself in a plot against a friendly power was bound to be exploited by the Republicans, even though the British ministry itself had behaved with strict propriety, but Adams did not hesitate to expose Blount. He sent the intercepted letter to the Attorney General, Charles Lee, and to two other prominent Philadelphia lawyers for their opinion on whether the activities of Blount constituted a crime and thus made him subject to impeachment before the Senate. All three agreed that it was a proper case for impeachment and Adams sent the letter with supporting documents to the Senate. When Jefferson read the incriminating document the chamber buzzed with astonished whispers. Blount was absent at the time, but as soon as he returned the letter was read once more. He turned ashen as he heard it. He had written a letter, he admitted, to a Mr. Cary, an interpreter for the Cherokee nation. He requested a copy of the letter so he could prepare his defense. It was given him and he promptly chartered a boat and decamped, leaving the Senate to decide his fate. That body voted to expel him as being guilty "of a very high misdemeanor, entirely inconsistent with his public trust and duty as a Senator." In the state of chronic crisis that beset the nation it was a small enough episode but, although Blount was a Republican, the incident was seized upon by the Jeffersonians as an instance of British interference in American internal affairs.

Another shadow darkening the spring of 1797 was Adams' growing breech with Jefferson. Busybodies informed the President of a letter written by Jefferson that was highly critical of his message to Congress. Adams angrily proclaimed it "evidence of a mind soured, yet seeking for popularity, and eaten to a honeycomb with ambition, yet weak, confused, uninformed, and ignorant."[7] To John Quincy, after detailing the Virginian's maneuverings, he declared: "You can witness for me how loath I have been to give him up. It is with much reluctance that I am obliged to look upon him as a man whose mind is warped by prejudice and so blinded by ignorance as to be unfit for the office he holds. However wise and scientific as philsopher, as a politician he is a child and the dupe of party!"[8]

Before Congress adjourned the Senate approved by a vote of sixteen to thirteen a bill to add twelve new frigates to the American navy; a few days later the House passed by seven votes a bill to strengthen coastal fortifications. However, a Senate measure to provide an army of fifteen thousand men was narrowly defeated just before Congress adjourned.

When Congress rose early in July, Adams was far from satisfied with its performance. A majority of the members were willing that American merchant vessels should be armed for the East Indies and the Mediterranean trade but not for the West Indies—a degree of nicety that baffled the President.[9] Yet half a loaf was better than none, and what was most important was that the executive had on the whole been supported by both branches of the legislature and some of the damage done by the session of the preceding spring thereby repaired. Adams had hoped for power to lay an embargo on the vessels of powers hostile to the United States as an act of retribution, but Congress rose without acting on his request, another evidence of its reluctance to take bold and resolute measures—"timidity" and "imbecility," Abigail called it.

With Congress adjourned, Adams longed to be back at Quincy but Wolcott and Pickering were uneasy at the prospect of the President being so far from the capital. The heat and the recurrent threat of the yellow fever made the city a perilous spot during the summer, and the exodus was so general that there was little business to be done at best. John and Abigail planned at first to take a place in the country until the dangerous months were over. Then, at the last moment, they decided to strike out for New England. The city weather was unendurable, "like a bake house." The whole family suffered from diarrhea and the sea breezes beckoned them north. Abigail wrote ahead to Mary Cranch asking her to prepare for their coming. She would like "some coffee burnt and ground, some bread and cake made," and if there were indications that they might be met on the road to Quincy by a reception committee of townspeople, there must be wine and punch to refresh them. The wine could be drawn from the casks in the cellar and the punch made by the gallon, of Jamaica rum and brandy. Mattresses should be put on the feather beds, two beds put up in the outchamber for the menservants, and the table set in the dining parlor.[10]

To Abigail's cousin William Smith went an order for a quarter cask of properly aged and decanted madeira wine, a barrel of the best flour, a quarter hundredweight of loaf sugar, a hundred pounds of brown sugar, twenty-five pounds of coffee, a pound each of the best Hyson and Souchong tea, a cask of crackers, and as many dozen lemons as he judged necessary for a large, thirsty household.[11]

The whole caravan—John and Abigail, the coachman, the Brieslers, Louisa Smith, and the servants—left Philadelphia July 19 in a shower of rain that fell upon them like a blessing after the stifling heat. But the next day it was so hot on the road that Abigail thought she would suffocate and twice within a few hours had to stop at inns along the way to undress and lie down until she no longer felt faint. The weather compounded all the usual inconveniences of travel—the poor food, the small rooms and uncomfortable beds, some of them no longer than one of Abigail's bolsters. Abigail, the insomniac, got little sleep.

At New York they picked up Nabby and the children and pushed on to Quincy, panting beneath the dog star, as Abigail expressed it.[12] The little troop reached home on the fifth of August with feelings akin to the crew of a ship that makes port after a trying and storm-tossed passage. Mary Cranch and Cotton Tufts had prepared everything for their arrival. The house was cool and pleasant-smelling, the larder stocked, the comfortable, familiar beds made up with fresh linen, the table set, the coffee in the pot, and John's favorite cigars in a jar on the parlor table. The farm was green and fruitful, showing the effect of Dr. Tufts' faithful supervision. Most of the cows had calved and the five young heifers grazed in the meadow. Caesar and Cleopatra, the coach horses, seemed as glad to be home as their master and cavorted in the field like colts.

A few days after their arrival a committee of Bostonians made up of Stephen Higginson, Benjamin Lincoln, Oliver Wendell, Jonathan Jackson, and Thomas Dawes addressed a letter to Adams, congratulating him on the firmness and resolution with which he had discharged his duties as President and inviting him to a dinner in his honor. In his acceptance of their invitation Adams spoke of "this period when disorder, indiscipline, and disobedience of every kind, fashioned into a kind of science, are vindicated as right and inculcated as duties." In such a time it was inevitable that some Americans should catch the contagion. He was especially troubled by the disposition in certain groups and individuals to try to undermine the confidence of the people in their government. If they succeeded it would mean an end to republican government in the United States, and its enemies everywhere would argue that it was a "demonstration that the people are not capable of such a government; and by the sudden introduction of wasting calamities, would soon convince the people themselves of the necessity of instituting another form for their own protection."[13] When he had finished the reply it was clear that he had dwelt too much on his own moral rectitude and on the turpitude of his opponents. On the advice of Benjamin Lincoln, whom he consulted, he toned down his remarks in a second draft, and even more in a third, until instead of an angry diatribe he presented a more restrained statement of his fears and hopes for the Republic. Placed side by side, the drafts suggest the strength of his own feelings and the difficulty which he invariably experienced in trying to adopt a moderate public tone.

While Abigail visited friends in Boston and took Mary Cranch with her on an expedition to Hingham to see their sister Eliza, now remarried to the Reverend Stephen Peabody, Adams was busy answering dispatches which arrived by every mail from Philadelphia. It would be months, of course, before the French negotiation was heard from. But the news from Pickering regarding the progress in extending United States jurisdiction into the lower Mississippi was encouraging. Surveys were being run, and troops sent into the area were meeting with a friendly reception from Indians and white settlers alike. The Secretary of State had prepared a strong letter of rebuke to the Spanish minister, Carlos d'Yrujo, for meddling in the Blount affair and he sent the letter to Adams for his approval. Adams termed it a "masterly composition" which would do honor to its author and "cast disgrace on the Spanish minister."[14]

Much of the correspondence concerned appointments and Adams devoted a disproportionate amount of time trying to assure himself that the best candidate for each position received the appointment. Although he clearly preferred applicants who were firm supporters of the government, he tried to keep rumors of personal opposition to him from coloring his judgments. Thus he approved Jonathan Williams, American agent at Bordeaux, "capable and upon the whole ingenious"—although there had been insinuations that Williams had opposed Adams' candidacy. He warmly recommended Benjamin Rush, whom he had "loved and esteemed these three and twenty years" for his "learning, ingenuity . . . and his public and private virtues," for some federal office.[15] Adams' position on appointments, at least as expressed by Abigail, was that he "would appoint to office merit, virtue, and talents, and when Jacobins possess these, they will stand a chance, but it will ever be an additional recommendation that they are friends to order and government."[16]

The summer, or what there was left of it, was gone all too quickly and, at the end of September, John and Abigail prepared for the long, tiresome journey to Philadelphia, indeed not knowing when they left Quincy where they would light. The capital was still possessed by the fever and if it did not abate rapidly Congress must convene elsewhere. Nabby's boys, William and John, were farmed out to Eliza Shaw Peabody as their uncles, Charles and Thomas, had been before them. Abigail sent wool for Betsy Shaw to knit them socks, ten dollars to have a little chest of drawers built for them, and detailed instructions as to their training and education. Nabby had returned to New York to await some word from the Colonel, who had gone off on another of those speculative ventures which were intended to establish his fortune beyond all the vicissitudes of chance.

As they traveled south the President and his lady were greeted everywhere with affection and respect. The inhabitants of the towns they passed through turned out to cheer and wave. The larger communities paraded their militia and set ceremonial tables. People seeing the President of the United States pass by without show or panoply had a renewed faith in the Republic. They remembered John Adams' long services to the Revolution and his reputation for standing solid as a block of New England granite for what he believed to be right and just. Recalling his simplicity and his independence, they were confident that this was not a man to quail before the rabid French or the imperious English. No one would budge that homely figure from his center. Everything that New England was, he was—as indigenous as a lichen-covered stone fence or a tough-grained maple. They loved him as one of their own and their love showed in their faces and rang in their voices. John and Abigail were touched to tears.

Abigail was especially moved by an old man with a shock of white hair who appeared at an inn where they were staying and asked to see the President. He was admitted, bowed respectfully, and asked if Abigail was the President's wife. "I came many miles this morning on purpose," he said. "I told my wife this morning that I would come, and she said, 'Why, ain't you afraid?' 'No,' said I, 'why do you think I should be afraid to go and see my father?'" "This was said with so much hearty sincerity," Abigail reported to Mary Cranch, "that to me it was of more value than the whole military cavalcade of Pennsylvania."[17]

The people, Adams reminded himself, was a fickle mistress. Yet to a man who for so long had thought himself maligned and misunderstood the outpouring of affection that followed his progress through his native region was sweet indeed. He must be careful to guard against its seduction. It was easy to see how a statesman, once he had tasted such wine, could become drunk on it, could sacrifice judgment, independence, and finally honor for fresh drafts. "The spirit of union and Federalism," he wrote John Quincy, "pervades every part of the New England, with very few exceptions. I have been assured from all quarters that there is but one mind and that mind is in support of our constitution and government. . . . On every occasion and opportunity they have shown their attachment to the government by personal respect to the Chief Magistrate, both by civil and military exhibitions which, however contrary" to his "taste and inclination," he must now submit to.[18]

John and Abigail stopped off at Eastchester with Nabby, while the Brieslers went ahead to open the house and prepare for their arrival. John wrote to Philadelphia inquiring about the state of the distemper in the city and soliciting from his Secretaries suggestions for his forthcoming address to Congress. While he waited in New York the citizens of the city put on a military parade and festival for him. The climax was an elegant dinner for three hundred people. This "splendid and magnificent" feast, and the numerous marks of "personal respect and satisfaction" accorded the President, helped heal some of the wounds inflicted by the radical journalists.

Before they left the farm word had arrived that John Quincy had been married to Louisa Catherine Johnson in July, and a few weeks later they got a letter from the happy groom telling them of the event. John Quincy's joy in his beautiful bride was for Abigail in painful contrast to Nabby's plight. The latter's house was remote and lonely; she had received no word from her husband since June, and lacked friends to offer her help or comfort. As always, she was quiet and reserved and Abigail's efforts to draw her out were unsuccessful. She would make no complaint or say anything critical of her absent husband. Abigail decided to take her and little Caroline to Philadelphia. It was more than her mother's heart could bear to leave her behind, "a prey to grief and misfortune."[19]

It was almost the middle of November before word came that Philadelphia was free of the plague and the Adamses pushed on to the capital. Six miles out of Trenton, New Jersey, the Governor of Pennsylvania with a large crowd of citizens and a troop of cavalry met the President's party. Adams was presented with an address and while Abigail went on to the Delaware ferry he replied, expressing his pleasure at returning to Philadelphia and urging unity against the enemies of the United States. In spite of the reception, Abigail was convinced that Pennsylvania could not "bear a comparison with New England." The state was too "clogged . . . by the spirit of Quakerism and cursed . . . by the spirit of Jacobinism. They are a house divided against itself."[20]

The day was raw and Adams caught a miserable cold from riding with the carriage windows down. It was the usual "great cold" or "Philadelphia cold" that invariably greeted him when he arrived in that city. This time he was in bed for a week. Abigail found the presidential mansion "in perfect good order, and all my old hands escaped . . . the pestilence . . . so that at present I could not wish to be better off than I am with respect to domestics, which greatly enhances the comfort of life."[21] The return of the President was a signal for "Ben" Bache to unlimber his journalistic artillery; he began by hinting that the city militia had been ordered by the President to salute his arrival and to be sure that the populace paid him proper respect.

Congress was slow assembling because of the uncertainty caused by the fever. By the fifteenth of November the House had a quorum but the Senate was unable to convene. Adams occupied himself preparing his opening address and adjudicating the matter of Tench Coxe, commissioner of the revenue in the Treasury Department, who had been charged by Wolcott with insolence and insubordination. Adams was doubtless glad for a pretext to get rid of a man who he felt had betrayed him, but he was scrupulous in reviewing Coxe's case and in collecting the opinion of the other Cabinet members on his conduct. Pickering, McHenry, and Lee were of the opinion that the Pennsylvanian had clearly been derelict in his duty and Adams promptly sacked him. Coxe's cause was taken up by Bache, who charged that he had been fired simply for having Republican sympathies. His expulsion, the editor declared, showed that the Adams administration was determined to make war upon Republicanism wherever found.

The President's address to Congress was based very largely on a draft submitted by the Secretary of State. Adams corrected and revised it extensively, but in general the form was Pickering's. When both Houses assembled on the twenty-second of the month, some of the resolution which had marked the special session had already evaporated, but the President's tone was as firm as it had been in the spring. There was a job to be done and he directed them firmly to its doing. The envoys had departed and presumably were at that moment carrying on their negotiations with representatives of the Directory. He joined in the common wish for their success. Yet it was simple discretion to be prepared for possible failure and Congress must once again consider how the energy and resources of the United States might best be mustered for national defense. Nothing had happened, indeed, since the adjournment of Congress almost six months ago to lessen the need for a respectable naval and military establishment. The fact was that, whatever the outcome of the current negotiations, Europe, and in consequence America, would face a period of stress and danger. The world was in a turmoil—"the sense of moral and religious obligations so much weakened, public faith and national honor . . . so impaired, respect to treaties so diminished, and the law of nations" so generally disregarded, that a simple sense of self-preservation required that America look to her defenses. It was very well to hope that peace and order might suddenly be restored by the discussions of reasonable and well-intentioned men; but it was only common prudence to be prepared for what indeed was far more likely—that the United States would have to maintain for years and perhaps decades a hazardous balance between warring nations. She could only hope to do so by making herself strong and respected. Power, not ac-commodating words and pious hopes, move the world, and if Americans were to sit in on this game they must be prepared to use cards the other players understood. Commerce was essential to the growth and prosperity of the United States. Even agriculture, fisheries, arts and manufactures depended on it. "In short," Adams declared, "commerce has made this country what it is, and it cannot be destroyed or neglected without involving the people in poverty and distress."

The Spanish, he pointed out, still clung to their garrisons in the Natchez region and foreign agents circulated on the frontier trying to stir up the Indians. The boundary line of the St. Croix was still being deliberated upon. The commissioners appointed to decide on the debts due British merchants by American citizens had not yet reached agree-ment, but they too were continuing their discussions. The commissioners appointed to consider the claims of citizens of the United States for losses and damages sustained by reason of irregular and illegal capture of American vessels had made several decisions and a number of claims had been paid. Finally there was the hard fact that the government was faced in the coming year with increased expenses and the House of Representatives must thus find new sources of revenue.

Adams' speech was received with praise or abuse depending on the party affiliation of the individual. The Republicans denounced it as tantamount to a declaration of war on France. To the Federalists it seemed a firm and moderate statement of the administration's deter-mination to defend the honor and integrity of the nation. Madison, retired leader of the House Republicans, deplored "those who tolerate . . . the fashionable sentiments," adding, "Let us hope that the tide of evil is nearly at its flood."[22] Albert Gallatin, Madison's successor, made clear his views by opposing the reply of the House to the President's address and leading a fight to establish the right of the popular branch to refuse appropriations for diplomatic expenses approved by the Pres-ident and Senate. He lost on both counts, serving only to underscore the Federalist superiority in the House.

But aside from Bache's daily flow of bile—referring to Adams as the Duke of Braintree and naming him and Abigail Darby and Joan, after an old country couple in a popular Yorkshire ballad—there was little public reaction. Rumors had already begun to circulate about the fate of the commissioners in Paris and there was a general disposition in both camps to wait and see what news the next packet from France might bring.

A letter from John Quincy, written shortly after the arrival of the special envoys, predicted that they would fail to make "any satisfactory arrangement" with the French government. The uprising against the Directory had resulted in the suppression of every moderate voice and placed at the helm of the French government "men without principle and without feeling, and the most inveterate enemies of America."[23]

The political lull meant no less work for the President, however. He was in constant consultation with his Secretaries and plowed through mountains of documents and dispatches. Indeed, work pressed so on him that he found no time for the walks and rides that afforded him such pleasure and relaxation. Word came early in January that Francis II of Austria had made a peace treaty with the Directory, by the terms of which he surrendered the Belgian provinces and the left bank of the Rhine to the victorious armies of Napoleon. The treaty left England standing alone and there were reports that Bonaparte was preparing a massive invasion of the island nation. The news cheered the Republicans. With proud England humbled in the dust, the French Revolution would be everywhere triumphant and the new day of liberty, fraternity, and equality would dawn over all Europe. The Federalists, deprived of their last resource, would have to abandon their implacable hostility to France and either watch powerless or join with the majority of their fellow citizens in embracing the principles and the program of the Revolution.

For Adams the French victories meant only more trouble. Flushed with success in Europe, that country would be more intractable than ever in her demands on America. His own feelings were reflected in Abigail's outburst to her sister. France sought not only the end of American "independence and liberty but a total annihilation of the Christian religions." Her laws were those of "robbers, murderers, scoffers, backbiters. In short," she added, there was "no crime however black or horrid to which they have not become familiar. America must be punished . . . for having among her legislatures men who sanction these crimes, who justify France in all her measures, and who would rejoice to see fire, sword, and massacre carried into the island of Great Britain until she became as miserable as France is wretched."

From William Vans Murray they heard discouraging news of the envoys. Murray had received a few lines from Marshall informing him that the commissioners had not been received and that he doubted if they would be. They were spied on and not permitted to go about or to converse with anyone. Under such circumstances they dared not even write, Murray reported.[24]

Addicted as he was to letters, those of his sons, especially John Quincy's, were Adams' particular delight. He derived both instruction and pleasure from Murray's able and intelligent communications and every item of news from his New England correspondents was prized by the President. Abigail indeed found her husband rather indiscriminate in his appetite for mail. When she went to his office one morning to see if the post had arrived she found him standing "very gravely" by the fire reading one of Mary Cranch's letters. Abigail gave him a scolding and a little lecture on the sanctity of private correspondence. She didn't open his mail and she would thank him not to open hers. John, resembling a small boy caught with his hand in the cooky jar, protested lamely that Sister Cranch's letters were worth a dozen others. "She always tells us so much about home. And if I don't look at them clandestinely I seldom see them," he said, making the best of a weak case. There were things, Abigail retorted, which passed between sisters that were just for their eyes and he must show greater respect for the United States mails. "The President has agreed that he will not open any more letters to me," Abigail wrote her sister, "and will be satisfied with such parts as I am willing to communicate."[25]

Soon afterward Abigail came on her husband writing a letter to Cotton Tufts. He looked so guilty that Abigail penetrated his secret at once. He was instructing the doctor to buy more land for him and he knew that Abigail would disapprove. She wished their savings to go into deferred stocks and every extra dollar she got her hands on she sent off to Tufts with instructions to buy securities. She accused him straight out and laughed with delight at John's startled expression. She knew him like a book, she declared in wifely triumph.[26]

Having made good her point about the inviolability of letters from Mary Cranch, Abigail cunningly suggested to her sister that she enclose letters from Dr. Tufts (which did not enjoy the same immunity) in her own letters, since "the doctor and I have some business transactions which are between ourselves."[27]

THE President fretted over the conduct of Congress. With a dozen pressing measures awaiting the consideration of the members of both houses, they occupied much of their time wrangling over the question of Blount's impeachment. A month and a half, off and on, was taken up with the Foreign Intercouse Bill intended to establish the diplomatic and consular service on a more substantial and comprehensive basis. The bill, introduced by Robert Goodloe Harper, a South Carolina Federalist, aroused the isolationist and states rights instincts of the Republicans, who were inclined to feel that United States foreign relations should stop with France. Any other contact would risk involvement in European politics and the pollution of American democracy. To John Nicholas of Virginia it was axiomatic that America "ought to have no political connection with Europe."

For the enemies of the administration the bill offered an irresistible opportunity to attack the President at what was perhaps his most vulnerable spot—his appointment of his son as minister to Prussia. The Foreign Intercourse Bill, Republican orators insisted, was designed by the executive department to steal power from the legislative branch. Nicholas was especially eloquent in analyzing the nefarious intent of the measure. It was clear that the President wished to be free to advance his eldest son to the top rungs of the diplomatic ladder and undoubtedly to find posts in the diplomatic corps for his younger sons, for his numerous nephews and cousins, and for a horde of Federalist office seekers. After the discussions of the bill had dragged on for several weeks Abigail observed dryly that the House of Representatives had "expended as much money by the length of the debate as would pay the salaries of our ministers for two years to come."[1]

At the end of January the House was further distracted by a bitter exchange between Roger Griswold of Connecticut and Matthew Lyon. When Griswold disparaged the Vermonter's military record Lyon, who was sitting close by, rose and spit in his face. Griswold restrained himself for the moment but, when it became apparent after almost two weeks of angry accusation and counteraccusation that the House would not expel Lyon, Griswold took matters into his own hands and attacked his enemy with a cane as he sat at his desk. Lyon snatched up a pair of fire tongs and the two men grappled and rolled on the floor until they were separated. Lyon, red and raging, shouted that he wished nothing better than to be left alone with his adversary.

The Federalist press doubled its denunciation of the Vermont Republican as "an unclean beast," "a brute," "a spitting animal," and demanded that he be expelled from Congress as the citizens of Philadelphia removed "*impurities* and *filth* from their docks and wharves." "That wild Irishman," Abigail called him, bemoaning the fact that there were "not to be found impartial men enough in the House to expel the wretch. . . . Oh, 'tis a pitiful business!" she wrote Cotton Tufts.[2]

One interlude that afforded some relief from the atmosphere of protracted crisis was the appearance at the President's mansion of the kings of three Indian nations. After paying their respects to the President they were presented to Abigail, nine tall, brown savages in full regalia. They sat in silence facing her for a few moments and then one arose and declared that "he had been to visit his father, and he thought his duty but in part fulfilled until he had visited also his mother, and he prayed the Great Spirit to keep and preserve them." That said, they all rose and shook hands solemnly and then had wine and cake, "much more civil," Abigail noted, "than the Beast of Vermont," Matthew Lyon.[3]

While the Lyon affair blazed away the President involved himself in another unhappy controversy. Washington's birthday had been marked every February 22 with a handsome ball and general festivities. John and Abigail had always disapproved of the birthday celebration. It seemed to them dangerously close to deification. They recalled that undue veneration for military heroes had helped to bring about the downfall of the Roman republic and felt that in the General's birthday observance a potentially dangerous precedent had been set. They reconciled themselves to the event, however, with the reflection that the lavish annual affairs honored the office as much as the man.

When a group of prominent Philadelphians sent them an invitation to a "ball . . . in honor of the birth of George Washington," Adams was indignant. He felt that he and the office he held had been insulted. The President of the United States was being asked to attend the birthday celebration of a private citizen. "However good, however great [the General's] character," it was most inappropriate to mark it in such a manner. "How could the President appear at their ball and assembly but in a secondary character . . . to be held up in that light by all foreign nations?" Abigail asked her sister. Adams wrote tersely across the face of the invitation "Declined" and fired off a curt note of refusal.

The word of the rebuff touched off a political storm. Bache was prepared to embrace the President as a democratic hero but many Federalists were deeply offended. As Abigail had predicted, the action was attributed to injured vanity and wounded self-esteem. The announcement that the President and his lady had declined threw a pall over the whole occasion. "Everyone was inquiring the why and the wherefore," in Abigail's words. Many who had subscribed decided not to attend and Jefferson, who had been pleased to note that it was the birthday of Washington the General and not Washington the President which was being commemorated, had second thoughts and stayed away himself. It would hardly do for the leader of the Republican party to appear at the birthday of a man whose administration he had criticized so often and so bitterly, while the Federalist President expressed his disapproval of the affair by refusing to attend. Adams, not penetrating so far into the Vice-President's motives, was grateful for what he felt was support for his position. Jefferson, for his part, was pleased at the bad feeling created by the whole episode. "The late birthnight has certainly sown tares among the executive Federalists," he wrote Madison. "It has removed the grain from the chaff. The sincerely Adamsites (or is it Adamites?) did not go. The Washingtonians went religiously, and took the secession of the others in high dudgeon."[4]

The whole incident was unfortunate. Adams, however exalted his motives might have been in fact, was shown in a poor light. To many people, not all of them his enemies, he appeared jealous and petty. The Federalists, already riddled with factionalism, had still another cause for dissension.

Throughout the month of February, Adams sent a flood of special messages to the Senate and House but both bodies seemed bogged down in trivial and irrelevant matters. The Republicans were determined to obstruct, as far as they were able, any efforts to strengthen the nation's defenses or provide for the arming of merchant ships. Every week brought reports of new seizures and indignities suffered by American vessels and seamen at the hands of the belligerents. A French privateer, the *Vertitude,* entered the harbor of Charleston and plundered and burned a British vessel anchored there, an act in direct violation of American sovereignty. The incident was only one among dozens of similar occurrences. But Congress was more concerned, as Abigail put it, with fighting "not the French, but the Lyon, not the noble British Lyon, but the beastly transported Lyon."[5]

To support the increased military establishment and finance the building of naval vessels, the preceding Congress had passed a stamp tax. To the Republicans the symbolism was evident. They launched a determined campaign to repeal the law, and their efforts were barely frustrated by the Federalist Senate. This action of the Republicans in the House, show-

ing as it did a willful and intractable spirit, dismayed Adams. Abigail put
the matter succinctly in a letter to her cousin, William Smith. The effort
at repeal, she wrote, comes "at a time . . . when revenue is wanted for
to defend the Southern states against the Indians, to form new treaties,
to purchase their lands . . . to put forts and garrison in repair . . . to assist in completing the *solitary* buildings in the Federal City." Every measure designed to strengthen the country was "bellowed against as a declaration of war," and Giles had declared "he would if he could destroy every
tax throughout the United States." Congress, in Abigail's words, was spin-
ning "a mere Penelopean web," destroying at one session the fabric they
had woven earlier.[6] She wrote to Eliza Peabody that she and the President were "sick, sick, sick of public life" with its endless demands, its
tribulations, its rancors, lies, and abuse.

The President was worn out with the constant strain, exhausted men-
tally and emotionally "by continual opposition and by constant exertions
to support order, harmony, and peace against ambition, disorder, and
anarchy."[7] To see the world in turmoil, the nation hanging on the edge
of war, confused, uncertain, and torn by faction while the national legislature wrangled and procrastinated and played the game of politics, maneuvering for party advantage, putting sectional interests ahead of national welfare, was like living in a kind of nightmare in which, while
disaster threatened, nothing was done to forestall it. The power to act,
to move, to respond, to strike back seemed lost, as in the strange sequences of a dream. Adams read reports, consulted with the Secretaries,
wrote urgent messages to Congress, but nothing happened. To anticipate
the failure of the mission to France, he canvassed the Cabinet again on
the question of war with that country. The Secretaries assured him that
there was a "general indisposition to war in the minds of the people
of the United States" and that they were "peculiarly averse to a war with
the French Republic." Therefore an actual declaration of hostility or a
formal rupture between the two countries would have the gravest consequences. The best course seemed "a mitigated hostility"—"a truly vigorous defensive plan, with a countenance still kept up to negotiate," a cold
war. Every effort should be made to bring home to Congress the dangers
which confronted the nation and the necessity "of ample provision of
revenue."

The tone of the President's communications to Congress should be
"cautious, solemn, grave, and perfectly derobed of all asperity or insult."
McHenry's recommendations revealed an abler mind than his own at
work. He had consulted with Hamilton and his reply to Adams' query
was largely the work of the New Yorker, whose advice, in this instance as
on the question of the envoys, conformed very nearly to Adams' own
views.[8]

On the fourth of March the long-awaited dispatches from the envoys arrived. Adams notified Congress at once. The bulk were in cipher, but one letter, dated January 8, 1798, was in plain hand and he enclosed copies for the information of both Houses. To Adams, especially as the deciphered documents were laid before him, the conclusion seemed, inescapably, war. War must be declared at once against France and the nation prepared for a long and bitter struggle. (That the President was convinced war was inevitable is indicated by Abigail's letter to William Smith ordering fifty pounds of coffee and a hundred and fifty pounds of brown sugar on the assumption that a declaration of war would bring a sharp rise in prices.) As the tale of the insults and indignities offered the commissioners unrolled, Adams' indignation increased. The French were knaves and madmen, drunk with their own power and the wild brew of revolution. Pinckney, Marshall, and Gerry had called several days after their arrival in Paris to present their credentials to Talleyrand, Foreign Minister to the Directory. After a wait of almost a week they were informed that the Directory was "greatly exasperated" at some parts of President Adams' Inaugural Address and "would require an explanation."

Four days later a French negotiator, referred to in the dispatches as "X," entered the picture. He had a message from Talleyrand, he whispered. The minister himself was friendly to the Americans, but unfortunately two members of the Directory were much offended at certain passages in Adams' speech "and desired that they should be softened," although how three emissaries of the President could modify the sentences of their chief was not clear. That was the problem of the commissioners. They would not be received until they had, in effect, repudiated the President's statement of his administration's policy. In addition Talleyrand and the Directory must have a "*douceur* for the pocket" of twelve million livres, fifty thousand sterling, and the promise of a large loan from the United States. The Americans indignantly rejected the suggestion and shortly two more agents, "Y" and "Z," became involved. Reading the commissioners' account, Adams could not suppress his irritation at the Americans' "pedantical, timorous" behavior. They should have insisted on seeing the minister and no one else. The "tittle tattle" of X "ought not to have been attended to," he noted, "nor any word said . . . till the envoys were received by the Directory."

But that was water under the bridge, the price that must be paid for having to use amateurs for the complex and exacting duties of professional diplomats. What remained was to decide upon the proper action. Again he circularized the Secretaries, sending them the dispatches and requesting their recommendations. Charles Lee replied first, advising Adams to declare war. "To me," he wrote, "there appears no alternative between actual hostilities on our part or national ruin." A declaration of war would make it possible to root out the die-hard adherents of France as traitors and muster the resources of the country in a spirited and effective way. Wolcott was ambiguous, recommending such measures (apparently short of war) "as are afforded by the ample resources of the country for the protection of the persons and property of our seafaring and commercial citizens." McHenry reiterated his earlier stand for "a qualified hostility."

Again, the Cabinet members had looked to Hamilton and Hamilton wisely advised against an immediate declaration of war. Pickering had written to the New Yorker suggesting a defensive and offensive alliance with Great Britain, but Hamilton rejected such a measure. The country would not accept it.

Despite the advice of his Secretaries, Adams felt that a declaration of war was called for if American honor was to be preserved. He thus sat down in a most belligerent frame of mind to draft "A Message Referring to a Decree of the Directory," apparently intended for Congress: "For defending our commerce . . . against this decree," he wrote, referring to an order of the Directory which declared that a ship was friendly or hostile according to the hands by which the cargo was manufactured, "every effort and every resource should be called into action, which cannot be done unless there be a formal declaration of war. To proceed no farther than the plan of arming vessels under regulations and restrictions is too insufficient of itself. . . . To me there appears no alternative," he added, borrowing Lee's sentence, "between actual hostilities on our part and national ruin."[9]

As he wrote, a lecturing, pedagogical note crept into his sentences. "The great source" of America's misfortunes, he declared, had been indulging in "too keen a resentment, too implacable a malignity against one nation and too fond a partiality for another." The best-informed men in the United States had not enough knowledge of European nations to enable them to judge "what forms of government they can bear, are fit for their use, or can be productive of their happiness." Americans, swept away by their emotions, had abandoned themselves to men and measures that they imperfectly understood or egregiously misinterpreted.

Those Americans who had so fanatically espoused the cause of France without understanding what they were about had helped to bring the United States to its present dilemma. They had encouraged the French government, "by professions . . . of unqualified devotion to the French Republic," to believe that a majority of Americans preferred the government of that nation to their own. Thus France had been tempted to her folly, believing that she could chastise United States citizens for having the effrontery to elect a President unacceptable to the Directory. Such treacherous Americans had succeeded only in producing the danger of "a final and irretrievable rupture between the two countries." Some indeed had gone so far as to set themselves up as French privateers to prey upon the ships of their fellow citizens and these were men of "a total depravity of principle and corruption of heart."

One final heresy he wished to extirpate, the "false" and "dishonorable" contention that the "principles of [the French] Revolution and ours were the same. . . . Ours was resistance to innovation, theirs was innovation itself, which we have no right to censure or applaud." The French must be their own judges. It was only necessary for Americans to understand that the two revolutions were as different as night and day.

Adams' resentment poured forth in a long list of grievances, among them the "open exertions and secret intrigues" of the ministers plenipotentiary from the French Republic who had attempted to involve the United States in war with Britain by "their cabals and corruptions . . . their patronage and employment of profligate printers and prostituted newspapers; their continual combinations with a disaffected party against the constitution and administration of our government." The conclusion was simple and devastating: If war was not to be declared, a law should be passed "prohibiting all commerce, intercourse, and correspondence with France and all its dominions in every part of the world, upon penalty of treason."

Such statements were tantamount to declaring war, not only on France but on the Republicans and with them a large portion of the American populace. Even as he wrote, Adams' anger subsided. The hot words, like a bleeding of hot and distempered blood, lowered his fever. The reaction of Congress, strong as it was, to the news of the mission's failure indicated clearly enough that they were not yet ready for such desperate measures. A recommendation for a declaration of war would never succeed unless Congress was told the full story of French insults and chicanery; to release the documents might bring a reaction from the Directory that could endanger the lives of the commissioners. (Abigail compared them to the three children in the fiery furnace—Shadrach, Meshach, and Abednego.) This, at least, was Charles Lee's view and, although McHenry made light of it, Adams decided to hold back the actual dispatches. It was, Abigail wrote, "a very painful thing" to the President not to be able to communicate to Congress the public dispatches.[10] This meant that he could not play his strongest card. Therefore he must settle for very much lower stakes—for McHenry's policy of a "vigorous defensive plan" and "a qualified hostility," or in effect a state of undeclared, unofficial war. Coming to such a position reluctantly, Adams became more and more conscious of its advantages. There must be time to ripen American opinion so that the vast majority of the country would unite behind the government's policy. The inevitable incidents that must occur between France and the United States should in time produce that firmness of spirit which would support a war or, what would be infinitely better, finally persuade the French to undertake negotiation in good faith.

In the midst of the crisis another event took place which perhaps inclined the President to move slowly. Word reached Pickering that Sweden, an important neutral power, was ready to renew its expiring treaty with the United States. Adams sent a message to the Senate on the twelfth of March nominating John Quincy as a commissioner to negotiate a new treaty of amity and commerce with the Scandinavian state. John Quincy's appointment as minister to Prussia had not yet been confirmed by the Senate and the new recommendation touched off an explosion among the angry and supicious Republicans. Senator Tazewell declared that the United States would be better off with no ministers in any foreign countries and Bache picked the item up at once and declared it "all a job in order to give Mr. Adams a new outfit and an additional salary at every court."[11]

"Tazewell," Jefferson reported to Madison with an edge of malice, "made a great stand against it [the appointment of John Quincy], on the general ground that we should let our treaties drop and remain without any."[12] But the Senator mustered only eight votes in support of his position. The next day he tried a new tack, arguing that the renewal was inexpedient. Defeated again, the Republican leader made a determined effort to nip the negotiation in the bud by lining up more than the third needed to prevent ratification of any treaty with Sweden that might be submitted to the Senate in the future. But the vindictiveness of Tazewell and his lieutenants was so patent that they failed by a wide margin in their ingenious scheme to reject a treaty which had not yet been drafted.

It was not unnatural in the face of such persistent harassment that Adams felt persecuted. "We have *renewed information,*" Abigail wrote Mary Cranch, "that [the Republican] system is to calumniate the President, his family, his administration until they oblige him to resign, and then they will reign triumphant, *headed by the Man of the People,*" the Vice-President.[13]

The President had a doughty defender in Peter Porcupine, who wrote, "All men now agree that Congress ought to do something, and that immediately, and if they do not they may expect to bring on themselves all the odium attached to such indecisive measures—I had almost said criminal—everyone knows that the snaillike mode of proceeding which we have long beheld is not the fault of the President. He has taken care that his character, either as an American or as the chief magistrate of America, shall not suffer, let the result be what it may." Abigail, however pleased, was a little uneasy at such a champion. "There is a strange mixture in him," she noted. "He can write very handsomely, and he can descend and be as low and vulgar as a fishwoman."[14]

On the nineteenth of March, Adams sent Congress a mild enough message, drafted by Wolcott, which declared that a review of the commissioners' correspondence gave him "no ground of expectation that the objects of their mission can be accomplished on terms compatible with the safety, the honor, or the essential interests of the nation. This result," the message declared, "cannot with justice be attributed to any want of moderation on the part of this government, or to any indisposition to forgo secondary interests for the preservation of peace." Under the circumstances Adams felt it appropriate to reiterate the recommendations which he had made at the beginning of the session for the protection of American shipping and the defense of the American coast. The one bold stroke was Adams' revocation of Washington's order forbidding American vessels to sail "in an armed condition."

Moderate as the communication was—termed "the insane message" by Jefferson—it still burst on Congress like a bombshell. On one hand there was "exultation . . . and a certainty of victory; while the other," Jefferson informed Madison, "is petrified with astonishment." In actual fact, the Republican ranks were thrown into confusion by the document. There were defections, among them Thomas Evans, a Representative from Virginia, who could not bring himself to vote against the message and, since he dared not vote for it, absented himself from the House.

Determined to contest the field, Jefferson and Giles hurried about rallying their demoralized forces. The language of the message was highly ambiguous, they argued. Closely read, it hinted at the truth—that the French had made such accommodations as the United States had the right to expect and the Federalists, fearful of having to make peace, were deliberately concealing the French terms. Jefferson had two suggestions: first, that the executive order authorizing merchant ships to arm be attacked as unconstitutional on the grounds that the power lay with Congress, not with the President; second, that Congress adjourn ("as to do nothing and to gain time is everything with us") on the pretext that its members must "go home and consult their constituents on the great crisis of American affairs now existing." Adjournment would allow time for the French under Napoleon Bonaparte to invade England and remove that country from the scale of international politics. Jefferson was convinced that the true aim of the Federalists was to use the peace negotiations to split the union into two great sections, North and South.[15]

Republicans at the seat of government sent off word posthaste to the hinterland requesting support for their resistance to war; half a dozen Massachusetts towns responded with resolutions protesting the right of the President to remove the ban on the arming of merchant ships. As petitions began to pour into the capital Jefferson and his cohorts took heart. Adams was dismayed. He had so far misjudged popular reaction that it had never occurred to him that there would be widespread opposition to measures of simple self-defense. The news of the temper of the Massachusetts town meetings made him furious. "You cannot conceive," Abigail wrote her cousin, "what mischief will result to our country from the interference of people who can have only a partial view of subjects of this nature. . . . The unfortunate movement in our state," she concluded, ". . . has given impudence to Bache, if it was possible to add to his former audacity, and damped the friends of government. It has given triumph to the Jacobins, it weakens the hands of government and has a hydra head of evils."[16]

On the twenty-seventh a caucus of Republican members of Congress proposed three resolutions to frustrate the administration's efforts to strengthen the country's defenses. The first was "that it is inexpedient to resort to war against the French Republic"; the second protested the legality of arming merchant vessels; and the third called for measures to protect the coastal areas against attack by any maritime power. Jefferson confessed his gloomy apprehensions that the first resolution would fail of a majority in the House where Robert Goodloe Harper and Thomas Pinckney "pronounced bitter philippics" against the motion and against France. To the Vice-President the issue of war or peace depended "on a toss of cross and pile." The Quakers were approached in an attempt to extract from them a declaration in favor of peace, but the Quakers would have none of it. Nonetheless the Republicans redoubled their efforts. Two or three new Republican newspapers were started in Massachusetts and Connecticut. These, taking their cue and much of their material from Bache, began to denounce the President as a warmonger devoted to making the United States subservient to Great Britain once more. Abigail was stung by such canards. "What benefit can war be to him?" she asked her sister. "He has no ambition for military glory. He cannot add by war to his peace, comfort, or happiness. It must accumulate upon him an additional load of care, toil, trouble, malice, hatred, and I dare say revenge."[17] In a letter to William Smith she poured out her concern over the dilemmas which faced her husband. "How different," she wrote, "is the situation of the President from that of Washington? The Vice-President never combined with a party against him and his administration, he never intrigued with foreign ministers or foreign courts against his own government and country. He never made Bache his companion and counselor."[18] "Lies and falsehoods were continually circulated, and base and incendiary letters sent to the house" addressed to Adams. Some contained threats and Abigail was disturbed about his safety. "With this temper in a city like this," she noted, "materials for a mob might be brought together in ten minutes." Adams' proclamation of a day of prayer and fasting brought only ridicule from the Republicans: another bit of Federalist flimflam intended to delude the people.[19]

But John Adams was made for crisis. It toned up his system and invigorated him, made the blood cruise more warmly through his veins. Immediately after his special message of the nineteenth, a motion had been made and tabled to call on the executive for all the papers relating to the peace commission. As the Republican counterattack gathered momentum Adams began to wish he had risked the necks of the commissioners and placed the dispatches before Congress. He was not in a position, however, to assume the initiative; he could not send the papers to Congress without a demand for them. To do so would render him liable to the charge that he acted in a partisan spirit. Some Federalists, having gotten wind of the nature of the correspondence, were as anxious as the deluded Republicans to have them made public. Jonathan Mason, a Boston Federalist, wrote to Harrison Gray Otis urging their publication. "We wish much for the papers if they can with propriety be made public. The Jacobins want them. And in the name of God let them be gratified; it is not the first time they have wished for the means of their destruction."[20]

On the second of April the House voted to call for the papers. The shrewder Republican leaders watched uneasily as the members voted overwhelmingly to request the dispatches. Gallatin—"the sly, the artful, the insidious Gallatin," as Abigail called him—suspected a trap and refused to join in the call. Giles was overheard saying to friends, "You are doing wrong to call for those dispatches. They will injure us." There was an irony in the situation that did not escape the more observant Federalists. Gallatin and Giles had been so successful in persuading their fellow Republicans that the President had misrepresented the nature of the dispatches for partisan purposes that they were powerless to prevent the House action. A number of Federalists, led by Thomas Pinckney, joined in the call but even this failed to alert the main body of Republicans to the trap that they were so intent on rushing into. Jefferson simply ascribed the Federalist participation to Hamilton's jealousy of Adams. The New Yorker wished to discredit the President, Jefferson reasoned, and he was using Pinckney as his creature.[21]

Adams responded to the request of the House with alacrity and relief. Here was the "proof as strong as Holy Writ" that the Republicans demanded. He would have been less than human if he had not enjoyed the consternation of his enemies. It is not, perhaps, going too far to call it panic; certainly it was demoralization. "The Jacobins were confounded, and the trimmers dropt off from the party like windfalls from an apple tree in September," Fisher Ames wrote gleefully, employing a classic New England metaphor.[22]

The *Aurora*, which had been the most strident voice calling for publication of the dispatches, reversed itself abruptly and declared that since the negotiations had not been concluded it was wrong to publish the correspondence. It was a Federalist trick; a betrayal of the American people; an act of aggression against the French. The blame was Talleyrand's and he was a monarchist and a friend of Hamilton. So Bache collapsed into contradiction and irrelevance. In the House the Republicans tried to retrieve what they could from the debacle by voting not to publish the correspondence, but the Senate opened the door that the House had closed by ordering the printing of fifty thousand copies and their distribution about the country.

"The Jacobins in Senate and House were struck dumb," Abigail wrote her sister, "and opened not their mouths, not having their cue, not having received their lessons" from the emissaries of Talleyrand.[23] Jefferson belatedly decided that it was his "duty to be silent." "Citizen Nicholas, Farmer Giles, and the polite Mr. Livingston" were reported to have said that they were convinced of the President's genuine desire to accommodate American differences with France and, as though in confirmation, the first two abandoned their posts and departed for Virginia, leaving their distraught followers leaderless.

"The Jesuit Gallatin," Abigail wrote, "is as subtle and as artful and designing as ever, but meets with a more decided opposition, and the party, though many of them as wicked as ever, are much weakened by some whose consciences will not let them go all lengths with them [the radical Republicans]."[24]

The Vice-President was made of sterner stuff. While he admitted that the dispatches had "produced such a shock in the Republican mind as had never been seen since our independence," he attributed the shock to "the artful misrepresentations" of the commissioners themselves. The fault was Adams' for ever having made references to France in his Inaugural Address, which that country quite rightly resented. If the "insult from our executive should be . . . wiped away," the French might still be willing to negotiate in good faith. Far from the negotiation being at an end, the dispatches showed it was "in its commencement only." It was absurd to suppose that the Directory, made up of high-minded and magnanimous men, had lent itself to any scheme of bribery. They were "above suspicion."[25] By such reasoning did Jefferson comfort himself, confident that in the coming congressional elections the "Whigs"—that is to say, the Republicans—would gain enough new strength in the House and Senate to reverse the fatal policy of the administration.

The reports that came in from around the country suggested a very different conclusion. "The effect of the publication . . . on the people . . . has been prodigious," Theodore Sedgwick related to Rufus King. "The leaders of the opposition . . . were astonished and confounded at the profligacy of their beloved friends, the French." Everywhere the Federalists observed "the most magical effects" on public opinion.[26]

Philadelphia, not unnaturally, was the first to feel the consequences of the publication of the dispatches. "The public opinion," Abigail noted, "is changing here very fast, and the people begin to see who have been their firm unshaken friends, steady to their interests and defenders of their rights and liberties." The merchants of the city held a meeting and prepared a special letter of thanks to the President "for his firm and steady conduct," and the French cockade which had decorated many hats a few days before virtually disappeared. Those who still dared to wear them risked having them snatched from their hats by indignant citizens. Adams was specially pleased at the report of "the common people" remarking that if Jefferson "had been our President, and Madison and Burr our negotiators, we should all have been sold to the French."[27]

The letter of the merchants was followed by one from the Philadelphia grand jurors, pledging their support to the government and praising the President's firmness and moderation. In Congress the chastened members proceeded to pass legislation providing for the defense of the country "with a degree of spirit which has not before appeared." Adams was literally overwhelmed with work. A packet from Europe brought a flood of dispatches from Rufus King in England, from Murray, and from the commissioners in France; Adams sat at his desk until late at night reading and digesting their contents. In addition he had "officers to appoint, naval and military," and piles of "recommending letters to read, weigh, and examine."[28]

Bache's *Aurora* and the Boston *Chronicle* continued to pour forth their venom. A writer in the latter paper declared that the President and his eldest son were profiteering at the expense of the people. They had received eighty thousand dollars between them in a two-year period. Together they would ruin and impoverish the country. "Bache has the malice and falsehood of Satan, and his vile partner the *Chronicle* is equally as bad," Abigail wrote her sister. "An abused and insulted public cannot tolerate them much longer. In short they are so criminal that they ought to be presented by the grand jurors. . . . Perdition catch them!" she concluded. "We had as good have no Devil if he does not claim his own. Forgive me if I have been rash. My indignation is excited at these hypocrites."[29]

Abigail was especially incensed at Bache's description of the President as "old, querulous, bald, blind, crippled, toothless Adams." Thus had the bad children mocked Elijah and felt the Lord's wrath in consequence, she recalled hopefully.[30] Steel themselves as they might, John and Abigail still writhed under "the . . . wicked and base, violent and calumniating abuse" leveled by Bache at the President. There must be some defense against lies and billingsgate. Criticism of the government and its officers could be borne—indeed a free press was the support of free government—but what about falsehood and deliberate misrepresentation? What about treacherous loyalty to a foreign government which had insulted and degraded the United States? In a republic the people must have access to the truth if they were to act wisely. But suppose the very springs of public information were poisoned by blind and malevolent partisanship; suppose many newspapers were controlled by men who wished to destroy the government itself. Certainly a free people had the right to protect itself, to insist that there was a valid distinction between liberty and license, that the right of a free press carried with it a responsibility to truth and decency. "Nothing will have an effect until Congress pass a sedition bill," Abigail declared, "which I presume they will do before they rise. . . . The wrath of the public ought to fall upon [the Republican editors'] devoted heads." If they and their lies were not suppressed, "we shall come to a civil war," Abigail affirmed to her sister.[31]

Her indignation at Bache was increased when the *Aurora* published a letter from Talleyrand to the envoys, a copy of which had evidently been sent by the French minister, having reached him and already been published before the Secretary of State had received the official document. At least it had the virtue of demonstrating the close ties between the American Jacobins and the French government, but Abigail observed that "in any other country Bache and all his papers would have been seized." They should have been in the United States, "but Congress are dillydallying about passing a bill enabling the President to seize suspicious persons and their papers."[32]

Despite or because of such billingsgate, Bache's paper lost readers by the hundreds and it and Mathew Carey's paper tottered "for want of subscriptions." "If these papers fall," Jefferson wrote Madison, "republicanism will be entirely browbeaten." With passions boiling over, the Vice-President felt he kept himself "cool and clear of the contagion," although in consequence he found few people to talk to. The taxes needed to support an increased military and naval establishment were "sedatives" which would soon cool the ardor for war, he assured a friend.[33] He arranged to have speeches by Gallatin and Nicholas, attacking the efforts to "establish a great navy," published and widely circulated. He detected hopeful signs of open insurrection in Pennsylvania and of "inquietude" in New Hampshire and New York. When Adams appointed Rufus King to make a treaty with Russia and dispatched William Smith, the Maryland Federalist, to Constantinople to negotiate one with the Turks, Jefferson saw the appointments as provocations to the French. The President was simply trying to irritate the Directory into declaring war on the United States.

Addresses of support for Adams' policy swelled to a flood as the days passed—from Yorktown, from the Mayor, aldermen, and lawyers of the city of Philadelphia, from New York and Baltimore, and smaller communities in between. French tunes had been all the rage for many months. At the New Theater in Chestnut Street, "*Ça ira*," the marching song of the French Revolution, had pre-empted the field; but with the rise of anti-French feeling the cry arose for a patriotic American song. "Yankee Doodle" was too light and "The President's March," so called, had no words. Joseph Hopkinson, son of Adams' friend Francis Hopkinson, provided the missing lyrics and Abigail, learning that it was to be played at the New Theater, got Samuel Otis to take a box and went off incognito with the Otises to observe the popular reaction. After *The Italian Monk* was performed, the actor and singer, Gilbert Fox, appeared on the stage to sing Hopkinson's work, "accompanied by the full band and a grand chorus." It was a thrilling and dramatic moment for Abigail. "At every chorus," she wrote Mary Cranch, "the most unbounded applause ensued." The song was encored four times; "it was enough to stun one," she added. On the last rendition the whole audience broke forth in the chorus, clapping their hands so loudly that Abigail's head rang.[31] A week later Adams attended by popular request and an even more tumultuous scene took place. These were exciting occasions—the President and his lady felt sustained and fortified by the wild, unreserved acclaim. It strengthened them in their conviction that once the people understood the issues they would respond in the proper spirit.

Every day brought more addresses attesting to the loyalty of the signers. Five came from Philadelphia and its environs in a period of ten days. They came from dozens and then hundreds of small towns—Sharpsburg, Pottstown, Plymouth, Charleston, Quincy, Little Egg Harbor, Shippensburg; from militia companies, grand juries, colleges, even from groups of young men of military age. "They breathe one spirit, they speak one language—that of independent freemen—approving the measures of government and expressive of full confidence in the wisdom, virtue, and integrity of the Chief Magistrate," Abigail wrote. The students of Princeton, Harvard, and Dartmouth sent addresses. Those from Harvard offered "the unwasted and unimpaired energies of our youth to the services of our country. Our lives," they declared, "are our only property; and we were not the sons of those who sealed our liberties with their blood if we would not defend with these lives that soil which now affords a peaceful grave to the moldering bones of our forefathers."

From Dartmouth College, "seat of science in the northern region of an extensive republic," came "a tribute of duty and respect from us, a band of youth . . . and that you would be assured of our love, our attachment, our confidence in your administration and the legislative bodies. At your command, illustrious MAGISTRATE of a great PEOPLE, we will hasten to the standard of freemen and warriors."

Adams, amid his miltitudinous duties, could not forbear to answer the addresses. Indeed, he most cheerfully undertook the herculean task. He was deeply touched by these largely spontaneous expressions of support, and he was determined to seize the opportunity to deliver hundreds of little lectures or sermons on the responsibilities of the citizens of a republic. In the process he could not refrain from disparaging those Americans who, in his view, had placed devotion to a foreign nation above allegiance to their own country.

The addresses and their replies were published in newspapers throughout the country. "By this means," Abigail wrote, the President "has an opportunity of diffusing his own sentiments more extensively and probably where they will be more read and attended to than they would have been through any other channel."[35]

But the Republicans never forgave the President for what they considered to be reflections on their loyalty. Their feelings were well expressed by a writer who signed himself "Cato" and declared that future generations would find it difficult to believe that Americans had elected as their President "a man capable of using such terms of reproach, or of indulging feelings so apparently intemperate, so unbecoming to the station he is placed in." Some friend should bid him put up his pen, warning him that he had "already . . . lost the confidence, respect, and esteem of every enlightened, dispassionate mind in America."[36]

Even Hamilton thought some of the replies "intemperate and revolutionary." "It is not for us, particularly for the government," he wrote Wolcott, "to breathe an irregular or violent spirit. . . . There are limits which must not be passed, and from my knowledge of the ardor of the President's mind . . . I begin to be apprehensive that he may run into indiscretion. . . . Some hint must be given, for we must make no mistakes."[37] For the time the Republicans could only watch in furious silence or take cold comfort from a few strident Anti-Federalist journals like the *Aurora* and the *Argus* which continued to denounce the government.

In his responses to the student addresses Adams touched a different chord: the need of the Republic for the services of its youth. To the Dartmouth students he wrote: "You cannot all be soldiers. Society must be supplied with the ordinary professions and faculties in time of war as well as in peace. Those of you who feel an inclination to a life of danger and glory may find employment for all the activity and enterprise of your genius in due time. Let me entreat you, and all my other young friends in America, whether students or men of business, not to be dazzled by the splendor or intimidated by the horror of modern events. Remember that the Roman republic was revived in the fourteenth century; that Rienzi was as famous as the modern heroes; that Petrarch was his friend and admirer; that atheism and blasphemy were as prevalent and fashionable then as they are now, at least in Italy." The rising generation must renounce such corruptions or the Republic would not endure.

The President's reply to the address of the people of Quincy, wrote Mary Cranch, was "so affectionate and tender" that many people who heard the Reverend Mr. Whitman read it "in a most pathetic manner" after his sermon were moved to tears and Deacon Webb, the town's leading Republican, "absolutely turned pale."[38]

The most impressive address was that delivered by eleven hundred young men of Philadelphia who came to the President's mansion in a body, marching two by two, to deliver their declaration. A vast crowd packed Market Street as far as the eye could see to watch the procession; the windows of the houses nearby were filled with spectators and some bolder spirits perched on the rooftops. "In great order and decorum the young men with each a black cockade marched through the multitude and all of them entered the house preceded by their committee," Abigail reported. The President, dressed in his uniform, received them in the Levee Room, heard their address, and gave his answer. The delegation then withdrew and as they appeared in the doorway the crowd gave three cheers. From the President's mansion the crowd surged on to the State House yard where the address was read once more and Joseph Hopkinson's new song was sung. At twelve o'clock that night John and Abigail were awakened by a group of the young men, glowing with wine and patriotism, who serenaded them with "Hail, Columbia."[39]

May 9 was set aside by presidential proclamation for "Public Humiliation, Fasting, and Prayer Throughout the United States." On the heels of the announcement of the fast day came rumors of a French plot "to set fire to several different parts of [Philadelphia] . . . to massacre man, woman, and child." Adams was informed of the supposed plot by an anonymous letter writer; still another letter found in the street contained a similar warning.

In spite of the uneasiness produced by the rumors, May 9 was observed "with much solemnity." The churches and meeting-houses were filled and the sermons dwelt on the duties of loyal Americans and the horrors of French atheism. The only untoward incident took place in the State House yard in the afternoon when some thirty young Republicans with tricolored cockades in their hats tried to tear off the black cockades worn by the supporters of the government. There was a sharp scuffle which ended when one of the attackers was carried off to jail. The episode, mild in nature, was still enough to alarm the city so that the light horse were called out, a guard posted before the President's house, and the streets patrolled all night long.

ABIGAIL, of course, worried about her husband. She had never seen him look so pale. He lost weight and clearly needed "a ramble in the clear air of the country, and a new scene." But she dared not tell him so and she had to admit that she had rarely seen him in better spirits. His appetite was good and he slept "in general tolerably well."[1] (She spoke of him proudly as "made of the oak instead of the willow. He may be torn up by the roots, or break, but he will never bend."[2])

Her own health held up surprisingly well. It was true she was seldom free from what she called her "rheumatism." It "floated about," sometimes in her head, sometimes in her chest or stomach, and she combated it with six grains of powdered niter, six parts of tartar emetic, and six parts of a grain of calomel, taken three times a day. She was often ill a day or two at a time, but nothing "worth mentioning," as she wrote Mary Cranch, "when compared to the weeks of confinement I have experienced."[3]

Mary Cranch was Abigail's "almoner," distributing her little gifts and stipends to the needy and the ailing—a cord of wood to Phebe Fields, the Negro woman who had served her faithfully, two dollars a month to old Mrs. Baldwin, crippled with arthritis, oranges and biscuits to Polly Palmer to cheer her in a wasting illness, a bottle of madeira from the cask in the cellar for poor, senile Parson Wibird. "It is a part of religion as well as morality," she wrote her sister, "to do justly and to love mercy and a man cannot be an honest and zealous promoter of the principles of a true government without possessing that good will towards man which leads to the love of God and respect for the Deity." A proper appreciation of the rights and duties of citizens was a prelude to a respect for religion and its institutions.[4]

Quincy and the farm were seldom far from Abigail's thoughts. She wanted some of Mrs. Pope's delicious butter, worried about the cheese, and plotted with Dr. Tufts to have two upstairs rooms made into one large, spacious room which would hold all John's books "and be a pleasant room for the President to do business in." She meant to have it all done as a surprise for her husband before they returned to Quincy. Adams, barred from reading Mary's letters, asked plaintively, "How does the farm look? Oh, that I could see it and ramble over it. Does not Sister Cranch say a word about it?"[5]

At the end of May the new 44-gun frigate, the *United States*, the first fruit of Adams' new navy, set sail to protect American shipping, and on the twenty-seventh of May a bill empowering American war vessels to capture all French cruisers and privateers which were found in American waters was passed, fifty to forty, by the House. With such authority, the *Ganges* and the *Delaware* took their stations soon after the *United States* put to sea. Adams, having offered the newly created post of Secretary of the Navy to George Cabot, who turned it down, tried Benjamin Stoddert of Maryland, who also refused. Adams renewed his request to Stoddert, pointing out the importance of the office and the need of finding a qualified candidate. If Stoddert did not feel that he could make the financial sacrifice involved, perhaps he would take the office for a short time until the navy had been put on its feet. Everything had gone badly in the building and equipping of the vessels. They were months behind and a firm hand was needed to expedite things. As Abigail put it: "These frigates must be got to sea; they are an immense expense without any benefit. The business has lagged along very heavily."[6] Stoddert finally accepted and Adams, breathing a sigh of relief, shifted "the responsible and painful task" of completing the naval establishment to the Marylander's shoulders.

In Congress the bill providing for a navy of twelve vessels passed by a comfortable majority and without the crippling amendments that the Republicans tried to attach to it. But a provision to raise a regular army of twenty-four thousand men had rougher going. When it finally passed early in May, the regulars were reduced in number to ten thousand.

The House, as was its wont, proceeded more slowly than the Senate, and Abigail, blaming Gallatin for the delay, wrote: "If it was not for that specious, subtle, spare Cassius, that imported foreigner, the House of Reps would proceed with energy and act with decision, but he is continually throwing down *balls* to them; and though no golden ones, they obstruct their cause and prevent their reaching their goal."[7] In spite of Gallatin's delaying tactics, the House voted in June to stop all intercourse with France.

In addition to the measures of the government, there were heartening instances of local initiative. Newburyport had voted to raise money to build a 20-gun ship and loan it to the government, and New York and Philadelphia followed suit. "We shall have a navy spring up like the gourd of Jonah," Abigail wrote John Quincy. "This city . . . has become *one* military school, and every morning the sound of the drum and fife lead forth."

After the March 19 message, Adams had ceased to consider recommending a declaration of war and, from what he heard from John Quincy, he felt sure that the Directory had no intention of declaring war on the United States. With each passing week, however, the failure of the commissioners to return made him more uneasy. The Republicans of course made their continued absence conspicuous. If the negotiations had indeed been broken off, where were the negotiators? There were disturbing reports of a division among the three envoys—that Elbridge Gerry had taken a different line from his colleagues and was attempting to carry on private discussions with Talleyrand. Indirect word finally confirmed the rumor that Gerry had remained behind to carry on further negotiations with Talleyrand, and Murray expressed the fear that the French would convert Gerry "into an innocent baby-engine against the government."[8]

Adams was dismayed at the news. "That vile intriguer Talleyrand," Abigail wrote William Smith, "I fear has entrapped him whom I should have supposed the most wary; like the serpent, he has charmed him, and like him, he will destroy his prey." Poor Gerry, she added, "always had a wrong kink in his head," though his heart was honest enough.[9] Even John Quincy could not forbear to chide his father for sending "that *one* . . . your particular friend and acquaintance—the special object of *your* choice, against whom even the warmest promoters of the American cause objected at the time of his appointment."[10] Talleyrand, according to Murray, had prevailed on Gerry to stay after the departure of his colleagues by implying that for all three of the envoys to return would cause an immediate rupture of relations between France and the United States.[11]

Whatever the reason, the continued absence of the envoys and the rumors that Gerry was still negotiating encouraged the Republicans in their delaying tactics and weakened the resolution of the Federalists. Adams once more started to think in terms of a declaration of war. There were so many complications and inconveniences attendant upon trying to wage even a defensive war without a formal declaration that Adams felt himself hampered and frustrated at every turn. Moreover the popular repsonse to the XYZ affair inclined him to believe that the real resources of the country could only be marshaled by war. Perhaps it was a characteristic of a democratic republic that its citizens could not be brought to a high pitch of energy and resolution and imbued with a deep concern for their honor and liberties except by war or its imminent threat.

The President was strengthened in this feeling by a movement among the Republicans to create a volunteer militia force of their own. An aftermath of the address of the young men of Philadelphia had been the formation of a "volunteer corps" which took the name of Macpherson's

Blues and pledged itself to support the government against any foreign power. Egged on by the *Aurora,* an effort was made to recruit a unit to be called the Republican Blues, captained by Benjamin Bache's brother. Report had it that the scheme was hatched by Alexander James Dallas, Secretary of the state of Pennsylvania, and Benjamin Franklin Bache, with the counsel and assistance of Gallatin. Its effect would clearly be to create two armed factions within the city, one committed to Adams' administration, the other to the cause of France. Although Governor Thomas Mifflin had given assurances that he would not commission officers for the Republican Blues, his Jacobin principles made his promise suspect.

A declaration of war, by making such an act treachery, would nip a dangerous enterprise in the bud. Moreover Adams was under heavy pressure from many members of his own party to declare war. Stephen Higginson was sure that "nothing but an open war can save us, and the more inveterate and deadly it shall be, the better will be our chance for security in the future."[12] Fisher Ames held similar views: "Though I do not wish Congress to *declare* war, I long to see them wage it," he wrote Oliver Wolcott. He wanted the legislative branch to "go to every proper length . . . as no time seems to promise such success to rendering Jacobin members obnoxious before another election."[13]

George Cabot praised the President for having awakened the country "from the fatal stupor into which it had sunk. . . . All men whose opinions I know are unbounded in their applause of the manly, just, spirited, and instructive sentiments expressed by the President in his answers to the addresses. I am persuaded that the good effects of these open declarations cannot be overrated." Another high Federalist described the President as a modern-day Pericles: "It is said of Pericles," a friend wrote Wolcott, "that he frequently repeated to himself, 'Remember, Pericles, that you command free men.' A greater and better man than Pericles seems to decide and act under the spirit of similar reflection . . . he will not be disappointed in the honorable opinion formed of his countrymen."[14]

Such support of course could be counted on only as long as the President seemed to be taking a line of active opposition to France. With Gerry still in Paris and negotiations thus not clearly at an end, it was impossible for Adams to recommend a declaration of war to Congress.

June brought distressing family news. James Greenleaf, whose brother John was married to Lucy Cranch, Richard's and Mary's daughter, had failed spectacularly in his land speculations. Greenleaf had employed Billy Cranch, Lucy's brother, in his Washington venture which ended in disaster. Now, in a new wave of failures, Dr. Thomas Welsh, who had managed some of John Quincy's business, went under, taking a number of investors with him. Abigail's cousin, William Smith, was reported to have lost eighteen thousand dollars, and Abigail felt sure that the money

John Quincy had sent the doctor for investment had also been lost. In addition Charles Adams had apparently been involved with Dr. Welsh, and Abigail was concerned about the fate of considerable sums of money that John Quincy had sent his brother with instructions to invest it in real estate. "What a besom of destruction is this spirit of speculation," she exclaimed to her troubled sister.[15]

Of much greater distress to Abigail were the deaths of a number of her family and close friends. Two of the children of her profligate brother William died within a year of each other, apparently of pneumonia. Suky Warner, Dr. Tufts' stepdaughter by his second wife, died in the spring of 1798; Mrs. Norton Quincy, Abigail's aunt, was a victim of a violent fever; and her niece, Betsy Shaw, was carried off by tuberculosis. "The longer we live in the world," Abigail wrote her sister, "the more do troubles thicken upon us; yet we hug the fleeting shadow. . . . . My path to Massachusetts is spread with sorrow and covered with mourning," she lamented; but she was grateful for the blessings which remained and never for a moment "unmindful that I hold all by a frail tenure."[16]

Philadelphia was oppressively hot and John and Abigail longed for the ocean breezes of Quincy. The streets of the city stank with refuse and litter, fish offal, rotting vegetables, and animal excrement. The morning air was stagnant—not a leaf stirred or a breath of air; there was a plague of flies. "I get up and drop in my chair," Abigail wrote her sister. She and the President had started taking cold baths as a relief from the heat.[17] In some parts of the city the dreaded fever appeared. The Adams household was attacked by "complaints of the bowels" and sore throats. One ailment began with stiffness and pain in the neck and back part of the head, lasted for several days, and left the victims weak and shaky. Congress was impatient to adjourn but there was too much to be done and Adams could only comfort himself with Mary Cranch's description of clover and barley fields. "He most sincerely pines after them," Abigail wrote, "but he is tied to his table nine hours of the day. . . . Some forenoons he is called from his room twenty times in the course of it, to different persons, besides the hours devoted to the ministers of the different departments, the investigation necessary to be made of those persons who apply for offices or are recommended, the weighing the merits and pretensions of different candidates for the same office, etc., etc., etc." Fortunately his eyes, which had given him so much trouble, were "quite well," and he was able to read for hours without a strain.

On June 18, John Marshall arrived at Philadelphia from New York and the city turned out to welcome him with the greatest fanfare in its history. A fleet of carriages and hundreds of men on horseback with three corps of cavalry in full uniform rode out to meet him six miles from the city. When he reached the city limits the church bells were all rung and the citizens lined the streets, cheering wildly and waving handkerchiefs.

The editor of the *Aurora* had bitter reflections as he watched the exultant crowds hailing Marshall as a hero. "Many pensive and melancholy countenances," Bache noted, "gave the glare of parade a gloom much more suited to the occasion, and more in unison with the feelings of Americans. Well may they despond; for though the patriotic Gerry may succeed in settling the differences between the two countries, it is certain that his efforts can be of no avail when the late conduct of our administration and the unprecedented intemperance of our chief executive magistrate is known in Europe."[18] Jefferson, convinced that the administration would give a partisan and doctored account of the mission, swallowed his pride and went to see the man he hated, but Marshall was absent and when he returned he replied coldly and formally to the note that Jefferson had left.

Marshall's report to Adams and Pickering gave them a different perspective on the French position. The Virginian was confident that France did not want war with the United States but thought, rather, that she could bully America into a compliance with her wishes. Adams, who had been prepared to ask Congress for a declaration of war before it adjourned, now decided to hold off. It might be that France, once she saw that the government was not to be intimidated and that a great majority of the people supported the government, would adopt a more reasonable line.

The night before Marshall's departure for Virginia the Federalists gave a dinner for their hero "as evidence of their affection for his person and their gratified approbation of the patriotic firmness with which he sustained the dignity of his country during his important mission." The Speaker of the House, Jonathan Dayton, the Justices of the Supreme Court, the field officers of the army, and the Roman Catholic and Episcopal bishops, James Carroll and William White, along with most of the members of Congress, were at the long, richly set table. Sixteen toasts "were drank with unbounded plaudits" by an increasingly convivial company. The first was to "the United States—'free, sovereign, and independent!'"; the second to "the people and the government—'one and indivisible!'"; then to "the President—'some other hand must be found to sign the ignominious deed' that would surrender the sovereignty of his country!" So they proceeded—to General Washington, to General Pinckney, (Gerry was conspicuously omitted), to the army and navy, to the militia, the heroes of the Revolution, and finally, in words that were to echo through the country in a glorious cry of defiance, "Millions for defense but not a cent for tribute!"

Jefferson's departure for Monticello—that remarkable marriage of abstract proposition and practical ingenuity so expressive of its builder—was not merely coincidental with the arrival of Marshall in Philadelphia. Giles, Nicholas, and Clopton had preceded him. Parker and Evans had defected to the enemy. The Vice-President, in abandoning the field to the Federalists, simply underlined the extent of the Republican demoralization. From this point on it was merely a question of what legislation the Federalist majority agreed to pass.

The day before Marshall left Philadelphia, Adams sent Congress a letter from Gerry explaining the latter's conduct—"his intentions and prospects. . . . . I presume," Adams wrote, "that before this time he has received fresh instructions . . . and therefore the negotiation may be considered at an end. . . . I will never send another minister to France," he added, "without assurances that he will be received, respected, and honored as the representative of a great, free, powerful, and independent nation."

Washington had written Adams, inviting him and Abigail to pay a visit to Mount Vernon and congratulating him on his success in meeting the French menace. Adams replied warmly, thanking the General for his proffered hospitality but pleading the excuse of business. If America weathered the storm it would "depend upon Heaven, and very little on anything in my power," he wrote. He had not decided, he added, whether to call on the seasoned generals of the Revolution or "to appoint a younger set. . . . I must ask you sometimes for advice. We must have your name, if you will in any case permit us to use it. There will be more efficacy in it than in many an army."[19]

Adams had been considering for some time the problem of finding a commander-in-chief for the army. He was aware of Hamilton's ambitions and determined, if possible, to forestall them. Washington was the obvious choice, indeed it would be hard to avoid offering the position to the General even if Adams had wished to do so. On the other hand, to appoint Washington would be to risk having Hamilton come in as the actual commander with Washington simply a figurehead. Hamilton himself was well aware of the various possibilities. He and his supporters pushed for him to have supreme command, presumably on the ground that the General was too old for active duty. If Washington himself could be brought to that view, the way would be cleared for the New Yorker. Cautious feelers were dispatched to the General, and all possible pressure was brought to bear on Adams by Hamilton's adherents. But to Adams the New Yorker, able as he was, was dangerously ambitious. He suspected him of a Caesar complex, and Abigail spoke for her husband when she confided to William Smith: "that man . . . would become a second Buonaparty if he was possessed of equal power. . . . . You can hardly conceive," she added, "what a powerful interest is made for Hamilton."[20]

Adams' delay in appointing a commander-in-chief was based in part on his preference for the naval over the military arm. The more fervent Federalists, out of hatred for France, devotion to Great Britain, or the desire to maintain their party in power by rigorously suppressing the Republicans as the party of traitors, pressed strongly for war and above all for a large standing army. But for Adams sentiment and reason combined to make a strong navy the *desideratum*. A war between France and America must be fought primarily on the sea. A large regular army would be expensive and dangerous. At every point Adams was dilatory about mustering up the army but pressed the establishment of an adequate navy as vigorously as possible.

Finally, at the end of June, with Congress restive and straining to be off for home, Adams realized that he must act on the appointment of officers for the projected army. Without consulting his Cabinet, whom he knew to be Hamilton partisans, he nominated Washington "Lieutenant General and Commander-in-Chief of all the armies raised or to be raised in the United States." Then, as soon as the nomination was confirmed by the Senate, he sent James McHenry off to Mount Vernon to offer the command to Washington.

In his letter of instruction to McHenry, Adams quite naturally requested Washington's advice on the formation of a list of officers. "The names of Lincoln, Morgan, Knox, Hamilton, Gates, Pinckney, Lee, Carrington, Hand, Muhlenberg, Dayton, Burr, Brooks, Cobb, Smith," he wrote, "may be mentioned to him, and any others that occur to you; particularly, I wish to have his opinion of the man most suitable for Inspector General, and Adjutant General, and Quartermaster General. His opinion on all subjects must have great weight."

Before the Secretary's arrival Washington had already given much thought to the selection of his second in command. In order of seniority, three men ranked: Knox, Pinckney, Hamilton. Attached as he was to Knox personally, Washington did not wish to appoint him second in command. In the General's mind the choice lay between Hamilton and Pinckney. Pinckney was an able and experienced soldier and a leader of the South Carolina Federalists. To place Hamilton ahead of him might very well be to lose his services. While Washington agonized over the choice, Pickering bombarded him with letters pressing the claims of Hamilton and implying that the latter would not accept any appointment other than second in command. "There is one man," he wrote, "who will gladly be *your second* but who will not, I presume, because I think he ought not, be second to any other military commander in the United States. You too well know Colonel Hamilton's distinguished ability, energy, and fidelity to apply my remark to any other man." Washington, in reply, agreed that Hamilton's services should be secured at "*almost* any price."[21] The "*almost* any price" seemed to Hamilton and his adherents to suggest a dangerous indecision. It was McHenry's task to put the issue beyond doubt. He thus went to Mount Vernon as Hamilton's devoted lieutenant, intent on serving his interest as best he could. He was armed with a letter from Pickering insisting that Hamilton must be second in command; and Hamilton himself, arriving in Philadelphia the day before McHenry set off for Virginia, seconded Pickering's letter with one of his own.

McHenry, after conferring with the General, wrote Adams that Washington had consented to serve. He would, McHenry continued, obtain from the commander-in-chief "the names of the persons he considers the best qualified for his confidential officers"; then he added, apparently as an afterthought, "and without whom, I think, he would not serve." Some time afterward, when the phrase had become the hinge of a sharp controversy, Washington asserted that it was included at his request. Under McHenry's persuasion Washington agreed to the choice of Hamilton as second in command; but in the list of officers forwarded to the President the Major Generals were simply listed in the order Hamilton, Knox, Pinckney, and nothing was said specifically about precedence. Adams, sending the names on to the Senate for confirmation, took the position that the order was merely fortuitous and that the rank of the new Generals would be determined by the date of their former commissions. Here, for the moment at least, the matter rested.

Wᴵᴛʜ the Republicans in retreat, Congress passed a naturalization act on the eighteenth of June 1798, extending the residence period required for citizenship to fourteen years. A week later a law entitled "an act concerning aliens" was passed; and on July 14 a statute providing punishment for sedition. The three laws together were known as the Alien and Sedition Acts. By the terms of the Alien Act the President was empowered in war or at the threat of war to seize, secure, or remove from the country all resident aliens who were citizens of the enemy nation. The principal defect of the act was that it did not go into operation unless war was declared or there was imminent danger of invasion. Meanwhile the country might teem with agents of a foreign power bent on subverting the United States Government. Moreover only enemy aliens could be deported and the United States, the Federalists felt, suffered greatly from refugee Irish and English aliens who made up some of the most zealous Jacobins in Republican ranks. The treason and sedition bill, introduced by Senator James Lloyd of Maryland, was designed to make up the deficiencies of the alien bills. The sedition bill provided the penalty of a fine of not more than five thousand dollars and imprisonment for not more than five years for any persons, aliens or citizens, who should undertake to oppose or defeat the operation of any law of the United States, "or shall threaten any officer of the United States Government with any damage to his character, person, or property, or attempt to procure any insurrection, plot, or unlawful assembly or unlawful combination." Similar penalties were reserved for those found guilty "of printing, writing, or speaking in a scandalous or malicious way against the government of the United States, either house of Congress, or the President, with the purpose of bringing them into contempt, stirring up sedition, or aiding and abetting a foreign nation in hostile designs against the United States." Truth was admissible in defense and the duration of the act was limited to two years.

While Adams had no hand in framing the bill or inspiring its introduction into Congress, he favored its passage. Perhaps he would have had second thoughts if he could have foreseen the Pandora's box the act would open up and the cloud it would come to cast over his entire administration. But even with such prevision he would doubtless have supported its enactment. The United States was at war *de facto* if not *de jure*. The simplest right of a nation in peril had always been and would remain self-preservation. A self-preservation, certainly, that remained within the limits of the constitution and the inalienable rights of Americans secured to them by its first ten amendments.

As revamped by the more moderate Federalists in the House, the law required that malice and intent be proved and that the jury judge of law as well as fact. The bill, which passed the House by a narrow margin, was immediately attacked by the Republicans as an infringement of the freedom of the press and the aggressive prosecution of Republican editors soon gave color to their accusation.

The Federalists replied heatedly that there was no "right" to sedition and therefore no infringement of a right. Even before the bill was passed, Richard Peters, Justice of the United States District Court, had issued a warrant for the arrest of Bache on the charge of having libeled the President and the government. Bache had asserted that the correspondence of Elbridge Gerry, submitted by the President to Congress, had been forged or doctored to give support to the administration's partisan views. To Adams, who was pleased to hear of Bache's arrest, the editor's accusation was of a piece with the innumerable lies and frauds which the man had published in his paper for years. Freedom of the press was one thing; deliberate distortion and falsehood that confused and misled the people was another. He saw no contradiction between his avowal that "a free press maintains the majesty of the people" and his endorsement of the Sedition Act. Nothing indeed would destroy a free press more quickly than its corruption.

If orderly government, the sanctity of the laws, and the union of the states were the hazards, it was simply Republican fuzziness to confuse proper restraints with animus to freedom. Adams would refer those who cried loudest about the curtailment of the freedom of the press to Revolutionary France, where they could observe what happened to newspaper editors who presumed to question the wisdom of a Robespierre, a Danton, or a Directory. If the American Jacobins succeeded in their dream of reproducing the French system in America, the freedom of the press would be only one of a number of freedoms whose loss they would come to regret.

As the Federalists were quick to point out in its defense, the Sedition Act was far milder than the provisions on libel contained in the common law. These last did not require proof of intent to produce disaffection or insurrection, nor did they admit the truth as defense. The fact of publication was enough to incriminate. "It was no matter," James Bayard declared, "how wicked the motive of an author might be, provided his publication was true, nor was it material how groundless the publication was, provided the motive was honest. It was the combination of wickedness and falsehood alone that was punished." Oliver Ellsworth, Chief Justice of the Supreme Court, underlined Bayard's arguments. The Sedition Act, by permitting "the truth of a libel to be given in justification, causes that [act], in some cases, not to be an offense which was one before."[1] Surely it did not seem excessive to ask that attacks on the government in a time of *de facto* war remain roughly within the bounds of truth.

The Alien and Sedition Acts have been used so persistently to indict the Federalists and the Adams administration that an effort to put them in their proper perspective is warranted. The new nation was in its infancy. Not ten years old, its existence was threatened by faction and dissension within and by the world's most formidable military power from without. As many as thirty thousand Frenchmen were estimated to be in America, many of them active agents of the Revolution. Indeed, the mere threat of the alien bill so alarmed the numerous French agents in the country that, according to Jefferson, they chartered a ship to carry as many of them as could crowd aboard back to France, since it was clear at last that the American people did not intend to depose their President in order to placate the Directory. In addition thousands of Irishmen and Englishmen, exiles from their native lands, troublemakers and revolutionaries by temperament and often by vocation, were loose in the country. Some were sincere and idealistic individuals, others were just such "desperate and profligate men" as the Federalists charged them with being. The press, through which many of them made their voices heard, was perhaps the most violent and vituperative that was to appear in a century and a half of American history.

Under such circumstances it was hardly surprising that the government took steps to protect itself and, as it felt, the country, by requiring that newspaper editors should tell the truth. A hundred and fifty years later, after generations of orderly and stable government, the greatest nation in the world, victorious in a global conflict but terrified by strange fantasies, hounded and harassed a handful of domestic Communists. Long instructed in the ways of freedom, powerful and united, the United States gave way in the twentieth century to panic fears, enacting legislation in the name of "internal security" that later historians may well judge far more harshly than the Alien and Sedition Acts. Those unhappy measures were neither unconstitutional nor, strictly interpreted, inimical to the freedom of the press. They were simply impolitic. Since it was left to weak and fallible men to enforce them, they were on a distressing number of occasions not strictly interpreted. Moreover, if they had been, they would have been largely nugatory. They were used in many instances as political weapons by frightened or vindictive men, or by persons who believed quite deeply and sincerely that they were saving their country from destruction.

We can leave the Alien and Sedition Acts to the periodic indignation of righteous historians who will be happy if their own nation and their own times show no grosser offenses against human freedom. The Adams administration was not so easily rid of the acts. They became eventually a festering sore in the side of Federalism, a sore which it could not heal or hide.

Jefferson, of course, viewed the Alien and Sedition Acts as the first step toward tyranny, as "merely an experiment on the American mind to see how far it will bear an avowed violation of the constitution. If this goes down," he announced, "we shall immediately see attempted another act of Congress, declaring that the President shall continue in office during life." This would be followed by a law making the presidential succession hereditary and the Senate elected for life. This was supposedly the aim of Adams, while the Hamiltonians were "playing their game for the restoration of His Most Gracious Majesty, George III." Nor could Jefferson assure himself that all this would not come to pass, considering "the dupery of . . . our countrymen." The only hope was that the people would rebel against the taxes required to maintain a wartime military establishment. In the meantime the Republican strategy must be to hammer away at the Alien and Sedition Acts, to argue that they were "against the constitution and merely void," and to urge other states to make similar declarations.

It was only in the state governments that some hope remained. They were "the very *best in the world*, without exception or comparison," while the national government, in the course of nine brief years, had degenerated into a tyranny worse than that of England itself; had, as Jefferson put it, grown more "arbitrary" and "swallowed more of the public liberty" than the English King and Parliament.[2]

When James McHenry came back from Mount Vernon he brought with him a list of general officers drawn up by Washington. Adams, as a conciliatory gesture, had proposed the names of certain Republicans, Aaron Burr and Muhlenberg among them, but now the only names on the returned list were those of staunch Federalists. McHenry may have carried to Washington word of Pickering's opposition to appointing William Stephens Smith as Adjutant General and supplied the arguments which convinced the General that Smith was not a suitable person for the position. In any event Colonel Smith's name was not included in the list of officers recommended by Washington. Adams was determined, however, to appoint his son-in-law Adjutant General and he included Smith's name among the list of officers sent to the Senate for confirmation. Pickering thereupon undertook to block the appointment in the Senate on the grounds that the Colonel was a Republican at heart and that he had participated in shady land deals.

Three members of Congress, all good Federalists, called on Adams and asked him to withdraw the Colonel's name. When Adams inquired the reason he was told that Smith was notorious as "a speculator . . . a bankrupt, and an Anti-Federalist." Adams replied that there were others on the list of whom the same thing could be said and that Smith, as a brave and experienced soldier, was entitled to a command. He would not, the President declared flatly, withdraw the nomination. The next day the Senate struck out Smith's name. "There were many secret springs at work," Abigail observed. Included in the opposition to the Colonel were Hamiltonians who were resentful because the President had passed over their champion to nominate Washington as commander-in-chief, and others who simply wished to strike at the President. Although Abigail refused to believe that the Colonel had been active in the election of Robert Livingston, the rabid New York Republican, she remarked to William Smith that "much of the unpopularity in which he [the Colonel] is placed is owing to his own folly and indiscretion, which has ever been condemned by the President and by me as fully as by others."[3]

Before it adjourned Congress formally abrogated the French treaty of 1778, but it disappointed Adams by not going on to a declaration of war. "The people throughout the United States, with a few exceptions," Abigail wrote John Quincy, "would have wholeheartedly joined in the most decided declaration which Congress could have made . . . but the majority in Congress did not possess firmness and decision enough to boldly make it."[4] In a letter written to Mary Cranch, she noted that Congress was "going on very well at the eleventh hour. Though timid they will do all but one thing before they rise." That "one thing" was a declaration of war which would free the President's hands to act with far more boldness and efficiency.

As though to underline the war theme, word reached the capital on the ninth of July that the *Delaware*, Captain Decatur commanding, had seized a 12-gun French privateer. The French Captain had thought that the *Delaware* was a British warship and when he discovered that she sailed under the American flag he asked with some surprise if the United States was at war with France.

"No," Decatur was reported to have answered, "but your country is with mine."

"Oh, but I have a commission for what I do," the Frenchman replied.

"And so have I," Decatur rejoined. When the French Captain saw the American flag hoisted over his ship he poured forth a stream of Gallic curses. *"Mon Dieu,"* he exclaimed, "I had rather see my ship sunk, or blown up in the air!"[5]

The Adamses prepared to dash for Quincy as soon as Congress arose. Young William Shaw, Abigail's nephew, soon to be graduated from Harvard, would be the President's summer secretary. Abigail sent him a handsome striped waistcoat for commencement and instructions to arrange the "book room" at Quincy with "strict order and method." He must file every letter and paper alphabetically "in desks and places designed for them" with "every different department relative to War Office, Marine Office, Secretary and Treasury Office distinct, so that no trouble occurs in searching for papers."

She wrote also to Mary Cranch asking her to buy tea, sugar, hard bread, coffee, brandy, nutmegs, cinnamon, mustard, pepper, cloves, bed ticking and beds for "four menservants," teapots "and a coffeepot or two, some teaspoons for the kitchen . . . yellow dishes and plates . . . knives and forks, half dozen pounds of spermaceti candles, flask of sweet oil."[6]

Scheme as they might, the President and his wife could not avoid ceremony and parade on their trip north. At every point along the way enthusiastic crowds cheered them. There were dinners and addresses and replies by the President. The weather turned hot and Abigail was exhausted and ill by the time the entourage reached Quincy. Even with Louisa's patient care she grew worse rather than better until her life seemed in danger. A small corps of doctors, summoned by Adams from Boston to attend her, confessed themselves at the end of their resources; emetics, bleedings, purges—nothing seemed to do any good: Abigail was desperately ill from a combination of diarrhea, "intermitting fever," and diabetes. The house was hushed and strained. The servants tiptoed about and John, miserable and distraught, neglected the affairs of state to hover by her bedside.

By the end of September, Abigail, though very weak, seemed out of danger, and Adams gave more time to the various details of administration that crowded in upon him. Of all the problems that beset him, that of the ranking of the Major Generals proved to be the most persistent and troublesome. McHenry had written a long, tedious letter about the difficulties of raising twelve regiments of infantry, listing dozens of officers who had been recommended for commands. He wished also to have authority to call on Knox and Hamilton to take charge "of particular branches of the service." Indeed, the Inspector General had already furnished "a system of tactics and discipline." Adams answered, authorizing a secretary and aides for Washington, but objecting to calling Hamilton and Knox into service until the question of rank had been settled. Adams had learned from Knox that the latter would not serve in a position subordinate to Hamilton. He had outranked Hamilton in the Revolution, and as a distinguished senior officer he did not mean to be superseded. "In my opinion, as the matter now stands," Adams wrote, "General Knox is legally entitled to rank next to General Washington, and no other arrangement will give satisfaction." Pinckney must also, in consequence, rank before Hamilton, the President added. If Washington would consent to the ranking Knox, Pinckney, Hamilton, the three officers might be called into the service at once. Otherwise there must be "long delay and much confusion."[7]

McHenry was alarmed at Adams' reply. The order of ranking, he pointed out, had "proceeded originally and exclusively from General Washington." McHenry protested (perhaps too much) that he had had "no agency direct or indirect . . . in deciding his mind." He neglected to mention, of course, that he had carried to Mount Vernon letters from both Pickering and Hamilton which constituted the strongest kind of pressure on the General. McHenry's solution was to sound out Knox about accepting a rank subordinate to Hamilton.[8]

Adams' answer to McHenry's letter was prickly and intractable. He would gladly resign the office of President to Washington but he had never suggested that while he held the office himself and was responsible for it the General should make his decisions. "He has always said in all his letters," he added, "that these points must ultimately depend upon the President." It was Adams' decision, ultimately, how the generals should be ranked and he wished them in the order Knox, Pinckney, and Hamilton. "There has been too much intrigue in this business," he declared, "both with General Washington and me. If I shall ultimately be the dupe of it, I am much mistaken in myself."[9]

McHenry professed to be much wounded at Adams' reference to "intrigues." It was, he declared piously, quite alien to his nature to do anything in secret and if Adams had him in mind he would "immediately retire."[10] Adams answered that as far as he knew the Secretary's conduct toward him had been "candid." "I have suspected however," he added, "that extraordinary pains were taken with you to impress upon your mind that the public opinion, and the unanimous wish of the Federalists, was that General Hamilton might be first and even commander-in-chief; that you might express this opinion to General Washington more forcibly than I should have done and that this determined him to make the arrangement as he did."[11] McHenry can hardly have failed to wince at the accuracy of the President's conjecture, but he satisfied himself with once more protesting his innocence.

While McHenry and Adams exchanged letters, the Hamiltonians, alerted by the Secretary of War, were busy behind the scenes. The President must be made to reverse his decision and Washington must be the instrument for bringing this about. Oliver Wolcott entered the controversy with a long letter to Adams arguing that perfect confidence must exist between the President and the commander-in-chief. Washington wished Hamilton to be second in command, Congress had assumed that from the order of the listing when the generals were nominated, and the public expected it.[12] George Cabot wrote supporting Hamilton in the strongest terms, stating that General Knox had been put up to refusing to serve under Hamilton by General Benjamin Lincoln and others who were opposed to the government.[13]

The fact was that the question reached far beyond a mere matter of precedence. With a great popular following, Adams found himself in the curious position of having his party's leadership defer to a man not even in the administration. To have his own administrative officers and the Federalist members of Congress looking to Hamilton for directions was galling enough. With Hamilton second in command to Washington and thus *de facto* commander of the army, Adams would be even more at the mercy of this ambitious intriguer. With Abigail's illness constantly on his mind, he felt hardly able to cope with the problem. Moreover, the longer the whole matter was delayed, the slower would be the recruitment and training of an army. Without an army to command, neither Washington nor Hamilton would present any problem. He wrote rather plaintively to Wolcott that Abigail's "dangerous sickness" had thrown his mind into such "a state of depression, agitation, and anxiety" that he felt unable to enter into a contention over the various arguments raised by the Secretary.

It was all very well to make a great point over the need for harmony between the President and the commander-in-chief; but the real issue, he continued bitterly, lay in "whether such jealousy, rivalry, and animosity will not be produced by the conflicting passions of powerful individuals as no authority in this country can possibly compose. . . . We have already on the list Pompey, Caesar, and Anthony." Adams, not aware of the letter from Washington, denied emphatically that it was the General's wish that Hamilton should be second in command. The General had certainly never indicated such an intention to him.

In a letter dated September 21, McHenry quoted Washington's reply to the news that Adams wished Hamilton to be ranked third. "I can perceive pretty clearly," the General wrote, "that the matter is or very soon will be brought to the alternative of submitting to the President's forgetfulness of what I considered a compact or a condition of acceptance of the appointment . . . or to return him my commission. . . . You will recollect too that, my acceptance being conditional, I requested you to take the commission back, that it might be restored or annulled according to the President's determination to accept or reject the terms on which I had offered to serve."[14]

Before Adams sent his reply to Wolcott a letter from Washington himself dispelled any illusion about the General's wishes. It was an Olympian rebuke to Adams for having appointed an Adjutant General without consultation with Washington after having agreed to make no appointments to the general staff without the General's concurrence. The loss of Hamilton, who would not serve except in the second place, would, in Washington's view, be "irrepairable."[15]

The letters were a blow to Adams, for he realized that in a contest with Washington the General held all the cards. If he stood firm and the General resigned over the issue of his second in command being Hamilton, the Federalists would be down around his ears in an angry swarm. Moreover he would lose much of his popular support in the country at large. He thus replied to the General's indignant letter by conceding that Washington could determine the order of rank. He would, moreover, consult with him in the selection of an Adjutant General. It was a bitter pill but Adams had no other choice than to swallow it.[16] The commissions went out with Hamilton first and Knox second. Knox promptly refused his, and Pinckney succeeded to second place. That much was accomplished. But Adams, as a result, was even less eager to push the mustering of the army. His feelings were suggested by his response to McHenry's complaint that the recruiting of the army was proceeding too slowly and that in consequence "the ardor of the country may soon subside to a temperature unfavorable to the attainment of soldiers."[17] "Regiments," Adams replied sharply, "are costly articles everywhere, and more so in this country than any other under the sun. If this nation sees a great army to maintain without an enemy to fight," he added, "there may arise an enthusiasm that seems to be little foreseen. At present there is no more prospect of seeing a French army here than there is in Heaven." In other words, a large and expensive army might well produce a reaction against the administration and the Federalists which would unseat them.[18]

Although bothered by his defeat on the issue of the major generals, Adams began to feel a cautious optimism at the news from abroad. Through the efforts of Talleyrand, the Directory on July 30 had revoked its decree authorizing depredations against American commerce. Victor Du Pont, whom Adams had refused to recognize as French consul general to succeed Letombe, had talked to Jefferson before his return to France and informed Talleyrand upon his arrival in Paris that American sentiment had swung sharply away from France in consequence of the XYZ affair and the orders in council. Talleyrand in turn warned the Directory that for France to go to war with the United States would be playing directly into the hands of the English. The Directory, realizing that its policy of threat and intimidation had failed, made its first gesture of conciliation with the revocation of the obnoxious orders. Adams was encouraged by this indication, small as it was, that his policy of firmness had succeeded and that France was coming to its senses. Richard Codman, a Boston merchant living in Paris, confirmed the softening attitude of the Directory. But most persuasive of all, Murray and John Quincy, maintaining the closest liaison with each other and writing, in addition to their official dispatches, directly to the President himself, testified to the changed mood of the Directory. Nothing, John Quincy insisted, should be left undone to avoid open war with France. The son's advice weighed heavily with his father, who credited him, quite rightly, with superior judgment in foreign affairs.

Moreover Adams was well aware, especially since Hamilton had won his fight to be second in command, that war or even the continuance of a state of hostility could only play into the hands of Hamilton and the faction that surrounded him. These men, with their implacable animosity to France and to the Republicans, were dangerous and must be kept in check. In addition Elbridge Gerry, returning home under a cloud, faced Adams with considerable courage and in seeking to exculpate himself helped to persuade the President of the French desire for peace. Adams' willingness to give Gerry an audience alarmed the Boston Federalists. Rather than being, as Stephen Higginson expressed it, "pushed into the shade with a strong arm immediately on his arrival," Gerry had gained the President's attention.[19]

Sewall, Higginson, and Cabot met with Harrison Gray Otis to discuss what could be done to forestall Gerry's visits to the President. It was decided that one of their company must travel out to Quincy to inform Adams that his "frankness" in receiving his old friend was causing alarm in Federalist ranks. It could not be Sewall because Adams was well aware of his hatred for Gerry. Cabot had also spoken so bitterly of the dilatory commissioner that he had disqualified himself for the mission. It thus fell to Otis to undertake the awkward mission. Adams heard him out politely enough but made it clear he thought it a presumptuous interference in his own affairs.

Cabot was beside himself at the President's obvious determination to be independent of the counsel of his party leaders. He clearly needed a keeper. Reporting to Wolcott on Otis' mission, Cabot burst out, "But, my dear sir, must there not be something more done? Must it not become a maxim, never to be violated, that the President shall always be accompanied by those whom he has selected to assist him in carrying on the executive government?" Cabot seemed inclined to treat the President like a child or a convict. If the President took time off for relaxation, care must be taken to see that he "does no business and gives no opinions." Otherwise there can be "no order and consistency" in Federalist affairs. The President would act an independent part and leave the party to shift for itself.[20]

Adams was distressed at the Secretary of the Treasury's account of the effects of the fever in Philadelphia. Fifteen hundred of the city's poor were camped on the common and fifty orphans whose parents had died in the plague had been taken in by the managers of the almshouses. John Ward Fenno, the Federalist newspaper editor, was dead and the disorder had appeared among the soldiers at Fort Mifflin.[21] Adams sent five hundred dollars to be distributed anonymously among the neediest cases.

To the requests of his Secretaries that he hurry to Philadelphia, Adams answered that his wife's health was still so uncertain that he could not bring himself to leave her until the last possible moment. "The last has been the most gloomy summer of my life," he wrote, "and the prospect of a winter is more dismal still."[22] Even so he was determined to be at the opening of Congress "or give up." Before he set out for Philadelphia he inquired of his Cabinet officers what he should include in his second annual message to Congress. Again one of his queries was "whether it will be expedient for the President to recommend to the consideration of Congress a declaration of war against France? . . . Another inquiry is, whether any further proposals of negotiation can be made with safety? and whether there will be any use or advantage, in Europe or America, by uniting minds more in our favor, by any such measure?" And if further negotiations seemed desirable, who should be sent: Patrick Henry, Judge Patterson of New Jersey, Senator Ross of Pennsylvania, Bayard of Delaware, Harper, or someone already in Europe such as Rufus King or Murray?[23]

The President's letter, posing the question of renewed negotiation, was received by the Secretaries with some consternation. A council was held which included Hamilton and several of the general officers, and Wolcott drafted a reply at Hamilton's instance. After reviewing the state of the undeclared war with France and its disadvantages and advantages, the Secretary expressed his view that a declaration of war was "inexpedient and ought not to be recommended." The government should continue on its present course and above all prevent the opposition from securing a "rallying point." Sending another minister "to make a new attempt at negotiation would be an act of humiliation to which the United States ought not to submit without extreme necessity; no such necessity exists." The Hamiltonians were determined above all else to prevent Adams from taking such a step. It seemed to them essential to keep the country on a war footing. Overtures of peace would be fatal to their policy.

EARLY in November, Adams set out with a heavy heart for Philadelphia. Abigail was much better but still far from being well enough to think of accompanying him. The faithful and patient Louisa went with him to act as his hostess and he also took William Shaw, Eliza Peabody's son, as his secretary. The trip was as always a refreshment to Adams. Although he was in constant pain from infected teeth—having lost several of his few remaining ones during the summer—and anxious about Abigail's condition, his spirits rose remarkably. The day-to-day account of his journey that he sent Abigail was quite jaunty. "We watered at Watertown," he noted. He missed his granddaughter, "the sprightly, charming Caroline," who had been such a delight to him at Quincy, but William Shaw was "very good, attentive, and obliging." At Marlborough they found a good inn before dark and were "very comfortable by a good fire, with good tea and brown toast. If I had less anxiety about your health," he wrote, "I should have more about public affairs, I suppose." In a curious way, his distress over Abigail's protracted illness—she had been in bed for eleven weeks—had given him a new perspective on the crisis that faced the country. His partisan feelings were dampened by his overriding concern for the person who was dearer to him than life. The clamors of party and faction, the bitter contentions of ambitious men, seemed suddenly small and remote beside the fear that haunted him, sleeping or waking, that troubled his dreams and distracted him as he sat at his desk trying to give his attention to affairs of state. To have been out of the capital, away from the cruel battering of the Republican press, muffled now to be sure, away from his Secretaries, who concerted their efforts to play upon his prejudices and lead him along the path that their master, Hamilton, had laid out for him to tread, this feeling of detachment had prepared him to act a resolute and independent part, and it had helped him to place himself firmly above the leadership of his party. George Cabot's anxieties were entirely justified. Adams had left Philadelphia in July regretting only that Congress had not declared war on France before its adjournment. He was returning in November, some three months later, in quite a different frame of mind. His commitment had always been to peace. But peace, he thought, could not be achieved by weakness and submission. Edmund Burke had put it well and wisely: "A great state is too much to be envied, too much dreaded, to find safety in humiliation. To be secure, it must be respected. Power and eminence and consideration are things not to be begged. They must be commanded and they who supplicate mercy from others can never hope for justice through themselves. . . . Often has a man lost his all because he would not submit to hazard all in defending it."

When Adams came upon these words of Burke's they had marvelously expressed his own views. This was his policy and it must be America's. Like a schoolmaster teaching a difficult lesson to a recalcitrant and obtuse student, he had labored long and late to drive the point home. Passionate as he was, he had almost succumbed to his own truth. That is to say, the stubborn resistance of others to his truth had tempted him to fanaticism. He had very nearly fallen victim to that political vice which he deplored—inveteracy, the unwavering devotion to a policy which, however necessary and right at the time of its initiation, may, if persisted in too long, become dangerous and destructive. The interval of suffering and anxiety, therefore, had been of much service to Adams and consequently to his country. There certainly had been more direct and practical considerations—his concern about Hamilton's bid for power and his defeat on the issue of the New Yorker's rank in the army, the revocation of the most offensive of the Directory's edicts against American commerce, the letters of Codman and John Quincy and Murray, the talks with Gerry, his isolation, which Cabot so deplored, from the most extreme and indefatigible Federalists. But these were all things that inveteracy might have blinded him to as it blinded so many others. Casting off inveteracy, he was able to see better and to judge more wisely.

So he went back into the den of lions and tigers with a curious lightness of heart. "Children, you know," he wrote Abigail, "when they are toothing, are somewhat fretful, and the toothing of the second childhood is equally apt to make peevish. But though my mouth is so sore as to give me a sore throat and an headache, I am neither fretful or peevish." The horses went "like birds." The frosty roads rang with their hoofs and the iron song of the carriage wheels. Clinken, he observed, full of a summer's grazing on sweet grass, "capers and rears and kicks and goes sideways enough to make Louisa fly out of the window." But he and William Shaw laughed at poor Louisa's alarm. The teeth bedeviled him. They were a scourge. "I ride and live in pain," he wrote, and would gladly give his few remaining teeth "to know whether you slept last night or will sleep tonight. . . . I want your society, advice, and assistance, however, so much that I should be willing to ride fifteen miles a day to obtain it."[1]

At Stratford, Connecticut, not far from Eastchester, Adams and William Shaw had just settled down in their bedchamber with tea and oysters when Nabby and Caroline "bolted in upon us." There was a happy reunion with his daughter and his "sprightly, charming Caroline." The girl and her mother were flushed and merry with the triumph of their surprise and for a time presidential dignity, the oysters, and tea were forgotten in a happy romp with the rosy, laughing child.[2]

At New York, Adams had an awkward meeting with Charles. Abigail had pressed him to try to get from Charles some statement as to what he had done with the money John Quincy had sent him to invest, but Adams could get no coherent story from his son. Charles had deteriorated alarmingly in appearance and manner and was vague and distracted. It was plain, as much from what Sally Adams did not say as from what she did, that her husband was in a dangerous emotional state. He was often away from home and frequently returned drunk and ill. His practice had been neglected and his creditors were beginning to harass him. The root of it all was his disastrous speculation, which had ruined thousands like him. His special agony was the betrayal of his brother, who had trusted him, and the distress of his parents. All his father's long letters of exhortation and encouragement had gone for nothing, all the years of patient work and study when he had seemed to throw off the instability that had first appeared at Harvard, all these had borne finally this bitter fruit. Like a character in a Greek tragedy, his fatal flaw had brought him down. Adams left him with a heavy heart.

The President arrived in Philadelphia on the twenty-fifth of November and found "all well and in good order." He was amused by Governor Mifflin's "terrible lamentations" that he had not heard of the President's coming in time "to draw out his horse and foot" soldiers for a grand parade. Briesler welcomed his master warmly but grumbled that in Abigail's absence he had no incentive to produce good dinners because "gentlemen never give any credit."[3]

There was a mountain of work to be done. Adams conferred with his Secretaries and reviewed their recommendations for his address at the convening of Congress, little more than a week away. McHenry recommended an immediate declaration of war against France as "indispensable" but then hedged the suggestion. Desirable as a declaration of war would be, the President was "engaged in a game of skill with the Directory" and with the Jacobin faction in his own country, and these opponents of the administration should not see "the cards we play with." It would thus be better for Congress to take the initiative in declaring war. The President's speech should simply provide the materials for such an action by Congress. To this end the President should make clear beyond question that he had no intention of sending another minister to

France until definite assurances had been given by the Directory that he would be received.

There was evidence that the Hamiltonians had for some time been concerned with a plan to seize the Louisiana territory from Spain and to this end had entered into correspondence with Francisco Miranda, a man once in the pay of the British Foreign Office. Adams had been informed of the scheme but had given it no encouragement. McHenry urged him, in his address to Congress, to request "such full powers . . . as would enable him to take effectual measures to counteract or render the designs of France to possess themselves of Louisiana and the Floridas as little injurious as possible to the United States"; or in other words to advance the plan of Miranda and those who had associated themselves with it.

Stoddert, with whom Adams discussed the content of the address at some length, felt also that a recommendation for a declaration of war was desirable in theory, but the danger was that Congress would refuse, that confusion and renewed rancor would result, and that in consequence the administration would lose prestige and weaken its authority. Pickering likewise doubted the willingness of Congress to declare war and gave it as his opinion that "the people of the United States are not yet convinced of the necessity of war." More time was needed to bring the pot to a boil.

Wolcott's reply to Adams' inquiry was the product of what Jefferson characterized as a military conclave. Hamilton's hand had guided it, and as a result it was the ablest and most comprehensive of the responses submitted to the President. Adams indeed took it as the basis of his own message, adding a paragraph commending the nation for the "spirit which has arisen in our country against the menaces and aggression of a foreign nation. A manly sense of national honor, dignity, and independence has appeared which, if encouraged and invigorated by every branch of government, will enable us to view undismayed the enterprises of any foreign power and become the sure foundation of national honor and prosperity." After expressing the desire of the President, "the other branches of the government, and of the people of the United States" for peace, Adams added, "I deem it a duty deliberately and solemnly to declare my opinion that whether we negotiate with [France] or not, vigorous preparations for war will be alike indispensable. These alone will give to us an equal treaty and ensure its observance."

Perhaps the President's most significant change in the Wolcott draft was his replacement of the sentence, "the sending [of] another minister to make a new attempt at negotiation would be an act of humiliation to which the United States ought not to submit without extreme necessity," with the statement that "to send another minister without more determinate assurances that he would be received would be an act of humiliation." The modification was slight but significant. It served warning to the Hamiltonians that despite their united front Adams had by no means closed the door to renewed negotiations when he decided that the time was ripe.

Meanwhile things went well enough for the moment. Adams had the Secretaries and the general officers to dine, and all was agreeableness and good humor. He missed "the precious and invaluable" time which he had spent every day with Abigail the previous winter and longed to have her with him, but she must not again endanger "a life that is dear to me beyond all expression."[4]

Billy Shaw, despite an immature hand and a certain youthful bumptiousness, made himself very helpful to the President. At first he found it difficult to sleep amid the noises of the city, "the watchman crying the hours of the night—the oysterman crying oysters, and the teams and horses" directly under his window kept him awake for hours on end, but he soon became accustomed to the racket and slept like a city man born and bred.

On the eighth of December, Adams delivered his second annual message to Congress before a crowded house. Despite the loss of his teeth, he spoke so clearly, Shaw reported, "that there was [not] a single word but what was distinctly heard."[5] Having made his point that a stout defense was the only realistic basis for negotiation and reviewed the measures that must be taken to make and keep the country strong, Adams informed Congress that Spain had at last begun the evacuation of the border posts; the boundary between the United States and Canada had been settled by the joint commission at the river Scoodiac; the commission to adjudicate the claims against Britain for the capture and condemnation of American vessels was proceeding toward a conclusion of its deliberations; and a similar commission to settle claims against Spain for the capture of American ships had made notable progress.

The response of the House to the President's address was prompt and firm and passed without opposition. It contained a cautionary note injected by the Federalist leaders. The President should not indeed "submit to the humiliation of sending another minister to France without assurances sufficiently determinate that he will be duly accredited." This was notably stronger than the President's own phrasing, and the reply of the Senate was more emphatic still. If the peaceful professions of France were carried by individuals rather than through approved diplomatic channels, they should be rebuffed as being intended to "separate the people from their government" and produce confusion and disorder. The reference was to the private diplomacy of a Dr. George Logan. Logan, armed with credentials from Jefferson, had secured an audience with Merlin, the President of the Directory, who had assured him of France's pacific intentions.

The Senate's reference to Logan's mission prompted Adams in reply to refer to the "temerity and impertinence of individuals affecting to interfere in public affairs between France and the United States, whether by their secret correspondence or otherwise," and to ask whether such conduct ought not to be inquired into and corrected.

The speech was generally well received. If the Federalists felt any uneasiness they suppressed it and satisfied themselves with rather pointedly reinforcing the President's statements about negotiation. Even Jefferson expressed surprise at Adams' address, "so unlike himself in point of moderation,"[6] and professed to see dark designs behind it. The President, he suggested, was deliberately keeping back communications from Murray which would show the conciliatory spirit of the French.

The House of Representatives, once it had replied to the President's address, plunged into a nerve-racking debate over the Alien and Sedition Acts. The Republicans were determined to get all the mileage they could out of the issue, and the Federalists listened glumly as they rang all the changes of tyranny, oppression, and a free press. Jefferson remained aloof in Monticello. "The dangerous Vice is not arrived," Adams wrote his wife, adding, "It is thought the v.p. stays away from very bad motives."[7] Some diversion was supplied by five "large, tall . . . well-built" Indians who came for a ceremonial visit with their Great White Father. Adams listened patiently through a lengthy and eloquent harangue—"Brother, although we are in your house and sheltered from the cold winds, still we are in the presence of God—from His view we cannot hide ourselves, nor can we deceive Him," and a great deal more. After the speech they presented the President with "a great quantity of wampum," smoked the pipe of peace, drank some wine, and "marched off appearing to be well pleased."[8]

Although things were for the moment calm enough, Adams was restless and uneasy. Submerged with work, he pined for Abigail and complained of the "thousands of sea letters, Mediterranean passes, and commissions, and patents" that he must read and sign. He had to live with "no company—idle, unmeaning ceremony, follies, extravagance, shiftlessness," his health sinking under his "troubles and fatigues." Prominent among the latter was the fact that his "relations have no scruple to put my feelings to the trial. Many of them are soliciting places." Nabby and the Colonel and Charles were constantly on his mind. "My daughter and one son will bring down my gray hairs with sorrow to the grave," he wrote Abigail, "if I don't arouse all my philosophy. . . . Unfortunate daughter! Unhappy child!" One of his bad colds served to increase his depression.[9] He had decided reluctantly to recommend his son-in-law for a commission as commander of one of the provisional regiments that was being formed. He informed Pickering of his intention and sent the nomination with others to the Senate for confirmation. Pickering once more took it upon himself to stir up opposition in the Senate, but this time the Senate accepted Smith's defense against the charges leveled at him and approved his appointment to a rank lower than that which he had held fifteen years earlier.

Adams wrote Smith, informing him that he had nominated him for a lieutenant colonelcy and adding bitterly: "Upon this occasion I must be plain with you. Your pride and ostentation, which I myself have seen with inexpressible grief for many years, have excited among your neighbors so much envy and resentment that, if they have to allege against you any instance of dishonorable and dishonest conduct, as it is pretended they have, you may depend upon it, it will never be forgiven or forgotten. . . . It is a great misfortune to the public that the office I hold should be disgraced by a nomination of my son-in-law, which the Senate of the United States think themselves obliged to negative."[10] "All the actions of my life and all the conduct of my children," he exploded to Abigail, "have not yet disgraced me so much as this man. His pay will not feed his dogs; and his dogs must be fed if his children starve. What a folly!"[11]

He had hoped that Smith would refuse the command but, John wrote Abigail, "his pride is so humbled he has accepted." If he was guilty of the charges against him he ought not to command a regiment; if he was not, he deserved a brigade "and more. . . . . My grandchildren," he added, ". . . are destined to be the poorest objects in the community." Then in final bitterness, thinking of Charles: "My children give me more pain than all my enemies."[12] It was one of the many ironies of life that the half-demented Royall Tyler, from whom Nabby had so narrowly escaped, had gone on to become a famous playwright, the author of the first important American drama, *The Contrast*, and later the popular and respected Chief Justice of the Supreme Court of Vermont, while his successful rival had turned out a failure and a wastrel.

It was all part of the cross Adams must bear. He felt the familiar twinge of self-pity. "I am old, old, very old," he wrote Abigail (he had just turned sixty-four), "and I shall never be very well—certainly [not] while in this office, for the drudgery is too much for my years and strength." He was troubled, moreover, by an eruption on his hands which made them sore and scaly. But all his complaints and dissatisfactions—the fact that life had no savor—could be traced to one cause: "I want my talkative wife," he teased. But she would never live, he feared, to talk beyond Worcester or Springfield, and if she arrived safe and sound in Philadelphia she would soon be so busy "scribbling" letters to her friends in Massachusetts that he would hardly get her to talk in any event.[13]

Abigail, convalescing slowly, began to "feel like a housewife again," and although Mary scolded her for going into "your kitchen to make puddens and pies too soon," she felt her strength and energy flowing back. She wrapped herself in a warm cloak "and ventured to meeting half a day. . . . . Tell me," she wrote wistfully, "who inquires after me as if they cared for me." She was flattered by regrets expressed in Porcupine's paper and in a Federalist journal in New York at her absence. "I suppose they think you will want somebody to keep you warm." The snow was piled about Quincy in drifts four or five feet deep and the hired hands were kept busy shoveling.

Thanksgiving Day was a lonely one in Quincy. There was no mince pie or plum pudding and there were no children or grandchildren to brighten the house. But Abigail, worried as she was about Charles and Nabby and separated from her husband, reminded herself firmly of her "many, very many causes for thanksgiving. . . . . I hope my heart is not ungrateful, though sad," she added. Her principal trouble was sleeping. How many times had she gone off with a sinking heart to do battle with her enemy, night. During her illness she had taken laudanum, a sedative and pain-killer. It was an addictive drug though, and she was too conscious of the ruin it had brought to Patrick Henry, reported to be often under its influence, to be easy about taking it. She would rather lie awake than fall into a drugged and bottomless slumber.[14]

She had John on her mind constantly, and she professed no surprise at his morose letters. "There is nothing so much to render a man fractious," she wrote airily, "as living without females about him. . . . They know how to temper the wind to the shorn lamb." She sent him frequent admonitions about his health: he must keep wrapped up, have a fire in his bedroom, keep the windows closed at night, and take his medicine—sulphur, cream of tartar, and honey—at the first sign of a cold. She rebuked him sharply for his complaints about his children. If the childless Washington had "not the anxiety," she wrote, "he also has not the pleasure." As for the grandchildren, if they were decently educated "they will be quite as like to rise up virtuous and distinguished characters as though they had been born to great expectations." No one should know better than John that to live was to suffer, to be vulnerable, to be wounded. To have children was to increase by that degree one's exposure, to give life hostages, to produce beings who, if they could charm and delight a parent's heart, could also inflict such pain and distress as lay in the power of no other creatures. She was ashamed for his weakness. "If my hopes are blasted," she wrote, "I must submit to it as a punishment, a trial, an affliction which I must bear, and what I cannot remedy I must endure."[15]

The day before Christmas, Adams broke away from his official duties and rode for fourteen miles across the winter landscape with his nephew. Christmas was a fine day and he celebrated by another long, invigorating ride that made him forget how very ancient and decrepit he was.

The news of Lord Horatio Nelson's spectacular naval victory at the Nile brightened the President's New Year's party where government officials, Congressmen and Senators, and the officers of the newborn army consumed thirty gallons of punch and wine, and cake in proportion. Nelson's success improved the position of the United States and undoubtedly put the Directory in a more amenable frame of mind. "The English," Adams noted, "have exhibited an amazing example of skill and intrepidity, perseverance and firmness at sea. We are a chip off that block."[16]

Thomas Boylston, after almost five years of service abroad as his brother's secretary, had set out for home. John Quincy's marriage had changed their relationship. Thomas was acutely aware of being outside the enchanted circle of the young couple, so much in love and so preoccupied with each other. John and Abigail were delighted at the prospect of his return, although they experienced anxious weeks at his delay in arriving in America.

At last he reached New York on January 10 and hurried on to Philadelphia. He arrived the evening of the President's Tuesday night reception. The crowd of guests was beginning to thin when Briesler came running into the room red-faced and beaming with pleasure and announced, "Sir, Mr. Adams is upstairs." Adams was scarcely less active than his steward in rushing off to see Thomas. His voice choked with emotion and tears running down his cheeks, he embraced his son and said, "I thank my God that you have returned again to your native country."

John found his son's mind, as he put it to Abigail, "well stored with ideas and his conversation entertaining."[17] There were so many questions —John Quincy's health and spirits, his wife's, the affairs of Europe, the prospects of peace—that they talked until morning. Thomas brought dispatches and letters from Murray and John Quincy, and even more important, a personal representation of the views of both. They were convinced that the mood of France had changed dramatically. Murray had had a series of strange interviews with Pichon, "Secretary of the Legation of the French Republic near Batavia." Murray had made clear that he had no authority to treat or even discuss and had insisted that any effort to reopen negotiations be made through formal diplomatic channels.

Pichon, when he returned to Paris, had sent Murray a letter to pass on to the President. The letter was conciliatory but vague. It indicated a willingness to receive any commissioners the President might send, but it gave none of the specific assurances that had been made the conditions for a new American effort at negotiation. Murray himself was at a loss to explain the eccentric character of his contacts with Pichon. "The mysteriousness of concealing these conversations and communications even from the chargé d'affaires here [The Hague]," Murray wrote, "is unaccountable to me unless it has arisen from the first peculiar origin of

these conversations and communications—and secondly from their pride."
For his part Murray had insisted that the French declaration "must be as
public as the two former refusals—and as solemn as your message." Moreover Murray gave a favorable account of Logan's peace efforts. The
President of the Directory had given a dinner at which Logan proposed
as a toast "An honorable peace with the U.S.!" to which Merlin had replied grandly, "No, sir, I shall give that myself." "This," Murray observed
dryly, "is all dramatic—yet," he added, "it is all very different from this
time last year, my dear sir! . . . The *nature* of the affairs of the U.S. and
the direction of her views are changed very much. At least great objects
present themselves that were dormant a year since."

Pichon had declared to Murray that "*the President has as much as
said that if T[alleyrand] gave him the assurances he would treat, and
we have anticipated this and given the assurances.*" Pichon assured Murray that the eyes of France were open—"that they saw how deeply deceived they had been—that they saw our relative importance and acknowledged it by their present conciliatory turn . . . that they knew if
they were guilty of such perfidy to the U.S. they must never expect her
friendship and that they would lose too much to hazard such a measure."
After this conversation Pichon asked for another interview with Murray
and showed him a letter from Talleyrand which that minister had instructed him to show Murray. Pichon showed the epistle on the condition
that none of it would be made public—"they *dread* our papers," Murray
noted. As far as he could recall the contents of the letter, it was "a sort of
assurance on some of the points of our conversation—pretty explicit and
soothing. . . . ."

"Rest assured of it," Murray wrote, "F. is impotent towards U.S.—or
she would not have knuckled of late." But, he added cautiously, "I can
easily suppose that her present condescensions have ambiguity within."
Murray was afraid that if the United States did not meet the French halfway the Directory would make public the concessions that it had proposed to him and try, by throwing the onus of bad faith on the administration, to split the American people. This would help to explain the
curious obliqueness of the French peace proposals. They should be
strong enough and convincing enough to persuade Americans that France
genuinely desired peace, but they should be so presented as not to meet
technically the conditions for negotiation stated by the administration,
specifically in the President's message to Congress of a year earlier. "If
the country seems cured and solid, a negotiation might be risked," Murray
thought, but if not—if the energy which America seemed to be displaying
was "from partial sources and . . . not solidly bottomed"—Murray would
not hesitate to choose war. On one point he was emphatic. He was convinced that the only motive of the French in indicating a willingness to

negotiate was self-interest. They would carry on a negotiation only as long as it suited them to do so, and they had been brought to the point of negotiation only by the growing military and naval strength of the United States. "At the first sign of weakness and division in America," he warned, "they would again be intoxicated and again be insolent."[18]

Most important perhaps was the opinion of John Quincy as conveyed by Thomas. His son endorsed Murray's judgments wholeheartedly. If France was bluffing in its intimations of peaceful intent, better to call her bluff than run the risk of having the administration maneuvered into the position of not seeming sincerely anxious to repair the breach between the two countries. The American policy of firmness and resolution, it appeared, had succeeded. Now was the time to reap the fruit.

Unraveling the tangled web that Pichon and Talleyrand had spun, and placing beside it other bits of evidence as dubious as Logan's mission and a long letter from Joel Barlow (whose *Columbiad* Adams had admired so inordinately) to Washington insisting that the Directory was prepared to negotiate, it seemed to Adams that a definite pattern emerged.[19]

The more Adams thought about it the clearer his course seemed. The only real opposition to renewed negotiations would come from the irreconcilable Federalists—generally speaking, the Hamiltonians. These men were not to be counted on in any event. To the Secretaries and such men as Cabot, Higginson, and Ames he owed nothing. They were Hamilton's creatures, committed to his policy of rule or ruin. It seemed the time to act. Several days after the arrival of Thomas and the dispatches he sent a note to Pickering asking him to prepare "the draft of a project of a treaty and a consular convention, such as in his opinion might at this day be acceded to by the United States, if proposed by France."[20]

Matters of state could not diminish the President's pleasure in the company of his son. "Thomas is my delight," he wrote Abigail. The young man ran about in his blue coat with his dark hair cropped short in the modern fashion, seeing much of his old Quaker friends, who greeted him, "Thomas, how dost thee do?" and listened to his European adventures. Judge Cushing of the Supreme Court and Mrs. Cushing sat in the Adams pew on Sundays and then had dinner at the presidential mansion with the Samuel Otises. At the President's ball John overheard Alexander James Dallas remark *sotto voce* that, while Washington liked the ladies very much, Adams did not seem to care for them and did not know how to talk with them. Abigail was pleased at the report. "To be a gallant, a man must have a little of the fop," she remarked, adding, "Nothing pleases and gratifies me so much as to know myself the sole monopolizer."[21]

Knowing how Abigail longed to see Thomas, Adams sent him off reluctantly at the end of January to visit his mother at Quincy, thus becoming once more "a solitudinarian," although he went occasionally to the theater with William Shaw. The President and his nephew saw *Secrets Worth Knowing* and *The Children in the Woods,* but found them poor fare.

SHORTLY after the turn of the new year Adams found himself involved in a dispute with Pickering over Gerry's dispatches and the
Secretary's comments thereon. Pickering, who was convinced of
Gerry's "*duplicity*" and "*treachery*," wished to accompany the publication
of the dispatches with a lengthy and scathing refutation. Adams felt it
was unsuitable to prolong the controversy and wished, moreover, to protect his friend as far as it was proper to do so. He accepted Abigail's
judgment that "whoever questions the integrity of Mr. Gerry's heart does
him an injury," and he was more and more inclined to agree with her
that Gerry's windiness and circumlocution made him as unsuitable for an
important diplomatic post as "a voluble old woman."[1] He caught indeed
at her reference to "a voluble old woman" and wrote that in his view
they, or handsome young women, often made the best ambassadors to
certain courts and government. "I wish some power or other would send
you to me in the first character," he added.[2]

In the meantime the legislative wheels ground small and slow. The
Federalists in Congress were determined to indict Gerry; the House still
wrangled over the impeachment of Blount and debated acrimoniously
the Kentucky and Virginia resolutions—"the mad resolutions of Virginia
and Kentucky," in Abigail's words. The Kentucky Resolution, framed by
the Vice-President, implied a threat of disunion and put forward for the
first time a theory that was to have a long and stormy life: the doctrine of
nullification—that a state might determine for itself whether it would
comply with acts of the national legislature which it judged to be unconstitutional.

The rumors of a change of attitude on the part of the French government, the publication of Gerry's dispatches, the word of Logan's mission,
and the revived activity of the Republican press all served to swing the
balance of public sentiment somewhat more toward the Jeffersonians.
Sensing the current, the Vice-President was convinced that opinion was

"about to fall into the Republican scale," and that the coming summer would be the time "for systematic energies and sacrifices. The engine is the press," he added. "Every man must lay his purse and his pen under contribution."[3]

The President kept his own counsel. He observed the resurgence of the Republicans and noted that they had found an effective issue in their loud opposition to the Alien and Sedition Acts. He felt once more the pressure of Pickering and the other Cabinet members who, under instructions from Hamilton, made plain their intention of holding him steady on an anti-French course. He noted uneasily the growing emphasis on the army. Making his own assessment of the situation, he determined on a bold stroke. On February 18, just after the Senate had provided for raising an army of thirty thousand in the event of war, Adams sent a message to the Senate enclosing Talleyrand's letter and nominating Murray "to be minister plenipotentiary of the United States to the French Republic." Jefferson, reading the message as presiding officer of the Senate and noting the dismay on the faces of Federalist Senators, was no less astonished. Adams had kept the secret well. He had consulted with no one, solicited no advice, reached his decision independent of Cabinet or counselors.

When Jefferson had recovered from his own initial surprise he set about to ensure that as little profit as possible should accrue to Adams and the Federalists in general. "The face they will put upon this business," he wrote Edmund Pendleton, "is that they have frightened France into a respectful treatment." But this was manifest nonsense. France knew America was powerless to hurt her and had acted out of simple good faith and a desire for peace. As for the President's motives, they were clearly bad. He had held back Talleyrand's letter as long as he dared and then sent Murray's nomination to the Senate, hoping that the Federalist Senators would take on the odium of rejecting him and frustrating the mission.

As soon as he had dispatched his message Adams wrote to Washington declaring that he had made up his mind to take the action primarily on the basis of Talleyrand's letter to Pichon, supplemented by "a multitude of other letters and documents, official and unofficial. . . . Tranquillity upon just and honorable terms," was undoubtedly the "ardent desire" of all good Americans, and Adams only hoped that "the babyish and womanly blubbering" for peace at any price would not persuade Americans to conclude a treaty less than that. There was not much sincerity in the "cant about peace," he added; "those who snivel for it now were hot for war against Britain a few months ago and would be now, if they saw a chance."[4]

Having thrown down the gauntlet to the Hamiltonians, Adams did not have to wait long for the storm to burst about his head. Peter

Porcupine, long his supporter, turned on him with the venom which he had formerly reserved for Republicans. Hamilton was reported to have declared him "a mere old woman and unfit for a President"; and George Cabot wrote bitterly of the "surprise, indignation, grief, and disgust" that had "followed each other in quick succession in the breasts of the true friends of our country."⁵ "The end [peace] being a bad one, all means are unwise and indefensible," Ames wrote to Pickering. Federalist Senators, Jefferson observed with satisfaction, were "graveled and divided; some are for opposing, others know not what to do."⁶ Some Federalist members of Congress threatened to resign, among them Uriah Tracy. "I have sacrificed as much as most men . . . to support this government and root out democracy and French principles," he wrote McHenry, "but . . . I feel it to be lost and worse. . . . I can and will resign if all must be given up to France."⁷ Stephen Higginson, beside himself with chagrin, blamed "the influence of . . . servile flatterers" on the President, men who had wooed him away from his more independent and experienced advisers.⁸ Pickering wrote to Washington with malice that Adams "was suffering the torments of the damned at the consequences of his nomination [of Murray]."

Abigail wrote her husband that the measure had "universally electrified the public. . . . It comes so sudden, was a measure so unexpected, that the whole community were like a flock of frightened pigeons: nobody had their story ready; some called it a hasty measure; others condemned it as an inconsistent one; some swore, some cursed." Wagers were laid that the Federalist-dominated Senate would not concur in the nomination.⁹ The comment that the President most enjoyed was that Mrs. Adams would never have let him take such action if she had been in Philadelphia. "This ought to gratify your vanity enough to cure you," he wrote.¹⁰

Thomas heard similar talk in Boston: "they wished the old woman had been there; they did not believe it would have taken place." Abigail was delighted at the story. "This was pretty saucy," she wrote John, "but the old woman can tell them they are mistaken, for she considers the measure a master stroke of policy. . . . It is a measure which strikes in the head Jacobinism. It came as unexpected to them as to the Federalists." Abigail had heard no comments on it; she had "revolved the subject on my pillow" and heartily approved. But the country's defenses should continue to be strengthened. "Pray am I not a good politician?" she added.¹¹ She wrote Eliza Peabody a summary of her philosophy and her husband's: "We should hold the sword in one hand and the olive branch in the other."¹²

From Boston, Thomas wrote his father that he had become the hero of the Jacobins, who hailed him as an inspired statesman and declared that there was no longer any need for ships or armies. The pro-British faction of the Federalist party was indignant, but there was a large group of Federalists who stood behind the President. Typical of these was General Knox, who wrote that "the great body of the Federal interest confide implicitly in your knowledge and virtue." Adams' action, in Knox's view, was "one of the most dignified, decisive, and beneficial ever adopted by the Chief Magistrate of any nation, soaring above all prejudice, and regarding the happiness of the nation as the primary object of his administration."[13]

Among the Cabinet members, Stoddert and Charles Lee supported the President's action. The latter was especially warm in his commendation, forwarding a letter from Marshall which praised Adams' wisdom and courage in nominating Murray minister plenipotentiary to France.[14] Adams replied to Lee's letter that the nomination of the Marylander had had the effect of revealing the true motives of the Hamiltonian faction. Certain Federalist Congressmen had demonstrated that they thought their role was to dictate policy to the President. But if vanity, he added, "had no limits, arrogance shall be made to feel a curb." If anyone thought that because Adams had been elected by a margin of three votes he would be the tool of a party, they would find he was as independent and aggressive a leader as the constitution would allow him to be. "If combinations of Senators, generals, and heads of departments" should be formed too powerful to resist, and measures were demanded of him that he could not in good conscience adopt, he would resign. "I will try my own strength at resistance first, however," he concluded.[15]

At least one Federalist was so enraged by the appointment of Murray that he wrote threatening Adams' life. "Assassination shall be your lot," an anonymous writer declared, signing himself "a ruined merchant, alas! with ten children!!! made beggars by the French."[16]

Although the President had certainly anticipated a strong reaction to his nomination of Murray from the Hamilton faction, he was disconcerted at the violence of the storm his action created in the Federalist camp. A measure which he had hoped would isolate the extremists threatened seriously to demoralize the entire party. "I have no idea I shall be chosen P. a second time," he wrote morosely to Abigail, adding, "The business of this office has been so oppressive that I shall hardly support it [for] two years. . . . Rivalries have been irritated to madness." The Federalists, in his view, deserved to feel the force of the Sedition Law as much as the Republicans ever did, and Peter Porcupine merited the Alien Bill. "But I will not take revenge," he concluded. "I don't remember that I was ever vindictive in my life, though I have often been very wroth." He felt neither "very angry . . . nor much vexed or fretted."[17]

Since a recent student of Adams' presidency has suggested that the nomination of Murray was a shrewd effort to preserve his standing in the country, especially with an eye to the election of 1800, it is worth dwelling for a moment on the implications of the President's letter to his wife.

Adams always insisted that his act was a completely disinterested one, done for the good of the country. Assuming that few, if any, political acts are *entirely* disinterested, it seems reasonable to conclude that Adams' was as close as politicians are apt to come. He certainly thought that the moment was propitious and that the action would be a popular one with the great majority of Americans. Undoubtedly he enjoyed the discomfiture of his enemies. But the presidential elections were not a popularity contest in the decade of the 1790s. The machinery of choosing electors was firmly in the hands of the party leaders. If Adams' action alienated the principal Federalists, as he had every reason to believe it would, popular support would do him relatively little good. The electors were far too subject to manipulation, as the elections of 1792 and 1796 had proved conclusively, for anyone to have confidence that the outcome in 1800 would reflect public sentiment in any very precise way. Adams, indeed, was dependent primarily on the Hamiltonians for his nomination.

The answer might be given that Adams' letter to Abigail was written three days after his dramatic announcement and that the furor it had stirred up in the Federalist party had made him pessimistic about the chances of his being chosen as the Federalist candidate in 1800. On the other hand, he insisted that he had foreseen the Federalist reaction to his nomination of Murray. If he had not he would have been remarkably obtuse and the secrecy with which he enveloped his decision would have been quite meaningless.

It is much more in keeping with what we know of Adams' impulsive and passionate nature to accept his action as one taken with little or no regard for its practical political consequences, at least as they affected his own future. We can assume that once he had decided that this particular course was the proper one for the United States he would have pursued it regardless of the outcome. As Abigail put it several months later: "He has sustained the whole force of an unpopular measure which he knew would excite the passions of many, thwart the views of some, and showered down upon his head a torrent of invective produced by ignorance and malevolence and jealousy." Yet thinking the measure necessary, "he took the step and braved the effect. As he expected, he has been abused and calumniated—by his enemies, that was to be looked for—but in the *house of his friends,* by those calling themselves *friends of their country*—they have joined loudest in the clamor."[18] It was an effective statement of the President's case.

In addition to the "squibs, scoffs, and sarcasms" in the Federalist newspapers, Adams was called on by a delegation of rebellious Senators—Sedgwick, Stockton, Read, Bingham, and Ross. The President was indignant at the confrontation, which he thought unconstitutional, but by a heroic effort he kept the better part of his temper. The Senators' first efforts were to persuade him to withdraw the nomination. This sugges-

PLATE 25

Courtesy of Mrs. Arthur Adams

Louisa Catherine Johnson (Mrs. John Quincy Adams) by **Gilbert Stuart.**

PLATE 26

National Gallery of Art, Washington, D.C., gift of Mrs. Robert Hon

John Adams by Gilbert Stuart. This is apparently the portrait commissioned by the Massachusetts Legislature to be hung in the House of Representatives, but Stuart failed to complete the portrait. John Quincy wrote to Copley in 1811 that Stuart "actually took a likeness to the face" but with the "prerogative of genius" failed to finish the portrait. It was probably finished by another artist.

PLATE 27

Courtesy of Mrs. John Adams

Abigail Adams by Gilbert Stuart. This was the portrait, painted in 1800, for which Abigail paid a hundred dollars. When she asked Thomas Boylston to try to get Stuart to finish the portrait, her son wrote, "I have no idea it will ever be finished, unless you should stimulate his attention by a letter . . . If you write a few lines of a complimentary nature to him, perhaps he may take it into his head to finish your picture . . ."

Photograph by George M. Cushing

PLATE 98

Photograph by George M. Cushing

PLATE 29

The Long Room in the Adams Mansion. The portrait over the fireplace is of Dr. Joseph Warren, the Adams' friend and physician, who was killed at the Battle of **Bunker Hill.**

The Metropolitan Museum of Art, gift of William H. Huntington, 1883

PLATE 30

John Adams by Charles Balthazar Julien Fevret de Saint Memin. This is a black and white crayon "physiognotrace" portrait made by use of an instrument which traced off the subject's profile. It was made in 1801.

PLATE 31

New York State Historical Association, Cooperstown

Life mask of John Adams at the age of ninety by John Henri Isaac Browere. Adams was amazed that the process involved so little discomfort—"without injury, pain or inconvenience," as he told John Quincy. Browere had made a life mask of Jefferson in the spring of 1825.

Frick Art Reference Library

PLATE 32

John Adams by Gilbert Stuart, painted in Adams' ninetieth year. Josiah Quincy quotes Adams as saying, "I should like to sit to Stuart from the first of January to the last of December, for he lets me do just what I please and keeps me constantly amused by his conversation."

tion he rejected so summarily that they passed to their next gambit. The Senate would refuse to confirm the appointment on the ground that Murray was not a man of sufficient stature and reputation to conduct such an important negotiation. To the threat to negative Murray's nomination, Adams replied with a counterthreat to resign as President and leave the succession to Jefferson. Finally, after a hot exchange, the committee agreed that the appointment of two additional members of greater prominence would meet their objections, although according to Sedgwick the President accepted the idea "with much apparent reluctance."[19]

To conciliate the Federalist leaders, Adams chose two other commissioners to join Murray if any further assurances of an inclination to negotiate were received from France. Patrick Henry and Oliver Ellsworth were nominated by Adams on February 25. The commissioners would not depart, however, until some assurance was received from the Directory that they would be properly received.

Still the ultras were unappeased; Abigail summarized the complaints of the Boston Federalists: "Mr. Murray is not a man of experience, not a man of talents. Then comes the new nomination. 'Aya, the Senate advised on that in order to defeat the measure, for Mr. Ellsworth is out of health, a hipped man, and P. Henry so old that he will not go.' 'But are not the Senate pointed out by the constitution as advisers to the President?' 'Why, yes.' 'Are there any others whom he is obliged to consult?' 'No, but Washington always did.' 'And was not he censured for being led by Hamilton?' 'But why was not the Secretary of State consulted?' 'Aya, there's the rub.' "[20]

In the months that followed the nomination of Murray, the Federalists gained strength everywhere. Georgia, for the first time in six years, elected a Federalist Congressman. In Virginia, John Marshall defeated the Republican war horse, John Clopton. Washington estimated that five Congressmen out of six from South Carolina were of Federalist persuasion, and almost half of the Virginia delegation. William Heth, a Virginia Federalist, wrote Hamilton exultantly, "We have obtained such an accession of numbers as well as of talents that I think we may consider Jacobinism as completely overthrown in this state."[21] John Taylor, one of the Republican champions, was ready to concede victory to the enemy.

Several Hamiltonian Federalists, among them Jonathan Trumbull of Connecticut, decided on the desperate measure of trying to prevail on Washington to come out of retirement to run against Adams for the presidency in 1800, but Washington was indignant at the suggestion. "Principles instead of men," he wrote sternly, should be "the steady pursuit of the Federalists."[22] Wolcott predicted "malign circumstances" if Trumbull succeeded in his efforts.

Congress adjourned March 4. On the sixth Adams issued a proclamation appointing the twenty-fifth of April "as a day of solemn humiliation, fasting, and prayer" to be devoted "to the sacred duties of religion in public and private," to repentance, thanksgiving, and the prayer that the Lord would protect the United States "from unreasonable discontent, from disunion, faction, sedition, and insurrection; that He would preserve our country from the desolating sword" and spread peace and prosperity among the nations of the earth.

As Jefferson had perceived from the first, the taxes imposed by the Federalists to support their program of building up the navy and the army became in time the principal cause of resentment against the Adams administration. The direct Federal property tax imposed by Congress in the summer of 1798, of all the taxes, was the most unpopular. Far more than the Alien and Sedition Acts, the taxes reversed the tide of public sentiment and finally set it flowing toward the Republicans. Alexander Graydon expressed it in these terms: "A provisional army was voted, volunteer corps invited, ships of war equipped, and as a part of the system of defense the Alien and Sedition Acts were enacted. But the most volcanic ground of all was yet to be trodden. . . . The simple, well-meaning Federalists . . . with no small degree of self-complacency . . . passed a law for a direct tax. . . . This tax on real property was the fatal blow to Federalism in Pennsylvania."[23]

This time the resistance to taxation came from eastern Pennsylvania, from the Germans who were inordinately suspicious of English influence. When a United States marshal arrested two Pennsylvania Dutchmen and a militia captain for refusal to pay their taxes, John Fries, an auctioneer, raised a company of several hundred armed men and led an assault on the prison to free the tax evaders. Word of the incident reached Philadelphia just as Adams was preparing to leave the city for Quincy. He promptly issued a proclamation denouncing the insurrection as "subversive of the just authority of the government." The rebels, he declared, had perpetrated "certain acts which I am advised amount to treason, being overt acts of levying war against the United States. . . . Wherefore I, John Adams, President of the United States, do hereby command all persons being insurgents as foresaid . . . to disperse and retire peaceably to their respective abodes."

The President followed his proclamation by an order directing regular troops and militia to hunt down the rebels in Northampton County. There were none to be found and Fries and several of his lieutenants were arrested and borne off to Philadelphia to be tried for treason. The Federalists hailed the prompt suppression of the "insurrection" as another instance of the power of the national government. Major General Hamilton declared, "Whenever the government appears in arms, it ought to appear like a *Hercules!*" Supreme Court Justice James Iredell reminded a federal grand jury that if traitors were not punished "anarchy will ride triumphant and all lovers of order, decency, truth, and justice will be trampled underfoot."[24] Many of the Federalists were convinced that the uprising was the logical outcome of the treasonous Kentucky and Virginia resolutions and they looked forward to making a terrible example of the unfortunate Fries.

As soon as Congress had adjourned Adams was impatient to be off for Quincy. His Secretaries hinted that he should remain at the seat of government whether at Philadelphia or, if the government was moved to Trenton because of the threat of fever, at the latter city, but Adams brushed the hints aside. Indeed, he had hardly left the city before rumors began to circulate among the Republicans that he had removed all the public money from the banks, made a bargain with the King of England, and run away to Canada. A Federalist friend warned the President that "public sentiment is very much against your being so much away from the seat of government, from a conviction that when you are there the public vessel will be properly steered, and that these critical times require an experienced pilot."[25] But the President was determined to be with Abigail at Quincy. He could keep in touch by letters and special dispatches as he had the previous summer. "The Secretaries of State, Treasury, War, Navy, and the Attorney General," Adams wrote in his own defense, "transmit me daily by the post all the business of consequence, and nothing is done without my advice and direction. . . . The post goes very rapidly, and I answer by the return of it, so that nothing suffers or is lost." He insisted there was no need for him to be at "the chief seat of the synagogue." The rumors about the reasons for his absence, he added, "give me no anxiety."[26]

Of course Abigail was delighted to have him back, "in better health," as she wrote Eliza, "than I feared he would, from the close application he was obliged to give to business for four months together."[27] Abigail's own health, though much improved, was still shaky and she was surrounded by the sick and ailing. Her housemaid had the worms and she dosed her with calomel and jalap. Mary Cranch had a persistent cold and cough. William Shaw had a running fever and rheumatic pain. Richard Cranch was poorly and Eliza's infant daughter had an alarming complaint which paralyzed one of her arms. A few hot days in May threatened Abigail with a recurrence of her illness—as she put it, "reduced my strength, prostrated my spirits, and I lost my sleep, my appetite, and was ready to give myself up." But steel powders mixed with Winter's bark restored her.[28]

As soon as she could get about she bought a book of moral precepts for her niece, Abby Peabody, the infant daughter of Eliza and her second husband, the Reverend Stephen Peabody. Reading it over before she sent it, she discovered that it accorded women a subordinate role in the world. She sent a cautionary note to her sister along with the book. "I will never," she wrote, "consent to have our sex considered in an inferior point of light. Let each planet shine in their own orbit. God and nature designed it so—if man is Lord, woman is *Lordess*—that is what I contend for."[29]

Released from the pressures that focused on him at the capital, Adams fell into one of his black moods. The dark tide of paranoia flooded his mind; he was depressed, hostile, and suspicious. General Knox, Jonathan Jackson, and Dr. Waterhouse, all old friends, riding out from Boston one baking, dusty July day to see John, found him sullen and uncommunicative. He sat in front of his guests and read a newspaper from cover to cover, including, Waterhouse noted, the advertisements, offered the hot and thirsty guests no refreshment, and made no protest when they rose to go, discomfited and indignant, after an awkward half hour.

He did attend the launching of the frigate *Boston;* at Abigail's urging went to hear the election sermon in the city, and afterward dined with the Ancient and Honorable Artillery Company who had sent a troop of handsomely caparisoned light horse to serve as an escort. He put in an appearance at the Fourth of July celebration and the Harvard Commencement, but there were no end to the invitations. "Boston folks think they can never have enough of a good thing," Abigail complained. The President went everywhere reluctantly and played his part in an obviously perfunctory and distracted manner.

A group of enthusiastic young Bostonians decided to commemorate the seventh of July as the day on which the French treaty was abrogated, and they appeared in Quincy at seven in the morning to "request the President of the United States to attend" their ceremonies. "Young men . . . total strangers," Abigail wrote disapprovingly, "without anybody to introduce them or make their names known." At almost the same time a carriage of officers from the *Constitution* arrived to pay their respects to the President, and Adams returned from his morning ride to find the yard filled with unexpected visitors. He sent them all packing with a rough and sharp-tongued lecture on the impropriety of their behavior. Abigail, watching, was dismayed at the tartness of her husband's language. Her heart went out to the young men, who looked so abashed and crestfallen. "Their motives . . . though not judicious, were well meant," she protested.

While Adams was often tactless, the two incidents were a barometer of his mood. He snapped at the hired hands and at Abigail herself so that it was a relief to have him closeted in his study poring over dispatches from the Secretaries and writing queries or instructions, for whatever his own emotional turmoil, he paid close attention to his presidential duties.

When he learned from Pickering that John Fries had been convicted of treason and condemned to be hanged—the Secretary of State expressed his "calm and solid satisfaction that an opportunity is now presented, in executing the just sentence of the law, to crush that spirit which, if not overthrown and destroyed, may . . . overturn the government"—Adams was deeply concerned. The power to pardon lay with the President and he at once gave the law in the case the "closest attention of my best understanding." He wrote to the Attorney General to get William Lewis' arguments against the charge of treason and set himself to study the common-law precedents in treason trials.

The President wished to know if Fries was native or foreign-born, "a man of property and independence, or . . . in debt?" What had been his previous life—"industrious or idle, sober or intemperate?" And to what degree had he been involved in a general conspiracy? Adams' guides would be, he declared, that "neither humanity be unnecessarily afflicted, nor public justice essentially violated, nor the public safety endangered."[30]

A petition for pardon from Fries and his fellows reached Adams at Quincy late in the summer. To his inquiry as to whether he should give a pardon to the rebels, the Cabinet replied unanimously in the negative. The law should be allowed to take its course and the country to witness the fate of those who defied the government.

One persistent problem which troubled Adams throughout his administration was the British policy of impressment. He directed Pickering to instruct Rufus King to protest, "with all the decision which may be consistent with decency and politeness," the right of the British navy to "take from our ships of war any men whatever, and from our merchant vessels any Americans, or foreigners, or even Englishmen." In his view there was "no principle under heaven" which could justify such measures.[31]

Again he found that the greater part of his time was taken up with applications for commands in the army, which at long last had gotten down to active recruiting on the company and regimental level. The bulk of the considerable correspondence that passed between him and McHenry was concerned with appointment of company and field grade officers who besieged Adams with requests for commissions.

It was also a time of waiting. The Hamiltonians clung to the hope that France would rebuff the new negotiation, and the Republicans waited uneasily lest the frustration of the President's effort should lead to a resurgence of anti-French feeling. The commissioners were not to sail until further assurances were given by the Directory that they would be properly received, so that the noise of partisan conflict subsided somewhat.

In an engagement between the recently commissioned *Constellation,* commanded by Captain Thomas Truxtun and the French ship, *L'Insurgente,* the American vessel forced her opponent to strike her colors.

L'Insurgente was brought into Boston soon after Adams arrived at Quincy and a Frenchman, living in Boston, rode out to ask the President if his captured countrymen "might have the liberty of residing in Boston." Adams replied with a characteristic combination of tactlessness and compassion that they might have the liberty of the city and for a radius of five miles around, but added, "I wish there was not a Frenchman suffered to live in America."[32]

Adams also kept a close eye on the negotiations between Pickering on the one hand and General Thomas Maitland and Robert Liston on the other, regulating British and American trade with Toussaint L'Ouverture and the island of Santo Domingo and providing for formal relations with Santo Domingo's ruler. The President feared they might impair America's neutrality and irritate Spain and Holland as well as France, but he declared himself "by no means . . . bigoted" and "disposed to concur in any rational expedient which can be reconciled to justice and sound policy. . . . Harmony with the English, in all this business with St. Domingo, is the thing I have most at heart," he wrote Pickering. "The result of the whole is in my mind problematical and precarious."[33]

ITH the issue of war with France at least temporarily in abeyance, the Republicans concentrated their fire on the Alien and
Sedition Acts. "Pennsylvania, Jersey, and New York are coming
majestically round to the true principles," Jefferson wrote a friend. Yet Jefferson too had learned a lesson. He no longer spoke of Revolutionary
France as the hope of the world and the natural ally of America, but
insisted that he abjured "all political connection with every foreign power.
. . . Commerce with all nations, alliance with none, should be our
motto," he declared.[1] The Republican technique was to initiate petitions
of protest against the Alien and Sedition Acts in every town and county.
Thus the issue was kept alive and the pot boiling. The program was aided
by the prosecutions under the Sedition Act, which were recounted in
lurid detail in the Republican press. The *Aurora,* whose new editor,
William Duane, was a fit successor to Bache, suggested that Adams was in
the pay of Great Britain, and Pickering passed on the paper to William
Rawle, the district attorney, for him to judge whether it was libelous.

In addition to the attacks of Duane and the *Aurora,* Thomas Cooper,
an English friend of Dr. Priestley and editor of the *Northumberland
Gazette,* had published a scurrilous pamphlet denouncing Adams, entitled *Address to the People of Northampton.* Cooper was a disappointed
office seeker who had applied to Adams for a position on the joint commission on British claims. According to Cooper, Adams was a mad despot, an enemy of the people and of the rights of man, a champion of
aristocrats and a tool of the wealthy bent on subverting American freedom.

Cooper's attack, when Adams read it, infuriated him. "A meaner, a
more artful, or a more malicious libel has not appeared," he wrote Pickering. "As far as it alludes to me I despise it. But I have no doubt it is a
libel against the whole government, and as such ought to be prosecuted."

For his old friend the English radical, Dr. Joseph Priestley, who had also attacked his administration in bitter terms, he sought some exculpation. "He is as weak as water, as unstable as Reuben, or the wind," he noted. "His influence is not an atom in the world."[2] On Adams' recommendation prosecution was started against Cooper and the latter, in consequence, became a Republican hero—surely a curious symbol of the freedom of the press, this master of invective and abuse. It seemed to Adams a poor justice to have wretched Fries and his fellow insurrectionists in jail, sentenced to hang for treason, while men such as Cooper who had incited them continued to pour forth their false and incendiary material.

Throughout the summer of 1799 the conviction grew among the rank and file of Americans, always inclined to a certain feckless optimism, that there would be no war. An ironic result of this conviction was the increasing resentment over always unpopular taxation and a distaste for the army which was being mustered up all about them, a host of parasites to feed—as the average American saw it—off the bounty of their neighbors. If there was to be no war why all this martial clamor, these arrogant young officers striding about, these expensive ships outfitting in every port? The army, volunteer corps and regulars alike, seemed more likely to be used to pursue delinquent taxpayers or suppress independent state legislatures than to engage an enemy force.

Adams himself was far from happy at the cost of maintaining a naval and military establishment. At Pickering's suggestion that six additional companies of cavalry should be raised, he burst out: "The system of debts and taxes is leveling all governments in Europe." It frightened him, he declared, "out of my wits. . . . We must ultimately go the same way. There is no practicable or imaginable expedient to escape it that I can conceive."[3]

Early in August the President received dispatches from Murray with a letter from Talleyrand enclosed, repeating his assurances that the American negotiators would be received by the Directory. It seemed to Adams a shabby way of doing things—these irregular channels and eccentric expedients. "That the design is insidious and hostile at heart I will not say," he wrote the apprehensive Pickering. "Time will tell the truth. Meantime, I dread no longer their diplomatic skill. I have seen it, and felt it, and been the victim of it these twenty-one years. But the charm is dissolved. Their magic is at an end in America." They could no longer count on a French party to do their bidding. As long as Adams was in office "candor, integrity, and . . . a pacific and friendly disposition" would mark the relations of the United States with France. "In this spirit I shall pursue the negotiation," he warned, "and I expect the co-operation of the heads of departments." America would not allow the slightest relaxation in its preparations by land and sea. Pickering was to notify Governor Davie of North Carolina regarding his appointment to replace Patrick Henry, who had declined to serve for reasons of health, and notify Davie and Ellsworth to "make immediate preparations for embarking."[4]

The Hamiltonian Federalists, after the first shock of Murray's nomination, placed their hopes on preventing or delaying the sailing of the other two commissioners. At Pickering's suggestion, no announcement had been made of Henry's refusal or of Davie's appointment to replace him. Adams' letter to Pickering, the contents of which were immediately communicated to Hamilton and his followers, caused a new flurry of alarm in that camp.

Ames wrote to Pickering that the mission was simply "a measure to *make* dangers and to nullify resources; to make the navy without object; the army an object of popular terror."[5] The government, he added, "will be weakened by the friends it loses and betrayed by those it will gain. It will lose . . . the friendship of the sense and worth and property of the United States, and get in exchange the prejudice, vice, and bankruptcy of the nation." The effect of "this miraculous caprice," he wrote, would be, "at home, to embroil and divide; abroad, to irritate and bring losses and disgraces." It seemed to Ames a cheap play for popularity by the President, and it had clearly been successful, for while "all good men, *una voce*, condemn the business," the multitude applauded it. Adams himself would suffer. His reckless act would be no less "fatal to the peace and reputation" of its author than to the solidarity of the Federalist party. Apparently the President had calculated that the dispatch of the mission "will procure and secure popularity, not only with the multitude, but with the pretended American party." After almost a month of reflection Ames advised Pickering to do his best to arouse among the Federalists a public opposition to the treaty negotiations with France. It must be done "to save the nation" even at the cost of wrecking the party.[6]

Stephen Higginson likewise was sure that "the Jacobin influence is rising and has been ever since the mission to France was determined on . . . if a treaty be made with France, [Republican] ascendancy will be sure."[7]

At the end of August, Stoddert wrote Adams urging him to come to Trenton to confer with the ministers before their departure for France. The Secretary of the Navy, along with Charles Lee, were the only members of the Cabinet favorable to the peace mission, and Stoddert was well aware of the maneuverings that were going on between Pickering, Wolcott, and McHenry to frustrate the whole enterprise. Adams' presence on the scene, though the Secretary of the Navy could not state it so bluntly, would thwart the plotters.[8]

But Adams demurred. For him to go to Trenton to confer with Ellsworth and Davie would give "more *éclat* to the business than it deserv[ed]." He was in no special hurry to expedite their departure, he added; and further, "if any information of recent events in Europe should arrive, which in the opinions of the heads of department . . . would render any alteration in their instructions . . . expedient," he was willing that their departure should be suspended until he could be informed of it or until he could go to Trenton.[9] Unfortunately the Secretaries took Adams' mention of a possible suspension of the mission as an invitation to work more aggressively than ever for that end. Indeed, a valid enough pretense to suspend the mission appeared almost at once in the news of a new upheaval in the Directory in which four members of that body had been deposed including Merlin, its President. Perhaps, Pickering suggested hopefully, this was just such "information from Europe" as might raise "some doubts of the expediency of an immediate departure of the envoys." The change in the Directory gave additional proof of the "instability and uncertainty in the government of France." A suspension of the mission, the Secretaries felt, would "place the United States in a more commanding situation" and enable the President to make such changes in the mission as circumstances might suggest would be desirable. Apparently the Jacobins were once more in the ascendancy and they were notorious for their hostility to the present administration of the United States.[10] Adams found the letter persuasive. Taking, as he did, a dim view of what passed for government in France, the word of its overthrow, or at the least of its radical alteration, caused him to consider suspending the mission until the dust had settled.

On the fourteenth of September the President received the new instructions to the ministers but without any indication of the views of the various Secretaries. He wrote to Pickering asking for these so that he might consider all together "and write my sentiments fully on the subject." Little time would be lost. "The revolution in the Directory," he wrote, "and the revival of the clubs and private societies in France, and the strong appearances of another reign of democratic fury and sanguinary anarchy approaching, seem to justify a relaxation of our zeal for the sudden and hasty departure of our envoys." They might indeed remain in the United States until the fall gales had blown themselves out and then their ocean passage would be safer and less arduous. At the same time, in reply to a letter from Ellsworth requesting permission to continue on the Vermont circuit, Adams wrote that "the convulsions in France . . . will certainly induce me to postpone for a longer or shorter time the mission to Paris." Ellsworth would hardly leave before the latter part of October.[11]

When Ellsworth sent this word to Wolcott it strengthened the latter's conviction that the mission would be suspended, and Ellsworth himself expressed his opinion that the suspension would, "under present aspect, universal opinion, I believe, and certainly my own," be entirely justified.[12] It was thus hardly surprising that Pickering, answering Adams' letters, should refer to "the temporary suspension [of the mission] which you have already deemed expedient," and that the Hamiltonians in general should take heart.

To send the commissioners or not to send them was a disturbing problem and Adams turned it over in his mind "with great anxiety." The mere fact that there had been a new upheaval in the French government did not in itself lessen the chances for successful negotiation. After all it was the Terror which had been, of all the French factions, "the most disposed" to reach an agreement with the United States. Certainly neither the royalists, nor the priests, nor the aristocrats were friendly toward the United States. A revolution of the right would not, therefore, produce any more conciliatory spirit in that nation. If there was a general peace conference in Europe to settle the conflict between England and France, America would have no reason to expect any consideration. Certainly there were two ways to view the matter. The agitation in the Directory might be just the revolution in the French government which would produce a greater spirit of conciliation.

Stoddert meanwhile refused to take Adams' "no" for an answer to his suggestion that the President should come to Trenton as quickly as possible. He pointed out that it was not just the matter of possible French negotiations; American relations with Great Britain were severely strained. After a long and able disquisition on Anglo-American relations, Stoddert arrived at what was probably his essential point. "Artful, designing men" might make use of the President's absence "from the seat of government . . . to make your next election less honorable than it would otherwise be."[13] He had written at too great a length, he feared, but these were urgent matters which directly involved both the nation's welfare and the fate of the Federalist party in the future as well.

Adams replied warmly to Stoddert's letter—"You need not to have apologized for its length; there is not a word in it to spare"—and made plans to leave for Trenton. The commissioners should be there when he arrived. In return he asked of Stoddert only one thing—that the whole subject of the election of 1800 "may be wholly laid out of this question and all others." He was determined to be a strong President "or no President at all." He would act as he thought best for his country, not as he thought best for his own political prospects.[14]

The President wrote to Pickering the same day that he was coming to Trenton the middle of October and would decide the fate of the mission when he arrived. He wished the Attorney General to meet with the other department heads. "We must all be together to determine all the principles of our negotiations with France and England," he wrote. "Any day between the twentieth and thirtieth of October is as good a time to embark for Europe as any part of the year. If our envoys are delayed so long at least, it will be no misfortune."[15]

The last sentence served warning to Pickering that he could not assume that the President would decide to suspend the mission. Moreover the Secretary of State was plainly alarmed at Adams' decision to come to Trenton. If the news from Europe, as expected, should "not only strengthen your reasons for the temporary suspension which you have thought already expedient," he wrote hopefully, but also determine him to abandon it for the time being, the President need not leave Quincy.[16] The Secretary's obvious reluctance to have him come to Trenton simply strengthened Adams' decision to go. Abigail would come on later with Briesler, Louisa, and the usual entourage. He would stop off briefly in New York to see Nabby and the children and Charles and Sally and then proceed to Trenton.

Adams was thinking as much about the English treaty as the French peace mission. The commission established to settle the British claims under the sixth article of the Jay treaty had disbanded amid charges of bad faith. Indeed, it was this that most immediately concerned him. He was determined, he wrote Pickering, that the treaty should be executed "in its full extent. . . . If it costs us four millions sterling when it ought not to cost us one," he wrote, "I had rather pay it than depart from good faith or lie under the suspicion of it." Some fair and equitable agreement must be reached promptly.[17]

As always Adams left the farm reluctantly. Carpenters were busy completing a cider house and putting the finishing touches on the barn. Tirrell and Porter were digging potatoes; neighbors' boys were picking apples in the orchard. Looking at the rich harvest weighing down the tree limbs, Adams estimated it would yield fifty barrels of cider. When he set out in the chariot with William Shaw the weather was delightful, clear and sunny, cool and sharp as hard cider, the trees a great explosion of color, their leaves crackling under the carriage wheels; the corn stalks like rows of Indian tents in the roadside fields; the hay stored safely in the barns—an autumn landscape of familiar beauty. The roads were smooth and hard and the chariot rolled along like a song while the President and his nephew read Ovid's *Metamorphoses*. At Worcester they spent most of Sunday in church, heard "two very good sermons and . . . music equal to the music of the spheres." It was apple season and at every tavern they were offered apple pie. Knowing how Louisa loved it, they were sorrry they could not collect them and send them all back to her.[18]

At Eastchester, Adams found things improved. Nabby and Caroline were well and the Colonel was busy at his encampment organizing his regiment—"in his element and therefore happy," Adams observed. Sally Adams and her two children were staying with Nabby and Charles had disappeared. For the first time Sally gave her father-in-law a full recital of Charles's terrible disintegration. "I pitied her, I grieved, I mourned," he wrote Abigail. It was the tale of man possessed. "I renounce him. King David's Absalom had some ambition and some enterprise. Mine is a mere rake, buck, blood, and beast." It was almost more than he could bear, and he hardly knew which emotions most possessed him—distress, humiliation, or rage. With every opportunity before him, a Harvard education, a sound legal training, the best of prospects, Charles had gone on his own mad course to destruction, while his agonized parents watched, powerless to arrest the descent. The President left New York without seeing his son and pushed on to Trenton "loaded with sorrow."

Arriving in that city with one of his "great colds," he located a small sitting room and bedroom at the Misses Barnes', two maiden ladies who were flustered but delighted to have the President of the United States as their lodger. They clucked like two hens over his cold, provided him with a down comforter, and dosed him with rhubarb, calomel, and a remedy of their own compounding which cured him with surprising speed. (When she heard of the cure Abigail was a little vexed that the Misses Barnes' cold remedy should have been so much more efficacious than her own.) Under their ministrations his spirits as well as his health revived.

At Trenton, Adams found a letter from Lee declaring that the Attorney General could not "perceive any sufficient reasons of the suspension" of the mission. Such a measure, he argued, "would exceedingly disappoint the expectation of America" and excite "jealousy and suspicion" of the President's sincerity in making the nomination in the first place.[19] Stoddert was of a similar opinion and there was no lack of anti-Hamilton Federalists to support the two Cabinet officers. It was clear enough to Adams by this time that Pickering, Wolcott, and McHenry were opposed to the mission on principle and would thwart it in every way that they could. Equally clear was the fact that a suspension of the mission would raise a storm in the country and to no good purpose. It was impossible to predict what the outcome of the new crisis in France might be, but no harm could possibly be done at this point by sending the envoys on their way. The more Adams thought about it the more convinced he became that there was no reasonable alternative.

Whether by chance or design, Hamilton turned up in the city soon after Adams' arrival and Robert Liston, the British minister, as well. Pickering, realizing that the concentration of British "interest" looked suspicious, insisted it was "purely fortuitous." Hamilton, in any event, came to see Adams to try to prevail on him to delay the mission. It was a strange meeting—the Puritan and the libertine, the short, stout President, little more than civil, and the Major General, gracious, charming, and subtle. The disturbance in the Directory, Hamilton argued, would bring about a restoration of the French monarchy by Christmas. "I should as soon expect that the sun, moon, and stars will fall from their orbits," Adams replied, "as events of that kind take place in any such period; but suppose such an event possible, can it be any injury to our country to have envoys there? . . . And if France is disposed to accommodate our differences, will she be less so under a royal than a directorial government? Have not the Directory humbled themselves to us more than to any other nation or power in contest with her? If she proves faithless, if she will not receive our envoys, does the disgrace fall upon her or upon us? We shall not be worse off than at present. The people of our own country will be satisfied that every honorable method has been tried to accommodate our differences." Hamilton, conscious that the stubborn little man before him would not bend or yield, offered his respects and withdrew.[20]

The conversation with Hamilton settled the matter in Adams' mind. As though in direct rebuff of the New Yorker's admonitions, he ordered Davie and Ellsworth to take passage for France by the first of November "or sooner." "As their visit to France is at one of the most critical, important, and interesting moments that ever have occurred," he wrote, "it cannot fail to be highly entertaining and instructive to them, and useful to their country, whether it terminates in peace and reconciliation, or not. The President sincerely prays God to have them in His holy keeping."[21]

The commissioners were instructed to claim full indemnification for the capture or destruction by the French of United States property. However, if the French waived their national claims, the American commissioners were empowered to waive those of the United States as a mutual concession. On the other hand, an essential condition of any treaty must be a provision for settling the claims of individual American citizens against France, such claims to be determined by a board. No alliance was to be entered into and no guarantee was to be given of French possessions in America.

The announcement that the envoys were to sail caused little comment except among the self-deluded Hamiltonian faction, who charged the President with having deceived them by design. Adams was pleased at their indignation. As with all his critical decisions, he made this one in a mood almost of euphoria which carried through the whole of the following week. The day after he wrote a facetious letter to Thomas, cautioning him against marriage and adding, "The source of revolution, democracy, Jacobinism . . . has been a systematical dissolution of the true family authority. There can never be any regular government of a nation without a marked subordination of mothers and children to the father." But his opinion, he cautioned Thomas, was a secret one, "between you and me." Let Abigail hear of such a heresy and it would "infallibly raise a rebellion." Then he added, more seriously, "I have been young, and know how tender 'tis to love. I have never dictated to my children. Perhaps it would have been better in two instances, if I had. I wish them to use a prudent consideration, and not to be led away by a very wild but a very fickle and transient passion."[22]

The twenty-fifth of October was the thirty-fifth anniversary of the marriage of John and Abigail Adams. "Few pairs can recollect so long a union," he wrote. The next winter would be the last they would ever spend in Philadelphia. The approaching election would "set us at liberty," he predicted, "from uncomfortable journeys."[23] While in Trenton, Adams attended the Episcopal church and found its service "more cheerful and comfortable" than the Presbyterian. Although he could dispense with the creeds (finding all that was needed for orthodoxy in the Scriptures), the ritual of the church seemed "very humane and benevolent, and sometimes pathetic and effecting." The church service set him to reviewing the events of his own life and his relation to the Almighty. "Benevolence and beneficence, industry, equity and humanity, resignation and submission, repentance and resurrection are the essence of my religion," he wrote Abigail. But, "alas, how weakly and imperfectly" had he fulfilled its duties. "I look back upon a long life very poorly spent in my own estimation. It appears . . . to have been much too idle, inactive, slothful, and sluggish. I fear it is too late to amend. My forces are too far spent." Yet, despite such a gloomy audit of his past, he could not help but be in sinfully good spirits.[24]

Early in November, Abigail, with Nabby and Caroline and the Otises, set out for Philadelphia. Stopping off in Eastchester with Nabby, remote from the centers of politics, Abigail wrote William Shaw that she could give him no news from that quarter. "I can tell you that the leaves wither and fall, beautifully variegated by the frost with all the colors of the rainbow. . . . The tide ebbs and flows, covering the meadow from the window of the chamber where I write, which enhances the beauty of the rural scene; that I walked out on Saturday, the weather was so fine and mild, that the birds sang like spring and I picked some new-blown flowers from the grass." She could tell of the pear tree at her window with both fruit and pear blossoms on it at the same time. "The dark and intricate field of politics" was not half so charming.[1]

From Eastchester, Abigail went on to New York to visit Sally Adams. Charles was absent, no one knew where, and Abigail took her two little granddaughters to her heart. Susan was three, an unusually quick, bright child who knew her alphabet and "goody goose" stories by heart and loved to have her grandmother Adams read to her. She would beg in a captivating, lisping way until Abigail gave in and read *The Renowned History of Giles Gingerbread,* which she had read to John Quincy thirty years before. Abby, the baby, was pretty as a doll, and walked at nine months. It made Abigail weep to see the two children and their pale, anxious mother.[2]

After a week with Sally, Abigail pushed on with her companions for Philadelphia, taking Nabby and Catherine with her. Adams met them at Brunswick from which they went to Trenton; then on the following day through a downpour to Philadelphia where the City Troop of Light Horse met them and escorted them to the presidential mansion. Abigail found much of her time taken up at once by a series of formal visits. Among the ladies who called was Madame de Tilly, Ann Bingham's fifteen-year-old daughter, married to a profligate French Count. The girl,

Abigail noted, had "all the appearance and dress of a real Frenchwoman, rouged up to the ears."

The Adamses fell readily if not easily into the round of Philadelphia life. Abigail received a shipment of codfish and invited a company of New Englanders to enjoy it. The President missed his white potatoes and cider so Abigail ordered twenty bushels of potatoes and six barrels of cider to carry him through the winter. Their arrival in the city was clouded only by the success of the Republicans in the state election, the first real evidence of the resurgence of that party since the XYZ debacle. The *Aurora* trumpeted the victory daily and prophesied the imminent downfall of the Federalists. "The Jacobins," Abigail noted, "having carried so triumphantly, as they say, their election, consider it as an auspicious omen of their future success." Americans, she concluded darkly, had to contend "against English democratic madness and monarchical hatred of Republicanism, as well as French anarchy and disorganization, American ambition, delusion, and frenzy. If New England does not keep its sober senses the ship will founder upon the rocks."[3]

For two weeks before Congress convened the city hummed with political activity. The Federalists were confident that they would be able to oust John Beckley, the Republican clerk of the House and the most resourceful and untiring political manager of his day. The Jeffersonians, encouraged by the turn of events in Pennsylvania, were determined to retain him. "The conduct of Great Britain towards our commerce," Abigail wrote, "gives us great reason to complain and put weapons into the hands of the Jacobins. . . . I am told that at the southward they pretend to believe the President strongly attached to the British," she added. "This falsehood is propagated to answer political purposes. . . . To do justice to all is the rule; and to be partial to none."[4]

Adams, as usual, solicited the views of his Secretaries on what should be included in his third annual message to Congress. With their reports before him, he worked on a succession of drafts. An early version was full of spleen about the "groundless discontent and seditious practices, long concealed in the darkness," which had erupted in Fries' rebellion. It was the work of "designing and malicious individuals" who had played upon "the groundless apprehensions of many citizens." The outburst was cut out of the final version of the speech, but it showed the rather painful steps by which the President was prevailed upon and brought himself to moderate his tone.

On December 3, Adams delivered his address to a joint meeting of both houses. In the audience were Nabby, Louisa, and Dr. Rush. Abigail wished to go but felt it would not be proper. Some people would not like the address, she predicted, "because it will not disclose enough about the mission to France. Others will growl because war is not waged against England, in words at least. They will grumble at all events and under all circumstances, and so let them."[5]

Adams reviewed Fries' rebellion, the French mission, the breakdown of the claims commission, and the state of the new Capitol being built at Washington. He reminded his listeners that the result of the negotiation with France was uncertain, and that "an obvious dictate of wisdom" was "perseverance in a system of national defense commensurate with our resources and the situation of our country. . . . Nothing short of the power of repelling aggressions will secure our country a rational prospect of escaping the calamities of war or national degradation."

The reply of the Senate, although drafted by "a New England man certain—no Southern man ever quotes Scripture," Abigail noted, was "cool and languid." The Federalist Senators were too much under the influence of Hamilton to express any enthusiasm for the President's message. On the other hand, the answer of the House, drafted by Marshall, not only contained "so full and unqualified an approbation of the measures of the President in his late mission [to France]" as to please Adams enormously but, even more heartening, it was approved unanimously. Indeed, it was received by that body "with more applause and approbation than any speech which the President has ever delivered," Abigail wrote her sister.[6]

Others were not so well pleased. George Cabot deplored "the intimations contained in the speech." Its spirit of moderation simply encouraged the Jacobins to raise their heads once more. Vindicated by the resumption of the negotiations, they "add the hope of getting rid of the army and the influence of some great men [Hamilton] connected with it, so that the pure principles of democracy may be no longer restrained but have a free course, as in France," he concluded sarcastically.[7]

Soon after the President's message Wolcott sat down to give Fisher Ames an account of the prospects for the Sixth Congress. The more intractable Anti-Federalists took the view that the President's decision to dispatch the mission had been forced on him, despite his reluctance, by popular opinion. "They admit, however," he wrote, "that considering all circumstances, the President has shown such respect for the voice of the people as justly to entitle him to an increase of their confidence."

Wolcott described John Marshall's role in the new House as a key one. Among the Federalists from the Southern states, Marshall was a natural leader. "A man of virtue and distinguished talents," he was possibly "too much disposed to govern the world according to rules of logic" and to expound the constitution "as if it were a penal statute." Henry Lee would be Marshall's strong right arm. Between the two of them the House should be securely if not rigidly Federalist. Some of the Northern Federalists would support the President "from personal considerations"; others because they believed he had acted wisely; "others consider it impolitic and unjust to withdraw their support, though they admit he has committed a mistake."

The President himself seemed determined to preserve a nerve-rackingly independent course. He had come, Wolcott confessed, to think of Pickering, McHenry, and himself as his enemies. He resented Hamilton and spoke darkly of a British faction within the United States in words clearly aimed at the dissident members of his Cabinet.

Adams had hardly turned to the knotty problems posed by the breakdown of the British claims commission when word reached Philadelphia of Washington's death on the fourteenth of December. In his brief message to Congress announcing the General's death, Adams spoke of "the purity of his character" and "the long series of services to his country" which had rendered him "illustrious through the world, . . . the most illustrious and beloved personage which this country ever produced. . . . . It remains for an affectionate and grateful people, in whose hearts he can never die, to pay suitable honors to his memory," the President concluded.

The House proceeded at one to the presidential mansion to express its condolence and distress; the Senate came in a body several days later to present a more formal statement of grief. In the absence of the Vice-President, Samuel Livermore, President of the Senate *pro tem,* read the reply. "Permit us, sir, to mingle our tears with yours. On this occasion it is manly to weep. To lose such a man at such a crisis is no common calamity to the world. Our country mourns her father. The Almighty Disposer of human events has taken from us our greatest benefactor and ornament. . . . Favored of heaven, he departed without exhibiting the weakness of humanity. Magnanimous in death, the darkness of the grave could not obscure his brightness. Such was the man whom we deplore. Thanks to God, his glory is consummated. Washington yet lives on earth in his spotless example; his spirit is in heaven. Let his countrymen consecrate the memory of the heroic general, the patriotic statesman, and the virtuous sage. Let them teach their children never to forget that the fruit of his labors and his example are their inheritance."

The deification of the dead Washington had already begun. As Adams listened he felt the eulogy was excessive. He had known the General, magnificent as he had been, as a man. What was the meaning of the sentence, "Washington yet lives on earth in his spotless example"? It was not necessary to turn him into a god to appreciate his greatness. But he replied nonetheless with deep feeling: "The life of our Washington cannot suffer by comparison with those of other countries who have been most celebrated and exalted by fame. . . . For himself he had lived enough to life and to glory. For his fellow citizens, if their prayers could have been answered, he would have been immortal. For me, his departure is at a most unfortunate moment. Trusting, however, in the wise and righteous domination of Providence over the passions of men and the results of their councils and actions, as well as over their lives," he continued, "nothing remains for me but humble resignation. . . . His example is now complete, and it will teach wisdom and virtue to magistrates, citizens, and men, not only in the present age but in future generations as long as our history shall be read."

Abigail's own assessment of the dead General was equally warm: "He never grew giddy, but ever maintained a modest diffidence of his own talents. . . . Possessed of power, possessed of an extensive influence, he never used it but for the benefit of his country. . . . When assailed by faction, when reviled by party, he suffered with dignity. . . . If we look through the whole tenor of his life, history will not produce to us a parallel," she wrote Mary Cranch.[8]

From a New England divine came, ironically, what was perhaps the most perfervid tribute of all. "Liberty's temple is rent in twain," the Reverend Rosewell Messinger exclaimed. "Her spotless high priest hath retired to rest, through the portals of everlasting fame. . . . Oh, Adams, thy grief must pierce the center of thy heart. . . . The prophet with whom thou hast walked hand in hand is now departed. Receive the mantle of thy brother. If the waters of death threaten to flood our country, divide them asunder . . . God will make thee Columbia's second Savior. . . . Though they said he was a god, he died as a man; let us not murmur, but rather wonder, that his great and immortal soul should be contented to reside in a human form so long"—a panegyric that Abigail scornfully referred to as "a mad rant of bombast. . . . Simple truth is his best, his greatest eulogy," she declared.[9]

The funeral procession took an hour and a quarter to move the short distance from Congress Hall to Christ Church through mud so thick that some gentlemen's shoes were sucked off and those following trod them deeper into the mire. Abigail went to the church at eleven o'clock and did not get home until twenty minutes to four. Then, exhausted as she was, she had to sit down with a company of thirty ladies and gentlemen at a formal presidential dinner.

While the country gave itself over to mourning for the dead hero, certain politicians took stock of how the General's death would affect their political fortunes. The most seriously affected was Hamilton. Hamilton's greatest political asset had been his close relationship with the ex-President, under whom he had served so ably in peace as well as in war. In a letter written in the first shock of sorrow and chagrin, he declared that Washington had been "an aegis very essential to me," and several days later he wrote Rufus King of "the irreparable loss of an inestimable man" which "removes a control which was felt and was very salutary." Hamilton's plans for managing Adams depended in a large degree upon

Washington. With Washington dead, a difficult task was made much more complicated. Wolcott shared Hamilton's view that the Virginian's character "afforded a recourse in an extreme case." Adams himself could not be "the arbiter of contending factions."[10]

Under the surface all kinds of schemes bubbled away. The President was especially indignant over the behavior of Pickering, who seemed to take great delight in his role as opposer of the President. Abigail spoke for her husband when she described the Secretary of State as a man whose "manners are forbidding, whose temper is sour, and whose resentments are implacable," who sought to dictate every measure of the administration. "I am mistaken if this dictator does not get himself ensnared in his own toil," Abigail wrote her sister. The President would indeed fire him in a moment if it was not for the fact that he was unwilling to give way to personal resentments. It was from Pickering that had flowed "all the unpopularity of the mission to France which some of the Federalists have been so deluded as to swallow large drafts of."[11]

The most extraordinary figure in the Sixth Congress was young John Randolph, a Virginia Republican. With the appearance of a girl and a high-pitched voice, this emasculated young man—"Little Johnny," his adversaries soon called him—made clear that he intended to be the scourge of Federalism. "This stripling comes full to the brim with his own conceit and all Virginia democracy," as Abigail put it. "He chatters away like a magpie."[12] Attacking the army, Randolph called it a group of mercenaries and ragamuffins. Several nights later at the theater two officers jostled and insulted him, whereupon the young Congressman wrote an angry letter to Adams, charging the President with personal responsibility for his treatment and demanding "that a provision commensurate with the evil be made."[13] Adams sent the letter to the Cabinet, who united in declaring that "the contemptuous language therein adopted required a public censure." Adams referred the whole matter back to the House where an investigation was made and a report submitted that "no evidence appeared sufficient to incriminate the officers with a design to insult Mr. Randolph," concluding that the style of the latter's letter to the President was "improper and reprehensible." Abigail was amused at the whole incident. "The *youth* will find that old *birds* are not caught with the chaff," she wrote William Smith.[14]

The Sixth Congress, which had opened in a spirit of good will and conciliation, soon degenerated into partisan bickering. The Republicans, looking toward the November election for President, were determined to squeeze all possible political advantage out of every issue that came before the House or that might, by one means or another, be brought before it. The members had wrangled for weeks over the censure of "Citizen Johnny Randolph," and when Adams sent the Prussian treaty

negotiated by John Quincy to the Senate at the end of February, one of
the Southern Senators asked to see the letters between the Secretary of
State and the American minister relative to the treaty, on the grounds
that he understood the minister had been critical of the policy of his
government. When the Senate resolution requesting the letters reached
him, Adams was furious at the petty harassment, but he sent the papers
and "the result was to the great mortification of the party."

Another effort was made to repeal the Sedition Law and it would
certainly have been better for the Federalists had it succeeded, but
James Bayard routed the enemies of the act by proposing that the common law should be substituted for it with the additional proviso that the
truth might be pled in defense. "The Antis were so terrified lest this
should be adopted," Abigail wrote John Quincy, "that they were glad
to let the old law remain by a vote of twenty-six members."[15]

In every state, but especially in the South where they were guided
and encouraged by the Vice-President, the Anti-Federalists pushed their
campaign to defeat Adams. A number of Republican presses were set up
in strategic towns and political barbecues were held everywhere. Typical
was one in Fayette County, Kentucky, which proposed, among its sixteen toasts, one to "Thomas Jefferson, the pride of Republicans and the
terror of aristocrats; may he be soon raised to the seat to which his
unfortunate country has been too long in elevating him!" Another was
to "the memory of Gen. Washington; may his illustrious actions and
services be faithfully recorded down to the year 1787, but no farther!"
and finally, "The President of the U. States; may he soon retire to
Quincy by general consent, accompanied by his *Defence of the American
Constitutions!*" The toasts brought a reference from a Federalist editor
to the "infamous sentiments" of the "drunken Republic of Kentucky."

To Jefferson the election of a Republican President was essential if
the country was to be saved from despotism—"the enemies of our constitution are preparing a fearful operation," he wrote his nephew.[16] The
Republican prospects everywhere were bright, however. New York would
be the decisive state and there the Republicans had in Burr, Livingston,
and Clinton three of the most astute party managers in the country. They
should put up Clinton himself, General Gates, "and some other old
Revolutionary characters" as electors, Jefferson suggested.[17]

Early in March the Jeffersonians, led by Livingston, Gallatin, and a
revived Nicholas, fastened on another issue which they were confident
would win votes for their party. An English sailor named Thomas Nash,
who had been a murderer and a mutineer on board a British warship,
was discovered in Charleston, South Carolina. At the request of the
British consul, Nash was seized and jailed under the twenty-seventh
article of the Jay treaty. Nash swore that he was not a British sailor but
an American citizen, Jonathan Robbins of Danbury, Connecticut. With

clear evidence that Robbins was not an American but the mutineer Nash, Adams requested the judge of the United States District Court of South Carolina to turn him over to the British consul for extradition to the West Indies to face trial for mutiny and murder. Although the House was in possession of papers which proved conclusively that Nash was what the British represented him to be, Edward Livingston and Gallatin were determined to use the case to try to indict the President. Various Republican orators rose to accuse Adams of truckling to the British and bartering away an innocent American citizen, of defying the constitution and interfering with the judiciary. Jefferson encouraged the effort to make political hay of the episode. "I think," he wrote, "no circumstance since the establishment of our government has affected the popular mind more. I learn that in Pennsylvania it had a great effect."[18]

Livingston's formal resolution charged that Adams' action constituted "a dangerous interference of the executive with judicial decisions," and stated that the Court's compliance was "a sacrifice of the constitutional independence of the judicial power."

John Marshall, indignant at the tactics of the Republicans—he wrote his brother that "every stratagem seems to be used to give this business undue impression"—gave what was perhaps the finest speech of his political career in defense of the President's action.[19] At its conclusion Livingston's resolution was over whelmingly defeated and the right of the executive to carry out extradition agreements established beyond cavil.

The Republicans were not the only ones who were busy. The Hamilton faction worked overtime making trouble for the President. Fenno and Peter Porcupine turned their guns on Adams and the irreconcilables left no prospect unturned in looking for a presidential replacement. Washington was dead. Perhaps General Pinckney could be squeezed in as Thomas Pinckney had almost been in 1796. While some of Hamilton's lieutenants sounded out Pinckney, others tried the name of Oliver Ellsworth, Chief Justice of the Supreme Court and special envoy to France. Adams was well aware of the plotting and scheming going on about him. An anonymous writer told him of the project "to have Mr. Ellsworth elected President" in Adams' stead and identified Sedgwick, Harper, Dayton, Wolcott, and Pickering as members of the "Cabal." Hillhouse and Wolcott, the writer declared, had sent "hundreds of letters to Connecticut on this subject." McHenry and Carroll were active on Ellsworth's behalf in Maryland. "Your real friends," he continued, "hope you will not be alarmed by the plot which has been contrived against you and shrink from another election. . . . Sedgwick and Dayton are violent in their opposition to you." If Adams could provide places for them or their friends, "the storm which threatens us might be dispersed."

His anonymous adviser urged the President to take some popular action, preferably disbanding the army, in order to rally support to his

standard. Hamilton and Wolcott were organizing the military and revenue officers, "under the direction of their respective chiefs," against him.
"The fear of your disbanding the army has of late given them much
uneasiness," the writer declared; "this measure would, they know, render
you popular amongst the great mass of the people and take from them
[the Hamiltonians] a powerful engine which, directed by its General,
will, they think, be very operative." The fear had passed, however, and
"Sedgwick's party do not now think you will disband the army prior to
the election." If he could not muster out the army he should take steps
to reconcile the rebels.[20]

Adams read the letters with mixed feelings. There were wheels within
wheels and he could not be sure the letters were not written by a Republican who wished to sow suspicion and hostility among the Federalists. Yet there was a ring of authenticity about them. The writer seemed
privy to the plans of the cabal. His statements checked to a degree with
what Adams already knew or strongly suspected. Ellsworth was a surprise
and Adams could not consider him a serious threat. Able as the man was,
he had no popular following, was old, in poor health, and not even in the
country.

KNOWLEDGE of the intrigues made Adams moody and irascible. He was surrounded by plotters and yet he hardly knew what course of action to pursue. To fire Pickering, Wolcott, and McHenry would be to tear the party to pieces on the eve of a vital presidential election. To suffer them to continue in office was to be continually frustrated and to know that the day-to-day affairs of his administration were passed along to his enemy Hamilton. There seemed nothing for it but to put up with the disloyal Secretaries until after the coming election. But the decision, once made, did nothing for Adams' disposition. He lived in a kind of continual rage, like a diminutive volcano that might erupt at any moment.

The eruption came unbidden in the late spring when he had weathered the long winter and had only a few weeks to go before he could escape to Quincy. He summoned McHenry to confer with him on a routine matter affecting the War Department. Seeing the Secretary standing before him, full as he had reason to suspect of a false deference, his indignation got the best of him. He had heard, Adams said, that the Secretary of War wished to retain his office after the coming presidential election. McHenry replied evasively and then, as he recalled the scene later, the President "with great warmth" declared that Hamilton had been opposing the administration in New York. "No head of a department shall be permitted to oppose me," he said, his face flushed with anger.

"I have heard no such conduct ascribed to General Hamilton and cannot think it to be the case," the frightened McHenry answered.

"I know it, sir, to be so. . . . You are subservient to him. It was you who biased General Washington's mind . . . and induced him to place Hamilton on the list of major generals, before Generals Knox and Pinckney."

Suddenly all of Adams' bitterness against Hamilton broke forth in a torrent. He was "an intriguant, the greatest intriguant in the world—a man devoid of every moral principle—a bastard and as much a foreigner as Gallatin." For himself, Adams would rather serve as Vice-President under Jefferson or resident minister at The Hague than be indebted "to such a being as Hamilton for the presidency." Washington had saddled him with three ministers all of whom were children in the vitally important field of foreign policy. Wolcott was an excellent Secretary of the Treasury but of no use as an adviser in the dangerous waters of international diplomacy. "How could such men," Adams demanded, growing more irate every minute, "dictate to me on such matters, or dare to recommend a suspension of the mission to France!"

The President's accumulated resentment, his suspicion, frustration, and disappointment poured over McHenry. The unhappy Secretary endured the tirade as best he could; when the President paused at last, he replied with what dignity he could muster that he would of course resign at once.

"Very well, sir," Adams said, already a little ashamed of his outburst. "For myself, I have always, I will acknowledge, considered you as a man of understanding and of the strictest integrity."[1]

The next day the shaken Secretary submitted his resignation and Adams accepted it. There was general agreement among those who, like Washington, Wolcott, and Hamilton, knew him best that McHenry was an inept Secretary of War. It was also clear that he was working at cross-purposes with the President; but even so Adams regretted that he had lost control of himself and subjected the man to such humiliation. The fact was that only a sadist and a bully would have summoned a man like McHenry to such an inquisition with the idea of badgering him into offering his resignation. Whatever Adams was, he was not that. Rude, tactless, and hot-tempered as he might be, he never tyrannized or browbeat a subordinate.

That Adams suffered from a bad conscience at his treatment of McHenry was borne out by Wolcott's report to that unfortunate gentleman, recounting how the President had raised the issue of the resignation and declared to Wolcott that "he was happy in understanding that your circumstances were affluent, and that the loss of your late office would not distress your family; and that if any suitable office should become vacant, he should with pleasure confer it on you."[2] These were not the words of a vindictive man, but rather of one who wished to right a wrong. Of course Adams in his later accounts of the firing of his Secretary could hardly have offered as an explanation the fact that he had lost his temper.

This interpretation would account for the fact that four days passed before Adams wrote Pickering asking for his resignation. Had Adams intended to ask McHenry to resign, the normal way would have been by letter, as he did later with Pickering, or by a simple statement of his charges against the Secretary of War followed by a request for his resignation. Adams was too well aware of how readily his temper could betray him to have trusted himself to such a meeting, which by its nature invited hasty and ill-considered statements. Reviewing McHenry's account of the episode, it is hard to escape the conclusion that the President was either utterly inept in the means that he chose to handle a difficult and unpleasant task or that his emotions betrayed him.

Having brought about the resignation of McHenry, the weakest of the Cabinet members, a man who in the President's view was simply a tool of Wolcott and Pickering, Adams had little choice but to oust Pickering. The fact that he failed to ask for Wolcott's resignation indicates that he had no intention of simply sweeping out those members of the Cabinet who had opposed his policies and worked behind his back to frustrate them. If he had stopped with McHenry it would have been generally assumed that he was afraid to take on the more powerful and arrogant Secretary of State. On the tenth of May, Adams requested Pickering's resignation. The Secretary of State was less amenable. Hinting at financial need, he refused flatly to resign and Adams, the same day, summarily dismissed him.

Pickering's own view of the nature of his office was expressed some years later in a letter to McHenry reviewing the circumstances of his firing. He had never thought, he wrote, that Cabinet officers should be bound by the rule of *"implicit obedience or resignation. On the contrary, I should think it their duty to prevent, as far as practicable, the mischievous measures of a wrongheaded President."*[3]

A recent study of the Adams administration has argued that the President was a shrewd politician whose actions in 1799 and 1800 can be read as carefully calculated moves to strengthen his bid for the re-election. The truth is quite otherwise. It was a basic tenet of Adams' political and moral creed that nothing must be done simply for the sake of securing votes. He would have betrayed the whole long course of his public life if he had allowed purely or even primarily political considerations to guide his actions. Indeed, rather the reverse was true—that he often threw away political advantage quite deliberately.

Adams was a superior politician only in the sense that he had a philosophy which provided an excellent basis for political analysis and a long experience in observing the "springs of human action," which is to say men's motives. But he invariably displayed a stiff-necked and often unrealistic rectitude which inhibited the most effective political action. Jefferson provided the contrast that gave dramatic emphasis to Adams' classical ideal of being somehow above politics. Adams saw himself as the suffering servant of the people, abused and reviled, but proceeding with unswerving determination on the course which he had set for himself. The attitude tempted him constantly to self-righteousness, as we have seen. It inclined him to conceive of leadership not primarily as the response to popular pressures but as a lonely search for the path that the leader's superior knowledge and understanding indicated as the right one. Of course in a democratic republic the leader was responsible to the electorate for a wise exercise of his powers. He must answer to them at the polls for his custodianship, but at the same time he must try to educate and inform, for if the action, taken after searching and reflection, was the right one, the people, when they understood the reasons for it, would see its rightness and support the leader.

Adams saw himself, like Washington, as a national leader, a reconciler of parties and factions, the President of Federalists and Republicans alike, and his policies and actions can best be understood in the light of such a conception of the presidency. This is not to say that Adams was unaware of public opinion. He knew very well that it set the limits of the possible, and that if public opinion could not be brought to support a policy, however wise and farsighted, the original policy must be compromised on the theory that half a loaf was better than none; or a new policy must be devised that would achieve the same ends.

All of this is simply to make the point that Adams persistently tried to act by only one standard—the country's welfare as he understood it. The firing of McHenry and Pickering was an embarrassment for many reasons. It was the first time under the new government that the executive had taken such a step, if we except the case of Edmund Randolph. It involved, moreover, a theory of the functioning of the executive branch. Were the heads of departments career officials whose tenure was based on efficiency rather than party affiliation, or were they essentially, like the President himself, political figures? Beyond that, were they men from whom the President could expect personal loyalty, loyalty to him as their superior rather than loyalty to the party or to a party leader who might not be the President?

The firing was bound to fan to a raging flame the fires of factional bitterness within the Federalist party. It would be interpreted as an unmistakable act of defiance to Hamilton and his supporters. The presidential elections were only some five months away. Embittered Hamiltonian Federalists could do far more to ruin Adams' chances of re-election than a few mollified Republicans could to ensure it. The President might enjoy a transient popularity with the less zealous Republicans because his policies, for the moment, seemed to conform to their dogmas, but he had no illusion that firing McHenry and Pickering would win votes as well as applause from the Jeffersonians.

Beyond this, there was the fact that Adams was certainly not a cold, hard man who made decisions with the chill detachment of a person insensitive to their human dimension. Both McHenry and Pickering were men he had trusted, confided in, thought of, if not as personal friends, at least as close associates. They had sat often at his table. They and their wives had been part of the small official family. He had been glad of their counsel and in many instances responsive to their advice. It seems clear enough that for the last time in his public career John Adams' emotions betrayed him and it might be argued that the betrayal cost him what he so much desired—a second term as President of the United States.

Adams first offered McHenry's position to Marshall, who wisely declined it; then to Samuel Dexter, the New England Senator, who after conferring with his wife accepted the post. Next he offered Pickering's chair to Marshall and the Virginian, after hesitating for almost two weeks, indicated his willingness to serve.

The dismay caused in Federalist ranks by the firing of McHenry and Pickering was somewhat assuaged by Marshall's appointment. Indeed, Wolcott expressed the opinion that if Marshall and Dexter had declined "rage, vexation, and despair would probably have occasioned the most extravagant conduct" on the President's part. Dexter and Marshall were, in truth, "state conservators—the value of whose services ought to be estimated not only by the good they do but by the mischief they have prevented."[4]

In the midst of public affairs there were private distractions. General Knox appealed to Adams about the fate of his son, a midshipman in the navy who had gotten into a scrap and been denied promotion by the Senate. Billy Cranch was bankrupt in Washington and had had to sell his lawbooks to feed his children and keep out of jail. John Quincy's father-in-law, Joshua Johnson, was also an applicant for a federal job. Cotton Tufts' nephew wished a commission and Dr. Welsh, wretched and penniless, begged for appointment as an army surgeon. The news of Charles at New York aroused his father's "unutterable indignation."

Abigail found her social life more crowded than ever before. The Philadelphia ladies, Abigail guessed, thinking that the President would be defeated for re-election and that "it will be the last opportunity they will have to show their personal respect," visited her in droves. "All these visits must be returned," she added, "and what with dining company always twice a week, frequently three times, I find my time altogether occupied." Fortunately her health held up and she had fewer sleepless nights than usual. When the intermitting fever came on, she had herself bled at once and the fever was thereby forestalled.

She followed the fashions closely—cambric muslin, embroidered with gold and silver, velvet cloaks and fur-trimmed bonnets of black, purple, red, or green—but noted with disapproval the tendency of some of the faster young ladies of the city to dress immodestly at balls and parties. They had taken, she wrote Mary Cranch, to exposing the greater part of their breasts, to wearing no stays or bodice, and dresses so loosely draped "as perfectly to show the whole form," while some were rouged "*à la mode de Paris*, red as a brick hearth." When such a lady came up to curtsy to Abigail, every eye in the room hung on her décolleté, "and you might literally see through her." Not satisfied with nature's charms, they had supplemented them until they looked "like nursing mothers."[5]

Everyone, young and old, had taken to wearing curls, and those who had no hairdresser wore wigs. Abigail was amused to hear Samuel Dexter, the new Senator from Massachusetts, say to Judge Cushing (who was somewhat deaf) that only two of the ladies were wearing wigs. "Sir," replied the Judge, "I thought we were all *Whigs* at table."[6]

Gilbert Stuart, that strange, improvident man who seemed constitutionally unable to finish what he had set his hand to, had been commissioned to paint a portrait of Abigail for one hundred dollars. Copley, wishing to have his portrait of the President engraved, wrote to Stuart from London asking him to sketch the President without his wig so that the engraving might be up to date.[7] Abigail, sitting intermittently for the unpredictable artist, was flattered by the report that Stuart had said, "I wish to God I could have taken Mrs. Adams' [likeness] when she was young. I should have had a perfect Venus." John, hearing the remark, added, "So he would."[8] But Stuart was such a dawdler that the picture was not finished when Abigail left for Quincy.

The winter was a mild one and spring came on prematurely at the end of February—"clear sunshine . . . the snow all melted, the rivers open and the weeping willow . . . putting on its first appearance of vegetation, a yellow aspect," Abigail noted, "which changes to a beautiful green in a few weeks." She suddenly felt an affection for the city which had so often held her in durance. They would move to the new capital in the fall and, whatever the shortcomings of Philadelphia might be politically, it was a noble contrast to the boggy flat beside the Potomac, named so grandly for Washington. "There is something always melancholy in the idea of leaving a place for the last time," she wrote her sister. "It is like burying a friend. I could have wished that the period of the first election might have closed in this city."[9]

Adams, in the spring of 1800, was in a state of acute irritability. Although he professed to believe that he would be defeated for re-election in the fall, the thought of his downfall was almost more than he could bear to contemplate. To have contended not only against the Vice-President and his party but against the Hamiltonians as well; to have preserved his country from war and internal conflict; to have given some order and direction to national policy; and despite all this, to face apparent defeat—this was too much to bear.

The results of the voting in New York confirmed his gloomiest apprehensions. There the Republicans scored a narrow but important victory. Against popular Republican candidates, the Federalists had been unable to find outstanding men to dispute the ticket and had fallen back on "the mechanics . . . men of no note, men wholly unfit for the purpose." It was a triumph for party management; for money (fifty thousand dollars was rumored to have been spent by the Republicans); and for prominent and appealing candidates.

As soon as she heard the news Abigail wrote to Mary Cranch that she was sure New York would be "the balance in the scaile, scale, skaill, scaill (is it right now? it does not look so)" in the coming election.[10] Apparently all the misery, all the blows and buffets, the long labors, the perils, the agonies were to go for nothing. The classic image of the statesman was a man of stoic aloofness, of detachment and resignation. But Adams was no stoic. His philosophy, unable to quench the fire of his passions, failed him. But if Jefferson persisted in believing that Adams' re-election would be fatal for the country, the New Englander thought better of his Republican rival. He was "far from considering [Jefferson] as a person inimical to the established government and constitution of the country," but Jefferson, lacking boldness and decision, would be surrounded by dogmatists and fanatics and "borne down with the opinions of others who are as wild and mad as the democrats of France have been."[11] The words were Abigail's but the sentiments were equally John's.

Abigail left for Quincy on the nineteenth of May. Adams had to make a trip of inspection to the "Federal City"—Washington—and before he left he must reach some conclusion in the case of John Fries and his lieutenants. He addressed fourteen questions to his Cabinet officers in regard to Fries' rebellion and the legal questions involved in the charge of treason. The Secretaries were unanimous in recommending that the sentence of death for treason be carried out on the three accused and Charles Lee concurred; but the more Adams thought about it the more convinced he was that it would be a disservice to the nation to extend the definition of treason so far. Fries' "rebellion" was to him no more "than a riot, highhanded, aggravated, daring, and dangerous indeed," but hardly treason. "Is there not great danger in establishing such a construction of treason as may be applied to every sudden, ignorant, inconsiderable heat among a part of the people wrought up by political dispute?" he asked.[12]

So reasoning, he decided to pardon Fries and all those implicated in the insurrection, to "take on myself alone the responsibility of one more appeal to the humane and generous natures of the American people." His proclamation of pardon discovered little generosity in the natures of the Hamiltonians. It was, they declared, simply another instance of the

President's weakness and of his desire to court popularity at the expense of sound principles. "Undue mercy to villains is cruelty to all the good and virtuous," Uriah Tracy wrote McHenry. "Our people in this state are perfectly astonished. . . . I am fatigued and mortified that our government, which is weak at best, would withhold any of its strength when all its energies should be doubled."[13] But most Americans approved the pardon and applauded the President for granting it.

The Republican attack, however, was not a whit diminished, and as the time grew shorter before the election, statements on both sides grew more extreme and bitter. It was a distressing spectacle to those who, without the assurance drawn from dozens of such contests which the nation would endure, feared for the stability of the Republic. Such rancor and bitterness, such lies and calumnies—there was no reckoning them. The story was told and believed that Adams had planned to marry one of his sons to a daughter of George III and thus start an American dynasty which would reunite the country with Great Britain. Before his death Washington, so the tale went, hearing of this enormity, had gone to Adams, dressed in a white uniform, to plead with him but the President had been adamant. The General had gone a second time dressed in black and renewed his arguments. When the President still refused to abandon his scheme Washington had visited him a third time dressed in his Revolutionary uniform and threatened to run him through with his sword if he did not renounce the project. Only then had Adams given up his cherished ambition to become King.

Another story, widely circulated, which amused Adams far more than it annoyed him, gave it out that Adams had sent General Pinckney to England in a United States frigate to procure four pretty girls as mistresses, two for the General and two for himself. "I do declare upon my honor," Adams wrote William Tudor, "if this be true General Pinckney has kept them all for himself and cheated me out of my two."[14]

The *Aurora* undertook in somewhat the same spirit to analyze the remodeled Cabinet. Wolcott was "scarcely qualified to hold the second desk in a mercantile counting-house," Charles Lee was simply "without talents," and the Secretary of the Navy was "a small Georgetown politician . . . cunning, gossiping . . . of no character or . . . principles." Dexter was no more qualified as Secretary of War than "his MOTHER," and Marshall was a "*rhetorician* and a *sophist*" rather than a statesman, a man pliant and insincere.[15]

James Callender, Republican journalist and hatchet man, published a book in the spring entitled *The Prospect Before Us*. The purpose of the work, the title page proclaimed, was to exhibit the "corruption of the federal government and the misconduct of the President, Mr. Adams." The work was a compilation of all the old canards: disunion and a war with France faced the nation unless Adams was turned out of office;

Adams was determined to make the country a monarchy and his children successors to the throne; Congress and the President had made a shambles of the constitution; the imprisonment of Matthew Lyon showed what happened to those who dared to make honest criticisms of the government; Lyon had been done in "by John Adams, by his war hawks, his paper jobbers, his federal judges, and his juries, appointed by himself."

Washington had been, Callender declared, "twice a traitor." The "tardiness and timidity of Mr. Washington were succeeded by the rancor and insolence of Mr. Adams"; the "successive monarchs of Braintree and Mount Vernon" had reduced the country to desperate straits and shackled freedom; Adams' administration had been "one continued tempest of *malignant* passions"; the President had labored "with melancholy success to break up the bonds of social affection and under the ruins of confidence and friendship to extinguish the only beam of happiness that glimmers through the dark and despicable farce of life." France was the proper model for the United States, Callender concluded: "The French are cheerful and powerful," their churches flourish, and "internal improvements are advancing faster in the Republic than in any part of the United States."

Of course it did not work just one way. The Federalist press gave almost as good as it received. Jefferson was depicted as an atheist, a Francophile, a revolutionist, a man devoid of morals whose election would deliver the country to licentiousness and debauchery. Rape, seduction, and blasphemy would stalk the land; the principles of the French Revolution would pervade the government and destroy the Union.

To party and factional bitterness was added that of sections—the North against the South, the middle states against both, the East against the West. It was small wonder that Abigail lamented the outpouring of "abuse and scandal, enough to ruin and corrupt the minds and morals of the best beople in the world."[16]

WHILE Abigail, having fired off a stream of preparatory instructions to Cotton Tufts and Mary Cranch, started north, Adams set out with William Shaw for Washington. The President, with a new coachman and two smart footmen, made his way over incredibly rutted roads, delayed by enthusiastic demonstrations of affection and respect. The southern Pennsylvania countryside was like "a perfect garden," the equal, Adams declared, to Flanders and to the lush landscape of England. As the presidential carriage approached Lancaster and York, troops of horsemen rode out to meet him and accompany him into town. "Tawny Town" was beautifully illuminated in his honor, and at Frederick Town the local militia joined in, the church bells were rung, "and every possible mark of veneration and respect paid." Everywhere people turned out, shop-keepers and farmers, lawyers, merchants, tavern-keepers, mothers with babies in their arms, pretty girls, and apprentice boys.

The President was met at the District line by a company of citizens on horseback and escorted to the Union Tavern in Alexandria where he was greeted with a salute fired by the militia of the city and a company of marines imported from Baltimore. At Georgetown he received and replied to an address of the townspeople expressing their respect and affection. The next day he passed over Rock Creek Bridge and entered the capital.

The city looked raw and unfinished. There were no paved streets and few private houses, but the President found the public buildings "in a much greater forwardness than he expected." One wing of the Capitol was nearly completed and the President's mansion, with "a sufficient number of rooms," would be ready by the fall when the Adamses returned from Quincy. Adams and William Shaw lodged at Tunnicliff's City Hotel with Samuel Dexter and Marshall, and the President was entertained at a dinner for seventy given by the leading citizens. They had dinner the following day with Joshua Johnson, John Quincy's father-in-law, and talked of the younger Adamses. Mrs. Johnson had invited a

company of friends to meet the President at tea but he put in a disconcertingly brief appearance—only long enough indeed to swallow a cup
of tea. Most of his Washington hosts suffered similar disappointments.
Adams was restless and ill at ease on such occasions and his appearances
were perfunctory.

The President visited Charles Lee and envied his Attorney General's
handsome home in Alexandria, just across the river. "Oh! that I should
have a home!" he wrote Abigail. "But this felicity has never been permitted me. Rolling, rolling, rolling into the bosom of mother earth." He
planned to visit Martha Washington at Mount Vernon to pay his respects and then he would travel north as fast as his old bones would
allow him—at perhaps twenty miles a day.[1]

Abigail on her way north stopped off at New York. There the news was
all bad. The provisional regiment that Colonel Smith had organized was
being disbanded. Smith had written Adams begging him for a commission and the President in turn had written to Hamilton asking his
opinion about commissioning the Colonel in the regular army at the rank
of brigadier general. Hamilton had advised against it because of Smith's
relation to the President, and the Colonel found himself once more without the means of providing for his dogs and horses. Nabby, in consequence, was gloomy and depressed though she tried not to let her mother
see it.

Most devastating of all to Abigail was Charles's condition. He had
returned home but he was clearly far gone in drink and dissipation. The
meeting was a painful one. Charles was pathetically happy to see his
mother; shame and humiliation reduced him to tears. He pulled himself
together enough to ask after his father's health and give a rambling and
incoherent account of the bad fortune which had brought him to his
present state. It was heartbreaking to Abigail to see her son, the once
charming and gay young man who had won everyone with his graciousness and high spirits, his singing and flute playing, his dancing and witty
stories, sunken in misery and despair. "Trials of various kinds seem to be
reserved for our gray hairs, for our declining years," she wrote Mary
Cranch. "Shall I receive good and not evil? I will not forget the blessings
which sweeten life," she added resolutely. She had heard so many lies
and falsehoods circulated about her husband on her trip that she felt
"disgusted with the world, and the chief of its inhabitants do not appear
worth the trouble and pains they cost to save them from destruction."
She confessed to her sister that she was "in an ill humor. . . . I heard a
sermon yesterday upon the subject of humility. I believe I do not yet
possess enough of that negative quality to make me believe that I deserve all that can be inflicted upon me by the tongues of falsehood." The

torrent of abuse directed at John, who had devoted his life to "the best interest of his country," seemed a sad reward for his services.[2]

The President, having completed his inspection of the new capital, set out for Quincy at breakneck speed, often making fifty miles or more a day. He arrived at the farm early in July, exhausted by his dash through the summer heat, and found Abigail ill in bed, but the sea air worked its restorative magic upon both husband and wife. John, touching his native earth, was strengthened as always and Abigail was soon "pretty spry . . . as we New England people say."[3] She busied herself about the painting and remodeling of the house and John gave what time he could take from public matters to completing the barn, which bid fair to be the finest structure in Quincy. Again he was criticized for leaving the capital, but in a day when it took from five to eight weeks for a dispatch to cross the Atlantic Ocean, a delay of six or seven days (which was the time needed for a letter to get from one of the Secretaries at Philadelphia to Adams at Quincy) was not a serious matter and Adams felt that his life, quite literally, depended on his getting back to his farm for a few months each year. Not only did he need it for his always precarious health, but he found that getting out of the press and confusion of the capital gave him a calmer, better perspective on the problems that faced him and his country.

He carried on a steady correspondence with Marshall on matters of state, and less frequently with Stoddert and Dexter. Letters passed back and forth every few days dealing with the depredations of the Barbary pirates, the vexatious problem of the British claims commission, the need for fresh instruction to the American envoys in France.

The farm, moreover, was by no means isolated from the outside world. Dozens of Massachusetts politicians made their way to Quincy during the summer to seek or give counsel and to offer their opinions about the prospects of the coming election. In all this coming and going, the Boston Federalists—Cabot, Sewall, Higginson, et al.—were conspicuous by their absence, and their desertion distressed Adams more than any other single incident in the bitter campaign. He had counted most of these men as his personal friends in better times. They were fellow New Englanders, blood of his blood and bone of his bone, in a manner of speaking. They were men who had enjoyed his hospitality, his confidences, and his favors. Prominent among them were Fisher Ames, George Cabot, John Lowell, Theophilus Parsons (John Quincy had served his law apprenticeship with Parsons), and Francis Dana, who had been like a member of the family, Adams' fellow envoy in Europe, and a kind of foster father to John Quincy. They had supported Washington's administration loyally and now, angry and unforgiving, they had turned on his successor, on one of their own. Politics, which for Adams at least was life, had brought him many disappointments but none more deeply felt than the loss of old friends who one by one dropped off, deserted him in the face of the enemy at the height of the battle. In his son's words these men now directed their "personal abuse and deadly animosity against the President," men who "have known him in public and in private life for thirty or forty years; who have acted with him in a variety of public capacities, and with some of whom he has been for many years in habits of friendship."[4]

Wolcott wrote Fisher Ames in August that, in his view, Adams should not be supported by Federalists. In a long comparison of Jefferson and Adams, the Secretary of the Treasury concluded that there was little to choose between them. "However dangerous the election of Mr. Jefferson may prove to the community," he wrote, "I do not perceive that any portion of the mischief would be avoided by the election of Mr. Adams. We know the temper of his mind to be revolutionary, violent, and vindictive; he would be sensible that another official term would bring him to the close of life. His passions and selfishness would continually gain strength; his pride and interest would concur in rendering his administration favorable to the views of democrats and Jacobins . . . the example of a selfish attention to personal and family interests would spread like a leprosy in our political system." Adams had irritated the British and shown little understanding of the financial needs of the country and little sympathy with the business and mercantile interests.

Wolcott made it plain that he had done all he could to advance the cause of General Pinckney but he had little hope of success because of the popular sentiment in the President's favor.[5] The Secretary of the Treasury concluded his letter by authorizing Ames to make what use of it he wished among the Federalists of Massachusetts and New England. "I shall do all in my power, consistently with truth and integrity, to promote the election of General Pinckney," he wrote McHenry a few weeks later, urging him to do what damage he could to the President by disclosing the circumstances which had attended his resignation.[6]

Cabot, reluctant as he was to support Adams, did not "see how it will be practicable to discard Mr. Adams as a candidate at this period without confounding us in this quarter, and consequently exposing the whole party to a defeat."[7] He wrote in a similar vein to Hamilton, warning him that "without a union of all the Federalists, neither Mr. A[dams] nor Mr. P[inckney] can probably be chosen. Hearing that Hamilton was at work on an indictment of Adams' "misconduct," Cabot reminded the New Yorker that the Federalists, in effect, had endorsed Adams and Pinckney as the party's candidates in a caucus at Philadelphia and to attack Adams now would be to go back on that pledge. It should be clear, therefore, in any assault made on the President that it was personal in nature and that the party officially preferred the election of Adams to

Pinckney.[8] One of the most persistent themes of the Hamiltonians was that Adams was superannuated, senile, too old and infirm for the duties of his office. They made much of his tremor, of his toothlessness and poor eyesight.

Meanwhile Adams could only watch helplessly while the leaders of his party undermined his strength. The Massachusetts Jacobins, Abigail reported to John Quincy, "are so gratified to see the Federalist[s] split to pieces that they enjoy in silence the game. . . . So much for elective government," she added bitterly; "if we pass the ordeal this time, I am satisfied from what I have seen and heard that it is the last time. God save the United States of America."[9]

Thomas, in Philadelphia, wrote in similar terms. If Jefferson got the presidency it would be the Federalists who put him there. There was much talk in the city about the weakness and inadequacy of the constitution, he reported. "It seems to me that nobody cares for the constitution—the framers of it are apparently in many instances disgusted with it—and all its original enemies . . . and all the Virginia tribe, as also the small folks *here* and in other parts of the Union, when they carry the day, will assuredly try to set up something else."

The ultra Federalists seemed to be embarked on a systematic effort to wreck the party. "Like the chief of the rebel angels described by Milton," Thomas Boylston noted, "it would assail the Almighty Chief of the skies, to drag Him from His throne, though sure to fall by failing in the attempt." Thomas summarized the Federalist grievances against the President: his appointment of Gerry to the first peace commission and his subsequent refusal to renounce him; his decision to dispatch the subsequent mission, "contrary to the wishes and opinions of all the Federal party, by which the strength of the democratic party has been increased and the hopes of the Federalists totally blasted"; the pardon of Fries and his lieutenants; the disbanding of the provisional army (which, though the act of Congress, Adams was blamed for); and finally his dismissal of the two Secretaries. From Maryland, the Jerseys, Pennsylvania, North Carolina—the story was the same. Adams had considerable personal popularity, but among most of the Federalist leaders there was "every symptom of languor and inactivity." The Republicans, on the other hand, were indefatigible in their efforts. Whatever differences existed among themselves were obscured in their common effort to unseat the President. They had more newspapers, more active workers, more pamphleteers, and more effective issues. They hammered away at the themes of excessive government spending and heavy taxation; the threat to liberty posed by the Alien and Sedition Acts; and the oppressiveness of a standing army. These were all classic campaign issues. Related as they were to the grievances which had brought on the Revolution, they touched a responsive chord in virtually every American

Moreover the Federalists had been in office for twelve years. Under the democratic system, the party in power falls heir to the accumulated complaints and irritations every citizen holds against his government or, indeed, to some degree against the world in general. The man with the shrewish wife or the improvident farmer came to feel subconsciously that things might be better with them if there was a change in the national administration. "Had Enough? Vote Republican!" was the inspired slogan of a later age after twenty years of Democratic rule.

Jefferson's platform was plain enough. As he saw it, the Federalists wished "to sink the state governments, consolidate them into one, and monarchize that." They were committed to a large standing army to intimidate and overawe the people; they were the party of banks and commerce, of war and the suppression of freedom; the party of big government and big spending. The Republicans stood for the opposite. The states should be left to manage all domestic problems themselves; the federal government should concern itself only with foreign affairs and thus be reduced "to a very simple organization and a very inexpensive one; a few plain duties to be performed by a few servants."[10]

Yet despite the skill of the Republicans in party management and the array of appealing issues which they presented to the voters, Adams was convinced that if the election were lost it would be by the divisions among the Federalists, and more particularly by the underhanded tactics of the Hamilton faction. "They must take the consequence," he wrote John Trumbull. "They will attempt to throw the blame upon me, but they will not succeed. They have recorded their own intemperance and indiscretion in characters too legible and too public. For myself, age, infirmities, family misfortunes have conspired with the unreasonable conduct of Jacobins and insolent Federalists to make me too indifferent to whatever can happen."[11]

As the time for the choosing of electors approached, there were a number of discouraging signs. "The Southern states are uncertain," Thomas Boylston reported; "the middle states suspicious or decidedly *wrong;* and the Northern . . . on this occasion are in some respects less steadfast than heretofore."

All this tempest swirled around the President's head, but at least in Quincy he was outside of the eye of the storm. The truth was that the country seemed demented. For anyone who had read Tacitus, or Plutarch, or Thucydides with his unforgettable account of the Corcyraean rebellion in which truth became lies and friends were transformed into bitter enemies, it seemed all too evident that the new Republic, begun with so much hope little more than ten years earlier, would hardly survive the ordeal ahead of it. Abigail naturally was convinced that "the peace, safety, and security" of the country rested "under God, in the re-election of one whom even the Jacobins cannot but respect." Yet she confessed that the outcome was "a mere hazard, a chance, a die. I am mortally certain we shall never have another. If Jefferson comes in, he will have a 'turbulent sea of liberty'; if Pinckney . . . he will not have a free hand nor dare to pursue measures which may be necessary for the peace and safety of the country."[12]

Adams was well aware that the Republicans were a coalition of "many sects." Once in office it would be apparent to the world that they were as divided as the Federalists. Jefferson would not be found "the man of all their people; no, nor a majority of them." He was not fanatical and zealous enough, Adams felt sure, to satisfy the extremists who dominated his party, just as Adams was not extreme enough to appease the Federalist ultras. "In short," he concluded, "one half the nation, the Federal half, has analyzed itself with eighteen months past, and the other will analyze itself in eighteen months more. By that time this nation, if it has any eyes, will see itself in a glass. I hope it will not have reason to be too much disgusted with its own countenance."[13]

There was word from New York that Hamilton, reviewing troops in his capacity as Inspector General, took the occasion to electioneer among the officers against Adams and for General Pinckney. He had inspected troops at New York, Boston, and Portsmouth, so the story went, and everywhere his message had been the same—that Adams was a weak and ineffective man who could not win on the Federalist ticket. His aides used similar language in Adams' own back yard—Massachusetts. The General was further reported as saying that it did not matter who was elected President in November because he would not have his head upon his shoulders long unless he had an army to back him up. "Thus," Abigail wrote Thomas, "has this intriguer been endeavoring to divide the Federal party—to create divisions and heart burnings against the President, merely because he cannot sway him or carry such measures as he wishes." Both Abigail and John were convinced that Hamilton was determined to try to engineer the election of General Pinckney on the ground that "a military man only should be President."[14]

As if all this were not enough, Hamilton, who was beside himself at the frustration of his plans and subject to misgivings of his own about the country's future that were quite as profound as those of his political rivals, Jefferson and Adams, wrote a peremptory note to the President on the first of August demanding to know if, as it had been reported, he had spoken "on different occasions of the existence of a *British faction* in this country . . . and that you have sometimes named me as one of this description of persons. . . . I must, sir, take it for granted," Hamilton continued, "that you cannot have made such assertions or insinuations without being willing to avow them, and to assign the reasons to a party who may conceive himself injured by them."[15] It was hardly the letter that the President of a great nation might expect to receive from his commanding general. Insolence spoke from every line. Adams was infuriated, as Hamilton knew he would be, by its tone.

That this "Creole bastard," this lecher and schemer with the cunning of a serpent, after his efforts, first to rob Adams of the presidency, and then to run or ruin his administration, could have the effrontery to address him in such a manner was incomprehensible. Mad with disappointment, Hamilton seemed bent on shattering the party and destroying whatever chance it might have to retain control of the government. Better Jefferson than a Federalist who presumed to act an independent part. Adams exploded into a fine, shaking rage. Of course he would not reply to the would-be Caesar, but the letter rankled nonetheless.

Even as Hamilton was demanding an explanation from Adams for the alleged statements made about him, the New Yorker was preparing an attack on the President which he felt confident would expose him once and for all as a weak and narrow man. In so doing he hoped to destroy henceforth among Federalists any good name or character left to Adams. Wolcott assisted by providing Hamilton with confidential government communications, and the embittered McHenry gave what aid he could. Yet even Wolcott had misgivings. Although he considered it "perfectly proper and a duty" to make known to the public Adams' "defects and errors" which had brought about "the present humiliation of the Federal party," he was concerned lest any attack by Hamilton redound to Adams' credit. When Hamilton tried to associate him openly with his campaign to denigrate the President, Wolcott replied that it would be pointed out that "the President has not injured me; that he has borne with my open disapprobation of his measures; and that I ought not to oppose his re-election by disclosing what some will term personal or official secrets." To protect himself from being accused of being a member of a "secret cabal," Wolcott declared, he had expressed his views about the shortcomings of the President to his colleagues. This, he apparently felt, freed him to work assiduously behind Adams' back to bring about his defeat.

While he did not discourage Hamilton from his project, Wolcott urged him not to publish it under his own name. "We must," he concluded, ". . . renounce our plan [to push Pinckney into office over Adams] or continue it without support. Mr. Jefferson will probably be elected, for I hold it impossible that men of sense should cordially support Mr. Adams, whatever they may affect."[16]

On the twenty-sixth of September, Hamilton sent Wolcott a copy of his "letter" attacking Adams, requesting his opinion and an acknowledging that much of it was inspired by material supplied by McHenry, Pickering, and Wolcott himself from the confidential papers of the government. "I hope from it two advantages," Hamilton wrote; "the promoting of Mr. Pinckney's election, and the vindication of ourselves." It was Hamilton's plan to distribute it "to so many respectable men of influence as may give its contents general circulation." Moreover he must do it over his own signature because "anonymous publications can now effect nothing."[17]

Wolcott promptly replied that the "style, temper, and spirit of the composition are well suited to the object and will do you honor." It should be sent to Federalists in other sections besides New England. "The letter ought and will influence the election," he added. Especially in Maryland it might draw off a few crucial votes for Pinckney by opening the eyes of some of the electors. Hamilton should at the same time explain that it was not personal motives but the good of the party which prompted his criticisms; that he was "seriously apprehensive of fatal consequences from a re-election of Mr. Adams," and simply wished to put the facts before "gentlemen of known respectability and prudence" who could decide dispassionately on the merits of the issues raised.

Still, having written all that, Wolcott was assailed once more with misgivings. If Adams seemed to have "popular sentiment" behind him, if Massachusetts seemed determined on its native son, perhaps the letter should be withheld. With the country "so divided and agitated as to be in danger of civil commotions," it might be better not to add further fuel to the fire. If the letter did not have a reasonable chance of ensuring Pinckney's election, it had better not be turned out into the world.[18]

But Hamilton, possessed by his own demons, had determined on a course that he refused to deviate from. His letter was too late to influence the choosing of the electors (indeed, it was not intended for that purpose), but it was not too late to influence the electors themselves. If only a few waverers were converted to Pinckney, Hamilton reasoned, the election might be swung to him. For a man as brilliant as Hamilton was, he could on occasion be curiously obtuse. He had tried his manipulation of electors at three previous elections, in 1789, 1792, and again, most recklessly, in 1796. Only in the first instance had he been successful and then it was merely in reducing the margin of Adams' victory. Yet he would not learn and, inflexible as he was, must hold his fatal course to the end.

The letter, intended only for private circulation, came, through the agency of Aaron Burr, into the hands of a Republican editor who was delighted to publish it and thereby advertise the division in Federalist ranks. In pamphlet form, it was scattered throughout the states to work its poison wherever it could.

To the familiar list of charges against Adams' administration, Hamilton added a devastating analysis of Adams' personal character. A man of undoubted integrity, the President nonetheless did "not possess the talents adapted to the *administration* of government." There were "great and intrinsic defects in his character which unfit him for the office of

Chief Magistrate." His boundless vanity and jealousy made it impossible for him to decide issues wisely and impartially on their own merits. He had "an imagination sublimated and eccentric, propitious neither to the regular display of sound judgment nor to steady perseverance in a systematic plan of conduct."

Once the pamphlet had appeared, Adams found staunch supporters, among them the Federalist newspaper editor and sometime lexicographer, Noah Webster, who wrote and published an able defense of the President, describing him as a man respected and beloved for his services to the Revolutionary cause and to the new union of the states, a strong candidate with a large popular following. "Under these circumstances," he wrote, "what extreme indiscretion was it to undertake an opposition from which, in case of success, would inevitably result an irremediable division of the Federal interest; and in case of defeat, complete our overthrow and ruin! Will not Federal men," he wrote, addressing Hamilton, "as well as Anti-Federal, believe that your ambition, pride, and overbearing temper have destined you to be the evil genius of this country?" On the basis of Adams' long public service, Webster noted, it was evident that he was "a man of pure morals, of firm attachment to republican government, of sound and inflexible patriotism, and by far the best-read statesman that the late Revolution called into notice." Contrasted with these qualifications, "his occasional ill humor at unreasonable opposition and hasty expressions of his opinion are of little weight. . . . Your conduct," Webster concluded, "on this occasion will be deemed little short of insanity."[19]

Uzal Odgen, in another pamphlet written and published at Salem, eulogized Adams for the "preservation of our Union and the suppression, as far as possible, of the *spirit* of *party*." William Pinckney, writing as Caius, called Hamilton's letter "the production of the malice of disappointed ambition, and the unintentional instrument of much good to Mr. Adams' election, by removing from the minds of all honest and discerning Democrats all apprehension of his [Adams'] harboring an unjustifiable bias towards England, and by convincing them that the most laborious and cunning investigation of his character have contributed nothing to lessen him in the eyes of those who discern and reflect."

But the defenses came too late; the damage could not be repaired. The man to whom a majority of Federalist leaders looked as the effective head of their party had disavowed that party's President, coming out at the eleventh hour in open opposition to his re-election. The division between the leaders inevitably infected the rank and file of Federalists. "I cannot describe . . . how broken and scattered your Federal friends are!" Troup wrote to Rufus King. "We have no rallying point; and no mortal can divine where and when we shall again collect our strength. . . . Shadows, clouds, and darkness rest on our future prospects." Even the Hamiltonians were dismayed. "Our friends . . . lamented the publication. . . . Not a man . . . but condemns it. . . . Our enemies are universally in triumph."[20]

Adams' reaction to the pamphlet was expressed in a merciless analysis of his enemy's character. "His exuberant vanity and insatiable egotism," he wrote of Hamilton, "prompt him to be ever restless and busy meddling with things far above his capacity, and inflame him with an absolute rage to arrogate to himself the honor of suggesting every measure of government. He is no more fit for a prompter than Phaeton to drive the chariot of the sun. If his projects had been followed they would absolutely have burnt up the world." Abigail reserved comment on "the little General's letter" until she should arrive at Washington. There she hoped she would "have more health to laugh at the folly, and pity the weakness, vanity, and ambitious views of as very a sparrow as Sterne commented upon in his *Sentimental Journey*, or More describes in his fables."[21]

Added to the President's political handicaps was the unfortunate Pinckney letter. When Thomas Pinckney, brother of General Charles Cotesworth Pinckney, had been appointed ambassador to Great Britain in 1792 as Adams' successor, the latter had written with characteristic indiscretion to Tench Coxe that he had a poor opinion of the South Carolinian. The Pinckneys, in Adams' view, had long coveted the post for a member of the family and had even been responsible for limiting Adams' own tenure to three years, "in order to make way for themselves to succeed me." Included also in the letter was a dark reference to "much British influence" in the appointment.

After Coxe was fired from the Treasury Department he dug up the letter and took it to William Duane, Bache's successor as editor of the *Aurora*. Duane thereupon wrote an editorial declaring that the federal government had "acted under the influence of British gold." The government initiated libel proceedings against Duane, and the editor in his defense produced the letter to Coxe. He asserted that it was the President of the United States who had by implication made the charge. Of course the letter said no such thing, but the prosecution was clearly embarrassed by its presentation as evidence. There was a hasty conference with the Attorney General; the indictment was withdrawn and Duane placed under an injunction not to publish the letter or reveal its contents.

Thus blocked at one point, Duane tried to use the letter to produce a rift in the Federalist party. He made three copies and put two of them in the hands of the Pinckneys and gave another to a Republican Senator. Thomas Pinckney, not unnaturally indignant, took the letter to the President. Adams' embarrassment was evident. The remarks were hasty and ill advised, he admitted. They were based on a rumor which he was now convinced had been wrong. He had not personally known any of the

Pinckneys at the time, and having come to know them subsequently, he had the highest respect for their ability and integrity. The explanation was accepted and the issue hopefully laid to rest.

But Duane had no intention of letting it lie. He published the letter and sent copies to Republican papers in every state. Pinckney, pressed to defend himself, stated it as his conviction that the letter was a forgery, although he knew that in substance at least it was correct. Duane responded by giving an account of the discussion over the letter which he alleged had taken place between the President and Pinckney the previous winter. The letter, Duane insisted, was genuine. Thus cornered, Pinckney asked for and received from Adams a recantation which was widely published. The President had no "particular" recollection of the letter. He had undoubtedly written some such comments but he certainly never intended to suggest that the influence of the British on the appointment of the ambassador was an improper one. Governments not infrequently let it be known that a certain gentleman would be acceptable to them. He had meant no more than that. As to the rest, he had been unacquainted with the Pinckneys and misinformed both as to their sentiments and their character. His suspicion, he declared, "of even that kind of influence" was "wholly unfounded in reality." The letter had been written in a "sportive, playful, careless" spirit and the President was happy to state that he knew "of no two gentlemen whose character and conduct are more deserving of confidence" than Thomas and Charles Cotesworth Pinckney.[22]

The damage was only partly repaired. Everything was grist for the political mill and Republican editors made all they could of the episode to split the Federalists and discredit the President.

IN SEPTEMBER, Quincy was racked by "a bilious intermitting fever" that started with the owner of a slaughterhouse and spread through the entire community. John and Abigail escaped it, but Abigail was prostrated by another attack of the rheumatic fever, as she called it, which had nearly taken her life two summers before. It was time for the President to make his way back to the new capital at Washington, and he despaired at the thought of having to leave her behind at the moment in his life when he most needed her. He did not dare to take her with him to the boggy swamp on the Potomac. But at the last moment his resolution failed. She wished to be by his side. For two old people, there were some things more important than the shreds of life remaining to them. It would be too dismal to be alone in the partly finished presidential mansion, separated by another hundred and fifty miles. Seeing him waver, Abigail determined to follow him "bag and baggage" as soon as possible, whatever it might cost her in bumpy, rutted roads, pain and discomfort, or life itself.

Adams' journey to Washington was attended by crowds as large and enthusiastic as those which had turned out after his election, and for a brief time his spirits rose. Perhaps all was not lost. But popular applause and approbation would not, of course, elect him President. The presidential electors were chosen in a variety of ways in the different states and, as we have seen, there was room for a vast amount of maneuvering and even chicanery. The election would be won or lost in the consciences of the individual electors, most of whom had been chosen because of their personal popularity rather than because of a hard and fast commitment to a particular candidate. The President smiled wryly when Thomas Boylston wrote that several Republicans had told him that "*next* to their idol Jefferson they would infinitely prefer him to any man in the country. . . . This language," Thomas added, "is humorous enough, and one hardly knows which it savors of most, rudeness or flattery."[1]

When he arrived in Washington, Adams found awaiting him the resignation of his Secretary of the Treasury—for personal reasons, Wolcott explained. Was it a case of abandoning a sinking ship, or had his conscience at last dictated what he should have done months before? Adams replied in a brief note expressing his reluctance to accept the resignation and thanking Wolcott for his services.

The new executive mansion, unfinished as it was, was an impressive building. Adams moved in with Briesler and made himself as comfortable as he could in the damp, echoing rooms. His first night there, he sat down to write Abigail. After telling of his journey from Philadelphia, he added, "Before I end my letter, I pray Heaven to bestow the best of blessings on this house and all that shall hereafter inhabit it. May none but wise and honest men ever rule under this roof."[2]

A week after her husband's departure Abigail left Quincy with a heavy heart. The bilious fever had stricken her sister, Mary Cranch, and the coachman had fallen ill, requiring her to find another driver. In New York she must visit poor Charles, and in Washington there would be the confusion and disorder of setting up the new quarters, coupled with the painful ordeal of living out the final months of an administration that apparently had been rejected by the people it had served so well. "My journey is a mountain before me, but I must climb it," she wrote Thomas.

At New York she found Charles destitute and desperately ill with a racking, consumptive cough, a liver infection, and dropsy. He had been given lodging by a friend and clearly did not have long to live. Abigail was overcome by pity and greatly distressed. Sally, who had taken the children to her mother's home, was with Charles to give him what comfort and nursing she could. Abigail said good-by to her son, knowing it was for the last time, feeling such heartbreak as only a mother can comprehend.

In Philadelphia she stayed at the former presidential mansion, now serving as a hotel. Even with things changed about, she felt at home, and with Thomas beside her and her friends coming by to call, she had a brief interlude of contentment and ease.[3] From Philadelphia she proceeded on to Washington, which as she expected had "houses scattered over a space of ten miles, and trees and stumps in plenty." The presidential mansion was "a castle of a house" on a slight hill with a beautiful view of the Potomac. The country round about was "romantic but a wild, a wilderness at present." The house itself was twice as large as the Quincy meeting-house but "built for ages to come." Not a single chamber was fully furnished and the rooms were so large and drafty that thirteen fires had to be kept going constantly to keep off the chill.

Settled in as well as could be with her retinue, Abigail could not but feel that she was in a foreign land. This was the South and it was as different from Quincy in tone and temper, mood and spirit as London was from Rome, or New England cider was from the imported wines of the Southern planter. It needed commerce and industry, in her view, before it would rise "to any degree of respectability." She saw everywhere the evidences of the slavery she deplored. From her bedroom she watched what seemed to her a classic Southern scene. Twelve Negro slaves were occupied with four small carts removing dirt from in front of the house. The four carts were all loaded at the same time; while four Negroes drove them to a dump about half a mile away, the other eight rested on their shovels and entertained each other. If the carts had been staggered in their trips, all twelve Negroes could have worked constantly. Indeed, she wrote Cotton Tufts, describing the scene, "two of our hardy N. England men would do as much work in a day as the whole twelve." It was a strange system that drove "slaves half fed and destitute of clothing . . . to labor, whilst the owner walked about idle, though his one slave is all the property he can boast."

The lower grades of whites were a class below even the Negroes "in point of intelligence and ten below them in point of civility." They looked like "the refuse of human nature," and were surly and insolent. Most maddening of all to Abigail's efficient New England spirit was the "want of punctuality" among all classes. Laborers who promised to come at eight appeared at noon. No one was ever on time or even apologetic for being late. The whole tempo of life was so casual and relaxed that it was a wonder anything ever got done, even as late and as badly as it did. In addition it was difficult to get many tasks done at all. With unwanted trees standing right in the middle of the so-called city, it was impossible to find someone to perform the simple labor of sawing them down and cutting them up into firewood. No one wished to take the trouble, and the most impoverished white scorned the job as "nigger's work."[4]

On the twenty-second of November, Adams delivered his fourth annual message, written largely by Marshall, to a joint session of the House and Senate, meeting for the first time in the new Capitol building. It was appropriate to ask God's special blessing on the occasion: "May this territory be the residence of virtue and happiness! In this city, may that piety and virtue, that wisdom and magnanimity, that constancy and self-government which adorned the great character whose name it bears be forever held in veneration!" One of the first questions before Congress would be the question of how the "local powers over the District of Columbia, vested by the constitution in the Congress of the United States," should be exercised.

Adams reported that the provisional army had been disbanded in conformity with the instructions of Congress, and once more recommended that a reform of the Court be an urgent item on the legislative agenda. The difficulties which had caused a suspension of the sixth article of the

Jay treaty had not yet been resolved, but every effort consistent with dignity and honor was being made to that end. Napoleon Bonaparte, the First Consul, had received the American envoys and appointed three persons to treat with them. Despite the favorable developments, in the President's opinion it was essential for the United States to maintain a naval and military establishment "adapted to defensive war." In the long run it would be the wisest economy and the best insurance of the future tranquillity and safety of the country.

The reply of the Senate was polite but noncommittal. It echoed the President's hope that the new city would prove worthy of the hero after whom it had been named, and observed that "it is not the least among our consolations that you, who have been his companion and friend from the dawning of our national existence, and trained in the same school of exertion to effect our independence, are still preserved by a gracious Providence in health and activity to exercise the functions of Chief Magistrate."

The response of the House was bolder and more extensive. Special mention was made of the "cheerfulness and regularity" with which the provisional army had disbanded, evidence "clear and conclusive of the purity of those motives" which had induced officers and men "to engage in the public service." Notice was also taken of the administration's policy of creating a respectable military and naval force. "At this period it is confidentially believed," the House declared, "that few persons can be found within the United States who do not admit that a navy, well organized, must constitute the natural and efficient defense of this country against all foreign hostility." The words were sweet to Adams' ears. If he had done nothing more than nourish and win popular acceptance for an adequate navy, it would in time be clear that he deserved the gratitude of the nation.

Equally worthy of comment and commendation was the "great and rapid increase of revenue" which had arisen "from permanent taxes." Here was "proof which cannot be resisted that those measures of maritime defense . . . which have produced such extensive protection for our commerce were founded in wisdom and policy. The mind must, in our opinion, be insensible to the plainest truths, which cannot discern the elevated ground on which this policy has placed our country."

The address of the House was the work of the moderate Federalist members of that body who, taking advantage of their soon-to-be-lost majority, testified to their appreciation of the President's leadership through four critical years. Adams received the address with "emotions which," as he put it, "it would be improper to express if any language could convey them." The presidency might indeed be lost to him, but in these affectionate and laudatory words there was infinite balm.

Outside the walls of Congress, Adams' message and the rejoinders of the House and Senate received little attention. People were too pre-occupied with the election to take notice of the exchange. Even the invective of the *Independent Chronicle* and the *Aurora* lacked its usual vehemence.

On the fourth of December the electoral colleges assembled in each state. Four days later the votes of Pennsylvania, Maryland, and New Jersey were known at the capital. The tally was nineteen for Adams and Pinckney, thirteen for Jefferson and Burr. (The Republicans charged that in a strong Jeffersonian district in Maryland the Federalists had set the woods afire on Election Day, thereby keeping many farmers from the polls.) On the ninth of December the votes from Delaware and Con-necticut came in, adding twelve to the Federalist side; those from New York, twelve to the Republicans. Something had gone awry in New York, for Burr, playing Hamilton's game, had arranged for one elector in that state to divert a vote from Jefferson and thus make Burr, the vice-presi-dential candidate, President.

When the votes from Massachusetts and Virginia were recorded the tally stood at forty-seven for Adams, forty-six for Jefferson. For a brief instant the Federalist hopes ran high. The vote in Pennsylvania had been split between the Republican and the Federalist ticket; with the votes of South Carolina, where Federalist sentiment was thought to be strong and where General Pinckney was expected to rally voters to the side of the administration, they could win after all. But on the sixteenth of December the crushing news arrived. South Carolina had gone Repub-lican. Jefferson led by one vote with two Republican states, Georgia and the new state of Tennessee, still to be heard from. Adams was certainly defeated although it was not yet clear whether Jefferson or Burr would succeed to the presidency. "The consequences to us personally," Abigail wrote to Thomas Boylston when she heard the South Carolina returns, "is that we retire from public life." She had few regrets. She would be far happier at Quincy. "Neither my habits, or my education or inclinations," she declared, "have led me to an expensive style of living. . . . If I did not rise with dignity, I can at least fall with ease, which is the more difficult task." Her only regret was that her husband's financial circum-stances were so limited that he could not in retirement "indulge himself in those improvements upon his farm which his inclination leads him to, and which would serve to amuse him and contribute to his health." She felt no "resentment against those who are coming into power, and only wish the future administration of the government may be as productive of the peace, happiness, and prosperity of the nation as the two former ones have made it. I leave to time the unfolding of a drama."

To the President, almost at the moment of the news of the loss of South Carolina and with it the presidency, came word from New York of Charles's death. Beside the pain of his son's tragic end, his own political fate seemed of small moment. He gave much time to prayer and to reflection on the inscrutable ways of God and of men. "Oh!" he cried out to Thomas, "that I had died for him if that would have relieved him from his faults as well as his disease." There was "nothing more to be said but, let the eternal will be done!"[5]

By the twenty-third of December the votes of Georgia and Tennessee were in and it was apparent that Jefferson and Burr were tied at seventy-three votes apiece while Adams had sixty-five. Whoever the President would be, Jefferson or Burr, the Republicans would take over the administration of government. Anticipation of the blow and personal sorrow had robbed it of much of its power to wound. "Seventy-three for Mr. Jefferson and seventy-three for Mr. Burr," Adams wrote Elbridge Gerry. "May the peace and welfare of the country be promoted by this result! But I see not the way as yet. In the case of Mr. Jefferson, there is nothing wonderful; but Mr. Burr's good fortune surpasses all ordinary rules, and exceeds that of Bonaparte. All the old patriots, all the splendid talents, the long experience, both of Federalists and Anti-Federalists, must be subjected to the humiliation of seeing this dextrous gentleman rise like a balloon filled with inflammable air over their heads . . . what an encouragement to party, intrigue, and corruption! What course is it we steer, and to what harbor are we bound?"[6] And writing to William Tudor, he noted: "Mr. Hamilton has carried his eggs to a fine market. The very two men of all the world that he was most jealous of are now placed over him." Adams derived a little cold comfort from the thought that Burr owed his eminence to the fact that he was "wellborn," a member of America's natural aristocracy, son of President Burr of Princeton College and grandson of the great Jonathan Edwards. He had predicted ten years before that the fame of his ancestors might one day make Aaron Burr President of the United States.[7] Now it looked as though his prophecy, most unhappily, might be fulfilled.

Analyzing the causes of the Federalists' defeat, Adams reflected: "No party that ever existed knew itself so little or so vainly overrated its own influence and popularity as ours. None ever understood so ill the causes of its own power, or so wantonly destroyed them. If we had been blessed with common sense, we should not have been overthrown by Philip Freneau, Duane, Callender, Cooper, and Lyon, or their great patron and protector. A group of foreign liars, encouraged by a few ambitious native gentlemen, have discomfited the education, the talents, the virtues, and the property of the country. The reason is, we have no Americans in America. The Federalists have been no more Americans than the Antis."[8]

He found consolation in John Quincy's assurance that "the sober decision of posterity" would be that his father had given a shining example "of a statesman who made the sacrifice of his own interest and influence to the real and unquestionable benefit of his country. . . . You have . . .

given the most decisive proof," his eldest son wrote, "that in your administration you were not the man of any party but of the whole nation."⁹

Assured of victory, the Republicans gave themselves over to rapturous rejoicings. Celebrations were held everywhere. Shouts and songs and cries of triumph rang in the streets and taverns of a hundred towns. At Lancaster, at Easton where a hill above the Bushkill was christened Mount Jefferson, and at the Green Tree Tavern in Philadelphia, happy Republicans joined their voices in toasts and in song to "Jefferson and Liberty!" The bad old days of monarchal government, of the suppression of freedom and hostility toward France, were over. The new day of liberty, equality, and the rights of man had dawned. All that was evil had been routed; all that was aristocratic, British, and un-American had been overthrown; and all that was honest and pure and splendid had been raised up. So chopfallen were the Federalists, a Republican writer crowed, that barbers were forced to raise their prices for shaving such long faces. In Pittsfield the town bell was rung so enthusiastically that the bell rope broke and pieces of it became treasured souvenirs of the overthrow of tyranny.

For most Federalists it seemed indeed as though the world, or at least their world, had come to an end. Confusion and anarchy must follow the elevation of either Jefferson or Burr to the presidency. Atheism, sponsored and encouraged by Republican fanatics, would triumph over religion; the political heresies of Revolutionary France would tear the country asunder. The Washington *Federalist* expressed a sentiment common to many members of that party when it reversed the eagle on its masthead and put under it the motto, *Pluria e Uno*, "Many out of One." The "Lunatic Party" under the "Moon of Democracy" was watching the eclipse of the Federal Sun; the Eagle of Freedom would soon be replaced by the Owl of rational skepticism.

"The die is cast!" the editor of the *Federalist* lamented. ". . . Our beloved ADAMS will now close his bright career. . . . Immortal sage! May thy counsels continue to be our saving Angel! Retire and receive . . . the . . . blessings of all *good* men. . . . Sons of faction! demagogues and high priests of anarchy! now have you cause to triumph. . . . Calumny, persecution, and banishment are the laurels of the hoary patriot. . . . Our constitution is our last fortress. . . . When this falls, our country is lost forever!"

Amid such tumults Adams managed to keep his head and, what was equally important, to hold it up. When the first shock of disappointment had worn off, both John and Abigail took a more optimistic view of things. Although stocks fell sharply at the news of the Federalists' defeat, Abigail advised Thomas not to sell but rather to buy. "I think they will rise again," she wrote. "I think when the election is over, unless the party are more mad and wild than I believe they will be permitted to be, things will not suddenly change." Abigail felt sure that Jefferson "will finally be agreed upon; neither party can tolerate Burr. Though he has risen upon stilts, they know it will be giving to America a President who was not thought of."[10]

Their own future, as well as that of the country, was constantly on the minds of both Adamses. A few days after the election results were known Adams wrote Cotton Tufts that he would be back at Quincy as early in the spring as the roads were fit for travel. "The only question remaining with me is what shall I do with myself?" he added. "Something I must do or ennui will rain upon me in buckets. . . . Will books and farms answer the end? I must go out on a morning and evening and fodder my cattle, I believe, and take a walk every afternoon to Penn's Hill—pother in my garden among the fruit trees and cucumbers and plant a potato yard with my own hand." He would go back to the bar, he declared, but "I have forgotten all my law and lost my organs of speech and besides that I have given my books away."[11]

Although he protested that he was not bothered at being rejected by the voters, Adams admitted to Joseph Ward that he was uncertain as to the effect a quiet and retired life might have upon his health. To change from "a life of long journeys and distant voyages, in one or another of which I have been monthly and yearly engaged for two and forty years," he wrote, and take up instead "a routine of domestic life without much exercise . . . may shake an old frame. Rapid motion ought not to be succeeded by sudden rest. But at any rate," he concluded, "I have not many years before me, and those few are not very enchanting in prospect."[12] But to Thomas, who wrote a letter full of grief and affection, he replied stoutly: "Be not concerned for me. I feel my shoulders relieved from a burden. The short remainder of my days will be the happiest of my life."[13]

Abigail's principal concern arose over how they would make out financially. It seemed unfair that a man who had devoted his life to the service of his country should not be able to spend his last years in some degree of leisurely comfort and convenience. "I lose my sleep often and find my spirits flag," she wrote her youngest son. She believed in her deepest soul that no sparrow fell to the earth without the notice of the Almighty, and likewise that the change in government was not the result of chance. But it was a severe test of her faith—that the Lord had so ordered it that her husband, an upright man and a faithful servant, should give way to one who, if not an atheist, came perilously close to it. "Can the placing at the head of the nation [of] two characters known to be Deists be productive of order, peace, and happiness?" she asked. Perhaps it was God's way of punishing the nation for its growing infidelity. Having written the paragraph, she crossed it out. She must not even express such a misgiving about the all-wise and all-knowing Father of the Universe.

Thomas tried to comfort his parents by pointing out that "the federal constitution has never yet had a fair experiment as a system of govern-ment." The force of Washington's personality had buoyed it up initially, and Adams' own stature as a Revolutionary patriot had worked to the same end. Now, with Jefferson or Burr in the President's chair, the government would show whether it could survive even in the hands of its enemies, so to speak.[14]

William Tudor's suggestion that Adams become an ambassador the Presi-dent rejected out of hand. "No. No! What a figure? A President of the United States descending from the head of the second commercial power of the world to become a minister plenipotentiary at a foreign court—haunting the levees of kings, queens, and ministers and taking rank after an ambassador from Sardinia, Naples, etc. No, no." He had decided, "I must be Farmer John of Stonyfield and nothing more . . . for the rest of my life." His only regret was that his financial circumstances would not permit him to entertain his friends as he would wish or to make those improvements on his farm "which require more expense than they repay in profit." But it was too late to repent. "I am not about to write lamen-tations or jeremiads over my fate, or panegyrics upon my life and con-duct," he added. "You may think me disappointed. I am not. All my life I have expected it. And you might be surprised perhaps to see how little it affects me." After a year he might, like the retired statesman in *Gil Blas*, see a specter of gloom and despair, but he did not expect to.[15]

But this was all a kind of whistling in the dark. Deep down there was no assuaging the pain. He had been pierced and hurt terribly in his inner-most self and he wished, like a stricken animal, to crawl away out of sight and die. For all his philosophy and his religion, he lived life too passion-ately, cared too intensely, was involved in its hopes and anguish too in-extricably to meet this final, most bitter defeat with equanimity. His re-jection inflicted a raw wound that would never entirely heal, that he would carry to his deathbed, that would torment him in the dark hours of innumerable nights to come. But he must put a good face upon it and carry on the routine tasks of his office for some six weeks until his successor, whoever he might be, should take over the presidency of the United States. This was the most difficult time. To accept with a pretense of graciousness the condolences, some certainly hypocritical, others sincerely meant, to go about, appear in public, answer letters and make decisions that in a sense no longer had any meaning for him—that was the severest test of all.

LXXXIII

THE question remains to trouble the historian as it troubled Adams all his days—why was he defeated? Political scientists have not yet perfected the techniques for analyzing political behavior. When the dust of battle had settled it was apparent that Adams, with everything against him, had come surprisingly close to victory. The switch of a few hundred votes in the key state of New York would have done the trick. So perhaps Abigail's immediate diagnosis, made in anticipation of the outcome, may be taken to be most nearly correct of the many that have been offered with the wisdom of hindsight by students of history in the years since. "The defection of New York has been the source [of defeat]," she wrote Thomas on the thirteenth of November. "That defection was produced by the intrigues of two men [Hamilton and Burr]—one of them sowed the seeds of discontent and division amongst the Federalists, and the other seized the lucky moment of mounting into power upon the shoulders of Jefferson."[1] Indeed, Jefferson himself gave principal credit to Burr for the Republican victory. "He has certainly greatly merited of his country and the Republicans in particular, to whose efforts his have given a chance of success," the Virginian wrote of the Republican victory.[2]

In an election as close as that of 1800—some enthusiastic historians of Jeffersonian persuasion have called it a revolution—it is obvious that any one of a number of things could have been responsible for the defeat: unpopular taxes, the capture of Pennsylvania by the Republicans (although the vote of that state was split), the fear of a standing army, hostility to Great Britain, the skill and enterprise of Burr and Jefferson and their lieutenants, the inactivity of the Federalists growing out of their inflexibility and dogmatism, the firing of the Secretaries, Adams' letter to Coxe, Hamilton's pamphlet, the Alien and Sedition Acts. Out of such an array, the historian may take his pick. He may choose one or a combination, according to his tastes. The liberal historian may select, as many have, the Alien and Sedition Acts. That they determined the outcome cannot be proved or disproved, and although the weight of evidence seems, on the whole, against such a supposition, who would dare to say that if they had never been passed Adams would have been defeated? Besides, to pin the blame on the Alien and Sedition Acts helps to make an improving moral: the freedom of the press must never be infringed because the liberty-loving American people will take their revenge on the administration that does so.

It seems more accurate, however, to say that the rancorous division among the Federalists, a division that defeat could not heal but rather augmented, was the basic cause of Adams' defeat—that and the untiring and ingenious efforts of the devious Burr. If the Federalists had supported Adams, even halfheartedly, the Alien and Sedition Acts would have weighed as a feather in the scale. As for the "revolution," it is a strange revolution indeed that is consummated by three hundred astutely managed votes in one state, for aside from New York Adams was stronger in 1800 than he had been in 1796. He was a popular figure with a stormy but successful administration behind him.

Here we must perhaps pause and defend our statement that his administration was a "successful" one. On this point the weight of many historians is against us. The standard mode has been to dismiss the Adams years as unfortunate ones, sandwiched in somehow between two great Presidents—Washington and Jefferson—and doomed to failure because of Adams' bad temper and inability to get along with his subordinates. In exculpation, it is noted that his Cabinet was loyal to Hamilton and to a policy that was not that of the chief executive himself. Then we pass on to the effects of the Jeffersonian revolution—the defeat of Federalism and the triumph of democratic liberalism.

Adams' presidency has been a cipher because of the very independence which he prided himself on as the principal strength of his administration. Sometimes it must seem to the student of the early national period of American history that it has been, in its various written versions, a kind of battleground over whose bloody margins the professorial champions of Hamilton and Jefferson have contended for victory. Back and forth they swayed, first one side dominating the field and then the other. For a while the Jeffersonians seemed victorious; then a turn in the tide of battle after the Civil War gave the Hamiltonians the ascendancy. In the early decades of the twentieth century the Jefferson warriors, spurred on during the thirties by Franklin Roosevelt, swept all before them and left the Hamiltonians shattered and demoralized. With the conclusion of World War II, however, a new generation of Hamiltonians appeared once more, well armed with monographs, formidable in numbers and in erudition, to contest the issue.

It need hardly be said that neither camp has had much regard for John Adams. To the Hamiltonians, the intractable New Englander was the agent of all their hero's woes. To the Jeffersonians, he was a prickly little man, an advocate of monarchy, out of tune with the true character of American democracy. Better certainly than Hamilton, he was simply the lesser of two evils.

If this burlesque account of the Hamilton-Jefferson warfare may be allowed to contain a certain degree of truth, it must also be said that the "philosophical temper" of those Americans who thought and wrote about our past has not been congenial to the ideas and attitudes held by Adams. Addressing ourselves to the particular question of Adams' stature as a President, it might be well to ask how the success of an administration had best be measured. Here one would assume the answer to be: by its accomplishments. According to this standard, it is possible to argue that Adams' administration deserves high marks. In the first place, he came to the presidency at one of the most critical periods in the nation's history. Only Washington's enormous prestige had prevented very serious divisions in Congress and in the country. The success of the new experiment represented by the federal constitution was so far from being assured that many thoughtful and devoted patriots despaired of its future. The country was on the verge of a ruinous war which, had it taken place, might well have resulted in domestic conflict and disunion. Adams, by the policies and measures which have been detailed, steered the Union through these perils, avoided war, maintained order, and reconciled the greater part of the country to him if not to his party. When he brought his administration to a close, there existed a small but effective navy, an augmented army, a solvent treasury, and above all peace. Quite properly, Abigail might hope that the next administration would do as well.

It is true that a study of Adams' presidency does not reveal great administrative skill, far-reaching reforms, shrewd and effective management of Congress, or, of greater import, a gift for binding his subordinates to him with ties of loyalty and affection—although he seems to have done so in the case of one of his ablest Secretaries, Benjamin Stoddert, and his Attorney General, Charles Lee. But the urgencies of the hour, not the abstract propositions and measuring sticks of historians, are the standard of successful leadership and here it seems clear enough that Adams' policy, or perhaps it should be said Adams' character, served his country well. Of the rightness of his basic policy—to make the country strong while continuing to negotiate for peace—there can be little question.

Though Adams was defeated, it was not clear who had won. Burr and Jefferson remained deadlocked at seventy-three votes each, and the Federalists at once realized their opportunity. They had enough strength in the House of Representatives to elect Burr if they wished. "Jefferson and Burr have seventy-three votes and . . . the Democrats are in a sweat," Uriah Tracy wrote to McHenry. The tie vote, Jefferson wrote a friend, "opens upon us an abyss at which every sincere patriot must shudder."[3]

Much as Hamilton hated Jefferson, he hated Burr more and he did all that he could to persuade the angry and vindictive Federalists to elect Jefferson rather than "the *Catiline* of America." But his party showed on this occasion little inclination to follow his lead. "The Federalists, almost with one mind, from every quarter of the Union say elect Burr," a friend wrote to McHenry, because "they must be disgraced in the estimation of the people if they vote for Jefferson, having told them that he was a man without religion, the writer of the letter to Mazzei, a coward, etc., etc."[4] Moreover the Federalists felt confidence that the opportunistic Burr could be prevailed upon in return for their support to adopt a more Federalist line. To their surprise he proved thoroughly intractable. "Every man who knows me," he wrote, "ought to know that I disclaim all competition. Be assured that the Federalist party can entertain no wish for such a change."[5]

Jefferson was more pliant. It was rumored that he had made certain assurances, if not concessions, to the Federalists which might swing the tide in his favor. Abigail was convinced that there was some truth to the story that the Virginian was bargaining for Federalist support while his rival stood firm and she wrote to Thomas Boylston that "this was bargain and sale business. . . . Is it not enough to give every considerate and reflecting person a surfeit of elective government [when] such proofs appear of corruption and of principle?"

Between Jefferson and Burr there was no question in Adams' mind whom he preferred. Jefferson, with all his liberal folly, was a man of principle and honor, a lifelong servant of his country and the unmistakable choice of the people of the United States to be their President. Burr was an opportunist and adventurer. Adams thought of resigning as President, in which case the office would have passed automatically to Jefferson and the Federalists in Congress would hardly have dared to cast their votes for Burr. But Abigail, ailing in body ("my constitution," she wrote Mary Cranch, "appears . . . to be much broken by repeated attacks of an intermitting kind. I patch it up, but it is hard work") and sick in spirit, persuaded him that "it would be best for him to leave to the people to act for themselves, and take no responsibility upon himself."[6]

As the weeks passed Abigail wavered in her preference for Jefferson. "I have turned and turned, and overturned in my mind," she wrote Mary Cranch, ". . . the merits and demerits of the two candidates." She found it hard to reconcile herself to seeing as President of the United States a man who was by his own admission not a Christian. "He believes religion only useful as it may be made a political engine," she wrote, "and that the outward forms are only, as I once heard him express himself,

mere mummery. In short he is not a believer in the Christian system."
Despite this, "her long acquaintance, private friendship . . . and full
belief" in the Virginian's personal integrity made her prefer him to Burr.
Yet having said that, she thought once more of his "visionary system"; of
his childish faith in the bloody and malignant French Revolution; of his
opposition to a strong government, a respectable navy, and taxes adequate to support the dignity of the United States; of his suspicion of
commerce and his determination to give the individual states supremacy
over the national government, and her heart failed her. Perhaps "the more
bold, daring, and decisive" Burr would serve the country better. At least
he was no doctrinaire.[7]

Abigail, it was decided, would return to Quincy ahead of her husband.
Before she set out the second week of February, Jefferson came by to see
her and wish her a good journey. They talked pleasantly enough. Jefferson rather put himself out to be charming. Nothing could give him greater
pleasure, he assured her, than to be of service to her, to Mr. Adams, or to
any of their family. He made special inquiries about John Quincy. Did
he like his post at Berlin? Was he in good health? "He never sees me but
he inquires with affection after him," Abigail wrote Thomas with obvious gratification. Was there a hint in the polite inquiries that John
Quincy's diplomatic career might flourish if the President could persuade
a few of his followers in the House to throw their votes to Jefferson? Certainly the Vice-President was at pains to make clear his admiration and
affection for the President's son. If there was such an implication it
escaped Abigail. But the point could hardly have been lost on Adams.[8]
Burr would have little inclination to support John Quincy's aspirations,
or those of his father for him.

John hated to see Abigail go, but in a month he could join her and the
long travail would be over. They would be together for the remainder of
their days. There was comfort, at least, in that. Traveling with Louisa,
Abigail arrived at Baltimore, "beat and banged," as she put it, not wishing a severer punishment for "the Jacobins and half-Feds who have sent
me home at this season" than to ride the roads that she had passed
over.[9]

On the eleventh of February the votes of the electoral college were
opened and the tie vote confirmed. It thus fell to the House to elect the
President and the members began to ballot at once. On the first ballot
eight states supported Jefferson and six Burr. Maryland and Vermont
were divided. After six ballots the total remained unchanged. All through
the afternoon and evening of the eleventh of February the balloting went
on amid mounting tension. As the voting continued some members sent
home for pillows and blankets and stretched out on the floor to sleep

between ballots while others wrapped themselves in greatcoats and shawls, and napped at their desks. At one o'clock and again at two and two-thirty the tellers stirred up the sleeping Congressmen and polled them. At four o'clock in the morning a postrider left the Capitol with word that there had been no conclusion to the balloting. Five more ballots were taken in the early hours of the day, the twenty-eighth at noon, and then the House adjourned after having agreed to take the twenty-ninth ballot the following day.

After the thirty-third ballot on Saturday, the fourteenth, the House decided not to take the vote again until Monday the sixteenth. In the interval the city buzzed with wild rumors—the citizens of Philadelphia had seized arms and were marching on the city; the French influence was being exerted for Jefferson; Adams was conspiring to make Burr President; and many others. A petition was circulated exhorting a Maryland Congressman representing the district in which the city of Washington lay to change his vote. A dozen men in a huge sled drawn by ten horses dashed about the city flying a banner inscribed "Jefferson, the Friend of the People!"

But when Congress convened on Monday for the thirty-fourth ballot the vote was still the same. James Bayard of Delaware, the Federalist floor leader, had employed his best efforts to swing a few embittered, last-ditch Federalist votes to Jefferson. He had received assurances from the Virginian, he declared, that the main achievements of the Federalists —the infant navy and the public credit—would be preserved. There would be no wholesale eviction of Federalist officeholders from their jobs. With such assurances, the Federalist Congressmen from Maryland, Delaware, and Vermont cast blank ballots and the election went at last to Thomas Jefferson.

Abigail was in Philadelphia when the news reached that city of Jefferson's selection by the House. It was ironical, she thought, that the bells of Christ Church were rung so wildly to celebrate the election of "an infidel."[10] She watched and listened with a heavy heart while the city gave itself over to a wild celebration. From the clamor one might be inclined to believe the Federalist jibe that the Republicans huzzahed "until they were seized with lockjaw" and that three hundred of them were drunk "beyond hope of recovery." Gin and whiskey, the *Gazette of the United States* reported, had "risen in price 50 per cent since nine o'clock this morning. The bells have been ringing, guns firing, dogs barking, cats mewling, children crying, and Jacobins getting drunk ever since the news of Mr. Jefferson's election arrived in this city." For Abigail it was a painful and discordant symphony.

Adams' relations with Congress did not end with the news of his defeat by Jefferson and Burr. On the fifteenth of December he sent a special message to the Senate, enclosing "for their consideration and decision" a proposed "convention" between the United States and France. Along with it went the journals of the envoys, explaining and detailing the course of the negotiations. This was his final gift—peace with the French Republic and an end to the undeclared war which had existed for almost three years.

The French had responded to the American demand for indemnification by insisting that the new treaty should be a kind of backhanded confirmation of the old. The instructions of the Americans forced them to refuse the French propositions. The negotiations had been delayed while the French ministers sent off to Napoleon in Italy for his directions. The answer came back promptly enough. The United States must confirm the old treaties as a basis for indemnification. Otherwise there would be no consideration of American spoliation claims. The earlier treaties had given the French privileges that they were as anxious to recover as the Americans were to deny them. The commissioners, after consultation with the Secretary of State, offered in a sense to buy off the most distasteful provisions of the previous treaties—the guarantee of French possessions in America, and the right of French privateers to take prizes into American ports. Although the negotiations seemed deadlocked, neither country wished to break off talks and return to the status of the undeclared war. In September, therefore, a "convention" was agreed upon in lieu of a treaty.

By its terms American property, seized but not yet condemned, was to be restored to its owners; commerce was to be free of any special restrictions; France was given a position in trade equal to that of the most favored nation; the familiar principle that free ships make free goods was affirmed by both powers, and the phrase "contraband of war" more explicitly defined. That was the best the commissioners could do. It was enough to launch the two countries on an uninterrupted course of peace that was to last for generations to come.

For almost two months the Senate debated the terms of the convention. Finally, on February 3 it was ratified with a limitation of eight years and the proviso that nothing in the convention should be construed to "operate contrary to any former and existing treaties between either of the parties and any other state or sovereign."

The illness and resignation of Oliver Ellsworth left the Chief Justice's chair open, and Adams at once offered it to his old friend the former Chief Justice, John Jay. If Jay refused it, Adams planned to offer it to Associate Justices Cushing and Patterson, in that order. Jay declined but Adams, recalling the age and infirmity of both Cushing and Patterson, had second thoughts. If the Court was to be a stronghold of Federalist principles, it would be necessary to have a vigorous Chief Justice, young enough at the very least to have a reasonable expectation of living through several Republican administrations. It was not yet certain whether Jefferson or Burr would become President, but if it should be the Virginian there would be a kind of huge and wonderful irony in leaving to dispute his passage John Marshall, fellow Virginian and bitter enemy. We do not know the path by which Adams arrived at his decision to nominate Marshall as Chief Justice, but certainly some of these thoughts occurred to him, for in answer to a letter from Elias Boudinot, Jr., urging that he appoint himself to the position, he spoke of having chosen "a gentleman in the full vigor of middle age."[11]

Adams thus offered the chief justiceship to John Marshall, and after a few days of reflection Marshall replied, accepting. "This additional and flattering mark of your good opinion has made an impression on my mind which time will not efface," the Secretary of State wrote. "I shall enter immediately on the duties of the office, and hope never to give you occasion to regret having made this appointment."[12]

The reform of the national judiciary which Adams had recommended in his annual message was pushed assiduously by a Federalist Congress. On February 13 a bill was passed which re-formed the judicial districts, established six circuits instead of the existing three, and in the process created some twenty-three new federal judgeships. The President began almost at once to submit nominations for the new offices to the Senate. He nominated John Lowell as "chief judge" of the District of Massachusetts, and Harrison Gray Otis to be District Attorney. Oliver Wolcott was named as a judge in the Second Circuit, and Charles Lee chief judge of the Fourth District. Theophilus Parsons was nominated to replace Lee as Attorney General of the United States, and James Bayard, the Federalist Senator from Delaware, was appointed minister plenipotentiary to the French Republic.

Adams also swallowed his pride and, doubtless at the prompting of Abigail, nominated Colonel Smith as Surveyor of the District of New York and Inspector of the Revenue. The nominations went to the Senate on the eighth of December, but it was the twenty-first of February before the Senate with obvious reluctance gave its consent.

Some of the judges whom Adams appointed refused the proffered positions. Charles Lee declined to serve as chief judge of the Fourth Circuit and was replaced by Philip Barton Key, whose son, Francis Scott, had a talent for setting original words to popular tunes. Jared Ingersol declined in the Third Circuit, and Adams tried first Edward Tilghman and then, when he also refused, his brother William.

On the last day of February, Adams sent the Senate the name of his nephew, William Cranch, as assistant judge in the District of Columbia; on the second of March he forwarded a number of appointments and promotions in the army, as well as forty-three nominees to the offices of justice of the peace for the District of Columbia and the county of

Alexandria. The latter names read like an honor roll of Federalism: Tristram Dalton, Benjamin Stoddert, Uriah Forest, Daniel Carroll, William Hammond Dorsey, William Fitzhugh, Robert Townsend Hooe . . .

The *Executive Journal* of the Senate shows no nominations on March 3 except those of Thomas Duncan and Hugh Barclay to be attorney and marshal of the Western District of Pennsylvania. The Senate was in session until nine o'clock, however, acting on nominations made earlier and not yet confirmed. The great bulk of these were the army officers and the justices of the peace for Alexandria and the District of Columbia. The only judges whose commissions were signed Tuesday evening, March 3, John Adams' last day as President of the United States, were the three judges appointed for the District of Columbia, among whom were Billy Cranch and William Hammond Dorsey, the latter appointed judge of the Orphans' Court in the District of Columbia.

Politics being politics in the eighteenth as in the twentieth century, it was entirely natural that Adams should wish to appoint loyal and deserving Federalists to offices that in his opinion they were far better qualified to fill than Republican claimants. But the Republican press took up the cry that the sly old President had stayed up half the night signing commissions for a host of Federalist placemen who, safely inured in judicial berths, would perpetuate the political principles which the people had rejected by their suffrages, freely and properly exercised. Regardless of the date of their approval by the Senate, the newly appointed jurists were labeled "The Duke of Braintree's Midnight Judges," and cited as an example of Adams' harsh and implacable spirit. Historians, for the most part, have repeated the story and thus given credence to the charge.

Adams certainly spent a portion of his last evening in the White House signing those commissions which the Senate had acted on that day. It is equally certain that he left Washington early the next morning and headed for Quincy, angry and bitter at his rejection by the people he had served so well. It would have been a courteous and gracious gesture on Adams' part to participate in the inauguration of his successor. In his defense, it might be pointed out that the formalities of the transfer of authority had not yet been shaped by a tradition. Indeed, the story was told (incorrectly) that Jefferson simply rode up to the Capitol at noon on the fourth of March, tied his horse to the picket fence, entered the chamber of the Senate, and took the oath of office.

The actual ceremony was not much more formal—a company of artillery and one of infantry, a rather disorderly but spirited crowd, "among whom were many members of Congress," marching to the Capitol, a discharge of cannon as the new President mounted the steps to enter the Senate chamber—that was about the extent of the ceremony. It may very well have been that Adams was not invited to take part and, sensitive as he was, preferred to absent himself rather than appear as a kind of uneasy ghost at his own political funeral.

Whatever the causes of his abrupt departure, the Republican press made pointed references to his flight and one editor, in a characteristic bit of hyperbole, reported that the ex-President had rushed off in such haste that he passed through New York the same day. Since that city was over two hundred and fifty miles from the capital over wretched roads rutted by spring thaws, John Adams would have had to travel by balloon to make such astonishing speed.

JOHN ADAMS came back to Quincy to die. By the standards of the day, he was an old man, and he felt old—toothless, palsied, bruised in spirit, defeated and rejected by the people he had loved and served. In the few years that might remain to him he would try to enjoy those rural pleasures that he had so often extolled; for the first time in thirty-five years he would settle down as a properly married man with his "best friend," his adored and adoring wife, to the simple routine of retired domestic life.

Certainly on his arrival at Quincy the weather did nothing to brighten his spirits. The heavens opened up and spilled an equinoctial downpour on the farm that lasted, with scarcely a letup, for ten days. Adams' despondency and withdrawal can be measured, to a degree, by his silence. Indefatigable letter writer that he was, he hardly put pen to paper for months on end. He was haunted moreover by the memory of Charles who, as he wrote Jefferson in reply to a note from the President, "was once the delight of my eyes and a darling of my heart." His son had been "cut off in the flower of his days, amidst very flattering prospects by causes which have been the greatest grief of my heart and the deepest affliction of my life."[1]

Adams gave much thought to the causes of his defeat in the months after his return to Quincy. It seemed to him that his decision to send the second peace mission to France in the fall of 1799 had been the cause of his downfall. The dispatch of the commissioners had been the "right" act, taken at the right moment. Shakespeare had expressed it perfectly: "There is a tide in the affairs of men, which, taken at the flood, leads on to fortune." But the victory belonged to the nation, not to Adams, except in the moral sense. He had seized the propitious moment and, disregarding the political consequences, acted as he thought best for his country. There was a kind of consolation in his subsequent defeat. He had performed a pure political act, an act that was sacrificial, an act that Thucydides or Tacitus or Polybuis would have applauded. For a man who had fed all his life on a sense of injustice and persecution, the election of 1800 was in a curious sense a vindication. In Adams' cosmology, if the right act was rewarded by victory, it was of necessity less pure, less disinterested and independent than if it brought defeat. The vanquished politician could draw comfort from his own sense of rectitude.

Yet Adams was too human ever to assuage entirely the pain of his rejection by such considerations. He got what comfort he could from them, and it was considerable but not enough. He would never exorcise the demons that his defeat summoned up. To the end of his life he would review in painstaking detail what seemed to him the essential cause of his undoing, recounting, explaining, and justifying. In retrospect it was, above all, the folly of the Federalists. Reflecting on the consequences of Jefferson's election, Adams compared the condition of the Federalists to "the party of Bolingbroke and Harley after the Treaty of Utrecht: completely and totally routed and defeated."[2] If the Federalists had only shown a little common sense, all the lies and libels of the Republican press, of Freneau, Duane, Callender, Bache, Greenleaf, Cooper, and Lyon could not have brought him down. Behind all the Federalists' missteps stood the sinister figure of Alexander Hamilton, who had pursued Adams unrelentingly from the moment of his return to American soil. "In this dark and insidious manner did this intriguer lay schemes in secret against me," he wrote, "and like the worm at the root of the peach did he labor for twelve years underground and in darkness to girdle the root while the axes of the Anti-Federalists, Democrats, Jacobins, Virginia debtors to English merchants, and French hirelings, chopping as they were for the whole time at the trunk, could not fell the tree."[3]

When Christopher Gadsden wrote a letter full of affection and sympathy, Adams was deeply touched. "While Wythe and Pendleton and McKean and Clinton and Gates and Osgood and many others . . . were arranged in political hostility against their old friend," he responded, "Gadsden was almost the only staunch old companion who was faithful found." What, he wondered, were the reasons "that so many of our old 'stanbys' are infected with Jacobinism? The principles of this infernal tribe were surely no part of our ancient political creed."

Adams revealed a good deal of his own frame of mind when he spoke of his fears of ennui which, "when it rains on a man in large drops, is worse than one of our northeast storms." He would try to find shelter in "the labor of agriculture and the amusement of letters," but his "greatest grief" was that he could not return to the bar. There he would "forget in a moment that I was ever a member of Congress, a foreign minister, or President of the United States." Then bitterly: "I know of no philosophy or religion but years which can reconcile man to life."[4] To Thomas he wrote: "If I were to go over my life again, I would be a shoemaker rather than an American statesman."[5]

There were from the first, however, many consolations. Shortly after Adams returned to Quincy the members of the Massachusetts Great and General Court rode out to Quincy to present him with an expression of esteem and gratitude for his long and devoted service both to his state and to his country. He was moved to tears, as he also was upon receiving John Quincy's affectionate letter offering all his property for the support of his parents.

Yet soon he was maintaining resolutely that he had never been so happy in his life as he was as a simple farmer. "How long this tranquillity will continue," he added cautiously in a letter to Billy Cranch, "I know not. Men are weak. No man can answer for himself; a loss of health, a family misfortune, any of the common accidents of life are sufficient sometimes *abattre le courage* of the firmest human minds, especially in old age."[6] Meanwhile he would immerse himself in the routines of the farm. He insisted that he had not been so cheerful "since some sin to me unknown involved me in politics." Abigail, writing to Mrs. Johnson, John Quincy's mother-in-law, declared that, "the beauties which my garden unfolds to my view from the window at which I write tempt me to forget the past and rejoice in the full bloom of the pear, the apple, the plum and peach, and the rich luxuriance of the grass plats, interspersed with the cowslip, the daffy, and the columbine, all unite to awaken the most pleasing sensations. . . . Envy nips not their buds, calumny destroys not their fruits, nor does ingratitude tarnish their colors."[7] She could not, she wrote John Quincy, see in his father or feel in herself "any animosity or resentment against the world, or even those individuals who have maligned and abused us."[8]

Abigail, hearing that Gilbert Stuart's paintings had been impounded by the sheriff for bad debts, commissioned Thomas Boylston to try to retrieve her unfinished portrait and that of John as well. Upon Thomas' assurance that the picture had been paid for, "the sheriff consented to withdraw your representation from the fangs of the law," he wrote his mother. He had left it with Stuart, "but I have no idea it will ever be finished," he added, "unless you should stimulate his attention by a letter. . . . If you write a few lines of a complimentary nature to him, perhaps he may take it into his head to finish your picture, but unless something is said to him on the subject he will never put a brush to it again."[9]

The "Adams Mansion," as it is now somewhat pretentiously called, was a comfortable country house, extended and added to until it suited its owner's needs very well. It was constantly filled with children and all too soon grandchildren and eventually great-grandchildren, together with orphaned nieces and nephews and improvident relatives. In addition there was, by modern standards, a large staff of servants who helped to make the house bulge at the seams. As one reads the voluminous family correspondence which recounts the comings and goings of this large and constantly multiplying clan, one wonders how they were ever provided for. Peace Field, Stony Field, or Montizello, as Adams variously called his farm, must have often been more like a busy hotel than a home.

Charles's widow, Sally, and her two children, Susanna Boylston and Abigail Louisa Adams, came to live at Stony Field, and the little girls helped to draw their grandfather out of his slough of despondence. Besides the Adams grandchildren, there were a multitude of young visitors. Josiah Quincy, a cousin and son of the Federalist Senator, was often invited to Sunday lunch when he was in the Reverend Peter Whitney's grammar school at Quincy. He was to recall in later years that "the President," as everyone in the family called Adams, was always lively and informal, full of little jokes and odd bits of information.

Children responded to his appetite for life, his wit and his genuine fondness for them. In a curious way it was with children and young people that Adams was at his best. Then, the reserve and awkwardness that were part shyness and part lack of small talk, the moodiness, the irascibility, the touchiness—all these disappeared. In their company his Puritan stiffness was utterly dissolved; he loved the young because they were full of the life he cherished, brimming over with exciting potentialities, still malleable and unfixed, open to experience.

Abigail, in her "rich silks and laces," was more formal, more the disciplinarian, the figure of authority and austerity. No less loving, no less susceptible to youthful charms and beguilements, she could not indulge herself as her husband did in play and frivolity. She was responsible for training and discipline. Adams might create a hilarious chaos by a frolic with three or four grandchildren; Abigail had to restore order. In the empire of the family he was the revolutionary, she the benevolent despot.

Josiah Quincy also recollected, a little painfully, the Sunday dinners. The first course was invariably boiled corn meal, followed by meat. Louisa Smith or Abigail always carved; the President's contribution was "good-humored, easy banter." Abigail presided over all this with her usual efficiency. Those who were there she mothered, instructed, guided, and fed; those who were absent she wrote wonderful long letters to, full of precept and advice, full of exhortation and encouragement to be virtuous, industrious, devout, and thrifty, to guard their health, take exercise, and say their prayers.

In the midst of this ordered turmoil Adams did not behave precisely like a man at death's door. He threw himself with his usual intensity into the endless and often exhausting chores of his farm. He was up at first light, ate a New England breakfast which armed him, as it had armed generations of his forebears, for whatever the day might bring. Then in his rusty work clothes with sweat and work-stained gloves on his strong, gnarled hands, he tackled whatever job lay at hand. It might be simply picking bugs off Abigail's roses and squashing the destructive little creatures; it might be an assault on the tent caterpillars that came forth every spring to do battle for his fruit trees; it might be to give special attention to his prized manure. (He wrote Samuel Dexter that he "had exchanged honor and virtue for manure.") He christened himself wryly, "Monarch of Stony Field, Count of Gull Island, Earl of Mount Arrarat, Marquis of Candlewood Hill, and Baron of Rocky Run." Duane would doubtless announce that the ex-President's preoccupation with "heaps of compost" was clear evidence of his predilection for royalty, and "all the Germans and all the Irish and all the Quakers and Anabaptists will say they believe him; and the Presbyterians will shake their heads and say it is too true," a "mathematical demonstration that my taste for agriculture is only a fruit of my arbitrary disposition and despotic principles," he wrote Thomas.[10]

At night he fell into bed exhausted from his labor and slept like a hibernating bear. Work was of course the best therapy for the shock and disappointment of his defeat. Unwittingly he healed himself in body as well as in spirit. The sea air, the unconscious rhythm of the farm, the dreamless nights, the good food, Abigail's care, the absorbing interest of his large, complex family—these gave him a new health, caught him up gradually and bound him to life. He no longer spoke or wrote as an old man tottering to his grave; he grasped existence again and, though his hands still shook, his iron grip was as tenacious as that of men twenty years his junior.

But his full involvement was slow and almost grudging. To his Dutch friend, Van der Kemp, writing from Oldenbarnveldt in New York State, Adams replied that his public engagements had left him no time "for the curious inquiries which now engage your attention."[11] But when Van der Kemp persisted, perhaps suspecting that Adams needed to be cozened and wheedled a little, the latter launched into a speculation on the reproduction of shellfish. "The little nautilus, or what sailors called the Portuguese man of war," in Adams' opinion, was "a shellfish in embryo." It was his guess that the spat or eggs were hatched by the sun on the surface of the water. "Whatever information you possess on this subject, I pray you to impart to me," he wrote.[12]

Speculations on nature, especially the principle of the magnet, "the arcana of nature," drew Adams on to the observation that "nature itself is all arcanum; and I believe it will remain so. It was not intended," he felt, "that men with their strong passions and weak principles should know much. Without a more decisive and magisterial moral discernment, much knowledge would make them too enterprising and impudent." The human spirit would always "be only of yesterday and know nothing." Its deepest secrets would remain a riddle, however much science might reveal of the natural world. Man had given no clear indication that he could use wisely the power that already lay at his command; to multiply that power hundreds or thousands of times over by scientific and technological means, without a concomitant growth in wisdom, would be to make the world a far more dangerous place than it had been in less enlightened times.[13]

The trouble with scientists was that they arrogantly assumed that their small systems comprehended man in all his mystery and variety. Buffon, the great French naturalist, was typical of the scientific fraternity in his insistence that the world consisted of nothing more than he or his fellows could observe through a microscope. According to the Frenchman, the world, natural and human, was simply made up of matter, "eternal and self-existent." All the "good and evil, intelligence and accident, beauty and deformity, harmony and dissonance, order and confusion, virtue and vice, wisdom and folly, equity and inequity, truth and lies," were a kind of cosmic incident that had existed from all time. "Planets and suns, systems and systems of systems," by this philosophy, "are born and die . . . and . . . this process will go on to all eternity." So thought Buffon, so thought D'Alembert, Diderot, and Condorcet. Adams was reminded of the German ambassador who had once said to him, "I cannot bear St. Paul; he was so severe against fornication." On the same principle Adams wrote, "These philosophers cannot bear a God, because He is just."

It seemed clear enough to him that man's only hope lay "in the wisdom, power, and goodness of our Maker." This was all the security man had, "roasting in volcanoes, writhing with the tortures of grief, stone, cholics, and cancers, sinking under the burdens of dray horses and hackney-coach horses to all eternity. Nature," he noted, "produces all these evils, and if she does it by chance, she may assign them all to us whether we behave well or ill, and she, poor hag, will not know what she does."[14]

To Van der Kemp's efforts to draw him into extended scientific inquiries, he replied a little abruptly that he was "too anxious for the precarious state of my country and for the afflicted and distressed state of my family [Abigail was ill] to be enough at ease for speculations about mammoths . . . fossil statues, or coins—these are all pitiful bagatelles when the morals and liberties of the nation are at hazard, as in my conscience I believe them to be at this moment."[15]

Susan Boylston Adams, daughter of the dead Charles, was a permanent member of the family and a source of considerable anxiety to Abigail. She showed an independence and self-will that dismayed her grandmother, and an alarming physical precocity—she had the full figure of a woman before she was thirteen years old—"a great misfortune," Abigail noted, "to have the body outgrow the mind." Susan was a sharp contrast to her cousin, Caroline Amelia, Nabby's daughter. Caroline, practically the same age, was still a child and a charming one, "soft in her manners, compliant in her temper and disposition . . . every way engaging." Susan was a restless, rather sullen girl, talkative to be sure but unhappy and impatient in her woman's body. "A thread would govern one, a cable would be necessary for the other," Abigail wrote, but remembering her own girlhood, "when I was young and very wild," she felt sympathy for Susan. Decades ago a family friend observing Abigail's rebellious and independent spirit, had declared, "Nabby, you will be a very bad or a very good woman." She would say the same for Susan. Intractable as the material might be, she would do her best to make her a very good one. "You have had a variety of tempers and dispositions to deal with," she wrote her sister; "how would you manage one upon whom you could not impress any subordination—any true deference to age or relation or rank in life?"

William Shaw, established in Boston, gave the appearance of a confirmed bachelor although Abigail, incurable matchmaker that she was, never ceased placing nubile young ladies athwart his path.

Thomas Boylston married Ann Harrod and prospered moderately. Often ailing, he had little of the fierce energy of his older brother, but in time he produced seven children and his father was gratified when the General Court appointed him to the Governor's Council. It was more an honorific office than an effective one, but Thomas did his duties faithfully and was a comfort to his parents.

Nabby and the Colonel were established on a small farm at Lebanon, New York, and John Adams Smith practiced law and served as postmaster and master in chancery in nearby Hamilton.

Adams' exile was cheered immeasurably by the return of John Quincy and Louisa Catherine from the court of Berlin in the fall of 1801. John Quincy preceded his wife to Boston. When she arrived several weeks later she brought with her the infant, George Washington Adams, their first child and John's and Abigail's seventh grandchild.

If the reunion at Quincy was a joyful one for the Adams clan, it was trying for Louisa Catherine. With her genteel nurture—raised in England and France—she found the Adams farm a disconcertingly primitive establishment. "Had I stepped into Noah's Ark," she wrote, recalling her first encounter with her in-laws, "I do not think I could have been more utterly astonished." Country dress and country manners, the nasal twangs, the Indian puddings and boiled potatoes all made her feel as though she had fallen in with a strange tribe. "I was literally and without knowing it a *fine* lady," she noted ruefully. Abigail clearly thought her a helpless poor creature, but Louisa found consolation in the fact that "the Old Gentleman took a fancy to me."[16] She gratefully returned the fancy. Between Abigail and her daughter-in-law a certain wariness remained. Yet they were not unalike in their strong wills, their intelligence, and their candor. Even as a letter writer Louisa was worthy of comparison with Abigail.

John Quincy had hardly settled down in Boston to the practice of law before he was appointed to the upper house of the Great and General Court. He then ran for the Boston seat in Congress but was beaten by his Republican opponent, William Eustis, by a majority of fifty-nine votes. In 1803 when a vacancy occurred in the United States Senate, he was put forward in opposition to Timothy Pickering and appointed by the Massachusetts legislature.

In the Senate, John Quincy led the Federalist opposition to the Louisiana Purchase, but once the purchase had been approved he refused (perhaps thinking of the Jay treaty) to join the irreconcilables in opposing the appropriation for carrying the treaty into effect.

One of the things that most concerned John Quincy was finding something to keep his father occupied and diverted. He longed to see him enjoy *"tranquillity of mind,"* as he wrote his brother. "I wish," he added, "it were possible he could see the course of things with more indifference. Try to engage his mind in something other than public affairs. For these will henceforth never affect him but unpleasantly, and the less he feels on this subject the more he will enjoy."[17] John Quincy's solution was to get his father started writing his autobiography.

When the idea was first broached to Adams he rejected it. It would, as he put it, "engage my feelings and inflame my passions. . . . It would set me on fire and I should have occasion for a bucket of water constantly by my side to put it out."[18] Nevertheless, beginning in 1804, he worked intermittently on an autobiography.

As ADAMS overcame his sense of alienation the pattern of his daily
life shifted perceptibly. He still worked around the farm as the spirit
moved him, but the manual labor he left largely to the hired hands,
whose activities he supervised closely. As long as he could mount a horse
he rode regularly, often along the shore, and every day he walked four
or five miles over the familiar paths in the Blue Hills.

More and more of his time was taken up with reading and writing.
In addition to the autobiography, his personal correspondence swelled
to a great tide. He maintained a lively and affectionate exchange with the
physician and scientist Benjamin Waterhouse until the latter's death in
1822. He wrote a series of letters to William Cunningham and to the
Boston *Patriot* reviewing the events of his administration. For the
Reverend Samuel Morse, an amateur historian, for James Lloyd, a United
States Congressman, and for Hezekiah Niles, editor of the *Weekly Regis-
ter,* he traced in detail the steps leading to the Revolution.

When John Taylor of Caroline wrote *An Inquiry into the Principles
and Policy of the Government of the United States,* which was very
largely an attack upon the *Defence,* Adams undertook to defend his own
political theories in a series of some thirty-two letters written in 1814–15.
He resumed his correspondence with Thomas McKean, Chief Justice of
the Pennsylvania Supreme Court, who once had been a stalwart Federalist and a close friend of Adams but had subsequently defected to the
Republicans. We wrote frequently to his Harvard classmate, David
Sewall, and to William Tudor. Van der Kemp remained until the end of
Adams' life an indefatigable correspondent, eccentric but always entertaining.

When we recall the difficulty with which Adams wrote, the volume of
his correspondence is extraordinary. As he himself said (doubtless with
some exaggeration), it took him as long to write a word as it once had to
write a page and, before he took to dictating in the last years of his life,
he had to use both hands to trace the letters. The bite and trenchancy of

expression remained, however, to the end. He had always, he wrote Rush, had "a little capillary vein of satire meandering about in my soul," which "broke out so strangely, suddenly, and irregularly that it was impossible ever to foresee when it would come or how it would appear."[1]

Perhaps even more remarkable was the insatiable appetite for reading. "Before I was twenty years old," he wrote John Quincy, "I resolved never to be afraid to read any book. From Hobbes and Mandeville to Diderot and Dupuis, I have kept my resolution, and I repent of none of my reading. It has all contributed to exalt my ideas of the universe and its Author, and of man and his destiny."[2] To Van der Kemp he wrote: "Can you give me any news of the millennium? Is it to commence soon enough for me to entertain a hope that I may live a thousand years longer? I want to study the Chaldean language, the Dialects, and all the books that are written in them. I want to read all the Christian Fathers and Ecclesiastical historians. I want to learn the Chinese language, and to study all the Asiatic researches!"[3]

The reading fell into three main categories. First there were the classics—Virgil, Terence, Horace, Cicero, and a dozen others. These he read and reread, and when his grandsons had grown old enough he undertook to guide them through the Greek and Roman authors who meant so much to him. Then there were historical and philosophic works —Destutt de Tracy, La Harpe, D'Argens, Grimm; and finally, the theological works—Barrows, Dupuis, the early Fathers of the Church. On everything he read, he made more or less extensive notations. Sometimes these were explosive marginal comments—"I understand nothing of this gallimauphry!" (in Priestley's *Early Opinions Concerning Jesus Christ*), or "A barbarous theory!" (a comment on a passage in Mary Wollstonecraft's *French Revolution*). But frequently they were lengthy observations entered in the commonplace book which he had kept since his days in Worcester.

In the entries in the commonplace book he argued and expostulated with the authors, challenged their remarks, dissected their logic. Of Dupuis he observed: "He is the historian of the opinions of others, and professes not to give his own. Yet in the progress of the work he frequently gives his opinions voluntarily, unnecessarily and indelicately, if not indirectly." Dupuis argued against revealed religion and Adams broke out indignantly: "If you neither love, honor, admire, or fear this, your own universe, you are an idiot and deserve no conversation or correspondence with rational beings!" Since it was evident that Dupuis did indeed "love, honor, admire, and fear" the universe, what was this "but true worship?"[4]

Halfway through D'Argens he noted: "I am very weary of these deep, profound, studious, elaborate vagaries and reveries of pagan philosophers, Christian divines, and modern philosophers. 'In pride, in reasoning pride our error lies:/All quit their spheres and rush into the skies,'" he quoted, adding, "To me there appears an immense preponderance of virtue and happiness even in this world, wicked and miserable as it is represented. . . . D'Argens, Voltaire, Johnson, ye are all models of ardent, restless, discontented minds! unsubdued by philosophy or religion." D'Argens dared to speak of "the worst of all possible worlds," but Adams could easily conceive of a worse one. "If the Master of the Universe," he wrote, "should commit to you the government of it, in one half hour you would make it infinitely worse than it is. And if your friend Voltaire and patron Frederick were associated with you in a triumvirate, you would make it, if possible, still worse. . . ."

The Manichaean idea of two contrary principles of good and evil, light and darkness, contending in the universe was a seductive but absurd concept. Nor would Adams accept the Leibnitzian notion that "man alone is the cause of evil. . . . You might have said that caterpillars, canker worms, mites in cheese, or animalcules in pepper water, or rose bugs or squash bugs, or fleas or lice were the cause of all evil," he exclaimed. God did not "interpose His power to prevent [evil] because this would destroy that liberty without which there could be no moral good or evil in the universe. Would you," he asked his unhearing adversary, "have had the universe a mere chemical process, a mere mechanical engine to produce nothing but pleasure?" Yet at the same time Adams could not entirely resolve "the existence of evil with infinite wisdom, goodness, and power." It was a problem whose solution must rest, ultimately, with God Himself. He emphatically rebuffed, as we have seen, the current disposition to reduce everything to matter. It was not even possible to tell what matter was. "Our microscopes, I fear, will never magnify sufficiently." The "atomical" theory of matter resolved no difficulties. Granted, "atoms are matter, have parts, are divisible, have active power; the question still remains, who and what moves them?" But if such questions were hopelessly complex, the duties of man were clear enough. "May I confine myself to them and discharge them to the utmost of my power!" he wrote.[5]

In his letters to Benjamin Rush, Adams was caustic about the general effects of Enlightenment thinking on the mass of the people. Priestley's notion of human perfectibility was especially insidious. Did these theorists mean that "chemical processes may be invented by which the human body may be rendered immortal and incapable of disease upon earth?" he asked. It was no extenuation to say that the Enlightenment philosophers were "honest enthusiasts carried away by the popular contagion of the times; for moral and political hysterics," he declared to Rush, "are at least as infectious as the smallpox or yellow fever." It seemed to Adams "humiliating to the pride of human nature that so frivolous a piece of pedantry should have made so much noise in the world and been productive of such melancholy and tragical effects."

The idea that man was perfectible, in short, was "mischievous nonsense." Man was not perfectible. But this stubborn, immutable fact of human existence should in no way lessen "our utmost exertions to amend and improve others and in every way ameliorate the lot of humanity: invent new medicines, construct new machines, write new books, build better houses and ships, institute better governments, discountenance false religions, propagate the only true one, diminish the vices, and increase the virtues of all men and women wherever we can," he wrote Van der Kemp.[6]

The vanity and presumption that exalted man against God could only bring misery and calamity to the world. The Bible contained all the wisdom man needed to guide and order his life. There could be found "the most perfect philosophy, the most perfect morality, and the most refined policy." It was "the most republican book in the world," because in its commandments were to be found the only preservative of republics. If, for instance, the prohibitions against fornication and adultery were widely and generally broken, a republic could not survive because its moral fiber would be eroded.[7]

His reading and his reflection made Adams more and more plainly Unitarian. He rejected the notion of the Trinity as superstition and with it the idea of the divinity of Christ. It was intolerable to think of the greatest power in the universe nailed by weak and sinful men to a cross. "The Christian religion, as I understand it," he wrote Rush, "is the brightness of the glory and the express portrait of the eternal, self-existent, independent, benevolent, all-powerful and all-merciful Creator, Preserver and Father of the Universe. . . . It will last as long as the world. Neither savage nor civilized man without a revelation could ever have discovered or invented it. Ask me not then whether I am a Catholic or Protestant, Calvinist or Arminian. As far as they are Christians, I wish to be a fellow disciple with them all."[8]

He wished for a "more liberal communication of sentiments" between all the nations of the world on the subject of religious beliefs. Each nation doubtless had something to contribute, since each might be assumed to have gained at least a partial apprehension of the Divine. "Translations of the Bible into all languages and sent among all people," he wrote David Sewall, "I hope will produce translations into English and French, Spanish and German and Italian of sacred books of Persians, the Chinese, the Hindoos, etc., etc., etc. Then our grandchildren and my great-grandchildren may compare notes and hold fast all that is good."[9] His conclusion from his reading was "universal toleration. Let the human mind loose. It must be loosed; it will be loose. Superstition and despotism cannot confine it."[10] In such an atmosphere Christianity, as the true religion, the most complete and effective revelation of God, would triumph, reinforced by such elements of other religions as could prove themselves in the court of reason and common sense.

It was the Jews, even more than his beloved Greeks, Adams felt, who had done the most to civilize men. "If I were an atheist," he wrote Van der Kemp, "and believed in blind eternal fate, I should still believe that fate had ordained the Jews to be the most essential instrument for civilizing the nations." They had preserved and propagated "to all mankind the doctrine of a supreme, intelligent . . . almighty Sovereign of the Universe, which I believe to be the great essential principle of all morality and consequently of all civilization. I can't say that I love the Jews very much neither. Nor the French, nor the English, nor the Romans, nor the Greeks. We must love all nations as much as we can, but it is very hard to love most of them," he concluded.[11]

Adams was also much concerned with what might be called the sociology of religion—how religion worked to give order and purpose and dignity to man's common life. His forebears, for instance, had not been great men but they had been honest and upright ones. "What," he asked Rush rhetorically, "has preserved this race of Adamses in all their ramifications, in such numbers, health, peace, comfort, and mediocrity?" It seemed to him it was religion, "without which they would have been rakes, fops, sots, gamblers, starved with hunger, frozen with cold, scalped by Indians, etc., etc., etc., been melted away and disappeared." It was the rigor and discipline of Calvinism that had preserved them in a hostile environment, that had given form and meaning to their lives and to those of all New Englanders.[12]

In the area of politics, although Adams had formally renounced them and no longer read political theory, he did not cease to speculate about the political behavior of man. He was reconciled at last to party bitterness and faction. "In the struggles and competitions of fifty or sixty years, in times that tried men's hearts and brains and spinal marrow, it could not be otherwise," he wrote Rush.[13] Parties provided a means of releasing, in a more or less systematic way, the passions generated in a democratic society.

Adams professed to see a pattern in party politics. There would be an alternation. One party, representing the more conservative side, would hold power for some twelve years and then there would be "an entire change in the administration," with the more radical side taking over for a similar period. Jefferson and his supporters, he thought, might hold power for sixteen years; but then, inevitably, there must be a reaction. "Our government will be a game of leapfrog of factions, leaping over one another's back about once in twelve years according to my computation," he predicted.[14] He observed that a party was frequently never so near defeat as when it had carried everything before it. Parties, like people, could not stand success. "When a party grows strong," he observed, "and feels its power, it becomes intoxicated, grows presumptuous and extravagant, and breaks to pieces."[15] Such had been the fate of the Federalists.

The old anxiety about the possibilities of a genuinely free society remained. "One is always in danger," he noted, "of adopting an opinion that human nature was not made to be free. No nation has long enjoyed that partial and imperfect emancipation that we call a free government. Banks, whiskey, panem and *circenses,* or some other frivolities, whims, caprices, and above all idolatries and military glories, luxuries, art, sciences, taste, mausoleums, statues, pictures, adulatory histories and panegyrical orations, lies, slanders, calumnies, persecutions, have sooner or later undermined all principles, corrupted all morals, prostituted all religion, and where then is liberty?" It was only by anticipating the loss of freedom that it could be preserved.[16]

Americans seemed to have the illusion that they enjoyed some special dispensation. It did not occur to them that the rules which governed the rest of mankind also applied to them. Other nations rose and fell, but the United States seemed to possess the happy illusion of immortality. "There is no special Providence for us," Adams insisted. "We are not a chosen people that I know of. If we are, we deserve it as little as the Jews. . . . We must and shall go the way of the earth. We ought to contend, to swim though against the wind and tide as long as we can; and the poor, injured, deceived, mocked, and insulted people will struggle till battles and victories and conquests dazzle the majority into adoration of idols. Then come popes and emperors, kingdoms and hierarchies."[17]

It was extremism that Adams envisioned as the principal threat to free government. He had seen it in various manifestations and considered it uniformly destructive: "the fanaticism of honor; the fanaticism of royalty; the fanaticism of loyalty; the fanaticism of republicanism; the fanaticism of aristocracy; the fanaticism of democracy; the fanaticism of Jacobitism and Jacobinism; the fanaticism of sans-culottism; the fanaticism of Catholicism and Protestantism, of Lutheranism and Calvinism, of Arianism and Socinianism, of common Quakerism and shaking Quakerism, of atheism and Deism, of philosophy and antipathy to learning, of peace societies and missionary societies."[18] All man's civilization was a thin veneer, maintained by law and religion. "When men are given up to the rule of their passions," he wrote Rush, "they murder like weasels for the pleasure of murdering, like bulldogs and bloodhounds in a fold of sheep."[19]

One of the most important political laws, Adams pointed out, was that man moved forward (or backward) in history, generally speaking, by the narrowest of margins. To take note of that fact was most important, for it reminded men of the precariousness of the human situation, and by so doing it encouraged the bolder and more resolute spirits to act decisively at critical moments. The Stuarts, for example, were turned out and William of Orange invited in by one or two votes in Parliament. Adams himself had been defeated for a second term by three votes in South Carolina, "not fairly obtained." Jefferson had defeated Burr by a single vote. The concept of the Trinity was approved in a general church council by one vote against a Quaternity: "the Virgin Mary lost an equality with the Father, Son, and Spirit, only by one suffrage. All the great affairs of the world, temporal and spiritual, as far as men are concerned in the discussion and decision of them, are determined by small majorities."[20]

Adams gave as much thought to history as to politics, stimulated by his constant review of the events which his own life had encompassed. Man's history, he told Dr. Waterhouse, was a record of "awakenings and revivals." People abandoned a religious or a political enthusiasm only to suddenly seize it up again, often in a frenzy of excitement. There were revolutions and counterrevolutions. After Napoleon came the Bourbons once more. It was thus impossible to say that something men had once believed in and fought for was irrevocably over and done with. Calvinism and the Catholic Church might equally reassert themselves and orthodoxy oust liberalism.

After the revolutions of the eighteenth century, in the name of popular and representative government, the world now witnessed the rise of a new despotism, supported by Metternich's system of alliances, which seemed about to carry Europe back to a new age of absolutism. "Cannot you and your friend Jenner," Adams asked Waterhouse, "discover some recondite inoculation to moderate its deleterious rage?"[21] "Sovereigns," he observed to another correspondent, "who modestly call themselves legitimate are conspiring in holy and unhallowed league against the progress of human knowledge and human liberty." The people were hopelessly divided while the ruling classes were united and held "all the artillery and all the bayonets in their hands."[22] The new reaction threatened "to destroy the rights of the people to constitute their own governments. But great is truth," Adams added, "and [it] will ultimately prevail." Bluster as "the crowned noodles" of Europe might, America would preserve her liberties and be a beacon light of freedom to the world.[23]

It seemed to Adams, as he looked back over the long sweep of the past, that it could safely be said that "men are at war with each other and against all living creatures. Beasts, birds, fishes, and insects are at war with each other and with all other species. It is a militant state in a militant planet." Consequently he viewed uneasily the efforts of idealists to organize societies for perpetual peace. To preach the doctrine of perpetual peace successfully would mean "no more nor less than everlasting passive obedience and nonresistance."[24] Men would always have to fight for the things they believed in.

When he was solicited to join a peace society being formed by idealistic New Englanders, Adams replied with characteristic bluntness: "It is very desirable that all wolves, bears, tigers, panthers, and lions should be tamed, civilized, and humanized," but it would not be advisable in the present state of the world "to instill in the minds of all mankind conscientious scruples about the lawfulness of defending ourselves against their ferocity by gun, drum, trumpet, blunderbuss, and thunder." As long as mankind remained aggressive and greedy, it was folly to talk of "universal and perpetual peace," for such talk, if accepted by the civilized, simply left them at the mercy of their more predatory neighbors, who could not be depended upon to sign the conventions of the peace-lovers or, even if they did sign, to observe them.[25]

He had one bit of advice for those who wished to recapture the authentic spirit of the past—seek out the sources. He advised his grandson, George Washington Adams, to read Hutchinson's *History of Massachusetts Bay*, Thomas Morton's *New English Canaan*, Cotton Mather's *Magnalia*, Locke's constitution for the colony of South Carolina, and similar works. It was there that the truth was to be found; not in the warmed-over accounts of later historians, superimposing their own biases on the events and characters of an earlier time.[26]

One of the most serious problems of historiography was the philosophy of the historian himself. Historians were always writing histories to prove something, generally something that had little or nothing to do with attitudes and aspirations of the times and people with which they were dealing. They wrote to prove that this or that historical figure was a demigod without blemish or imperfection (like John Marshall's *Life of Washington*); or they wrote a history of philosophy to prove that God did not exist (Dupuis); or an account of the reign of Louis XIV to confirm the divine right of kings. If history was indeed, as the ancients had said, "philosophy teaching by examples," then the philosophy which written history professed to teach must determine the validity of the history. For Adams, "every history must be founded on some philosophy and some policy." If he himself were to write a history he would base it "on the morality of the Gospels and leave all other philosophy and policy to shift for itself."[27] Written history's most essential task was to do justice to the motives and aspirations of individuals and groups of earlier ages, and in so doing to keep viable those principles and ideals which had drawn man upward on his long climb from barbarism. Man must learn from his errors, lest he repeat them; he must repeat his triumphs, lest he fall into error. History, as man's collective memory, must above all distinguish truth from falsehood.

WHEN the bitterness of defeat faded and time worked its proverbial therapy, Adams turned to some of the relationships which had meant much to him before and which had been strained by political battles. The first of these was that with Benjamin Rush, family doctor and friend, goodhearted, emotional , flighty, and, at least in Adams' view, politically naïve. Adams had been Rush's benefactor appointing him head of the Mint despite the doctor's Jeffersonian principles. When he took up his pen, early in 1805, to renew contact with the Phila-delphian, it marked a large step on the road back to a frank and generous spirit of reconciliation with his former friends and later political oppo-nents. "It seemeth unto me that you and I ought not to die without saying good-by," he wrote, "or bidding each other adieu. Pray how do you do? How does that excellent lady, Mrs. Rush? How are the young ladies? Where is my surgeon and lieut.? How fares the lawyer?" (The references were to Rush's sons and daughters.)

Then, to tease his friend, he asked: "Is the present state of the nation Republican enough? Is virtue the principle of our government? Is honor? Or is ambition and avarice, adulation, baseness, covetousness, the thirst of riches, indifference concerning the means of rising and enriching, the contempt of principle, the spirit of party and of faction, the motive and the principle that governs us? These are serious and dangerous questions. But serious men ought not to flinch from dangerous questions."[1]

Rush replied promptly: "Your letter of the 6th instant revived a great many pleasant ideas in my mind. I have not forgotten—I cannot forget you." Travelers from Quincy had brought news from time to time of the ex-President's good health, that he showed his "usual good spirits, and that upon some subjects you are still facetious." The doctor confessed he was quite disillusioned with the course of the Republican adminis-tration. He was one of those liberal spirits who expect everything to go well and are quick to be dismayed when their heroes behave like mortals.

"My children are often the witnesses of my contrition for my sacrifices and of my shame for my zeal in the cause of our country," he wrote.

He felt, he told Adams, like a stranger in his own state of Pennsylvania. His medical theories were rejected by the profession; his patients were his only companions, and his books his only friends. Like Adams, he had experienced "the injustice and cruelty" of his contemporaries for heterodox opinions.[2]

Rush's reply provided the perfect basis for a warm exchange—the recantation of his Jeffersonian heresies, and the same sense of persecution that Adams felt so strongly. ("Rush! every persecuted man, persecuted because he is envied, must be an egotist or an hypocrite," Adams wrote. "You and I must therefore cordially embrace the character of egotists and acknowledge the imputation of vanity."[3]) The correspondence between the two men became the principal pleasure and resource of each. They ranged over a vast field of subjects—the characters and opinions of various leaders of the Revolutionary era; the course of contemporary events, foreign and domestic; the philosophy of the French Revolution; the rise of "new" men in business and politics; the decline of morality and virtue. In a series of letters they debated the ingredients of fame with particular attention to the "myth" of George Washington, whose countrymen had not been content to applaud him as a mere man but appeared compelled to make him into a god. "I loved and revered the man," Adams wrote, "but it was his humanity only that I admired. In his divinity I never believed." Rush could still not bring himself to credit the General with greatness, and Adams explained at length just what the elements of the Virginian's genius were.[4] Above all else the General had "possessed the gift of silence. This I esteem as one of the precious talents. He had great self-command. It cost him a great exertion sometimes, and a constant constraint; but to preserve so much equanimity as he did required a great capacity."[5]

But Adams mocked the "adorations of Divus Washington." At the celebrations of the Fourth of July held in his own Boston at Faneuil Hall, there was a huge portrait of Washington behind the "table of the principal magistrates" and, most offensive of all, facing it an equally large picture of Hamilton "in the most conspicuous spot in the whole hall, while the pictures of Samuel Adams and John Hancock are crowded away in two obscure corners." Thus, he wrote caustically, is Faneuil Hall, "which ought to be as sacred in Boston as the Temple of Jupiter was on the Capitol Hill in Rome, made the headquarters of fornication, adultery, incest [references to Hamilton's notorious affairs], libeling, and electioneering intrigue."[6]

It was useless, Adams admitted, to oppose the process of deification. The popular mind would have heroes, democracy or no democracy. Not content with acknowledging Washington's true and great gifts, they would turn the man into a god. The pilgrimages to Mount Vernon would in time become like those to Mecca or Jerusalem, Adams predicted.

He also watched Hamilton's cult grow. (Indeed, many Americans worshiped at both shrines.) The Federalist newspapers insisted that "Hamilton was the soul and Washington the body, or in other words that Washington was the painted wooden head of the ship and Hamilton the pilot and steersman."[7] There was talk among Hamilton's admirers that the New Yorker had planned a history which would have revealed Washington as his instrument. The story filled Adams with indignation. Hamilton was "an insolent coxcomb who rarely dined in good company where there was good wine without getting silly and vaporing about his administration, like a young girl about her brilliants and trinkets. . . . I lose all patience," he wrote Rush, "when I think of a bastard brat of a Scotch peddler daring to threaten to undeceive the world in their judgment of Washington, by writing a history of his battles and campaigns. This creature was in a delirium of ambition: he had been blown up with vanity by the Tories, had fixed his eye on the highest station in America, and he hated every man young or old who stood in his way."[8]

Rush wrote of his dreams and Adams, charmed, analyzed them. Dreams had a special fascination for both men. In them time and space were annihilated and the dreamer broke loose into a world of symbolic richness and transcendent freedom.

The country, the world, and man with all his foibles and vanities passed in review through a correspondence wonderfully rich in wisdom, humor, and insight. They shared, for example, a common detestation of banks and banking. "The banking infatuation pervades all America," Adams wrote his friend. "Our whole system of banks is a violation of every honest principle of banks. There is no honest bank but a bank of deposit. A bank that issues paper at interest is a pickpocket or a robber. But the delusion will have its course. You may as well reason with a hurricane. An aristocracy is growing out of them that will be as fatal as the feudal barons, if unchecked in time. . . . Think of the number, the offices, stations, wealth, piety, and reputation of the persons in the states who have made fortunes by these banks, and then you will see how deeply rooted the evil is."[9] "Who could compute the amount of the sums taken out of the pockets of the simple and hoarded in the purses of the cunning in the course of every year? Yet where is the remedy? The Republicans are as deep in this absurdity and this guilt as the Federalists."[10]

On one subject the two friends differed sharply. Rush believed that Greek and Latin should be banished in favor of a more practical, vocational curriculum for the schools. "I do most cordially hate you," Adams wrote his friend, "for writing against Latin, Greek, and Hebrew. I will never forgive you until you repent, retract, and reform. No! Never! It is impossible!"[11] Rush had developed a "tranquillizing chair" designed to quiet lunatics. If Adams had sovereign power over the doctor's hospital, he warned, he would place the physician in his own "tranquillizer, till I cured you of your fanaticism against Greek and Latin." The world had never seen a Milton, he declared, "if a Homer and a Virgil had not lived before him."[12]

Writers of letters, they were also readers and critics of others' missives. Pliny's were "too studied and too elegant," Adams declared, while Cicero's had the "perfect simplicity, confidence, and familiarity" of the best letters. Madame de Sévigné had created "a sweet, pretty little ancient world out of nothing." But Pascal's *Provincial Letters* "exceeded everything ancient or modern," the products of "infinite art." Federick the Great's letters to Voltaire and D'Alembert were "sickish and silly," and his adulation of Voltaire "babyish." "Have mercy on me, posterity, if you should ever see any of my letters," he concluded.[13] His letters were too rambling and formless to merit the accolades of that severest judge. There was nothing "more ridiculous than an old man, more than three quarters of a hundred, rattling like a boy of fifteen at school or at college." Yet rattle he must, from one subject to another, chasing enthusiasms like an eccentric lepidopterist chasing butterflies.[14] Even so, he was plainly flattered by the praises of Miss Jerusha Lyman, a literary young lady and a friend of the Rush family who read some of Adams' letters and declared: "This gentleman is too great an object to be fully seen and known while he *is near us.* Such minds require the distance of centuries to be perfectly understood and fully appreciated." "With all my childish vanity," he noted warily, "I have not an enemy that thinks more humbly of my life than I do."[15]

Abigail and Mrs. Rush enjoyed the correspondence almost as much as their husbands, although they teased them about it from time to time. The friends exchanged letters, Mrs. Rush declared, "like two young girls about their sweethearts." Adams promptly replied that the decadence of the modern world was due "to the general relaxation of family discipline." Wives no longer showed any respect for their husbands, and his wife had been so bold as to inform him a few days before: " 'When you write to Dr. Rush, you string together epithets and adverbs and substantives just as boys string their robins' eggs on long rows in the spring.' Ought not some measures to be taken," he asked, "to teach these ladies more reverence for their lords?"[16]

Adams was fascinated by Rush's book on mental disease. It proved "us all to be a little cracked," he declared. "Vanity," he reminded Rush, "is one of your diseases of the mind. You and all the world know to what a scandalous degree I have been infected with it all the days of my life."[17]

Rush, like John Quincy, urged Adams to write his autobiography, and Adams professed to be tempted. "I do not know but I shall take your advice and write my own worthless life, merely to keep myself out of idleness," he answered Rush, failing to mention that he was already launched on the enterprise. But he was appalled at the chaos of his voluminous papers. "Of all men who have acted a part in the great affairs of the world," he observed, "I am afraid I have been the most careless and negligent in preserving papers. [This is not a negligence which is apparent to his biographer.] I must write many things from memory and oftentimes facts to which there is no other witness left alive." Moreover the task of rooting through his papers was "so extensive that I have not time left to persecute it. To rummage trunks, letterbooks, bits of journals and great heaps and bundles of old papers is a dreadful bondage to old age, and an extinguisher of old eyes." Beyond this, the papers concealed "follies, indiscretions, and trifles enough and too many," along with a depressing tale of the "jealousy and envy of those who have been my most intimate friends, colleagues, and coadjutors." There had been, he confessed to his friend, many times in his life when he had been "so agitated in my own mind as to have no consideration at all of the light in which my words, actions, and even writings would be considered by others. . . . The few traces that remain of me must, I believe, go down to posterity in as much confusion and distraction as my life has been passed. Enough surely of egotism!" he exclaimed.[18]

Any hesitation that Adams might have felt about plunging into the fearful mass of papers he had accumulated throughout the years was dissipated by the publication of Mercy Otis Warren's *History of the Revolution* in 1805. The work manifested a strong Republican bias, and John's old friend was outspoken in her criticism of his presidency and policies. She castigated him for his monarchal and aristocratic leanings, even quoting her husband's charge that his years in Europe had corrupted his revolutionary principles.

Adams' notion that he had accommodated himself to a life of forbearance and resignation was quickly dispelled by the book. His response was a great bellow of rage and indignation. "Corrupted! Madam!" he exclaimed. "What provocation, what evidence, what misrepresentation could [General Warren] have received that would prompt him to utter this execrable calumny? Corruption is a charge that I cannot and will not bear—I challenge the whole human race, and angels and devils too, to produce an instance of it from my cradle to this hour!"[19]

Mercy's book, he charged, was chock-full of errors. He would point them out to her "in the spirit of friendship, that you may have an opportunity, in the same spirit, to correct them for any future edition of the work." One of the first errors was Mrs. Warren's statement on page 392 that "'Mr. Adams' passions and prejudices were sometimes too strong for his sagacity and judgment.' "I will not, I cannot say that this is not true," he replied. "But I can and will say with the utmost sincerity that

I am not conscious of having ever in my life taken one public step or performed one public act from passion or prejudice, or from any other motive than the public good." If she would make such a statement she must support it by specific instances; otherwise it was little better than slander.

Adams was equally firm in rejecting the charge of "partiality for monarchy," and of having an attachment to Great Britain. Mrs. Warren, if she doubted his rebuttal, should read his *Defence*. "The limited equipoised monarchy of England" he had always considered as "the only government which could preserve political and religious liberty . . . in any of the great populous, commercial, opulent, luxurious, and corrupted nations of Europe." But he had never advocated a government for America with a hereditary executive and hereditary Senate, nor had he ever favored the British cause.

The first letter was followed by a succession of others, explaining, correcting, rebuking. Indeed, Adams began a review of his whole political career, supporting his arguments with documents exhumed from the great jumble of his correspondence. Mercy had written in her history that he had first appeared on the political scene in 1774, whereas in fact he had been conspicuous in the patriot ranks for half a dozen years before. It was a small point to be sure, but it betrayed "a malignity of heart and a disposition to lessen me as much as you could in the opinion of your readers, both in present and future times"—an attitude, he declared, which ran through the whole work.[20]

Every day throughout the latter part of July and the greater part of August was given over to the interminable vindication—dozens and dozens of pages written with incredible effort, patient, detailed explication, with only here and there an outburst of bitterness: "If Mrs. Warren is determined to be enrolled in the glorious list of libelers of John Adams, she is welcome. Ned Church, Lloyd, Freneau . . . Ben Bache, Duane, Porcupine, John Fenno, Junior, McDonald and his satellites, Callender, Hamilton, Wood . . . and the nameless crew of the [*Independent*] *Chronicle*. But most of these have already come to a bad end, and the rest will follow," he forecast ominously.[21]

Mercy Warren, virtually inundated, answered with asperity, protesting the flood of letters. But Adams continued doggedly on until, in his view, he had put the record straight.

ALL Adam's fear about Jefferson's administration seemed to be confirmed. Encouraged by the President, Congress repealed the judiciary act which the Federalists had passed, dumping Adams' appointees unceremoniously out of office to the accompaniment of fine rhetoric about the former President's duplicity in appointing "the midnight judges."

The army and, what was far worse, the navy were dismantled. In place of Adams' proud frigates the Republicans decided to pin their hopes on unseaworthy scows—gunboats—designed to protect American ports. American diplomacy became a matter of words, not weapons, of exhortations to the nations of Europe to be wise and reasonable, fair and just, because the Americans wished them to be so. Economic sanctions rather than naval power were to be the means of rendering a Napoleon or a Canning more tractable. Such tactics were self-defeating. "Commerce will decline," Adams warned, "and the revenue will fail. . . . I mourn over the accumulated disgraces we are bringing on ourselves but I can do nothing."[1]

At the same time that he foresaw the consequences of his successor's feeble and vacillating foreign policy, his belief in his country's future revived. "Although I have sometimes been staggered in my faith for a moment," he said in reply to an invitation to attend a banquet at Plymouth, "by the license of calumny, I still entertain a pleasing hope that this nation will long enjoy a continuance of felicity and prosperity under their pure principles and representative governments."[2] He told Rush: "I love the people of America and believe them to be incapable of ingratitude. They have been, they may be, and they are deceived. It is the duty of somebody to undeceive them."[3]

Although, as Adams wrote Rush, he "must soon travel into another country, to return no more," still he could not "throw off the habits of this world so entirely as to be indifferent to the future fate of my friends, country, and species. I love them all and would cheerfully sacrifice my-

self to promote their happiness." But he was powerless; he could "do
nothing more than pray for their prosperity and weep over their follies
and misfortunes. I am not, however, very prodigal of my tears," he added,
"for I am determined to make the best of everything as long as I can."
Rush, "as wise as a serpent and as harmless as a dove," refused to discuss
politics at all. But Adams, by his own fireside, "dogmatized" to his heart's
content. The newspapers, he confessed, "sometimes make me scold, and
in dogmatizing, laughing, and scolding I find delight . . . no one is the
worse for it, and I am the better."[4]

He began to read the debates in Congress and there found confirmation of his gloomiest prognostications. Macon, Early, and other Republican Congressmen took the line "that the moment you raise a public
force you give up your liberties; and therefore there must be neither
an army, navy, fortifications, a select militia, or even a revenue, because
if any of these exist they must be entrusted to the executive authority,
establish a system of patronage, and overthrow the constitution." This
was all very well, Adams observed, but it would "fly like chaff before
the wind as soon as any nation, by a series of insults and depredations,
shall excite a serious national resentment."[5]

Adams was dismayed not only by the course of the administration but
by the wild cant that continued to circulate in the country about what
was termed "democracy." These democratic champions wished to level
every form and order in society and every institution that did not conform
to their enthusiastic dogmas. They clamored against the judicial branch
of the government, criticized the executive—nothing, it seemed, would
satisfy them but the unicameral legislature extolled by the French philosophers. They must have the French Revolution in America at once, with
all its mad bloodshed and sorrow. "Have you such a set in Connecticut,
as we have in Massachusetts," he inquired of his old friend John Trumbull, "of strange, awkward, and outlandish vagabonds running about in
every town in the character of lay preachers, schoolmasters, peddlers, day
laborers, and beggars watching every opportunity to preach democracy
and propogate all the lies and slanders of Duane and the other editors
of his feather? Or is the mere sound of Liberty a magical talisman?"[6]

Suddenly the course of events, which after all had seemed rather remote from Quincy, veered close to home. The Spaniard, Francisco
Miranda, a dashing and romantic revolutionary of whom Napoleon was
reputed to have remarked, "The man has a sacred fire in his soul," enlisted Colonel Smith in a mad adventure to free Venezuela from Spanish
rule. The Colonel not only raised money and enlisted recruits for the
expedition, but he sent along his oldest son, William Steuben Smith,
as a lieutenant of Miranda's.

The undertaking ended in disaster. Young Smith was captured with
most of his companions at Caracas, and there awaited trial for conspiracy

against the government. Adams was indignant when he heard of the venture. Perhaps worse than risking his life was the fact that his grandson had dropped out of Columbia College a few months before his graduation. "I saw the ruin of my only daughter and her goodhearted, enthusiastic husband," he wrote in despair to Rush when he learned of the expedition, "and I had no other hope or prayer than that the ship with my grandson in it might be sunk in the Gulf Stream."

Nor would Adams intercede with the Spanish ambassador, the Marquis d'Yrujo, to ask clemency for William. He must share the fate of his companions. "New York has been the box of Pandora to me and my family," he declared. But however "pungent my grief or mortifying my disappointment, I do not complain. It is enough for me to suffer in my own heart and never torment others with endeavors to excite their compassion. I have no reason to hope that my name will contribute in the smallest degree to save the life of my grandson." He had little sympathy for Colonel Smith who, when the story of the expedition and his role in it became known, was summarily dismissed from his post as Surveyor of the Port of New York. "The absurdity of his conduct throughout the whole business cannot be too severely reprobated," Adams wrote Rush.

The whole matter of South American independence, in his view, should be approached with extreme caution. Independence "would increase and multiply the distractions of the world, already too numerous," and "occasion convulsions and reverberations over the whole globe." "The human universe is asleep"; he asserted on another occasion, again referring to South America, "but it must awake. . . . The whole human race is interested, deeply interested in it. Let us be cool and sober if we can. It is a more difficult question than our own independence."[7] A South America independent of Spain would be "governed by a dozen royalists, independent of each other, and each of them ruling by a system of priestcraft, superstition, and despotism, frequently at war with each other, and each of them seeking alliance in Europe and in the United States."[8] The South American people were not yet ready for the demanding task of establishing free and stable republics, and would not be for generations to come.[9]

In June 1807 the British frigate *Leopard* fired on the United States frigate *Chesapeake* when Commodore Barron refused to permit a search for alleged deserters from the British navy. Three American sailors were killed, eighteen others wounded, and the *Chesapeake* badly damaged. The incident caused a flare-up of bitter anti-British feeling. British warships were ordered to leave United States territorial waters, and the British replied with orders for more energetic impressment of British deserters on neutral vessels.

The British action aroused Adams' sharpest resentment: "My old acquaintance, King George, has broke his word," he wrote. "He promised he would be the last to disturb our independence." He questioned his grandson, John Adams Smith: "Can American seamen bear? Ought they to bear? Ought they to submit to the tyranny of British seamen? Will not such impressments break their hearts and put petticoats on them all? Can we ever expect to have a navy that will stand against foreign seamen, if ours are habituated tamely and patiently to bear such indignities and injuries?"[10] England saw America "through a mist of passions and prejudices, such a mixture of contempt, jealousy, fear, and hatred," that she would never act fairly unless she was forced to.[11]

Jefferson met the British intransigence with a Nonimportation Act directed against British goods; when this failed to wring any concessions he followed it by an Embargo which in effect closed American ports. Adams watched uneasily. The Embargo seemed quite the wrong measure to him. If it was prolonged for more than six months it would produce a violent reaction in the country at large, especially among those classes who depended on commerce for their livelihood. The result must be the collapse of some prices and the inflation of others, acute hardship for many Americans, and finally either abandonment of the Embargo or war. In his view, the British proclamation affirming the right of impressment was a virtual declaration of war on neutral shipping. "I agree with you," he wrote Rush, "we ought not and cannot suffer this new encroachment. Nor do I know how we can take a stand against it. . . . Impressment of seamen by the law of nations! What a daring act of despotism! What imprudence!" This was the bitter fruit of downgrading the navy, the consequence of the administration's "hydrophobia," as Adams put it. "Hail Massachusetts, New York, and Pennsylvania!" he exclaimed. "Sacrifice loyally your commerce and clank your chains in harmonious concert with Virginia! She tells you commerce produces money, money luxury, and all three are incompatible with republicanism! Virtuous, simple, frugal Virginia hates money and wants it only for Napoleon, who desires it only to establish freedom through the world!"[12]

"We are taught," he observed to Rush a few months later, "to be cowards both by Federalists and Republicans. Our gazettes and pamphlets tell us that Bonaparte is omnipotent by land, and Britain is omnipotent at sea."[13] Adams was convinced that the Embargo must be removed. "If it is kept on till Doomsday it will not bend France or England. We are in a shocking delusion not only in our own opinion of the efficacy of the Embargo but in our unaccountable aversion to naval preparations. The one thing needful is a navy!"[14]

It seemed to Adams that in addition to its mistaken policy the administration was lacking in candor. There was no clear executive leadership. As a consequence the country drifted along with increasing confusion and bitterness. "My friend!" he broke out to Rush. "Our country is in masquerade! No party, no man dares to avow his real sentiments. All is disguise, vizard, cloak. The people are totally puzzled and confounded. . . . If I was only forty years old, I would as I did at that age set all disguise and fear at defiance, and once more lead my country." But it would be madness to attempt any such thing now. "I have not," he wrote, "any confidence in my own judgments. My strength of body and capacity of application to business or study are gone." As the country faced the uncertainty of the approaching election of 1808, Adams expressed himself as "determined to rally round the standard of the President, as far as I can in honor, whether Mr. Pinckney, Mr. Clinton, or Mr. Madison be the man. I will engage," he concluded, "in no systematical and universal opposition to any man. . . . Commerce and wealth have produced luxury, avarice, and cowardice. . . . Our beloved country has become a miser and a spendthrift," unwilling to spend the money to build a strong naval and military force but more than ready to squander money in high living and dissipation. "Corruption is coming in like a flood accelerated by the English influence to the greatest degree, and by the French . . . and still more by the eternal internal struggle between debtor and creditor which has overturned every republic from the beginning of time."[15]

Rush, from having been the fervent advocate of Jeffersonian principles, now that he had had a chance to observe them in action, wondered whether "such a country is worthy of the patriotism of honest men?" Adams reproved him. "Our people," he declared, "are like other people. Our obligations to our country never cease but with our lives. We ought to do all we can. Instead of being Frenchmen or Englishmen, Federalists or Jacobins, we ought to be Americans, and exert every nerve to convince and persuade our country to conquer its sordid stinginess, to defend our exposed cities and prepare a national force. This must be our ultimate resort." The judgments of heaven could not be averted, "but Dr. Rush can mitigate the yellow fever, and he can do much to guard against that avarice which is our national sin. . . . Aristocracy of wealth without any check but a democracy of licentiousness is our curse. . . . The eternal intrigues of our monied and landed and slaved aristocracy are and will be our ruin."[16]

"Mingled rage and fear" were "now the predominant passions of our nation," he noted in 1808. The "still, small voice of reason" could no longer be heard. New England ships rotted at their moorings; sailors lacking ships to sail roamed the streets, hungry, dissatisfied, and rebellious; merchants sank into penury, cursing the doctrinaire Virginian who sat in the White House. Congress, dominated by the Southerners, rigid and uncompromising, held to its course. The Republicans were not alone to blame. From the first, the Federalists had been "intolerant" and unco-operative. Adams had no patience with the growing talk of separation, of breaking the Union into north and south. "Americans, I fondly hope and candidly believe, are not yet arrived at the age of Demosthenes or

Cicero. If we can preserve our Union entire we may preserve our Republic. But if the Union is broken we become two petty principalities, little better than the feudatories, one of France and the other of England." If it rested with him, he would pass a law against foreign influence, "though it should raise a clamor as loud as my Gag Law or your Grog Law or Mr. Jefferson's Embargo. . . . We may have all our republican virtues put to a trial. I am weary of conjectures but not in despair," he concluded.[17]

Clearly, Adams did not hesitate to lay the major part of the blame for the sad state of the nation at the feet of Jefferson. "He must know," John wrote Rush at the end of the Virginian's administration, "that he leaves the country infinitely worse than he found it, and that from his own error or ignorance. I wish his telescope and mathematical instruments, however, may secure his felicity."

Adams assured Rush, not very convincingly, that he had "no resentment" against the President, "though he has honored and salaried almost every villain he could find who had been an enemy to me."[18] He had always known that Jefferson's ideas were inaccurate and superficial. He had "studied natural history more than politics and . . . labored more to acquire a sweetness of style than to explore the profound and muddy bottoms of the policy of modern or ancient nations." But he had no question about his rival's sincerity or good intentions, and he maintained to Cunningham that he was "not much disposed harshly to condemn him and still less to blacken and slander him for being carried away by the public opinion which was at the same time so flattering and delightful to himself." The only thing for which Adams could not forgive or excuse Jefferson was his repeal of the judiciary act.

Callender, who had abused and vilified Adams, turned eventually on Jefferson and accused him of being the father of certain young Negro slaves at Monticello, by Sally Hemings, the woman who years before, when little more than a child herself, had accompanied Polly Jefferson to Europe. Adams accepted the story without question. It was "a natural and almost unavoidable consequence of that foul contagion in the human character—Negro slavery." A lady who knew the South well had told Adams that "she did not believe that there was a planter in Virginia who could not reckon among his slaves a number of his children." But he regretted the circulation of the story by Callender. It served no purpose to blacken the President's character.

One of the administration's measures earned Adams' unqualified approval. The Louisiana Purchase seemed most expedient to him because he was convinced that "if the union of the Northern, Southern, and Western states was to continue, the free navigation of the Mississippi was essential to its preservation."

In the election of 1808, James Madison, as a member of the "Virginia dynasty," was the leading candidate to succeed Jefferson. The New England Republicans nominated George Clinton, Jefferson's Vice-President, while the Federalists once more chose Charles Cotesworth Pinckney, their perennial candidate. The story was spread about New England that Adams, as he put it, had "changed his politics; has come quite round; has altered his system; has become a Democrat, a Jacobin, a Disorganizer, a Republican, a Turncoat, an Apostate, etc., etc., etc." This, he wrote his grandson John Adams Smith, "is an imaginary wonder; indeed, a wonderful wonder of wonders as ever this wondering world wondered at." Just as the primitive savage thought the sun revolved around the earth, so the "ignorant vulgar" believed Adams had budged, when in fact it was they who had revolved. His system had always been the same: strict neutrality as long as that was possible with honor; then, when aggressors rendered peace intolerable, to proceed resolutely to war.[19] "The Hyper-Federalists are become Jacobins," he declared, "and the Hyper-Republicans are become Federalists. John Adams remains, *semper idem*, both Federalist and Republican in every rational and intelligible sense of both these words."[20]

Both Federalists and Republicans seemed mired in petty bickerings. "Our parties at present," he asserted, "resemble the ladies of easy virtue, in whose quarrels and scoldings one reproaches the other with a lover last night, and the other retorts, 'You are worse than I, for you committed adultery the night before and put horns on your husband.' Unfortunately, there is too much truth in both."[21]

The Southern states and the Northern states appeared to Adams "to be all going wrong, to the utmost danger of our Union as well as independence." The Northern states were acting treasonably, and the Southern states had "inflamed them all by venturing on measures which cannot be justified. . . . Fury instead of reason will soon determine what shall be done if a change does not take place in our councils." If the North was driven to the edge of secession, it was Virginia and Kentucky who had taught her that dangerous doctrine.[22]

Yet Adams confessed to Senator Varnum "that in all the intricate combinations of our affairs to which I have ever been a witness I never found myself so much at a loss to form a judgment of what the nation ought to do, or what part I ought to act." Although he revered "the upright and enlightened general sense of our American nation," Americans were as capable of errors as any other people. Their most remarkable error probably was the illusion "that it is in our power to bring foreign nations to our terms by withholding our commerce."[23]

Indignant as he was over the behavior of the government and many of the citizens, he had faith in the durability of the Union. It was not, he told Rush, "a palace of ice, not a castle of glass. There must be an intense heat to melt it and very hard blows to break it. One war will not dissolve it. Deep and strong are its roots in the judgments and hearts of the people."[24]

For thirty-six years he had heard incessant prophecies of disunion, but the Union was still "the rock of our salvation." "However little we may think of the voice of people," he wrote Josiah Quincy, "sometimes they not infrequently see further than you or I in a great many fundamental questions." On the subject of the Union, for instance, the people of the United States were of a remarkably common mind. Whatever their leaders might say, they envisioned the Union as the guardian of their liberties, and they did not intend to see it dismantled.[25]

"I pity poor Madison," Adams wrote Rush when it was clear that the Virginian had been elected President. "He comes to the helm in such a storm as I have seen in the Gulf Stream."[26] Madison gave immediate evidence of his foresight and wisdom by nominating John Quincy as ambassador to Russia. The Senate at first rejected the nomination, thus demonstrating to the senior Adams its "constant inclination . . . for twenty years to interfere with the President in appointments to foreign embassies." He found consolation in the thought that he would continue to see his beloved son (who had resigned from Congress and was practicing law in Boston) often, visits that he would not exchange "for any office in or under the United States." They were the principal joy of his life.[27]

The Senate, however, capitulated after a show of resistance, and John and Abigail watched with heavy hearts as their son departed with his wife for the infinitely remote St. Petersburg. The mission was certainly an important one. "Russia," Adams wrote, "has been thawed out of her eternal snow and has crawled or stalked over all Europe, a tremendous power whose future influence cannot be foreseen. In one point I am clear—we ought to cultivate a good understanding with this power. There ought to be a new *consulato del mare*."[28] Nonetheless, it was hard on his parents that John Quincy must be the one to try to cultivate such an understanding. "This embassy," Abigail wrote Eliza, "sits heavy at my heart." There was at her age "very little expectation of meeting [her son] again upon this mortal theater."[29] John had been "the prop and support" of his parents' declining years. "His judgment, his prudence, his integrity, his filial tenderness and affection" had made his company "peculiarly dear" to his mother and father.

John Quincy and Louisa left the boys, George Washington, John, and the infant, Charles Francis, at Quincy. These youngsters, with their bright and lively ways, did much to amuse and divert their grandparents.

In 1809, Adams, spurred by Mercy Otis Warren's misrepresentations, began a series of letters to the Boston *Patriot* reviewing his motives and actions in the French mission which he had dispatched in 1799, against the advice of his Cabinet and to the rage of the Hamiltonian faction of his party. The letters, interspersed with official documents, were an effort to establish once and for all the facts surrounding the revived negotiation with France. He described his undertaking as an attempt "to throw off that intolerable load of obloquy and insolence" that had been heaped upon him by his enemies, or "perish in the struggle."[30] At nearly the same time Adams commenced his correspondence with William Cunningham, son of an old friend, in which (trusting to Cunningham's "sacred confidence") he retraced the main events of his presidency, and then went on to review his whole political career.

In his constant reviews and analyses of the causes of the Revolution, Adams persisted in pointing out that the rupture with the Mother Country did not come about suddenly in 1775. "The Revolution," he declared, "was indeed effected in the period from 1761 to 1775. I mean a complete revolution in the minds of the people. A . . . change of the opinions and affections of the people and a full confidence in the practicability of a union of the colonies. All this was done and the principles all established and the system matured before the year 1775." James Otis had launched the fateful ship of independence with his attack upon the Writs of Assistance, at that long past but unforgettably luminous moment when young lawyer Adams, dimly aware that a new nation was being called into existence, scribbled frantic notes. (If Patrick Henry was the Demosthenes and Richard Henry Lee the Cicero of the American Revolution, James Otis was "Isaiah and Ezekiel united," Adams declared.)

The Stamp Act, three years later, had in a sense completed the first phase of the Revolution. Almost to a man, with a unanimity that they would never show again, the colonists rose to resist the principle of parliamentary taxation. If England had not backed down there would have been a revolution then and there. Such, at least, had been the opinions of Charles Chauncey and Jonathan Mayhew, two of the most prominent Massachusetts divines. "If my more extensive familiarity with the sentiments and feelings of the people in the eastern, western, and southern counties of Massachusetts may apologize for my presumption," Adams wrote the Reverend Samuel Morse, "I subscribe without a doubt to the opinions of Chauncey and Mayhew." In 1765 "the colonies," he insisted, "were more unanimous than they ever have been since, either as colonies or states. . . . The resistance in America was so universal and so determined that Great Britain with all her omnipotence dared not attempt to enforce her pretensions."[31]

As the country drifted closer to war with England, Adams became increasingly impatient with the old die-hard Federalists who continued to whine and complain. "They," he wrote his grandson and namesake, "must call on the mountains to cover them. I mean the American mountains." If war came, the American character would appear in its true light, "brave as honesty herself, prudent as reflection, humane and tender as a woman, persevering as a Christian. Oh, my God!" he concluded, "I humbly and devoutly pray that this character may be preserved. That neither mercantile or military or priestly or judicial ambition or avarice may be permitted to corrupt or debase it."[32] When Josiah Quincy lamented the decadence of the present time, comparing it to the great days of the Revolution, Adams answered: "As far as I am capable of comparing the merit of different periods, I have no reason to believe that we were better than you are. We had as many poor creatures and selfish beings in proportion among us as you have among you; nor were there then more enlightened men, or in greater number in proportion, than there are now."[33]

The Republican policy from the first had been to avoid war at all costs. Such a course, Adams pointed out to Rush ("my sensible and humorous friend"), had its dangers. Demoralizing as war might be, it could not be as bad as a humiliating peace. Indeed, he would put it more strongly: "I cannot be of the opinion," he wrote the Philadelphian, "that frequent wars are as corrupting to human nature as long peace. In a peace of a hundred years, and sometimes fifty, and I have been suspicious of twenty-five, a nation loses its honor, integrity, and most of its other virtues. It sinks into universal luxury, voluptuary, hypocrisy, and cowardice. War necessarily brings with it some virtues, and great and heroic virtues too."[34]

Nor would Adams accept the glib equation of democracy and peace. Orators never tired of extolling the peace-loving character of Americans, but the truth was that democratic societies from Athens to the United States had been among the most belligerent in history. "Our people in America," he wrote a friend, "have been more inclined to a war than their government for these fifteen years past. There has been no year within that period when they would not have gone to war with England with pleasure."[35] The government was like a fire company which ever since 1789 had been constantly spouting "cold water upon their own habitations—built, if not of hay and stubble, [then] with wooden timbers, boards, and clapboard and shingles—to prevent its being scorched by the flames from Europe."[36] By seeking to avoid war at all costs the Republicans had only succeeded in making it inevitable.

THROUGH all the political storms of the outside world, life continued on its own course at Quincy. Abigail, of course, worked much too hard. She seemed to have no thought of her health or respect for her years. Although she was frequently indisposed, she insisted upon keeping her firm hand on the guide reins. Only by her constant attention could things run smoothly in such a large and complicated household with so many guests and visitors coming and going. Moreover she had to watch every penny. The farm provided little more than subsistence. If it had not been for the interest on the securities that Abigail had bought surreptitiously for years through Dr. Tufts, they would have been in very straitened circumstances. As it was, only care and thrift would make ends meet. When her friends expressed concern over the multitude of cares and duties that she took upon herself she replied: "I had rather have too much than too little. Life stagnates without action. I could never bear to merely vegetate."

There were also the little frictions and tensions that are part of every marriage. John was not selfish or overbearing, but to a large extent the household revolved about him. He was especially prone to undermine his wife's strict discipline with the grandchildren, romping with them and indulging them when they should have been set to tasks that would do more to shape their character and temper their childish exuberance. Moreover certain qualities in Adams that had once aroused her protective instincts came during their long "retirement" to abrade Abigail's sensitive nerves. But through the inevitable small conflicts and irritations their love remained the center and ballast of their lives.

"You and I, my dear sister," Abigail wrote Eliza Peabody, "have gone through a long life—with as few rubs of a maternal nature as falls to the lot of humanity." She could not lay claim to any special virtue, she wrote, "for I have sometimes insisted upon my own way and my own opinion, and sometimes yielded silently." Eliza's husbands, like Adams, had been somewhat inflexible. "You know all this," Abigail wrote. "Who is always in the right? Yet after half a century," she added, "I can say my first choice would be the same if I again had youth and opportunity to make it." The endorsement was firm but hardly enthusiastic. It partly bespoke Abigail's reticence and partly the relationship of two strong-willed old people, one of whom must have his way and the other who must bend to it.[1]

Abigail nursed children, grandchildren, and domestics through various illnesses and ailments, fussed over her husband, who read and wrote too much, neglecting his health, and she delighted in the good gifts of nature —the summer sun that brought the grains to ripeness, and the rains which "revived the languishing fruits of the earth, made the hills to rejoice and the valleys to sing—the husbandman to rejoice and give thanks with a grateful heart."[2]

"I bend to disease, totter under it, but rise again for a while, recover a degree of health and spirits, feel grateful, I hope, for the reprieve and wish so to number my days as to apply my mind to wisdom," she confided to Eliza.[3] At Christmas, barely recovered from an attack of fever, she set out to make pastry ("I am really so self-sufficient as to believe that I can do it better than any of my family"). The kitchen was chilly and the water cold, so that she was "punished for my self-conceit and vanity," and had to take to her bed again.[4]

Mary Cranch was ill with some wasting fever and Abigail felt full of apprehension for her sister. In addition there was some alarming news from Nabby. She had a cancerous growth in her breast which was painful and made it difficult for her to move her arm. Throughout the summer of 1811, Mary Cranch sank slowly but steadily while Abigail and Louisa took turns nursing her. "What a wreck does age and sickness make of the human frame!" Abigail exclaimed, gazing at her wasted sister. Life clung tenaciously to life and Abigail comforted herself with the thought of the "glorious prospect" that lay beyond: "This corruptible shall put on incorruption, and this mortal shall put on immortality." Abby Shaw, Abigail's namesake and niece, came on to help with the nursing and Susan Boylston, rather unexpectedly, was a pillar of strength. Mary wore herself out talking, and since she could not bear to be alone there must be a constant vigil by her bedside. Richard Cranch also fell ill and needed as much attention as his wife.

In the midst of such a scene of sickness, Nabby arrived "through all the dust and heat" of July in an open carriage with John and Caroline. There was a happy reunion after almost three years of separation, a reunion clouded by the threat of cancer, "one of the most to be dreaded of all complaints."[5] Some operations had been done on cancers and tumors, but such surgery was uncertain at best. The pain was severe and the results often negative. Adams wrote to Rush for advice and the latter, knowing the sole alternative was slow and agonizing death, recommended the operation. The senior Dr. Warren performed the surgery with his son and Dr. Welsh in attendance. The operation itself took twenty-five minutes and the dressing of the wound another hour. The "morbid substance," all the physicians agreed, was "totally eradicated and nothing left but flesh perfectly sound." Despite the apparent success of the operation, Adams, as he wrote Rush, "knowing the uncertainty that still remains" (that the cancer might reappear), rejoiced "with trembling."[6] Colonel Smith came on to be with Nabby through her convalescence. The wound healed cleanly; she could not use her arm and even mild exertions left her exhausted, but she was patient and cheerful and the prospects of recovery seemed excellent.

At the end of October, Richard Cranch died after a wasting illness of many months; two days later Mary expired peacefully in her sleep. It was a blessing. They had been married fifty years and had "fulfilled the age allotted to man." Both "had lived to every useful purpose upon earth and were not permitted to become burdensome and helpless to themselves or others," as Abigail expressed it. To the end Mary had been calm and lucid. She had given directions about her will, about the post office and the management of the farm. She recognized Adams when he went in to see her and spoke to him "with as much cheerfulness and spirit as usual."[7]

The faithful black Phebe—"our good old domestic," Abigail called her —fell ill and Abigail nursed her as devotedly as she had Mary Cranch. Phebe had "high African blood . . . in her veins," and old and sick as she was, she had "much of the sovereign yet"—dignity and poise and pride. "I love and respect and venerate her," Abigail wrote Eliza, "and would not see her want while I had bread to divide with her." It was almost impossible to find a "sober and prudent" white person to nurse Phebe, so most of the burden fell on Abigail. Betsy Smith and Lucy Cranch spelled Abigail, and when the latter's turn was over, Phebe held her by the hand and could not bear to have her go.[8] The deaths and illnesses in her family served warning to Abigail to keep her own "lamp . . . trimmed and burning." Like her husband, she still found a preponderance of good in life. "I bless God," she declared to Eliza, "that I have not yet lived to those days in which there is no pleasure."[9]

In the midst of so much suffering and death, Adams stumbled over a stake and tore the skin off his shank. It was a long, nasty wound and the doctor, "with his baths, cataplasms, plaisters, and bandages, hovered about daily," as John put it; "and poor I, deprived of my horse and my walks, have been bolstered up with my leg horizontal on a sofa."[10]

Under such circumstances it was not surprising that Abigail, looking at herself in the mirror, was depressed by the ravages of age. She looked "old, withered, feeble, and most good for nothing." She was reminded that Parson Wibird used to ask, "What is an old woman good for?" The only answer she could give was "that she would do to set off against an old man."[11] She herself had been plagued by a lung infection that lasted for months, finally culminating in a skin eruption "which," as she wrote her sister, "with its disagreeable qualities, gave me one pleasure—that of scratching."[12]

With several family crises, George and John were neglected, and Abigail decided to ship them off to Eliza in New Hampshire. There they would benefit from a regular regimen and the skillful instruction of the Reverend Mr. Peabody. George was a "good-tempered child," Abigail informed her sister, and might be "managed by reasoning"; John was inclined to "a quickness of passion and a stiffness which requires subduing." George was to study Latin and Greek and his younger brother reading and especially writing.[13]

In the "household of affliction" Adams made out surprisingly well. He was pleased by Colonel Smith's election to Congress in the fall of 1813. It was evidence of the esteem of his neighbors. "He must now meet on the same floor the most malicious and insidious tool in Tim Pickering," John wrote his son-in-law.[14]

Adams' correspondence with Rush continued to be his main intellectual indulgence. "I am such a miser," he told the doctor, "that I cannot suffer a letter of yours to remain a day unanswered, because my answer procures me an interest of eight per cent a month."[15] He continued to expound his ideas, political and theological, to his friend in the familiar spirit of righteousness. "How is it," he asked, ". . . that I, poor, ignorant I, must stand before posterity as differing from all the great men of the age? Priestley, Price, Franklin, Burke, Fox, Pitt, Mansfield, Camden, Jefferson, Madison! So it is. I shall be judged the most vain, conceited, impudent, arrogant creature in the world. I tremble when I think of it. I blush, I am ashamed."[16] And, he might have added, "convinced that I am right and they are wrong." Conscious of the peril of speaking too candidly of men and events, past and present, he assured Rush that he had become as reserved as the "old Scot with his mitten muffled tongue."[17]

The world must have progress but as an old man he would hold fast to the old pleasures. When John Quincy tried to convince him of the superior heating qualities of a Franklin stove or, if he could not abide that name, one of Count Rumford's models, Adams replied a little testily: "They may all be economical, but I would not surrender the beauty, the vivacity and light of a handsome blaze for all their dull heat."[18]

Adams continued to think of himself as a frail vessel. "My constitution," he noted, "is a glass bubble or a hollow icicle. A blast from the southwest or northwest may break or dissolve it in an hour. A slight irregularity or one intemperate dinner might finish the catastrophe of the play."[19] But there was no sign of any diminished zest for such life as might be left to him. His only serious complaint was the continued absence of his adored son. The news that John Quincy intended to remain for another winter in Europe, he related to Rush, "pierced his mother's heart and produced a pathetic exclamation that tortured mine beyond all expression."[20]

The palsy that had afflicted Adams so long grew worse each year. His shaky hands put him in mind of an anecdote which he relayed to his friend. "A wild Irish boy" who worked for Thomas Boylston had let a horse run away. When Thomas asked him why he did not cry out, the boy replied, "I was seized with such a quiveration that I could not speak." The word charmed Adams. It described his palsied hands exactly. He spoke of his ailment henceforth as his "quiveration." His eyes and his hearing held up remarkably well, though he had to use glasses to read; but his "organs of speech" were gone. The words that issued from his toothless mouth were hardly intelligible. When his old friend, Robert Treat Paine, now over eighty years old and hard of hearing, visited him, their efforts to communicate made Adams roar with laughter.[21]

"It has become fashionable to call me 'the Venerable,'" he grumbled in a letter to Waterhouse. "It makes me think of the Venerable Bede, the Venerable Mead . . . the Venerable Savonarola, the Venerable Wesley. . . . The gentlemen of the Navy Yard at Washington have lately called me the modern Nestor. I like that title much better. Pray change the title and say the Venerable Washington, the Venerable Jefferson, and the Venerable Madison; I have worn it too long. It has become threadbare upon me. Do not however, I pray you, call me 'the godlike Adams,' 'the sainted Adams,' 'Our Savior Adams,' 'Our Redeemer Adams.' . . ."[22] He even came to terms at last with his ancient nemesis—vanity. Josiah Quincy recorded that Adams had said to him: "They say I am vain. Thank God I am so. Vanity is the cordial drop which makes the bitter cup of life go down."[23]

The year 1811, which had been clouded by so much illness and death, ended on a happy note. Dr. Rush, who had maintained his friendship with Jefferson even though he expressed disillusion with the Virginian's administration, had dreamed of drawing the two old warriors together once more. He could not bear to think of these titans of the Revolution living out their years, if not in enmity, at least in coolness. Thus, with quite transparent guile, he wrote his two correspondents, appealing to them to bury ancient animosities and revive the friendship which had once meant so much to both. To Adams he sent some carefully edited sentences from one of Jefferson's letters. A New England visitor to Monticello had quoted Adams as saying, "I always loved Jefferson and still love him." "This," Jefferson had written to Rush, "is enough for me.

I only needed this knowledge to revive towards him all the affections of the most cordial moments of our lives. It is known to those who have heard me speak of Mr. Adams that I have ever done him justice myself and defended him when assailed by others, with the single exception as to his political opinions; but with a man possessing so many estimable qualities, why should we be separated by mere differences of opinion in politics, religion, philosophy, or anything else?"

The emotional doctor ended his letter to Adams with a dramatic flourish: "Fellow laborers in erecting the great fabric of American independence!—fellow sufferers in the calumnies and falsehoods of party rage!—fellow heirs of the gratitude and affection of posterity . . . embrace—embrace each other! Bedew your letters of reconciliation with tears of affection and joy. . . . Were I near you, I would put a pen into your hand and guide it. . . . 'Friend and fellow laborer in the cause of the liberty and independence of our common country, I salute you with the most cordial good wishes for your health and happiness!'"[24]

Adams was touched and amused by the letter. It was so typical of Rush, the careful stratagem, the physician's impulse to heal an old lesion, the final fervent exhortation. "I perceive plainly enough, Rush," replied John, "that you have been teasing Jefferson to write to me, as you did me some time ago to write to him." There had never been any hostility on his part, he declared, so there was no call for "negotiations of peace." While it was true that he deplored many of Jefferson's measures as President, he had "raised no clamors." All their differences had come to hardly more than this: "Jefferson and Rush were for liberty and straight hair. I thought curled hair was as republican as straight." He insisted that he had never thought of Jefferson as his enemy: "If I ever received or suspected any injury from him, I have forgiven it long and long ago and have no more resentment against him than against you. . . . Of what use can it be for Jefferson and me to exchange letters?" he concluded. "I have nothing to say to him, but to wish him an easy journey to heaven when he goes. . . ."[25]

After a characteristic exercise in self-justification, Adams wrote to Jefferson a few days later. John Quincy's *Boylston Lectures on Rhetoric and Oratory* had just been published in two volumes. The proud father took the occasion to send his former friend "two pieces of homespun, lately produced in this quarter by one who was honored in his youth by some of your attention and much of your kindness." The letter arrived ahead of the package and Jefferson, puzzled and not surprisingly missing the point, wrote a little treatise on the domestic manufacture of cloth in Virginia. Then he added graciously, "A letter from you calls up recollections very dear to my mind." It reminded him of the days when "laboring always at same oar . . . we rode through the storm with heart and hand, and made a happy port." He was confident that the nation would "continue to grow and multiply and prosper until we exhibit an association, powerful, wise, and happy, beyond what has yet been seen by men." He had abandoned politics, he wrote, adding, "I think little of them and say less; I have given up newspapers in exchange for Tacitus and Thucydides, for Newton and Euclid; and I find myself much the happier." He rode horseback three or four hours every day superintending his plantation, but he could not walk the distances that Adams could. He wished to get a letter, "like mine, full of egotisms," with news of "your health, your habits, occupations, and enjoyments."[26]

Adams was delighted with Jefferson's reply. He plunged into his own answer with gusto, rambling from one topic to another—Newton, the means of preserving the Union, the nature of fame, the virtues of Thucydides and Tacitus ("When I read them," he noted, "I seem to be only reading the history of my own times and my own life"). Nor would he let pass Jefferson's remark about preferring the "savage over civilized life." He would have something to say about this. It was the sentimental heresy of the *philosophes,* of Rousseau, Condorcet, Diderot, and the rest of that addled tribe.[27]

Having written to Jefferson and received an answer, Adams wrote Rush to give him the news. "Mr. Dreamer . . . Mr. Mediator! You have wrought wonders! You have made peace between powers that never were at war! You have reconciled friends that never were at enmity! You have brought again Babylon and Carthage, long since annihilated, into fresh existence! Like the Witch of Endor, you have called up spirits from the vast deep of obscurity and oblivion to a new acquaintance with each other. Mr. Conjuror! In short the mighty defunct potentates of Mount Wollaston and Monticello, by your sorceries and necromancies, are again in being." Four letters had already passed between him and Jefferson, those from Jefferson "written with all the elegance, purity, and sweetness —I would rather say, mellifluity or mellifluidity—of his youth and middle ages, and what I envy still more, with a firmness of finger and a steadiness of chirography that to me is lost forever."[28]

If Jefferson's disavowal of any interest in politics was a hint to his correspondent to avoid that tender subject, Adams soon made it clear that he had no intention of doing so. Tact had never been his strong point, and soon in his direct, blunt way he was inviting Jefferson to admit he had been wrong about France and that Adams had been right; that the Embargo, the Nonimportation, and the Nonintercourse measures had been a disastrous failure; that America's principal deficiency had been the want of a respectable navy to defend its commerce against the depredations of England and France; and that the repeal of the judiciary had been an unwarranted if not an unconstitutional act. It was as typical of Jefferson to evade such issues as it was of Adams to drag them out into the light. The nation, it was true, had supported Jefferson and Madison;

but "neither your authority nor that of the nation has convinced me," Adams declared, "nor, I am bold to pronounce, will convince posterity."[29]

In his enthusiasm Adams poured out a flood of letters. The country was on the verge of war and the ex-President's refusal to condone talk of New England secession from the Union had brought him into bad grace once more with the Federalist ultras. He wanted Jefferson to be sure to understand that it was the fruit of the former's weak and short-sighted foreign policy which had put the nation in such an unhappy state. "Money, mariners, and soldiers would be at the public service if only a few frigates had been ordered to be built. Without this our Union will be brittle as [a] china vase."[30] Jefferson ignored his friend's probes and pricks, devoting his letters to learned disquisitions on the customs, social forms, and theology of the American Indians or the military strategy of Genghis Khan.

In one letter Adams compared the doctrines of Oriental and Egyptian philosophers with those of Plato and Philo. Plato's Logos to him seemed to "resemble, if it was not the prototype of, the *Ratio and its Progress* of Manilius, the Astrologer; of the *Progress of the Mind* of Condorcet; and the *Age of Reason* of Tom Paine." He had given years to poring over the reflections of the greatest thinkers in history and he professed himself "weary of philosophers, theologians, politicians, and historians. They are immense masses of absurdities, vices, and lies," he wrote. Montesquieu had hit the mark when he declared "that all our knowledge might be comprehended in twelve pages of duodecimo. . . . I could express my faith in shorter terms: he who loves the Workman and His work, and does what he can to preserve and improve it, shall be accepted of Him."[31]

The correspondence between the two men was fitful. Sometimes as much as six months would pass, with three or four letters from Adams, before Jefferson replied. When he did, Adams would almost invariably dash off an answering letter within a few days.

WHILE his life centered on the farm, Adams was by no means circumscribed by Quincy and its environs. As President of the American Academy of Arts and Sciences, and of the Massachusetts Society for Promoting Agriculture, and a member of the Board of Visitors for the professorship of natural history at Harvard, he had to travel frequently to Boston. The Board of Visitors of the college met the last Saturday of each month. Every one of Adams' fellow board members was a "staunch Anti-Jeffersonian. . . . These are all real gentlemen," he added sardonically, "all but me very rich, have their city palaces and their country seats, their fine gardens and greenhouses and hothouses, etc., etc., etc.—men of science, letters, and urbanity."[1] He was invited to dine with Commodore Rogers, whom he had appointed many years before "as the second first lieutenant in the Navy," and a number of high-ranking officers; it proved to be a happy and sentimental evening. The officers fed his "mental disease," vanity, by calling him their father; and he, warmed by the wine and company, talked animatedly and then reproached himself later for an old man's garrulity.[2]

In many ways 1812 was the most active and stimulating year of Adams' retirement. It marked a kind of culmination in his long journey back to full vigor and complete involvement in a world that had used him, as he felt, very badly. Now in his seventy-seventh year, he found at last a kind of equipoise, a balanced government of his own strong passions. It was not a "serenity" or a "mellowness" to be sure, for the "capillary vein of satire" remained; but for the first time in his life he rose "above the battle." When he had done this he was ready for a reconciliation with old enemies and warring creeds.

In all this he was helped by his conviction that history had finally vindicated him. Eighteen-twelve was the year of Madison's re-election, and the year of the outbreak of war with England—the war that Jefferson's policy had made inevitable. Adams had wished for Madison's re-election. The Virginian had "genius, talents, learning, industry," he wrote Rush, as well as "more correct ideas than his predecessor." Unfortunately, since he had been "borne up under the wing of Mr. Jefferson," he had been "always shackled with Mr. Jefferson's visionary prejudices."[3] Out from under Jefferson's influence, Madison at long last had learned that national power must be based on adequate military and naval forces rather than proclamations and pious resolutions. He had found the courage to declare war on America's tormentor, Britain.

The President opened the new Congress with a message that Adams might have written himself. The only important omission that Adams noted was a recommendation for the establishment of a naval academy "in which young gentlemen should be taught every science subservient to maritime purposes." After more than five years of wandering in the wilderness of Nonimportation and Embargo, the country had finally come to the policies which Adams had always advocated and which the majority of his country had just as emphatically rejected. Americans, in their vanity, had thought "themselves masters of the drama of Europe and its actors and actresses. Good souls," Adams exclaimed to Rush, "they are ignorant as Fisher Ames" had been in his rigid Federalism. His own system had been based on the realities of international power politics.[4] "Who destroyed this system?" he asked, and answered: "The Congress[es] of the nineteenth century who by repealing the taxes have emptied their Treasury, who by mud-docking my navy have disarmed themselves at sea, who by a shallow, superficial, thoughtless policy have involved themselves in embarrassments and distress enough to make them objects of universal pity. . . . Weak, shortsighted, shallow, superficial children," he concluded, "you ought to have foreseen all this fourteen years ago as the madly ambitious, the profligate, 'the strong-featured John Adams' did, to his and his country's cost."[5]

The navy, of course, through the years of neglect, was much too small. It is "so lilliputian," he wrote his grandson, John Adams Smith, "that Hercules after a hasty dinner would sink it by setting his foot on it; I had like to say that Gulliver might bury it in the deep by making water on it. Fie, for shame, millions of rich people, so stingy or so cowardly!"[6] When Congress voted at last to augment the navy Adams greeted the news sarcastically: "Oh! the wisdom! the foresight and the hindsight and the rightsight and the leftsight; the northsight and the southsight, the eastsight and the westsight that appeared in that august assembly," he burst out to Rush.[7]

The war at first did not go well. An ambitious plan for a three-pronged invasion of Canada resulted in disaster, "a perfect comedy of bungling and error, a complete concatenation of absurdities," and Rush wrote despairingly to Adams listing the American blunders. Adams acknowledged them readily, but he refused to be discouraged. "We do not make more mistakes now than we did in 1774, 5, 6, 7, 8, 9, 80, 81, 82, 83," he assured his friend. "It was patched and piebald policy then, as it is now, ever was, and ever will be, world without end. The essential stamina remains and will remain. Health will be restored; the main pillars are founded on a rock. Winds and floods will not shake them. . . . What are you and I to the family of man? . . . We project everything, we conduct everything as well now as we did in our war, and we are now better united than we were then. . . . Such is the destiny of man in his terrestrial existence that nothing good is to be obtained but by much tribulation," he insisted. The war was "just and necessary," and Adams was "determined to stand or fall with the national government."[8] For him the setbacks in Canada were more than compensated for by a series of brilliant naval victories. He was exultant, considering "the commanders in our navy as my sons, and enjoy [ing] every laurel they acquire as much as if it were obtained by my own sons by nature."[9]

The country had responded to the war with a spirit that filled Adams with pride and gratitude. It proved the truth of his adage: "Human nature cannot bear prosperity. . . . Adversity is the great reformer." He found a country metaphor to illustrate his feelings about America. On his way to Weymouth to visit Dr. Tufts he had met a man who tried to sell him a three-year-old colt, "seventeen or eighteen hands, bones like massy limbs, ribbed quite to his hips, every way broad, strong, and well fitted in proportion, as tame, gentle and good-natured and good-humored as a . . . lamb. This noble creature," he wrote Rush, "is the exact emblem of my dear country." This would be his hobby horse—America. He rode him every day. "But I should shudder," he added, "if he should ever discover or feel his own power. By one vigorous exertion of his strength he might shake me to the ground, on the right hand or the left, pitch me over his head, or throw me back over his rump."[10]

The only unhappy note, and it was certainly a loud and discordant one, was the behavior of the New England Federalists. They opposed the war bitterly and talked of secession. A group of these irreconcilables, the so-called Essex Junto, met in a convention at Hartford, Connecticut, to decide what measures might be taken to give effect to their opposition to the war and the administration of Madison. Adams was full of scorn and derision. It was "a conclave of philosophers, divines, lawyers, physicians, merchants, farmers, fine ladies, peddlers, and beggars. . . . It is ineffably ridiculous," he wrote William Plumer. It was the most absurd and pathetic of political sights, an enterprise promoted by intelligent and honest men who had lost touch with reality.[11] "The debates in convention," he noted, "will be nothing more or less than the writings of Tim Pick and Jack Lowell, unskillfully abridged and coldly repeated. Even Otis' volubility can produce nothing better."[12]

In the spring of 1813 word reached Adams that John Quincy had been appointed a peace negotiator with, of all people, that insidious foreigner, Albert Gallatin. Jonathan Russell and young Henry Clay were also commissioners. The news excited Adams and started a series of letters to his son, reviewing his own diplomatic career and urging John Quincy not to surrender the fisheries under any circumstances. He longed to see his son, "once a day or even once a week," to discuss the impending negotiation as well as the general principles of diplomacy.

Although the Treaty of Ghent was inconclusive and left the issues in dispute between the United States and Great Britain largely unresolved, Adams like most Americans was pleased with the war and its consequences. The country had blundered through gloriously. "Mr. Madison's administration," Adams wrote a friend, "must be accorded by historians, notwithstanding all the errors, blunders, confusion, distractions, disasters, and factions with which it has been tarnished, as the most glorious period of the history of the United States." If the war had not settled impressment or even the issue of the fisheries, it had "laid the foundations of American prosperity . . . settled many points and decided many questions." It had proved "that a President can declare war and can conclude peace without being hurled from his chair. . . . It has proved that we can raise taxes. . . . It has proved that the Western and Southern states are as warlike as the Northern; and it has exalted the reputation of this nation in the eyes of all Europe by the only means with which it can be exalted or maintained, i.e., by splendid victories by sea and land; it has proved that our generals, admirals, and ambassadors are equal to any in the world in policy, and superior in wisdom and humanity."[13] "All things considered," he wrote his son-in-law, "we have got out the scrape very cleverly. This country is a cat that always falls upon her feet, whoever throws her up."[14]

The announcement of the peace produced wild rejoicings in New England. The "dongle" of the bells seemed to linger on for days in Adams' ears. If "dongle" was not in Johnson's dictionary, he, Adams, had as much right to make a word "as that pedant, bigot and cynic and monk."[15]

The spring of 1813 brought an unexpected and crushing blow to Adams. Early in April, Benjamin Rush died of typhus. When Adams had received the news he cried out in distress: "Oh, my friend, my friend, my ancient, my constant, my unshaken friend, my brother, art thou gone, gone forever?"[16] He told Elbridge Gerry: "As a man of science, letters, taste, sense, philosophy, patriotism, religion, morality, merit, usefulness, taken all together Rush has not his equal in America nor in the world that I know."[17] Abigail spoke of the doctor's death as being like "severing a limb." "An unchangeable friendship of thirty-eight years had grappled this friend of his country, his species, and his God to my heart with hooks of steel," Adams wrote James Madison. He had come to depend, as one of the props of his life, upon the constant flow of correspondence with his friend in Philadelphia. All that kindliness, good humor, wit, and engaging eccentricity was lost to him until they both should be united in a better world.[18]

Rush had left Adams a special legacy, the correspondence with Jefferson. After the first flurry of letters the exchange had languished. Both Jefferson and Adams had found their principal epistolary outlet in Rush. With the Philadelphian's death, they turned to each other for consolation and for intellectual stimulus. Yet Adams, as always, was prickly. He could not resist taking the Virginian to task for his opposition, fifteen years before, to the alien law. Adams' defense of the law was based on two somewhat contradictory points: that it was a proper and necessary law for a nation *de facto* at war—there was never "a government which had not authority to defend itself against spies in its own bosom"; and on the other hand, that he, Adams, had not prepared or invoked the law. The war with England had resulted in an alien law more severe than that of 1798. By its terms aliens must report their names and obtain certificates once a month. A Scotsman employed by Adams had to walk every month to Boston to renew his certificate from the marshal.[19]

Above all else, it was Jefferson's ability to ignore the dangers, hazards, and alarms that were such a conspicuous part of man's terrestrial existence that Adams was unable to reconcile himself to. The Virginian persisted in speaking and writing of mankind as though they were reasonable and rational creatures who needed only education to achieve true enlightenment, and presumably in time perfection. When Jefferson brushed aside the violence and turmoil of the 1790s, Adams accused him of having been "fast asleep in philosophical tranquillity."[20]

"Your character in history may easily be foreseen," he wrote with a poignant prescience. "Your administration will be quoted by philosophers as a model of profound wisdom; by politicians as weak, superficial, and shortsighted. Mine, like Pope's woman, will have no character at all."[21]

Adams also reminded Jefferson that in their bitter-end Federalism the Northern states were simply "servile mimics" of the Southern states between 1797 and 1800, when (though he did not say it), encouraged by Jefferson and Madison, the latter group had declared the right of secession. "Their newspapers, pamphlets, handbills, and their legislative proceedings," he reiterated, referring to the Essex Junto, "are copied from the examples set them by Virginia and Kentucky. I know not which [Federalists or Republicans] has the most unblushing front, the most lying tongue, or the most impudent and insolent, not to say seditious and rebellious pen."

This was strong stuff and it was to Jefferson's credit that he did not take offense. Adams followed it with almost a letter a day for several weeks. "Never mind it, my dear sir," he wrote, "if I write four letters to your one; your one is worth more than my four. . . . I never know when to cease, when I begin to write to you."[22]

Jefferson's comment that there was nothing new to be said on the subject of government touched Adams on a sensitive nerve. That might well be, he replied, but the things he had said in his *Defence* and *Davila* were new at least to Locke, Harrington, Hume, Montesquieu, Rousseau, Turgot, Condorcet, "to Franklin and to yourself, and at that time to almost all Europe and America." His "system" had enabled him to predict accurately the course of the French Revolution from its inception. "The French patriots" had appeared to him "like young scholars from a college, or sailors flushed with recent pay or prize money mounted on wild horses, lashing and spurring, till they would kill the horses and break their own necks. . . . . Let me ask you very seriously, my friend," he continued unrelentingly, "where are now in 1813 the perfection and perfectibility in human nature? Where is now the progress of the human mind? Where is the amelioration of society? where the augmentation of human comforts? where the diminution of human pains and miseries? . . . You and I ought not to die before we have explained ourselves to each other."[23]

Jefferson received the tide of letters with characteristic courtesy and urbanity. He had read them with "infinite delight," he told Adams. They opened a "wide field for reflection," but he must confine himself to a single topic. So saying, he picked up a stricture of Adams' on the doctrine of the Trinity, expressing his hearty agreement. It was certainly "too late in the day for men of sincerity to pretend that they believe in the Platonic mysticisms that three are one and one is three."[24]

To make his point about man's natural inequality as he came "from the hand of God," Adams suggested that Jefferson "pick up the first 100 men you meet, and make a republic. Every man will have an equal vote. But when deliberations and discussions are opened, it will be found that 25 by their talents (virtues being equal) will be able to carry 50 votes. Every one of these 25 is an aristocrat, in my sense of the word," he continued, "whether he obtains his one vote in addition to his own by his birth, fortune, figure, eloquence, science, learning, craft, cunning, or even his character for good-fellowship and a bon vivant." Then, to tease his friend, he added that the United States was far from the corruptions that had destroyed other governments. "Our pure, virtuous, public-spirited federative republic will last forever, govern the globe, and introduce the perfecting of man, his perfectibility being already proved by Price, Priestley, Condorcet, Rousseau, Diderot, and Godwin."[25] Again Jefferson's reply was polite and noncommittal. He was much more comfortable discussing Botta's *History of the American Revolution* or the histories of North Carolina. He had never had a taste for controversy.

When rumors of the correspondence between the two ancient rivals got about, Adams' Federalist friends asked him how he could possibly be on friendly terms with a man who had maligned and in a sense betrayed him. Adams replied a little sharply: "I do not believe that Mr. Jefferson ever hated me. On the contrary I believed that he always liked *me*, but he detested Hamilton and my whole administration. Then, he wished to be President of the United States, and I stood in his way. So he did everything he could to pull me down. But if I should quarrel with him for that, I might quarrel with every man I have had anything to do with in life. This is human nature. . . . I forgive all my enemies and hope they may find mercy in heaven. Mr. Jefferson and I have grown old and retired from public life. So we are upon our ancient terms of good will."[26]

On the family front there was ominous news that summer from Nabby. After being apparently free of cancer for over a year, she had once more been "afflicted with distressing pain and lameness" so that she hardly felt up to her projected visit. Indeed, there were few months in which death did not claim an old friend or a member of the large Adams clan. John Quincy's infant daughter, Louisa Catherine Adams, born in St. Petersburg, died when only a few months old. Although Adams had never seen the child, her death recalled to his mind with a terrible vividness the death of his own infant daughter, Susanna, many years before. Thomas Boylston's infant daughter died in the room where Adams had been born. Looking down upon the dead child, her grandfather could not help but weep. "Why was I preserved three quarters of a century, and that rose cropped in the bud?" he cried out in distress.[27]

Nabby, desperately ill, set out on an agonizing journey from Lebanon to Quincy. Knowing she was going to die soon, she was determined at whatever cost to be with her parents. She arrived at the farm with the signs of approaching death clearly upon her. Abigail put her to bed and gave her all the comfort she could in the final weeks of her illness. While Nabby lay dying, Sally Adams, Charles's widow, was laid low with an advanced case of consumption. She was put in the room next to Nabby's, and Abigail, nursing the two of them with the devoted help of Lucy Greenleaf and Louisa, was soon "worn down with care."

Three weeks after her arrival at Quincy, Nabby died, enduring intense pain with the same patient courage that she had shown all her life. Adams, writing to Jefferson, broke off: "I can proceed no further with this letter. Your friend, my only daughter, expired yesterday in the forty-ninth year of her age . . . forty-six of which she was the healthiest and firmest of us all; since which she had been a monument to suffering and to patience."[28] John Quincy wrote of his sister years later:

Her days were short and chequered o'er
With joys and sorrows mingled store,
    And Fortune's treacherous game—
But never since creation's hour,
Forth from Heaven's Almighty power
A purer spirit came.

Elbridge Gerry died in December of 1814, a few months after Robert Treat Paine. Adams was saddened by the news. "I am left alone," he wrote Rufus King. "While Paine, Gerry, and Lovell lived, there were some that I seemed to know; but now not one of my contemporaries and colleagues is left." Gerry, who had married late, left a widow and nine children poorly provided for, and Adams was deeply concerned over their fate.[29]

Throughout the winter and spring of 1814, Adams himself suffered a prolonged siege of ill-health: "head loaded, eyes almost blind, horrid churchyard cough! high fever! Feet almost stumbling on the dark mountains!" he wrote Van der Kemp. He was on a strict diet—"no veal cutlet, no old hock, no old or young madeira, no meat, no spirit, nothing but Indian porridge, water gruel, mutton broth, lemonade, five and twenty segars, much sleep and a little mercury and . . . bark."[30]

Mercy Warren, hearing he was ill, wrote expressing her concern. Adams replied graciously, thanking her for the "obliging letter," and reminiscing about her brother, James Otis, and the early stages of Revolutionary agitation.[31] Mercy answered and invited her old friends to visit her at Plymouth, but Adams declined with thanks. He had reached the age when he would not sleep out of his own bed for any inducement.[32]

In the spring of 1815, Eliza Peabody died. Dear, generous, kindly sister, faithful wife to two ministers, mother of three children and foster mother for a dozen more, she had spent her days unsparingly in the service of others. Charles and Thomas Boylston especially had been almost as much her children as Abigail's, and she had mothered another generation in John Quincy's sons, George Washington and John.

So it was that the bonds that held John and Abigail to life snapped, one at a time. Sisters could not have been closer or more devoted than Eliza, Abigail, and Mary Smith. Eliza's death was indeed "a deep affliction." Of the friends and family of their own generation, only Dr. Tufts was left and John's "dear blind and deaf brother," Peter Boylston. Nevertheless, Adams in writing to the Reverend Mr. Peabody regarding the news of Eliza's death, concluded, "I yet delight and rejoice in life."[33]

At the end of 1815, Cotton Tufts died after a brief illness and John and Abigail felt more alone than ever. The death of their "most ancient, venerable, and most beloved friend" was another of the irreparable losses which advancing age brought. The doctor had been part of the fabric of their lives, adviser and mainstay to Abigail during her husband's long absences, a faithful steward in the years when the Adamses were in England, and the reliable executor of a thousand small and large commissions for Abigail or John, from shipping Braintree cider to Richmond Hill, to buying stocks clandestinely for Abigail, or land for John.

A few months after Cotton Tufts' passing, Colonel Smith died with his daughter Caroline at his bedside. Adams wrote John Quincy, "Be to his virtues ever kind, to his faults a little blind," adding, "The world will never know all the good or all the evil he has done."[34]

Y
ET WITH all the death there was an abundance of new life. The charming Caroline had been married in the fall of 1814 to John Peter de Wint, "modest and discreet" and wealthy, who had been a classmate of her brother's at Columbia. When Adams heard of the engagement he wrote to young De Wint and sent love to his numerous sisters. "Tell them," the old man added, "I love them all, sight unseen, not only as your relations but for their kindness to my tender, my delicate, my lovely Caroline." He anticipated a "plentiful crop" of great-grandchildren, adding, "Keep this from Caroline—she will be shocked."[1]

It was a happy and fruitful marriage. Caroline, after the requisite nine months, began to produce children and continued to do so until she had brought twelve into the world. The first child, a girl named Caroline Elizabeth, was born on John Peter de Wint's and Adams' birthday, October 19. It seemed a happy augury. "Tell her," Adams wrote his grandson-in-law, "that her great-grandfather is but a little older than her, only eighty years, and that is but a span; but that although life is short, yet it is a very precious blessing, and every moment of it ought to be employed and improved to the best advantage."[2]

Soon after Caroline's marriage to John Peter de Wint, sixteen-year-old Abigail Adams, daughter of Charles and Sally, became engaged to Alexander Johnson, a young man from Utica, New York. "I am as little an advocate for enthusiasm in love as I am in politics or religion," he wrote his granddaughter, inquiring of her fiancé's profession, residence, "condition of his family . . . his means of subsistence, etc., etc."[3]

When he had satisfied himself of the young man's suitability he wrote him in a light and affectionate spirit: "Tell my little, lovely hussy Abby ——'What!' says Abby. 'Why does my grandfather descend from his dignity to apply such a familiar, such a vulgar word to me? Hussy?' Tell her hussy means housewife. And I hope she will know how a pot should be boiled and a spit turned, as well as how cakes and puddens and pies and tarts should be made."[4] Hussy was at least better than spouse when applied to a girl scarcely sixteen years old. "Nothing but a poet," he told Johnson, "will be wanting to make your Utica as famous as Ithaca, the kingdom of Ulysses."[5]

Adams was delighted when Abby Johnson promptly produced a boy. "Do you take care to make him a scholar," he admonished the proud father, "for without this, although the false trumpets of fame may sound him . . . a great man, he can intrinsically be good for nothing."[6]

Both John and Abigail suffered over John Quincy's absence. ("Oh! my son," Adams wrote, "you know not the grief that your long absence of almost five years has given me!") But George Washington, John, and Charles were a constant delight to them. "My sheet would not hold the history of their studies, their sports and frolics," Adams informed their father. Charles was his "little jewel," George his "friend and companion," who knew his books as well as he himself did, copied letters into the letterbook, and fetched volumes from the library. John was the most high-spirited of the three, and the most active sportsman. Together they made serious inroads into Abigail's "strawberries, raspberries, cherries, currants, plums, peaches, pears, and apples"; and, what was worse, the two younger boys got into their grandfather's bedchamber and "disarranged all the papers on my writing table."[7]

Louisa and John Quincy, held fast in England during the tortuous negotiation of the commercial treaty, desired to have the boys with them. Both of them indeed were in danger of being total strangers to their own children; five years is an infinity of time in the life of a young child. The boys must be sent to London.

The grandparents watched them depart with sinking hearts. Adams, especially, would miss the noise and excitement that they generated. He dispatched them with pocketfuls of admonitions and exacted from them promises to write faithfully. They must remember their "youth and inexperience," he warned, and always be "modest, ingenious, teachable, never assuming or forward." They should "treat all people with respect" and "preserve the character of youthful Americans." They should always carry a pencil in their pockets and be prepared to make notes on any unusual or extraordinary thing they saw or heard. "A journal, a diary is indispensable," Adams added; ". . . without a minute diary your travels will be no better than the flight of birds through the air. . . . I have burned bushels of silly notes in fits of impatience and humiliation which I would now give anything to recover."[8]

Charles was such a sober child that his grandfather enjoined his older brothers to teach him how to play. To George, inclined to trifle and daydream, Adams wrote: "Studies! George. Studies and virtues make men! All the rest are brutes."[9] The country houses of England were that country's glory. "I was fascinated with admiration," he noted, "but in the end I was wearied, disgusted with the endless repetition of artificial magnificence and expense. The surface of this earth is not our permanent abode and, however we may refine, decorate, and polish it, can never give us satisfaction."[10] Nonetheless, the "great models of the fine arts in architecture, painting, sculpture, statuary, gardening, music, etc.," which George would see in England should give "an entirely new turn to your mind."[11]

Adams concerned himself especially with John's ambition to be a sailor, debating the subject with him in a dozen letters. Finally he gave his blessing, on condition that his grandson would "make a covenant with yourself and your God never to do injustice or be guilty of insolence or inhumanity to subordinates, equals or superiors, whether friends or enemies. Upon these conditions I consent that you should leap at the moon and seize her by the horns when necessary, as your grandfather and father have done before you."[12]

John Quincy's diplomatic mission was constantly on Adams' mind. "My great and good son," he wrote, ". . . such are the collisions of interest, passions, prejudices, and caprices between the two nations that I am apprehensive you will lose in England, as I did, all the popularity you have acquired by such hazards, such labors, such services." Adams wrote his son "incessantly," advising, praising, and exhorting. "Reserve! Reserve! of which I know not whether your nature is capable, will be indispensable," he warned. His heart was too full to say all he felt.[13]

"I want to write to you every hour," he said a few months later, "but I . . . dare not write anything to you. I never take my pen but with the utmost anxiety lest I should hurt your feelings, embarrass your employments, give you unnecessary solicitude for your country, or excite a useless gloom on the prospects before mankind."[14]

Abigail was sick throughout most of the winter of 1816 but revived with the coming of spring, while John, who described himself as "good for nothing all year round," managed to read fifteen volumes of the Baron Grimm's history of the rise of the French Revolution "with more interest, amusement, and instruction than all the writings of Condillac and La Harpe." The work, in his view, "provided an indispensable key to the character of the century that was unfolding before them."[15]

Adams was delighted to see his wife "restored to her characteristic vivacity, activity, wit, sense, and benevolence." But he was indignant to see her at once "take upon herself the duties of her granddaughter, niece, maids, husband, and all." She was of course interminably writing letters to all of her far-spread tribe.[16] Throughout the spring and summer they rode out together whenever the weather was fair, an old man and his wife, bound together by a multitude of things, by love grown into habit and habit graced by love so that even the small details of daily life had a sacramental quality about them. They rode in the carriage over roads whose every bump and curve was as familiar to them as Abigail's garden paths, through a countryside inhabited by friends and relatives whose lives they knew with a firsthand intimacy, whose joys and misfortunes they had shared for five generations.

Adams took "great delight" in these excursions but he constantly fussed and fretted at Abigail's "uncontrollable attachment to the superintendence of every part of her household. . . . . Alas!" he concluded, "how few minutes either us have to live!"[17] It was, indeed, a kind of Indian summer for both of them. The household had been reduced, by death and marriage, to relatively simple dimensions. Abigail felt better than she had for years and Adams' own energy, fed by books and letters, burned undiminished. They rode to Boston to have dinner with Harrison Gray Otis and his wife, "in the neatest company imaginable," Boston's upper crust of Lymans, Minots, Thorndykes, and Boardmans. Adams professed to be astonished at being invited to dine with the high priests of Boston Federalism. "Do you ascribe it to the eclipse of 1816, to the comet, or to the spots in the sun?" he playfully asked John Quincy.[18]

"You cannot imagine of how much importance I am become," he wrote on another occasion; ". . . I am lately invited into all societies and much caressed." He and Abigail were guests at the Marstens' where "all the polite people, all the well-bred, all the well-educated people . . . the bon ton of our beloved town of Quincy" were in attendance. "Bless my heart!" he added, "how many feet have your mother and your father in the grave and yet how frolicsome we are?"[19]

One of Adams' greatest pleasures was the visits of Caroline and John Peter de Wint. They came in the fall of 1816, making the trip from New York to Boston with astonishing speed. One of the new steamboats had transported them in only forty-eight hours—a trip that used to take a full week. They brought along with them the infant Caroline to charm and amuse her great-grandfather and -grandmother. It was the first of their great-grandchildren that John and Abigail had seen, and although Caroline was "a little fractious from teething," Adams described her as "a pretty little, active, sprightly pet, puppet, baby! what shall I call her?" and promised himself "many a gambol with her."[20] John Peter and Caroline produced some peach and cherry trees for the orchard, and a side of smoked beef which, Adams noted, "will enable me to treat my military and naval friends now and then with a sandwich."[21]

In the fall of November 1816 the newspapers announced that John Quincy was being called home to be Secretary of State. John and Abigail, of course, were overjoyed. Here was a stage ideally suited to their son's remarkable capacities. Moreover he would be back in America where he belonged. Nor did the father fail to reflect that Madison had succeeded to the position of President from his office as Secretary of State under Jefferson; and that the chances were excellent that Monroe, Madison's Secretary of State, would succeed him as President in the forthcoming election of 1816. When Monroe had served out his two terms John Quincy might well be next in the line of succession.

With John Quincy and Louisa established in Washington and the boys attending school in Quincy, Adams wrote every few days to his son and daughter-in-law, telling them of the boys' progress—of the activities of John and Charles, and of George's experiences as a freshman at Harvard. He yearned to know every detail of John Quincy's public and private life, and Louisa and her husband were faithful correspondents. Adams was devoted to his daughter-in-law; he addressed her as, "wonderful woman, wife of a wonderful man!"[22] Her grace and gentleness had captivated him from the first, and as he grew to know her better her unusual intelligence and strength of character consolidated the victory which her charm had already won. "Tell Louisa I love her better and better every week," he wrote at the end of a letter to his son.[23] At Washington, he told his daughter-in-law, she was at the point of the Archimedean fulcrum. "From that station," he wrote, "the world will be moved. It is the greatest theater ever erected on this globe. If as great orators as Demosthenes, as great poets as Homer, as great statuaries as Phidias, as great painters as Apelles, are not produced, it must be because nature has not given to American brains the same firmness of texture which she gave to Grecians."[24]

I N OCTOBER of 1818, the month of their marriage fifty-four years before, Abigail fell seriously ill. A stroke came quite unexpectedly, after more than a year of excellent health and high spirits. For days she could neither move nor speak. When it was clear that she was dying, the town of Quincy was possessed by grief and by sympathy for Adams. It was almost tangible, a vast outpouring of love and affection for the great but simple lady whose Christian charity, goodness, and strong but gentle will the town had felt for more years than most of the inhabitants could remember. The terrible poignance of death, which everyone in Quincy knew well, suddenly seemed more stark and vivid than before. The burden of nursing quite appropriately fell on Louisa (to call her "the faithful Louisa" was to cover with a cliché what could not be described —the way her life had been intertwined and nourished by her aunt's and uncle's lives and theirs in turn by hers). A classic spinster, self-effacing, efficient, a bulwark in every crisis, it was she who most closely attended her aunt, aided by Susan, the strong-willed, impetuous young woman of whom Abigail had at times despaired, who was another casualty in the extensive family that Abigail had redeemed from some forlorn fate. Lucy Cranch Greenleaf was likewise a pillar of strength during Abigail's final illness; the Quincys were like "sons and daughters"; Billy Shaw, odd, crabbed bachelor that he was, came to offer his services; and the boys, George, John, and Charles, helped out as best they could.

Adams himself was stunned. Abigail was ten years younger than he; she had survived so many serious sicknesses that subconsciously he had come to think of her as indestructible. He had assumed that she would be around as long as he lived and probably for years after he had gone to the grave, presiding over generations of offspring with the same patient, loving, rather formidable efficiency on which he had depended for the better part of his life.

Abigail died easily and quietly on the tenth of November 1818, surrounded by her family, by children and grandchildren to the second and third generation. What was there to say of such a lady? The Reverend Mr. Norton was certainly not up to it, but that was not the good man's fault. The ritual observances of men in the face of the mysteries of life and death are inadequate enough. What could a country parson say that would illuminate a life his auditors knew far better than he? As much as she had loved this world, Abigail Adams had gone on to a better one where she would be reunited with the host of her friends and relatives, with her parents, her sisters, her son Charles, all the company of the blessed.

"The bitterness of death is past," Adams wrote his son; "the grim spoiler so terrible to human nature has no sting left for me." It had taken from him what was dearest. The great music was over. The strongest tie still binding him to life was cut. He would continue to live on, to enjoy life almost as much as he always had; but now he waited, sometimes impatiently, for death.

Jefferson wrote to express his grief and sympathy for a wound whose only medicines were "time and silence," a wound which words could not assuage. If he had doubts about life after death, he suppressed them and spoke of the not very distant time when both of them "must ascend in essence to an ecstatic meeting with friends we have loved and lost, and whom we shall still love and never lose again. God bless and support you under your heavy affliction," he concluded.[1] The letter was a comfort to Adams. "While you live," he wrote, "I seem to have a bank at Monticello on which I can draw for a letter of friendship and entertainment when I please."[2]

Slowly Adams picked up the threads of his life. There were the three boys, Louisa, the cook and two maids; but the house seemed terribly empty without Abigail. John Trumbull, Adams' old friend from his European days, had been commissioned by Congress to paint four scenes of the Revolution for the rotunda of the Capitol. Before the pictures were hung Trumbull took them on an exhibition tour. His painting of the signing of the Declaration of Independence was hanging in Faneuil Hall; Trumbull, Billy Shaw, and Josiah Quincy rode out to Adams' farm and carried him off to Boston to view the masterpiece. There in the great hall he saw the picture. He himself, Jefferson, and Franklin were in the foreground, the most prominent of the Signers. If he felt a rush of emotion and a resurgence of old memories, he made no mention of it. His only comment on the expedition was that he had foolishly taken off his hat in the drafty hall "and caught the pip." "The air of that hall is changed," he observed to John Quincy slyly. "I never caught cold there before."[3]

Louisa Adams, knowing how bereft and lonely her father-in-law must be, sent him a daily record of their life in Washington—"a reviving cordial," Adams called it, watching eagerly for each new installment and thanking her for the comfort they afforded him "in my desolation and solitude." Her letters admitted him "into the character of statesmen, politicians, philosophers, orators, poets, courtiers, convivialists, dancers, dandies, and above all ladies of whom I should know nothing without your kind assistance."[4] But the greatest solace of all was a visit from George Washington Adams during the winter vacancy. He was charming and affectionate, lively and entertaining as always. Although he had neglected his Greek for less austere studies, and spent too much precious time smoking his grandfather's "segars" and playing the flute, Adams could not find it in his heart to rebuke him.[5]

Adams now could no longer write without great pain, and he had "to borrow hands" to carry on his correspondence—Louisa Smith, John or Charles or George, a visiting friend or relative. Moreover dictating was awkward and unfamiliar. His correspondence, in consequence, grew more sporadic, briefer and less expressive. He wrote or dictated letters regularly to John Quincy, and followed in detail his son's brilliant career as Secretary of State. It could almost be said that there was an Adams dynasty in American diplomacy. In a nation which showed an unhappy propensity for muddled idealism in the realm of international relations, the son, like his father before him, was remarkable for the tough-minded realism with which he approached the problems confronting the United States. John Quincy had learned all that his father could teach him, and while he might lack the taciturnity of a Washington, he had far more reserve and self-control than his volatile parent.

Adams especially admired his son's skillful negotiations with the Spanish in the acquisition of Florida, "a blessing to the U.S. beyond all calculation or foresight." The treaty with Great Britain was another blessing, an accomplishment which would equally reflect credit upon the Secretary of State wherever careful students gave the subject their attention.[6]

John Quincy had spoken of writing a biography of his father, and Adams, obviously captivated by the idea, started to put his papers in some kind of order. They were scattered through trunks, boxes, and desk drawers that had been locked up for thirty years, and whose keys had long been lost. "The huge pile of family letters," he warned his son, "will make you alternately laugh and cry, fret and fume, stamp and scold as they do me."[7]

When Caroline and her husband and the children came to visit, she pitched in cheerfully to help her grandfather work his way through the piles of dusty papers; when she and her family left for New York, Thomas Boylston and his wife and their numerous brood of children moved in with Adams. The children would be nearer the schools and serve as "a comfort and amusement" to their grandfather.

He responded to the news of the arrival of Abigail Johnson's third son with warm congratulations. It was always "a pleasure," he wrote, "to be informed of the multiplication of my posterity." He trusted that they would all be "good soldiers, good sailors, good carpenters, good farmers, good tailors, good clothiers, good shoemakers, good woodcutters—or good something or other—the world is wide enough for them all."[8] When Caroline de Wint wrote him of the birth of another daughter he expressed the hope that "the lovely little creatures" would all imitate their mothers and grandmothers from the seventh and eighth generation. "Such a race of mothers," he added, "has rarely existed in this world, I believe." They might, he reflected, be the wives of ministers, lawyers, merchants, or "some of your Western landholders" who were bringing a whole vast continent under cultivation.[9]

The self-willed and unpredictable Susanna Boylston Adams, daughter of the dead Charles, had married an impecunious young man, Charles Clark, and then produced a daughter, Susanna Maria. Shortly thereafter the unfortunate Clark expired, and Susan, who had married against the emphatically expressed wishes of her grandparents, was left virtually destitute with a young child. She was too proud to apply to her grandfather for help so she turned to Louisa Catherine, who wrote Adams to find out if Susan and her child would be welcome at Quincy. "I can only say," the old man replied, "that if Susan will return here with her child and live in my complicated family she will be welcome to my heart—I will protect her at all hazard, as long as I live." At the same time he was determined to have peace in his household. Susan must check her temper. "She must return to me," he concluded, "and there must not and shall not be family bickerings."[10] He wrote promptly to Susan herself. His house, full as it was, had room enough for her and her "dear babe—and maid—and if you think these heterogeneous ingredients can be amalgamated together so as to live in harmony, come here and make part of the group."[11]

There were already nine children in the house, six of Thomas Boylston's and three of John Quincy's, although John and Charles were more men than children and George was a sophomore at Harvard. But the young people were a pleasure to Adams. He enjoyed "their exercises, sports, and amusements as much as they do," he wrote Louisa.

The news that his daughter-in-law had set out to translate Plato from Greek into English aroused feelings of "curiosity, astonishment and, excuse me, risibility," he wrote Louisa, assuring her that she "could not have hit upon a subject more to my taste."[12] When she sent him her translation of Alcibiades he was full of admiration and awe. "How is it possible," he asked, "that a gay lady of Washington, amidst all the ceremonies, frivolities, and gravities of a court and of a legislature, can find time to write so many and so excellent letters to me, to her children, and at the same time translate Plato's *Dialogues?*"[13]

There were, to be sure, difficult days and weeks to get through. The thoughtfulness of Louisa Smith and the attentions of his grand-children could not compensate for the loss of Abigail. His spirits flagged. He found his correspondence a burden; even the supervision of projects on the farm—"digging canals and ditches, building bridges, erecting long lines of stone-wall fence, carting gravelly knolls into bog meadows"—was a burden. He was flooded with letters inquiring about historical events in which he had been involved, with newspapers "which I cannot read, and prospectuses of projects of a thousand various sorts," including solici-tations for subscriptions to publications which he would never live long enough to read. Depressed and disconsolate, he wrote Van der Kemp: "my house is a region of sorrow. . . . Never in my whole life was I more perplexed or distressed than at this moment."[14] To Louisa he lamented: "The world falls to pieces round about me—my friends and my enemies disappear."[15]

He felt and struggled against the selfishness and self-absorption that accompany old age. The very old, like the very young, were inclined to draw into themselves, viewing the rest of the world with indifference if their own needs were provided for. Adams was reminded of the story of Fontenelle, who was visited by an old friend. There was to be aspara-gus for dinner and Fontenelle, knowing his guest liked his asparagus cooked in butter while he himself preferred it in oil, gave instructions to his chef to cook half in oil and half in butter. A few minutes later the guest fell dead with an apoplectic fit and Fontenelle, rushing into the kitchen, cried to the cook, "The whole in oil!" Such were the dangers of age.

Even so, Adams followed national and international events closely. He was pleased at Monroe's election in 1816. His own country had never been so united and so prosperous. It entered gratefully into the calm waters of the Monroe administration and Adams, with the political storm abated, began to think more often of death. He had, he wrote John Quincy, "the comfortable prospect of dying peaceably in my own bed, surrounded by amiable and affectionate children, kind neighbors, and excellent friends."[16]

The only cloud on the domestic horizon was the Missouri question, which Adams followed closely. The territory of Missouri was pressing to become a state. The issue before the nation was whether Congress could prohibit slavery in the state or whether Missouri would be added to those states which made up the slaveholding bloc. Adams was strongly opposed to the extension of slavery, with its great plantations and "great hordes of black serfs." It would discourage immigration by "the middle class of people" which made up the real strength of the country. "The Missouri question . . . hangs like a cloud over my imagination," he wrote Louisa Adams. The issue, of course, went far beyond Missouri:[17] "I shudder when I think of the calamities which slavery is likely to produce in this country. You would think me mad if I were to describe my anticipations," he observed. "If the gangrene is not stopped, I can see nothing but insurrection of the blacks against the whites . . . till at last the whites will be exasperated to madness—shall be wicked enough to exterminate the Negroes as the English did the Rohillas."[18]

Adams read the debates in Congress and was both amused and annoyed at the fulminations of John Randolph—"Jacky Cracky"—whom he had once compared to a "boy with a mischievous syringe in his hand, full of dirty water."[19] As a champion of compromise, he readily accepted Henry Clay's ingenious plan and, like the majority of his countrymen, put the troublesome slavery question out of his mind. The "Era of Good Feelings" induced him to sound a note of cautious optimism. "The nineteenth century appears to me," he wrote John Adams Smith, "likely to produce greater changes than the eighteenth has done. May the progress of knowledge of physical and intellectual liberty increase as time rolls on and the nations of the earth become better acquainted with each other as civilization advances."[20]

To view the younger generations with alarm and disfavor and refer to the period of their own youth and early maturity as a kind of golden age is characteristic of the elderly. Not so Adams. While he continued to worry about the materialism of Americans, he wrote to Thomas McKean that he contemplated "with pleasure the rising generation. As much as I am secluded from the world, I see a succession of able and honorable characters, from members of Congress down to bachelors [of arts] and students in our universities, who will take care of the liberties you have cherished and done so much to support."[21]

In March 1820, Quincy was struck by the most severe hurricane that anyone could remember. The Adams farm suffered with the rest, fruit trees and sturdy ancient oaks, fences and sheds, but for the Duke of Montizello there was "one mitigation"—"the most splendid winter scene that ever was beheld." Every drop of rain "was frozen wherever it fell on the trees and along the limbs and sprigs as if it had been fastened by hooks of steel; the earth was never more universally covered with snow, and the rain had frozen . . . a crust on the surface which shone with the brightness of burnished silver. The sickles on every sprig glowed in all the luster of diamonds—every tree was a chandelier of cut glass. I have seen a Queen of France," he wrote Peter de Wint, "with eighteen millions of livres of diamonds upon her person—and I declare that all the charms of her face and figure, added to all the glitter of her jewels, did not make an impression upon me equal to that presented by every shrub. The whole world was glittering with precious stones." It was a deadly beauty,

for it bore the limbs of bush and tree to the ground or snapped them off
and showered icy crystals on the snow. The old man sat at his study
window and reveled in "the sublimity, beauty, and novelty of the scene."
As long as life offered such "splendor and glory" he was content to survive.[22]

A few months more and he could watch "the blossoms upon the plum
and the cherry . . . opening." Nature and man continued to delight him;
he resisted remarkably well Fontenelle's disease of old age. Such was his
appetite for life that he could not escape it if he would.

That summer the corn grew especially tall and fine in the field before
the house. Adams could look up from his desk and see it, "more brilliant
. . . than the finest brigade of an army that I ever saw drawn up."[23] "I
enjoy life and have as good spirit as I ever had, but my fabric has become
very weak, almost worn out," he wrote Charles Carroll.[24] Yet he continued, with the aid of his stout cane, to "ramble" in the garden and
even farther afield.

"I am not tormented with the fear of death; nor though suffering under
many infirmities and agitated by many afflictions, weary of life," he declared to David Sewall. ". . . we shall leave the world with many consolations; it is better than we found it—superstition, persecution, and
bigotry are somewhat abated, governments are a little ameliorated,
science and literature are greatly improved and more widely spread. Our
country has brilliant and exhilarating prospects before it."[25]

IN THE spring of 1820, Adams received a visit from his old flame of years past, Hannah Quincy, now Mrs. Ebenezer Storer, a widow. It was the classic encounter between two old people who had been lovers more than half a hundred years ago. When Hannah Storer entered the room, Adams' face lighted up and he said impishly, "What! Madam, shall we not go walk in Cupid's Grove together?" Cupid's Grove was the local lovers' lane where John and Hannah had strolled long ago, and poor Mrs. Storer looked momentarily nonplused at this breezy salutation. Then with a kind of ancient mockery of coquettishness she answered, "Ah, sir, it would not be the first time that we have walked there." To Josiah Quincy, who was a fascinated spectator of the meeting, "the flash of old sentiment was startling from its utter unexpectedness."[1] He suddenly saw the decrepit old man as a bold and ardent lover and felt his humanity as he had never felt it before.

Josiah Quincy recalled other occasions that give an engaging picture of life in the Quincy farmhouse. He went one evening with thirteen young ladies and six gentlemen of Quincy to "President Adams'." One of the girls played the piano while the others danced with Josiah and his friends, and the President "gave the girls a fine account of the ancient belles and beaux" of the town.

A year later Josiah went with two of his friends, George Otis and Sam Phillips, to visit Adams and found him "well and lively," and as always, full of good conversation and entertaining anecdotes. Adams gave an especially droll account of his encounter with the Tripolitan ambassador in London years before—the customs, the ceremonial pipes, the ambassador's colorful retinue. From diplomacy the President moved on to dogmatic theology, the New England fisheries, and the Treaty of Ghent.

By the fall of 1820, Adams bestirred himself once more. For almost two years, since Abigail's death, he had hardly moved from the "narrow periphery" of the farm. Now he ventured with George Washington Adams to visit David Hyslop at Brookline. Hyslop was the owner of the old Boylston estate and for years Adams had wanted to visit the ancestral home of his mother. Susanna Adams had often taken him there as a child; he could still remember playing in the orchard and in the luxurious garden, thick with roses and phlox, and climbing the ancient elms and buttonwood trees. The day of the expedition was bright and clear. At Brookline Mr. Hyslop warmly welcomed Adams and his grandson and guided them to the roof of a summerhouse on the top of Brookline Hill. From here they saw a wonderful prospect of the Massachusetts shore line: "Land and sea conspired together to produce an assemblage of beauties—the grand city of Boston and the town of Charleston, the Castle, the islands, the rivers, the ponds of water, the orchards and the groves were scattered in . . . profusion over this great scene." Adams could see White's Mill, the home of his great-grandfather and the birthplace of his grandmother, the Charles River, and the distant Blue Hills.[2]

The year 1820 had another pleasure in store for Adams. The Massachusetts constitution which Adams had drafted forty years before had stood the passage of time remarkably well—it had given the state more than a generation of stable and orderly government—but it was clearly in need of revision. A convention was called to meet in Boston in late fall to frame a new constitution that would take into account some of the strains and stresses created by a rapidly changing society. The town of Quincy unanimously elected its patriarch, John Adams, as its representative to the convention. Adams was pleased and flattered, considering his election "the purest honor of my life." He had lately believed himself hardly able to travel as far as Weymouth, but he wrote Louisa that he was "sufficiently advanced in my dotage to have accepted the choice." Perhaps he would die dramatically on the floor of the convention in the midst of a speech like the Earl of Chatham in Parliament. He felt little "like a maker or mender of constitutions," but he would contribute his mite for what it was worth.[3] Certainly no one would any longer dispute the proper division and balance between the executive, legislative, and judicial branches of the government. That principle was as thoroughly accepted by Americans as any of the ten commandments.

For the period of the convention, Adams moved to Boston and stayed at the home of a Mr. Crufts in Pearl Street within easy walking distance of the State House. The delegates to the convention wore their hats after the practice of the day, and when Adams entered to take his seat they rose and removed their hats as a mark of respect until the representative from Quincy had been seated on the right of the presiding officer. To Josiah Quincy the scene recalled the Roman Senate in the days of the Republic, and the political talents of the men assembled were in his opinion comparable to those to be found "in the best days of the ancient republics."[4]

Adams found the long sessions tiring and, with his difficulty in enunciating, he seldom spoke. However when the question of universal suffrage versus a property qualification came up, Adams rose to speak in favor of a property qualification. He struck some of the old fire when he described the horrors of the French Revolution and reviewed the excesses of unlimited democracy in various historical eras. A relative equality of property was the basis of the Republic. If there was a small property qualification it would be an added incentive for people to own property and thus result in a wider and fairer distribution. Moreover, without a property qualification, the rich would exercise an undue influence over the poor, using their money to buy votes and corrupt the electorate. His ancient, muffled voice was that of a past era. The dogmas of democracy carried the day and Adams accepted defeat with good grace. If universal suffrage would work anywhere, it would have its best chance in the United States.

Adams took a keen interest in the men and the issues of the convention and agreed with his old classmate, David Sewall, that the members were "as wise, learned, and patriotic" a group "as ever convened in New England—and I will add, or in Old England—and I may add in the Old World." He felt for them much of the feeling of a proud father for his sons. If Washington was the father of his country Adams in a sense was the father of the state of Massachusetts, and these were his children.[5] But he paid a heavy price for his "romantic expedition to Boston" and his "daring attendance in the convention." He contracted a fever which put him to bed for almost two months. It was the middle of February before he could even venture out to church.[6]

In the spring, when Adams was fully recovered, he went to town meeting with Thomas Greenleaf to defend and explain the changes recommended by the convention. There, in the midst of the deliberations, Adams' brother, Peter Boylston, with "two or three octogenarians, half deaf," began talking and laughing so loudly that the meeting was almost disrupted. Peter Boylston, impish as always, announced to one of his companions in a stage whisper: "There is our John and Tom Greenleaf, Moses and Aaron, delivering the law from Mount Sinai. John can't speak very well; so he makes Tom his spokesman. However I don't know that we can do any better than vote with them."[7]

On the fourteenth of August 1821 the West Point corps of cadets, two hundred strong, having come to Boston from the military academy, marched out to Quincy to see the ex-President. The company fell out by the stream at the foot of the hill and the hot cadets refreshed themselves; then they formed up and paraded past the Adams house with flags flying and the band playing. After this the young men went through close- and extended-order drill in the field across the road while Adams stood on the porch to observe them. Following their maneuvers, the cadets stacked arms and marched into the courtyard where Adams addressed them. Although palsied by age, he could not resist greeting them, he declared, speaking of duties and obligations which faced them as the future military leaders of America. Washington should be their model and their ideal. A great country must have an efficient and well-trained military force but the officers of such a body must never aspire to have weight in the political councils of the nation. A good officer needed far more than merely military training; he needed a background in philosophy and in science. He must master the liberal arts as well as the arts of war. As he began to talk the President's voice was low and tremulous but it grew stronger as he warmed to his subject.

When the address was over the cadets feasted on a cold buffet spread under an awning in the courtyard; after lunch the commander of the corps, Major Worth, tried to persuade Moniac, the Indian cadet, to be introduced to Adams, but Moniac was too bashful to step forward. When the cadets had reassembled the band took up its position under the great chestnut tree that shaded the lawn and played "Adams and Liberty" and "other patriotic airs" for the President while the old man beat time along with them.

Following the band concert, the cadets filed by, one at a time, and shook the gnarled and palsied hand. The ceremony completed, they executed a few final "military movements" with admirable precision and marched off to Boston, carrying with them, as a memento of their visit, a copy of Adams' address.[8]

The review of the West Point cadets was Adams' last public appearance. His strength failed so badly that he could do little more than move from his bedroom to the comfortable old chair in his study. (Writing to Ward Boylston, he compared his condition to an old watch, "its spring and wheels so completely worn out that it can clip no longer. The hour, minute, and second hands all useless."[9])

In the study his grandchildren took turns reading to him and writing occasional letters at his dictation. George, now a young lawyer in Boston, paid his grandfather frequent visits and John, expelled from Harvard with the entire senior class for rioting and insubordination, built a little "guilded car" in which he insisted on driving Adams out when the weather was fine. The jolting of the carriage almost killed him, Adams confided to a friend, but he did not have the heart to disappoint John after the boy had worked so hard on the vehicle.

Although Adams was very conscious of having failed, Josiah Quincy, riding out to keep the President's eighty-ninth birthday with him, noted: "I scarcely ever saw him look better or converse with more spirit."[10] Taking his turn reading to the old man from Cicero's *De Senectute* (an essay which Adams declared he read every year), Quincy came to the passage in which the Roman orator argued against the idea that the approach of death was an evil, because those who died would meet later in the Elysian Fields. Here Adams broke in: "That is just as I feel. Nothing would tempt me to go back. I agree with my old friend Dr. Franklin, who used to say on this subject, 'We are all invited to a great entertainment. Your carriage [may] come first to the door; but we shall meet there.'"[11]

If the body was impaired, the mind remained as sharp as ever. From religion, Adams turned once more to New England history. Members of the large household, working in shifts, read him Hubbard's *History of New England,* Johnson's *Wonder-Working Providence,* "the original writings of Winslow, Bradford, Gookin, Eliot, and twenty others—the most ancient memorials of emigrations to America." As Adams put it, "all the superstitions, fanaticism, quaintness, cant, barbarous poetry, and uncouthness of style have not prevented this reading exciting in me as ardent interest . . . as I ever felt in reading Homer or Virgil, Milton, Pope, or Shakespeare. Silence then, ye revolutionary heroes, patriots, and sages! Never boast of your superiority for services or sufferings or sacrifices. Our Hancocks and Washingtons never exceeded in disinterestedness dozens of emigrants to America two hundred years ago. In short the whole history of America for two hundred years appears to me to exhibit a uniform general tenor of character for intelligence, integrity, patience, fortitude, and public spirit. One generation has little pretensions for boasting over another."[12]

By 1822, Adams had a new interest and a new incentive to live longer. There was already talk of Monroe's successor. John Quincy was an obvious candidate but so were Henry Clay, the framer of the Missouri Compromise, De Witt Clinton, the second of the Clinton dynasty to be Governor of New York, and Andrew Jackson, the hero of New Orleans. The opponents of John Quincy were busy spreading the story that he could not be elected because of Southern bias against New England. It made Adams furious. Was the United States to be in permanent thralldom to Southern slaveholders and aristocrats?[13] "Poor New England," he wrote George, "thou hast been for two hundred years an object of jealousy and hatred to all the world. The atheists and Deists hate thee because thou art a believer. The Catholic world hate thee because thou art a Protestant and, what is worse in their sight, because thou art a puritanical Protestant. The Church of England hate thee because thou art a dissenter. . . . All Europe dislikes thee because thou art part of a country which is an asylum for emigrants. Thy prudence, thy patience, thy perseverance, and thy valor have hitherto preserved thee under the protection of a kind Providence for two centuries and they will preserve you for two more and I hope to all ages, but you will have as hard struggles for ages to come as you ever have had." All of which was true enough and would have been truer if Adams had added: "All the world hates thee because thou art so often self-righteous."[14]

John Quincy's candidacy brought a fresh attack on Adams himself. Bitterness and party malevolence, it seemed, must pursue him to the grave. Years before he had written a series of letters to William Cunningham in which he had spoken with complete candor of the events of his presidency. Because of the frankness of his statements, Adams had pledged Cunningham not to publish the letters during his lifetime. Cunningham committed suicide in 1823 and his son, a rabid Jacksonian, promptly published the letters (which contained strong aspersions on Jefferson), hoping thereby indirectly to discredit John Quincy. Adams waited apprehensively for Jefferson's reaction. The Virginian refused to let the publication of the letters poison their friendship, "coeval with our government. . . . . It would be strange indeed," he wrote, "if, at our years, we were to go an age back to hunt up imaginary or forgotten facts to disturb the repose of affections so sweetening to the evening of our lives."[15]

To the grateful Adams it was "the best letter that was ever written," generous, noble, and magnanimous.[16] He was glad to bury his "peevish and fretful effusions" and reaffirm his affection for his old friend. He shared with Jefferson an interest in the political fortunes of "our John"— "our John" because when they had lived together in Paris "he appeared to me to be almost as much your boy as mine."[17]

Almost eclipsing the presidential campaign in the fall of 1824 was the arrival of General Lafayette. The Marquis had a triumphal procession through the streets of Washington and then north through New York to Boston, hailed everywhere as the symbol of Franco-American friendship and the hero of the Revolution. Adams, who had sent John and George Adams to invite him to Quincy, was full of admiration for the General's courage in venturing on such a taxing journey. If he had ever had any reservations about his French friend they had vanished long ago. He praised him as "a character that has no parallel in history," and looked forward eagerly to his visit.

From Boston, Lafayette made the journey to Quincy and sat for a time talking with Adams of ancient battles and faded glories. After the General, on whom time and his extraordinary adventures had left their mark, had gone Adams professed himself "highly delighted" with the visit, but he remarked privately: "That was not the Lafayette I knew." The General, in turn, was reported to have come away saddened, declaring, "That was not the John Adams I knew."

All of Adams' waning strength and attention were focused on the coming presidential election. It was an absorbing and nerveracking spectacle. Party distinctions had been virtually dissolved by the "Era of Good Feelings," and in the absence of any regular nominating procedures it was left to state legislatures and self-appointed nominating caucuses to put forward candidates. John C. Calhoun of South Carolina had announced his candidacy as early as 1821. The Tennessee legislature nominated the "frontier" hero, Andrew Jackson; Kentucky nominated Clay; John Quincy was nominated by a caucus at Boston; and a group of Congressional delegates designated William Crawford as a fifth candidate.

Crawford was eliminated from serious contention because of a paralytic stroke and Calhoun withdrew to run for Vice-President on both the Adams and the Jackson tickets. John Quincy and Jackson, as the leading candidates, represented a dramatic and indeed symbolic contrast. John Quincy was all restrained passion and intellectual brilliance, with the possible exception of Jefferson and his own father the most learned man ever to be a candidate for the office of President of the United States. He bore plainly the stigmata of New England, a certain aloofness, a certain stiffness of manner and cold austerity. With a mind as sharply honed as a surgeon's scalpel, he cut straight to the heart of the most complex problems; John Quincy Adams was perhaps as much of a refined brain as it is given men to be.

Jackson was everything that his rival was not. A man who depended more on the right instinct than right reason, he embodied the qualities of physical hardihood and personal bravery that Americans of all generations have admired. A frontier aristocrat and slaveholder, he made much of being one of the people, their voice, their spokesman, their champion against the "privileged orders" of society; against banks and merchants and monopolizers. For a country growing rapidly into an exuberant democracy, General Andrew Jackson, the man who had singed the lion's mane at New Orleans, was the perfect hero.

Adams, who admired Jackson inordinately, watched the course of the campaign anxiously. The General was not to be compared in gifts and capacity with his wonderful son, but the old man was well aware of the hero's power to attract votes. When the electoral college met, Jackson had indeed ninety-nine votes to eighty-four for Adams. The ill and incapacitated Crawford had forty-one and Clay thirty-seven. Since no candidate had a majority, the election was thrown into the House of Representatives. There Clay prevailed upon the Congressmen from Kentucky to defy the instructions of their own legislature and cast their votes for Adams. In such a manner did John Quincy Adams become the sixth President of the United States, the first New Englander to hold the office since his father and the last until Calvin Coolidge, almost a hundred years later.

For the senior Adams it was a satisfaction beyond reckoning, a compensation for every buffet and tribulation, a balm for old wounds, a final vindication for himself and his beloved New England. He derived special satisfaction from the fact that Braintree and Quincy cast unanimous ballots for John Quincy, while in Weymouth and Milton he got every vote but three.

Josiah Quincy and his mother, riding to Montizello to congratulate Adams on the outcome of the election, found the President, in Quincy's words, "considerably affected." Mrs. Quincy compared him to the old man, pronounced by Solon to be the happiest of mortals, who expired soon after learning of his son's victory in the Olympic Games. Hearing the story, Adams wept; it was true that his life was crowned with this special joy.[18]

Jefferson wrote promptly to congratulate him on the election of John Quincy as President. "It must excite ineffable feelings" in Adams to see the son to whose education he had contributed so much chosen as the leader of his country. The rancor of the campaign would soon die away. "Nights of rest to you and days of tranquillity are the wishes I tender you," concluded the Virginian.[19] "Every line from you exhilarates my spirits and gives me a glow of pleasure," Adams replied. ". . . I look back with rapture to those golden days when Virginia and Massachusetts lived and acted together like brothers."[20]

In the winter of 1825, Gilbert Stuart, himself in his seventieth year, came to Quincy to paint Adams' portrait once more. Adams consented to sit primarily because of his liking for the painter. "Speaking generally," he said to Josiah Quincy, "no penance is like having one's picture done. You must sit in a constrained and unnatural position, which is a trial to the temper. But I should like to sit to Stuart from the first of January to the last of December, for he lets me do just what I please and keeps me constantly amused by his conversation." There was no question about it, the painter was a marvelous talker and Adams looked forward to his visits.[21]

The finished painting, like the subject, was a happy triumph over age and infirmity. Stuart caught, as he always did at his best, the spirit of his subject, the old man's indomitable will, the resignation and inwardness of extreme age, the sense of a great life and long history fully lived, of a patient waiting for death and a still keen pleasure in life. It was more than a picture of Adams; it was a picture of old age, painted with tenderness and sympathy.

Young Josiah Quincy had planned a pilgrimage to Monticello in the winter of 1826 and Adams wrote him a letter of introduction to Jefferson, reaffirming his readiness to meet "the great and solemn event" of death. Jefferson, in turn, sent his grandson, Thomas Jefferson Randolph, to Quincy and Adams was delighted with the tall young Virginian. "How happens it," he asked, "that you Virginians are all sons of Anak?"—"the giants, the sons of Anak," as the chronicler called them—beside whom New Englanders were pygmies.[22]

From New York, Adams received in May a gold and a silver medal commemorating the opening of the Erie Canal, which was to link the Northeast and the vast and growing granary of the Middle West. He was pleased to have such mementos "of the pride and wonder of the age." He might have recalled his heroic image, drawn years ago, of America— a man as big as a mountain, guiding a mighty pine for a plow yoked to a hundred oxen, cutting westward through hills and forests, propelled by inchoate energies. The Erie Canal might well be taken as the furrow of this allegorical plow, binding the nation together, opening up the interior of a vast continent that moved with the elemental force of nature toward its unperceived destiny.

In June a committee in Boston making arrangement for the celebration of the fiftieth anniversary of independence waited on Adams to request his attendance. His presence would put a noble cap on a noble day. He declined reluctantly. He was too weak to go. He could not stand the carriage ride or sit in a chair through the ceremonies. He dictated a note to the committee expressing his regrets. The Declaration of Independence would become more memorable with the passing years. "Not the United States alone, but a mighty continent" was "destined to date the periods of their birth and emancipation from the Fourth of July 1776." Through all man's folly and vanity, he could see prospects for "the better condition of the human race."

The plans for the celebration put all Boston in a bustle. The Reverend Henry Ware, a brilliant young pulpit orator, had been chosen to give the address, but at the last minute he fell ill and Josiah Quincy, Sr., was prevailed upon to take his place. Half the city of Boston seemed to have collected on the Common to hear the bands, watch the Ancient and Honorable Artillery Company and the Boston militia pass in review, and listen to Quincy's oration, which seemed even longer than it was to the citizens who stood, closely packed, under the relentless July sun. Much of it was given over to describing the growth and progress of the country since that historic moment half a century ago when it had thrown off its ties with Great Britain. Then there was a special reference to John Adams, "that ancient citizen of Boston, that patriarch of American independence," the sole survivor of "New England's worthies." "He, indeed," Quincy continued, ". . . hears not our public song or voice of praise, or ascending prayer. But the sounds of a nation's joy, rushing from our cities, ringing from our valleys, echoing from our hills, shall break the silence of his ancient ear."

In Quincy, John Adams was dying. With family and friends gathered about him, as he had wished it might be, he sank into a coma and slept through the long, sultry morning. Near noon, aware that death was close, he roused himself briefly to say, with obvious effort, "Thomas Jefferson survives," and then dropped once more into unconsciousness. George Adams had gone to Boston for the festivities. When it was apparent that his grandfather was dying, he was sent for. As he entered the bedchamber Adams, regaining consciousness, tried to speak but could not.

At six on the evening of July 4, 1826, run down, as he himself had put it, like an old watch, the proud and passionate heart ceased to beat. Life which he had so loved could delight or wound him no more; the vast appetite was sated; the last tenacious fiber cut. At Monticello, five hundred miles away, Thomas Jefferson had preceded his friend to "the great and solemn event" by a scant few hours.

Two days after participating in an impressive celebration of the Declaration of Independence at Washington, President John Quincy Adams received word that Jefferson had died on the Fourth. "A strange and very striking coincidence," he noted in his journal. On the eighth of July he received a letter from Susan Clark, informing him that his father was failing rapidly and one from Thomas, written on the morning of the Fourth, confirming Susan's brief message. He started immediately for Quincy with his son, John, in a four-horse carriage. Having breakfast at Waterloo, Maryland, a few miles from Baltimore, he learned from the innkeeper, who had come that morning from the city, that his father had died the afternoon of the Fourth.

"I immediately took the determination," John Quincy wrote, "to proceed as speedily as possible to Quincy. . . . My father had nearly closed the ninety-first year of his life—a life illustrious in the annals of his country and of the world. . . . He had served to great and useful purpose his nation, his age, and his God. He is gone, and may the blessing of Almighty Grace have attended him to his account! . . . The time, the manner, the coincidence with the decease of Jefferson has the visible and palpable marks of divine favor, for which I would humble myself in grateful and silent adoration before the Ruler of the Universe. For myself, all that I dare to ask is that I may live the remnant of my days in a manner worthy of him from whom I came and, at the appointed hour of my Maker, die as my father has died in peace with God and man, sped to the regions of futurity with the blessings of my fellow men."

It was almost a week before word spread through the country, from Georgia to Maine and westward beyond the Mississippi, that the two last great surviving figures of the American Revolution had both died on the Fourth of July, fifty years to the day after the resolution of independence. It could not be said that Americans were struck dumb; rather the opposite. They were struck into an outpouring of wonder and astonishment. A great cry of amazement and awe arose, as it were, from the nation. For those Americans of a religious persuasion, it seemed, as it had to John Quincy, a peculiar instance of the intervention of that divine Providence which had guided the United States from its inception. Even hardened skeptics were shaken in their disbelief. One irreconcilable Boston Federalist wrote a friend that he had it on good authority that Jefferson had taken an overdose of laudanum so that he would expire on that sacred day. The Virginian had thus stolen some of the glory that belonged exclusively to Adams. But the country as a whole could only meditate aloud from pulpit and newspaper, from stump and platform, on the significance of the death of the ancient heroes. It was as though America, the giant plowman, had checked his oxen on their irresistible course and paused for a moment in mid-continent to look back to the place and manner of his birth, that birth which must perpetually define his purpose and express his meaning if he was not to become a blind and bewildered colossus. In that extraordinary moment America somehow came of age. Considering what it had been, it understood better what it was and what it had pledged itself, in time, to become. Adams and Jefferson together encompassed the Revolutionary experience. Their lives were a statement of the principles which America must stand for; even their conflicts suggested the tension inherent in the continuing colloquy of free men. The burden that they laid down, successive generations must pick up anew. This was what their death taught. If our history is the means by which we define ourselves, John Adams must be even more relevant to us today than he was in his own lifetime. "People and nations," he said, "are forged in the fires of adversity." Forged or broken; and so it will be with the nation that Adams loved and labored to build.

BIBLIOGRAPHICAL NOTE

Compared with his distinguished contemporaries, John Adams has attracted the attention of few biographers. The comparative neglect of Adams is undoubtedly due in part to the fact that his papers were not accessible to scholars until 1954 when Part I of the Papers were made available on microfilm through the Adams Trust set up by the family to supervise their reproduction, distribution and publication. Three more major installments of microfilmed letters and papers of John Adams and his descendants (the last issued in 1959) brought the total to 608 reels.

Although Charles Francis Adams published a portion of the letters and papers, as well as the diary and autobiography of his grandfather in a ten-volume edition, *The Works of John Adams, Second President of the United States with a Life of the Author* (Boston, 1856), it seems reasonable to assume that interested historians were inhibited by the fear that without access to the papers, they might miss important evidence which would prevent them from drawing an accurate picture of their subject.

But beyond the inaccessibility of the papers of John Adams there was the perhaps ultimately more important fact that Adams was an uncongenial figure during the period when America's counterparts of the "Whig historians" dominated the field of historical writing in the United States. Americans have preferred other heroes—Washington, Jefferson and Hamilton among them—to the prickly and outspoken New Englander.

In this century only one historian of note, Gilbert Chinard, has undertaken a biography of John Adams. Chinard's *Honest John Adams* (Boston, 1933), now long out of print, is a sound and sympathetic book. Catherine Drinker Bowen's novelized biography, *John Adams and the American Revolution* (Boston, 1950) helped to break down the image of Adams as a stiff and rather shadowy figure.

Correa Moylan Walsh, *The Political Science of John Adams* (New York, 1915) examined the provenance of Adams' political ideas. Manning J. Dauer, *The Adams Federalists* (Baltimore, 1953), concentrated on Adams and those Federalists who shared his political views as opposed to the Hamiltonian faction. The best treatment of Adams as a political theorist is Zoltán Haraszti's *John Adams and the Prophets of Progress* (Cambridge, 1952). Stephen G. Kurtz, *The Presidency of John Adams* (Philadelphia, 1957), is, as the title suggests, primarily a study of Adams' administration.

In addition to the *Works*, Charles Francis Adams edited the *Letters of Mrs. Adams, the Wife of John Adams* (Boston, 1840) which went through four editions in eight years. This was followed by his *Letters of John Adams, Addressed to His Wife* (Boston, 1841), 2 vols. and then in 1876 the famous *Familiar Letters of John Adams and his Wife Abigail Adams, during the Revolution.* Abigail's granddaughter, Caroline Amelia (Smith) De Windt, published the *Journal and Correspondence of Miss Adams, Daughter of John Adams* (New York and London, 1841) and the following year the *Correspondence of Miss Adams, Daughter of John Adams.*

An excellent edition of the *New Letters of Abigail Adams, 1788–1801* edited by Stewart Mitchell, was published in 1947. More recently Lester J. Cappon's splendid edition of the *Adams–Jefferson Letters* (University of North Carolina Press, 1959) has made this famous correspondence available in full.

In 1961, the first four volumes of the Adams Papers, edited by Lyman Butterfield and containing the Diary and the Autobiography were published. In these volumes and the ones to follow we will have the definitive edition of the writings of John Adams.

The following symbols are used in the notes:

MHS	Massachusetts Historical Society
APS	American Philosophical Society
HSP	Historical Society of Pennsylvania
NYHS	New York Historical Society
LCP	Library Company of Philadelphia
BPL	Boston Public Library
LC	Library of Congress
NYPL	New York Public Library

NOTES

CHAPTER XLIV

1. July 26, 1784, APm.
2. *Journal and Correspondence of Miss Adams,* edited by her daughter (New York, 1841), I, viii.
3. Auteuil, September 5, 1784, *Letters of Mrs. Adams* (Boston, 1840), II, 45–53; and to Cotton Tufts, September 8, 1784, APm.
4. March 8, 1785, APm.
5. *Letters of Mrs. Adams,* September 5, 1784, II, 53–56.
6. AA/Mrs. Charles Storer, January 15, 1785, APm.
7. AA/Tyler, January 4, 1785, APm.
8. January 11, 1785, APm.
9. September 1784, APm.
10. February 20, 1785, *Letters of Mrs. Adams,* II, 81–83.
11. January 3, 1785, APm.
12. AA/Lucy Cranch, Auteuil, January 24, 1785, *Letters of Mrs. Adams,* II, 78–81.
13. To John Thaxter, May 8, 1785, MHS.
14. January 4, 1785, APm.
15. April 28, 1785, APm.
16. April, n.d., 1785, APm.

CHAPTER XLV

1. November 4, 1784, MHS.
2. December 12, 1784; January 31, 1785, APm.
3. November 8, 1784, APm.
4. November 4, 1784, APm.
5. Cambridge, January 20, 1785, APm.
6. Jamaica Plain, January 7, 1784, APm.
7. Newburyport, April 6, 1784, APm.
8. December 15, 1784, APm.
9. JA/Jonathan Jackson, March 18, 1785, MHS.
10. Gerry/JA, February 14 and 24, 1785, APm.
11. March 5, 1785, APm.
12. Congress/JA, March 7, 1785, APm.

13. May 2, 1785, APm.
14. April 28, 1785, APm.
15. April 28, 1785, APm.
16. May 6, 1785, APm.
17. May 6, 1785, W-A, II, 255–56.
18. *Papers,* III, 175–76.
19. To Eliza Shaw, May 8; to Storer, May 18, 1785, APm.
20. May 18, 1785, APm.
21. JA/Richard Cranch, April 27, 1785, APm; May 8, 1785, *Letters of Mrs. Adams,* II, 93.
22. May 22 and 23, 1785, *Adams-Jefferson Letters,* I, 21–23.

CHAPTER XLVI

1. JA/Jay, London, June 2, 1785, *Works,* XIII, 255–59.
2. JA/Jay, June 10, 1785, APm.
3. June 6, 1785, A-J, I, 28.
4. AA/Mary Cranch, Bath Hotel, June 24, 1785, *Letters of Mrs. Adams,* II, 96–106.
5. June 26, 1785, APm.
6. Boston, April 19, 1785, APm.
7. New York, June 4, 1785, APm.
8. Boston, August 6, 1785, APm.
9. JA/Cotton Tufts, September 9, 1785, APm.
10. June 26, 1785, *Works,* VIII, 273–76.
11. July 19, 1785, *Works,* VIII, 279–83.
12. July 22, 1787, *Works,* VIII, 445.
13. June 7, 1785, A-J, I, 31–32.
14. June 21, 1785, A-J, I, 33–36.
15. AA/Elizabeth Smith, August 29, 1785, MHS.
16. August 15, 1785, *Letters of Mrs. Adams,* II, 106–8.
17. AA/Thaxter, Auteuil, March 20, 1785, BPL.
18. May 21, 1786, *Letters of Mrs. Adams,* II, 136–40.
19. July 14, 1786, APm.
20. November 21, 1786, *Letters of Mrs. Adams,* II, 158–62.
21. October 17, 1785, A-J, I, 79–80.

22. AA/Mary Cranch, September 30, 1785, *Letters of Mrs. Adams*, II, 116–20.
23. August 1, 1785, APm.

CHAPTER XLVII

1. January 7, 1786, APm.
2. Nabby/JQA, September 24, 1785, APm.
3. Nabby/JQA, July–August 1785, APm.
4. June 26, 1785, APm.
5. *Papers*, III, 195.
6. St. John's, September 21, 1787, APm.
7. August 1785, APm.
8. AA/William Smith, September 1785, APm.
9. AA/JQA, August 11, 1785, APm.
10. Bath Hotel, London, June 6, 1785, *Works*, VIII, 259–61.
11. August 25, 30, 1785, *Works*, VIII, 302–14.
12. JA/Jay, December 3, 1785, *Works*, VIII, 350–56.
13. October 21, November 4 and 24, 1785, *Works*, VIII, 325–33, 335–37, 345–47.
14. AA/Isaac Smith, London, May 27, 1786, MHS.
15. May 14, 1786, APm.
16. Jefferson, November 5, 1785, *A-J*, I, 90–94.
17. JA/Jefferson, February 17, 1786, *A-J*, I, 121–23; Nabby/JQA, February 8, 27, 1786, APm; JA/Jay, February 20, 1786, *Works*, VIII, 374–76.
18. August 18, 1785, APm.
19. July 15, 1785, APm.
20. JA/Jay, December 6, 1785, *Works*, VIII, 356–57.
21. Cotton Tufts/JA, Weymouth, December 25, 1785, APm.
22. Sullivan/JA, October 1785, APm.
23. November 1, 1785, APm.
24. November 23, 1785, APm.
25. October 24, November 4, 1785, *A-J*, I, 85–86, 88–89.
26. October 18, 1785, APm.
27. February 28, 1786, APm.
28. May 25, 1786, *Works*, VIII, 394–96.

CHAPTER XLVIII

1. New York, August 3, 1785, APm.
2. AA/JQA, April 25, 1786, APm.
3. July–August 1785, APm.
4. Haverhill, September 7, 1785, APm.
5. July 4–August 11, 1785, APm.
6. September 5, 1785, APm.

7. October 15, 1785; Mary Cranch/AA, October 1785; Eliza Shaw/AA, November 6, 1785, APm.
8. December 12, 1785, APm.
9. March 22, 1786, APm.

CHAPTER XLIX

1. AA/JQA, London, February 16, 1786, APm.
2. *Journal and Correspondence of Miss Adams*, 82.
3. December 5, 1785, APm.
4. December 29, 1785, APm.
5. AA/JQA, London, February 16, 1786, APm.
6. JQA/JA, April 2, 1786; and JQA/AA, December 28, 1785, APm.
7. July 24, 1786, APm.
8. July 24, 1786; December 23, 1785, APm.
9. March 18, 1786, APm.
10. JQA/AA, Cambridge, April 2, May 15, 1786, APm.
11. April 24, 1786, APm.
12. March 22, 1786, APm.
13. March 18, 1786, APm.
14. Undated, apparently sent 1786, APm.
15. March 19, 1786, APm.
16. April 2, 1786, APm.
17. July 21, 1786, APm.

CHAPTER L

1. March 4, 1786, *Letters of Mrs. Adams*, II, 124–28.
2. Jefferson/John Page, Paris, May 4, 1786, *Jefferson Papers*, ed. Julian Boyd, IX, 444–46.
3. See "Notes on a Tour of English Gardens," *Jefferson Papers*, ed. Boyd, IX, 369–73.
4. *Papers*, III, 184–87; and *Jefferson Papers*, ed. Boyd, IX, 369–73.
5. AA/Mary Cranch, June 13, 1786, APm.
6. *Journal and Correspondence*, 84; AA/Lucy Cranch, July 20, 1786, *Letters of Mrs. Adams*, II, 140–45.
7. *Works*, III, 403.
8. Accounts of the trip by both John and Abigail are in the *Papers*, III, 196–209; also Nabby/JQA, July 27; AA/JQA, September 27, 1786, APm.

CHAPTER LI

1. Leyden, August 15, 1786, *Correspondence of Miss Adams*, II, 53–57.
2. Amsterdam, August 23, 1786, *Corre-*

spondence of Miss Adams, II, 57–59.
3. The Hague, August 1786, *Correspondence of Miss Adams*, II, 60–64.
4. Lucy Cranch/AA, July 4, 1786, APm.
5. July 10, 1786, APm.
6. Higginson/JA, Boston, July 1786; Dalton/JA, Boston, July 11, 1786, APm.
7. April 30, 1786, *W-A*, II, 271–73.
8. August 27, 1787, MHS.
9. November 30, 1786, *A-J*, I, 156.
10. New York, November 14, 1786, APm.
11. December 16, 1786, APm.
12. November 25, 1786; February 27, 1787, *Letters of Mrs. Adams*, II, 170–72.
13. January 29, February 22, 1787, *A-J*, I, 160–69, 172–73.
14. July 4, 1786, *W-A*, II, 276–78.
15. November 30, 1786, APm.
16. November 22, 1786, APm.
17. *A Defence of the Constitutions of Government of the United States of America* (London, 1787), I, i.
18. Nabby/JQA, December 23, 1786, APm.
19. December 25, 1786, APm.
20. December 30, 1786, APm.
21. January 20, 1787, *Letters of Mrs. Adams*, II, 162–69.
22. December 30, 1786, APm.
23. AA/JQA, London, March 20, 1787, APm.
24. April 9, October 8, 1787, APm.
25. July 2, 1788, APm.
26. June 14, 1787, APm.
27. July 4, 1787, APm.
28. March 1, 1787, *A-J*, I, 175–76.
29. March 1, 1787, *A-J*, I, 175–77.
30. AA/JA, June 7, 1787, APm.
31. AA/JQA, January 17, 1787, APm.

CHAPTER LII

1. September 28, 1786, APm.
2. February 9, 1787, APm.
3. April 22, 1787, APm.
4. March 20, 1787, APm.
5. Mary Cranch/AA, April 22, 1787; JQA/Nabby, February 9, 1787, APm.
6. December 1786, APm.
7. JQA/Nabby, February 9, 1787, APm.
8. March 10, 1787, *Shaw Papers*, LC.
9. March 10, 1787, *Shaw Papers*, LC.
10. London, March 1, 1787, *A-J*, I, 175–77.
11. February 3, 1787, *Works*, VIII, 428–29.
12. May 8, 1787, *Works*, VIII, 438–39.
13. March 12, 1787, MHS.

14. April 25, 1787, APm.
15. June 7, 1787, APm.
16. JA/AA, Amsterdam, June 1, 1787, APm.
17. June 26 and 27, 1787, *A-J*, I, 178–79.
18. July 6 and 10, September 10, 1787, *A-J*, I, 183–98.
19. AA/Jefferson, July 10, 1787, *A-J*, I, 185–87.

CHAPTER LIII

1. *Journal and Correspondence of Miss Adams*, II, 84–85.
2. Account of the trip from Nabby's *Journal and Correspondence*, 84–94; and AA/Mary Cranch, September 15, 1787, *Letters of Mrs. Adams*, II, 180–90.
3. June 30, 1787, APm.
4. June 30, May 20, 1787; Tufts/JA, May 24, 1787, APm.
5. JQA/AA, June 30, 1787, APm.
6. Jay/JA, July 4, 1787, APm.
7. August 1, 1787, APm.
8. Eliza Shaw/AA, Haverhill, July 22, 1787, *Smith Papers*, LC.
9. January 23, 1788, APm.
10. July 1, 1787, APm.
11. Mary Cranch/AA, Braintree, September 23, 1787, APm.

CHAPTER LIV

1. August 25, 1787, *A-J*, I, 191–92.
2. August 30, 1787, *A-J*, I, 194–96.
3. AA/JQA, October 12, 1787, *Letters of Mrs. Adams*, II, 197–201.
4. October 12, 1787, *Letters of Mrs. Adams*, II, 197–201.
5. JA/Jay, London, November 20, 1787, *Works*, VIII, 462–64.
6. October 9, 1787, *A-J*, I, 202–3.
7. September 22, 1787, *Works*, VIII, 451–52.
8. September 23, November 15, 1787, *Works*, VIII, 453–55, 459–61.
9. November 30, 1787, *Works*, VIII, 462–64.
10. May 24, 1782, APm.
11. November 13, 1787, *A-J*, I, 211–12.
12. December 7, 1787, *A-J*, I, 213–14.
13. London, February 10, 1788, APm.
14. February 12, 1788, APm.
15. December 16, 1787, *Works*, VIII, 464–66.
16. October 18, 1787, APm.
17. *Journal and Correspondence of Miss Adams*, 95.
18. December 10, 1787, *A-J*, I, 214–15.

19. February 16, 1788, *Works*, VIII, 478–79.
20. March 11, 1788, APm.
21. Amsterdam, March 16, 1788.
22. Isle of Wight, AA/Nabby, April 9, 1788, *Letters of Mrs. Adams*, 67–69; Abigail's journal is in *Papers*, III, 212–15.

CHAPTER LV

1. Boston, May 7, 1788, APm.
2. AA/Nabby, July 7, 1788, APm.
3. July 16, 1788, *Correspondence of Miss Adams*, II, 87–89.
4. July 16, 1788, *Correspondence of Miss Adams*, II, 87–89.
5. July 27, 1788, *Correspondence of Miss Adams*, II, 89–91.
6. July 2, 1788, *Letters of Benjamin Rush*, I, 468–69.
7. August 8, 1788, APm.
8. Charleston, November 26, 1788, MHS.
9. October 5, 1788, *Correspondence of Miss Adams*, II, 101–4.
10. November 11, 1788, *Correspondence of Miss Adams*, II, 105–6.
11. November 2, 1788, *Works*, VIII, 484.
12. November 11, 1788, *Correspondence of Miss Adams*, II, 106–7.
13. November 23, 1788, *Works*, ed. Henry Cabot Lodge, VIII, 203.
14. November 9, 1788, Hamilton, *Works*, VIII, 211.
15. December 2, 1788, *Letters of John Adams Addressed to His Wife*, ed. Charles Francis Adams (Boston, 1848), II, 113–14; hereinafter cited as *LJA*.
16. January 25, 1789, *Pennsylvania Magazine of History and Biography*, XXIX, 210–11.
17. November 24, December 15 and 18, 1788, *New Letters of Abigail Adams*, ed. Stewart Mitchell (Cambridge, 1947), 3–7; hereinafter cited as *New Letters*.
18. December 13, 1788, APm.
19. December 13, 1788, APm.
20. AA/JA, December 15, 1788, APm.
21. May 17, 1789, APm.
22. March 2, 1789, *LJA*, II, 305–6.
23. William Maclay, *Sketches of Debate in the First Senate of the United States*, ed. George W. Harris (Harrisburg, 1880), 79.
24. May 1789, APm.
25. Maclay, 13.

CHAPTER LVI

1. Maclay, 63.
2. New York, May 8, 1789, APm.
3. Maclay, 41.
4. JA/Tudor, New York, May 9, 1789, MHS.
5. May 3, 1789, MHS.
6. July 5 and 24, 1789, BPL.
7. July 5, 1789, BPL.
8. April 18, 1790, APm.
9. June 19, 1789, APm.
10. Maclay, 87.
11. Maclay, 48.
12. May 27, 1789, MHS.
13. JA/Thomas Crafts, New York, May 25, 1790, APm.
14. June 7, 1789, APm.
15. April 25, 1790, APm.

CHAPTER LVII

1. Mercy Warren/JA, Plymouth, May 7, 1789; JA/Mercy Warren, May 29, 1789, *W-A*, II, 310–14.
2. Lincoln/JA, April 1789; Francis Dana, York, June 26, 1789, APm.
3. May 22, 1789, APm.
4. June 26, 1789, APm.
5. Dana/JA, Boston, July 31, 1789, APm.
6. September 14, 1789, APm.
7. AA/Eliza Shaw, Richmond Hill, September 27, 1789, *Shaw Papers*, LC.
8. May 5, 1789, APm.
9. May 14, 1789, *LJA*, II, 115.
10. May 13, 1789, APm.
11. June 14, 1789, APm.
12. May 24, 1789, APm.
13. JA/Tudor, New York, May 3, 1789, MHS.
14. Maclay, 71.
15. Maclay, 93.
16. June 18, 1789, APm.
17. May 22, 1789, APm.
18. June 28, 1789, APm.
19. September 8, 1789, MHS.
20. July 14–16, 1789, APm.
21. July 9, 1789, APm.
22. June 28, 1789, *New Letters*, 11–14.
23. Maclay, 130.
24. September 18, 1789, MHS.
25. July 9, 1789, APm.
26. July 4, 1790; October 4, 1789, *New Letters*, 53–54, 26–29.

CHAPTER LVIII

1. JA/Roger Sherman, June 17, 18, and 20, 1789, APm.
2. Maclay, 107–10.

3. Maclay, 122–24.
4. September 16, 1789, APm.
5. AA/Mary Cranch, Richmond Hill, September 1, 1789, *New Letters*, 22–26.
6. September 1, 1789, *Works*, VIII, 493–94.
7. JA/Trumbull, March 14, 1790, APm.
8. JA/William Smith, New York, May 20, 1790, APm.
9. JA/Jabez Bowen, New York, June 26, 1789, APm.
10. April 19, 1790, APm.
11. October 4, 1789, *New Letters*, 25–29.
12. Pensfield, October 14, 1789, APm.
13. Mary Cranch/AA, November 1, 1789, APm.
14. JA/AA, November (no day), Sunday, 1789, APm.
15. Cotton Tufts/AA, December 1, 1789, APm.
16. November 14, 1789, APm.
17. November 1, 1789, *New Letters*, 31–32.

CHAPTER LIX

1. AA/Mary Cranch, January 5, 1790, *New Letters*, 34–36.
2. March 27, 1790, HSP.
3. April 19, 1790, APm.
4. JA/Major A. Jardine, New York, June 1, 1790, APm.
5. June 11, 1790, APm.
6. January 9, 1790, APm.
7. Maclay, 158.
8. March 14, 1790, APm.
9. Maclay, 165.
10. February 6, 1790, APm.
11. March 9, 1790, APm.
12. March 9, 1790, APm.
13. March 14, 1790, APm.
14. March 30, 1790, APm.
15. JA/Van der Kemp, New York, March 27, 1790, HSP.
16. April 18, 1790, APm.
17. APm.

CHAPTER LX

1. April 28, 1790, *New Letters*, 46–48.
2. Maclay, 208.
3. Maclay, 204.
4. Maclay, 215.
5. Maclay, 218.
6. September 9 and 13, 1790, APm.

CHAPTER LXI

1. August 14 and 20, 1790, APm.
2. October 4, 1790, APm.

3. October 23, 1790, APm.
4. February 19, 1790, APm.
5. September 13, 1790, APm.
6. March 14, 1790, APm.
7. AA/Mary Cranch, New York, August 8, 1790, *New Letters*, 56–57.
8. August 29, 1790, *New Letters*, 57–58; AA/Mrs. Rogers, New York, September 1790, APm.
9. September 12, 1790, APm.
10. October 18, 1790. APm.
11. October 3, 1790, *New Letters*, 59–60.
12. AA/Nabby, November 21 and 28, 1790, *Letters of Mrs. Adams*, II, 207–10.
13. AA/Mary Cranch, December 12, 1790, *New Letters*, 65–67.
14. AA/Mary Cranch, December 1790, *New Letters*, 67–68.
15. AA/Nabby, February 21, 1791, APm.
16. January 8, 1791, *Letters of Mrs. Adams*, II, 212–14.
17. JA/Peter Thacher, February 25, 1791, APm.
18. January 8, 1791, *Letters of Mrs. Adams*, II, 212–14.
19. Maclay, 286.
20. Maclay, 288.
21. February 14, 1791, APm.
22. March 15, 1791, MHS.
23. Maclay, 301–2.
24. March 12, 1791, *New Letters*, 69–71.

CHAPTER LXII

1. Jefferson/Washington, May 8, 1791, Jefferson, *Writings*, ed. Ford, V, 328–30.
2. Philadelphia, May 8, 1791, Jefferson, *Writings*, ed. H. A. Washington, III, 257–58.
3. July 17, 1791, *A-J*, I, 245–46.
4. July 29, 1791, *A-J*, I, 247–50.
5. Philadelphia, August 30, 1791, *A-J*, I, 250–52.
6. JA/unknown correspondent but apparently Trumbull, Philadelphia, January 10, 1792, APm.
7. December 18, 1791, *New Letters*, 74–76.
8. AA/Tufts, Philadelphia, December 18, 1791, APm.
9. October 21, 1791, APm.
10. March 10, 1792, *Correspondence of Miss Smith*, II, 118.
11. February 19, 1792, APm.
12. June 16, 1792, Jefferson, *Writings*, ed. Ford, V, 78–79.

13. Hamilton/Col. Edward Carrington, May 26, 1792, Hamilton, *Works,* VIII, 251, 255.
14. April 20, 1792, *New Letters,* 81–84.
15. April 29, 1792, *New Letters,* 84.
16. Nabby/JQA, July 13, 1792, APm.

CHAPTER LXIII

1. Extracts from the diary of Nathaniel Cutting, November 3, 1792, *Proceedings* of Massachusetts Historical Society, XII (1871), 68.
2. September 9, 1792, APm.
3. October 30, 1792, APm.
4. JA/Rufus King, Quincy, October 11, 1792, HSP.
5. JA/Rufus King, Quincy, October 11, 1792, HSP.
6. December 2, 1792, APm.
7. September 24, 1792, W. C. Ford, "Some Papers of Aaron Burr," *Proceedings* of the American Antiquarian Society, n.s., XXIX (1919), 97.
8. Beckley/Madison, October 17, 1792, *Madison Papers,* New York Public Library, quoted, Noble Cunningham, *Jeffersonian Republicans* (Chapel Hill, 1957), 46.
9. December 5, 1792, APm.
10. Jefferson/William Short, Philadelphia, January 3, 1793; Jefferson/Thomas Mann Randolph, January 7, 1793, Jefferson, *Writings,* ed. Ford, VI, 153–57, 157–58.
11. January 2, 1793, APm.
12. JA/AA, January 8, 1793, APm.
13. JA/AA, December 7, 1792, APm.
14. December 26, 1792, APm.
15. December 26, 1792, APm.
16. January 24, 1793, APm.
17. February 3, 1793, APm.
18. February 18, 1793, *Belknap Papers,* MHS.
19. February 17 and 27, 1793, APm.
20. February 9, 1793, APm.
21. JA/AA, February 3, 1793, APm.
22. February 3, 1793, APm.
23. JA/JQA, January 27, 1793, APm.
24. March 2, 1793, APm.

CHAPTER LXIV

1. Quincy, November 26, 1792, APm.
2. January 7, 1793, APm.
3. January 24, February 4, 1793, APm.
4. AA/Nabby, Quincy, February 10, 1793, APm.
5. April 25, 1793, APm.
6. Alexander de Condé, *Entangling*

Alliances (Durham, 1985), 297–302.
7. March 16, 1793, APm.
8. May 12, 1793, APm.
9. November 28, 1793, APm.
10. December 11, 1793, HSP.
11. JA/AA, December 19, 1793, APm.
12. January 2, February 10, January 9, 1794, APm.
13. January 12, 1794, APm.
14. JA/AA, January 9, 1794, APm.
15. December 12, 1793, APm.
16. JA/AA, December 19, 1793, APm.
17. December 30, 1793, APm.
18. December 19, 1793, *LJA,* II, 132–33.
19. December 22, 1793, APm.
20. December 26, 1793, APm.
21. January 6, 1794, APm.
22. January 3, 1794, APm.
23. JA/AA, January 6 and 9, 1794, Apm; JA/Van der Kamp, February 18, 1794, HSP.
24. March 12, 1794, APm.
25. January 24, 1794, APm.
26. December 2, 1794, APm.
27. February 2, 1794, APm.
28. March 26, April 11, 1794, APm.
29. March 11, 1794, APm.
30. April 1 and 3, 1794, APm.
31. April 10, 1796, APm.
32. January 12, 1794, APm.
33. January 14, 1794, APm.
34. January 5, 1794, APm.
35. January 26, 1794, APm.
36. JA/AA, April 7 and 22, 1794, APm.
37. JA/JQA, April 23, 1794, APm.
38. May 12, 1794, APm.
39. March 12, January 24, 1794, APm.

CHAPTER LXV

1. March 12, 1794, APm.
2. February 8, 1794, APm.
3. April 15, 1794, APm.
4. JA/JQA, May 2; JA/AA, February 9, 1794, APm.
5. March 19, 1794, APm.
6. JA/AA, March 11, 1794, APm.
7. February 9, 1794, APm.
8. JQA/TBA, February 13, 1794, APm.
9. April 3, 1794, APm.
10. May 10, 1794, APm.
11. April 7, May 26, 1794, APm.
12. April 19, 1794, APm.
13. May 5, 1794, APm.
14. May 10, 1794, APm.
15. May 17 and 19, 1794, APm.
16. May 24, 1794, APm.

17. JA/JQA, May 26, 29, and 30, 1794, APm.
18. Quoted by Miller, *Federalist Era*, 158.

CHAPTER LXVI

1. JA/AA, November 17, 1794, APm.
2. JA/AA, November 18, 1794, APm.
3. November 8 and 9, 1794, APm.
4. Madison, *Writings*, ed. Gailliard Hunt, VI, 222.
5. JA/AA, Philadelphia, November 26, 1794, APm.
6. JA/AA, December 14, 23, and 28, 1794, APm.
7. November 26, 1794, APm.
8. December 5 and 7, 1794, APm.
9. JA/AA, January 20, 1795, APm.
10. December 30, 1794; January 1, 1795, APm.
11. December 6, 1794, APm.
12. December 14 and 2, 1794, APm.
13. December 28, 1794, APm.
14. December 14, 1794, APm.
15. December 6, 1794; January 20, 1795, APm.
16. January 16, 1795, APm.
17. February 9, 1795, APm.
18. JA/AA, January 26, 1795, APm.
19. February 9, 1795, APm.
20. February 2, 1795, APm.
21. February 15, 1795, APm.
22. March 26, April 21 and 26, 1795, APm.
23. April 26, 1795. APm.
24. June 9 and 17, 1795, APm.
25. AA/JA, June 18, 1795; JA/AA, June 19, 1795, APm.
26. June 11, 1795, APm.
27. June 21, 1795, APm.
28. JA/AA, December 12, 1795, APm.
29. JA/JQA, Quincy, August 25, 1795, APm.
30. June 19, 1795, *LJA*, II, 184–85.
31. Nabby/JQA, New York, October 26, 1795, APm.
32. December 28, 6, and 12, 1795, APm.
33. December 12, 1795, APm.
34. January 20, 1796, APm.

CHAPTER LXVII

1. JA/AA, January 5 and 23, 1796, APm.
2. January 5, 1796, APm.
3. January 7, 1796, APm.
4. January 3, 1796, APm.
5. January 20, 1796, APm.

6. January 26 and 29, February 8, 1796, APm.
7. January 21, 1796, APm.
8. February 20, 1796, APm.
9. March 1, 1796, APm.
10. February 14, 1796, APm.
11. January 31, 1796, *A-J*, I, 258–59.
12. February 28, 1795, *A-J*, I, 259–60.
13. February 28, 1796, *A-J*, I, 259–60.
14. May 27, 1795, *A-J*, I, 258.
15. JA/AA, February 6 and 8, 1796, APm.
16. February 2, 1796, APm.
17. February 8 and 6, 1796, APm.
18. February 15, 1796, APm.
19. April 9, 1796, APm.
20. May 5, 1796, APm.
21. JA/AA, January 12, 1796, APm.
22. JA/AA, February 13, 1796, APm.
23. February 10, 1796. APm.
24. January 29, February 2, 1796, APm.
25. March 1, February 2, 1796, APm.
26. JA/AA, March 3, 1796, APm.
27. JA/AA, March 11, 1796, APm.
28. March 13 and 15, 1796, APm.
29. March 29, 1796, APm.
30. March 7, 1796, APm.
31. AA/JA, April 25, 1796, APm.
32. March 19, 1796, APm.
33. April 18, March 2, 1796, APm.
34. AA/TBA, March 10, 1796, APm.
35. March 11, 1796, APm.
36. JA/AA, April 21, 1796, APm.
37. March 25, 1796, APm.
38. JA/AA, April 16, 21, and 19, 1796, APm.
39. JA/AA, April 28, 1796, APm.
40. JA/JQA, May 19, 1796, APm.
41. June 10, 1796, APm.

CHAPTER LXVIII

1. *Papers*, III, 227–28.
2. *Papers*, III, 232.
3. *Papers*, III, 238.
4. November 4 and 8, 1796, APm.
5. Ames/Oliver Wolcott, September 26, 1796, *Memoirs of the Administrations of Washington and John Adams*, ed. George Gibbs (New York, 1846), I, 384; hereinafter Gibbs, *Memoirs*.
6. November 11, 1796, APm.
7. December 27, 1796, Jefferson, *Writings*, ed. Ford, VII, 93–94.
8. January 4, 1797, *Rush Letters*, II, 784–85.
9. Noble Cunningham, *Jeffersonian Republicans*, 97.
10. Cunningham, 98–99.

11. *Aurora*, November 18, December 2 and 6, 1796.
12. *Pennsylvania Gazette*, November 2, 1796.
13. November 16, 1796, APm.

CHAPTER LXIX

1. JA/AA, Stratford, November 27, 1796, APm.
2. December 1, 1796, APm.
3. December 8, 1796, *LJA*, II, 233–34.
4. JA/JQA, December 5, 1796, APm.
5. December 4, 1796, *LJA*, II, 231–33.
6. JA/JQA, December 5, 1796, APm.
7. January 15, 1797, APm.
8. Philadelphia, December 7, 1796, APm.
9. December 8, 1796, APm.
10. December 12, 1796, APm.
11. December 31, 1796, APm.
12. January 9, 1797, APm.
13. January 28, 1797, APm.
14. December 20, 1796, APm.
15. December 30, 1796, APm.
16. December 23, 1796. APm.
17. December 27, 1796, APm.
18. January 3, 1797, APm.
19. December 28, 1796, *A-J*, I, 262–63.
20. January 1, 1797, APm.
21. JA/AA, January 3, 1797, APm.
22. Liston/Grenville, Philadelphia, February 13, 1797, quoted, Bradford Perkins, *The First Rapprochement* (University of Pennsylvania Press, 1955), 58–59.
23. Adet/Minister of Foreign Affairs, March 10, 1797, Frederick Jackson Turner, *Correspondence of French Ministers to the U.S., 1791–1797*, AHA, *Annual Report*, 1903 (Washington, 1904), 978–80; 993–94.
24. December 16, 1796, APm.
25. JA/AA, December 20, 1796, APm.
26. January 11, 1797, APm.
27. January 9, 1797, APm.
28. January 1, 1797, APm.
29. January 15, 1797, APm.
30. January 18, 1797, APm.
31. January 19, 1797, APm.
32. JA/AA, January 31, 1797, APm.
33. JA/AA, January 14, 1797, *LJA*, II, 240–41.

CHAPTER LXX

1. February 24, 1797, APm.
2. January 16, 1797, APm.
3. February 4, 1797, APm.
4. January 29, February 19, 1797; December 23, 1796, APm.

5. February 20, 1797, *Works*, VIII, 529–30.
6. November 25, 1796, APm.
7. March 9, 1797, APm.
8. March 5, 1797, APm.
9. March 15, 1797, APm.
10. March 27, 1797, *Jefferson Papers*, LC, quoted, Stephen G. Kurtz, *The Presidency of John Adams*, 226.
11. March 5, 1797.
12. McMaster, *History of the United States*, II, 308.
13. February 13, 1797, *Works*, VIII, 522–24.
14. May 3, 1797, BPL.
15. January 31, 1797, APm.
16. March 22 and 27, 1797, APm.
17. April 1, 1797, APm.
18. March 14, 1797, APm.
19. Philadelphia, April 15, 1797, APm.
20. April 6, 1797, *Works*, VIII, 538–40.
21. April 3, 1797, APm.
22. April 6, 1797, APm.
23. February 13, 1797, APm.

CHAPTER LXXI

1. April 8, 1797, APm.
2. JA/AA, April 6, 7, and 11, 1797, APm.
3. April 13, 1797, APm.
4. April 21, 1797, APm.
5. May 5, 1797, APm.
6. Cambridge, April 25, 1797, APm.
7. May 4, 1797, *LJA*, II, 254–55.
8. AA/Eliza Peabody, May 16, 1797. *New Letters*, 89.
9. TJ/Colonel Thomas Bell, Philadelphia, May 18, 1797, Jefferson, *Works*, ed. H. A. Washington, 174.
10. AA/Eliza Shaw, May 24, 1797, *New Letters*, 91–92.
11. *Aurora*, May 18 and 19, 1797.
12. To Wolcott, Jr., May 24, 1797, Gibbs, *Memoirs*, 536–37.
13. *Aurora*, May 19 and 20, June 6, 1797.
14. *Aurora*, May 23 and 22, 1797.
15. AA/Mary Cranch, May 24, 1797, *New Letters*, 91–92.
16. May 30. 1797, HSP.
17. July 3, 1797, APm.
18. July 8 and 17, 1797, *Works*, VIII, 547–48, 549.
19. July 15, 1797, APm.
20. June 2, 1797, APm.
21. November 3, 1797, APm.
22. AA/William Smith, June 10, 1797, MHS.

CHAPTER LXXII

1. AA/Mary Cranch, June 3, 1797, *New Letters*, 93–95.
2. AA/JQA, June 23, 1797, APm.
3. June 8, 1797, *New Letters*, 996–98.
4. AA/Mary Cranch, Philadelphia, July 6, 1797, *New Letters*, 100–2.
5. AA/William Smith, July 1, 1797, MHS.
6. AA/Mary Cranch, June 23, July 6, 1797, *New Letters*, 96–102.
7. JA/Uriah Forrest, Philadelphia, June 20, 1797, *Works*, VIII, 546–47.
8. November 3, 1797, APm.
9. AA/William Smith, June 10, 1797, MHS.
10. July 27, 1797, *New Letters*, 106–7.
11. July 29, 1797, MHS.
12. AA/Mary Cranch, July 27, 1797, *New Letters*, 106–7.
13. August 7, 1797, APm.
14. JA/Pickering, September 4, 1797, LC.
15. JA/Pickering, Quincy, September 15 and 22, 1797, *Pickering Papers*, LC.
16. AA/Mary Cranch, February 1–5, 1797, *New Letters*, 126–28.
17. November 15, 1797, APm.
18. November 3, 1797, APm.
19. AA/William Smith, October 23, 1797, MHS.
20. AA/William Smith, November 21, 1797, MHS.
21. November 15, 1797, *New Letters*, 110–11.
22. Madison/Monroe, December 17, 1797, *Madison Papers*, LC, quoted, Kurtz, *Adams*, 291.
23. September 21, 1797, APm.
24. AA/Mary Cranch, January 20, 1798, *New Letters*, 124–25.
25. November 15, December 26, 1797, *New Letters*, 110–13, 119–20.
26. AA/Cotton Tufts, February 6, 1798, APm.
27. March 14, 1798, *New Letters*, 144–46.

CHAPTER LXXIII

1. AA/Mary Cranch, March 3, 1798, *New Letters*, 138–39.
2. February 6, 1798, APm.
3. AA/Mary Cranch, March 14, 1798, *New Letters*, 144–46.
4. March 2, 1798, *Jefferson Papers*, LC.
5. AA/Mary Cranch, March 5, 1798, *New Letters*, 132–33.
6. February 28, 1798, MHS.

7. February 13, 1798, *Smith Papers*, LC.
8. February 15, 1798, *McHenry Papers*, LC.
9. APm, no date.
10. AA/Mary Cranch, March 20, 1798, *New Letters*, 146–47; AA/William Smith, March 20, 1798, MHS.
11. AA/Mary Cranch, March 20, 1798, *New Letters*, 146–47.
12. March 15, 1798, Jefferson, *Writings*, ed. Ford, VII, 220–21.
13. March 20, 1798, *New Letters*, 146–47.
14. AA/Mary Cranch, March 13, 1798, *New Letters*, 142–44.
15. Jefferson/Monroe, March 21, 1798, Jefferson, *Writings*, ed. Ford, VII, 221–22.
16. AA/William Smith, March 30, 1798, MHS.
17. March 27, 1798, *New Letters*, 147–49.
18. AA/William Smith, March 24, 1798, MHS.
19. AA/Mary Cranch, April 7, 1798, *New Letters*, 153–55.
20. March 30, 1798, Samuel Eliot Morison, *Harrison Gray Otis*, 93.
21. Jefferson/Madison, Philadelphia, April 5, 1798, Jefferson, *Writings*, ed. Ford, VII, 230–32.
22. Ames/Gore, December 18, 1798, Fisher Ames, *Works*, ed. Seth Ames, I, 245–46.
23. April 4, 1798, *New Letters*, 150–53.
24. AA/Mary Cranch, April 22, 1798, *New Letters*, 160–63.
25. Jefferson/Madison, Philadelphia, April 6 and 12, 1798; Jefferson/P. Carr, April 12, 1798, Jefferson, *Writings*, ed. Ford, VII, 234–40.
26. *Life and Correspondence of Rufus King*, ed. Charles R. King (New York, 1894–1900); Sedgwick/King, May 1, 1798; Troup/King, June 3, 1798, II, 319, 329.
27. AA/Mary Cranch, April 13, 1798, *New Letters*, 155–57.
28. AA/Cotton Tufts, April 13, 1798, APm.
29. April 21, 1798, *New Letters*, 157–60.
30. AA/Mary Cranch, April 28, 1798, *New Letters*, 167–68.
31. AA/Mary Cranch, April 26, May 10, 1798, *New Letters*, 164, 172.
32. Quincy, June 19, 1798, *New Letters*, 193.
33. April 26, 1798; James Lewis, Jr.,

Philadelphia, May 9, 1798, Jefferson, *Writings*, ed. Ford, VII, 245, 249–50.
34. April 26, 1798, *New Letters*, 164–66.
35. AA/Mary Cranch, May 18, 1798, *New Letters*, 174–76.
36. *Aurora*, August 28, 1798.
37. June 5, 1798, Gibbs, *Memoirs*, II, 50.
38. May 24, 1798, APm.
39. AA/Mary Cranch, May 10, 1798, *New Letters*, 170–72.

CHAPTER LXXIV

1. AA/Cotton Tufts, June 8, 1798, MHS.
2. AA/Mary Cranch, June 8, 1798, *New Letters*, 187–90.
3. May 21, 1798, *New Letters*, 178.
4. May 26, 1798, *New Letters*, 179–82.
5. AA/Mary Cranch, April 22, May 29, 1798, *New Letters*, 160–63, 182–83.
6. AA/William Smith, June 9, 1798, MHS.
7. AA/Cotton Tufts, June 8, 1798, APm.
8. Murray/JQA, June 8, 1798, quoted, Beveridge, *Marshall*, II, 363.
9. June 4 and 9, 1798, MHS.
10. April 15, 1798, APm.
11. Murray/JQA, April 17, 1798, APm.
12. Higginson/Wolcott, Boston, July 11, 1798, Gibbs, *Memoirs*, II, 70–71.
13. Ames/Wolcott, Dedham, June 8, 1798, Gibbs, *Memoirs*, II, 51.
14. Cabot/Wolcott, June 9, 1798, Gibbs, *Memoirs*, II, 53–54.
15. May 7, 1798, *New Letters*, 169.
16. June 1 and 27, 1798, *New Letters*, 183–84, 197–98.
17. June 25, 1798, *New Letters*, 196–97.
18. *Aurora*, June 21, 1798.
19. June 22, 1798, *Works*, VIII, 572–73.
20. July 7, 1798, MHS.
21. July 11, 1798, *Washington Papers*, XXXVI, 323–27.

CHAPTER LXXV

1. *Annals of Congress*, X, 407; Ellsworth to Pickering, December 12, 1798, Pickering MSS, MHS.
2. To Stephens Thompson Mason, Monticello, October 11; to John Taylor, Monticello, November 26, 1798, Jefferson, *Writings*, ed. Ford, VII, 282–83, 309–12.
3. July 23, 1798, *Townsend-Smith Papers*, MHS.

4. July 20, 1798, APm.
5. AA/Mary Cranch, July 9, 1798, *New Letters*, 199–201.
6. July 12 and 17, 1798, *New Letters*, 205–7.
7. JA/McHenry, August 14, 1798, *McHenry Papers*, LC.
8. August 22, 1798, *McHenry Papers*, LC.
9. August 29, 1798, *McHenry Papers*, LC.
10. September 6, 1798, *McHenry Papers*, LC.
11. September 13, 1798, *McHenry Papers*, LC.
12. September 17, 1798, APm.
13. September 29, 1798, APm.
14. September 21, 1798, APm.
15. September 25, 1798, APm.
16. October 9, 1798, *Works*, VIII, 600–1.
17. October 15, 1798, APm.
18. October 22, 1798, APm.
19. To Wolcott, September 11, 1798, Gibbs, *Memoirs*, II, 107.
20. October 10, 1798, Gibbs, *Memoirs*, II, 110–11.
21. Wolcott/JA, September 14, 1798, Gibbs, *Memoirs*, II, 107.
22. JA/McHenry, October 22, 1798, APm.
23. JA/Pickering, October 20, 1798, *Works*, VIII, 609.

CHAPTER LXXVI

1. Flagg's at Weston, November 12; Suffield, November 14, 1798, APm.
2. JA/AA, Stratford, November 16, 1798, APm.
3. JA/AA, November 25, 1798, APm.
4. November 28, 1798, APm.
5. December 8, 1798, APm.
6. To Madison, January 3, 1799, Jefferson, *Writings*, ed. Ford, VII, 313.
7. December 31, 1798, APm.
8. William Shaw/AA, December 20, 1798, APm.
9. JA/AA, December 13, 1798, *Letters*, 256–57.
10. December 19, 1798, *Works*, VIII, 617–18.
11. JA/AA, January 5, 1799, APm.
12. December 31, 1798, APm.
13. January 1, 1799, *LJA*, II, 258–59.
14. November 29, 1798, APm.
15. January 6, 1799, APm.
16. January 1, 1799, *LJA*, II, 259.
17. Shaw/AA, January 15, 1799; JA/AA, January 16, 1799, APm.

18. Murray/JA, September 7, 11, and 18, October 7, 1798, APm.
19. October 2, 1798, APm.
20. January 15, 1799, *Works*, VIII, 621.
21. Shaw/AA, January 21; AA/Shaw, February 2, 1799, APm.

CHAPTER LXXVII

1. January 25, 1799, APm.
2. February 4, 1799, *LJA*, II, 260–61.
3. To Madison, February 5, 1799, Jefferson, *Writings*, ed. Ford, VII, 342–45.
4. February 19, 1799, *Works*, VIII, 624–26.
5. To King, March 10, 1799, King, *Correspondence*, II, 551.
6. To Madison, February 19, 1799, Jefferson, *Writings*, ed. Ford, VII, 361–63.
7. Tracy/McHenry, September 2, 1799, quoted, Beveridge, *Marshall*, II, 425.
8. To Wolcott, March 29, 1799, Gibbs, *Memoirs*, II, 229–30.
9. March 3, 1799, APm.
10. February 25, 1799, APm.
11. February 27, 1799, APm.
12. April 7, 1799, *Smith Papers*, LC.
13. March 5, 1799, *Works*, VIII, 626–27.
14. March 14, 1799, *Works*, VIII, 628–29.
15. March 29, 1799, *Works*, VIII, 629.
16. Quoted by Charles Francis Adams, *Works*, VIII, 652–53n.
17. February 22, 1799, APm.
18. AA/Eliza Peabody, April 7, 1799, *Smith Papers*, LC.
19. Sedgwick/Hon. Rutherford, Philadelphia, March 1799, APm.
20. AA/JA, March 9, 1799, *Smith Papers*, LC.
21. May 11, 1799, *Hamilton Papers*, LC, quoted, Kurtz, *Adams*, 381.
22. Washington/Trumbull, July 21, August 30, 1799, *Writings*, XXXVII, 312–13.
23. *Memoirs of a Life Chiefly Passed in Pa.* (Harrisburg, 1811), 407–9.
24. *Life and Correspondence of James Iredell*, ed. Griffith J. McRee (New York, 1867–68), II, 551.
25. Uriah Forrest/JA, April 28, 1799, *Works*, VIII, 637–38.
26. JA/Uriah Forrest, May 13, 1799, *Works*, VIII, 645–46.
27. April 7, 1799, *Smith Papers*, LC.
28. AA/TBA, June 20, 1799, APm.
29. July 19, 1799, *Smith Papers*, LC.
30. JA/Pickering, May 17; JA/Wolcott,

May 17; JA/Charles Lee, May 17, 1799, *Works*, VIII, 648–70.
31. June 7, 1799, *Works*, VII, 655–56.
32. To Dr. Waterhouse, October 23, 1802, APm.
33. July 2, 1799, *Works*, VIII, 661.

CHAPTER LXXVIII

1. To Thomas Lomax, Monticello, March 12, 1799, Jefferson, *Writings*, ed. Ford, VII, 373–74.
2. August 13, 1799, *Works*, IX, 13–14.
3. JA/McHenry, Quincy, July 27, 1799, *Works*, IX, 4–5.
4. Quincy, August 6, 1799, *Works*, IX, 10–12.
5. November 5, 1799, Ames, *Works*, I, 260–61.
6. Ames/Pickering, Dedham, October 19, 1799, November 5 and 23, 1799, Ames, *Works*, I, 257–73.
7. Higginson/Pickering, April 16, 1800, *Annual Report*, AHA, 1896, I, 836.
8. Stoddert, Trenton, August 29, 1799, *Works*, IX, 18–19.
9. JA/Stoddert, Quincy, September 4, 1799, *Works*, IX, 19–20.
10. Trenton, September 11, 1799, *Works*, IX, 23–25.
11. September 22, 1799, *Works*, IX, 34–35.
12. Ellsworth/JA, Windsor, October 5, 1799, *Works*, IX, 37–38.
13. Trenton, September 13, 1799, *Works*, IX, 25–29.
14. September 21, 1799, *Works*, IX, 33–34.
15. September 21, 1799, *Works*, IX, 33.
16. September 24, 1799, *Works*, IX, 36–37.
17. September 23, 1799, *Works*, IX, 35–36.
18. Shaw/AA, October 6, 1799, APm.
19. Winchester, October 6, 1799, *Works*, IX, 38.
20. AA/Mary Cranch, December 30, 1799, *New Letters*, 224–25.
21. JA/Pickering, Trenton, October 16, 1799, *Works*, IX, 39.
22. October 17, 1799, APm.
23. October 24 and 25, 1799, APm.
24. October 27, 1799, APm.

CHAPTER LXXIX

1. October 28, 1799, *Smith Papers*, LC.
2. AA/Mary Cranch, October 31, 1799, *New Letters*, 210–12.
3. AA/William Smith, Philadelphia,

November 19, 1799, *Townsend-Smith Papers*, MHS.

4. AA/Cotton Tufts, November 22, 1799, APm.

5. AA/Mary Cranch, Philadelphia, December 4, 1799, *New Letters*, 217–19.

6. December 11, 1799, *New Letters*, 219–22.

7. To Wolcott, Brookline, December 16, 1799, Gibbs, *Memoirs*, 312.

8. December 22, 1799, *New Letters*, 222.

9. January 28, 1800, *New Letters*, 228.

10. To Ames, December 29, 1799, Gibbs, *Memoirs*, 313–16.

11. AA/Mary Cranch, December 11, 1799, *New Letters*, 219–22.

12. AA/JQA, February 8, 1800, APm.

13. January 11, 1800, APm.

14. January 16, 1800, *Townsend-Smith Papers*, MHS.

15. February 8, 1800, APm.

16. To Thomas Mann Randolph, February 2, 1800, Jefferson, *Writings*, ed. Ford, VII, 421–24.

17. Jefferson/Madison, March 4, 1800, Jefferson, *Writings*, ed. Ford, VII, 429–34.

18. Jefferson/Pinckney, October 29, 1799, quoted, Beveridge, *Marshall*, II, 459.

19. Marshall/James M. Marshall, February 28, 1800, Beveridge, *Marshall*, II, 463.

20. Anonymous/JA, March 11 and 19, 1800, APm.

CHAPTER LXXX

1. McHenry/JA, May 31, 1800, *McHenry Papers*, LC.

2. August 26, 1800, Gibbs, *Memoirs*, II, 410.

3. February 13, 1811, *Life and Correspondence of James McHenry*, ed. Bernard C. Steiner (Cleveland, 1907), 568.

4. Wolcott/Ames, August 10, 1800, Gibbs, *Memoirs*, II, 401–2.

5. March 18, 1800, *New Letters*, 239–42.

6. AA/Hannah Smith, January 30, 1800, *Townsend-Smith Papers*, MHS.

7. Copley/JA, London, March 4, 1800, APm.

8. Shaw/AA, May 25, 1800, APm.

9. February 27, 1800, *New Letters*, 234–36.

10. May 5, 1800, *New Letters*, 251.

11. AA/JQA, May 15, 1800, APm.

12. May 20, 1800, APm.

13. May 6, 1799, quoted, Beveridge, *Marshall*, II, 430.

14. December 13, 1800, *Tudor Papers*, MHS.

15. *Aurora*, June 12, 1800.

16. AA/Mary Cranch, May 4, 1800, *New Letters*, 250–52.

CHAPTER LXXXI

1. June 13, 1800, APm.

2. May 26, 1800, *New Letters*, 252–53.

3. AA/TBA, July 12, 1800, APm.

4. TBA/JQA, October 12, 1800, APm.

5. To Fisher Ames, Washington, August 10, 1800, Gibbs, *Memoirs*, II, 400–5.

6. August 26, 1800, Gibbs, *Memoirs*, II, 409–10.

7. Cabot/Wolcott, Brookline, August 23, 1800, Gibbs, *Memoirs*, II, 406.

8. August 21, 1800, Gibbs, *Memoirs*, II, 407–8.

9. September 1, 1800, APm.

10. To Gideon Granger, Monticello, August 13, 1800, Jefferson, *Writings*, ed. Ford, VII, 450–53.

11. September 10, 1800, *Works*, IX, 83–84.

12. AA/TBA, October 12, 1800, APm.

13. JA/AA, November 15, 1800, APm.

14. July 18, 1800, APm.

15. AH/JA, New York, August 1, 1800, APm.

16. September 3, 1800, Gibbs, *Memoirs*, II, 416–18.

17. September 26, 1800, Gibbs, *Memoirs*, II, 421–22.

18. October 2, 1800, Gibbs, *Memoirs*, II, 430–31.

19. Webster signed himself "Aristides." *A Letter to General Hamilton occasioned by his letter to President Adams*, by a Federalist (New York, 1800).

20. October 1, November 9, 1800, King, *Correspondence*, III, 315, 331.

21. AA/Mary Cranch, November 10, 1800, *New Letters*, 254–55.

22. October 27, 1800, APm.

CHAPTER LXXXII

1. TBA/AA, October 19, 1800, APm.

2. November 2, 1800, APm.

3. AA/Mary Cranch, November 10, 1800, *New Letters*, 254–55.

4. November 28, 1800, APm.

5. December 17, 1800, APm.

6. December 30, 1800, *Works*, IX, 575–76.
7. December 13 and 25, 1800, *Tudor Papers*, MHS.
8. JA/Stoddert, Quincy, March 31, 1801, *Works*, IX, 582–83.
9. Berlin, November 25, 1800, APm.
10. January 3, 1801, APm.
11. December 26, 1800, MHS, *Proceedings*, XX, 361.
12. February 4, 1801, *Works*, IX, 96–97.
13. December 17, 1800, APm.
14. TBA/AA, January 24, 1801, APm.
15. January 20, 1801, *Tudor Papers*, MHS.

CHAPTER LXXXIII

1. APm.
2. Jefferson/Pierce Butler, August 11, 1800, Jefferson, *Writings*, ed. Ford, VII, 449–50.
3. To John Breckenridge, December 18, 1800, Jefferson, *Writings*, ed. Ford, VII, 468–69.
4. Hindman/McHenry, January 17, 1801, McHenry, *Correspondence*, 489–90.
5. Burr/Smith, December 16, 1800, quoted, Beveridge, *Marshall*, II, 539.
6. January 15, 1801, *New Letters*, 262–64.
7. February 3, 1801, *New Letters*, 265–66.
8. February 3, 1801, APm.
9. AA/JA, February 13, 1801, APm.
10. AA/JA, February 21, 1801, APm.
11. January 26, 1801, *Works*, IX, 93–94.
12. February 4, 1801, *Works*, IX, 96.

CHAPTER LXXXIV

1. Stony Field, March 24, 1801, APm.
2. JA/Benjamin Stoddert, March 21, 1801, APm.
3. JA/Mercy Otis Warren, July 20, 1807, APm.
4. April 16, 1801, APm.
5. September 9, 1801, APm.
6. May 23, 1801, APm.
7. May 8, 1801, APm.
8. May 30, 1801, APm.
9. May 31, 1801, APm.
10. September 15, 1801, APm.
11. July 13, 1801, APm.
12. August 20, 1801, APm.
13. JA/David Sewall, January 12, 1803, APm.
14. To Van der Kemp, March 3, 1804, APm.

15. November 5, 1804, APm.
16. "The Adventures of a Nobody," written July 1840 and later, APm.
17. November 16, 1804, APm.
18. November 6 and 22, December 7, 1804, APm.

CHAPTER LXXXV

1. February 27, 1805, APm.
2. January 22, 1817, APm.
3. June 5, 1812, APm.
4. APm, reel 188.
5. APm, reel 188.
6. To Van der Kemp, August 23, 1806, APm.
7. JA/Rush, September, July 23, 1806; February 2, 1807, APm.
8. JA/Rush, January 21, 1810, APm.
9. November 4, 1815, APm.
10. JA/JQA, November 15, 1816, APm.
11. JA/Van der Kemp, February 18, 1809, APm.
12. July 12, 1812, APm.
13. January 9, 1812, APm.
14. February 5, 1805, APm.
15. JA/Rush, May 1812, APm.
16. JA/Rush, August 1, 1812, APm.
17. JA/Rush, October 22, 1812, APm.
18. To Waterhouse, December 25, 1817, APm.
19. August 1, 1812, APm.
20. To Rush, June 12, 1812, APm.
21. December 19, 1815, APm.
22. JA/Madison, June 17, 1817, APm.
23. JA/Oliver Wolcott, November 17, 1823, APm.
24. To Noah Webster, February 6, 1816, APm.
25. To Judge Dawes, February 3, 1818, APm.
26. December 15, 1815, APm.
27. To Van der Kemp, April 20, 1812, APm.

CHAPTER LXXXVI

1. February 6, 1805, APm.
2. Philadelphia, February 19, 1805, *Letters of Benjamin Rush*, II, 890.
3. September 16, 1810, APm.
4. July 24, 1805, APm.
5. April 15, 1808, APm.
6. February 25, 1808, APm.
7. JA/Rush, February 25, 1808, APm.
8. January 25, 1806, APm.
9. December 27, 1810, APm.
10. July 3, 1812, APm.
11. September 16, 1810, APm.

12. October 13, 1810, APm.
13. JA/Rush, December 27, 1812, APm.
14. February 26, 1812, APm.
15. August 1, 1812, APm.
16. Rush/JA, June 4, 1812, *Letters of Benjamin Rush*, II, 1138; JA/Rush, June 24, 1812, APm.
17. January 15, 1813, APm.
18. July 23, 1806, APm.
19. July 20, 1807, APm.
20. July 27, 1807, APm.
21. August 15, 1807, APm.

CHAPTER LXXXVII

1. To Nabby, September 26, 1802, APm.
2. To Joshua Thomas et al., December 21, 1802, APm.
3. February 27, 1805, APm.
4. March 9, 1806, APm.
5. To Rush, June 22, 1806, APm.
6. February 6, 1805, APm.
7. JA/Rush, May 14, 1810, APm.
8. JA/JQA, January 8, 1818, APm.
9. JA/Rush, January 22, 1806, APm.
10. April 15, 1808, APm.
11. JA/JQA, February 5, 1806, APm.
12. JA/Rush, December 28, 1807, APm.
13. July 26, 1808, APm.
14. January 23, 1809, APm.
15. June 20, 1808, APm.
16. April 18, 1808, APm.
17. September 27, 1808, APm.
18. April 18, 1808, APm.
19. December 14, 1808, APm.
20. June 21, 1811, APm.
21. JA/William Cunningham, February 22, 1809, APm.
22. JA/Rush, February 20, 1809, APm.
23. December 26, 1808, APm.
24. December 28, 1807, APm.
25. October 13, 1811, APm.
26. March 4, 1809, APm.
27. March 23, 1809, APm.
28. JA/William S. Smith, March 2, 1814, APm.
29. July 18, 1809, *Shaw Papers*, LC.
30. JA/William Cunningham, April 24, 1809, APm.
31. December 5 and 22, 1815, APm.
32. December 22, 1811, APm.
33. February 1, 1811, APm.
34. March 23, 1809, APm.
35. JA/William Heath, December 14, 1807, APm.
36. JA/Van der Kemp, April 4, 1811, APm.

CHAPTER LXXXVIII

1. February 10, 1814, *Shaw Papers*, LC.
2. June 13, 1810, *Shaw Papers*, LC.
3. September 1, 1810, *Shaw Papers*, LC.
4. AA/Eliza Peabody, December 29, 1811, APm.
5. AA/Eliza Peabody, July 10, 1811, *Shaw Papers*, LC.
6. October 15, 1811, APm.
7. AA/Eliza Peabody, October 22, 1811, *Shaw Papers*, LC.
8. September 11, 1812, *Shaw Papers*, LC.
9. April 20, 1812, *Shaw Papers*, LC.
10. JA/Rush, November 2, 1811, APm.
11. AA/Eliza Shaw, April 2, 1811, *Shaw Papers*, LC.
12. June 10, 1807, *Shaw Papers*, LC.
13. November 8, 1811, *Shaw Papers*, LC.
14. To W. S. Smith, January 15, 1813, APm.
15. May 26, 1812, APm.
16. August 17, 1812, APm.
17. May 15, 1812, APm.
18. JA/Van der Kemp, February 5, 1813, APm.
19. JA/Rush, January 15, 1813, APm.
20. May 26, 1812, APm.
21. June 21, 1811, APm.
22. JA/Waterhouse, August 16, 1812, APm.
23. Josiah Quincy, *Figures of the Past*, 78.
24. Rush/JA, *Letters of Benjamin Rush*, II, 1110–11.
25. December 25, 1811, APm.
26. January 21, 1812, *A-J*, II, 290–92.
27. February 3, 1812, *A-J*, II, 293–96.
28. February 10, 1812, APm.
29. May 1, 1812, *A-J*, II, 300–1.
30. June 28, 1812, *A-J*, II, 308–11.
31. June 28, 1812, *A-J*, II, 308–11.

CHAPTER LXXXIX

1. JA/JQA, December 27, 1812, APm.
2. JA/Rush, January 20, 1813, APm.
3. JA/Rush, May 14, 1812, APm.
4. April 22, 1812, BPL.
5. June 24, 1812, APm.
6. June 15, 1812, APm.
7. JA/Rush, December 8, 1812, APm.
8. 1812, APm.
9. JA/Amason Stetson, December 7, 1812, APm.
10. December 8, 1812, APm.

11. December 4, 1814, BPL.
12. JA/William Stephens Smith, November 27, 1814, APm.
13. JA/Rush, August 26, 1815, APm.
14. JA/William Stephens Smith, February 22, 1815, APm.
15. JA/Mrs. Catherine Rush, February 22, 1815, APm.
16. AA/Mrs. Benjamin Rush, April 24, 1813, photostat, MHS, original in possession of Lyman Butterfield.
17. April 26, 1813, APm.
18. April 24, 1813, APm.
19. June 14, 1813, APm.
20. June 30, 1813, APm.
21. July 1813, APm.
22. July 13, 1813, APm.
23. July 15, 1813, APm.
24. August 22, 1813, A-J, II, 367–68.
25. November 16, 1813, APm.
26. Figures of the Past, 79–80.
27. JA/Rush, July 19, 1812, APm.
28. August 14, 1813, APm.
29. December 14, 1814, APm.
30. JA/Van der Kemp, July 5, 1814, APm.
31. July 15, 1814, APm.
32. August 17, 1814, APm.
33. April 21, 1815, APm.
34. June 26, 1816, APm.

CHAPTER XC

1. November 22, 1814, APm.
2. November 8, 1815, APm.
3. October 26, 1814, APm.
4. November 1814, APm.
5. January 11, 1815, APm.
6. October 10, 1815, APm.
7. August 27, 1815, APm.
8. JA/George and John Adams, May 3, 1815, APm.
9. November 12, 1815, APm.
10. November 17, 1815, APm.
11. September 6, 1815, APm.
12. June 27, 1816, APm.
13. March 14, 23, and 26, 1815, APm.
14. August 30, 1815, APm.
15. JA/JQA, May 10, 1816, APm.
16. JA/JQA, June 26, 1816, APm.
17. JA/JQA, July 6, 1816, APm.
18. August 26, 1816, APm.
19. July 26, 1816, APm.
20. JA/JQA, September 5, 1816, APm.
21. JA/De Wint, May 1, 1817, APm.
22. January 14, 1823, APm.
23. January 29 1818, APm.
24. February 1, 1824, APm.

CHAPTER XCI

1. November 13, 1818, A-J, II, 529.
2. December 8, 1818, APm.
3. December 7, 1818, APm.
4. April 2, 1819, APm.
5. JA/JQA, February 3, 1819, APm.
6. JA/Louisa Adams, April 8, 1819, APm.
7. December 24, 1818, APm.
8. JA/Alexander Johnson, May 13, 1819, APm.
9. December 18, 1823, APm.
10. June 11, 1819, APm.
11. June 22, 1819, APm.
12. June 11, 1819, APm.
13. June 25, 1819, APm.
14. September 25, 1819, APm.
15. May 8, 1820, APm.
16. November 13, 1817, APm.
17. December 23, 1819, APm.
18. January 13, 1820, APm.
19. JA/Rush, May 14, 1810, APm.
20. October 11, 1819, APm.
21. November 16, 1815, APm.
22. March 15, 1820, APm.
23. JA/Ward Nicholas Boylston, August 10, 1820, APm.
24. July 12, 1820, APm.
25. May 22, 1821, APm.

CHAPTER XCII

1. Figures of the Past, 64–65.
2. JA/Ward Nicholas Boylston, September 16, 1820, APm.
3. October 21, 1820, APm.
4. Figures of the Past, 86–87.
5. January 10, 1821, APm.
6. JA/Van der Kemp, February 12, 1821, APm.
7. JA/Ward Nicholas Boylston, May 4, 1821, APm.
8. Figures of the Past, 90–93.
9. June 23, 1823, APm.
10. Figures of the Past, 73.
11. Figures of the Past, 75.
12. JA/Richard Peters, April 2, 1822, MHS.
13. JA/George Adams, July 25, 1822, APm.
14. JA/George Adams, January 12, 1823, APm.
15. October 12, 1823, A-J, II, 601.
16. November 10, 1823, APm.
17. January 23, 1825, APm.
18. Figures of the Past, 73–74.
19. February 15, 1825, A-J, II, 608–9.
20. February 25, 1825, APm.
21. Figures of the Past, 82–83.
22. April 17, 1826, APm.